UNIVERSIT
UW-STEVE  P9-AQE-221

13.75

HOW EFFECTIVE ARE YOUR COMMUNITY SERVICES?
Procedures for Monitoring the Effectiveness of Municipal Services

HARRY P. HATRY
LOUIS H. BLAIR
DONALD M. FISK
JOHN H. GREINER
JOHN R. HALL, JR.
PHILIP S. SCHAENMAN

THE URBAN INSTITUTE
AND
THE INTERNATIONAL CITY MANAGEMENT ASSOCIATION

Copyright © 1977
The Urban Institute
2100 M Street, N.W.
Washington, D.C. 20037

LC 77-90431
ISBN 87766-206-1
UI 225-1211-4
Please refer to URI 19500 when ordering.
List price: $10.00
A/77/10M

HD
4605
.U72
1977

BOARD OF TRUSTEES

William D. Ruckelshaus
    Chairman
Warren E. Buffett
William T. Coleman, Jr.
Anthony Downs
Daniel J. Evans
John H. Filer
Eugene G. Fubini
William Gorham
Katharine Graham
Vernon E. Jordan, Jr.
Richard Llewelyn-Davies
Bayless A. Manning
Robert S. McNamara
Arjay Miller
Lois D. Rice
Herbert E. Scarf
Henry B. Schacht
Irving S. Shapiro
Franklin A. Thomas
John G. Veneman
James Vorenberg

THE URBAN INSTITUTE is a nonprofit research organization established in 1968 to study problems of the nation's urban communities. Independent and nonpartisan, the Institute responds to current needs for disinterested analyses and basic information and attempts to facilitate the application of this knowledge. As a part of this effort, it cooperates with federal agencies, states, cities, associations of public officials, and other organizations committed to the public interest.

The Institute's research findings and a broad range of interpretive viewpoints are published as an educational service. The interpretations or conclusions are those of the authors and should not be attributed to The Urban Institute, its trustees, or to other organizations that support its research. The research and studies forming the basis for this report were supported by grants from The National Science Foundation, The U.S. Department of Housing and Urban Development, and The National Center for Productivity and the Quality of Working Life.

Contents

Contents

EXHIBITS

Foreword

We believe this publication represents an important advance in the field of evaluating local government services. It provides a solid foundation on which others can build. In each of nine functional areas it raises issues that should make department heads and other local officials sensitive to the needs of the citizens they serve. It gives officials some new ways to think about city services and their role in handling them.

The topic is not new. Over 30 years ago Clarence E. Ridley and Herbert A. Simon, in *Measuring Municipal Activities* (1943), suggested types of information local governments might collect to monitor and control their services. They were far ahead of their time. The concept, rarely applied by practitioners, was all but forgotten by public administration theorists.

Interest in performance monitoring has come to life recently, however. This apparently stems from a combination of pressures on local officials—pressures from budget squeezes, pressures from citizens who demand accountability, and pressures to achieve professionalism with more sophisticated managerial tools (among others, management by objectives, program-planning-budgeting, performance auditing, and most recently, zero-base budgeting). Seldom debated any longer is whether effectiveness measures are needed. Rather, the concern of local administrators is how to develop practical techniques for collecting and analyzing pertinent data.

To tackle this problem, the International City Management Association, The Urban Institute, and the local governments of St. Petersburg, Florida, and Nashville-Davidson County, Tennessee, cooperated for the past few years in a project to develop and apply effectiveness measures. This work, building on earlier state-of-the art efforts undertaken by the Institute, breaks new ground in local government management. The project produced two reports. The first, *Measuring the Effectiveness of Basic Municipal Services: Initial Report* (1974), provided an overview of the kind of measurement system that could be used. This report complements the earlier one by providing more detailed material designed to help local officials develop and apply specific effectiveness measurement procedures in their own communities.

Mark Keane, *Executive Director*
International City Management Association

William Gorham, *President*
The Urban Institute

Washington, D.C.

Acknowledgments

This report is based on a cooperative effort of The Urban Institute, International City Management Association (ICMA), and the governments of St. Petersburg, Florida, and Metropolitan Nashville-Davidson County. The work was supported by funds from the Research Applied to National Needs program of the National Science Foundation and from the Office of Policy Development and Research of the Department of Housing and Urban Development. The National Center for Productivity and the Quality of Working Life also contributed support through its project with ICMA on municipal productivity improvement. The views expressed herein are, of course, those of the authors and not necessarily those of the sponsoring agencies.

ICMA provided both guidance for the project and on-site personnel to work with the two governments in testing the measurement procedures. For ICMA, James L. Cavenaugh and John Pazour worked on the project efforts in St. Petersburg and Nashville, respectively. Mr. Cavenaugh also provided special help in reviewing the final text. Donald Borut, Steve Carter, and George Barbour were coordinators of the work for ICMA and provided reviews of various drafts. George Barbour also was a coauthor of Appendix 14.

St. Petersburg, Florida, and the Metropolitan Government of Nashville-Davidson County (hereafter designated as Nashville) were major participants in the development and testing of the effectiveness measures and procedures discussed in this report. Their vital role cannot be overemphasized. For St. Petersburg, Paul Yingst was the overall project coordinator; he was assisted by William Owens. Mr. Yingst also provided extensive reviews of the draft material. For Nashville, Tom Finnie was the overall project coordinator, assisted by Martha Groomes, Richard Brant, and Jon Seaman. All of these persons also provided valuable reviews of the draft material.

On specific chapters, we received considerable assistance either in the development of the procedures or reviews of manuscripts from the following persons:

Solid Waste Collection:
  Herman Mueller and Attileo Corbo, St. Petersburg; and Vijay Alsii and Eugene Melgaard, the District of Columbia.

Solid Waste Disposal:
  Dave Holihan and Herman Mueller, St. Petersburg; Fred L. Smith, Jr. and Cindy McLaren, Environmental Protection Agency; and Richard Sullivan, American Public Works Association.

Recreation:
  Charles Spears, Ruth Allen, and Chris McLean, Nashville; Jack Puryear, Ruth Stenger, and Susan Warren, St. Petersburg; Robert Fiore, William Spitzer, and Merle J. Van Horne, Bureau of Outdoor Recreation; Peter Verhoven, National Recreation and Parks Association; and Diana R. Dunn, Temple University.

Library Services:
  De Lyle Runge and Patricia Broad, St. Petersburg; Sheila Douglass, Nashville; Ellen Altman, University of Toronto; Mary R. Power, American Library Association; and Judy Fair and Carol Pyke, The Urban Institute.

Crime Control:
  A. Lee McGehee, Lt. John Schrive, and Richard Smith, St. Petersburg; Lt. R. Kirschner, Jr., Nashville; Joseph Lewis, Police Foundation;

Ralph Anderson, Norman Darwick and John Quinn, International Association of Chiefs of Police, and Peter B. Block, The Urban Institute.

Fire Protection:
Chief Jerry Knight, St. Petersburg; Joe Swartz, Michael Karter, and Dave Novak, National Fire Protection Association.

Transportation:
Jim Anderson, St. Petersburg; and Milton Tharp and Francis May, Nashville.

Water Supply:
Elroy Spitzer, American Water Works Association; Richard Sullivan, American Public Works Association.

Citizen Complaints and Requests:
Milton Reese, Don Donley, and William Bateman, St. Petersburg; and Camille Cates, Sunnyvale, California.

Citizen Surveys:
Sidney Hollander, Jr., Sidney Hollander Associates (Baltimore, Maryland); Jack Vernon of Suncoast Opinion Surveys, Inc. (St. Petersburg, Florida); Carol H. Weiss, Bureau of Applied Social Research, Columbia University; and Robert Sadacca, The Urban Institute.

Survey of Businesses:
Ivan Elmer, U.S. Chamber of Commerce.

Efficiency:
Milton Weiss, the city of Charlotte, North Carolina; and W. E. Vickery, Research Triangle Institute.

The project team received considerable assistance in the early stages of the study from the project advisory group, which included David A. Burkhalter, city of Charlotte, North Carolina; James L. Cap-linger, city of Kalamazoo, Michigan; Comer Coppie, Washington, D.C.; Stanley R. Cowle, Hennepin County, Minnesota; Corwin S. Elwell, town of Brattleboro, Vermont; Robert E. Goldman, National Science Foundation; Ray Harbaugh, city of St. Petersburg, Florida; Cole Hendrix, city of Charlottesville, Virginia; Whitney Shartzer, city of Dayton, Ohio; George A. Sipel, city of Palo Alto, California; Stanley Stern, city of Indianapolis, Indiana; John Thomas, National Association of Counties; Robert Thomas, Orange County, California; Joseph Torrence, Nashville-Davidson County, Tennessee; Richard Wall, city of Boston, Massachusetts; Robert Wilson, Fairfax County, Virginia; and Ward Wright, National League of Cities. In addition, Jerry Coffman and Milton Weiss of the city of Charlotte, North Carolina, provided important advice.

The overall research effort was directed by Harry P. Hatry, who was also the author of Chapters 1, 12, and 14-17 and coauthor of the chapters on recreation, libraries, and police. The following Urban Institute personnel were authors or coauthors of chapters in this report: Louis H. Blair—Solid Waste Collection, Trained Observers, and Citizen Surveys; Donald M. Fisk—Recreation, Library Services, and Solid Waste Collection; John M. Greiner—Citizen Complaints and Requests, and Transportation; John R. Hall, Jr.—Solid Waste Disposal, Water Supply, and Fire Protection; and Philip S. Schaenman—Police, Fire Protection, and Transportation chapters. Other participants from The Urban Institute were as follows: Alfred Schainblatt assisted in preparing the chapter on Fire Protection; Lynn Bell provided major inputs for the Survey of Businesses chapter; Richard Winnie contributed to the Transportation chapters; Alfred I. Schwartz helped with the Solid Waste Collection, Trained Observers, and Police chapters; and Winstanley Luke and Harold Parker provided assistance in a number of program areas.

How Effective
Are Your
Community Services?

Chapter 1

Introduction and Scope

Officials and citizens alike are frequently frustrated in their attempts to determine how well local government is serving the public. Complaints of poor service may be reported in the media or brought directly to the attention of city or county offices. Success stories may come to light in a similar haphazard fashion. Typically, however, a comprehensive view of the effectiveness of basic services is not available. Appropriate data are not collected or are improperly used for a regular check on whether local government operations are providing what the public needs.

This report provides suggestions by which city and county governments might regularly obtain information on the effectiveness and quality of their services.

The suggestions herein provide an initial "menu" of ideas from which local governments can select for trial those that appear most applicable to their needs. The procedures presented vary considerably in the degree of testing they have received. As more experience is gained, many of the procedures may well need modification. Indeed, this material is intended to encourage individual governments to develop effectiveness measurement procedures tailored to their own special needs.

Background

The measures and data collection procedures described here have been developed from a number of efforts. The single most extensive one was an eighteen-month effort in 1973 and 1974 sponsored by the Research Applied to National Needs Program of the National Science Foundation and by the Office of Policy Development and Research of the Department of Housing and Urban Development. Principal participants were St. Petersburg, Florida, and Metropolitan Nashville-Davidson County, Tennessee; the International City Management Association, which provided guidance on national measurement needs as well as on-site project coordinators in both "test" cities; and The Urban Institute, which provided overall coordination and technical guidance.

This report also draws on other Urban Institute experiences in developing effectiveness measurement procedures, especially those for solid waste collection and recreation undertaken in cooperation with the District of Columbia and Rockford, Illinois, and for fire protection and transportation services. This report also draws from experiences of other local governments that have worked on similar procedures, including those of Palo Alto, California; Savannah, Georgia; Randolph Township, New Jersey; Dallas, Texas; and Sunnyvale, California.

An initial report was published in February 1974.[1] It provides an overview of various aspects of local government effectiveness measurement, including criteria for the selection of measures, uses for such measurement, identification of measures for each service area covered, a brief discussion of citizen survey procedures, and the early findings on implementation. This second report details specific measures and data collection procedures. It is in-

1. *Measuring the Effectiveness of Basic Municipal Services: Initial Report* (Washington, D.C.: The Urban Institute and the International City Management Association, February 1974).

tended to supplement rather than supersede the 1974 report.

Measures and data collection procedures are discussed for the following basic services provided by city and county governments:

- Solid waste collection
- Solid waste disposal
- Recreation
- Libraries
- Crime control
- Fire protection
- Local transportation—both public transit and other ground transportation activities
- Water supply
- Handling of citizen complaints and requests for services

In addition, measures were identified and limited testing of procedures was undertaken on storm and wastewater disposal, but the findings were not deemed sufficiently informative to merit inclusion in this report. A preliminary list of measures for these services, however, is presented in the 1974 initial report.

The procedures identified here, such as the use of citizen or business surveys and of trained observers, can also be adapted for services *not* discussed in this report or for aspects of services not covered here. Because of their potential importance for a number of government services, three procedures—citizen surveys, the use of trained observer ratings, and the survey of businesses—are subjects of separate chapters.

Measures of government efficiency, although an important element in any effort to measure government performance, are not a focus of this report. Chapter 16, however, discusses efficiency measures as they relate to effectiveness measurement. Improvements in unit costs or, conversely, output per unit of input, achieved at the expense of quality of service, can be said to represent an improvement in efficiency only by twisting the meaning of that term. The effectiveness measurements discussed in this report can help local governments develop comprehensive efficiency measurement procedures that include checks on whether quality is at least being maintained.

Although most of the suggested measures have been used, as of this writing, by only a few governments, the measures should not seem foreign to local officials or to the public. Most, if not all, of the service characteristics covered by the suggested measures should be familiar and readily accepted as being of interest and concern to them. Indeed, two

major sources used to identify the service characteristics for which measures should be developed were citizen-complaint files and preliminary interviews with a small number of citizens. Because some of the *procedures* for collecting data for the measures depart from current government procedures, however, they may, at least initially, seem somewhat strange, or at least unusual, to many local governments.

For each local government service, a statement of objectives of what that service is intended to provide to the people and to the community is identified. A list of associated effectiveness measures is then drawn up to match each of the objectives. Next, procedures are suggested for obtaining data as a basis for giving factual content to the measures. The sources used to help identify the objectives and measures presented in this report include (1) statements of goals, objectives, and lists of measures currently in use, such as those displayed in program budgets; (2) suggestions by professionals in each service area, obtained from discussions with agency personnel and representatives of national professional organizations; (3) citizen complaint files from several local governments; (4) citizen concerns as expressed in newspaper articles and in a number of open-ended interviews with citizens administered by project staff; (5) professional literature; and (6) suggestions by reviewers of draft reports. These same sources might also be used by local governments to identify additional measures for themselves.

The measures and data collection methods in this report focus on those procedures appropriate for periodic measurement in order to permit tracking of problems, progress, and trends. These procedures were not developed to identify *why* conditions are as they are, nor *what should be done* about them. Accurate information about the outcomes of a service is, however, likely to be of significant help to local decision makers. Such information should aid in identifying priorities for necessary in-depth program evaluations or analyses.[2]

This report focuses on services and the specific outcomes associated with them, rather than on indi-

2. Discussions of procedures for program evaluations (to determine the impacts attributable to specific *existing* programs) or for program analyses (to estimate the likely effects of program *options*) are *not* within the scope of this report. For discussions of these procedures and for other bibliographic references on these topics, see Harry P. Hatry, Richard E. Winnie, and Donald M. Fisk, *Practical Program Evaluation for State and Local Government Officials* (Washington, D.C.: The Urban Institute, 1973); and Harry P. Hatry, Louis Blair, Donald M. Fisk, and Wayne Kimmel, *Program Analysis for State and Local Governments* (Washington, D.C.: The Urban Institute, 1976).

vidual government agencies. For most of the services examined, however, a single government agency is associated with the service, such as the fire department with fire services, or a park and recreation agency with recreation services. This means that a specific agency can reasonably be assigned primary responsibility for the measures of outcome associated with each service. Of course, in many, if not all, cases, *other* government agencies can also affect the outcomes of the service. Transportation services, for example, can affect outcomes in recreation accessibility, recreation services can affect crime, and housing and code enforcement agencies can affect fire services outcomes. Also, numerous external factors, such as weather conditions and various social conditions, can have substantial impacts. This is a fact of life for governments. No single agency is likely to have complete control over the effectiveness measures associated with the services it provides.

Some important impacts of local services are not captured by the measures and data collection procedures described in this report. These include such secondary, but important, impacts as the effect of government services on economic development, on property values, and on the jurisdiction's tax base. The estimation of such complex interrelationships seems more appropriate for in-depth studies than for the regular monitoring procedures discussed in this report.

Criteria for Selection of Measures and Data Collection Procedures

In selecting measures of effectiveness and data collection procedures, the following criteria were used:

1. *Appropriateness and Validity.* Does the measure relate to the government objectives for that service and does it really measure the degree to which a citizen need or desire is being met—including minimization of detrimental effects?
2. *Uniqueness.* Does it measure some effectiveness characteristic that no other measure encompasses?
3. *Completeness.* Does the list of measures cover all or at least most objectives?
4. *Comprehensibility.* Is the measure understandable?
5. *Controllability.* Is the condition measured at least partially the government's responsibility? Does the government have some control over it?

6. *Cost.* Are cost and staffing requirements for data collection reasonable? The answer to this will depend partly on the government's funding situation and its interest in a particular measure.
7. *Timeliness of Feedback.* If the information is needed for specific decisions—possible launching of new programs, setting budget levels for the coming year, and the like—will the data and analysis become available before the decision makers reach their deadline?
8. *Accuracy and Reliability.* Can sufficiently accurate and reliable information be obtained? This is a problem not only with procedures that use samples, such as citizen surveys, but with many government statistics, such as crime rates.

Local governments that wish to select their own tailor-made measures of effectiveness might well use these same criteria.

Keeping a Manageable Number of Measures

For each service area, approximately fifteen to twenty-five measures are presented. Each measure is intended to address some service characteristic not covered by any other measure. The monitoring of multiple measures is desirable to avoid excessive focus on one aspect of a service at the expense of others. Yet the cost of data collection and analysis and the need to prevent information overload are reasons for keeping the number to a minimum.

In some instances, data for a number of the measures can be gathered as part of the same collection procedure. For example, if a survey of citizens is undertaken, additional questions, each providing data for different effectiveness measures, can be included at little extra cost.

To reduce the burden of a large number of measures, there are four basic alternative approaches:

- Include only the more "global" measures, deleting those focused on narrow service characteristics. One can, for example, obtain information on citizens' overall level of satisfaction with public transit services rather than asking citizens for specific ratings of transit frequency, accessibility, and comfort. The global measures provide an important overview to upper-level local officials such as municipal managers, major executive officers, and council members.

- Include measures focused on specific service characteristics and eliminate the global measures. Individual operating agencies are likely to find measurements of specific service characteristics more useful in determining needed actions. However, because relatively few global measures are proposed, their deletion would not significantly reduce costs or managerial overload.

- Include both global and specific measures but reduce their coverage. One way to do this is to exclude service characteristics judged to be of minor importance. Another possibility is to exclude measures of conditions that are deemed unlikely to change substantially from one period to another.

- Minimize the potential information overload by having staff personnel provide summaries for management focusing on key measures and on those that, for the period under review, show unusually high or low values (see Chapter 12).

Focus on Implications of Services to Citizens, Not on "Immediate" Outputs

This report emphasizes effectiveness as related to citizen-client concerns. This means that the measures in some instances will seem less directly useful to lower-level supervisors. For example, park maintenance supervisors may be more immediately concerned with whether the grass is cut on schedule than with citizens' ratings of park appearance. Citizens, however, are more likely to be concerned with overall park appearance. Sensitizing supervisors to client concerns can in the long run lead to improved services.

An Additional Need: Periodic Auditing of Effectiveness Data

It is desirable to review data collection procedures periodically to assure that data collected continue to be of satisfactory quality. This applies to data based on citizen surveys (even when a survey is conducted by a professional survey firm) as well as to data collected internally. Government data collection proce-

dures and the data collected should be checked for possible sources of error and bias; citizen survey questions should be checked for possible ambiguities and biases; and survey procedures should be reviewed with survey firms that have been hired.

Application to Small Communities

The various service characteristics and the associated measures identified for each service (and presented in Chapters 2-11) should apply to smaller as well as larger governments if the government is responsible for the particular service. Small communities have fewer dollars and staff persons available for measurement procedures and analysis, but they will probably find their measurement needs correspondingly smaller. The volume of records, the number of streets, and the number of different population groups for which data are needed are likely to be smaller than those for larger jurisdictions. Many of the procedures can be scaled down to fit the needs of these smaller governments. Even the citizen survey procedure can be scaled down considerably, although required sample sizes depend less on the size of the population than on its homogeneity.[3] A citizen survey similar to the one proposed here has been undertaken by a number of small communities, including Randolph Township, New Jersey (1970 population, 13,300); Falls Church, Virginia (10,800); Zeeland, Michigan (5,000); and Washington, North Carolina (9,000).[4]

The Need to Differentiate Results for Various Client Groups

A major use of the data collected is to provide information on the effectiveness of services for various population groups in the community, in order to obtain a perspective on the need for, and equitableness of, services. Thus measurement values for major population groups as well as aggregate jurisdiction-wide totals are needed. Populations have tradition-

3. Because there are likely to be fewer (if any) service districts, fewer distinctive neighborhoods, and possibly fewer population groups, only 100 to 300 interviews may be required. The number of questions and length of interviews probably can also be reduced.
4. These communities used reasonably sophisticated procedures but were able to obtain volunteer help to keep costs down.

ally been grouped by age, sex, approximate income level, and race. Grouping by geographical areas is also generally very important for government services. For measurement purposes, the community could be divided into a small number (for example five to ten areas) with effectiveness data displayed for each area.[5] Residential neighborhoods are one useful way to divide a jurisdiction geographically. Other geographic groupings might be made by police, fire, and sanitation districts, or by city or county council districts. Groupings of census tracts or census enumeration districts could be used; often these can be assembled in different ways to form various types of districts.

These demographic and geographic categories appear to be relevant to most government services. For measuring some individual services, other client-group breakouts seem appropriate. For example, measures of the adequacy of transportation services should distinguish families with and without automobiles. Such special breakouts are suggested when appropriate in the individual chapters.

Many data collection procedures discussed in this report permit the separation of measurement data for various client groups. Citizen surveys, for instance, obtain data on age, sex, race, income, residence location, and automobile ownership. But some measures rely on collection procedures that do not obtain such data. For example, citizen complaints about various services are likely to provide information on location of residence but not on the age, race, or income category of the complainant. Examples of summary formats displaying breakouts by various population groups within a jurisdiction are presented in Chapter 12.

Principal Data Collection Procedures

Four principal types of data collection procedures are recommended throughout this report:

1. Data from existing government records, although often with suggested modifications as to data elements and ways to group the data.
2. Ratings of conditions by "trained observers" using specific predesignated rating criteria to

maximize the likelihood of obtaining reliable and consistent ratings.
3. Surveys of samples of the general population and perhaps of businesses in the community, to obtain ratings of specific aspects of individual services as well as certain factual data, such as extent of use of government facilities and programs.
4. On-site surveys of samples of users of specific government facilities (such as parks or libraries) or services (such as complaint handling) to obtain user ratings of specific aspects of these facilities or services.

Separate chapters are provided to discuss aspects of the trained observer, general citizen survey, and business survey procedures because they are suggested for use in measuring a number of government services. Although there is no separate chapter on "user" surveys, much of the discussion on citizen surveys is also applicable to user surveys, and detailed procedures are presented in the particular chapters in which use of such surveys is suggested. The specific applications of these procedures are discussed in the individual service chapters.

Organization of the Report

The next ten chapters (2-11) discuss the specific measures and data collection procedures suggested for consideration for specific municipal government services, including information on limitations, costs, and special validity problems. Chapter 12 discusses a number of the uses for service effectiveness data, provides some suggestions as to how the data might be usefully summarized for government officials, and briefly discusses some basic analysis that can be done to make the best use of the data. Chapters 13-15 deal with the three special data collection procedures, namely, the trained observer ratings, the citizen survey, and the survey of businesses. Chapter 16 attempts to categorize the various types of efficiency measures, discusses their relationship to effectiveness measurement, and illustrates the various types of efficiency measures. The report concludes in Chapter 17 with a brief discussion of some key issues on the implementation of effectiveness measurement procedures.

This report is not intended to be read from cover to cover. Rather, because each chapter discusses specific procedures in detail, it should perhaps be considered a handbook of local government effec-

5. St. Petersburg divided the city into five areas and Nashville, ten, for purposes of obtaining and analyzing data from their citizen surveys.

tiveness measurement procedures. The reader interested in only a particular service area should read the chapter on that service area plus Chapters 12 and 17, and those on special procedures that apply, such as Chapters 13, 14, and 15.

For the convenience of the reader, the exhibits have been coded with the chapter number rather than numbered consecutively throughout the book.

Chapter 2

Solid Waste Collection

How clean are streets, alleys, sidewalks, and vacant lots? Are they cleaner or dirtier than they were last year? To what extent? How do these conditions vary among areas of the community? What progress is being made to overcome undesirable conditions? How well are private collectors under contract to the government performing and how can they be held accountable? How often do solid waste collection crews miss collecting from households? To what extent are citizens and business persons satisfied with their solid waste collection services?

In most communities, one looks in vain for answers to such questions. Current measurement practices in most local governments focus on effort expended—households served, tons of refuse collected, number of special pick-ups, and miles of streets swept. These pieces of information are important for controlling operations, but they say little, if anything, about the resulting quality of the service. Complaints sometimes are tallied and the results used as an indicator of performance. But citizen complaints rarely indicate the views of the whole community—only of those who know how to complain and are sufficiently motivated or incensed to take the trouble to complain. Virtually all sanitation officials have opinions, based on their personal observations, of the cleanliness or dirtiness of streets and alleys in the various neighborhoods. But such opinions are difficult to quantify. They vary among observers; they can be based on observations of only a portion of the neighborhood—such as a main street—that may not be representative of the neighborhood; and officials relying solely on memory would probably have difficulty distinguishing levels

of cleanliness and degrees of differences among various parts of the community and changes that occur over time.

This chapter presents suggested measures and data collection procedures for regularly obtaining more comprehensive and reliable information on the effectiveness or quality of solid waste collection services. Most of the measures and data collection procedures have been tested and used in at least one municipality. Local governments considering setting up a measurement system can obtain additional information from a prior report, *How Clean Is Our City?*[1] The basic measurement concepts presented in this chapter have been drawn from that earlier work.

Objectives and Related Effectiveness Measures

The following basic objectives for solid waste collection appear appropriate for most communities, whether the service is provided by the government

1. Louis H. Blair and Alfred I. Schwartz, *How Clean Is Our City? A Guide to Measuring the Effectiveness of Solid Waste Collection Service* (Washington, D.C.: The Urban Institute, 1972). A more detailed presentation of the procedures is contained in Louis H. Blair and Alfred I. Schwartz, *Measuring the Effectiveness of District of Columbia Solid Waste Collection Activities* (Washington, D.C.: The Urban Institute report to the District of Columbia, September 1971).

Exhibit 2-1
OBJECTIVES AND PRINCIPAL EFFECTIVENESS MEASURES FOR SOLID WASTE COLLECTION

OVERALL OBJECTIVE: To promote the aesthetics of the community and the health and safety of the citizens by providing an environment free from the hazards and unpleasantness of uncollected refuse with the least possible citizen inconvenience.

OBJECTIVE	QUALITY CHARACTERISTIC	SPECIFIC MEASURE	DATA COLLECTION SOURCE/PROCEDURE
Pleasing Aesthetics	Street, alley, and neighborhood cleanliness	1. Percentage of (a) streets, (b) alleys the appearance of which is rated satisfactory (or unsatisfactory).	Trained observer ratings
		2. Percentage of (a) households, (b) businesses rating their neighborhood cleanliness as satisfactory (or unsatisfactory).	(a) Citizen survey (b) Business survey
	Offensive odors	3. Percentage of (a) households, (b) businesses reporting offensive odors from solid wastes.	(a) Citizen survey (b) Business survey
	Objectionable noise incidents	4. Percentage of (a) households, (b) businesses reporting objectionable noise from solid waste collection operations.	(a) Citizen survey (b) Business survey
Health and Safety	Health hazards	5. Number and percentage of blocks with one or more health hazards.	Trained observer ratings
	Fire hazards	6. Number and percentage of blocks with one or more fire hazards.	Trained observer ratings
	Fires involving uncollected waste	7. Number of fires involving uncollected solid waste.	Fire department records
	Health hazards and unsightly appearance	8. Number of abandoned automobiles.	Trained observer ratings
	Rodent hazard	9. Percentage of (a) households, (b) businesses reporting having seen rats on their blocks in the last year.	(a) Citizen survey (b) Business survey
	Rodent bites	10. Number of rodent bites reported per 1,000 population.	City or county health records
Minimum Citizen Inconvenience	Missed or late collections	11. Number and percentage of collection routes not completed on schedule.	Sanitation department records
		12. Percentage of (a) households, (b) businesses reporting missed collections.	(a) Citizen survey (b) Business survey

(Exhibit continued on next page)

Exhibit 2-1 continued

OBJECTIVE	QUALITY CHARACTERISTIC	SPECIFIC MEASURE	DATA COLLECTION SOURCE/PROCEDURE
Minimum Citizen Inconvenience (continued)	Spillage of trash and garbage during collections	13. Percentage of (a) households, (b) businesses reporting spillage by collection crews.	(a) Citizen survey (b) Business survey
	Damage to private property by collection crews	14. Percentage of (a) households, (b) businesses reporting damage to property by collection crews.	(a) Citizen survey (b) Business survey
General Citizen Satisfaction	Citizen complaints	15. Number of verified citizen complaints, by type, per 1,000 households served.	Sanitation department records

or by private contractors under government regulation:

To promote the aesthetics of the community and the health and safety of the citizens by providing an environment free from the hazards and unpleasantness of uncollected refuse with the least possible citizen inconvenience.

The suggested measures of effectiveness relating to these objectives, and the proposed sources of data on them, are summarized in Exhibit 2-1. They are discussed in four groups:[2]

- Pleasing aesthetics—clean streets (Measures 1-4);
- Health and safety (Measures 5-10);
- Minimum citizen inconvenience (Measures 11-14); and
- General citizen satisfaction (Measure 15).

The measurements can be undertaken for the community as a whole, and for individual areas of the community. These measures appear appropriate for both commercial and residential collection services and for monitoring services whether they are provided directly by the government or by private contractors under government regulation.

The measures apply primarily to household and commercial refuse collection and street- and alley-cleaning services. But some measures can be used, or at least adapted, for such specialized activities as abandoned automobile removal and code enforcement. The findings from some measures—such as the trained observer ratings of street cleanliness and

2. The order of the measures does not necessarily indicate their relative importance.

citizen ratings of neighborhood cleanliness—are affected jointly by street-cleaning and refuse collection operations. Through the collection of supplementary information as part of the procedure, a government can use the measurement data to help identify specific responsibility and possible action for correcting undesirable conditions.

Principal Measures and Measurement Procedures

Since solid waste collection is intended to remove unsightly and unsanitary wastes, the chief measurement issue is how to measure (a) the resulting cleanliness and (b) the extent of any health and safety hazards on streets and alleys in the community. Two complementary approaches are described here.

1. The first suggested procedure relies on trained observers employing a photographic rating scale of "1—very clean" to "4—very dirty" to rate the cleanliness of streets and alleys in the community. Observers also note the presence of health and fire hazards, abandoned autos, and miscellaneous bulk items. This procedure has been tested fairly extensively in Washington, D.C.; New York City; St. Petersburg, Florida; Nashville, Tennessee; and Savannah, Georgia. It can provide the government with reliable information as to the nature and location of unsightly conditions in small or large areas of the community, depending on the scope of the measurement effort undertaken.

2. The second principal procedure is that of telephone or personal interviews with a sample of
citizens, and possibly businesspersons, in the
community. The interviews can obtain representative viewpoints on neighborhood cleanliness as well as ratings on refuse collection service
including the frequency of missed collections,
trash spillage during collections, incidents of objectionable noise during solid waste collection,
odors from uncollected refuse, and rat sightings.
Although citizen perceptions are subject to memory limitation and inaccurate observation, they
are important as an indicator of how the responding clients view their service. This interview procedure becomes especially useful if the survey
undertakes to obtain feedback on a number of
services in addition to solid waste collection. This
procedure has been used in St. Petersburg,
Nashville, the District of Columbia, and a
number of other cities as well.

Individual Measures

Pleasing Aesthetics—Clean Streets (Measures 1-4)

Keeping streets and alleys clean—maintaining a
satisfactory appearance—is a major aim of solid
waste collection. In addition, keeping sidewalks,
off-street parking areas, vacant lots, and yards free
from accumulations of unsightly or hazardous
wastes (such as abandoned autos, discarded furniture and appliances, garbage, or extensive amounts
of combustible litter) is a government responsibility
often shared by code enforcement, street-cleaning,
and refuse collection personnel. Sanitation data
used by most local governments, however, do not
provide reliable, regular information on cleanliness
and appearance. The occasional observations of collection personnel and other public officials are not
systematically collected; moreover they provide
little useful data for comparative assessments of improvement or degradation in appearance as, for
example, from one year to the next. Complaints from
citizens often identify specific problems. But many
persons do not complain because they don't like to,
don't know how to, or don't feel it would do any good.
Often complaints are not valid—they misrepresent
the condition. Complaint data cannot be depended
on as reliably representing either actual conditions
or the views of all the jurisdiction's citizens.

But can more reliable, quantitatively based
measurements of cleanliness be provided? Two com-

plementary approaches to such measurement have
been tested and seem appropriate. One or the other
of the approaches were operational on a regular
basis in at least four cities as of early 1977. The
approach discussed in Measure 1 is based on a photographic rating scale used by trained observers to
make objective ratings of actual conditions. The approach presented in Measure 2 is based on subjective
citizen perceptions of neighborhood cleanliness.

*Measure 1:   Percentage of (a) streets, (b) alleys, the
appearance of which is rated satisfac-
tory (or unsatisfactory) on a visual rating scale.*

Here ratings are based on visual ratings by a
specially trained observer. The cleanliness and
appearance of a street or alley are graded in accordance with a set of photographs and written descriptions that cover a range of litter conditions
generally found throughout the community. An
example of a typical set of grades is shown in Exhibit
2-2. Trained observers driving along the streets (or
through the alleys) assign to each block face a numerical rating that corresponds most closely to a
grade described in the photographs and written descriptions.[3] The observer does not have to leave the
car to make the ratings.

These ratings constitute a readily understood
measure, especially when results are presented with
examples of the photographs on which the rating
scale is based. Under proper supervision, the trained
observer program provides a reliable way to measure aesthetic impacts on the community and
changes in cleanliness over time. Photographic rating scales for cleanliness have been used by the governments of Washington, D.C., New York City,[4]
Savannah,[5] Nashville, and St. Petersburg.

Cleanliness and appearance problems can arise
from a number of sources; among them are litter
dropped by transients, inadequate household or
commercial storage practices, slipshod collection

3. A block face is defined here as the area bordered by the
center line of the street, the property line on the right-hand side
of the street and the center lines of the cross streets at either end
of the block. It is an area that the public agency is generally
responsible for keeping clean.

4. For a summary of this effort see "Project Scorecard: Purpose, Function, Method, and Structure," Fund for the City of New
York, 1975, and monthly reports on cleanliness of streets and
sidewalks in fifty-eight districts comprising New York City, issued by the Fund for New York.

5. For Savannah's presentation of the product of this work
see "City of Savannah Community Renewal Program," Office of
the City Manager (June 1973), pp. 2-15; and "Responsive Public
Services Program: Savannah," Report of the City Manager to the
Mayor and Aldermen, August 19, 1974.

Exhibit 2-2
EXAMPLES OF STREET LITTER CONDITIONS

Condition 1=Clean; 2=Moderately clean; 3=Moderately littered; 4=Heavily littered

Exhibit 2-3
ILLUSTRATIVE DISPLAY OF STREET
CLEANLINESS RATINGS
BY TRAINED OBSERVERS,
NASHVILLE, 1974

NEIGHBORHOOD	PERCENTAGE OF STREETS WORSE THAN 2.0	AVERAGE STREET LITTER RATING[1]
A	28	2.1
B	33	2.1
C	6	1.9
D	8	1.7
E	31	2.1
F	12	1.9
G	41	2.2
H	14	2.0
I	34	2.2
J	37	2.3
Total City	24	2.05

1. Since the rating grades ("1," "2," "3," and "4") are not based on "absolute" cleanliness levels, many standard statistical manipulations, such as calculations of averages, are not literally correct.

SOURCE: Statistics provided by Metropolitan Nashville-Davidson County Finance Office.

services, spillover from private property, or construction debris. To distinguish the specific type of problem in the dirtier areas and to help identify corrective strategies, trained observers can be asked to identify the apparent nature or source of the refuse. In Washington, D.C., the trained observers regularly use a series of codes to note problems such as refuse not in containers, construction or excavation debris, overflowing public trash containers, or discarded bulky items. In Savannah, trained observers categorize uncollected trash as "loose litter," "trash piles, junk appliances, etc.," or "junk cars." Special technical aspects of establishing a litter-rating index are discussed later in this chapter.[6]

Cleanliness-rating information can be tabulated to indicate cleanliness by neighborhood, by sanitation service area, or for the entire city. This is illustrated in Exhibit 2-3. Alternatively, such data can be mapped to identify problem areas, as illustrated in Exhibit 2-4; this exhibit shows changes over time in cleanliness by sanitation district.

Special Validity Considerations for Measure 1. The visual rating procedure, despite its attractive features, can quickly degenerate into an unreliable procedure unless proper care—particularly in supervising inspectors—is taken. Over time, inspectors may forget the definitions, become careless

6. More detailed discussions of the trained observer concept are also contained in Chapter 13 of this volume and in Blair and Schwartz, *How Clean Is Our City?*

in their application, or even make up ratings. In one city, the ratings of one inspector gradually retreated into so narrow a spectrum that he did not use the extreme ratings regardless of the circumstances. (This scale compression is relatively common when inspectors do not adhere to photographic or written standards.) A second city was not able to use its ratings after it discovered that independent but virtually simultaneous inspections of the same scenes had resulted in wide rating disparities—disparities that had not been promptly corrected by retraining the inspectors.

Experiences to date indicate that several actions are needed, particularly after implementation of the rating system, to ensure that the data are reasonably reliable. These include the following:

1. The development of the visual, photographic rating scale should be undertaken systematically (as described later in this chapter) to assure that the rating scale can reliably distinguish the different levels of cleanliness.
2. Adequate training of observers in the use of the rating procedure, both for new observers and periodically in the form of retraining for experienced observers, should be provided to prevent deterioration in rating skill.
3. Regular checking of sample ratings should be undertaken to determine whether observers maintain sufficient accuracy in their ratings. Perhaps 10 to 15 percent of each inspector's ratings would be replicated by the supervisor. The local government should set reliability targets; for example, 75 percent of the inspector's ratings could be required to agree with those of the supervisors, and 90 percent to agree within one-half point. These targets appear reasonable, based on experience in the cities noted earlier. If the checks do not indicate sufficient accuracy, immediate retraining of raters and possibly further refinement of photos and written standards for the ratings should be undertaken.

Measure 2:   Percentage of (a) households, (b) businesses rating their neighborhood cleanliness as satisfactory (or unsatisfactory).

Another important perspective on the cleanliness of the community and, by implication, on the satisfactoriness of solid waste collection services, is provided by the perceptions of citizens and business establishments. This information can be obtained from a survey of a representative sample of the community. The same survey can be used to provide

Exhibit 2-4
NEW YORK CITY CLEANLINESS REPORT
COMPARISON IN THE 58 SANITATION DISTRICTS OF STREET AND SIDEWALK CLEANLINESS FOR OCTOBER AND NOVEMBER 1975

Difference in Percent of Blocks rated "Acceptable" to "Clean"

Major improvement	+15.0% or more
Moderate improvement	+5.0% to +14.9%
Stable	−5.0% to +4.9%
Moderate decline	−5.0% to −14.9%
Major decline	−15.0% or more

MANHATTAN

Sanitation Dist.	Percent of Blocks rated "Acceptable" to "Clean" Oct 1975	Nov 1975	Difference	Citywide Rank* Oct 1975	Nov 1975
1	72.0	65.2	− 6.8	34	36
2	50.8	48.3	− 2.5	48	49
3	63.1	57.0	− 6.1	39	43
4	75.7	61.3	−14.4	33	42
5	65.8	61.8	− 4.0	37	41
6	89.0	84.0	− 5.0	14	17
7	58.9	55.4	− 3.5	43	46
8	51.3	47.2	− 4.1	47	51
9	65.5	43.2	−22.3	38	53
10	43.5	18.8	−24.7	52	58
Man.	64.8%	54.8%	−10.0%		

BRONX

Sanitation Dist.	Oct 1975	Nov 1975	Difference	Rank Oct 1975	Rank Nov 1975
20	62.3	38.6	−23.7	40	55
21	43.2	33.2	−10.0	54	56
22	48.2	62.3	14.1	50	39
23	33.7	48.5	14.8	57	47
24	86.6	90.4	3.8	17	11
25	41.8	45.3	3.6	55	52
26	82.0	86.8	4.9	22	14
27	58.6	41.0	−17.6	44	54
28	95.3	79.6	−15.8	7	23
29	71.2	78.5	7.4	35	28
Bronx	70.6%	68.8%	−1.8%		

QUEENS

Sanitation Dist.	Oct 1975	Nov 1975	Difference	Rank Oct 1975	Rank Nov 1975
50	80.5	79.7	− 0.8	26	22
51	81.6	83.4	1.8	24	19
52	76.6	67.4	9.2	32	33
53	93.6	86.8	6.8	8	15
54	81.0	85.7	4.7	25	16
55	95.6	91.2	4.5	6	10
60	92.1	96.8	4.7	10	4
61	87.7	96.8	8.8	15	5
62	99.0	96.1	2.9	1	6
63	98.2	100.0	1.0	3	1
64	89.5	99.4	10.0	13	2
65	83.7	89.3	5.6	21	12
66	81.6	92.8	11.2	23	9
67	77.8	79.5	1.7	31	24
68	84.6	70.6	−13.9	20	31
69	77.9	98.4	20.5	30	3
Queens	86.7%	89.1%	2.3%		

STATEN ISLAND

Sanitation Dist.	Oct 1975	Nov 1975	Difference	Rank Oct 1975	Rank Nov 1975
70	90.5	83.7	− 6.7	12	18
71	87.1	87.1	− 5.0	16	13
72	98.3	93.2	− 5.0	4	8
73	97.4	93.9	− 3.5	2	7
S.I.	94.3%	90.5%	− 3.4%		

BROOKLYN

Sanitation Dist.	Percent of Blocks rated "Acceptable" to "Clean" Oct 1975	Nov 1975	Difference	Citywide Rank* Oct 1975	Nov 1975
30	57.8	65.6	7.8	45	35
31	40.2	63.7	23.5	56	38
32	85.4	79.0	− 6.4	18	25
33	79.8	80.9	1.1	27	21
34	85.1	82.0	− 3.1	19	20
35	70.0	75.4	5.4	36	30
36	31.6	55.5	23.9	58	45
37	43.2	69.9	26.7	53	32
38	43.5	55.5	12.0	51	44
39	54.9	48.3	− 6.5	46	48
40	50.1	28.5	−21.6	49	57
41	60.3	47.7	−12.6	41	50
42	79.2	64.9	−14.2	28	37
43	60.3	61.9	1.6	42	40
44	78.4	66.2	−12.2	29	34
45	96.2	78.8	−17.4	5	27
46	91.5	78.8	−12.7	11	26
47	92.4	77.4	−14.9	9	29
Bklyn.	70.2%	67.3%	−2.9%		

	Oct 1975	Nov 1975	Difference
CITYWIDE AVERAGE	79.1%	77.4%	− 1.6%

*The 58 Sanitation Districts are ranked each month from cleanest (#1) to dirtiest (#58). Source: Project Scorecard, Fund for the City of N.Y.

data for several other solid waste collection measures. Questions such as number 47 of Appendix 1 (for residents) ". . . would you say that your neighborhood is usually: very clean, fairly clean, fairly dirty, or very dirty" and number 26 of Appendix 2 (for businesses) can be used to obtain these data.[7] Satisfaction with cleanliness in these examples is expressed in terms of how clean the respondents rate their neighborhoods rather than directly in terms of how "satisfied" they are. Nashville and St. Petersburg considered neighborhood cleanliness as "satisfactory" if persons polled responded "very clean" or "fairly clean."

Because the citizen survey procedure is covered in Chapter 14, it will not be discussed in detail here. A government will probably find the citizen survey to be most practical if it simultaneously obtains information on a number of other local government services. If a wide-ranging citizen survey is not undertaken, the sanitation department might conduct its own annual survey to monitor a number of aspects of collection operations. Such a survey has been conducted by the District of Columbia.[8] A low-cost, five-minute telephone survey seems to be a feasible option.[9] If so, Questions 47-52 and 66-79 of Appendix 1 could be used. (Questions 48-52 would obtain information on other solid waste collection measures, as discussed below, and numbers 66-79 would obtain demographic information.)

Special Validity Considerations for Measure 2. Although Chapter 14 discusses the potential validity factors applicable to any survey of households or businesses in a community, there is an additional concern here about the wording of the question used to collect data on this measure. The survey question on rating of neighborhood cleanliness is straightforward, but it can be difficult to decide what types of corrective actions are appropriate. Are the respondents' ratings based solely on litter on streets

7. We suggest that citizens be asked about *neighborhood* cleanliness rather than the cleanliness of the street or alley adjacent to their residence. Comparison of responses of twenty-eight pairs of citizens living on twenty-eight different blocks in Washington, D.C., showed that the two members of the pair agreed about two-thirds of the time on neighborhood cleanliness, but only about one-third of the time on street or alley cleanliness. See Blair and Schwartz, *Measuring the Effectiveness,* vol. 3, pp. 77-78.

8. The findings of the survey of eighty households in the Anacostia section of Washington were described in a report by Vijay Alsi, "A Telephone Survey of Residents of Service Area 3 and Service Area 34" (Washington, D.C.: Operations Analysis Division, Department of Environmental Services, 1973).

9. Additional information on such procedures can be obtained from Blair and Schwartz, *How Clean is Our City?* Chapter 4. A telephone survey questionnaire is included, pp. 40-41.

and alleys and other public areas where the sanitation department can correct conditions? It seems likely that the ratings will also take into account the litter on private property and possibly even the condition of buildings and yards over which the department has little or no direct control. Buildings needing paint or repairs or unkept lawns can make an area look dirty. Citizens responding "somewhat dirty" or "very dirty" might be asked, "Why do you say that?" or "What contributes most to the neighborhood's being dirty?" The replies would help identify the specific nature of the problem. This was not done in the surveys in St. Petersburg and Nashville; in both jurisdictions the emphasis was on avoiding such open-ended questions with their subsequent coding difficulties, and only a small amount of interview time could be allocated to sanitation service questions.

Citizen Perceptions Versus Trained Observer Ratings. Measures 1 and 2 are treated separately on the assumption that they measure different aspects of service effectiveness, that is, citizen perceptions of neighborhood cleanliness as opposed to an "objective" physical evaluation of street and alley cleanliness. However, if the results for these two measures are highly correlated and seem likely to remain so under most conditions, it would be adequate to employ only one and use that measure as a proxy for the other. Comparisons of the methods have been made in three cities. (The summary data appear in Appendix 3.) First came a comparison of visual inspection ratings and citizen survey responses in Washington, D.C., in 1971. About two-thirds of the time citizen ratings were found to agree with those of the inspectors. In 1973, in St. Petersburg, comparisons of aggregate ratings for four areas showed a general match. Those districts that the citizens viewed as dirty were generally rated as littered by the visual inspection process. A comparison of results for ten areas of Nashville in 1974 brought less conclusive results. In some cases the match between citizen perceptions and visual ratings was good, but in other cases it was poor. With respect to the four urban areas of Nashville-Davidson County, however, citizen and visual inspection ratings generally agreed.[10]

10. This finding suggests the need to reexamine the visual inspection procedures and possibly the citizen rating procedures as they apply to rural areas. The survey was conducted in the winter, the visual inspections in the summer. Thus seasonality factors (such as high weeds in ditches and gutters along the road in rural areas) rather than inadequate rating procedures might have been responsible for the differences.

These findings suggest that some correlation exists but that it cannot be fully depended on.[11] Pending more extensive studies, our opinion is that Measures 1 and 2 measure different aspects of cleanliness and that it is desirable to collect information for both. For places where a local government finds the outcomes for the two measures quite different, the data might provide clues to corrective action. They could indicate (1) whether physical conditions had actually changed or whether the problem appeared to be a perceptual change or (2) that conditions on streets and alleys had changed but not those on private property (or vice versa).

Measure 3: Percentage of (a) households, (b) businesses reporting offensive odors from solid wastes.

Improperly stored organic solid wastes, particularly food wastes, can decompose and putrefy in a few days in warm weather, creating noxious odors and causing possible health hazards. Low-income housing areas or dense, inner-city residential areas frequently seem to suffer from such odors in warm weather. The prevalence of odors can be estimated by surveying citizens and businesspersons concerning their perceptions and recollections of odors caused by solid wastes, as part of the household or business surveys previously mentioned. Question 50 of Appendix 1 (households) and number 33 of Appendix 2 can be used to obtain the data.

The measure's validity may be affected by certain limitations. Citizens may not be able to identify the source of odors in their neighborhoods, especially in areas with polluted waterways or with extensive commercial operations that emit odors. Even if respondents are able to identify an odor as coming from solid wastes, much of the waste might be on private property or in buildings over which the sanitation agency has no control. Furthermore, the season when the survey is conducted will affect the results. Odors are likely to be more pronounced in warm weather, but if the survey is conducted in winter or spring, the respondents might not remember vividly the problems experienced during extended warm periods.

Measure 4: Percentage of (a) households, (b) businesses reporting objectionable noise from solid waste collection operations.

Household refuse collection and street cleaning can be noisy. Noise levels can be measured with appropriate equipment, but it is difficult to relate noise levels to impacts on citizens and to measure citizen dissatisfaction. The extent to which noise is objectionable to citizens depends not only on the absolute noise level, but on such factors as the following: whether the noise is sharp or dull, constant or intermittent; the proximity of the residence or business to the collection operation; the extent of other noises; the time of day the noise is made; and whether citizens have become conditioned to collection noises. Surveys should indicate the extent to which the noises are considered to be objectionable.[12] If a citizen survey or survey of businesses is being conducted by the local government, questions such as number 49 of Appendix 1 (households) and number 32 of Appendix 2 (businesses) can be used to obtain the data.

Health and Safety Measures (Measures 5-10)

Measure 5: Number and percentage of blocks with one or more health hazards.

Avoidance of environmental health problems caused by uncollected, improperly stored refuse is perhaps the single most important purpose of solid waste collection. Solid waste often contains organic wastes and food scraps which provide breeding areas for insects in hot weather. Piles of discarded food containers or furniture offer food and harborage for rats. Discarded refrigerators or extensive amounts of broken glass may become inviting dangers to children.

The extent of these hazards can be estimated from ratings by trained observers inspecting for block-face and alley cleanliness (Measure 1). Many of these hazards are found on private property—backyards, vacant lots, and other privately owned illicit dumping areas where the sanitation department may have little power to correct conditions. The department will have to decide whether the inspection will cover these areas. Because the local government will probably want to act immediately to correct a situation posing serious danger to health—or have the health or zoning department

11. A scatter diagram and simple regression line, using the eight data points representing the four 1973 St. Petersburg areas and four 1974 urban Nashville areas in Appendix 3—of "percentage 'fairly,' 'usually,' or 'very' dirty" against the percentage of streets with ratings worse than 2.0—indicate a close straight-line fit. But these eight observations are far too few to permit any meaningful statement as to the general relationship.

12. If the survey uncovers a noise problem in one or more areas of the community, noise-measuring equipment might then be used to describe the nature of the problem more accurately.

issue a citation—the location of all health hazards detected should also be recorded.

There is as yet no generally accepted definition for how large an accumulation has to be to constitute a health hazard. The term might be defined as the presence of any of the following: abandoned bulk items (such as stuffed chairs, mattresses, and appliances), to be noted separately; dead animals; abandoned autos (also counted in Measure 8); piles of organic refuse exceeding some minimum size shown in a photograph; or, piled rubbish (such as boards, boxes, or brush) that appear to harbor rats. Each local government should attempt to provide and adhere to a specific definition so that counts taken in different parts of the community, by different inspectors, and at different times, will be at least roughly comparable.

The decision whether to note health hazards on private property will probably depend on the amount of responsibility the department has for removing such hazards. The inspection of private property can become quite time consuming because of the need (1) to drive slowly, (2) to examine a much larger area than just the street or alley, and (3) to drive through alleys to note conditions in backyards (where fences may block the view).

Health hazards (and fire hazards—see Measure 6) are likely to be correlated with certain street or alley litter ratings. One examination in Washington showed that such hazards were almost never present when the litter rating was 1 or 2.[13] Yet hazards do not always occur with high litter ratings. Because of public concern about health hazards and because of their potential impact on the public, it seems desirable to include this measure.

Measure 6: Number and percentage of blocks with one or more fire hazards.

A fire hazard is defined here as an accumulation of combustible solid wastes which, if ignited, would probably cause substantial property damage or which would cause a blaze of such a size that a prudent citizen would call the fire department. Fire hazards on the public way can be detected by trained observers as part of the procedure used for Measure 1. If the information is to be used only for sanitation department purposes, the inspections can probably be confined to the public way and the information gathered with virtually no additional effort. If the information is also to be used by the agency responsible for private property (such as the fire marshal),

13. Blair and Schwartz, *Measuring the Effectiveness,* vol. 3, p. 48.

then substantially more time-consuming inspections of private property will be required.

Probably few of the fire hazards on streets and alleys will lead to fires, even when not removed for weeks or months. Measure 7 is included to provide estimates of this "ultimate outcome." Still, because of the potentially serious nature of fire hazards, reporting the number and specific locations of fire hazards seems appropriate to encourage any needed correction actions. Fire hazards can have a seasonal aspect (piles of brush or leaves not collected promptly in thenfall constitute an example), so special attention might be devoted to this measure during such periods.

Measure 7: Number of fires involving uncollected solid waste.

One direct measure of solid waste problems is the number of fires that originate in refuse. In many localities the fire department investigates each fire to determine its cause. Some departments summarize the fires by cause and location. In all but the largest cities a review of fire incident records probably could be conducted with a maximum of one or two employee-days of effort to determine the number and geographical areas of fires from solid wastes on the public way. In Washington, D.C., approximately 14 percent of all reported fires in one year involved uncollected solid wastes—trash and brush, trash containers, or abandoned autos.[14] It might be hard to determine whether the accumulation was located in a place from which it should have been collected by sanitation personnel or whether it was on private property where it should have been detected and cited by sanitation inspectors. Data collection could be simplified if fire department personnel were to specify which fires involve solid wastes on the public way. The fires might be additionally classified according to the size of fire or the severity of damage.

Measure 8: Number of abandoned automobiles.

Abandoned automobiles are ugly, are sometimes fire hazards, often harbor rats, and are inviting nuisances for children. The same trained observer inspection procedure discussed earlier can be used to collect data on abandoned autos. If the sanitation agency wants to know the exact location of such vehicles—perhaps to direct automobile collection operations—trained observers will have to inspect all blocks: streets, alleys, and perhaps even private property. Results of such an inspection could be presented as in Exhibit 2-5; data could also be

14. Ibid., p. 87.

Exhibit 2-5
ABANDONED MOTOR VEHICLES LOCATED DURING VISUAL INSPECTION OPERATION

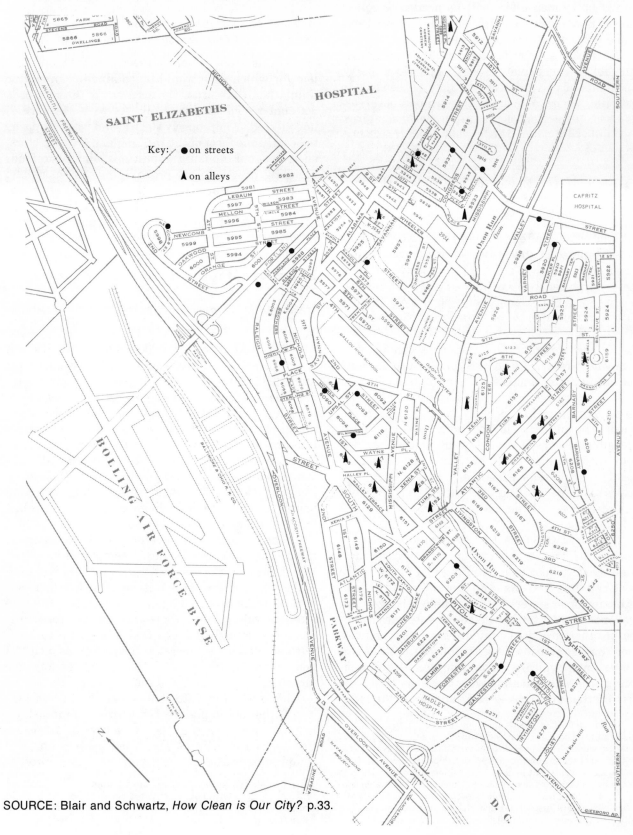

SOURCE: Blair and Schwartz, *How Clean is Our City?* p.33.

summarized by area. If the agency just wants an estimate of the number of abandoned vehicles to determine how much effort will be needed to collect them or how effective collection efforts have been, sample inspections will be adequate.

When the agency is responsible for removing automobiles from private as well as public property, inspections of private property may be needed. In Nashville, where a team of two trained observers was used, inspection of private property for abandoned autos did not markedly slow down the inspection process.

Measure 9:   Percentage of (a) households, (b) businesses reporting having seen rats on their blocks in the last year.

Solid wastes often provide refuge and food for rats. Estimates of the presence (or at least visible evidence) of rats over some interval of time can be obtained inexpensively with the citizen or business survey using Question 52 of Appendix 1 (households) and Question 28 of Appendix 2 (businesses). Although the responses are impossible to translate into *numbers* of rats, the responses can identify areas where rats are seen most often; such data appear adequate for tracking the rat problem.[15]

It is not known how accurate citizens' memories will be of such sightings, especially for long recall periods. The questions in Appendix 1 assume that it is feasible to survey once a year; hence they ask about rat sightings over the past twelve months. Questions could refer to sightings over shorter time periods to increase the accuracy of the responses, but then responses will be more sensitive to seasonal variations.

Rat infestations are not necessarily the result of improper solid waste collection practices of the sanitation agency. Poor food handling and food storage practices by citizens and commercial establishments, open sewers, and buildings with ground-level openings for unobstructed rat entry are examples of other practices that attract rats. Agencies other than sanitation departments, such as health departments, typically have responsibility for enforcing ordinances dealing with these matters. This measure therefore provides an estimate of the effec-

tiveness of both the sanitation agency and of related health inspection activities.

Measure 10: Number of rodent bites reported per 1,000 residents.

This is a more dramatic measure of the rat problem for which data would be obtained from city or county health records. The accuracy of these records was not tested in this study. As with Measure 9, uncollected or improperly stored solid wastes appear to be only one facet of the rat problem. Other factors, such as poor housing conditions and poor food-handling practices, are probably more responsible. Thus, this measure reflects the combined effectiveness of many local activities including those of the departments of health, housing or zoning, and sanitation.[16]

Measures of Citizen Inconvenience (Measures 11-14)

Measure 11: Number and percentage of collection routes not completed on schedule.

A missed collection is poor service. Refuse left on the streets or in alleys and awaiting collection is unsightly, and scattering of it produces dirty streets and alleys. Customers become irritated. There seem to be four principal data collection sources for information on missed collections. They are: (1) information provided by crews and their foremen, (2) tallies of citizen complaints on missed collections, (3) citizen responses in a sample survey, and (4) observations by trained observers spot-checking collection points shortly after scheduled collections. The last two are discussed under Measure 12.

Many agencies require each crew to report at the end of the day whether it completed its route; this information is the data source for this measure. Although this measure has been included, reservations remain regarding its value, unless the government takes pains to ensure accurate reporting. Some crews might be reluctant to report a route as uncompleted if they feel it will be taken as a sign of poor crew performance. Another drawback for some jurisdictions is that the data will probably not be available when private firms make the collections.

Tallies of complaints from citizens of missed collections can be used as an alternative data source. Because not all citizens, for a variety of reasons, will complain, the counts are likely to underrepresent

15. In some cities health department officials inspect blocks to determine if there are droppings, tunnels, or other signs of rats. Such inspections could provide data for this aspect of evaluation. The trained observers on their inspections discussed earlier could look for signs of rats, but to do so would probably require them to leave their vehicles, which would slow down the inspection process. No data have been available to permit correlations between health department inspections and citizen responses so that the findings of these two procedures can be compared.

16. Also, the incidence of rat bites is likely to be small. In 1975 there were only twelve reported incidents of rat bites in Washington, D.C., but rodent control personnel estimated that fewer than half of the rat-bite incidents were reported.

the number of missed collections. Nevertheless, the ready availability of this information makes it an attractive, if crude, measure. (A complaint-count gauge has been included as Measure 15, which considers complaints for all reasons, not just missed collections.)

Measure 12: Percentage of (a) households, (b) businesses reporting missed collections.

The measurement data here are likely to be more credible in one important respect than are the data from the previous measure because they do not depend on self-appraisals—sometimes negative—by public or private collection personnel.

Questions on client surveys such as number 48a of Appendix 1 (households) and number 29 of Appendix 2 (businesses) can be used to obtain the data.[17] These surveys can also inquire about the dependability of special pickups. To obtain feedback on its tree limb and brush pick-up service, Nashville used Question 51 of Appendix 1.

There are some special validity problems with the data for this measure:

- Some residents might not be aware of a missed collection. Residents of multi-family apartment units with a central storage/disposal facility would probably not know if collections are missed occasionally; these responses should be separated from those of single-family householders (as by using the instructions to the interviewers for Question 48 in Appendix 1).
- Sometimes citizens will set out refuse late, after the refuse collection team has passed through, and then blame the collectors for missing them.
- Memories of respondents may be poor, especially if asked about periods as long as twelve months.

Because of the memory problem, responses with regard to the specific number of missed collections

17. An alternate, but probably more time-consuming, way to obtain data on missed collections (untested in this study) is to use trained observers to sample collection points shortly after scheduled collection. They could check to see if the collection took place, if all of the refuse properly set out was collected, if any spillage was not cleaned up (for Measure 13), and if containers were returned to their proper places (if this is a sanitation function). The inspectors could select blocks at random, determine the collection time, then make a few (perhaps two to four) inspections on each block within a few hours of the scheduled collection. At least fifty to seventy inspections—spread over a few weeks if possible—would need to be made in each district to estimate with reasonable accuracy the percentages of missed collections, spillage, and so forth.

should be considered as only rough estimates. The particular ranges used (0, 1-2, 3-4, 5-6, and over 6 times), which are illustrated in Appendix 1, may be too narrow. If the respondent is asked about a period as long as twelve months, perhaps wider ranges (such as 0, 1-5, 6-10, and more than 10) would suffice without affecting substantially the utility of the data.

Measure 13: Percentage of (a) households, (b) businesses reporting spillage by collection crews.

Spillage of refuse leads to dirty streets, causes irritation and inconvenience to households and businesspersons, and represents an attraction for rats. Scattering can be the fault of the collectors or of the customers who do not use proper containers.

The prevalence of spillage can be estimated by asking questions on citizen surveys such as number 48b of Appendix 1 (households) and number 30 of Appendix 2 (businesses).[18] Responses should be considered rough estimates because there are problems of memory and knowledge, similar to those described under Measure 12. Moreover, a person who shares a central collection point with other households may not know if spillage was caused by sloppy handling of refuse by the collectors or by other householders. Therefore, as for Measure 12, it appears that the narrow ranges for responses used in the examples in the appendices (0, 1-2, 3-4, 5-6, and more than 6 times) should probably be widened.

Measure 14: Percentage of (a) households, (b) businesses reporting property damage caused by collection crews.

Collection crews sometimes damage refuse containers, shrubbery, and parked vehicles while pick-

18. If spillage appears to be a serious problem as indicated by inspection, by responses to the annual survey, or by complaints, a trained observer might conduct special inspections just before and just after collections at a random sample of perhaps fifty to seventy collection points to determine the following:
Just Before Collection
- Are proper solid waste containers being used?
- Are the refuse set-out areas clean, except for properly containerized refuse awaiting collection?
Just After Collection
- Has refuse been scattered or has spillage occurred during the collection?
The postcollection rating could be undertaken with the check for missed collections, discussed in note 17. The precollection rating might be conducted in conjunction with a street and alley rating activity. This should be a rapid inspection process, and the extent of spillage or missed collections on a particular route or in a particular district could be estimated with perhaps about two hours of inspection time. Such an inspection might be conducted on a neighborhoodwide or citywide basis or only on those routes where there are frequent complaints of missed collections.

ing up refuse. Although rarely a major problem, this practice can irritate customers. This measure might be of particular interest if a major change is made in collection procedures or if collectors frequently go onto private property. Complaints would probably be made only for the more serious incidents of damage; thus reported complaints seem likely to underestimate the frequency of incidents. When the service is provided by a private contractor, the government may receive almost no complaints, even if the government has some regulation authority.

Questions such as number 48c of Appendix 1 (households) and number 31 of Appendix 2 (businesses) can be used to obtain the data. It will be hard to be certain that the damage actually was caused by collection forces. Damage caused by vandals or irresponsible persons could be attributed by the respondent to collectors. If a survey of citizens or businesses is already being conducted, however, the cost of the added question on damage should be minimal.

Measure of Overall Citizen Satisfaction

Measure 15: Number of verified citizen complaints, by type, per 1,000 households served.

Some governments use reported complaints to evaluate the quality of service for a number of the problems covered by some of the measures previously discussed. As already noted, reported complaint tallies have the drawback that only the highly motivated or the most angry persons tend to complain.

Another drawback with counts of reported complaints is that some might not be justified, such as, for example, a complaint of missed collections when the refuse had been set out after collection.[19] Yet complaints, when tabulated by type and compared with complaints in previous time periods, can indicate important trends and emerging problems. The data tallied could exclude complaints found to be invalid after investigation by the government, perhaps by having an inspector examine the complaint to see if the condition really exists and if it is the responsibility of the sanitation agency.[20]

19. In the District of Columbia, The Urban Institute made cleanliness ratings for sixteen randomly selected locations that had been classified as complaints of a dirty street or alley. For twelve of the complaints the street or alley rating (on a four-point scale) was 3 or 4; in only one case did there appear to be no cleanliness problem. The twelve complaints were of such severe litter conditions that they were also health hazards and were considered to be promiscuous dumps. In five of the twelve cases, the problem concerned primarily private property. This suggests that although most complaints about unsatisfactory conditions are valid and, in fact, relate to severe conditions, they are often conditions that the department alone cannot control.

20. This process itself introduces questions as to possible biases of those doing the investigations if they belong to the same agency as that being evaluated.

Citizen complaint data should be summarized regularly, perhaps monthly or quarterly by type of complaint, by neighborhood, or by sanitation district; then they should be compared with data from previous periods to help identify problems and trends.

Although not included in the list of measures in Exhibit 2-1, an additional option would be to include on the general citizen survey a question as to respondents' ratings of their overall satisfaction with the solid waste collection service. Beginning in its 1974 survey St. Petersburg has asked respondents for their overall ratings of (a) "garbage collection" and (b) "cleanliness of city streets."

The Photographic Litter-Rating Procedure

This section discusses various aspects in the development and implementation of a photographic litter-rating procedure—used particularly for Measure 1 but also for Measures 5, 6, and 8.[21]

How to Develop a Photographic Rating Scale

A local government could utilize one of the scales already developed (such as those of the District of Columbia, Nashville, St. Petersburg, or New York City). Conditions among many cities or counties appear sufficiently similar that this seems a meaningful option. Each of these four cities, however, developed its own rating scales, because officials there felt more comfortable with scales that used photographs taken of actual local conditions. Yet Savannah has used the set of photos developed for the Washington, D.C., system. If a community prefers its own rating scale, the scale has to be developed carefully to assure that the photographs used to represent the various levels of cleanliness do indeed convey an impression of significantly different cleanliness levels that observers can reliably distinguish.

Each city that developed its own photographic rating scale also wrote its own definitions to accompany its photographs. As an example, those for Nashville are shown in Appendix 13.

The procedure used for developing the rating scales for the District of Columbia, Nashville, and

21. More details of the procedures are found in "Solid Waste Litter Visual Inspection and Reporting System," District of Columbia, Office of Environmental Services, by E. M. Melgaard (Washington, D.C., May 1974) and in Blair and Schwartz, *How Clean Is Our City?*

St. Petersburg, which appears applicable for other jurisdictions, is as follows:

1. Take a large number of photographs of scenes representative of the range of existing litter conditions on streets and alleys, and of the variety of backgrounds, structures, and land uses in which the conditions occur. A number of black and white photos should be taken to represent the various litter conditions encountered. Following a review, additional photographs to give complete coverage should be taken if necessary.

2. Have a number of "judges" separate the photographs into four groups corresponding to four different levels of litter conditions, from the cleanest to the most-littered categories. The judges should be persons who have varied backgrounds and who are not associated with the measurement activities. Photographs on which there was complete or nearly complete agreement concerning the category labels would be included in the set to be used as the visual inspection standard.

3. Use trained observers to field-test the set of photographs—and the written definitions—to determine if the set provides sufficient guidance for making ratings and for obtaining close agreement among ratings in a trial test.

Washington, D.C., took about 400 photographs; a panel of nineteen "judges" then classified them. Nashville took about 200 photographs, and a panel of six was used to classify them. In St. Petersburg, a photographer spent two days taking 150 pictures, and an analyst spent ten days constructing the final photographic rating scale. In Washington and Nashville additional photographs and guidelines were needed to help observers differentiate between condition "2" and condition "3" situations. (See Exhibit 2-2.)

Several different scales have been used in the photographic rating system. Washington, D.C., started with a four-point scale, went to a ten-point scale because of the inability of the inspectors to agree, and then dropped back to a seven-point scale. The city now uses a nine-point scale. The scale uses five major points (1.0, 2.0, 3.0, 4.0, and 5.0) that are tied to photographs, and four midpoints (1.5, 2.5, 3.5, 4.5) that are used when an observer cannot decide between the major points. St. Petersburg and Nashville used a seven-point scale, with the four major points tied to photographs and three midpoints used to resolve cases in which the inspector was unable to decide on the main points. New York City has been using a scale with four points (1.0, 1.5, 2.0, and 3.0) tied to photographs. Intermediate rat-

ings (1.2, 1.8, and 2.5) are assigned to conditions that do not conform to the photo standards. Ratings of 1.5 or lower are considered acceptable according to a public survey and to the agency's own standards.[22]

How Often Should Inspections Be Made?

The answers depend on local conditions and the expected uses of the information. Litter conditions in large areas normally change little from day to day and from week to week.[23] But there can be strong seasonal effects on cleanliness, such as leaves in the fall, brush and other vegetation in the summer, and more street litter in tourist seasons. If the government wants to know about cleanliness during the seasons—perhaps to help direct cleaning efforts—quarterly inspection may be appropriate. Washington, D.C., has a full-time inspection force which usually inspects the entire city quarterly. If the litter information is used in the more or less day-to-day direction of cleaning forces, more frequent inspection is necessary. Weekly inspections are used in New York's most littered areas, but the cleaner areas are inspected one to three times a month—depending on their level of cleanliness. If a government wants to know only if there are inequities among areas or if conditions are generally improving (or degrading), an annual inspection, probably in midsummer, should be sufficient. Nashville conducted its annual inspections in the summer.

How Many Block Faces or Alleys Should Be Inspected?

The decision as to how many streets or alleys should be inspected depends largely on what use is to be made of the information and how much statistical confidence is required. If the information is to be used to direct crews to specific locations or to evaluate the performance of individual crews, it will be

22. New York City started with a seven-point scale with four points tied to pictures and the midpoints used without pictures. The 1.0 rating was reserved for no litter, a condition rarely found. As a result there were a large number of 1.5 ratings. In an attempt to decrease the clustering about 1.5, a new rating of no litter (0.5) was introduced. Although this had the desired effect of reducing the number of 1.5s and increasing the number of 1.0s, it also meant that the new averages could not be compared with the old averages because of the shift in scale. Thus, after some discussion, the raters decided to return to the old scale but added pictures to the 1.5 rating to further define the point. This seems to have resolved the problem. At the same time, however, they dropped the 4.0 rating, claiming that there were so few 4s that it was not worth collecting information in this area. There is a question as to whether, by eliminating one end of the scale, the entire scale becomes too compressed.

23. A statistical analysis of cleanliness-rating data collected over a ten-week test period in Washington, D.C., showed little day-to-day or week-to-week variation in overall cleanliness in each service district. For a more thorough discussion see Blair and Schwartz, *Measuring the Effectiveness*, vol. 3, pp. 41-48.

necessary to inspect almost all streets and alleys, at least in those areas of the community generally known to have problems. If the information is only to detect changes in conditions over time or differences among areas, inspection of a sample of 50 to 70 block faces or alleys in each area, randomly selected in advance of the inspection, should be sufficient in most cases.[24] Washington and New York inspect virtually all streets. Nashville inspected 50 randomly selected block faces per service area in 1974 and 150 per service area in 1975. St. Petersburg inspected 50 to 180 per area, depending on the cleanliness level of the area.

Who Should Make the Ratings?

Persons with a wide variety of educational backgrounds and experience have been able to make trained observer ratings. In Washington, D.C., regular city sanitation inspectors were used. St. Petersburg used sanitation supervisors. In Nashville, summer interns from a local university were used. New York City contracted with an independent, nonprofit firm that, in turn, used ex-addicts and ex-offenders to make the ratings. Any of these approaches seems appropriate, as long as inspectors are properly trained and ratings are periodically checked (as discussed later). This activity might be an excellent use of employees obtained on a short-term basis, perhaps as part of a public employment program.

Can Cleanliness Ratings Be Made for Private Property?

Some governments may want to measure the cleanliness of private property, perhaps as a check on health and litter-code enforcement activities. Nashville used a four-point rating scale for yard cleanliness, and ratings for yard cleanliness and street cleanliness were made for every block face

inspected. Washington, D.C., inspectors made a separate notation of exceptionally bad conditions on private property (litter ratings of 3.0 or worse, or health and fire hazards).

As has been noted, making ratings on private property does slow down the inspection process. It is doubtful that many communities will find a combined cleanliness rating of public and private property useful because the agency responsible for maintaining the cleanliness of public property will probably be different from the one responsible for private property.

What Rating Should Be Set as a Criterion for an "Unsatisfactory" Condition?

As with all measures of effectiveness, the criterion for what constitutes an "unsatisfactory" condition probably should be set by each local government itself. The District of Columbia, Nashville, and St. Petersburg used a rating of "worse than 2.0." (Each had slightly different photographs depicting and written guidelines defining a rating of "2.0.")

Another way to present cleanliness-rating data is to compute average ratings for each area and for the jurisdiction as a whole. New York, Washington, and Nashville officials felt that the percentage of ratings exceeding some level of satisfactory conditions was a more meaningful term than the average litter rating.[25]

Costs and Staffing Requirements for Implementing and Maintaining the Data Collection Procedures

Many factors will affect measurement costs. These include the size of the community, the number of measures for which data are being collected, the fre-

---

24. Samples of this size would enable a government to determine, with a 90-percent confidence level, that the actual percentage of all streets or alleys exceeding a certain rating was within 7 percentage points of the percentage in the sample. A government could conclude that differences of 10 percentage points or more between two samples (inspections in the same area in different years or among different areas) indicated actual differences and not sampling uncertainties. For more details on the sample size to select and test for determining if differences between percentages are statistically significant, see Blair and Schwartz, *How Clean Is Our City?*, particularly pages 65-67.

The amount of resources available will also affect the number of block faces inspected. In the District of Columbia, inspectors have been able to inspect 200 block faces or 75 alleys in a day. However, when a random sample of blocks is selected and inspectors have substantial travel time between inspection points, 30 to 60 block-face or 20 to 40 alley inspections per day (rates similar to those achieved in Nashville) for each inspector or inspection team are probably the most that can be comfortably achieved.

25. The use of an "average" rating has a special technical problem. Results from certain statistical manipulations such as averages can be difficult to interpret because of a nonlinear relationship among grades—that is, the difference in the amount or impact of litter between grades 1 and 2 will not necessarily be the same as that between grades 2 and 3, or 3 and 4. If averages are used, the government officials using them should recognize that they are somewhat artificial. The use of the "average" rating has one advantage over the "percentage" of streets or alleys with an unsatisfactory cleanliness rating. Generally, about thirty block faces would have to be rated in each area to yield a 90-percent confidence that an observed 0.25 difference in average cleanliness condition between two samples reflects an actual difference in average ratings and was not due to "the luck of the draw." This contrasts with about fifty to seventy block faces that would need to be rated to give 90-percent confidence that an observed difference of ten percentage points in the "percentage of blocks with an unsatisfactory rating" (the other version of the measure) was not due to the luck of the draw.

quency of inspections, the number of service districts from which sample blocks or sample households are selected, the intensity of inspection (all blocks or only a sample), the extent to which survey and trained observer operations can be shared among other government agencies, local pay rates, the use or diversion of existing staff rather than out-of-pocket expenses for additional staff or consultants, and the extent of analysis of the data that are collected.

Exhibit 2-6 identifies some of the factors which affect the requirements. Exhibit 2-7 presents some estimates of measurement activity costs for several city sizes and for two basic types of inspections—one involving inspection of a randomly selected sample of streets and alleys and one involving an inspection of virtually all streets and alleys. These include set-up costs such as training inspectors, taking photographs, and preparing inspection forms, maps, and procedure manuals. Costs in succeeding years would be somewhat lower. If more than two sets of inspections are conducted or if a number of conditions (for example, cleanliness of private property, road surface conditions, or street signs) in addition to street and alley cleanliness are rated, or if traffic congestion particularly impedes inspection operations, costs could be substantially higher. Out-of-pocket costs would be reduced to the extent that existing personel can be used.

Exhibit 2-6
COST AND STAFFING FACTORS FOR SOLID WASTE COLLECTION MEASUREMENT

ACTIVITY	STAFF INVESTMENT	ACTIVITY	STAFF INVESTMENT
1. *Set-up:* Selecting measures; establishing neighborhood boundaries; preparing procedures manual, photographs for trained observer ratings, and maps; training staff; establishing data collection and reporting procedures	3 to 4 person-months of staff personnel (possibly 2 to 4 months in addition would be needed to develop data processing capability)	4. *Report preparation:* Preparing a report with tables, charts, and appropriate narrative descriptions of conditions, changes over time, variations among neighborhoods	1 to 2 person-months of time for each report
2. *Trained observer ratings:* • Initial and annual retraining	1 person-week per inspector	5. *Program evaluation and program analysis:* Determining specific causes of problems; developing alternative strategies for more productive collection operations; evaluating performance of special cleaning operations, equipment, programs, and so forth	½ to 1 person (full-time equivalent)
• Inspections, if only a sample is to be inspected	1 inspector-day for every 30 to 60 block faces, or 20 to 40 alleys inspected		
• Inspections, if continuous inspection of all block faces or alleys is wanted	1 inspector-day for every 200 to 250 block faces or every 60 to 90 alleys inspected		
• Supervisory replication of ratings	1 person-day of supervisory time for each 4 to 6 person-days of inspector time		
• Clerical support (setting up and preparing routes, transcribing ratings)	1 person-day of clerical time for each 2 to 3 person-days of inspection time		
3. *Telephone surveying of citizens or businesses:* • Setting up, deciding on questions, making arrangements with other government agency or with private survey firm to carry out (alternatively, training internal staff to conduct)	1 person-week of staff personnel		
• Conducting survey (100 responses per neighborhood or sanitation service area)	$3 to $5 per response (1976 cost estimate) if only for solid waste collection or if prorated among other services in a general citizen survey		

Exhibit 2-7

ESTIMATED ANNUAL COSTS FOR SOLID WASTE COLLECTION MEASUREMENT PROCEDURES[1]

CLASSIFICATION	LOCAL GOVERNMENT DEPARTMENT SIZE		
	SMALL	MEDIUM	LARGE
Population	Less than 250,000	250,000-750,000	More than 750,000
Number of blocks	Less than 1,500	Approximately 5,000	More than 9,000
Number of sanitation employees	100	300	1,500
Refuse collection operating budget	$1.0 million	$4.0 million	$20.0 million
Sample inspection option[2]			
Annual cost	$7,500	$15,000	$20,000
Percentage of operating budget	Less than 1 percent	Less than 1 percent	Less than 1 percent
Person-years of effort	0.25	0.5	1.0
Number of visual inspections	2 sample inspections per year	2 sample inspections per year	2 sample inspections per year
Citizen survey effort	Conducted by other city department (no cost to sanitation department)	Conducted by other city department (no cost to sanitation department)	Conducted by other city department (no cost to sanitation department)
Complete inspection option[3]			
Annual cost	$30,000	$45,000	$75,000
Percentage of operating budget	3 percent	1 percent	Under 1 percent
Person-years of effort	2	3	5
Number of visual inspections	2 complete inspections per year	2 complete inspections per year	2 complete inspections per year
Citizen survey description	By sanitation department telephone survey of 400 households	By sanitation department telephone survey of 600 households	By sanitation department telephone survey of 1,000 households

1. The costs shown include set-up costs (such as developing procedures and training inspectors) as well as regular measurement activities. Costs in succeeding years would be somewhat lower.
2. This option assumes that only a randomly selected sample of streets and alleys would be inspected.
3. This option assumes that all streets and alleys would be inspected.

Chapter 3
Solid Waste Disposal

The effectiveness measures of solid waste disposal presented in this chapter are intended to cover the environmental impacts, both physical and aesthetic, of solid waste disposal processes. The effects of such disposal services on the public are somewhat different from those of the other services discussed in this volume. Because most disposal takes place at relatively isolated sites, only those few persons living, working, or traveling near the sites are exposed visually and aesthetically to disposal operations.[1] However, certain potential environmental effects are of concern to the whole community.

Performance measurement in solid waste disposal has tended to focus on comparisons with established practices of site selection and facility operation. These are appropriate management concerns, but they do not in themselves indicate the actual environmental effects of solid waste disposal on the community. For example, current local government assessment procedures generally call for noting the presence or absence of screens to reduce problems with paper that blows away. However, those procedures do not focus on the actual visibility of blown paper at the site periphery. Similarly, other procedures call for noting the presence of proper site grading and appropriate drainage channels, but until recently these procedures rarely required actual measurement of the water quality of site runoff. Regular, direct measurement of these effects does not occur in most communities.

1. Solid waste collection activities, which are directly observable by most citizens, are discussed in Chapter 2.

Objectives of Solid Waste Disposal

Following is the statement of solid waste disposal objectives used to identify appropriate effectiveness measures in this report:

To provide for solid waste disposal in a safe, environmentally sound, and aesthetically acceptable manner.[2]

The next section summarizes the major recommendations, followed by more detailed discussion of the individual measures.

Principal Recommendations for Measuring Solid Waste Disposal Effectiveness

The complete list of suggested measures is shown in Exhibit 3-1, while Exhibit 3-2 shows a format for

2. Recycling is not included. This is because the short-term evaluation of recycling tends to be expressed in terms of efficiency and profitability rather than in terms of impacts on the environment. Further, the long-term values of recycling—extended landfill life, reduced energy usage, and reduced pressure on natural resources—tend to be spread over so long a period of time and to involve so many controversies over true costs and benefits that no annual local measurement procedure is likely to be adequate. A measure of the degree of recycling is suggested, but the larger question of the relative value of various levels of recycling has been left to later analysis by other interested parties.

Exhibit 3-1
EFFECTIVENESS MEASURES FOR SOLID WASTE DISPOSAL SERVICES

OVERALL OBJECTIVE: To provide for solid waste disposal in a safe, environmentally sound, and aesthetically acceptable manner.

OBJECTIVE	QUALITY CHARACTERISTIC	SPECIFIC MEASURE	DATA COLLECTION PROCEDURE
Environmental Soundness	Impact on groundwater (for operations involving land disposal)	1. Number of days per year that tests for leaching indicated imminent danger to nearby groundwater users.	Chemical testing of water quality characteristics affected by leaching
	Impact on surfacewater (for operations involving land disposal)	2a. If landfill runoff is captured and treated before release: Number of days per year that landfill runoff released to nearby bodies of water failed to meet standards on quality. *or* 2b. If landfill runoff is not captured and treated before release: Number of days per year that any body of water in the community failed to satisfy quality standards for its class, due to landfill runoff contamination.	Chemical tests of landfill runoff
	Impact on groundwater and surface water (for operations involving land disposal)	3. Number of sites of previous groundwater or surface water use rendered unusable by contamination from landfill sites.	Department or city records
	Impact on air (for operations involving controlled burning)	4. Number of presumed days per year that stack emissions from incinerators exceeded federal or state standards.	Automated monitoring or periodic inspections
		5. Number and percentage of trained observer site inspections that detected smoke, dust, or ash problems, for all sites and for each site.	Trained observer ratings
		6. Number of valid complaints per year about smoke, dust, ash, or other airborne emissions from solid waste disposal sites.	Agency records
	Extent of recycling	7. Number of pounds and percentage of all waste, by weight, reused for productive purposes.	Agency records on sites with recycling operations
Aesthetics	Appearance, odors, and noise around disposal sites	8. Number and percentage of all trained observer site inspections that detected odor, noise, or appearance problems attributable to site, for all sites, and for each site, overall and by type of problem.	Trained observer ratings. A "problem" is a rating of 3 or more on a four-point scale

(Exhibit continued on next page)

Exhibit 3-1 continued

OBJECTIVE	QUALITY CHARACTERISTIC	SPECIFIC MEASURE	DATA COLLECTION PROCEDURE
Aesthetics (continued)		9. Number of valid citizen complaints per year on odor, noise, and appearance problems arising from site.	Agency records
Safety	Safety hazards and pest control	10. Number and percentage of all trained observer site inspections that detected problems with pests, health hazards, or other hazards, for all sites and for each site, overall and by type of problem.	Trained observer ratings
	Safety incidents	11. Number of incidents of citizen injury and damage requiring repair or replacement of citizen property.	Tabulation of reports of such incidents to department
Overall Site Conditions		12. Number and percentage of all trained observer site inspections that detected any of the problems considered in Measures 5, 8, and 10.	Trained observer ratings

displaying data for those measures. Principal suggestions are as follows:

- A variety of technical tests seem highly desirable to measure the effects of disposal operations on ground and surface water. Currently, these impacts appear to be checked only irregularly by most local governments. To summarize the results of these tests for public officials, measures are suggested such as "the number of days a problem condition was known to have existed" (Measures 1 and 2), and one relating to the extent of real damage caused by contamination (Measure 3). Measures 1 and 2 focus on the duration of hazardous conditions, while Measure 3 focuses on their severity. Because this type of testing has yet to be perfected, it may often be hard to identify minor problems, but severe ones can be spotted.

- Regular inspection of each disposal site by trained observers is recommended as a means of obtaining ratings of air quality conditions (the presence of smoke, dust, and ashes); aesthetic conditions (unsightly appearance, odors, or noise) and safety conditions (pests, other health hazards). The sample rating scales presented here have been shown to be understandable by a small test group of sani-

tation officials, but local governments will want to review any scales they use with their own personnel.

The scales presented have not been tested for reliability in practice—in other words, to discover if ratings of the same factor at the same place by two independent observers are sufficiently similar. Thus, local governments wanting to use the procedures will need to provide for a test period prior to actual use to check their reliability and, if necessary, revise the scales. For regular use, local governments should provide (a) training in the use of the procedures for trained observers and (b) periodic checks of each inspector's ratings by another "judge" to assure the continued reliability of the observers.

Individual Measures

The measures are grouped for discussion into four categories as follows:

- Environmental soundness (Measures 1-7);
- Aesthetics (Measures 8-9);
- Safety (Measures 10-11); and
- Overall site conditions (Measure 12).

Exhibit 3-2

ILLUSTRATIVE SUMMARY REPORT: SOLID WASTE DISPOSAL SERVICES

EFFECTIVENESS MEASURE	THIS QUARTER	THIS YEAR TO DATE	ANNUAL TARGET	YEAR TO DATE AS PERCENTAGE OF TARGET	SAME QUARTER LAST YEAR	LAST YEAR TO DATE
1. Number of days of leaching danger evidence (a) Landfill A (b) Landfill B (c) Overall (Measure 1)						
2. Number of days of contamination evidence at surface water or runoff test points (a) Landfill A (b) Landfill B (c) Overall (Measure 2)						
3. Number of water sites where previous use was curtailed by contamination evidence (a) Landfill A (b) Landfill B (c) Overall (Measure 3)						
4. Number of days of stack emission violations (incinerator) (Measure 4)						
5. Number of valid complaints—smoke, dust, odors, appearance, etc. (Measures 6 and 9)						
6. (a) Number of pounds recycled (b) Percentage of pounds recycled (Measure 7)						
7. Number of incidents of citizen injury or damage to citizen property (Measure 11)						
8. Percentage of inspections of disposal sites that found pollution, aesthetic, or safety problems (a) Landfill A (b) Landfill B (c) Incinerator (d) Overall (Measure 12)						

NOTE: Measures 5, 8, and 10 are not included in this summary because they are covered on another form (see Exhibit 3-4).

Measures Related to Environmental Soundness

Impacts on Ground and Surface Water (Measures 1-3)

Measure 1:   *Number of days per year that tests for leaching[3] indicated imminent danger to nearby groundwater users.*

Measure 2a: *If landfill runoff is captured and treated before release: Number of days per year that landfill runoff released to nearby bodies of water failed to meet standards on quality.*

or 2b: *If landfill runoff is not captured and treated before release: Number of days per year that any body of water in the community failed to satisfy quality standards for its class due to landfill runoff contamination.*

Measure 3:   *Number of sites of previous ground or surface water use rendered unusable by contamination from landfill sites.*

These measures apply to land disposal techniques. Measures 1 and 2 each call for an annual sum of "violation days"—the number of days between the first test showing a problem and the first subsequent test showing no evidence of a problem. (Note that the "number of days" form does not imply daily testing. Periods of up to a week or more will be required to complete some tests, and daily testing is not needed for most characteristics.)

A measure in this form is a conservative estimate of the duration of the problem, since there will be no way to know exactly how long the contamination was present before the "unacceptable" test result showed up. The criteria for an unacceptable test result for Measure 1 should take account of the contaminants, strengths at the test point, the speed and direction in which goundwater is moving at that point, and the distance to the nearest point of groundwater use. (Generally, only the contaminants' strengths and the speed of movement will change from one test to the next.) Our project did not develop or test these criteria, but most local officials should be able to develop such standards for their sites, with the aid of technical personnel from the

U.S. Geological Survey (USGS).

These criteria must be tailored to the particular circumstances of each site, and they should make use of a background survey of groundwater quality before creation of the disposal site, if possible. The criteria for an unacceptable test result for Measure 2 will be based on set standards for the same contamination-related water quality characteristics as in Measure 1 plus, in the case of Measure 2b, some specified procedure for identifying the source of contamination. Exhibit 3-3 shows how a calculation of violation-days might be made.

The "number of days" measure represents a departure from current practice in local government. This recommended change is motivated by the belief that for these kinds of effects the *duration* of undesirable conditions is usually more important than the *degree* of contamination.

In addition, the "number of days unacceptable" measure is recommended over that of "percentage of tests failed" because the former appears to be better designed to give comparable results across different testing frequencies. Nevertheless, one drawback of a measure in this or any similar form is that its values are sensitive to the frequency of measurement. This fact raises a serious validity problem; managers could improve their probable ratings by reducing the frequency of measurement, thereby endangering the community. This incentive occurs because the period of time (of unknown length) that unacceptable conditions existed before they were discovered is not charged against the agency's performance.

On the other hand, if the entire period prior to the test showing a problem (back to the time of the last test that showed no problem) were counted as a violation, there would be an incentive to make measurements *more* frequently than is necessary or desirable. Still, the less frequent the measurement, the less valid and meaningful the measure will be. Recommended measurement frequencies were not identified in this project and will likely depend upon local conditions, such as soil permeability.

None of the suggested measures has been used on a regular basis in a local government, although they have been used in special studies. In recent years, the USGS and several state health departments have been putting more emphasis on the need for positive proof that groundwater and surface water near landfills is not contaminated. Realizing the gaps that exist in present knowledge about the leaching of pollutants into groundwater, the USGS has, in the past few years, installed experimental test wells in a number of landfills serving areas with high water tables. These wells have been checked

3. Leaching is the process by which moisture in the waste, or rain water infiltrating through the soil cover and the waste, may carry contaminants through the underlying soil into groundwater below and around a landfill. Water contamination characteristics attributed to leaching include changes in five-day biological oxygen demand (BOD_5), coliform count, dissolved solids, conductance, and alkalinity.

Exhibit 3-3
AN EXAMPLE OF HOW TO CALCULATE MEASURES OF "NUMBER OF DAYS OUTSIDE ACCEPTABLE CONDITIONS"

TEST FOR LEAD CONTAMINATION OF RUNOFF

January

Date	1	2	3	4	5	6	7	8	9	10	11	12	13	14	15	16	17	18
Reading	.01							.06	.06	.04	.03				.07	.06	.05	.03
Did test show satisfactory conditions?	Yes							No	No	Yes	Yes				No	No	Yes	Yes
Cumulative number of violation-days during the year								1	2						3	4		

Scenario: Normally, testing is performed weekly with a standard for lead contamination of 0.05 mg/liter. The test on January 8 showed a violation. Steps were taken to cure the problem; at the same time, the testing schedule was accelerated to monitor the success of corrective actions. The January 9 test still showed violation, but the test on the following day indicated that the standard was again being met. The days on which the last test showed a violation are January 8 and 9, leading to a value of "two days." Subsequent tests on January 15 and 16 revealed contamination and two more violation-days.

several times a year for evidence of leaching, but there has been little effort to move from these experiments to a systematic measurement program for general use in decision making.

The chemical test procedures required by the measures have been tested and used extensively and can be considered reliable, within the limits indicated by the APHA's *Standard Methods*.[4]

Almost all states now have standards for the quality of their bodies of water; these could be used for Measure 2b. A few states have recently added the requirement that all runoff into those bodies of water meet the standards of the receiving body of water; this could be used for Measure 2a.[5] The standards generally are based on the U.S. Class 1, 2, and 3 system, which specifies the water quality required for certain uses (for example, fishing compared to no fishing).

The two versions of Measure 2 are somewhat interchangeable. Measure 2b provides a better

4. American Public Health Association, *Standard Methods for the Examination of Water and Wastewater,* 13th ed. (Washington, D.C.: American Public Health Association, 1971).

5. The particular quality characteristics of concern include coliform, BOD₅, and suspended solids. It is necessary to take account of mixing because contaminated runoff may be well mixed into receiving bodies of water before any contact or use occurs. In contrast, leaching into groundwater involves the percolation of contaminants into the water across a broad front without substantial opportunity for mixing. State codes vary considerably as to how much mixing is permitted before the water quality criteria must be met.

measure of actual impact, but it involves much greater problems of control and interpretation, including the issue of deciding whether, or to what extent, solid waste site runoff is to blame for existing conditions. This measure will involve checking the effluent streams of all sources that might have contributed to the problem, so that particular pollutants found in source effluents and at the point of use can be correlated. Even then, a positive determination of the cause of problems may not be possible, in which case a government may need to press for improvements in effluents from all possible sources of the problem.

By comparison, Measure 2a (condition of runoff water from landfills) gives a poorer picture of direct citizen impact because the runoff is not directly re-used; but this measure does vastly simplify the problem of attributing responsibility for existing conditions.

Both Measures 1 and 2 use the same battery of tests on water samples; they differ only as to the points at which those samples are taken. The Environmental Protection Agency (EPA) estimated in 1973 that this battery of tests would take about four employee-hours for any one location, once the samples are in the lab. EPA prices the tests at $30 in 1973 (or about $40 in 1976 figures) using the personnel cost formulas and materials costs prevailing at EPA labs.

The actual cost to a particular local government

will depend on how it has its tests done (for example, in its own lab or through contracts with local private labs or USGS facilities). Local costs may be much higher than the EPA figures, but the employee-hour figures should apply generally. The annual lab-test cost for weekly testing of Measures 1 and 2, assuming seven test wells[6] for groundwater and one test site to sample landfill runoff, would be ten employee-months, for an estimated total cost (employee time and materials) of about $17,000 in 1976 dollars. Additional test wells or additional samples from runoff points would mean higher costs.

There also may be start-up costs for (1) Measure 1 in placing the test well (an estimated $1,000 to $5,000 depending upon the depth required to reach the water table and the nature of the material that must be drilled through), and for (2) Measures 1 and 2 in acquiring chemical testing equipment (which may cost up to $100,000), although most local governments will already have established their own test labs or made contracts with local private labs to perform other tests—those needed by the water, sewer, health, or environmental protection services.

These costs may seem high, but this information is essential to the safe operation of a disposal site, and the collection of much of it is, or probably soon will be, required by law. The added cost of converting the information to the form of these measures for easy managerial review is slight. If standards for surface water contamination do not exist or are judged to be too loose, standards will have to be set—possibly those of a neighboring state can be borrowed—before test results can be interpreted.

Measure 3 is a crude gauge of the ultimate impact of failures to control water pollution at solid waste disposal sites. The measure calls for a tally of the number of sites where previous use of either groundwater (for example, wells on a nearby farmer's property that are used for water supply) or surface water (for example, a creek running through a landfill and nearby farm property or a lake located near the site) has rendered the sites unusable because of contamination. The judgment as to "unusability" may be made by applying specified water quality criteria for the use involved.

Testing of nearby water use sites could be either a regular part of the city's performance measurement activities or a special act triggered by certain findings at the solid waste disposal site test wells and test runoff-sampling points. If readings at those points indicated danger, the endangered water use

site would be tested; otherwise it would not. This would obviate the problem of trying to conduct regular testing on private property.

Impacts on Air (Measures 4-6)

Measure 4:   *Number of presumed days per year that stack emissions from incinerators exceeded federal or state standards.*

Measure 5:   *Number and percentage of trained observer site inspections that detected smoke, dust, or ash problems for all sites and for each site.*

Measure 6:   *Number of valid complaints per year about smoke, dust, ash, or other airborne emissions from solid waste disposal sites.*

Each of these measures covers a somewhat different aspect of the problem. Measure 4 applies only to incinerator disposal facilities, while Measures 5 and 6 apply to both incinerator and landfill disposal sites.

The development of procedures for Measure 4 has been hampered by the lack of an inexpensive, reliable way of measuring stack emissions. At present, data for this measure cannot be collected at a reasonable cost, and the technology required for daily monitoring of particulates is in the developmental stage. The only generally available equipment must be attached to the incinerator stacks; this process involves several days and several thousand dollars.[7] Standards do exist for stack emissions of both particulates and sulfur oxides, though both sets of standards were developed primarily for use at power plants. Because refuse generally is low in sulfur content and because no simple procedure exists for measuring it, no regular measurement of this characteristic is recommended.

Many local governments may want to await the development of new technology and thus will prefer to use Measures 5 and 6 to keep track of visible emissions until that new technology becomes available. The cost of collecting data for Measure 4 will depend on the ultimate output of current developmental research.

Measure 5 is included to provide a reliable indicator of disposal site smoke, dust, and ash problems.

6. Multiple test wells are needed to gauge the speed and direction of leachate flow and to keep track of how well the groundwater is cleaning itself as it moves away from the site.

7. An alternative procedure of untested validity and reliability would be to measure the ambient air quality in the vicinity of the incinerator, using the concentration of particulates per cubic meter as the measure and the EPA ambient air quality standards for reference.

Data are collected by the trained observer inspection procedure described later in this chapter. The form of Measure 5 presented here omits two factors: the duration of problems (which might be captured by converting to a measure such as "number of days after trained observers detected problems until inspections showed these problems were corrected") and the size of the population affected by the problems (which would be hard to capture but might be handled to some extent by indicating what proportion of the site's observation points[8] revealed problems). Only experience will indicate whether these aspects need to be incorporated into the measures in order for those gauges to be meaningful. Information on costs and testing experience is discussed later.

The trained observer inspections for smoke, dust, and ash examine only the visible aspects of these airborne pollutants. Hence, such inspections, when used at incinerator sites, do not adequately substitute for direct tests of stack emissions for particulates (see Measure 4).

Measure 6 requires that tallies of valid complaints on smoke, dust, or ash problems be routed annually to a central location. This measure, along with Measure 9, is not expressed in terms of complaint rates per 1,000 population (as is done with complaint measures in other services) because there are likely to be a very few complaints in a year. Also, the geographic isolation of most disposal sites makes it less likely that the number of complaints will grow with the population. At any rate, the cost of this procedure should be fairly low.

Validation of citizen complaints will involve efforts by agency personnel to determine whether the facts are as stated by the complainant and particularly whether problems result from a solid waste disposal site. Validation may involve asking about the color or odor of emissions in order to check out the possible sources. If the complaint refers to a continuing problem or one occurring at the time of the complaint, validation may involve a direct inspection by agency personnel for confirmation.

A complaint probably should be counted as valid unless it is proved invalid. Many local governments have some kind of validation procedure for this kind of data, and some already provide regular tallies on such complaints. However, these tallies do not seem sufficient because they are subject to various biases, including the reluctance of some citizens to use the complaint process, the problem of chronic complainers, and citizen confusion about how to use the complaint process. These problems render complaint

8. See Appendix 4 for a discussion of the procedure for clarifying what the observation points are.

tallies unreliable as sole indicators of problems.[9] At the same time, it appears likely that substantial changes in the number of valid complaints generally will be associated with changes in underlying conditions, making a regular complaint tally appropriate as a general indicator.[10] For years the two test cities involved in this study had received no complaints about air pollution originating at disposal sites. The limited trained observer inspection tests undertaken also did not find any air pollution problems there.

Extent of Recycling (Measure 7)

Measure 7: Number of pounds and percentage of all waste, by weight, reused for productive purposes.

Recycling objectives are very difficult to express in terms that lend themselves to annual measurement by a local government. Measure 7 provides information on the amount of recycling; these data may then be interpreted according to any context deemed appropriate by local officials. However, that context could at least include relevant information on the availability of local markets for the recycled material. Officials are also likely to want to use additional measures, such as the net cost or profit from recycling.[11]

Obtaining data for this measure should not be difficult because figures on the total weights of waste recycled and disposed of by other means are sometimes available as part of the routine accounting records for the site involved. But estimates of the percentage of wastes recycled by material type are seldom recorded. Therefore, breakdowns on nonrecycled waste, by weight and type of material, probably should be estimated so that percentages of waste recycled may be calculated for each material type.[12]

9. It is also true that some potentially dangerous airborne pollutants are not detectable by the citizens' unaided senses. Only Measure 4, which is not yet feasible, will overcome that problem.

10. See Chapter 11 for suggestions on the use of complaint measures.

11. There is some controversy as to whether recycling operations should be required to make money or break even and, if so, over what time period and with what cost formula. Although many local governments conduct some recycling operations, very few treat them as sources of revenue and those that do often use an incomplete cost picture. In any event, our approach has been to treat recycling as valuable in itself; its economies are not the subject of this report.

12. Such estimates would require some periodic (probably quarterly at most) sampling of refuse composition, but this sampling should not require more than a few employee-days per sample, given the relatively broad categories to be used. (The city of Los Angeles, for example, performs weekly analyses of a sample of all refuse collected, at a cost of about two employee-days per analysis. A sample consists of a truckload from a specified area.)

Effects of Aesthetics Around Disposal Sites (Measures 8 and 9)

Measure 8: Number and percentage of all trained observer site inspections that detected odor, noise, or appearance problems attributable to site, for all sites and for each site, overall and by type of problem.

Measure 9: Number of valid citizen complaints per year on odor, noise, and appearance problems arising from site.

These measurements are inherently difficult because of the subjectivity of any aesthetic judgment.

The approach suggested for Measure 8 is to use trained observer procedures that can produce reliable data on the presence or absence of objectionable odors, noises, and visible objects, such as blowing paper. The same basic inspection procedure used to obtain data for Measure 5 would be applied here; the details of the procedures are discussed at the end of this chapter. As with Measure 5, neither the duration nor the population affected is captured by this form of the measure.

Measure 9 requires that complaints be handled and validated, as in Measure 6. The cost of this process should be fairly low. The number of complaints alone does not appear sufficient to measure site aesthetics because citizens differ widely in their sensitivity to particular odors, noises, and sights. They also differ tremendously in their willingness to register a formal complaint when they find some condition unacceptable.[13] Finally, in the tests of this procedure the places around the disposal site that had poor ratings on odors, noise, or appearance affected only citizens in moving vehicles, and there is reason to believe people are less inclined to complain about momentary annoyances experienced while driving.

Safety Impacts (Measures 10 and 11)

Measure 10: Number and percentage of all trained observer site inspections that detected problems with pests, health hazards, or other hazards, for all sites and for each site, overall and by type of problem.

Measure 11: Number of incidents of citizen injury and damage requiring repair or replacement to citizen property. (Separate on-site incidents and off-site incidents attributed to site operations.)

Measures 10 and 11 reflect the presence of potential hazards that could lead to injuries or damage. These measures can be used to suggest the need for preventive action to government officials.

Data for Measure 10 would be collected using the same trained observer procedures required for Measures 5 and 8; these procedures are discussed at the end of this chapter. As with Measures 5 and 8, Measure 10 does not indicate the duration of problems nor the size of the population affected. However, as noted previously, variations can be constructed that may reflect these aspects if experience indicates this is desirable.

The incidents of citizen injury or property damage to be included to Measure 11 include not only the familiar incidents of children injured by hazardous objects on the site or cars damaged by the roughness of access roads to citizen dumping areas, but also such off-site incidents as the following: rat infestations of private property that are traceable to the site; traffic accidents at or near the site entrance that are caused by sanitation vehicle drivers; waterborne infections contracted from water polluted by site leaching or runoff; and airplane encounters with gulls drawn to the site. Because such incidents are likely to be few in number and because comparability across different kinds of incidents is very difficult to establish, it generally will be useful to have the incidents listed on backup material to the measures, along with notes on any corrective actions taken or settlements made. A special problem here is that, as with complaints, citizens may choose not to report such instances for a variety of reasons.

The collection of data for Measure 11 requires tabulation and, if necessary, validation of reported conditions. Because the number of incidents is likely to be very small in any given year, the cost of collecting data should be quite low. In the two test cities, no incidents had occurred within the range of the officials' memories. However, cities that still use open dumps or permit the use of disposal sites by private citizens are more likely to have such incidents and to be concerned with tracking the values for this measure.[14]

---

13. An alternative we have recommended for other municipal services is to include service-related questions in a general citizen survey. However, we do not recommend that questions relating to disposal sites be included because a citywide sample of citizens would probably contain too few citizens living near or driving past disposal sites to provide valid or significant results.

14. Local governments should consider the continued use of measures that consistently indicate no problem, particularly if the data-collecting costs are small. Such measures help assure a more balanced picture of service performance than will occur if only measures showing problems are reported.

Overall Disposal Site Conditions

Measure 12: Number and percentage of all trained observer site inspections that detected any of the problems considered in Measures 5, 8, and 10.

This summary measure covers all site problems checked for in trained observer inspections—smoke, dust, ash, odors, noise, unsightly appearance, pests, and other health and safety hazards. If a problem with even one of these characteristics occurred, the measure would register a problem inspection. As with Measures 5, 8, and 10, Measure 12 does not reflect the duration of the problem or the population affected, but it may be modified to do so. This measure could be used to pinpoint problem sites.

The basic data for this measure would be obtained from the trained observer site inspection procedures used for Measures 5, 8, and 10.

Other Measures

The following two measures were considered but have not been included in the suggested set of measures because of severe difficulty in problem definition, and in data collection and interpretation. However, some governments may want to consider these measures.

1. *Number of fires and number of fire-days per year at landfills.*

Because fires at landfills are generally evidence of poor management and because uncontrolled fires can cause pollution, the number of fires per year and the number of days when fires occur (or fire-days) per year are of potential importance. However, fires vary greatly in both their spread and their impacts on citizens. They may be ignited by hot or smoldering refuse just brought in; in such cases, the fire is usually small, quickly extinguished, and of little or no consequence to citizens. Some landfills burn dead vegetation, using controlled-burning devices such as "air curtain destructors," which are designed to keep smoke and other airborne pollutants from escaping. Such devices, when sanctioned by local health officials, can prevent vast, uncontrolled fires at dumps.

Finally, there is the problem of collecting the data. Unless an independent observer is stationed at the site to check for fires, the records would have to be kept by landfill personnel, who might be inclined to minimize the number of fires reported. Hence, it is suggested that fire detection be handled through trained observer procedures and citizen complaints (see Measure 5). Some local governments may also wish to track the number of citations for fires made by local health authorities, who may conduct inspections matching those of the trained observers in frequency. These health inspections would provide another source of data on fires at landfills.

2. *Number of years of expected lifetime remaining at currently owned solid waste disposal sites.*

This is not a measure of current impact, but one that may reflect future impact. The measure is of interest because of the long lead times required to select and acquire appropriate new sites for solid waste disposal. Because this gauge does not measure current performance and depends on forecasting highly variable trends, it is not recommended here. However, if adopted by a city, the measure would involve projecting a figure such as the tons per week expected over time (possibly assuming a fixed percentage growth in population and waste per person); converting that figure to cubic yards by using the compression ratios being achieved; and comparing the result with the amount of space available. Aerial photographs also could be used to determine the use of space in a landfill site over time.

The Trained Observer Rating Procedure at Disposal Sites

Trained observer ratings are called for in Measures 5, 8, 10, and 12. The general requirements for trained observer operations, discussed in more detail in Chapter 13, are applicable here in the solid waste disposal area, particularly in terms of the following steps:

- Developing and documenting standards that specifically define each of the values or ratings of the conditions to be measured, and

- Developing and documenting procedures to select rating locations.

This section presents a number of suggestions for local governments to use in establishing trained observer rating systems for solid waste disposal services. However, each government will probably want to adopt its own set of procedures and standards to reflect local conditions, with these suggestions serving as a starting point.

These procedures and guidelines have been developed and given some testing for feasibility in St.

Exhibit 3-4
ILLUSTRATIVE FORMAT: RESULTS OF TRAINED OBSERVER RATINGS
AT SOLID WASTE DISPOSAL SITES
(ABC Landfill)

CHARACTERISTIC	RATINGS OF 3 OR WORSE[1]						RATINGS OF 4[1]					
	THIS QUARTER		TWELVE-MONTH FLOATING TOTAL[2]		PREVIOUS YEAR FLOATING TOTAL[2]		THIS QUARTER		TWELVE-MONTH FLOATING TOTAL		PREVIOUS YEAR FLOATING TOTAL	
	Number	Percent	Number	Percent	Number	Percent	Number	Percent	Number	Percent	Number	Percent
Cleanliness of areas near site												
Appearance of site from areas nearby												
Presence of odors near site												
Presence of noise near site												
Presence of at least one of the above aesthetic problems (Measure 8)												
Smoke, dust, or ash (Measure 5)												
Pests												
Health hazards												
Other hazards												
The presence of pests or hazards of some kind (Measure 10)												
The presence of at least one of the above conditions (Measure 12)												

1. An inspection gets a rating of 3 or worse on a particular characteristic when any of the areas on or near the site where that characteristic is checked are rated 3 or worse. The inspections with ratings of 4 are defined similarly.
2. The twelve-month floating total covers all inspections in the twelve-month period ending this quarter. The previous year floating total covers all inspections in the twelve-month period ending this quarter last year.

Exhibit 3-5
TRAINED OBSERVER RATING SCALES AT SOLID WASTE DISPOSAL SITES

CHARACTERISTIC	RATING SCALE
1. Cleanliness of areas near site	1.0 to 4.0, based on photographic standards (see Chapter 2 for details).
2. Appearance of site from areas nearby	1.0 View from the perimeter point has no unattractive features of the disposal site in foreground; any unattractive features are visible only in the distant background. ("Unattractive features" are any of the items listed in the definitions of ratings 2, 3, and 4 as unattractive.) 2.0 The only unattractive features in view are raw earth or sanitation trucks. 3.0 Sanitation equipment (excluding trucks) can be seen either parked or in motion, or queues of sanitation equipment trucks delivering refuse to the site can be seen extending outside the site perimeters into areas of substantial general traffic. 4.0 Uncovered refuse (loose or in bags or containers) or blowing paper can be seen.
3. Odors	1.0 No odor detectable. 2.0 Odor detected could be from site but cannot be confirmed; or is part of pattern of similar odors and is not principal component. 3.0 Odor detected, confirmed as principally coming from site, but not offensive enough to cause an individual to take steps to avoid it. 4.0 Odor detected, confirmed as principally coming from site, and is offensive enough to cause an individual to seek to avoid it.
4. Noise	1.0 No noise detectable. 2.0 Noise detected could be from site but cannot be confirmed; or site noise is part of pattern of similar noise and is not principal component. 3.0 Noise detected, confirmed as principally coming from site, but is not offensive enough to cause an individual to take steps to avoid it. 4.0 Noise detected, confirmed as principally coming from site, and is offensive enough to cause an individual to seek to avoid it.
5. Smoke, dust, and ash	1.0 No blowing dust, no burning; for incinerator sites, no ashes stored in exposed places or in open containers where they can be blown by winds. 2.0 No blowing dust, no visible smoke escaping from area of burning operation (defined as five feet from burning material); for incinerators, some ashes stored in exposed places or open containers where they could be blown by winds but no ashes currently being blown. 3.0 Considerable blowing dust, or some visible smoke does escape area of burning operation; or for incinerators, intermittent blowing dust, ash, or visible smoke. 4.0 Visible smoke is escaping from burning area continuously or almost continuously; for incinerators, blowing dust or ash or visible smoke is in evidence continuously or whenever wind blows.
6. Pests	1.0 No evidence of rats or insects. 2.0 Evidence of insects but no evidence of rats. 3.0 Evidence of rats but no rats seen. 4.0 Rats seen.
7. Health hazards	1.0 No uncovered wastes. 2.0 A few scattered items, but no uncovered food waste, toxic wastes, dead animals, or bulky goods providing potential shelter for pests. 3.0 A few scattered items of uncovered, unprocessed[1] waste including food waste, toxic wastes, dead animals, or some bulky goods providing potential shelter for pests. 3.5 For landfill: widespread uncovered waste, but no piles of wastes and most of the ground is visible; for incineration: widespread, uncovered, unprocessed[1] waste, but no piles of waste and most of the ground is visible. 4.0 Uncovered or (for incineration) unprocessed[1] wastes either cover large areas of the ground or are in piles.

(Exhibit continued on next page)

Exhibit 3-5 continued

CHARACTERISTIC	RATING SCALE
8. Other hazards	1.0 Restricted area.
	2.0 Unrestricted area but no hazards.
	3.0 Unrestricted area with some hazards but none likely to lead to serious injury. Hazards included are small amounts of broken glass, metal furniture, and other structures; and improper or inadequate directions on access roads used by citizens, but no hazards likely to lead to damage, even if citizens inadvertently ride over or walk on them.
	4.0 Unrestricted area with some hazards capable of leading to serious injury. Hazards included are refrigerators with doors still attached, places where steep falls to the sludge bed are possible for citizens disposing of refuse on their own, uncontrolled fires, large amounts of broken glass, and rusty nails.

1. Unprocessed wastes require same-day covering with earth to prevent insect and rodent problems. Wastes processed through incineration or milling, by contrast, may often be disposed of without the need for daily earth covering.

Petersburg, Florida, Nashville, Tennessee, and Fairfax County, Virginia. A government using these procedures will need to test their reliability to assure that local inspectors are able to make ratings with sufficient reliability.

The trained observer inspections are aimed at obtaining ratings on the following characteristics: the presence of airborne emissions such as smoke, dust, and ash (for Measure 5); the presence of odors, noise, or unsightly appearance (for Measure 8); and the presence of pests and other health and safety hazards (for Measure 10). Exhibit 3-4 illustrates how the trained observer ratings might be summarized for management use. Note that the format used assumed that ratings are reported quarterly.

The inspection procedure consists of two parts: (1) an external inspection of the entrance and selected perimeter points around the disposal or incineration area (to obtain ratings on appearance, odors, and noise), and (2) an internal inspection of the landfill or incineration area (to obtain ratings on other characteristics).

Exhibit 3-5 indicates the candidate rating scales for the inspections. Details on the trained observer rating procedures are presented in Appendix 4.

Frequency of Trained Observer Inspections

The principal considerations in determining frequency are the cost per inspection, the variable impact of weather, and the variability in ratings from one inspection to another. High temperatures, high humidities, and high winds all tend to aggravate one or more of the problems associated with disposal operations, such as odors or blowing dust and paper. If inspections are made once every two weeks or more frequently, there will probably be sufficient variety in weather conditions to provide an overall picture of site conditions. However, if inspections are made monthly, quarterly, or annually, weather conditions

should be considered in setting the times of inspections. (A procedure for accounting for weather is given in Appendix 4.)

If conditions vary considerably over time, more inspections will be required to obtain an accurate, representative overall assessment of the site than will be required if the ratings vary only slightly from inspection to inspection. To take account of this factor, the initial inspections might be done on a weekly basis, followed by a shift to less frequent inspections if the range of ratings over the initial period is narrow.[15]

Trained Observer Costs

In the four brief trials of this procedure, landfill inspections never required more than about two hours (and generally much less time), with much of that time taken up in transit to perimeter points. St. Petersburg continued using the procedure after the test, as discussed below, and found that the observers continued to require only one and one-half to two hours in the field per inspection. Inspection of incineration sites also should not take longer than two hours. The time required to perform and record the observations at each of the perimeter points and at the operation within the facilities will be only a few minutes.

The estimated annual cost per site for performing trained observer inspections once every two weeks, as suggested in this chapter, is about thirteen employee-days, assuming that the disposal sites are reasonably close to the jurisdiction concerned. Analytical and clerical time will be addi-

15. For example, the rule might be that if initial ratings varied by no more than two steps and if at least half of the ratings were within one step of the average rating, then one rating every two weeks or possibly less would be sufficient. If the ratings varied by as much as three steps or if at least half of the ratings were more than one step away from the average rating, weekly or even semiweekly ratings could be undertaken.

tional and will probably bring the total to about thirty employee-days per site. The precise cost will depend upon the size and remoteness of a disposal site and the dispersion of its activities.

Trained Observer Procedure Testing

Four brief trials of the trained observer procedures were undertaken. These were at four different landfills in three different localities (St. Petersburg, Nashville, and Fairfax County). The first three tests were aimed primarily at refining the detailed rating scales and procedures.

The fourth test, conducted at the St. Petersburg landfill, involved four employees of the city's environmental sanitation department who already were serving as trained observers rating street cleanliness and had a few months' experience in that activity. A training session of about two hours' duration was held to acquaint them with the measurement procedures.

Each of the four observers made independent ratings. No disagreements arose in the internal inspection phase. However, differences in ratings did occur at two of the four perimeter points, once each on the appearance, odor, and noise ratings. Each discrepancy involved a one-step difference in the rating. In each of the three cases, the disagreement arose because the rating turned on the presence or absence of some item (such as visibility of trucks, recognizable odor, constant noise) that one observer had missed through casual observation. There were no disagreements over what the rating should be once these missed items were pointed out. This finding suggests that the principal reliability concern in this measure is how carefully inspectors check the scene, rather than how the different raters interpret items on the rating scales.

After the test was completed, St. Petersburg continued to use the inspection procedure on a regular basis for about a year and a half. For the first four to five months they inspected weekly, and after that, monthly. Later, the inspections were dropped because they tended to produce the same readings each time (except just after high winds or substantial rains), and the inspectors had higher priorities and competing demands elsewhere. The official in charge felt the use of the procedure had made city officials more aware of the site's external appearance, which they worked to improve.

This testing experience is not sufficient to demonstrate the reliability of the measurement procedures. More extensive testing is needed to determine whether observers can maintain the required attention, whether their reliability declines over time, and how frequently, if at all, retraining sessions may be needed.

Potential users should test the procedures themselves to ascertain that the terms used in the rating definitions apply to their sites and to assure that a reasonable level of reliability can be maintained among different trained observers. This testing should be done before full implementation of the procedure. A number of points at sites that are rated should be rerated independently by a second person, so the ratings can be compared. A high percentage—at least 75 percent—of the ratings should be identical if the procedure is to be considered operational. (See Chapters 2 and 13 for more discussion of this issue.)

A period of approximately three months should be allowed for initial preparations, such as setting up the rating forms and identifying the observation points at the sites where ratings will be taken. An additional period of three months is advisable to train the observers, check their reliability, and note the reasonableness and meaningfulness of the range of ratings obtained. After that, if rater reliability is satisfactory, regular operations can be undertaken.

Measuring the effectiveness of recreation services is not completely new to most local governments, but current procedures have major deficiencies. Past evaluation of local government park and recreation activities has tended to focus more on inputs such as the number of acres of land, the number of facilities, and the number of arts-and-crafts programs provided rather than on outputs such as the number of persons served and their satisfaction with those services. The park and recreation agencies of most local governments lack information on even the most fundamental facts: What percentage of the population is being served? How satisfied are citizens with recreation services? Who does not use the services and why not? To what extent do such factors as accessibility, dislike of the facility, fear of crime, or lack of knowledge about recreation opportunities affect the use of facilities and programs?

The work reported here builds on earlier efforts, especially in Washington, D.C., to develop better procedures by which local governments can measure the effectiveness of their recreation services. The park and recreation agencies in Nashville, Tennessee, and St. Petersburg, Florida, tested some of the procedures developed in the Washington, D.C., effort. With only limited help from the project team, three other jurisdictions have tested some of the same procedures: Rockford, Illinois, in 1972; Palo Alto, California, in 1973; and Birmingham, Alabama, in 1974.

The information provided in this chapter sup-

plements earlier publications,[1] which should be consulted for a complete picture of the work undertaken thus far.

The objectives, measures, and data collection procedures in this chapter focus on recreation opportunities for individual citizens. Recreation is considered for the purposes of this report as an end in itself, not as a means to some other end such as reducing juvenile delinquency or improving mental and physical health. (Measures of juvenile delinquency, however, are included in Chapter 6.)

Objectives and Related Effectiveness Measures

A basic objective for recreation services, one that seems common to most communities, is:

To provide for all citizens a variety of enjoyable leisure opportunities that are accessible, safe, physically attractive, and uncrowded.

A set of indices to help measure progress toward

1. See the U.S. Bureau of Outdoor Recreation, *How Effective Are Your Community Recreation Services?* (Washington, D.C.: U.S. Government Printing Office 1973), and Harry P. Hatry and Diana R. Dunn, *Measuring the Effectiveness of Local Government Services: Recreation* (Washington, D.C.: The Urban Institute, 1971).

Exhibit 4-1
EFFECTIVENESS MEASURES FOR RECREATION SERVICES

OVERALL OBJECTIVE: To provide for all citizens a variety of enjoyable leisure opportunities that are accessible, safe, physically attractive, and uncrowded.

OBJECTIVE	QUALITY CHARACTERISTIC	SPECIFIC MEASURE[1]	DATA COLLECTION PROCEDURE
ENJOYABLE-NESS	Citizen satisfaction	1. Percentage of households rating neighborhood park and recreation opportunities as satisfactory.	General citizen survey
	User satisfaction	2. Percentage of those households using community park or recreation facilities who rate them as satisfactory.	General citizen survey or survey of users (of particular facilities)
	Usage—participation rates	3. Percentage of community households using (or not using) a community park or recreation facility at least once over a specific past period, such as three months. (For nonusers, provide the percentage not using facilities for various reasons, and distinguish reasons that can be at least partly controlled by the government from those that cannot.)	General citizen survey
	Usage—attendance	4. Number of visits at recreation sites.	Attendance statistics; estimates from general citizen survey
AVOIDANCE OF CROWDED-NESS	User satisfaction	5. Percentage of user households rating crowdedness of community facilities as unsatisfactory.	General citizen survey or survey of users (of particular facilities)
	Nonuser satisfaction	6. Percentage of nonuser households giving crowded conditions as a reason for nonuse of facilities.	General citizen survey
	Crowding factor	7. Average peak-hour attendance divided by capacity.	Attendance statistics and estimates of carrying capacity
PHYSICAL ATTRAC-TIVENESS	User satisfaction	8. Percentage of user households rating physical attractiveness as satisfactory.	General citizen survey or survey of users (of particular facilities)
	Nonuser satisfaction	9. Percentage of nonuser households giving lack of physical attractiveness as reason for nonuse.	General citizen survey
	Facility cleanliness	10. Percentage of user households rating cleanliness as satisfactory.	General citizen survey or survey of users
	Equipment condition	11. Percentage of user households rating condition of equipment as satisfactory.	General citizen survey or survey of users
SAFETY	Injuries to participants resulting from accidents	12. Number of serious injuries (for example, those requiring hospitalization) per 10,000 visits.	Accident and attendance statistics
	Criminal incidents	13. Number of criminal incidents per 10,000 visits.	Criminal incident statistics of some park and recreation agencies and most municipal police forces; attendance statistics
	User satisfaction	14. Percentage of user households rating safety of facilities as satisfactory.	General citizen survey or survey of users
	Nonuser satisfaction	15. Percentage of nonuser households giving lack of safety as a reason for nonuse of municipal facilities.	General citizen survey

(Exhibit continued on next page)

meeting the various parts of this objective is presented in Exhibit 4-1.

The objectives and measures identified in this chapter are intended to assist in evaluating the total recreation system. Most of the procedures can be used to assess recreation effectiveness in major geographic areas of the community. To a more limited degree, these measures can also be used to assess specific agency functions (such as park maintenance or public information about recreation opportunities), or specific activities (such as swimming or arts and crafts). Some of the data collection procedures suggested here, such as the on-site surveys of users, will provide large enough samples to draw conclusions about specific facilities.

Although these measures focus on public facilities and activities, private and quasi-public efforts (such as voluntary youth-serving agencies) in-directly influence some of the measured values. For example, data on the accessibility of swimming opportunities can include the availability of private but nonrestricted facilities. The measure of "households rating neighborhood's recreational opportunities as satisfactory (or unsatisfactory)" reflects both private and public opportunities. As such, the measure can be used to indicate the adequacy of, and the need for more or different, public facilities.

Grouping Measurement Data by Population or Client Characteristics

The different perspectives of various population or client groups are very important, and the per-

Exhibit 4-1 continued

OBJECTIVE	QUALITY CHARACTERISTIC	SPECIFIC MEASURE[1]	DATA COLLECTION PROCEDURE
ACCES-SIBILITY	Physical accessibility	16. Percentage of citizens living within (or not within) 15 to 30 minutes' travel time of a community park or recreation facility distinguished by type of facility and principal relevant mode of transportation.	Counts from mapping latest census tract population figures against location of facilities, with appropriate travel-time radius drawn around each facility
	Physical accessibility—user satisfaction	17. Percentage of user households rating physical accessibility as satisfactory.	General citizen survey or survey of users
	Physical accessibility—nonuser satisfaction	18. Percentage of nonuser households giving poor physical accessibility as a reason for nonuse.	General citizen survey
	Hours/days of operation—user satisfaction	19. Percentage of user households rating hours of operation as satisfactory.	General citizen survey or survey of users
	Hours/days of operation—nonuser satisfaction	20. Percentage of nonuser households giving unsatisfactory operating hours as a reason for nonuse.	General citizen survey
VARIETY OF INTERESTING ACTIVITIES	User satisfaction	21. Percentage of user households rating the variety of program activities as satisfactory.	General citizen survey or survey of users
	Nonuser satisfaction	22. Percentage of nonuser households giving lack of program variety as a reason for nonuse.	General citizen survey
HELPFULNESS OF STAFF	Staff helpfulness—user satisfaction	23. Percentage of user households rating helpfulness or attitude of staff as satisfactory.	General citizen survey or survey of users
	Staff helpfulness—nonuser satisfaction	24. Percentage of nonuser households giving poor staff attitude as a reason for nonuse.	General citizen survey

1. Many of the measures inquire into percentages of citizens or users who find conditions "satisfactory." Local officials may wish in some instances to focus more directly on the amount of *dissatisfaction,* in which case the word "satisfactory" would be changed to "unsatisfactory."

formance of each group should be distinguished whenever data collection procedures permit. Eight factors seem particularly important to recreation decisions: age, sex, area of residence, income, race, education, existence of handicap, and ownership of or access to an automobile. The last characteristic is important because of potentially important variations in accessibility, and thus potential differences in the character, variety, and level of satisfaction with recreation experiences between those with and those without access to automobiles or public transportation.

The data collection procedures suggested in this chapter generally permit performance data to be grouped by the characteristics cited above—if not too many categories for any one characteristic are sought. For example, the citizen survey sampling procedures can probably permit a government to distinguish perhaps five to ten different geographic areas or age groups within a jurisdiction but would not permit twenty or more to be distinguished with any reasonable precision.

The particular clientele groupings used should be related to the specific characteristics of those groups for which programs and activities are planned and operated by the park and recreation agency. For example, Washington, D.C., used six age groupings—less than 6 years old, 6 to 13, 14 to 19, 20 to 34, 35 to 64, and 65 and over—because it operated programs specifically aimed at these age groups. In selecting age groupings, it also is helpful to choose those for which census information is readily available. This will aid in the calculation of several measurements, such as physical accessibility, and will facilitate checking the representativeness of sample survey results.

Principal Recommended Measurement Procedures

1. A major need in measuring the effectiveness of recreation services is to obtain reliable indicators of community satisfaction with available public recreation services. A regular (perhaps annual) survey of a sample of the community's citizens is recommended to obtain information on their satisfaction with recreation services. Reasonably reliable information can be obtained with survey techniques that obtain feedback from a relatively small (a few hundred households) but representative cross section of the community. Infor-

mation can be obtained from the survey both as to overall satisfaction with recreation opportunities and ratings of such characteristics as accessibility, cleanliness, safety, helpfulness of personnel, and condition of the equipment.

The same survey can also be used to obtain figures on the percentages of the community using and not using recreation facilities. For those who do not use government recreation services, the survey can also produce estimates of the apparent reasons for nonuse. This will enable recreation planners to distinguish reasons that could be affected by the government (for example, inaccessibility of recreation areas, lack of safety, lack of knowledge about recreational opportunities, and the types of recreational opportunities available) from reasons that, for the most part, cannot be affected by government (such as lack of interest or preference for nongovernmental recreation opportunities).

Data for twenty of the twenty-four measurements of effectiveness proposed in Exhibit 4-1 can be collected by the citizen survey. Pilot measurement efforts in Nashville, St. Petersburg, Palo Alto, Birmingham, Rockford, and Washington, D.C., have drawn heavily on that survey to collect information on citizen experiences and perceptions. In each of these six cities, park and recreation agency personnel were heavily involved. In all jurisdictions except Palo Alto, city personnel handled the survey but with considerable outside technical advice.

The efforts in Nashville and St. Petersburg relied on internal personnel to undertake the surveys because the departments did not feel that the necessary funding (approximately $5,000) could be made available to hire a professional survey firm. Although park and recreation agencies were able to handle the survey, they found it a larger undertaking than they had expected.

Substantial outside assistance to undertake the survey seems necessary in order for regular surveys of this type to be feasible in most communities. If a jurisdiction is unable to support a full citizen survey on recreation alone, a fallback position is to include a reduced number of recreation questions on a multiservice citizen survey, a procedure recommended in other chapters of this report to deal simultaneously with a whole range of local services.

Each of the surveys except Palo Alto's was conducted by telephone. Appendix 5 shows an example of a questionnaire used in a recreation citizen survey.

2. Annual surveys of *users* of recreation programs and facilities should be considered. These can be conducted on site, and they provide citizen feedback on satisfaction with the specific programs and facilities. Nashville, St. Petersburg, and Palo Alto, which conducted such surveys, found the resulting information to be of particular interest to park and recreation management.

   User surveys can produce data on twelve of the measures of effectiveness. Unlike the general citizen survey, user surveys probably can be handled primarily by recreation staff personnel, and because they are administered at recreation sites they place less burden on the staff than does the household survey. To avoid pitfalls such as poorly worded questions and sloppy surveying techniques, some outside assistance is recommended. An example of a questionnaire for use in a survey of users of recreation facilities is provided in Appendix 6.

   Although these user surveys probably provide the best way to collect data on users' behavior patterns and perceptions, they do not provide information on nonusers and their reasons for nonuse. For these latter purposes, the general citizen survey discussed in (1) above is necessary.

3. To gauge physical accessibility to facilities—a crucial factor contributing to facility use—a mapping technique is suggested. This technique, which plots a community's population distribution against the location of existing recreation facilities, permits a calculation of the percentages of the population within or beyond a convenient time or distance (such as fifteen minutes) of a neighborhood recreation facility.

4. Basic community records also should be tracked on such factors as attendance (where obtainable), crowding (measured as estimates of average daily attendance divided by carrying capacity), and rates of injuries and criminal incidents. Thus comparisons can be made over time, among various areas, and of particular facilities in the community.

Resource Requirements for Measurement Procedures

A local government with a park and recreation department of about 100 full-time employees is esti-mated to require about one and a half person-years of effort to pursue effectiveness measurement on an ongoing basis. A smaller department with forty or fewer employees might require one person-year of effort. A large department with 500 or more employees would probably consume two person-years of effort.

Because of the sampling procedures involved, the cost of measuring effectiveness is not directly proportional to the size of the park and recreation department involved. Effectiveness measurement is likely to be easier to fund in medium-size and larger departments than in smaller departments simply because the task consumes a smaller percentage of the operating budgets in departments of medium and larger size. However, there are ways to reduce the cost of regular effectiveness measurement; these include using community volunteers and reducing the number of measurements and the frequency with which they are obtained.

Individual Measures

This section discusses the rationale for the measures shown in Exhibit 4-1 and describes procedures that appear usable in collecting data for each measure. Because most of the measures use data from either general citizen surveys or surveys of recreation users, procedural discussions are kept to a minimum in this section. Subsequent sections of this chapter discuss in more detail each of these two principal data collection approaches.

The measures are arranged in seven groups:
- Enjoyableness (Measures 1-4);
- Crowdedness (Measures 5-7);
- Physical attractiveness (Measures 8-11);
- Safety (Measures 12-15);
- Accessibility (Measures 16-20);
- Variety of interesting activities (Measures 21 and 22); and
- Helpfulness of staff (Measures 23 and 24).

Measures of Enjoyableness

Measure 1: Percentage of households rating neighborhood park and recreation opportunities as satisfactory.

Measure 2: Percentage of those households using community park or recreation facilities who rate them as satisfactory.

Measure 3: Percentage of community households using (or not using) a community park or recreation facility at least once over a specific past period, such as three months. (For nonusers, provide the percentage not using facilities for various reasons, and distinguish reasons that can be at least partly controlled by the government from those that cannot.)

Measure 4: Number of visits at recreation sites.

This set of measures uses two approaches to gauge enjoyableness. Measures 1 and 2 are direct indices of satisfaction; they call for obtaining citizens' ratings of the level of satisfaction with their recreation opportunities. Measures 3 and 4 attempt to get at enjoyableness more indirectly by measuring attendance or usage by citizens.

Measure 1 is the more comprehensive of the direct satisfaction measures. Using the general citizen survey (discussed in detail later), it produces a rating from a representative cross section of all households in the community. Measure 2 focuses only on those citizens who have actually made use of at least one local government-operated recreation facility during a recent time period. If the data are obtained from a general citizen survey, the findings should be representative of a cross section of the whole population of users in the community. If feedback from a sample of users of specific facilities is obtained, these individuals will be representative of users of all government facilities to the extent that the user surveys cover all programs and facilities or at least are representative of them.

All measures that inquire into "satisfactory" ratings by citizens or users may be changed to focus on "unsatisfactory" ratings if these would appear more meaningful to a local jurisdiction.

Data Collection. Data for Measure 1 can be obtained by surveying a representative sample of households in the community. A question such as Number 3 in Appendix 5 can be used to obtain the data. For ratings by users (Measure 2), either a general citizen survey or surveys of users of specific facilities can be employed. If a general citizen survey is used, a question such as Number 12vii in Appendix 5 could obtain the data. If a survey of users is undertaken, a question such as Number 21 of Appendix 6 can be used.

One problem is how to define a "user." The questionnaire in Appendix 5 somewhat arbitrarily defines a user as any household which has used a facility at least once in the past month (see Question 4, Appendix 5).

Measure 3 defines the period as three months. A government may prefer to alter the definition to consider a longer time period (such as twelve months) or to require more uses during the given time before considering the household a "user." Another possibility is to tally responses for households with various amounts of usages.

In the Nashville survey, a period of three months was used as the reference period. Because of seasonal problems, it can be argued that the individual should be asked about the full period between surveys, which might normally be twelve months. However, the longer the time period asked about, the more difficult it may be for some respondents to remember experiences and impressions with sufficient accuracy.

There is little direct evidence on the memory problem. However, the evidence available (see Chapter 14 and the section later in this chapter on the recreation general citizen survey) indicates that even if the survey is taken only at annual intervals, citizens can reasonably be expected to respond to questions covering longer periods of time, such as six or twelve months. The memory problem is of less concern for "satisfaction" questions than for questions asking for frequency of usage of recreation facilities.

For Measures 3 and 4, estimates of attendance or usage, the assumption is that people "vote with their feet"; that is, by using programs or facilities they indicate their satisfaction with them. Others may argue that citizens, particularly the less affluent, have few choices and in effect are a captive audience. To the extent that this is true, attendance or participation rates will not indicate the degree of enjoyableness of the facilities. Then, too, users of facilities will have different degrees of satisfaction. But usage is clearly important information to government officials, and represents an important indicator of the value of recreation activities.

The traditional method for estimating usage is by attendance figures, as in Measure 4. Most agencies keep some statistics, such as the numbers of persons attending classes and using facilities with controlled access, such as community centers. Generally lacking are attendance counts at open facilities such as city parks and playgrounds. In the latter cases, attendance estimates are sometimes obtained using various formulas often based on counts at peak periods. For example, the National Park and Recreation Association has offered a "peak count" formula to determine summer playground attendance. This procedure calls for multiplying a factor of 1.8 by the peak-time morning attendance count, 2.5 by the afternoon peak count, and 1.8 by the evening peak count. These figures are then added to produce the estimated daily attendance. Developed in 1938, this formula was retested nationally in 1960 and supported by the test findings.[2]

The general citizen survey provides an additional way to estimate total recreational attendance and to estimate for those few facilities specifically asked about in the survey.[3] The user survey provides a way to collect attendance statistics at several specific facilities. Both Nashville and St. Petersburg found their reported attendance counts differed from estimates based on the general citizen and user surveys. (Drawing on the user data, Nashville held a series of meetings with community center supervisors to improve attendance taking.) At this stage of knowledge, however, there has been too little analysis of the data and probable reasons for differences to make firm conclusions or recommendations as to the most accurate procedures for estimating attendance.

What is clear is that attendance counts do not indicate how many *different* persons or families use the facilities because those attending may be repeat users. The general citizen survey is a better way to obtain participation rates. That is the purpose of Measure 3, which provides an estimate of the percentage of households which have (or have not) used community facilities. A question such as Number 4 in Appendix 5 can be used to obtain this information in a general citizen survey.

As discussed under Measure 2, the definition of use and nonuse is important; but there is no clearcut, preferred definition. The one-month recall period used in Appendix 5 may provide for more accurate responses, but it does not seem to cover a large enough period, especially if the surveys are taken only annually. As indicated under Measure 2, a six- or even twelve-month period seems more appropriate in order to cover a greater amount of the respondents' recreational experiences. Usage can be defined as meaning at least one use during the referenced period, but some communities may prefer a higher threshold, such as three uses or more.

Decisions on length of recall period and number of uses will affect the values derived for the measure. As long as the decisions are used consistently, however, any choices should provide adequate information for making comparisons on participation rates from one time period to another, from one geographical section of the community to another, or from one facility to another.

Reasons for nonuse are likely to be critical in measuring objective of reaching all citizens who desire to be served. Thus it is important that the nonuse rates be broken down by reason for nonuse. Questions such as Numbers 13 and 14 in Appendix 5 can be used to obtain this information; the latter question includes a checklist of reasons for nonuse.

Governments testing these procedures have found it particularly helpful to group the reasons for nonuse into those that are "potentially within government control" and those that are "probably beyond government control." Exhibit 4-2 lists a sample set of reasons grouped by these two categories. In addition, the exhibit presents, for illustrative purposes, the frequency of individual reasons given by citizens for nonuse in three surveys.

Most of the reasons for nonuse that are categorized as "potentially within government control" are also used as the basis for subsequent indicators of effectiveness—that is, Measures 6 (crowded conditions), 9 (lack of physical attractiveness), 15 (safety problems), 18 (inaccessibility), 20 (inconvenient hours), 22 (lack of interesting programs), and 24 (poor staff). Two other reasons for nonuse also could be added: lack of information or knowledge about the facility or programs and the cost of using facilities or programs. Data for these latter characteristics can be obtained through questions such as 14a and 14f of Appendix 5.

A note of caution is in order in directing action based on reasons for nonuse. Experiences in other service areas, particularly in the use of public transportation, suggest that actions based primarily on reported reasons for nonuse did not necessarily produce usage. Thus, government officials using these data should be careful to treat them as approximate and tentative, more indicative than definitive. Such information does appear on the surface to be useful for guiding government action, but confirming information should be sought.

Measure 3 could be expressed as either household participation rates or individual participation rates, or both. The questions illustrated in Appendix 5 ask about the respondent's own participation and that of each of the other members of the household. With this information, participation

2. See George Butler, "Summer Playground Attendance Formula," *Recreation* (April 1961), and International City Managers' Association, *Municipal Recreation Administration,* 4th ed. (Chicago, 1960), p. 347. (The latter suggests slightly different factors.)

3. See U.S. Bureau of Outdoor Recreation, *How Effective Are Your Community Recreation Services?* pp. 57–63, for a discussion of this procedure and a fuller discussion of recreation attendance figures.

Exhibit 4-2
REASONS GIVEN BY CITIZENS FOR NONUSE OF ROCKFORD, ILLINOIS, ST. PETERSBURG, FLORIDA, AND WASHINGTON, D.C., RECREATION FACILITIES

(Responses in Percentages)

	ROCK-FORD	ST. PETERS-BURG	WASH-ING-TON, D.C.
CAUSES POTENTIALLY WITHIN GOVERNMENT CONTROL			
Facility unknown	10	12	26
Too far away	13	5	10
Activities not interesting	3	13	5
Too dangerous	4	4	3
Too crowded	5	2	2
Inconvenient hours	3	1	1
Not attractive	2	0	1
Costs too much	1	1	0
Total	41	38	48
CAUSES PROBABLY BEYOND GOVERNMENT CONTROL[1]			
Too busy	21	20	18
Poor personal health	1	} 19	6
Too old	3		5
Don't like other users	4	2	2
Total	29	41	31
No opinion—Won't say	31	21	21

1. An additional category not used in these surveys could be "Satisfied with nongovernmental recreation facilities."

SOURCE: Statistics compiled from citizen surveys in Washington, D.C., (June 1972); Rockford, Illinois (August 1972); and St. Petersburg, Florida (September 1973).

rates can be calculated for respondents, households, or both. The accuracy of respondents' reports on usage by other household members is not clear. This issue is discussed further in the section on the recreation general citizen survey and in Chapter 14.

In the process of obtaining citizen ratings on overall satisfaction, it seems highly desirable for the government also to obtain ratings on particular aspects of the facilities. These include hours of operation, cleanliness, condition of equipment, helpfulness and attitude of personnel, crowded conditions, safety, accessibility, and parking availability. Question 12 of Appendix 5 and Questions 6 through 18 of Appendix 6 illustrate how such data would be obtained. Most of these ratings are used in subsequent measures and are discussed below.

Measures of Crowded Conditions

Measure 5: Percentage of user households rating crowdedness of community facilities as unsatisfactory.

Measure 6: Percentage of nonuser households giving crowded conditions as a reason for nonuse of facilities.

Measure 7: Average peak-hour attendance divided by capacity.

These three measures cover three perspectives. Measure 5 obtains ratings of crowdedness directly from persons who have used the community facilities, based on either the general citizen survey (for example, see Question 12v of Appendix 5) or user surveys (see Question 10 of Appendix 6). Measure 6 provides the percentage of nonuser households which give crowded conditions as a reason for nonuse, as obtained from a question such as 14d in Appendix 5. Because citizen perceptions of crowded conditions may be quite different from actual conditions, the citizen ratings obtained from Measures 5 and 6 seem particularly important in assessing crowdedness.

Measure 7 provides a statistic based on actual attendance records; it attempts to relate attendance counts to an estimate of the "capacity" for various recreation sites. For some facilities, such as tennis courts and swimming pools, the capacity can be defined with some precision. However, the problem is more difficult for playgrounds, open space, and multiple-use facilities.

In order to consider all facilities rather than each individually, Measure 7 could be transformed into a form calling for the "number of recreational facilities in which average daily attendance exceeded the capacity." However, this measure still reflects the problem that the average figures may hide the specific frequency of occasions when capacity was exceeded. Preferably, there would be an estimate of the number of occasions, perhaps in number of hours, when capacity was exceeded. The feasibility of gathering such information comprehensively, given the current state of the art of attendance measurements, seems questionable. The data collection seems feasible, however, for selected kinds of activities such as swimming, golf, tennis, and various recreation classes, in which attendance counts, waiting times, and possibly the number of turnaways can be feasibly monitored, especially during peak use periods.

Measures of Physical Attractiveness

Measure 8: Percentage of user households rating physical attractiveness as satisfactory.

Measure 9: Percentage of nonuser households giving lack of physical attractiveness as reason for nonuse.

Measure 10: Percentage of user households rating cleanliness as satisfactory.

Measure 11: Percentage of user households rating condition of equipment as satisfactory.

Similar to the measures for crowdedness, Measures 8, 10, and 11 provide ratings, from households which have used recreation facilities, of overall physical attractiveness (Measure 8) or such specific aspects as facility cleanliness (Measure 10) and equipment condition (Measure 11). To obtain this information either general citizen surveys or user surveys can be used. Examples of appropriate questions are Questions 12ii (cleanliness) and 12iii (condition of equipment) in Appendix 5 (no direct rating was requested from users on overall physical attractiveness in that survey) or Questions 7 (cleanliness), 8 (condition of equipment), and 12 (physical attractiveness) in Appendix 6.

Although not explored as part of this investigation, it should be possible to develop "objective" measures of facility cleanliness (Measure 10) and equipment condition (Measure 11). In both cases, it should be possible to develop a trained observer rating by using procedures such as those described in Chapters 2 and 13 for solid waste collection.

Measure 9 provides an estimate of the percentage of nonuser households giving lack of physical attractiveness as the reason for nonuse (based on a question such as 14e, Appendix 5). The same qualifications already mentioned in the discussion of Measure 3 on reasons for nonuse also apply here.

Measures of Safety

Measure 12: Number of serious injuries (for example, those requiring hospitalization) per 10,000 visits.

Measure 13: Number of criminal incidents per 10,000 visits.

Measure 14: Percentage of user households rating safety of facilities as satisfactory.

Measure 15: Percentage of nonuser households giving lack of safety as a reason for nonuse of municipal facilities.

Measures 12 and 13 use basic government statistics, whereas Measures 14 and 15 employ ratings from the citizen or user surveys.

For legal and administrative reasons, most park and recreation agencies keep detailed statistics on reported injuries (Measure 12), and all local police departments keep statistics on criminal incidents (Measure 13). Some park and recreation agencies also have their own police forces, which maintain crime statistics. What is lacking in most of these agencies, however, is any attempt to track the statistics through time to see if the situation is changing.[4]

When making comparisons of the number of injuries or criminal incidents over various time periods, among recreation districts, or by facility, it is highly desirable to relate the number of incidents to some indicator of the population at risk. (After all, the playground or swimming pool with the fewest number of injuries would be the one that is not used at all!) An approach that seems appropriate is to divide the number of injuries or incidents in a given time period by the attendance or number of attendance hours during that period.

Although losses because of vandalism are not included in the list of measures in Exhibit 4-1, some governments may also want to track the dollar amount of these losses. Vandalism records normally will be kept by most agencies for purposes of reporting to the police, scheduling repairs, and justifying budgets. Again, generally lacking are procedures to track these data through time and across geographic areas. In making comparisons about vandalism losses, it is desirable to relate the amount of loss to the amount of property at risk, such as the total value of the property. Thus, the vandalism loss measure might be expressed as "dollar value of vandalism losses per $1,000 of property value." In making comparisons from one year to the next, adjustments for rising costs would also be appropriate.

Measure 14 estimates the percentage of households using recreation facilities who rate their safety as satisfactory (or unsatisfactory), using questions such as 12vi in Appendix 5 (general citizen survey) and Number 11 in Appendix 6 (user survey) to obtain these data.

Measure 15 provides estimates of the percent-

---

4. Ibid., pp. 63–66, for a more extensive discussion of safety measures.

age of nonuser households giving lack of safety as a reason for nonuse of municipal facilities. These estimates can be reached by asking a question such as Number 14g of Appendix 5 in a general citizen survey. The same qualifications noted elsewhere for such surveys apply here.

An additional concern for Measures 12 and 13 is that not all injuries resulting from accidents or criminal incidents are likely to be reported. The citizen and user surveys could be employed to ask citizens whether they were involved in any recreation area accidents or criminal incidents that were not reported. Estimates of frequency of unreported incidents could then be added to tallies of the reported incidents. The unreported crimes in recreational areas could be included in the series of questions on victimization discussed in Chapter 6 and illustrated in Appendix 1. However, the small number of citizens who both (1) use park and recreation facilities and (2) are victimized means that the estimates from the small samples discussed in Chapter 6 would provide only a crude estimate of the extent of victimization at those facilities.

Measures of Accessibility

Measure 16: Percentage of citizens living within (or not within) 15 to 30 minutes' travel time of a community park or recreation facility, distinguished by type of facility and by the principal relevant mode of transportation.

Measure 17: Percentage of user households rating physical accessibility as satisfactory.

Measure 18: Percentage of nonuser households giving poor physical accessibility as a reason for nonuse.

Measure 19: Percentage of user households rating hours of operation as satisfactory.

Measure 20: Percentage of nonuser households giving unsatisfactory operating hours as a reason for nonuse.

The concept of accessibility is complicated. It includes factors such as physical accessibility, problems due to various forms of explicit or implicit discrimination, lack of transportation, inconvenient hours of operation, excessive waiting (see crowdedness measures), or inadequate parking space. Measures 16–18 provide indications of physical accessibility, whereas Measures 19 and 20 focus on hours of

operation. No specific measures of the extent of discrimination or parking problems are included, but such elements could be included in questionnaires such as those shown in Appendices 5 and 6. Question 15 in Appendix 6 illustrates how the question of parking might be included in the ratings sought in user surveys.

Measure 16 focuses on the proximity of the population to recreational facilities and can be obtained by a mapping technique. Measure 17 focuses on ratings by user households, employing a user survey question such as Question 17 of Appendix 6. In the St. Petersburg recreation general citizen survey shown in Appendix 5, no rating was sought from users on physical accessibility, although this could be added—as part of Question 12 in Appendix 5. Measure 18 provides an estimate of the percentage of nonuser households which give poor physical accessibility as a reason for nonuse based on a question in a general citizen survey such as 14c ("too far away") in Appendix 5.

Measure 16 requires more discussion. Ease of accessibility is one of the crucial factors contributing to facility use. Two important considerations in examining accessibility are first, how close the individual citizens are to the facilities and second, the extent of the individuals' mobility. For many potential users of recreation facilities, such as youths and others without access to automobiles, mobility is a problem and the geographic distribution of facilities in a community is important. Therefore, the measurement of accessibility will vary somewhat with the mobility characteristics of the intended user group.

One way to measure accessibility is to calculate the percentage of the total population (or of a particular potential user group) residing within a given distance of a facility. These data provide a useful adjunct to citizen perceptions of physical accessibility and a check against them.

Specific procedures for the mapping technique in Measure 16 are described in detail in a previous report.[5] Here these procedures are briefly summarized. Exhibit 4-3 illustrates the steps involved.

1. Obtain appropriate maps, such as those prepared locally or by the U.S. Census Bureau. Census population statistics are keyed to census tracts, with block group and block numbers printed on the maps. Several census map sheets will probably be needed to cover each city, plus a "fringe

---

5. Ibid., pp. 39–56. This report also discusses the results of initial trials of this procedure undertaken for the District of Columbia.

Exhibit 4-3

MAPPING TECHNIQUE FOR MEASURING PHYSICAL ACCESSIBILITY

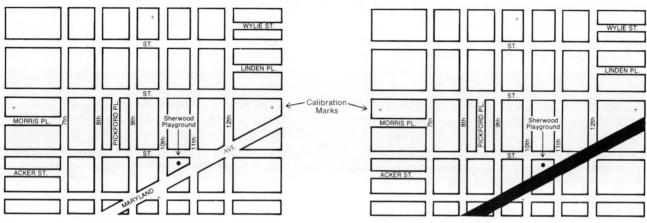

Step 1. Obtain base map.

Step 2. Identify and mark physical barriers on base map.

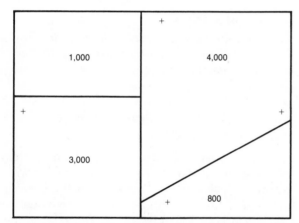

Step 3. Tabulate population; plot on map overlay.

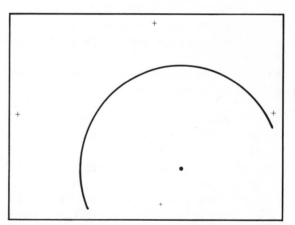

Step 4. Plot facility and activity locations on map overlay.
Step 5. Draw physical accessibility circles around each location.

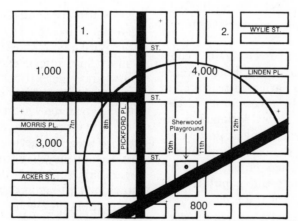

Step 6. Assemble overlays on base map. (For clarity, only overlays for population by block groups and facility are shown.)

Source: U.S. Bureau of Outdoor Recreation, *How Effective Are Your Community Recreation Services?*, p. 59.

area" of at least three-fourths of a mile around its political boundary. Calibration marks, such as four "+"s, should be placed on the base map. These marks will guide aligning the map overlays described in succeeding steps.

2. Identify on the maps physical barriers that would affect accessibility to recreation areas. These barriers, including freeways, railroads, industrial zones, and rivers, should be marked on the base maps. An examination of the local transportation planning agency highway map, or even a common street map, along with government personnel's knowledge of the city, are all helpful in determining locations of barriers. On-site checks may be desirable in some instances.

3. Plot the population distribution on an overlay. Use the basic population data tabulations (from census statistics or planning information) to prepare population overlays on tracing paper or acetate. Place the population overlay on the base map. Write population data on the overlay for the appropriate census tracts, block groups, or blocks.

4. Plot the location of recreation facilities on an overlay to the base map.

5. Draw an accessibility circle on the facility location overlay around each plotted facility. The radius used for these circles should reflect the mode of transportation persons are assumed to use and the estimated maximum travel time. We suggest fifteen- and thirty-minute travel times, or three-fourths and one and one-half miles. In order to account for the effect of physical barriers and any other identifiable barriers to access, the areas blocked from access to facilities should be eliminated from the circles.

6. Assemble overlays on base map, using the calibration marks on the maps and overlays to permit rapid alignment.

7. Estimate the "number and percentage of people living within" the physical accessibility circles. The proportion of the population in tracts or in blocks that are split by the accessibility circles should be estimated by visually estimating the percentage of the census tract or block group area lying within each physical accessibility circle and then splitting the population proportionately.[6] This method assumes that the population is evenly distributed throughout the area.

Note that separate sets of overlays will be necessary to distinguish different population

6. The estimate may be further refined if unpopulated areas of blocks or tracts can be identified and excluded from the percentage calculations.

segments—for example, to consider accessibility for various age groups. In addition, car-oriented facilities such as golf courses or major city or county parks will require riding-time accessibility circles, whereas neighborhood facilities will require walking-time circles. (For client groups without access to automobiles, transit-time accessibility might be needed to estimate accessibility to major local recreation facilities, with such access plotted around transit stops. See Chapter 8 for more on this.)

For Measure 19, user-household ratings of the hours of operation can be obtained from questions such as Question 12i in Appendix 5 (the general citizen survey) and Question 6 in Appendix 6 (the recreation user survey).

For Measure 20, the proportion of nonusers giving hours of operation as a reason for nonuse, data can be obtained from the general citizen survey by asking Question 14b in Appendix 5.

Measures of Variety

Measure 21: Percentage of user households rating the variety of program activities as satisfactory.

Measure 22: Percentage of nonuser households giving lack of program variety as a reason for nonuse.

Two perspectives are provided on variety. Measure 21 obtains a rating from households which used the facilities using a question in the user survey such as Number 13 in Appendix 6. (No question on variety was included in the St. Petersburg questionnaire shown in Appendix 5, but one could easily be added.) For Measure 22, the percentage of nonuser households giving lack of program variety as a reason for nonuse, data can be obtained from the general citizen survey using a question such as 14j ("activities not interesting") in Appendix 5. At the same time, information could be obtained on the particular activities of interest to the nonuser households by asking "What would be interesting?" as shown under Question 14j.

A measure such as "the average number of different program activities per facility" was considered as an easy way to gauge program variety. However, this appears to measure input more than results, so it has not been included in our list of suggested effectiveness measures.

Measures of Helpfulness of Staff

Measure 23: Percentage of user households rating helpfulness or attitude of staff as satisfactory.

Measure 24: Percentage of nonuser households giving poor staff attitude as a reason for nonuse.

In the process of providing recreational services, considerable interaction often occurs between government employees and the clients of recreational activities. Some feedback seems appropriate on the degree to which such government employees are helpful and courteous to clients. Measure 23 provides a perspective on user households through questions such as Question 12iv of Appendix 5 in a general citizen survey and Question 14 of Appendix 6 in a user survey. Measure 24 provides estimates of the percentage of nonuser households giving poor staff attitudes as a reason for nonuse. This reason was not included as a choice in the St. Petersburg general citizen survey as part of Question 14 (Appendix 5). This factor seldom appeared in early surveys asking respondents about "other" reasons for nonuse. Such a question, however, could be included.

The Recreation General Citizen Survey

These surveys, if properly carried out, produce knowledge difficult to obtain in any other way. First, the surveys provide a way to obtain a representative citizen evaluation of facilities and programs. Second, the surveys are probably the most efficient way to gather usage-participation data on urban parks and playgrounds that lack controlled access points. Third, they provide a means for probing the behavior of various classes of recreation users and nonusers alike.

Problems do exist in using general citizen surveys to assess recreational effectiveness. Surveys such as those discussed in this chapter require significant resources, and most park and recreation agencies will need outside expertise to set up, conduct, and analyze survey results.

Recreation citizen surveys have been used to obtain the types of evaluation information discussed in this report in a number of cities, including Washington, D.C.; Rockford, Illinois; Nashville, Tennessee; Palo Alto, California; St. Petersburg, Florida; and Birmingham, Alabama. Data for twenty of the twenty-four effectiveness measures listed in Exhibit 4-1 can be obtained through a citizen survey. In addition, the survey also obtains demographic and supplementary diagnostic information to help interpret the data.

Included in an earlier report are detailed discussions of the survey procedures, along with instructions and procedures for conducting a telephone survey such as that used in Rockford and Washington, D.C.[7] Many citizen survey issues that apply regardless of the government service are discussed in Chapter 14. The St. Petersburg questionnaire is presented in Appendix 5.

Interviewing Method

St. Petersburg, Nashville, Washington, D.C., and Rockford used telephone interviewing. This method has some advantages over face-to-face interviews: Travel costs for interviewers are substantially reduced, interviews can be more closely controlled as to quality if a central location is provided for the interviewers and a supervisor monitors the interviewing effort, call-backs can be made with a minimum of trouble, and problems with households' refusing to allow interviewers into their homes are avoided. An important disadvantage is that some families, often lower-income ones, may not have telephones. If a significant percentage of the community's population lacks telephones, telephone surveys will not be appropriate. Otherwise, it appears that telephone interviewing may be the most appropriate method for local government park and recreation agencies.

Birmingham used a combination of face-to-face and telephone interviewing. The goal was 100 face-to-face interviews, but because of difficulty in reaching the respondents, the city was able to complete only twenty-five, with two call-backs. The 300 telephone interviews were completed without problems. The same interviewers conducted both types of interviews and used the same questionnaire.

Length of Interview and Response Rate

The St. Petersburg, Washington, D.C., Rockford, and Birmingham interviews took an average of eight minutes to complete. However, some took as long as thirty minutes and others were completed within five minutes. In Nashville, where many additional questions were added, the average time was fifteen minutes, with a number of interviews lasting thirty minutes; a few took up to an hour. Completing interviews, even with the longer questionnaire, did not prove to be a problem, but doubling the interview time, of course, raised the cost of the survey. The basic completion rate was about the same in

7. U.S. Bureau of Outdoor Recreation, *How Effective Are Your Community Recreation Services?*, especially Chapter 3 and appendices. See also U.S. Bureau of Outdoor Recreation, *How to Conduct a Recreation Effectiveness Telephone Survey* (Washington, D.C.: U.S. Government Printing Office, 1974).

Nashville as in the other cities where the shorter questionnaire was used.

The rates of cooperation in Nashville, St. Petersburg, Washington, D.C., and Rockford ranged from 74 percent to 86 percent. (Some additional interviews were not obtained because the numbers called were not answered—see Exhibit 4-4.) This is a somewhat poorer rate than those often quoted by professional survey firms. At least two reasons may account for the poorer response rates in these four cities. First, professional interviewers were not used. Although some of the park and recreation personnel had 90-percent completion rates or higher, many had 50-percent or even lower rates. Second, the interviewers were instructed not to press for an interview if the citizen did not want to participate. Professional survey firms have somewhat greater freedom to pursue a survey interview.

Who Should Undertake the Survey?

The set-up, interviewing, and data tabulation were handled by city personnel in St. Petersburg and Nashville, but outside technical assistance was provided to each jurisdiction on survey details, including training of the interviewers. In Birmingham a combination of park and recreation personnel, volunteers, and students were used in the set-up and interviewing. Limited outside assistance was provided in that city. Even the interview training was conducted by agency personnel, with the help of a videotape of the Nashville training session.[8]

As in the projects in Rockford and Washington, D.C., about half the prospective interviewers in Nashville and St. Petersburg dropped out after the initial training sessions. In both St. Petersburg and Nashville, interviewers tended to bog down after an initial burst of enthusiasm. About one-third of the forms were completed in the first three days, the next third took about twice as long, and the last third took a massive push to complete on schedule. In St. Petersburg, the survey was completed by bringing in a half-dozen of the best interviewers at night and paying them overtime to complete the interviewing. In Nashville, the supervisors had to complete the interviewing. Both jurisdictions indicated that in the future they would restrict themselves to a few good interviewers.

For long-term continuity, a government would probably need to use outside help, such as a survey firm, for interviewing. However, the government

may want and need to undertake the first survey primarily in house, with only outside technical guidance.

Use of an Introductory Letter

Both Nashville and St. Petersburg mailed an introductory letter to the prospective respondents before telephoning. Some survey professionals believe that such a letter increases the interview response rate. A question was included in the St. Petersburg survey as to whether the respondent had seen the introductory letter from the park and recreation department; for those persons who had, the successful completion rate was about twice that of those who had not. This finding suggests that the letter had some beneficial influence. However, the overall response rate in both Nashville and St. Petersburg was about the same as it was in Washington, D.C., and Rockford, where the introductory letter was not used.

Another reason for using the letter was that it tended to put the interviewers more at ease. Indeed, a number mentioned that it had made their job easier. A further advantage of using the introductory letter is that of identifying prospective respondents who have moved. Postal authorities were asked not to forward letters but to return them to the park and recreation agency if the addressee had moved. Approximately 5 percent of the letters were returned in both jurisdictions. In these cases, new households were added to the sample as replacements.

Both the Nashville and St. Petersburg letters asked the citizens to call the park and recreation agency if they wanted to be interviewed at a specific time, and each jurisdiction received a few requests for interviews. St. Petersburg received four calls, including one long-distance call from a citizen on vacation. The other calls came from residents who were leaving town on trips and wanted to be interviewed before departing.

Nashville and St. Petersburg officials estimated the cost of preparing and mailing the introductory letter at about $100 and two person-days of effort. Finally, it is important to note that an introductory letter can be used only when addresses of respondents are available in advance. If random digit dialing is used for the survey (to cover households with unlisted telephone numbers), letters cannot be sent out in advance.

Survey Flexibility

The citizen survey can be used to collect a variety of information. It could be used to ask respondents

---

8. This tape is available as of this writing to other local governments that wish to use it in training sessions. Interested governments should contact their regional office of the U.S. Bureau of Outdoor Recreation for additional information.

Exhibit 4-4

INTERVIEW COMPLETION RATES FOR GENERAL CITIZEN TELEPHONE SURVEYS ON RECREATION IN ST. PETERSBURG, WASHINGTON, D.C., ROCKFORD, AND NASHVILLE

CATEGORY	ST. PETERSBURG RANDOM SAMPLE OF TELEPHONE DIRECTORY		WASHINGTON RANDOM SAMPLE OF ALL TELEPHONE NUMBERS		ROCKFORD RANDOM SAMPLE OF TELEPHONE DIRECTORY		NASHVILLE RANDOM SAMPLE OF CITY DIRECTORY	
	Number	*Percent*	*Number*	*Percent*	*Number*	*Percent*	*Number*	*Percent*
(a) Completed usable interviews	384	48	836	58	415	58	402	50
(b) Interview rejections	138	17	139	10	116	16	106	13
(c) Bad telephone numbers	164	21	307	21	80	11	152	19
(d) Lost forms	54	7	31	2	0	0	16	2
(e) No answer[2]	58	7	107	8	102	15	128	16
(f) Unusable interview forms	2	—	17	1	0	0	0	0
Total numbers dialed	800	100	1,437	100	713	100	804	100
Nonrefusal rate: Completed as a percentage of total households answering call: $\frac{a}{(a+b)}$	$\frac{384}{522}$ =	74	$\frac{836}{975}$ =	86	$\frac{415}{533}$ =	78	$\frac{402}{508}$ =	79
Completion rate: Completed as a percentage of "good" numbers attempted: $\frac{a}{(a+b+e)}$	$\frac{384}{580}$ =	66	$\frac{836}{1,082}$ =	77	$\frac{415}{633}$ =	66	$\frac{402}{636}$ =	63

1. This category includes nonworking or disconnected numbers, business numbers, address changes, telephone number changes, and respondent on vacation.

2. As many as six call-backs were made in St. Petersburg, Washington, D.C., and Rockford. In Nashville, as many as nine call-backs were made.

Source: St. Petersburg, Florida, September 1973 survey; Washington, D. C., June 1972 survey; Rockford, Illinois, August 1972 survey; and Nashville, Tennessee, November 1973 survey.

about selection of recreation programs as well as about facilities. St. Petersburg, Birmingham, and Nashville have all used the inherent flexibility of the survey to collect information on issues of special interest to them. For example, St. Petersburg added questions on the type of programs preferred by respondents. That city also incorporated a series of questions on respondents' interest in a public golf course, an important issue for the city when the survey was conducted. Nashville extended its questionnaire to include questions about the general recreational interests of Nashville residents.

The few questions added to the St. Petersburg and Birmingham surveys added only a minute or two to the total survey time, but in the case of Nashville, the additional questions increased the average survey time from about eight to fifteen minutes.

Identifying Facilities

A somewhat complicating aspect of the questionnaire involved asking respondents about specific facilities in their neighborhoods. In Washington, D.C., each respondent was questioned about the three facilities closest to his or her residence, while in Nashville respondents were asked about the closest park and community center. In Rockford and St. Petersburg, respondents were asked about the closest park, pool, and community center; they were also asked whether they used any other local government facility, and, if so, which one. The interviewers, who were park and recreation employees, then determined whether the facilities mentioned by the respondents were operated by the park and recreation agency. (Questions 4 and 6 in Appendix 5 illustrate the format used.)

The problem with this approach is that the interviewer must identify the specific facilities before asking further questions. For telephone interviews when the interviewer does not know the respondent's address prior to the call (as with random digit dialing procedures), the interviewer must (1) obtain the respondent's address on the first call and then make a second call after determining the appropriate facilities to ask the respondent about, or (2) work very fast while on the telephone to identify the appropriate facilities on the spot. For at-home or telephone interviews, for which addresses are available ahead of time, this is less of a problem.

The need to call twice adds about ten minutes to each completed interview. Because of this added time and expense, random dialing procedures which would require this added effort were not used in St. Petersburg or Nashville (where about 12 percent of the telephones were unlisted). Washington, D.C., did use random digit dialing, so interviewers there had to obtain the address and make the second call after identifying the appropriate facility. About 100 of the 836 interviews completed in the District of Columbia were with respondents who said that their telephones were unlisted. The responses showed no significant differences in recreation behavior or perceptions between those respondents with unlisted and those with listed numbers.

A simpler alternative is to ask the respondents whether they had used *any* public park, pool, community center, or other facility during the time of interest without determining which ones. The respondents would be asked to rate the facilities of each type they had used or to indicate why they had not used the other types of facilities. Although this approach would prevent the government from obtaining information (such as reasons for nonuse) on *specific* facilities, it would considerably reduce the required survey effort and cost. Of course, it also has the drawback that some of the recreational experiences drawn on by respondents for their ratings might be for facilities not under the government's jurisdiction. If a jurisdiction has one or a few major facilities intended for communitywide use, those facilities could be specifically asked about in the survey.

Frequency and Timing of the Survey

The St. Petersburg survey was conducted in September; the Nashville survey, in early December; and the Birmingham and Palo Alto surveys, in May. The month selected in each city reflected staff availability rather than a deliberate attempt to conduct the survey at a particular time. However, an effectiveness measurement survey ideally should be tied into a government's budgeting cycle. For recreation, it is desirable that the survey encompass all seasons, or at least those seasons in which the government sponsors activities and those in which activities are likely to differ.

The St. Petersburg and Birmingham surveys asked respondents about one-month periods, the Nashville survey about three months. This time factor would not be a problem if respondents had perfect memories or if information were available on their memory span. However, research-based information is lacking as to citizen memory of recreation experiences. Studies in the areas of health and crime suggest that several factors are involved, including the length of time since the incident, the importance or frequency of the event in the respondent's life, and the respondent's motivation to report accurately.[9] Further research is needed.

If interviews are conducted at intervals throughout the year (for example, 150 every three months rather than 600 during one month), timing would be of less concern because respondents would need to be asked only about the period involved. Presumably, then, the full sample for the year would cover all seasons and all recreational experiences during that year. However, such a procedure can be an administrative headache.

It is more likely that these surveys will be undertaken only on an annual basis. If so, one guiding principle is to conduct the survey at approximately the same time each year so that the amount of change is reliable even if absolute levels are not.

Sample Size

This issue is discussed in somewhat greater detail in Chapter 14. Sample size depends heavily on the precision desired and the funds available. A third important factor is the number of data groupings the jurisdiction wants. As a crude guideline, a minimum of approximately 100 interviews should be sought for each group surveyed, whether that group is identified by geographic location, income, or whatever.

Validation of Survey Results

Full validation of survey responses—that is, determining that the measurements resulting from the data collection procedures truly reflect what was intended to be measured—was beyond the scope of this project. Nevertheless, certain steps were taken to maximize the likelihood that valid information was obtained. These steps should be undertaken by other governments using the survey:

1. Adjust the questionnaire wording for local conditions and pretest for local ambiguities.
2. Check sample procedures. Nashville drew its sample from the city directory. Careful counts were kept by neighborhood, and survey planners

---

9. See Chapter 14 for further discussion of this issue and references to existing research on the memory issue in terms of government questionnaires.

discovered that one part of the city had been excluded from the directory. Thus it was necessary to obtain numbers for that area from a different source.

3. Check demographic sample results. The demographic characteristics of the Nashville sample matched those of other samples and of the census quite closely. The St. Petersburg survey matched except for income, which suggested that the sample was biased toward high-income families. Interpreters and users of survey findings should consider such issues.

4. Check results for reasonableness. A number of approaches can be used to do this. In St. Petersburg, for instance, survey personnel spent an entire morning with the park and recreation director and his immediate staff reviewing the survey results for reasonableness. There was general agreement that the results were reasonable. The participation and attendance rates seemed reasonable, and they varied in the expected direction for different geographic areas.

Recreation Survey Costs and Staffing Requirements

The St. Petersburg survey involved interviews with 384 households by telephone, using a survey form

that took an average of eight minutes to complete. The project required thirty-six person-weeks of effort. In addition, St. Petersburg had an out-of-pocket cost of about $300 for printing, mailing, and contracting with a professional survey firm to provide the training. In Nashville, where the average survey time was fifteen minutes, fifty-three person-weeks were needed to complete the 402 questionnaires. Nashville spent approximately $900 for printing, mailing, training, and data processing; about $500 of the $900 was for keypunching and computer processing of the results. The survey in St. Petersburg was hand-tabulated.

Exhibit 4-5 summarizes the staffing and cost requirements for those surveys. Survey costs for St. Petersburg were similar to those incurred in Washington, D.C., and Rockford. Nashville costs were about 50 percent higher than those in Washington and Rockford, chiefly because of the longer survey questionnaire.

On a per completed-questionnaire basis, the staffing requirements were 3.7 hours per completed survey in St. Petersburg, 5.3 hours in Nashville, and 3.5 hours in the Washington, D.C., and Rockford experiences.

The elapsed time from the beginning of the set-up for the survey to the final report was thirteen

Exhibit 4-5
STAFFING AND DOLLAR EXPENDITURES, 1973 RECREATION TELEPHONE SURVEY—ST. PETERSBURG AND NASHVILLE

SURVEY ELEMENTS	ST. PETERSBURG (AVERAGE INTERVIEW = 8 MINUTES)			NASHVILLE (AVERAGE INTERVIEW = 15 MINUTES)		
	CALENDAR TIME IN WEEKS	DOLLARS EXPENDED	PERSON-WEEKS EXPENDED	CALENDAR TIME IN WEEKS	DOLLARS EXPENDED	PERSON-WEEKS EXPENDED
Set up—get ready						
Design questionnaire	4		2	6		4
Select random sample	3		2	4		4
Prepare survey material	4		12	4		15
Printing		50			100	
Postage		100			100	
Conduct survey						
Train interviewers	2		14	2		20
Conduct survey	2		14	2		20
Professional trainer		150			200	
Tabulation and analysis						
Check and code data	—	—	—	2	—	7
Tabulate data	2	—	4	3	—	—
Prepare report	1	—	2	3	—	3
Keypunch	—	—	—	—	200	—
Computer runs	—	—	—	—	300	—
Total	13[1]	300	36	18[1]	900	53

1. Some of the survey elements overlap so the total calendar time required is less than the sum of the individual elements.

Source: St. Petersburg, Florida, September 1973 survey; Nashville, Tennessee, November 1973 survey.

weeks in St. Petersburg and eighteen weeks in Nashville. These figures correspond to estimates based on the Washington, D.C., and Rockford experiences.[10]

We estimate that subsequent surveys by the same governments would cost about one-third less than the initial surveys. The saving is based on the two-part assumption that the same questionnaire would be used and that, if interviewing is done by government personnel, most of the same individuals would be involved in subsequent surveys. But this basic assumption, at least as it relates to personnel, can be questioned. In both St. Petersburg and Nashville, three of the persons most intimately involved with the park and recreation survey had moved to other jobs within a year of the surveys.

Finally, park and recreation managers should expect to spend time on a recreation survey. In Nashville and St. Petersburg, top managers devoted several days each to their survey efforts.

Options for Simplifying the Survey

As already noted with regard to Nashville, St. Petersburg, Washington, D.C., and Rockford, recreation personnel themselves undertook most survey aspects, including interviewing, rather than contracting with a professional survey firm. In part, this action was taken to save direct expenditure outlays. Recreation is a service area that seldom has funds for such contracting and few sources of outside support, such as federal dollars, for this type of activity. In addition, agency heads felt that their personnel would benefit from doing the interviewing, thereby gaining an increased understanding of citizen viewpoints.

Although accurate estimates were made in advance and city personnel were warned of the commitment required to undertake a citizen survey of this type, each agency was surprised at the intense effort required over the three- to four-month period required to complete the survey. Participants had to work extremely hard during this period and by the end were generally exhausted.

The likelihood of a recreation agency's undertaking this effort regularly, such as annually, seems small. Some options should, therefore, be considered. These include the following: (1) simplifying the questionnaire, especially by avoiding the requirement for the interviewer to determine the nearest community recreation facilities for each respondent (as discussed in the section on identifying facilities); (2) contracting out the survey; (3) using volunteers

10. See U.S. Bureau of Outdoor Recreation, *How Effective Are Your Community Recreation Services?*, p. 36.

outside the government, such as various citizen groups, to undertake the survey; or (4) if the government is already undertaking a citizen survey for other government services, participating in that survey and settling for considerably less detailed information.

The contracting option involves the problem noted earlier—that recreation agencies are likely to find the funds hard to obtain annually.

The fourth option would require selection of a small set of questions for the multiservice general citizen survey. The citizen survey is suggested in other chapters of this report to provide citizen feedback simultaneously on a number of local government services. Because the recreation departments in our project undertook separate citizen surveys (which is the more desirable procedure), the multiservice citizen surveys did not contain recreation questions during the initial trials. (Appendix 1 presents the multiservice questionnaire used by Nashville in 1974; Question 27 of that appendix concerns recreation and would provide data for Measure 1.)

St. Petersburg switched to using the multiservice survey for recreation; Appendix 7 abstracts the recreation questions in that effort. However, the drawback of the multiservice approach is the likelihood of space for only a small number of recreation questions. The questions in Appendix 7 provide data only for Measures 2 (overall user satisfaction) and 3 (participation and nonparticipation rates, including reasons for nonparticipation). The questions do not provide ratings of specific characteristics such as crowding or physical attractiveness.

Primary candidates for inclusion in the multiservice survey, if time were available, would be such questions from Appendix 5 as numbers 3 (overall rating), 4 (asking about usage of each type of recreation facility, rather than about specific facilities), 12 (ratings of various facility characteristics), and 14 (reasons for nonuse).

The Recreation User Survey

A number of park and recreation agencies in the United States, particularly at the state and federal level, have conducted on-site surveys of persons who use park and recreation facilities. Such surveys are much less common at the local government level, but they have been used by a number of city and county park and recreation agencies. Generally, these surveys have been one-time efforts that focused on the overall satisfaction of users and any modifications they would like made. User surveys have not been employed to collect regular information on the effectiveness of current services, at least not in a systematic way that permits annual comparisons.

The surveys described in this section focus on service effectiveness. They ask about users' recent past experiences and attitudes toward existing facilities and activities. When administered annually, these surveys can be used to provide time-trend information on both program and individual facility effectiveness.

The suggestions presented here are based on on-site user surveys undertaken in 1973 or 1974 in Nashville, St. Petersburg, and Palo Alto. The Nashville survey was restricted to community centers, but the St. Petersburg survey included those centers and selected parks as well. The Palo Alto survey involved only golf course users. A sample user survey questionnaire (adapted from the Nashville and St. Petersburg questionnaires) is presented in Appendix 6.

On-site user surveys offer the following advantages over general citizen surveys:

1. They provide an efficient way to collect data directly related to users' actual experiences.
2. They produce, at low cost, sample sizes large enough for statements to be made about the effectiveness of specific facilities or programs. This is in contrast to general citizen surveys, in which, because of cost, it is not usually feasible to have large enough samples to make precise statements about individual facilities and programs.
3. They permit individuals to speak for themselves. In most household surveys, by comparison, time and cost factors mean that one person is asked to speak for the entire household.
4. They seem well within the capability of the average recreation department to conduct on its own.

There are three principal disadvantages to user surveys:

1. They do not permit a department to collect data on nonusers and their reasons for not taking advantage of recreation services.
2. From the information provided by a user survey it is difficult to estimate with any precision the percentage of different users in a community.
3. User surveys are difficult to conduct where the site is large and lacks controlled access, such as a large park.

The user surveys discussed here can produce data for ten of the twenty-four measures shown in Exhibit 4-1. Those ten measures are listed in Exhibit 4-6.

In addition to client ratings, questions should also be included on the survey to produce demographic and diagnostic data. These data include such factors as age, sex, and income range of respondents; how far the individual traveled to reach the facility; the mode of transportation used; and perhaps the length of time spent in transit (see Questions 1–5 and 23–27 in Appendix 6).

Interviewing Method

There are two basic interviewing approaches: face-to-face interviewing and self-administered forms. The former requires an interviewer to read each question and record the answer. With self-administered surveys, users complete the questionnaire themselves. Most park and recreation agencies will find a combination of the two procedures to be advisable. Both Nashville and St. Petersburg used such a combination, with face-to-face interviewing used only in the case of young children or others unable to complete the form themselves. The Palo Alto golf survey relied solely on the self-administered questionnaire.

Length of Interview

The type of questionnaire suggested should require less than ten minutes to complete. In Palo Alto the average time to complete the questionnaire was six minutes; in St. Petersburg, five minutes; and in Nashville, four minutes.

Exhibit 4-6
DATA COLLECTED BY USER SURVEY FOR RECREATION EFFECTIVENESS MEASURES

PERCEPTION (SUBJECTIVE) MEASURES	MEASURE NUMBER[1]	SURVEY QUESTION NUMBER[2]
User satisfaction	2	21
Crowded conditions	5	10
Physical attractiveness	8	12
Facility cleanliness	10	7
Equipment condition	11	8
Safety	14	11
Physical accessibility/ convenience	17	17
Hours/days of operation	19	6
Variety of interesting activities	21	13
Staff helpfulness	23	14

1. See Exhibit 4-1.
2. These are the questions shown in the illustrative user survey in Appendix 6.

Special Validity Issues

Essentially the same questions can be raised with the user survey as with the general citizen survey concerning the validity of citizen responses: Does the survey questionnaire obtain valid information from respondents? General validity problems are discussed in Chapter 14; some special recreation validity issues were discussed earlier in this chapter. However, in several respects, user surveys present less severe problems than do citizen surveys. First, in user surveys, individuals speak only for themselves; they are not asked to respond on behalf of other members of their families as well. Surveys in the health field show that, at least for health-related questions, this factor improves accuracy.[11] Second, sampling is much less of a problem. There should be little or no bias introduced by sampling if fairly simple procedures are followed.[12] Third, the user is more likely to be interested in the survey and as a result to give more accurate answers.[13] Fourth, the questions do not rely heavily on respondent's memories.

Who Should Undertake the Survey Operations?

With only limited outside assistance, government personnel in Nashville, St. Petersburg, and Palo Alto designed their own survey questionnaires, pretested the forms, conducted the surveys, and tabulated the results. Although most governments should have professional advice, particularly for the initial survey and questionnaire design, local governments should be able to handle most aspects of a user survey by themselves.

There is a question as to whether the use of recreation personnel to handle the interviewing produces a bias in the results. There are two sources of potential bias. First, recreation personnel may unintentionally encourage responses that correspond to their own perceptions. Second, if the persons being interviewed felt park and recreation personnel were being rated on the basis of their responses, the interviewees might respond more favorably to facility conditions than they otherwise would. St.

11. U.S. Public Health Service, *Reporting of Hospitalization in the Health Interview Survey* (July 1965).

12. Nashville did find that some of its centers failed to complete the survey as instructed. Only six centers out of twenty-seven conducted the survey entirely as instructed; another three completed the survey with minor errors (e.g., a few interview forms without a date or time); sixteen partially completed the survey; and two centers did not participate at all. Although St. Petersburg and Palo Alto completed the user survey as planned, supervising personnel in the two cities reported that it was necessary to visit those carrying out the survey frequently—that is, several times a day. Otherwise, interviewers tended to skip individuals and failed to check the completed survey forms properly.

13. U.S. Public Health Service, *Reporting of Hospitalization*.

Petersburg attempted to overcome this potential problem by assigning its personnel to facilities other than those where they would normally work.

It also may be possible to use interviewers outside the park and recreation agency. Possibilities include other government personnel; volunteers from groups such as the League of Women Voters, Park and Recreation Board, or Health and Welfare Council; or paid outside help. The Palo Alto survey was administered entirely by volunteers of the local golf club and League of Women Voters. Washington, D.C., used Neighborhood Youth Corps personnel to help with a swimming pool survey. When such outside personnel are used, close supervision is particularly important.

Frequency and Timing of the Survey

Since seasonal differences are important in recreation, it may be advisable to conduct a survey at the end of each major recreational season. Governments interested in evaluating a particular program, such as summer activities, may want to conduct the survey at the end of that season.

Seasonality would not be a problem if users could be counted on to recall the experiences over an extended period. Unfortunately, information on citizen recall of recreation experience is scanty (see the discussion earlier in this chapter and that in Chapter 14). The issue seems to be most important for the more objective type of information, such as the frequency of attendance and length of stay. It is probably less important for subjective information such as ratings of recreational opportunities.

The Palo Alto golf survey asked respondents about their use over a period of twelve months, as does the questionnaire illustrated in Appendix 6 (see Question 4). The St. Petersburg community center and park survey asked about a two-month period. The Nashville community center survey did not specify a time on its questionnaire. It may be that the time period has little effect on the responses, but research on this problem is needed.

The survey is intended to cover a representative cross section of users. Because the kind of user is likely to vary by the time of the day and the day of the week, a survey should cover all the periods that a facility is open. In Palo Alto and Nashville, the survey was run for a complete week. The St. Petersburg survey, which was restricted to three days by resource constraints, sampled one low-attendance day, one medium-attendance day, and one high-attendance day. In each of the three cities, the survey was conducted from opening to closing time on each survey day.

Sample Size and Selection

Sampling is much less of a problem for a user survey than it is for a household survey because the users come to the site and to the interviewer. Hence it is a relatively simple task to select those to be sampled. The factor that primarily determines the cost of the user survey is not the absolute sample size but rather the number of different facilities covered and the number of survey hours and days spent at each facility.

The sample size should be sufficiently large at each site to permit grouping the user responses into desired categories, such as age, sex, race, and location or residence. In St. Petersburg, the sample design called for 100 completed interviews from each center. In total, there were 1,207 interviews at fourteen facilities. At some places where the expected attendance was small, everyone was interviewed. At other sites, every other person or every third person was selected; at one busy facility, every fifteenth person was selected to complete a questionnaire.

Essentially the same procedure was used in the Nashville community center survey. The average weekly attendance for a recent month was used as the basis for selecting a sample that would yield about 150 interviews per center. In the Palo Alto golf course survey, everyone at the site was interviewed; 908 responses were collected. Added costs of increasing the sample size for a user survey are likely to be small, particularly if computer processing is used to tabulate the data.

Interviewing the Users

The user surveys in Nashville, Palo Alto, and St. Petersburg were conducted at sites where access was controlled. No surveying took place at open-access parks and playgrounds, sites that introduce a more complicated sampling problem not investigated in the course of this study.

At each facility, tables were set up for the survey team, which generally consisted of two individuals. In Palo Alto, each user was stopped and asked to complete the survey form. In Nashville and St. Petersburg, a separate sample was designed for each site, based on the number of expected visitors. Every third, ninth, or fifteenth person through the gate was asked to complete the survey form; these numbers were based on the estimated interval required to obtain the desired 100 interviews from the attendance expected during the period when the in-

terviews were to be conducted.[14] When users were not old enough to complete the form by themselves, a member of the survey team read the questions and helped complete the form. Respondents were asked to put their completed form into a ballot box.

Tabulating and Analyzing the Results

If the survey is larger than several hundred interviews, it is probably advisable to precode the survey questionnaire, keypunch the results directly from the survey forms, and tabulate by computer. Several computer programs facilitate a variety of tabulations and statistical manipulations. Nashville, Palo Alto, and St. Petersburg each used the Statistical Package for Social Sciences (SPSS) in tallying the results of their surveys. Of course, the results can always be hand tabulated, but this is an onerous task and increases the possibility of error.

Use of survey results requires more than simple tabulations. Analysis of the data and consideration of their meaning by recreation personnel are both needed if the full potential usefulness is to be mined from the data. In Palo Alto, a special analysis was prepared for the city council, which had requested information on the golf course. In Nashville and St. Petersburg, the results of the survey were documented in a series of site reports for the responsible recreation supervisors. (An example of one of these site reports is presented in the last section of this chapter.) In addition, a series of discussions on the results was held with site supervisors. A report was also prepared summarizing the data from all survey sites.

User Survey Staffing and Timing Requirements

Exhibit 4-7 shows the estimated staff time required for a user survey. Based on the experiences in Nashville, St. Petersburg, and Palo Alto in 1973 and 1974, it appears that designing the questionnaire, conducting the survey, and tabulating results take about one person-hour for each completed survey questionnaire. The amount of staffing and time will vary, depending mainly on the number of different sites and the number of hours over which the survey is conducted. Less important for user surveys is the number of questionnaires completed at any one facility.

14. It would not be appropriate to conduct such sampling of persons already in the park rather than those entering. The former procedure could bias the sample by making persons remaining longer at the facility more likely to be surveyed. See Robert C. Lucas, "Bias in Estimating Recreationists' Length of Stay from Sample Interviews," *Journal of Forestry* 61(12):912–14.

Exhibit 4-7

ESTIMATED TIME REQUIREMENTS
FOR USER SURVEY

For 100 interviews at each of 10 facilities open 10
hours per day for one week

TASK	TIME REQUIRED	
	ELAPSED CALENDAR TIME (WEEKS)	PERSON-WEEKS
(1) Select topics, specify accuracy, and design management plan	½	½
(2) Design and pretest questionnaire	1	1
(3) Design sampling plan and prepare material	1	1
(4) Recruit and train interviewers	½	½
(5) Conduct survey	1	15
(6) Edit, code, keypunch, and tabulate	2	2
(7) Analyze and prepare written findings	4	4
TOTAL	8[1]	24

1. Because some of the survey elements overlap, the total time required is less than the sum of individual elements.

Repeat surveys in future years should cost somewhat—but not much—less, as the only saving would be in the design and pretesting of the questionnaire. Staffing for a survey at ten facilities (seventy survey hours) would probably require one survey leader, one computer programmer, one management analyst, and twenty interviewers. It is possible that a single person can handle more than one of these tasks.

The total elapsed time from the decision to go ahead until the time the results are available will be about two to three months. In the Palo Alto, Nashville, and St. Petersburg experiences, the greatest time delay came in getting data keypunched and run on the computer.

Costs and Staffing Requirements for Measurement Procedures

Earlier publications have presented the cost and staffing requirements for measuring the effectiveness of recreation services.[15] Based on the experi-

ences in Nashville, Palo Alto, and St. Petersburg, there appears to be no reason to change the earlier overall cost and staffing estimates. Exhibit 4-8 summarizes the estimated annual costs for each of the measurement procedures. Exhibit 4-9 provides estimates of the total costs for three agency sizes and three measurement levels.

The overall effort needed to collect the data on the measurements outlined in Exhibit 4-1 is likely to be a little less than one person-year of effort for a department with an operating budget of $500,000 or less; about one and one-half person-years of effort for a department with a budget of approximately $1 million; and about two person-years for a department with a budget of $10 million or more.

The actual *added* operating expenditure required to support these effectiveness measurement procedures in any jurisdiction will depend on a number of factors—in particular, the current availability of staff and data. In Nashville, Rockford, St. Petersburg, and Washington, D.C., recreation personnel handled much of the work, thus reducing considerably the out-of-pocket cost to the park and recreation agency. The actual added expenditures in each city were small, less than $1,000. Also, it is not necessary for a jurisdiction to adopt all of the measurement procedures. Government managers may be more interested in certain elements than in others. Finally, the frequency of reporting will have an important impact on the overall cost of the system.

Using the Recreation Effectiveness Information

The utilization of effectiveness measurement information is the subject of Chapter 12. Presented here, however, are some findings related particularly to the recreation field. Park and recreation officials with whom we have discussed measures of effectiveness have generally demonstrated a lively interest in information that can be collected through citizen surveys—both the general citizen survey and the on-site user surveys.[16] However, when presented with information from the general citizen survey, some have expressed disappointment because it did not provide data on individual programs or facilities; the sample sizes were large enough to provide meaningful data only on major districts in the cities or

15. U.S. Bureau of Outdoor Recreation, *How Effective Are Your Community Recreation Services?*, by Donald Fisk (Washington, D.C.: Government Printing Office, April 1973) pp. 73–79; and Hatry and Dunn, *Measuring the Effectiveness*, pp. 42–44.

16. For an example of the reports provided, see Metropolitan Nashville-Davidson County Government, Board of Parks and Recreation, "Summary Report of Citizen Surveys of Metro Park and Recreation Opportunities in Nashville-Davidson County" (May 1974). This document reports on both the general citizen survey and the community center users' survey.

Exhibit 4-8

ESTIMATED COST OF ESTABLISHING AND OPERATING A RECREATION EFFECTIVENESS
MEASUREMENT SYSTEM, MEDIUM-SIZE CITY

(250,000 population; 100 full-time recreational employees, medium level of measurement)

MEASUREMENT TOOL OR TECHNIQUE	FIRST YEAR		SUBSEQUENT YEARS	
	PERSON-HOURS	COST	PERSON-HOURS	COST
Data collection				
General citizen survey				
One survey per year[1]				
(400 households)	1,400	$12,500	1,200	$ 6,250
User survey				
One survey per year				
(15 recreation sites)	950	5,250	725	3,650
Other measurements				
Physical accessibility	300	2,000	150	700
Attendance	100	500	50	250
Safety	50	250	25	100
Crowdedness	100	750	25	100
Subtotal	2,900	$21,250	2,175	$11,050
Data analysis				
Subtotal	1,100	$18,750	825	$13,950
Total collection and analysis	4,000	$40,000	3,000	$25,000

1. Actual out-of-pocket expenditures can be reduced significantly if current government personnel undertake certain tasks, such as interviewing. Costs also can be reduced if survey designers adopt the options discussed in the text, such as avoiding the requirement for interviewers to identify the nearest community recreation facilities for each respondent, or including a more limited set of questions on a multiservice survey.

Source: Adapted from U.S. Bureau of Outdoor Recreation, *How Effective Are Your Outdoor Recreation Services?*, Exhibit 32, p. 75, with revisions based on 1974-75 experiences in Nashville and St. Petersburg. (See further details in the respective sections of this chapter.) Cost estimates are based on 1975 salary levels.

counties. Recreation managers found such information difficult to interpret and insufficiently relevant to their needs. The information they seem to have found most interesting thus far is that collected by the user survey. These data can be tied to specific facilities, programs, and individuals. Thus, the user surveys can provide feedback to individual facility managers as well as higher level officials on the effectiveness of their operations. This feedback provides a way to establish accountability in the park and recreation field.

Nashville and St. Petersburg prepared short reports on the user survey results for each facility manager. Exhibit 4-10 presents an example of such a report. As a result of the survey, one Nashville manager discovered that his program had been serving people predominantly outside the center's immediate geographic area. He then redirected the program to seek to attract the residents surrounding his center.

Probably the greatest interest in the Nashville and St. Petersburg survey results (both user and general citizen surveys) came from the park and recreation supervisors. For the first time, they were provided with systematic feedback on citizen's viewpoints about operations in their individual geographic areas.

Both Nashville and St. Petersburg conducted meetings involving center supervisors, area supervisors, and the program analysts responsible for preparing the user survey results. Such meetings can be used to discuss issues that have escaped the notice of department managers and program analysts, and they can provide a forum for outlining steps to take corrective action where needed. Often the meetings may simply highlight problems that supervisors already knew existed. For example, one center in St. Petersburg was cleaned and repainted after the survey. Until discussions were held with the program analyst and area supervisor about survey results, the center supervisor did not realize that he had to initiate the work order to have the center painted. Similarly, custodians in Nashville were told that citizens' ratings would be taken into account in evaluating custodial performance. (However, we have no current information on the effects of this policy.)

Despite its limitations in terms of data on specific facilities or programs, the general citizen survey does provide a comprehensive perspective on

Exhibit 4-9
ESTIMATED ANNUAL RECURRING COST
OF A RECREATION EFFECTIVENESS
MEASUREMENT SYSTEM
(Three city sizes and three measurement levels)[1]

CLASSIFICATION	RECREATION AGENCY SIZE		
	SMALL	MEDIUM	LARGE
Population	Fewer than 100,000	Approx. 250,000	More than 500,000
Agency operating budget	$500,000	$1,000,000	$10,000,000
Number of full-time employees	40	100	500
Low Budget			
Update of measurements	Annual	Annual	Annual
Number of user surveys per year	1	1	1
Total staff-years of effort	0.5	0.75	1.0
Total yearly cost	$10,000	$15,000	$20,000
Percentage of operating budget	2%	1.5%	.02%
Medium Budget			
Update of measurements	Seasonal	Seasonal	Seasonal
Number of user surveys per year	1	1	1
Total staff-years of effort	0.75	1.5	2.0
Total yearly cost	$15,000	$25,000	$30,000
Percentage of operating budget	3%	2.5%	.03%
High Budget			
Update of measurements	Monthly	Monthly	Monthly
Number of user surveys per year	2	2	2
Total staff-years of effort	1.0	2.0	2.5
Total yearly cost	$20,000	$30,000	$40,000
Percentage of operating budget	4%	3%	.04%

1. All options shown include a general citizen recreation survey. Actual out-of-pocket expenditures can be reduced significantly if current government personnel undertake certain tasks, such as interviewing. Costs also can be reduced if survey designers adopt the options presented in the text, such as avoiding the requirement for interviewers to identify the nearest community recreation facilities for each respondent, or including a more limited set of questions on a multiservice survey.

Source: Adapted from U.S. Bureau of Outdoor Recreation, *How Effective Are Your Outdoor Recreation Services?*, Exhibit 31, p. 74, with revisions based on 1973-74 experiences in Nashville and St. Petersburg.

recreation services. This type of survey reflects, for example, both nonuser attitudes toward existing recreational services and the extent of nonusage.

At least two recreation supervisors in the District of Columbia produced and distributed information on their programs to the surrounding community after discovering from the citizen survey that the citizens were unaware of D.C. facilities and program offerings. Officials in St. Petersburg used survey results to justify the need for more tennis courts, to speed up the construction of a swimming pool, to justify an addition to a community center, and to clean a facility that the citizens identified as dirty. Although each of these actions probably would have taken place without the survey results, in at least two cases it seems likely that the survey results speeded up official action. Top agency officials in St. Petersburg devoted an entire morning to a review of the survey results; although there was disagreement with some of the citizen responses, officials generally agreed that their perceptions matched those of the citizens.

Effectiveness information is but one class of data—albeit a very important one—needed before major government actions should be taken. The information generated by the procedures discussed in this chapter and throughout the report does not indicate why conditions are bad or good nor what should be done about them. That information indicates only the results of government services. It is necessary to compare results obtained from effectiveness data with other available information and with managers' experience. A major problem in implementing park and recreation measures of effectiveness in local government is the lack of analytical personnel. Few recreation agencies have the staff needed to carry out measurement procedures or analysis of the data obtained. Where such staff people are available, they are generally used to the maximum; the test cities reported on here were no exception.

Based on the experiences discussed here, it appears that when persons with analytical skills are recruited by park and recreation agencies they may not remain for long. (Most of those with the necessary skills were young and highly mobile.) Thus, one of the test cities began using a person from within the park and recreation agency to carry on the measurement work. This employee knew the agency and its staff and was apparently successful in understanding and using effectiveness measurement information.

The lack of analysts to examine effectiveness measurement and other relevant data seems to be a major constraint on the full use of that information. Many of the outputs and procedures for collecting the data are new and unfamiliar to managers. For example, managers are not accustomed to questioning staffs or encouraging them to consider the implications and improvements suggested by the data. In the long run, such an orientation seems necessary in order for governments to get the most out of effectiveness measurement information.

Exhibit 4-10
EXAMPLE OF USER SURVEY RESULTS (For one community center and park)

NEIGHBORHOOD CHARACTERISTICS

Kirkpatrick is located on South 9th Street on 7.75 acres in East Nashville. The J. A. Cayce Homes, public housing for low-income persons, are located behind the center. The Community Center has a gym, two club rooms, a game room, and a kitchen. The Community Center Director has determined that this center should serve the immediate neighborhood bordered on the west by South 7th Street, to the east by South 15th, Lenore Street to the south, and Woodland Street to the north. The areas served by Kirkpatrick and East Community Centers correspond to Census Tracts 120, 123, and 124. These Census Tracts reported a racial composition (1970) of 14 percent nonwhites, 86 percent whites. In age distribution there were 36 percent children to 18 years, 51 percent adults to 64 years, and 13 percent 65 and older. Forty-seven percent of the population is male, 53 percent female. The median family income (the average of three medians) is $4,819.

USER CHARACTERISTICS (1973)

The characteristics of users from the December 1973 sample were as follows, based on the 47 persons filling out forms: 66 percent of those stated their race was black, and 33 percent white; 58 percent of users were male and 42 percent female. In age composition, 38 percent were from ages 6 to 12, 45 percent 13 to 17, 14 percent 18 to 34, and 2 percent 35 to 59. That is, 83 percent were children and teen-agers and 16 percent were adults. No elderly persons were users that week. The predominant mode of transportation of Community Center users was walking (62 percent), although 30 percent did use a car to get there. For the majority of users, time spent traveling to the center was ten minutes or less (74 percent). For those traveling by car, length of travel time ranged from five to thirty minutes.

Day of the week and hour of arrival were also sampled. Users were sampled from Monday through Thursday only; no data were collected on Friday and Saturday, which were identified as the least frequented days. About 43 percent of users arrived between 6:30 and 10:00 p.m. The average length of stay was about 3½ hours. The attendance was higher on Tuesday and Thursday because of league basketball games.

USERS' RATINGS

Users' favorite activities were basketball for both boys and girls; only 28 percent of the males and 44 percent of the females listed other activities. Among things respondents liked about the center were "basketball," "everything," and "the staff." Most people said they disliked "nothing" about the center. A few complained that the center closed too early and had too many league basketball games. Forty-five percent of the users learned about the Community Center through friends, relatives, or neighbors.

The center received the following satisfactory ratings, listed in order from best to worst ratings:

	PERCENTAGE OF SATISFACTORY RATINGS	
	CENTER RATINGS	*AVERAGE ALL CENTERS*
Helpfulness and attitude of staff	96	81
Amount of supervision	93	78
Cleanliness	89	68
Conditions and safety of equipment	86	71
Feeling of security	74	70
Amount of space	72	64
Convenience to your home	68	73
Hours and days open	67	74
Variety of programs and activities	63	73

In summary, the center received high ratings for staff, supervision, and cleanliness. The lowest ratings were for convenience, hours and days open, and the variety of programs.

PARK USERS

The random sample telephone survey included only two household members who had used Kirkpatrick Park; therefore, there are no results to report.

CONCLUSIONS AND RECOMMENDATIONS

The neighborhood surrounding the center is a low-income one, 86 percent whites and 14 percent blacks. Thirty-six percent of the population are children (to 18), 51 percent are adults (to 64 years), and 13 percent over 65. Among the users, 83 percent were children (to 17 years), 16 percent were adults (to 59 years), and there were no elderly. *It is concluded that the center is not meeting the needs of its adult and elderly populations.* The center is serving a high proportion of females (42 percent), although these are mainly teen-age blacks who come more as spectators than participants.

It is recommended that more programs should be offered for the adults and the elderly population. It is also recommended that more of a variety of programs and activities should be offered to the eighteen-and-under age groups because of the low "variety" rating the center received in the users' survey. In order to facilitate the development of more programs for the elderly, some type of transportation is needed. They live a few blocks from the center and there is a perceived and actual danger involved in walking because of muggers and other street crime. Another possibility is to initiate a recreation program within apartment dwellings in community rooms. A number of adult and elderly men have expressed interest in playing croquet on the outdoor area provided in the park, if a shade or cover is added to provide protection from the sun.

Source: Based on the 1974 Nashville Users Survey and Nashville-Urban Observatory, *Leisure Services: The Measurement of Program Performance* (June 1974), pp. 73–77.

Chapter 5
Library Services

Most public libraries report on various aspects of their operations, but few do so systematically from the perspective of users and potential users. Most library systems lack information on (1) the level of citizen satisfaction with library operations, including the comfort of facilities, hours of operation, speed of service, and helpfulness of the library staff; (2) the availability of materials sought by the users; and (3) the percentage of households using the system, with estimates of reasons for nonuse by those not using the system.

Some libraries have, on occasion, collected such information through special studies. But there has been no regular collection of such information and systematic tracking of it over time.[1]

Objectives and Related Effectiveness Measures

A basic objective for library services that seems applicable to most communities is:

1. There is considerable research and writing in the area of library measurements. In addition, consultants, citizen groups, and library staffs themselves have made a number of studies of individual libraries. See Ernest R. DeProspo, Ellen Altman, and Kenneth E. Beasley, *Performance Measures for Public Libraries* (Chicago: American Library Association-Public Library Association, 1973) for a review of the literature. The bibliography in DeProspo's appendix provides a list of a number of other relevant studies. These are useful sources of ideas for measures and procedures for regular collection of data by local governments. The in-library measurement suggestions (Measures 6-8) draw heavily upon DeProspo et al.

To present library services that, to the extent possible, provide the greatest satisfaction to citizens, including timely, helpful, and readily available services that are attractive, accessible, and convenient.

A set of measures to assess progress toward meeting this objective is presented in Exhibit 5-1. The data collection procedures for most of these measures were tested in St. Petersburg and Nashville.

The objectives and measures listed here are for evaluating the overall library system, but in many cases the measurement procedures can also provide information on specific units such as individual branches, or on individual activities such as reference, circulation, or special collections. Except for measures that use data from a survey of the general population and the measures on physical accessibility (which are concerned with accessibility of the public to the *set* of library facilities rather than individual facilities), most of the measures and associated data collection procedures readily lend themselves to tallying by individual facilities. To evaluate special programs, such as mobile or outreach programs or libraries for lawyers or schools, some measures would need to be modified. For example, the measurement procedure for "diversity and currentness of book holdings" would probably have to be modified for special libraries, and the measurement procedures for "physical accessibility" would need to be modified for mobile or outreach programs. But many measures, such as those for "overall citizen satisfaction" and "helpfulness and courtesy of the staff," apply to special operations as well as to the overall system.

Exhibit 5-1
MEASURES OF EFFECTIVENESS FOR LIBRARY SERVICES

OVERALL OBJECTIVE: To present library services that, to the extent possible, provide the greatest satisfaction to citizens, including timely, helpful, and readily available services that are attractive, accessible, and convenient.

OBJECTIVE	QUALITY CHARACTERISTIC	SPECIFIC MEASURE[1]	DATA COLLECTION PROCEDURE
Overall Citizen Satisfaction	Citizen satisfaction	1. Percentage of citizens rating library as satisfactory.	General citizen survey
	User satisfaction	2. Percentage of clients using city libraries that rate them as satisfactory.	Library user survey or general citizen survey
	Use—Household	3. Percentage of households using (or not using) a public library a minimum number of times, such as 4 times over past 12 months—with reasons for nonuse.	General citizen survey
	Registration—Household	4. Percentage of households with (or without) a valid registration card.	Statistics from public library or general citizen survey
	Use—Visitation	5. Number of visits to library facilities per capita (or per household).	Library counts of number of users with population estimates from city planning department
	Use—Circulation	6. Circulation per capita by type of material—e.g., fiction, nonfiction, records, film—divided between internal and external use.	External circulation figures, kept by most public libraries. Internal figures, estimated from periodic sampling
Comprehensiveness/ Timeliness/ Availability of Holdings	Diversity and currentness of book and periodical holdings	7. Probability of owning (a) books, and (b) periodicals published during given time period (e.g., last 5 years).	Random sample of (a) books published from the *Book Publishing Record* (BPR) or other bibliographic catalog, or (b) citations published in one of common periodical indexes—compared with library holdings
	Availability of book holdings	8. Probability of a user's obtaining (a) a book or (b) a periodical when it is wanted.	Random sample of (a) books or (b) periodicals held and checked against availability in the proper area
	Speed of service	9. Percentage of users who rate speed of service as satisfactory.	Library user survey or general citizen survey
Helpfulness of Staff	Helpfulness— Courtesy of staff	10. Percentage of persons using library who rate helpfulness and general attitude of staff as satisfactory.	Library user survey or general citizen survey
	Helpfulness— Quality of reference service	11. Percentage of persons using library reference services who rate them as satisfactory.	Library user survey or general citizen survey
Attractiveness of Facility	User satisfaction with comfort, crowdedness, noise, etc.	12. Percentage of persons using library who rate comfort, crowdedness, noise, cleanliness, and temperature/ventilation as satisfactory.	Library user survey or general citizen survey
	Nonuser satisfaction	13. Percentage of nonusers who cite lack of comfort, crowdedness, noise, cleanliness, or temperature/ventilation as reasons for nonuse.	General citizen survey
Accessibility and Convenience	Physical accessibility, convenience	14. Percentage of users rating convenience as satisfactory.	Library user survey or general citizen survey
		15. Percentage of nonuser households who give poor physical accessibility as a reason for nonuse.	General citizen survey
		16. Percentage of citizens who live within a specific travel time (such as 15 minutes) of a public library.	Counts from mapping latest census tract population figures against location of facilities with appropriate travel time radius drawn around each facility
	Hours of operation	17. Percentage of users rating hours of operation as satisfactory.	Library user survey or general citizen survey
		18. Percentage of nonuser households who give poor hours as a reason for nonuse.	General citizen survey

1. Officials who wish to focus on amount of local *dissatisfaction* may substitute "unsatisfactory" for the term "satisfactory" in many of these measures.

Principal Measures and Measurement Procedures

Exhibit 5-1 lists eighteen effectiveness measures suggested to help in assessing library services. When data on these measures are collected regularly—at least annually—progress can be tracked over time and emerging problems identified. The principal suggestions can be summarized as follows:

1. A prime indicator of the quality of public library services is the overall satisfaction of the citizens of the community with those services. Both an annual survey of a random sample of citizens in the community and a random sample of library users are suggested. Data from a survey of a representative sample of citizens throughout the community[2] can be used to obtain a reasonable estimate of the satisfaction level in the community. Information on how satisfactory the users find the library can be obtained from a sample of users in the library.

2. The general citizen survey can also be used to obtain information on the percentage of households in the community that have used a public library a minimum number of times during a specific period, such as within the previous twelve months. From nonusers, the survey can obtain information as to reasons for nonuse. Tallying the reasons for nonuse can help guide public officials toward improvements in the attractiveness and effectiveness of library services.

3. A number of specific qualities of library service important to library management and other public officials should be measured, including speed of service, helpfulness and courtesy of staff, comfort of the facilities, and physical accessibility and convenience (including hours of operation) of library services. Data to measure these qualities can be obtained from the same surveys of users and the general population used to obtain overall satisfaction and usage information. Such ratings by citizens appear to be the most direct way to obtain feedback on the quality of services, and are important for library service assessment.

4. The availability and comprehensiveness of materials such as books and publications are important aspects of library service. An American

2. The practicality of a local government's undertaking an annual survey of a representative sample of the community is greatly enhanced if the survey simultaneously covers a number of local services (not just one service such as the library). The multiservice citizen survey is suggested throughout this report.

Library Association-sponsored effort has promulgated procedures that were tested in the two test cities. These measure the "probability of the library's owning recent books and periodicals," and the "probability of a user's obtaining a book or periodical owned at the time the user wants it." The comparison of a list of library holdings with a random sample of titles drawn from a comprehensive bibliographic catalog can provide data on the first measure. A search of the library shelves for a random sample of books or publications owned by the library can provide data on the second measure. An alternative, untested, procedure would be to sample library users in the library to determine whether they had found the materials they sought. (The latter procedure is more direct and inclusive, but cumbersome. It would be less cumbersome if it could be included as part of the survey of library users.)

The individual measures and procedures for collecting data for them are discussed in the following sections.

Individual Measures

This section describes the rationale for the various measures shown in Exhibit 5-1 and indicates the procedures for collecting data for each. Because data for many of the measures can be collected by a survey of a sample of library users and many others by a survey of a sample of citizens throughout the community, these procedures are discussed in more detail in a later section.

The measures are grouped for discussion into five major categories:

- Overall citizen or client satisfaction (Measures 1-6);
- Comprehensives, timeliness, availability (Measures 7-9);
- Helpfulness of staff; attractiveness of facility (Measures 10-13); and
- Physical accessibility and convenience (Measures 14-18).

Measures of Overall Citizen/Client Satisfaction (Measures 1-6)

Two types of measures appear appropriate for obtaining information on citizen and patron satisfaction with public library services: ratings by citizens and clients as to their overall satisfaction (Measures 1 and 2) and estimates of actual usage of libraries (Measures 3-6).

Usage measures (Measures 3-6) assume that because use of libraries is voluntary, the amount of usage is an indication of citizen satisfaction with the library services. Citizens in effect "vote with their feet." Unlike users of many other government services, citizens do not have to use the libraries if they do not want to. Those who use library services, however, may have various levels of satisfaction with the service. Moreover, it can be argued that because the alternatives to using existing public libraries are (1) to buy the materials or (2) to forego them completely, those inherently interested in library services comprise at least a partially captive audience. Thus Measures 1 and 2 also appear important.

The two types of measures—satisfaction and usage—are complementary; using one without the other would cause a major gap in information on the quality of library services. Together, the measures provide a more comprehensive picture of library quality.

Measure 1: *Percentage of citizens rating library service as satisfactory (or unsatisfactory).*

Measure 2: *Percentage of clients rating library service as satisfactory (or unsatisfactory).*

Measure 1 is intended to provide a composite estimate of the overall satisfaction level of a representative sample of the whole population of the community. This is done through a survey of a random sample of all citizens in the community. Measure 2 is intended to provide estimates of the overall satisfaction level of only those who have used the library. The data for Measure 2 can be obtained by a special survey of library users (generally conducted at the library facilities), or by questions included in the survey of a random sample of all citizens. A survey of users is more efficient for reaching those who have used the services; furthermore, this procedure permits obtaining satisfaction levels for users of individual branches for library systems that have more than one facility.

The general citizen survey, however, has the advantage of permitting the government to obtain ratings of library services from those who did not use the libraries (or used them only a few times). Although ratings of specific aspects of library services by nonusers are unlikely to have so sound a "factual" basis as those of library users, nonusers' perceptions are of interest to government officials, and if reasons for nonuse can be obtained (as discussed below) they should provide important information for program and policy decisions.

Question 21 of Appendix 1 (the multiservice citizen survey) and Question 17 of Appendix 8 (the library user survey) can be used to obtain the data for Measure 2. Question 21 would provide data for Measure 1.

To obtain data on library user satisfaction from the general citizen survey for Measure 2 it is necessary to distinguish the ratings provided by persons who have used the library system from those who have not. This could be done by making a cross-tabulation of Question 21 (satisfaction) in Appendix 1 against Question 23 (frequency of use). Both types of surveys can provide simultaneously not only an overall rating of library service, but also ratings on specific aspects of the service. These opportunities are discussed later in this chapter.

Exhibit 5-2 illustrates the kind of information that can be obtained—here split out by region of the community. Note that the overall community totals can hide some large differences in satisfaction among various regions. For example, regions A and D particularly appear to merit closer examination by the library system since a relatively large proportion of the respondents rated the service as only fair or poor (35 percent and 30 percent for the two regions). The format of Exhibit 5-2 can be used to dis-

Exhibit 5-2
RESPONDENT RATING OF NASHVILLE PUBLIC LIBRARY SERVICE
(February-March, 1974, General Citizen Survey of About 1,000 Households)

	RESPONDENT RATINGS[1]			
	EXCELLENT + GOOD (PERCENT)	FAIR + POOR (PERCENT)	DON'T KNOW[2] (PERCENT)	FAIR + POOR AS A PERCENTAGE OF THOSE PROVIDING A RATING
Total city	55	9	36	14
Region of city				
A	39	21	39	35
B	51	11	37	18
C	53	8	40	13
D	32	14	55	30
E	68	4	27	6
F	63	14	23	18
G	46	6	48	12
H	64	8	29	11
I	77	5	18	6
J	68	6	26	8

1. The question asked was: "How would you evaluate Metro public library services? Would you rate them excellent, good, fair or poor?" (Question 21 of Appendix 1).

2. The substantial percentage of "don't knows" is in part a reflection of the fact that 49 percent of the households interviewed indicated that they had not used the library system at all during the past year.

play the results of the ratings obtained from the general citizen survey or the library user survey.

Measures 3-6: Various Usage Counts. Measures 4-6 use actual library tallies of the number of persons with registration cards (Measure 4), number of visits (Measure 5), or number of items circulated (Measure 6). None of these measures, however, indicates how many different households actually use the library. Visit and circulation figures will be affected by repeated use by a small group of citizens.[3] Registration figures do not reflect actual usage, may be out of date, and may contain many multiple-card households.

Measure 3, "the percentage of households using or not using a public library a certain minimum number of times, such as four or more times over the past twelve months," is included to provide estimates of the number and percentage of different households who actually use the library services. A question such as Question 23 of Appendix 1 can be used to obtain the data in a general citizen survey. For example, the information from the general citizen surveys in St. Petersburg in 1973 and Nashville in 1974 indicated that 57 percent and 49 percent, respectively, of the households had not used the public library in the past year. There were, however, wide differences among different groups within each city. In St. Petersburg, 74 percent of the households with incomes less than $5,000 per year were nonusers, while only 30 percent of those with incomes above $15,000 were nonusers. In Nashville, the comparable figures were 77 percent and 23 percent.

Measure 3 also provides an opportunity to obtain information on reasons for nonuse of the library facilities as part of the citizen survey procedure. A particular concern is to identify the percentage of persons whose reasons for nonuse can be affected by the government (such reasons as libraries' lacking materials of interest, being too noisy, having too little parking, or being inaccessible), as distinguished from reasons that are outside the government's control (such as the citizen's poor health, general lack of interest, or preference for purchasing needed materials). Examples of specific questions

that could be used to collect these data in a general citizen survey are shown in the various parts of Question 25 of Appendix 1. Exhibit 5-3 illustrates the classifications that might be used and the types of data obtainable.

The St. Petersburg 1974 and Nashville 1974 and 1975 citizen surveys yielded results very similar to those shown in Exhibit 5-3 for St. Petersburg in 1973.[4] These data indicate that in both cities the citizens' reasons for nonuse apparently related generally to factors over which the government has little control. However, more detailed questioning might be desirable to pinpoint further the specific nature of reasons for nonuse. Library officials will probably find it useful to separate out reasons for nonuse by certain demographic data collected on the survey, such as by income class as illustrated in Exhibit 5-3.

Because procedures for collecting data on Measures 4 and 5 (registration cards and visits per capita) are relatively routine, they appear to require no special attention. However, Measure 6, "circulation per capita," has one unusual feature. Most libraries already collect statistics on the amount of materials checked out of their facilities. It is also desirable to capture in-library circulation, that is, material used within the library. A test run in St. Petersburg indicated that about 25 percent of all circulation was in-library use. In other words, circulation figures which included both in-library and out-library use would have been about one-third higher than figures currently recorded (out-library only). In St. Petersburg we found the mix of in-library versus out-library circulation to vary dramatically by library facility. DeProspo and associates found these same conditions in the twenty libraries included in their study.[5]

Library staff personnel can estimate in-library circulation by counting items being used by patrons as well as items left on tables. During the sampling period, signs would be posted asking users not to reshelve materials. The materials would be counted and reshelved periodically by library pages. In St. Petersburg, a count was made in each branch once each hour on each of two consecutive work days.[6] The items can be classified in a number of different ways, such as by type of material. St. Petersburg

3. The 1973 St. Petersburg citizen survey found that 20 percent of the responding households reported having used the library system at least once a month; the 1974 and 1975 surveys, which added a frequency category of "at least once a week," found that 9 percent and 8 percent of responding households used it this frequently. The 1974 and 1975 Nashville citizen surveys found 21 percent and 23 percent of the households reporting usage at least once a month. We weighted the frequencies that were reported by the percentage reporting them for the 1973 St. Petersburg and 1974 Nashville surveys; about 20 percent of the respondents accounted for approximately 65 percent of the users of the library system. This confirms the expected importance of repeat users in visitor counts.

4. All the percentages in each of these three other surveys were within four percentage points of the totals shown in Exhibit 5-3 for each category: "reasons potentially within government control" (9 percent), "reasons probably beyond government control" (74 percent), and "other reasons or no opinion" (17 percent).

5. DeProspo et al., *Performance Measures*, p. 39.

6. St. Petersburg, Florida, "Report on Library User Survey 1974" (Management Improvement Department, October 1974), p. 7.

Exhibit 5-3
"MOST IMPORTANT" REASONS FOR NONUSE OF ST. PETERSBURG PUBLIC LIBRARY
(As Percent of Respondents Classified as Nonusers)

REASON	TOTAL CITY	INCOME CLASS			
		0-$4,999	$5,000-$9,999	$10,000-$14,999	$15,000 +
Reasons potentially within government control					
Hard to get to	6	7	3	7	5
Wrong books-material	1	1	1	2	0
Don't know about the library	2	1	1	6	0
TOTAL	9	9	5	15	5
Reasons probably beyond government control					
Too busy	27	23	27	33	37
Buy own books-material	21	19	29	18	21
Poor health[1]	14	19	13	6	2
Not interested	12	12	12	13	12
TOTAL	74	73	81	70	72
Other reasons or no opinion	17	18	14	15	23

1. St. Petersburg has a significant percentage of older persons, many on low incomes, which may explain these large percentages of "poor health" responses. (If so, this would suggest the possible need for a special library outreach service for the elderly. If a substantial proportion of these have reading or related difficulties, however, the outreach program might not be useful or at least might require use of special aids.) This illustrates that here, as with all measurement data, the data can raise questions and issues, but further analysis should be performed before specific program or policy action is taken.

Source: St. Petersburg general citizen survey (September 1973). Respondents who indicated they had used the library less than four times a year were asked to give their reasons for nonuse.

used these categories: reference, fiction, nonfiction, periodical, newspaper, document, telephone book, microfilm, microcard, slide, film strip, vertical file, and other.

Special Validity Considerations for Measures 3-6. Data from both general citizen surveys and surveys of library users will have the various potential accuracy problems discussed later in this chapter and in Chapter 14. Some validity issues related specifically to these particular measures are discussed here.

1. The validity of respondent information on reasons for nonuse is uncertain. Do respondents give accurate reasons? Can they give accurate reasons? Studies of nonuse of another government service, public transit, have indicated service changes designed to remedy the reasons for nonuse have not always resulted in increased usage. Currently, there is available no information on the validity of reasons given for nonuse of libraries. Some of the reasons listed in the questions used to date (see Question 25 of Appendix 1) appear somewhat ambiguous. For example, "Too busy to go to the library" may mask a problem—such as excessive travel time to get to libraries or to find parking—that is at least partly controllable by the government.

Individual local governments may want to attempt more in-depth questioning on reasons for nonuse, at least during the initial testing of their survey questions. The check list of possible reasons for nonuse illustrated in Question 25 of Appendix 1 was developed from a number of interviews, which included "open-ended" questions on reasons for nonuse, as well as from examination of check lists used by other researchers and the judgments of local officials. Questions remain, however, so the check list is not fully satisfactory.

2. The accuracy of data obtained for Measures 4-6 by various library tallies varies with the care taken in their collection. As the procedures themselves are relatively routine, they received no special attention. Several problems with library registration figures (Measure 4) as a measure of current satisfaction did emerge, however. First, many libraries do not keep registration figures up to date. Some households will have left the community or otherwise not be active users of the library. This problem worsens if the interval between registration renewals is long or if renewal is not required. Also, as noted earlier, the total number of households with library cards cannot be accurately deduced from totaling the number of cards issued, since many households contain more than one cardholder.

This problem could be solved by devising a sampling procedure to estimate the number of households with more than one library card. This figure can then be divided by the total number of households in the community to derive the percentage of households with cards.[7]

Measures of Comprehensiveness, Timeliness, and Availability (Measures 7-9)

Measures 1-6 obtained information on overall library quality as reflected by citizen satisfaction. The remaining measures consider specific aspects of library performance.

The procedures suggested for Measures 7 and 8, as well as in-library circulation estimates for Measure 6, are based on procedures described and tested in a number of libraries by DeProspo and associates in their extensive work for the American Library Association.[8] Both St. Petersburg and Nashville also tested adaptations of these procedures as part of this project.[9]

Measure 7: Probability of owning (a) books and (b) periodicals published during a given time period (such as within the last five years).

This measure reflects the comprehensiveness and currentness of library holdings. The following procedure can be used to provide estimates for Measure 7: A sample of approximately 500 titles can be drawn at random from the *American Book Publishing Record* (BPR) covering the desired number of years (St. Petersburg used four years, DeProspo and associates, five). These are not titles "recommended" for ownership by the library, but simply a group of titles published within the specific time period. The card catalog can then be searched to determine which of these books are in the collection of the library system. Earlier editions of books on the search list could be counted (as DeProspo and associates recommended) or not (as in the St. Petersburg test).

The same procedures can be used for periodicals. The list of periodicals might be obtained from any of a number of common indexes, such as the *Reader's Guide, Art Index,* or *Education Index.*

The measure might also be usefully split into the ownership of adult-audience, as distinct from juvenile-audience, materials.

Measure 8: Probability of a user's obtaining (a) a book or (b) a periodical when it is wanted.

There are four procedural variations to obtain values for Measure 8. Each gives a somewhat different measurement. The first two are (tested) ways to determine the availability of a preselected sample of books or periodicals. The last two are possible (but not fully tested) procedures for estimating availability based on materials that actually have been sought by citizens.[10]

Approach 1. The availability of the BPR sample drawn for Measure 7 would be determined. The library shelves would be searched at randomly selected times to ascertain how many of the items in the BPR sample found to be owned by the library were actually available to users. The availability can then be determined by dividing the "number of books actually available" by the "number of books in the sample owned." This provides an estimate of the likelihood that any book published within the past few years that is owned by the library is available.

Approach 2. To determine the probability of a library user finding *any* item owned by the library on the shelves at a given time, a sample of 500 titles could be drawn from the library's catalog (rather than from the BPR). In St. Petersburg, 500 individual cards were selected (using uniform intervals established by dividing total inches of shelves by number of titles in the catalog), thereby providing a selection of titles representative of the library's collection. The shelves can be searched to determine how many of the titles thus selected are available to users. The probability of availability can be calculated by dividing the number of books found by the

7. Can the possession or lack of possession of a library card be used as an indicator of household usage during the year, that is, as a substitute for Measure 3? The St. Petersburg 1975 general citizen survey results showed that of those saying that some member of the household had a library card (cards are good for three years), 94 percent reported that someone in the household had used the library system in the past twelve months. For those reporting that their household did not have a library card, 18 percent report usage (2 percent said they didn't know). The 1974 St. Petersburg library user survey found that 20 percent of the users sampled reported that no one in their household had a library card. As expected, there was clearly a strong relation between having a card and library usage; however, the problems noted in the text and these findings suggest that card registrations can be used as only a very approximate measure of library usage.

8. DeProspo et al., *Performance Measures.* For additional procedural suggestions, see Ernest R. DeProspo, Ellen Altman, Phil M. Clark, and Ellen Connor Clark, *A Data Gathering and Instructional Manual for Performance Measures in Public Libraries* (Chicago: Oberon Press, 1976).

9. For a description of the results of the 1974 St. Petersburg, Florida, efforts, see St. Petersburg, Florida, "Report, 1974."

10. Note that there is a direct trade-off between the probability of availability of library materials and circulation (Measure 6). The probability of availability tends to increase as circulation decreases.

number of books searched for (in this example, 500).[11]

In addition, ownership of the material and its current availability on the library shelves should be considered together. One means of combining both factors would be to combine Measures 7 and 8 using the BPR sample.[12] This would yield the probability that an item in the BPR was both owned and available. For example, if 20 percent of the BPR sample were owned and 80 percent of the owned items were found on the shelves, the overall availability of the BPR sample would be 16 percent. But this still does not consider the actual requirement of users.

Approach 3. Approaches 1 and 2 have the drawback that they do not provide estimates of the actual experiences of users in finding items that they want. A better measure (not tested in our project) would be to sample actual users' searches for materials to determine how many items users were able to locate. Persons leaving the library could be sampled to see whether they had been looking for a book or periodical and, if so, whether they had been able to find the item(s). If the library system undertakes a user survey, those surveyed might be asked to report on their success in finding materials sought then or on previous visits to the library. This approach also provides an opportunity to cover material provided the user through inter-library loan.

A variation is to include a question such as Number 9 of Appendix 8 in the library user survey, which asks the respondent to rate whether the "availability of material you want is excellent, good, fair, or poor?" Testing of this third procedure would be desirable, at least initially, to determine whether the information obtained from the less obtrusive procedures in Approaches 1 and 2 will be approximately the same.

Approach 4. Another alternative is to ask respondents on the general citizen survey for their ratings of availability of materials they had wanted (Question 24b of Appendix 1). This question might be asked only of persons who had used the library some minimum number of times (at least four times in the past year in the St. Petersburg and Nashville general citizen surveys). Since the question may be asked some time after users' actual experiences, responses may be subject to variation in the memories of the respondents.

This measure might also usefully be split into availability of adult- versus juvenile-audience material.

Some Illustrative Results of Measures 7 and 8.[13] For Measure 7, St. Petersburg found that the municipal library system owned 17 percent of the BPR sample of titles published over the previous four years. DeProspo and associates found a range of 14 percent to 58 percent in large cities ($750,000 to $3,499,999 budget), 16 percent to 29 percent in medium cities ($250,000 to $749,999), and 8 percent to 18 percent in small cities ($100,000 to $249,999).

For Measure 8 (Approach 1), St. Petersburg found 63 percent of the BPR sample owned to be available on the shelves. (This, when combined with Measure 7, produces an availability of 11 percent of the BPR sample—0.63 × 0.17.) For Approach 2, a random sample of all books it owned, 85 percent were available. DeProspo and associates found a range of 55 percent to 81 percent for BPR ownership (from five previous years) for their twenty-library sample and 58-percent to 89-percent range of availability for all titles owned by the libraries (library size did not appear to alter the ranges greatly for Measure 8). For Approach 4 of Measure 8, the 1974 Nashville citizen survey found that 73 percent of the respondents rated the availability of reading materials that they wanted as excellent or good, 17 percent fair, and 4 percent poor. The remainder indicated that they didn't know.

Special Validity Considerations for Measures 7 and 8. There are three important validity issues for these measures. (1) For Approaches 1 and 2 of Measure 8, does a random sample of titles adequately represent the availability probabilities for the books that users actually want? For example, many users tend to concentrate on current best sellers. Thus, the probability of a random title being available might be higher than the probability of the books that users want being available when they want them. (This would depend in part on the number of copies the library has.) (2) For Measure 7 there is the related question of whether the book and periodical lists chosen for the sample in fact reflect the interests of clients. (3) Validity can be affected considerably by how carefully the sampling procedures and tallies are undertaken.

A Summary of Measures 7 and 8 In summary, Measures 7 and 8 present several ways of determining the availability, comprehensiveness, and currency of materials. The procedures in Measure 7 and Approaches 1 and 2 of Measure 8 are perhaps the easiest for a library to use. However, Approach 3, and to a lesser extent Approach 4, which attempt to

---

11. St. Petersburg, Florida, "Report, 1974," p. 73.
12. DeProspo et al., *Performance Measures,* p. 34.

13. St. Petersburg, Florida, "Report, 1974," p. 7, and DeProspo et al., *Performance Measures,* p. 47.

reflect users' wishes for materials, appear preferable if the clients' immediate interests are of principal concern. It can be argued that the experience reflected in Approaches 3 and 4 may ignore the value of having a wide range of literature available, which can be assessed better by the other measures. Both types of approaches are recommended, as they seem to be complementary, and neither appears to be costly if annual citizen and library user surveys are already being conducted.

Measure 9:   Percentage of persons using library who rate speed of service (e.g., book retrieval and checkout) as satisfactory (or unsatisfactory).

Even though books and materials are available on the shelves, library patrons may still encounter annoying delays in finding materials and in checking them out. This measure attempts to provide an estimate of the degree to which users are satisfied with the speed of service.

If a periodic survey of library users is undertaken, patrons sampled can be queried to obtain ratings of the speed of service they have experienced during the period under review. The general citizen survey can also obtain similar information. (See Questions 13 and 14 of the library user survey in Appendix 8 and Question 24f of Appendix 1 for the general citizen survey.)

An alternative, or additional, procedure would be to provide a more objective estimate of delay times. This would involve sampling lines at the checkout counter at randomly selected times during the library year.[14] Either size of lines or length of waiting times plus checkout times could be sampled. These procedures have not been tested, but they appear to present no major difficulties other than the relatively modest resources required to undertake the sampling. Note that the measurements of delay times provide only indirect measures of client satisfaction, because it is not known to what extent satisfaction correlates with waiting times.

Measures of Staff Helpfulness (Measures 10 and 11) and Physical Attractiveness of theLibrary (Measures 12 and 13)

Each of the following four measures attempts to obtain citizen ratings of specific aspects of staff helpfulness or the physical attractiveness of the library facility.

14. Since libraries may operate for long hours during the week, it may well be more efficient to make counts only during peak periods—if peak hours can be predicted reliably in advance. However, if staffs are reduced during off-peak hours, long waits may occur sufficiently often to warrant such counts.

Measure 10:   Percentage of persons using library who rate helpfulness and general attitude of library staff as satisfactory (or unsatisfactory).

Measure 11:   Percentage of persons using library reference services who rate them as satisfactory (or unsatisfactory).

Measure 12:   Percentage of persons using library who rate the comfort, crowdedness, noise, cleanliness, and temperature/ventilation as satisfactory (or unsatisfactory).

Measure 13:   Percentage of nonuser households who cite lack of comfort, crowdedness, noise, cleanliness, or temperature/ventilation as reasons for nonuse of facilities.

Characteristics of library service such as staff helpfulness, quality of reference services, comfort, noise, cleanliness, and crowdedness are reasonably straightforward and need little explanation. Measures 10-13 obtain information either by querying a sample of users of the library (with the library user survey) or by using the general citizen survey. (In the latter case, it appears appropriate to obtain ratings on these specific issues only from those indicating they have used the library.)

In general, the user survey is the more efficient way to obtain feedback on Measures 10 and 12 as long as the primary focus is to obtain ratings from those who have actually used the libraries. As indicated under Measure 3, about half of the households interviewed in St. Petersburg and Nashville in the general population survey had not used the public library in the past year. Nevertheless, if the municipality undertakes a general citizen survey annually for other government services, the addition of library questions is likely to add little to the cost. Further discussion of these procedures is presented later in this chapter and in Chapter 14.

Examples of the specific questions that can be used to obtain data on Measures 10-12 include the following: For Measure 10 on helpfulness of the staff, see Question 12 in Appendix 8 and 24e in Appendix 1. For Measure 12, see Question 10 in Appendix 8 and 24c in Appendix 1. Both of these questions cover comfort and cleanliness. Questions on crowdedness, noise, and temperature/ventilation could be asked separately or together. The term "comfort" is ambiguous and probably encompasses such concerns as ventilation and crowdedness. For

Measure 11 on the quality of the library reference service, a question such as number 16 of Appendix 8 can be used. The general citizen survey does not appear to be appropriate for Measure 11, because too few citizens in a general sample would be likely to have used the reference service.[15]

Measure 13, the nonuser households' ratings of discomfort, crowdedness, and similar complaints as reasons for nonuse of library facilities, would need to be obtained from the general citizen survey. A question such as number 25i of Appendix 1 can be used to collect this type of information, although it asks only about noise and crowdedness. Only about 1 percent of those providing a rating in both Nashville and St. Petersburg indicated that noise or crowdedness restricted their library use; the maximum for any of the client subgroups examined was 4 percent. This suggests that the question, and possibly this measure, may be of marginal use other than to indicate that the libraries are performing very well on these conditions.

Measures of Physical Accessibility and Convenience (Measures 14-18)

Library patrons and would-be patrons are concerned not only with the quality of service their library offers, but also with the accessibility and convenience of the service. In both the Nashville and St. Petersburg general citizen surveys, of those reasons over which a government has some potential control, the principal reason offered for not using libraries was difficulty in getting to the facility (see Exhibit 5-3). About 25 percent of library users in the Nashville general citizen survey rated the convenience from their residence as "fair" or "poor." Measures 14-18 attempt to measure various aspects of this quality.

Measure 14: Percentage of users rating convenience as satisfactory (or unsatisfactory).

This measure provides information on library users' perception of the convenience of the library system. Data can be obtained from either the library user or general citizen survey. Questions 24d (convenience to home) and 24g (ease of parking) of Appendix 1, and Questions 11 and 15 of Appendix 8

illustrate questions that can be used to obtain the data.

Parking problems, along with "convenience to your home," were the characteristics rated worst in the Nashville general citizen survey. (For example, in the 1974 survey, 13 percent rated ease of parking poor and another 10 percent rated it fair; in some areas of the county, poor and fair ratings were considerably higher.) To reflect the extent to which inadequate parking space relates to nonuse, an additional measure similar to Measure 18, asking about parking, could also be included (see Question 25k of Appendix 1).

Measure 15: Percentage of nonuser households who give poor physical accessibility as a reason for nonuse.

Whereas Measure 14 measures library user ratings of convenience, this measure considers nonuser views. Data must be drawn from the general citizen survey. A question such as 25h of Appendix 1 can be used.

Measure 16: Percentage of citizens who live within a specific travel time (such as 15 minutes) of a public library.

This provides a more "objective" measure of physical accessibility, but it is not necessarily a "better" measure, since citizen perceptions of accessibility may be more meaningful than physical proximity. This measure calls for calculation of the percentage of household residents within a given distance or travel time of a public library.[16] This measure can be calculated by plotting population locations from the latest census data on a city or county map. Contours representing perhaps fifteen minutes' travel time can then be drawn from the map around each of the branch libraries. The population contained within the contours would then be used to calculate the percentage of the total city population within this travel time or distance. Although these procedures were not tested in this project, similar procedures on accessibility to recreational facilities have been tested and appear adaptable for this measure. These procedures are discussed in some detail in Chapter 4.[17] Calculating the

---

15. Even the library user survey in the jurisdiction's main library may not provide a sufficient number of persons who can rate library reference services. However, in the St. Petersburg 1974 library user survey, about 75 percent of those surveyed did provide a rating. Based on past frequency of personal visits to each library's reference service, a jurisdiction can estimate whether, for the sample size planned for the survey, there are likely to be enough users of the reference service in the sample to warrant a question asking for a rating.

16. Travel *distance* might also be used as a version for this measure. The 1973 St. Petersburg user survey found that the median travel distance reported was ten to twenty blocks or one to two miles. However, for one branch, the median was less than five blocks and for another it was five to ten blocks. Questions 18-20 of Appendix 8 can be used to obtain this information.

17. Those who want to use this measure should review U.S. Bureau of Outdoor Recreation, *How Effective Are Your Community Recreation Services?* by Donald M. Fisk (Washington, D.C.: U.S. Government Printing Office, 1973), pp. 39-56.

procedure for ten or fewer libraries should require no more than one employee-week of effort. To carry out this measure requires population data for small areas such as blocks or block groups. Census tract data can be used but they introduce additional error.[18]

One must decide whether travel times for walking, biking, busing, or driving should be used. The population distribution could be separated by age group; for example, for measurement of convenience to children, a fifteen-minute walking distance could be used, whereas in measurements relating to adults, driving time might be used.

A problem with this measure is that at least some persons counted in these tallies will not be interested in using these library services regardless of geographic convenience. Measures 14 and 15 should therefore be considered along with Measure 16 to provide an improved perspective on physical accessibility.

Measure 17: Percentage of user households rating hours of operation as satisfactory (or unsatisfactory).

Measure 18: Percentage of nonuser households who give poor hours as a reason for nonuse.

Data for Measure 17 can be obtained from either the library user survey or the general population survey. Such questions as Numbers 7 and 8 on hours and days of operation, respectively, of Appendix 8 and Question 24a of Appendix 1 can be used.

Data on Measure 18 should be obtained from the general citizen survey with a question such as 25g of Appendix 1.

The Library User Survey

An annual survey of a sample of library users has been mentioned as a source of data for eight of the measures.

A number of public libraries have conducted user surveys. Generally these have been one-time efforts focusing on overall user satisfaction and on opinions as to desirable modifications in library services. So far as we know, surveys have seldom, if ever, been used to collect information regularly and systematically on the effectiveness of current services.

The survey described here focuses on service ef-

18. U.S. Bureau of Outdoor Recreation, *How Effective,* p. 47.

Exhibit 5-4
LIBRARY USER SURVEY

SERVICE QUALITY MEASURED	MEASURE NUMBER[1]	SURVEY QUESTION NUMBER[2]
Overall user satisfaction	2	17
Availability of materials	8	9
Speed of service	9	13, 14
Helpfulness or courtesy of staff	10	12
Quality of reference service	11	16
Comfort of facilities	12	10
Convenience to home	14	11
Hours of operation	17	7, 8
Ease in parking	14	15

1. See Exhibit 5-1.
2. See Appendix 8.

fectiveness. It obtains information on users' recent experiences and attitudes toward existing services. When administered annually, a survey of this type can be used to provide time-trend information on library services, including the effectiveness of branch operations.

The discussion here is based chiefly on experiences with the user survey conducted by St. Petersburg and its library system in 1974. Similar surveys were undertaken again in St. Petersburg in 1975 and in Nashville in 1974. The questionnaire used in the 1974 St. Petersburg survey is included as Appendix 8. It includes questions both on the measures and on demographic matters. The latter permit a variety of cross tabulations on the measurements for various client groups such as those categorized by age, sex, race, or income.

The wording of the questionnaire in Appendix 8 should by no means be considered final. Alternatives, some of which have been noted in previous sections, are likely to be desirable to meet the special needs of each library system.

User surveys offer some advantages over general citizen surveys. (1) They provide an efficient way to collect data if a government is interested primarily in the interests and actions of users. For example, as already noted, 56 percent of those interviewed in the St. Petersburg general citizen survey had not used the library at all during the previous twelve months and therefore could not be asked for user ratings. In Nashville, the figure was 49 percent. (2) User surveys seem within the capability of the average or even small library system to conduct. (3) At relatively low cost, interviews can be obtained at each branch permitting sample sizes large enough

Exhibit 5-5
ILLUSTRATIVE USER RATINGS—FOR ONE BRANCH LIBRARY[1]
(In Terms of Percentages of Responses)

MEASURE NUMBER	MEASURE	QUESTION NUMBER[2]	EXCELLENT	GOOD	FAIR	POOR	DON'T KNOW
2	Overall user rating	17	52	43	4	0	1
8	Availability of material	9	31	42	22	1	1
9	Ease in finding material	13	45	38	14	3	1
9	Ease in checking out material	14	69	28	3	0	1
10	Staff helpfulness and courtesy	12	73	22	2	0	3
11	Reference help	16	45	40	8	1	7
12	Comfort and cleanliness	10	49	38	12	1	1
14	Convenience to home	11	70	24	5	1	1
17	Hours of operation	7	64	34	1	0	2
14	Ease in parking	15	35	43	17	1	4

1. Numbers across rows may not add to 100 percent because of rounding.
2. See Appendix 8 for the specific wording of the questions.

SOURCE: Data from May 1974 St. Petersburg Library User Survey.

for statements about the effectiveness of individual branch operations. This is in contrast to communitywide household surveys which may become quite expensive if samples must be large enough to permit precise statements about individual library operations. (For example, in the 1974 Nashville general citizen survey, which interviewed about 1,000 individuals, respondents were asked which library they used most often; a number of library branches were mentioned by fewer than twenty persons.)

The user survey has three disadvantages: First, it does not permit a library system to collect data on nonusers. Second, it provides inadequate information to estimate Measure 3, the percentage of different users within a community, with any precision.[19] Third, it requires special time, effort, and probably dollars.

Exhibits 5-5 and 5-6 illustrate some of the types of data obtainable from a library user survey. Exhibit 5-5 shows the ratings for one branch library (1974 St. Petersburg library user survey). Exhibit 5-6 illustrates how the findings can be summarized to compare branches (1974 Nashville library user survey). Such summaries can help to highlight both problem areas and areas of high performance. Tables comparing ratings for different age, sex, race, or income groups can also be prepared. After data are obtained for more than one time period, comparisons of performance for different time periods can also be presented.

The St. Petersburg questionnaire presented in Appendix 8 also contains a number of other questions, such as frequency of use, length of stay, mode of transportation to the library, distance between

19. The same persons may use different library branches, and users will have varying frequencies of library use.

home and library, and open-ended questions on respondent likes, dislikes, and suggestions for changes in library services. These are peripheral to the effectiveness-measurement data but can provide additional interpretative information to library and other officials. Special questions could also be added to the questionnaire to obtain feedback on special issues of concern to library officials at the time of the particular survey.

Survey Procedures

Administration of Questionnaire. The questionnaire shown in Appendix 8 requires an average of about four minutes to complete. In the two cities where it has been administered, users were canvassed at library facilities. Both children and adults should be included in the survey. There are two variations for administering the questionnaire: (a) In the interview, an interviewer reads each question and records the answer. (b) In self-administered surveys, users complete the questionnaire themselves. A combination of the two procedures was used in St. Petersburg. Most users were happy to complete the questionnaire without assistance, but some of the younger children and some of the elderly with poor eyesight needed the questions read to them and the forms completed by a member of the survey team. Respondents were asked to place completed forms in a "ballot" box. Names were not requested.

Sample Size and Selection. The sample size should be large enough at each site to permit grouping of user ratings by age, sex, race, and library branch. In St. Petersburg, the sample design called for 100 completed interviews each day for two days in each library. Different sampling proportions were

Exhibit 5-6
ILLUSTRATIVE USER RATINGS—COMPARING LIBRARY BRANCHES
(Percentage Rating the Characteristics as Either "Fair" or "Poor" Rather Than
"Excellent," "Good," or "No Comment" for Each Branch)

MEASURE AND NUMBER	BRANCH												
	1	2	3	4	5	6	7	8	9	10	11	12	OVERALL
Overall rating (#2)	4	3	4	4	3	10	2	3	10	0	3	2	3
Availability of material (#8)	14	13	9	15	22	(33)	20	16	18	11	24	16	18
Ease in finding material (#9)	6	5	14	8	14	4	3	7	0	2	7	7	8
Ease in checking out material (#9)	4	1	6	5	1	0	1	2	6	0	3	3	2
Staff helpfulness and courtesy (#10)	4	3	4	4	3	7	1	2	6	1	2	3	3
Reference help (#11)	9	6	5	2	10	15	4	7	4	3	8	8	9
Comfort and cleanliness (#12)	13	11	10	14	15	(54)	4	11	20	(37)	23	17	15
Convenience to home (#14)	14	7	17	20	21	9	12	(45)	21	12	13	16	(28)
Ease in parking (#14)	20	10	11	5	14	(26)	2	(72)	8	17	6	4	(27)

Note: To illustrate how selected findings might be emphasized, we have (somewhat arbitrarily) circled all entries that reveal "dissatisfaction" levels of 25 percent or more. Clearly, inconvenience to home and ease in parking were the major overall problem areas.

Source: Nashville, Tennessee, November-December 1974 Library User Survey findings.

used in each library. At one branch where the expected attendance was small, everyone was requested to complete the survey form. At the main library every twelfth person was interviewed. At the other two branches every second or fifth person was interviewed. (In all, 664 interviews were completed; the individual library sample sizes were 64, 180, 209, and 211.) Nashville used a similar approach for its twelve branches.[20]

Large numbers of repeat patrons can somewhat bias the results. One branch operation in St. Petersburg found from the survey that almost 25 percent of its patrons came daily, and 64 percent came at least once a week. Such patrons will have a larger probability of being in the sample than others, and thus the findings will tend to be weighted more toward the perceptions of the more frequent patrons. (Some may believe this is desirable.) Because this survey is intended to identify the re-

sponses of different users, however, no individual should be interviewed more than once.

Frequency and Timing of the User Survey. The survey should obtain interviews from a representative cross section of the users. Since the type of user is likely to vary by the time of the day and the day of the week, the survey should cover all periods that a facility is open. In St. Petersburg the survey was restricted to two days because of personnel shortages. The two days picked represented one day of high use and one day of low use, and during those two days, the survey was run from opening to closing. The days were selected after consultation with library staff and an examination of daily circulation statistics.

It seems likely that seasonal differences affect the responses, so it would be desirable to conduct the survey more than once a year if the additional costs and administrative effort are acceptable. One survey might be conducted at the end of the summer season and another in mid-winter. Seasonal variations would be no problem if users can be counted on to recall their experiences over an extended period. Information on citizen recall of experiences with any government service is scanty (see Chapter 14). The matter of citizen recall is most troublesome for factual data, such as the number of visits and length of stay, but these are not emphasized in the user surveys. Memory is probably less important for "perception-type" information such as ratings of library operations, but recent experiences are likely

20. With such a procedure, the proportion of those given questionnaires at each library may not correspond to each library's true proportion of total system activity. It is then necessary to weight the responses from each branch to arrive at *systemwide* results. It might be done, as in St. Petersburg, by multiplying the sample interval by the number of questionnaires distributed to obtain the total number of persons using each library during the survey period. The number of users thus calculated for each library is divided by the total number of library system users, to arrive at the percentage of the total system that each library represents. These weighting factors can then be applied against the percentages giving each response. The resulting weighted percentages would be totaled to produce the percentage of the entire system's users giving that response. See St. Petersburg, Florida, "Report, 1974," p. 65.

to influence replies more than are remote experiences.

Survey Flexibility. If a library wants information on mobile services or telephone reference services, a somewhat revised questionnaire and set of interview procedures will be needed.

All the interviewing in St. Petersburg was conducted at fixed library facilities. No interviewing was undertaken at mobile vans or bookmobiles, and no attempt was made to interview persons requesting reference service by telephone.

The survey can also be used as an opportunity to obtain various other kinds of feedback from clients. For example, Nashville in its 1974 survey queried users about the days of the week they found most convenient to use the library, the hours of operation they favored, the types of books or other materials they would like to see added to the particular library, and what they considered to be the greatest need for improvement in the particular library. St. Petersburg asked users about changes they would like to see made in the library (see Question 23 of Appendix 8), their length of stay when visiting the library (Question 6), and the activity that brought them to the library (Question 3).

Who Should Undertake the Survey? Library personnel should be involved in the selection of the questions included in the user survey (as well as the library questions included in the general citizen survey discussed in the next section). They not only have firsthand knowledge of the issues, but they are also likely to be the principal users and interpreters of the responses.

In St. Petersburg and Nashville, library personnel with outside technical assistance participated actively in designing and pretesting the questionnaire, conducting the survey, and tabulating the results. Library pages were used, particularly for conducting the survey. In Nashville, a central staff office took the lead in designing the survey; library personnel reviewed the questionnaire and handled most of the remaining work. Most library systems should use outside professional advice, particularly in the first survey, for determining the final wording, pretesting, and training interviewers. Local government personnel can probably handle most aspects of later surveys themselves.

Special Validity Considerations

Much of the discussion of validity issues in the discussion of the general citizen survey in Chapter 14

also applies to user surveys. Here three issues are discussed.

a. Some individuals may refuse to complete the survey questionnaire. Refusal from many persons can pose a major threat to validity of the findings. In St. Petersburg, 17 percent of the respondents selected for sampling refused. At the main library the figure was 18 percent, and the largest refusal rate at any of the four branches was 21 percent.[21] A record was kept of the reasons for refusal. Most prevalent were "too busy" or "no time." Others refused because they came in to "use the phone," "use the toilet" (both of which seem valid reasons for exclusion from the sample), and "didn't have glasses." In Nashville, the refusal rate was 11 percent, and the principal reason was "no time."

Because of the danger that those who refuse may have different views and behavior patterns from those who complete the questionnaire, an effort should be made to keep the refusal rate down to about 10 percent. The use of experienced or at least well-trained persons to work with the persons sampled can help reduce refusal rates.

b. There is a question as to whether survey results are biased if library personnel conduct face-to-face interviews. There is some question of bias if the questionnaire is self-administered and left at the library (even if an "anonymous" ballot box is used). There are two sources of potential bias. First, the library personnel may intentionally or otherwise encourage responses along lines that correspond to their own perceptions. Second, the persons interviewed may respond more favorably than they normally would if they suspect that the library personnel will see their individual responses.

This problem can be alleviated if (1) it is made clear to the respondent before completing the questionnaire that it is not to be signed and is to be placed in a secure receptacle such as an anonymous ballot box, and (2) persons known not to be library employees—such as members of the League of Women Voters, an appointed Library Board, clubs such as Friends of the Library, other government personnel, or paid professional personnel—conduct the interviews. It is not recommended that respondents be allowed to complete the questionnaires at home and mail them to a nonlibrary office—another option—because many of the questionnaires may not be returned.

21. See ibid.

c. In one important respect the validity problem is less severe in user surveys. Sampling and finding respondents is relatively easy. Fewer biases are introduced by sampling since the sample population is simply the persons who actually visit the facilities. Also, because library users are more likely to be interested in the library questions, they will provide more thoughtful answers. But sampling problems still occur; as should be emphasized again, users at various times of the day, days of the week, and (ideally) seasons of the year should be properly represented.

Library User Survey Cost, Staffing, and Training

The number of different library facilities covered in the survey and the number of survey hours and days as well as the sample size in any given facility are important determinants of cost and staffing requirements.

Exhibit 5-7 presents rough estimates, based on the experiences in St. Petersburg, of the time and costs required to complete a library user survey of four facilities. The total cost is likely to be about $4,000. Repeat surveys should cost slightly less; savings in the design and pretesting of the survey form would reduce the work time for subsequent surveys by about sixty employee-hours and the elapsed calendar time by about two or three weeks. Costs can be reduced by using existing staff members and volunteers.

A survey at four facilities would require one survey leader, eight interviewers, one computer programmer, and one management analyst, most of whom would work part time. One person may be able to handle more than one of the tasks.

Exhibit 5-7 also provides estimates of total elapsed time from the decision to go ahead until the results are available—about two to three months, if the process goes smoothly. In St. Petersburg, keypunching and running the data through the computer caused more delay then had been anticipated. If this particular task can be speeded up, it may be possible to complete subsequent annual user surveys more quickly.

The General Citizen Survey

An annual survey of a sample of citizens in a community can be used to obtain data on the various measures listed in Exhibit 5-8. The 1974 Nashville Citizen Survey Questionnaire presented in Appendix 1 illustrates specific questions that might be used to collect these data. Exhibit 5-8 matches questions on that questionnaire with relevant measures.

Exhibit 5-7

ESTIMATED STAFFING, COST, AND TIME REQUIREMENTS FOR LIBRARY USER SURVEY

		TOTAL STAFF TIME (HOURS)	ELAPSED CALENDAR TIME (WEEKS)
Number of facilities covered by the survey:	4		
Days and hours covered by the survey:	10 hours per day for 2 days		
Number of completed questionnaires:	700		
Tasks			
Design survey		40	1½
Design questionnaire and pretest		40	1
Select and train interviewers		40	1
Conduct survey		120	2½
Code and tabulate results		80	1
Analyze and document results		80	2
Total time		400	9
		COSTS	
Dollars expended (excluding the above staff time)			
Questionnaire printing		$100	
Keypunch		300	
Computer processing		400	
Total		$800	

Note: These estimates are based on the St. Petersburg library user survey results. The costs would be slightly less for recurring surveys.

Exhibit 5-8
MEASURES OF EFFECTIVENESS DATA COLLECTED BY GENERAL CITIZEN SURVEY

SERVICE QUALITY MEASURED	MEASURE NUMBER[1]	SURVEY QUESTION NUMBER[2]
Overall citizen satisfaction	1	21
User satisfaction	2	21
Usage by households	3	23
Nonuse—by reason	3	25
Usage as indicated by registration card	4	22
Availability of material	8	24b
Speed of service	9	24f
Helpfulness—Courtesy of staff	10	24e
Comfort—User rating	12	24c
Comfort—Nonuser rating	13	25i
Convenience—User rating	14	24d
Accessibility—Nonuser rating	15	25h
Hours of operation—User rating	17	24a
Hours of operation—Nonuser rating	18	25g
Ease of parking—User rating	14	24g
Ease of parking—Nonuser rating	—	25k

1. See Exhibit 5-1.
2. See Appendix 1.

The wording of questions presented in Appendix 1 should not be considered final. Alterations, some of which have been noted in earlier sections, are desirable to meet the special needs of individual library systems.

Data for all the measures listed in Exhibit 5-8 have been collected from the general citizen survey in Nashville (1974) and for some of the measures in the 1973 St. Petersburg survey. The St. Petersburg survey provided 626 and the Nashville survey 1,002 completed interviews.

Survey Procedures and Special Validation Issues

Because citizen survey procedures are detailed in Chapter 14, they are not repeated here. However, some validation problems and related procedural issues especially pertinent to libraries will be discussed:

1. For the questions on use of public libraries and reasons for nonuse, the least expensive approach is to ask the respondent to give information covering all members of the respondent's household (see Questions 22, 23, and 25 of Appendix 1). But how accurately can respondents answer for the experiences of the others in their households? Research in the fields of health and crime suggests that persons speaking for all household members tend to understate actual occurrences. We know of no research concerning this issue in the area of public library use, and no information collected in the Nashville or St. Petersburg surveys shed light on this question.

   Ideally, each person in a household would be interviewed, but this procedure is likely to prove too expensive for most jurisdictions. Although some survey experts believe that the housewife is the best person to respond for the family on questions such as library use, housewives were not deliberately singled out for interview in the St. Petersburg and Nashville surveys because it seemed desirable that other questions— especially rating questions and questions on other government service areas—should be addressed to a cross section of all adults interviewed. (The general citizen survey cannot generally cover the satisfaction levels of children. The user survey, which does provide for childrens' responses, could be used for this purpose.)

2. The questions on the use of library facilities rely heavily on the memory of the respondents, especially those asked about their use of libraries over the past twelve months. This issue is less important for questions that ask for the respondent's *current* perceptions as to the rating of a specific aspect of the library service. Fortunately, precise information on the number of uses is not required. The suggested response categories for Question 23 of Appendix 1 have wide ranges—for example, "at least once a month" means twelve or more uses per year; "at least once every three months" can mean from four to eleven uses.

3. The questions aimed at rating specific aspects of the quality of library services (such as speed of service and helpfulness of staff for Measures 9 and 10) should be asked only of those respondents who indicate that they have used the library and thus have direct experiences on which to base their ratings. Thus, the question arises as to how many visits during the past twelve months should be considered sufficient experience to provide a rating. A good case can be made for even one visit, but the Nashville and St. Petersburg surveys set a minimum of at least four during the

previous twelve months.[22] Question 23 in Appendix 1 illustrates how this question could be handled procedurally, with some answers directing the interviewer to proceed with user ratings while other answers call for skipping those ratings. This choice appears primarily judgmental; we know of no significant data bearing on this question.

4. In communities such as Nashville where there are a variety of libraries (public, private, school, and university), the problem arises as to whether the respondent knows which are public libraries. It is intended that respondents' ratings apply to the public libraries that this particular measurement process is attempting to assess. One way to check whether there is confusion is to include a question such as Number 24 of Appendix 1, which asks the respondent to name the library facility the respondent uses most often. In Nashville, because respondents mentioned only libraries operated by the city, the question wording was apparently adequate on this point.

General Citizen Survey Cost and Staffing Requirements

The cost of a general citizen survey of a representative sample of the community's population is likely to be impractical for most communities if undertaken solely for the library system, especially if it is to be conducted annually. If library questions are included as part of a multiple-service, multiple-agency survey, the costs to the library system and the added cost to the government should be quite small. The general citizen survey questions on libraries in St. Petersburg and Nashville were part of communitywide citizen surveys concerning a number of services. (Appendix 1 contains the full set of questions covering all services included in the Nashville survey.)

In both cities, library personnel helped formulate the questions and reviewed the answers, but they were not involved in the survey mechanics. Nor did the libraries provide funding for any part of the survey.

22. In the Nashville survey, about 48 percent of the approximately 1,000 respondents indicated they had used the library at least once during the past year; 37 percent indicated they had used the library four or more times. Thus the user rating questions were asked of about 370 rather than 480 persons.

If a city or county library system sponsors its own community citizen survey, it would probably require less than thirty minutes per completed interview, including set-up, interview, and tabulation time. The actual interview time should be about five minutes. The questionnaire could consist of questions such as 21-25 and 66-79 of Appendix 1. The latter questions are to obtain demographic information to permit the library system to identify measurement data for various client groups identified by such characteristics as area of residence and age, sex, race, and income group. For a sample telephone survey of 400 households, the cost could run to $4,000 (1975 prices) or more, including data processing costs.

Whether a survey is conducted by volunteers or library personnel, expert advice and direction will be needed. It would be very unusual for local government libraries to have on-board expertise and talent to conduct properly a citizen survey such as suggested here. Assistance such as this is available from private survey firms and many universities.

Costs and Staffing Requirements

The estimated cost to a medium-size public library system (four facilities and 100 employees) of undertaking effectiveness measurement procedures, as outlined in this chapter, is roughly $6,900, including eighteen person-weeks, per year. Exhibit 5-9 breaks down the cost by major component. These estimates assume that the user survey and in-library measurements will be handled by the library and that any citywide, multiple-purpose household survey that includes library services will be conducted at no cost to the library.

About 30 percent of the expenditure included in Exhibit 5-9 is for data analysis. To be fully useful, the data obtained from the measurement procedures should be given at least some in-depth analysis.

To the degree that a library system already collects the data needed for effectiveness measurement, or can use currently available staff or outside volunteers, out-of-pocket costs shown in Exhibit 5-9 can be reduced.

Exhibit 5-9

ESTIMATED ANNUAL COST OF LIBRARY EFFECTIVENESS MEASUREMENT PROCEDURES FOR A MEDIUM-SIZE CITY

(250,000 Population, Four Library Facilities, 100 Full-Time Employees)

TASK	EXPENDITURES	
	EMPLOYEE-WEEKS	DOLLARS
Data collection		
Citizen survey[1]—Once a year	Negligible	Negligible
User survey[2]—Once a year by library, two days at each facility; 700 interviews (total)	10	4,000
In-library measurements		
Circulation	½	150
Holdings[3]	—	—
Physical accessibility	1	300
Book ownership and availability	1	300
Periodical ownership and availability	½	150
Data analysis	5	2,000
Total data collection and analysis	18	6,900

1. Assumes that library questions are included as part of a communitywide, multiservice survey at negligible cost to library.
2. Assumes that a data collection questionnaire similar in length and type to Appendix 8 is used.
3. Assumes that these data are already tabulated.

This chapter focuses on the role of police in crime prevention and deterrence and, for those crimes not prevented, on apprehension of offenders. Measures for corrections, prosecution, and adjudication functions are not included except to the extent that they are reflected implicitly in the suggested measures.

Crime control is a police responsibility, but it is influenced by other local government agencies, including those responsible for street lighting, narcotics treatment, recreation, and, in the long run, city planning, housing programs, and job development programs, as well as corrections and the courts. Crime control is also influenced by factors largely not under local government control, such as the community's population characteristics.

Many police activities such as traffic control and emergency medical aid do not involve crimes and are not treated in this chapter.[1]

Crime Control Objectives

For purposes of developing a set of effectiveness measures, the overall police objective in crime control is assumed to be the following:

To promote the safety of the community and a feeling of security among the citizens, primarily through the deterrence/prevention of crime and the apprehension of offenders, providing service in a fair, honest, prompt, and courteous manner to the satisfaction of the citizens.

1. Traffic control measures are included in Chapter 8.

Principal Measures and Measurement Procedures

The following principal measurement procedures are suggested as possibilities for annual tracking. The specific measures are listed in Exhibit 6-1.

1. A regular "victimization" survey of representative samples of citizens and businesses should be considered, perhaps annually. This would correct for the current inadequacy of information on the total incidence of crime due to the reliance on data pertaining to *reported* crimes.[2] Victimization surveys will yield estimates of the number of unreported crimes in various major categories. These can help show whether changes in the reported crime rates result from changes in the degree of reporting or represent true changes in actual rates of crime. The survey can also identify locations and characteristics of those parts of the population most victimized to help police develop better crime prevention programs. Because it is hard to obtain fully accurate information from respondents, these data should be regarded as imprecise estimates. They will be valuable primarily for making comparisons over time and among various groups within the community. The same survey can be used to obtain other information as discussed below.

2. The term "reported crime data" is used in this chapter when referring to the number of criminal incidents reported to a police department. Some studies prefer the term "recorded crime data," since police may not always report all incidents that are reported to them.

Exhibit 6-1
MEASURES OF EFFECTIVENESS FOR CRIME CONTROL SERVICES

OVERALL OBJECTIVE: To promote the safety of the community and a feeling of security among the citizens, primarily through the deterrence/prevention of crime and the apprehension of offenders, providing service in a fair, honest, prompt, and courteous manner to the satisfaction of the citizens.

OBJECTIVE	QUALITY CHARACTERISTIC (OR SERVICE ASPECT)	SPECIFIC MEASURE	PRIME DATA SOURCES
Prevention of Crime	Reported crime rates	1. Number of reported crimes per 1,000 population, total and by type of crime.	Incident reports
	Victimization rates	2. Number of reported plus nonreported crimes per 1,000 households (or residents or businesses), by type of crime.	General citizen survey
	Different households and businesses victimized	3. Percentage of (a) households, (b) businesses victimized.	General citizen survey, business survey
	Physical casualties	4. Number and rate of persons (a) physically injured, (b) killed in course of crimes or nontraffic, crime-related police work.	Incident reports
	Property loss	5. Dollar property loss from crimes per 1,000 population (or, for businesses, per $1,000 sales).	Incident reports
	Patrol effectiveness	6. Number of crimes observable from the street per 1,000 population.	Incident reports
	Inspection effectiveness	7. Number of crimes per 1,000 businesses in relation to time since last crime prevention inspection.	Incident reports, inspection records
	Peacekeeping in domestic quarrels and other localized disturbances	8. Percentage of domestic quarrels and other disturbance calls with no arrest and no second call within "x" hours.	Dispatch records, incident reports
Apprehension of Offenders	Crimes "solved" at least in part	9. Percentage of reported crimes cleared, by type of crime and whether cleared by arrest or by "exception."	Incident reports
	Completeness of apprehension	10. Percentage of known "person-crimes" cleared, by type of crime.[1]	Incident reports, arrest reports
	Quality/ effectiveness of arrest	11. Percentage of adult arrests that survive preliminary court hearing (or state attorney's investigation) and percentage dropped for police-related reasons, by type of crime.	Arrest and court records
		12. Percentage of adult arrests resulting in conviction or treatment (a) on at least one charge, (b) on highest initial charge, by type of crime.	Arrest and court records
	Speed of apprehension	13. Percentage of cases cleared in less than "x" days (with "x" selected for each crime category).	Incident report, arrest reports
	Stolen property recovery	14. Percentage of stolen property that is subsequently recovered: (a) vehicles; (b) vehicle value; (c) other property value.	Incident reports, arrest or special property records
Responsiveness of Police	Response time	15. Percentage of emergency or high-priority calls responded to within "x" minutes and percentage of nonemergency calls responded to within "y" minutes.	Dispatch records
	Perceived responsiveness	16. Percentage of (a) citizens, (b) businesses that feel police come fast enough when called.	General citizen survey, business survey, and complainant survey
Feeling of Security	Citizen perception	17. Percentage of (a) citizens, (b) businesspersons who feel safe (or unsafe) walking in their neighborhoods at night.	Citizen survey, business survey
Honesty,[2] Fairness, Courtesy (and general satisfaction)	Fairness	18. Percentage of (a) citizens, (b) businesses that feel police are generally fair in dealing with them.	General citizen survey, business survey, and complainant survey
	Courtesy	19. Percentage of (a) citizens, (b) businesses who feel police are generally courteous in dealing with them.	General citizen survey, business survey, and complainant survey

(Exhibit continued on next page)

Exhibit 6-1 continued

OBJECTIVE	QUALITY CHARACTERISTIC (OR SERVICE ASPECT)	SPECIFIC MEASURE	PRIME DATA SOURCES
	Police behavior	20. Number of reported incidents or complaints of police misbehavior, and the number resulting in judgment against the government or employee (by type of complaint (civil charge, criminal charge other service complaints), per 100 police.	Police and mayor's office records
	Citizen satisfaction with police handling of miscellaneous incidents	21. Percentage of persons requesting assistance for other than serious crimes who are satisfied (or dissatisfied) with police handling of their problems, categorized by reason for dissatisfaction, and by type of call.	Complainant survey
	Citizen satisfaction with overall performance	22. Percentage of (a) citizens, (b) businesses rating police performance as excellent or good (or fair or poor), by reason for satisfaction (or dissatisfaction).	General citizen survey, business survey, and complainant survey
VICE, DRUGS, AND SIMILAR OFFENSES[3]			
Apprehension	Level and focus of arrest activity	23. Number of arrests for vice- and drug-related crimes, by type of crime (e.g., prostitution, gambling, narcotics possession, narcotics sales, etc.) and type of drug, and by "big fish" or "little fish," if possible.	Booking records
	Quality of arrests	— Measures 11 and 12.	Arrest and court records
Citizen Satisfaction	Citizen perception of seriousness of problem	24. Percentage of citizens who feel that (a) pornography, (b) prostitution, (c) gambling, (d) soft drug usage, (e) hard drug usage, or (f) sale of drugs is a major problem in their neighborhood or community.	General citizen survey
Apprehension	Illegal materials seized	25. Quantity and street value of illicit drugs seized.	Police property records
	Availability of drugs	26. Retail and wholesale prices for illicit drugs, by type and quality.	Vice squad intelligence data

1. One person committing four crimes or four persons committing one crime would be four "person-crimes." When the number of offenders involved in a crime is unknown, as may frequently happen with such crimes as burglary, "one" criminal can be assumed for this statistic (or the historical average number of offenders for that type of crime could be used).

2. A satisfactory approach to measuring the degree of corruption, malfeasance, or negligence is lacking. Data on the number of complaints received by the city on these problems should be examined, particularly when their number increases substantially.

3. These offenses have special measurement difficulties, so measures for them have been grouped separately.

2. Current apprehension measures such as clearance rates and number of arrests appear to have major deficiencies, so the use of some form of the measure "percentage of arrests that survive preliminary court hearing" is suggested. This will provide an important check on the quality of arrests. Moreover, if the reasons for dropping arrests are identified and tallied, the "number of arrests dropped, by reason for being dropped," would provide additional useful information to police and courts. These new measures require procedures for obtaining data from the court or prosecution offices. Initial tests indicate that such procedures are feasible, but methods and definitions must be carefully developed.

A related improvement is to count the "percentage of 'person-crimes' committed that are cleared," so that if more than one suspect is identified, credit would be given when (or withheld until) the other suspects are brought to justice.

Better yet, but more complicated, would be a measure of the "percentage of 'person-crimes' committed leading to an arrest that survives a preliminary hearing."

3. The citizen survey that collects victimization data can also be used to obtain representative citizens' perceptions of the adequacy of various aspects of police service including feelings about security in their neighborhoods and about the speed of response, courtesy, and fairness of their police. In addition, a survey by telephone or mail (if properly followed up) of persons who have requested help would enable the government to assess its performance on calls that are for nonserious requests for assistance—the great majority of all calls.

4. Some small but potentially helpful modifications can be made of current, reported crime statistics.

These include providing crime rates separately for businesses and for residences, considering transient as well as residential populations in determining crime rates, and identifying rates for those crimes usually susceptible to police deterrence (such as crimes visible from the street). Many problems accompany the introduction of such changes, but the long-run cost should be small.

Individual Measures and Data Collection Procedures

Exhibit 6-1 presents a set of effectiveness measures for consideration by local jurisdictions.[3] These measures, and the procedures for collecting necessary data, are discussed in this section under four major headings:

- Measures of crime prevention (1-8);
- Measures of apprehension success (9-14);
- Measures of police responsiveness and citizen satisfaction (15-22); and
- Measures of performance on vice, drugs, and similar offenses (23-27).

Measures of "Crime Prevention" (Measures 1-8)

Measure 1. Number of reported crimes per 1,000 population, total and by type of crime.

This is the standard crime measure, but many variations are possible. The following should be considered by local communities for use in addition to the standard procedures required for FBI crime reporting:

1. Aggregate crime rates might be reported using three different groupings of crimes: (1) FBI "index" crimes, (2) FBI "Part I" crimes, and (3) a locally defined group of all crimes considered serious.[4] The first two groupings will generate crime rates that permit inter-city comparisons. The last grouping, tailored to local judgments, might include (a) all Part I crimes: the seven index crimes (homicide, rape, robbery, aggravated assault, burglary, larceny, and auto theft) plus negligent manslaughter, and (b) those Part II crimes with di-

rect, unwilling victims: arson, forgery and counterfeiting, fraud, embezzlement, vandalism, child neglect or abuse, kidnapping, blackmail, extortion, stolen property trafficking, and other related crimes. The local grouping might exclude the following: Part II sex offenses, narcotics possession, gambling, nonviolent offenses against the family, liquor law violations, driving under the influence of alcohol or drugs, drunkenness, disorderly conduct, vagrancy, runaways, loitering, and so forth.[5] The additional crime categorization would not require any additional data collection, but it does require another tabulation of data.

2. To the extent feasible, crime rates should be refined to reflect offenses against various populations at risk. Included in crime totals are offenses against businesses and against nonresidents (such as commuters) located in the city at the time of the offense. Thus, crime rates based on residential population (that is, crimes per 1,000 population) can be somewhat misleading. For example, the crime rate will be inflated artificially in those jurisdictions, or portions of a jurisdiction, that have proportionately more businesses or more employees and shoppers commuting from outside.[6] To reduce the problem of defining and measuring comparable groups of crimes and populations at risk, the following separate crime rates might be calculated:

- "The number of reported crimes against residents (or residences) per 1,000 residents (or residential units), defined to include all crimes against the person when the person is a resident and all property crimes involving residential property." Property crimes against businesses owned by residents could be counted here and in the next measure (the double counting that would result from some incidents[7] is not necessarily bad here). Resi-

5. St. Petersburg, Florida, adopted the following three-part division for aggregate reporting of its crime rates: (1) all Part I crimes, (2) the Part II crimes suggested for inclusion above, and (3) all other nonvice crimes. Vice crimes (including narcotics-related offenses) are reported separately as an indicator of department activities in that field.

6. We examined a sample of 100 Part I crimes in one city for January 1974. It showed that eighteen were against businesses and seven against nonresidents. Thus the overall crime rate as usually computed was one-third higher than the actual rate of crimes against residents (as residents). Some of the businesses may have been owned by residents, however.

7. An assault against a resident that occurs within a business would be counted as against resident. If a store was robbed, the crime would be counted as against both business and resident if the owner is a resident. Note that for crimes against the person, each person victimized constitutes a separate crime by FBI definitions, so that mixtures of residents and nonresidents involved in those crimes need not involve double counting.

3. References such as those listed in the selected bibliography are worth consulting in developing measures of police effectiveness and productivity.

4. Local governments might also wish to consider groupings of violent crimes, crimes against property, and other crimes with direct victims.

dential population estimates between censuses are often available from the local planning department.

- "The number of crimes against businesses per 1,000 businesses or the number of crimes against businesses per 1,000 employees." The latter version would reflect the increased population at risk presented by larger establishments and reduce the problem of defining a single business. An estimate of the number of businesses is often available from the license department, the treasurer's office, or one of the government's offices responsible for inspections, such as for fire and safety conditions. The measurement data might be categorized by type of business (banks, motels, and the like).

- "The rate of crimes per 1,000 equivalent daily population," with "equivalent daily population" defined as the total number of residents and nonresidents in the city on an average day. The "equivalent daily population" is likely to change with the season for communities with large visitor populations or with seasonally varying employment, and averages would need to be computed for annual figures. The chamber of commerce often has estimates of visitor populations, but since these may represent rough guesses, they should be investigated before use. In particular, they often cover only visitors staying in hotels or motels. Better estimates of "average daily population" might be developed by some centralized local agency such as the planning department, inasmuch as they will be useful to many agencies (for example, police, fire, transportation).

3. Report crime rates by age, race, sex, and neighborhood of victims (for nonbusiness crimes) and by general type of business and neighborhood (for business crimes). This practice will identify more clearly those groups with the most severe problems and may provide clues as to the direction needed for prevention procedures.

Special Validity Considerations. One major problem with the use of reported crime rates is that many crimes are unreported. According to the 1973-74 general citizen surveys in St. Petersburg and Nashville, unreported crimes in those cities represented 40 to 50 percent of total crimes. Surveys by the federal government have shown a range from 33 to 66 percent.[8] Measures 2 and 3, which include estimates of underreporting, are included to counteract this problem.

Another important problem with measures of reported crimes concerns the differences that develop among police officers or from year to year in the application of definitions for various crimes.[9] To cut down on differences in defining crimes, a government can provide officer-training programs that emphasize the importance of accurate records and clarify confusing categories, conduct regular supervisory review of incident reports, establish clearer departmental policies (when the law affords discretionary choice), and have an independent agency periodically check the accuracy of tabulations of a sample of incidents.

Measure 2: Number of reported plus unreported crimes per 1,000 households (or residents, or businesses), by type of crime.

Underreporting causes at least two major problems. First, it may mislead officials and the public about the total magnitude of crimes. Second, when a government undertakes activities that lead to increased crime reporting by citizens, the higher *reported* crime figures that result are likely to be misinterpreted as an increase in crime.

The degree of underreporting varies considerably by type of crime.[10] It may also vary as citizens gain or lose confidence in the police, and as they are encouraged to report, or dissuaded from reporting, crimes.

Data Collection. Obtaining reliable estimates of unreported as well as reported crimes is more easily said than done. An approach that appears feasible for many governments is to survey periodically a random sample of households and businesses to provide estimates of the number and percentage of

8. See, for example, U.S. Department of Justice, Law Enforcement Assistance Administration, "Criminal Victimization Surveys in Thirteen American Cities" (Washington, D.C., June 1975).

9. For example, practices may differ with regard to recording crimes involving youths, especially the lesser crimes.

10. Evidence from federal and local victimization surveys indicates that underreporting is particularly large for incidents involving little or no loss or harm, such as attempted forcible entry, attempted robbery without incident, and attempted assaults without weapon. However, rape and other assaults also appear to have unreported rates of over 50 percent. Detailed findings of completed federal victimization surveys are contained in U.S. Department of Justice, Law Enforcement Assistance Administration, *Criminal Victimization Surveys, Crimes and Victims: A Report of the Dayton/San Jose Pilot Survey of Victimization* (Washington, D.C., June 1974), and *Criminal Victimization Surveys in the Nation's Five Largest Cities* (Washington, D.C., April 1975).

households (or individuals) and businesses which have been the victims of unreported crimes.[11]

The U.S. Law Enforcement Assistance Administration (LEAA) has developed victimization survey questionnaires for use by the U.S. Bureau of the Census in a number of cities. These surveys ask detailed questions about many types of crimes to aid the memory of the respondents and to avoid relying on citizens' knowledge of the legal definition of each type of crime.[12] Unfortunately, few local governments are able to afford the lengthy interviews and large sample size of the LEAA surveys (about 10,000 households contacted per city) at all, much less for annual collection. Such surveys could easily cost $250,000 or more.

The victimization survey proposed here poses fewer questions, employs smaller samples (500 to 1,000 households), and probably uses procedures less sophisticated than those of the U.S. Bureau of the Census. It is drawn up in such a way that it could easily be part of a survey that covers other government services as well as crime control. The smaller sample size reduces the accuracy of the estimates, but the results are still useful.

This more limited approach to household surveys was used (and as of this writing is still being used) by St. Petersburg, Nashville, Palo Alto, and other cities. The victimization questions tested in Nashville are numbers 31 to 36 in Appendix 1. A similar set of questions was used in St. Petersburg.[13] Other governments may want to use these questions as a starting point for developing their own surveys. The questions generally follow the wording of the LEAA questions but inquire about fewer categories of crime and obtain fewer details about each crime. Interviewers administering questions on victimization must be trained to understand thoroughly the definitions of the categories of crimes included in the wording of the questions (such as when assault is "serious" or "not serious"). For example, see Question 34 in Appendix 1. Moreover, care must be taken to match survey questions with the categories of reported crimes already in use in the jurisdiction if

11. Another approach that has been suggested is to use insurance data on crimes with property loss or injuries to estimate total crime trends. However, this presents other validation problems such as lack of insurance for the poor (who are often heavily victimized), underreporting of even insured losses to the insurance companies themselves, and the lack of full information on nonproperty crimes, plus the difficulty of obtaining data from insurance companies.

12. A layman might call a burglary a robbery, for example.

13. See Questions 26 to 33 of the St. Petersburg questionnaire in "Measuring the Effectiveness of Basic Municipal Services: Initial Report" (Washington, D.C.: The Urban Institute/ICMA, February 1974).

victimization information yielded by the survey is to be compared with crime rates reported by the police.

Businesses as well as households can be surveyed to discover the extent of their unreported victimization. The Census Bureau questioned commercial establishments as part of the LEAA victimization survey. For annual data collection by local governments, however, it is recommended, as with the household survey, that a few victimization questions be included on a general citizen survey along with questions on other government services. A survey of businesses is discussed in Chapter 15; an illustrative, but untested, questionnaire is presented in Appendix 2. Questions 14 to 18 illustrate questions that might be used to estimate the number and percentage of unreported criminal acts against businesses.

The estimate of the total number of reported plus unreported crimes can be calculated in several ways; three are outlined here:

1. Estimate the total residential victimization rate by multiplying the per capita (or per household) victimization rate calculated from the survey by the total population of the jurisdiction. The number of commercial crimes could be estimated similarly from the business survey. (Less satisfactorily, business crimes could be estimated from police records, though this would omit unreported business crimes from the overall total.) This calculation will not include an estimate of victimizations of transients, who are not covered in the residential surveys. If the number of reported incidents involving transients is determined from police records, this could be added.

2. Estimate the amount of unreported residential incidents (and commercial incidents, if the survey of businesses is used) by multiplying the per capita (or per household) nonreported crime rates obtained from the survey by the total population. Add this to the number of crimes reported in police records. The resulting estimate will include no estimate of the underreporting of crimes involving transients (because, as noted above, these incidents are not covered by the residential surveys), but will include reported crimes involving transient victims.

3. Multiply the ratio of unreported-to-reported residential incidents, as obtained from the survey, by the number of crimes reported from police records to estimate the number of unreported incidents. Add this number to the number of crimes reported in police records. This method assumes that the nonreporting rate will be roughly the same for transients as for residents.

We have no evidence to suggest which approach will prove most accurate. Regardless of which approach is selected, the procedures should be used consistently to permit meaningful comparisons from one time period to another.

Finally, tallies of the reasons for nonreporting are desirable. This information—such as frequent mention of "fear or retaliation"—should provide the jurisdiction with clues as to necessary corrective action. Question 31c in Appendix 1 illustrates how such data might be collected.

Special Validity Considerations. The potential problems in the sample survey approach are discussed in full in Chapter 14, but one particular concern for this measure is the ability of respondents to recall accurately their victimization experiences.[14] The questions used in our city tests, such as those shown in Appendix 1, ask about a twelve-month period. Alternatively, respondents could be asked about shorter periods and the resulting data used to project annual amounts of nonreporting. Another problem concerns the validity of responses in cases in which one person in a household (or business) may be asked to recall crimes committed against anyone in the household.[15] Those efforts that have been undertaken to check on the validity of crime victimization responses suggest that surveys have problems but yield data accurate enough for gross monitoring.[16]

It is our judgment that, with proper survey procedures, estimating the total crime rate is likely to be a more accurate guide to a community's overall progress than merely relying on reported crime data.[17] With the use of the less detailed and less expensive procedures, however, estimates of the number of unreported crimes for a given type of offense are likely to be imprecise because of the occasional difficulty of determining the proper category of crime for a given incident. Thus, these abbreviated victimization surveys are not likely to collect enough detailed information on each crime to estimate reliably the crime rate by type of crime.

If the same survey questions are used from year to year, the survey should help indicate relative changes in the magnitude of the crime rate as well as possible changes in the degree of underreporting over time.

Measure 3: Percentage of (a) households, (b) businesses victimized.

Victimization measures are usually calculated as shown in Measure 2: the *total* number of crimes divided by the total population (or number of households). A potentially useful variation is Measure 3, which indicates the size of the victim population. The total number of crimes divided by the number of households is *not* equivalent to this measure, since many households are victims of more than one crime. For example, in the 1973 St. Petersburg survey, 31 percent of the respondent households indicated they had experienced at least one crime, but a division of the total number of crime incidents by the total number of households responding yielded 67 percent. The corresponding figures in the 1974 Nashville survey were 33 percent and 62 percent.[18] This measure is particularly useful as a rough indicator of possible inequities in the provision of crime-prevention services; it can be helpful for the police to know if a small number of households and businesses are experiencing a disproportionate share of the crimes. If characteristics of the frequently victimized households and businesses can be identified, local authorities may be able to use such information in redesigning and retargeting crime prevention programs.

Data Collection. The number of households and businesses victimized at least once would be esti-

14. The memory problem has two major components. On the one hand, respondents may forget incidents; on the other hand, they may include incidents that occurred prior to the period they are being asked about. Little evidence exists on the size of either of these problems and their net effect. The primary research on this to date of which we are aware is a study by LEAA in 1970 in Santa Clara County, California. See U.S. Department of Justice, Law Enforcement Assistance Administration, *San Jose Methods Test of Known Crime Victims* (Washington, D.C.: National Institute of Law Enforcement, Criminal Justice Division, June 1972). It reported a 74-percent recall rate when the inquiry was for "the past 12 months" and concluded that "a reference period of 12 months is not worse than one of 6 months for simply assessing whether a crime occurred." LEAA has been using twelve-month recall periods for victimization surveys of twenty-six large central cities, but six months for its national "panel" survey.

15. This problem can be eliminated by a local government if the more expensive survey procedures are used in which each member of the household is interviewed—perhaps including school-age children. The Bureau of the Census in its victimization surveys interviews all persons fourteen years or older in the surveyed households.

16. For a recent examination of the accuracy of victimization surveys see Alfred J. Tuchfarber and William R. Klecka, *Random Digit Dialing: Lowering the Cost of Victimization Surveys* (Washington, D.C.: Police Foundation, December 1976). Previous references on this issue, such as LEAA's tests in San Jose and Dayton, are listed in the selected bibliography.

17. See Roger B. Parks, "Complementary Measures of Police Performance: Citizen Appraisals and Police-Generated Data," *Studies in Political Theory and Policy Analysis* (Bloomington: Indiana University Department of Political Science, 1973), pp. 24 ff., for a review of studies supporting this view.

18. The 1974 Nashville survey found that 39 percent of the households which indicated that they had been victimized at least once had also been victimized more than once.

mated from general citizen surveys, using the same questions as those used for Measure 2. The "number victimized more than once" can also be obtained.

Special Validity Considerations. This measure may prove more generally reliable than Measure 2 (estimated total crime rate) because it is easier for a respondent to remember whether there were any crimes at all than to remember the exact number of crimes for a given period.

Measure 4: Number and rate of persons (a) physically injured, (b) killed in the course of crimes or nontraffic, crime-related police work.

In statistics relating to fire protection, fire-related casualties are routinely reported, but the situation in crime statistics is different. Except for the deaths by murder and manslaughter, statistics on other citizen injuries or deaths related to crime are rarely compiled.

There are problems in defining what constitutes an injury. It can be argued, for example, that all crimes—or at least all crimes against the person and most robberies—cause some degree of psychological, if not physical, injury. For this measure it is suggested that only those physical injuries requiring medical attention be included. (This will have the added benefit of allowing comparability with fire and traffic accident injuries, for which similar definitions are used.)

Although tempting, it is inappropriate to estimate this measure by summing the number of "crimes against persons." Many jurisdictions make no distinction between assaults that result in injury and those that do not. For example, aggravated assault may be an attack resulting in serious injury or a threat with a gun that is not fired. Also, injuries associated with crimes such as robbery and injuries to bystanders, whether caused by offenders or police, often do not result in separate formal charges for assaults.

Data can be grouped by the following categories:

- By role of person injured (victim of crime, bystander, suspect, or police);
- By cause of injury (actions of suspect, police, bystander, or victim; or accident associated with the crime—for example, a fall); or
- By severity of injury (death, injury that required hospitalization, other injury likely to require medical attention).

To obtain these data a display format for this information such as the following might be added to the incident report:

	TO VICTIM	TO POLICE	TO SUSPECTS	TO BYSTANDER/ OTHERS	CAUSE
Number of Injuries					
Number of Deaths					

Special Validity Considerations. This measure has not been tested in this project. Because it represents mainly a reformulation and summary of existing data, often reported in narrative form on incident reports, it probably presents no special validation problems—except for the definition of injuries, which is a longstanding problem in traffic and fire statistics.

Measure 5: Dollar property loss from crimes per 1,000 population (or, for businesses, per $1,000 sales).

Minimizing property loss is another basic objective in crime prevention. The amount of total property loss depends on the average loss per crime as well as on the number of crimes. Prevention education, inspections, and other police activities may help cut the "take" per crime whether or not they reduce the number of crimes.

Data Collection. Procedures for data collection must be standardized. Property losses for each crime should be established according to (a) victim estimates or (b) a periodically updated catalog of prices for new and used products of the kinds most frequently stolen, supplemented by victims' estimates. Insurance company estimates of the value of stolen articles can sometimes be used, but not all property is insured, and an insurance company may not follow a full-value reimbursement policy.[19]

To facilitate comparisons over time, summary statistics on losses should be presented in dollars adjusted for price-level changes as well as in current dollars.

Distinguishing between losses of residents, businesses, and nonresidents can be useful to demonstrate the relative magnitude of the problem within each group. Per capita losses to residents

19. See U.S. Department of Justice, Federal Bureau of Investigation, *Uniform Crime Reporting Handbook* (Washington, D.C., January 1974), pp. 52-55, for additional suggestions on valuation of stolen property.

might be compared to per capita tax dollars spent on police. For businesses, the dollar loss per $1,000 sales might be compared to the local taxes per $1,000 that go to police protection.

Special Validity Considerations. Validity problems can arise from having nonstandardized procedures for estimating the value of property loss, from losses that are unreported or incorrectly reported, and, for comparisons over time, from not adjusting for price changes.

Victimization surveys could be used to improve the data on losses relating to unreported crimes, but this information is likely to be less reliable than the data on the number of unreported crimes because the respondent has to recall even more specific information, that is, the value of the property lost.[20] Also, crimes involving high property loss are less likely to go unreported than are those with low loss; one reason often cited by respondents for not reporting crimes is that they were too unimportant.[21]

Measure 6:   Number of crimes observable from the street per 1,000 population.

This measure provides information on the types of crime most likely to be prevented by police patrol units. Crimes on the streets and alleys, or visible from them, should be more easily deterred by the presence of patrol units than most other crimes.

The effectiveness of patrol in deterrence has been the subject of much debate.[22] Widespread use of the street crime measure might throw useful light on this debate.

Data Collection. Standardized departmental guidelines defining the circumstances that characterize a visible crime would need to be developed. Outdoor crimes would obviously be included, but the

definition of visible crimes should probably also embrace such an offense as illegal entry, when the evidence of entry (for example, a broken window) would have been visible from the street.

Special Validity Considerations. A check of incident reports in St. Petersburg and Nashville showed that the distinction between outdoor and indoor crimes was already being made in those cities, and those occurring outdoors could be easily tallied. For most indoor crimes, however, visibility from the street could *not* be inferred from the reports. A workable set of definitions and procedures for collecting reliable data remains to be tested. Meanwhile, merely distinguishing indoor and outdoor crime probably is worthwhile and may indicate at least to some degree the effectiveness of patrol.

Measure 7:   Number of reported crimes per 1,000 businesses in relation to time since last crime prevention inspection.

Some jurisdictions inspect commercial premises to determine their safety and to suggest improved precautions against crime. In a few communities, these inspections are performed by public safety agents who simultaneously inspect for crime and fire hazards. The effectiveness of the inspections can be assessed partially by comparing the crime rate in inspected properties to the crime rate in similar properties that have not been inspected. Inspection of all properties of a given risk class would preclude comparison of inspected and uninspected properties, but it might still be possible to see whether recently inspected properties have substantially lower crime rates than properties that have not been inspected for some time.[23]

Special Validity Considerations. These procedures have not been tested, but analogous measures of the influence of inspection on fire rates have been tested.[24] The procedures are probably feasible, but they involve considerable effort and might be more appropriate for occasional special studies than annual use. Also, groups of properties at similar risk must be compared. When only a limited police inspection effort is possible, it is likely to be directed toward properties of highest risk, and these cannot be compared directly with properties of lower risk.

20. See Law Enforcement Assistance Administration, *San Jose Methods Test*, p. 16, for a comparison of losses per crime from incident reports and victimization surveys. Which is the more accurate data source is not clear.

21. For example, in the 1974 Nashville survey, 41 percent of the reasons given for nonreporting were that the respondents "didn't think it was important enough." (The second largest reason given was that they "didn't think it would do any good"—21 percent.) For the 1973 St. Petersburg study the corresponding figures were 31 percent and 29 percent.

22. See, for example, George L. Kelling, Tony Pate, Duane Dieckman, and Charles E. Brown, *The Kansas City Preventive Experiment: A Summary Report* and George L. Kelling et al., *The Kansas City Preventive Patrol Experiment: A Technical Report* (both Washington, D.C.: Police Foundation, 1974). For critiques of the study see the June 1975 issue of *Police Chief*. Other experiments involving police saturation patrols have shown reductions in some crime rates, at least in the short run, while also at the same time they suggest that crimes were perhaps being shifted to neighborhoods outside the saturated areas.

23. Some local governments may also want to measure the extent to which compliance has occurred within a ninety-day period following an inspection in which a deficiency was identified.

24. See John R. Hall, Jr., "Measuring the Effectiveness of Fire Inspections" (Washington, D.C.: The Urban Institute, March 1976). Working Paper.

Measure 8: Percentage of domestic quarrels and other disturbance calls with no arrest and no second call within "x" hours.

Domestic quarrels, quarrels among acquaintances, and the like are often precursors of serious crimes. They have received growing attention from the police because they often result in violence, sometimes with injuries to the officers responding. How well police defuse such situations is a key aspect of police effectiveness in deterrence. No other measure directly addresses this police activity.

This measure makes the assumption that, in many cases, police are able to defuse the situations which prompt these types of calls—without the need to make an arrest and in such a way as to prevent second calls for at least a certain period of time. This period (the value of "x" in the measure) might be the duration of a tour of duty, twenty-four hours, or perhaps even a week—the selection is here left to local judgment.

There will, of course, be occasions when an arrest is appropriate on the first call. On other occasions, a police officer may, exercising reasonable judgment, avoid making an arrest on the initial call, but circumstances beyond his control could prompt a second call. To the extent that such uncontrollable circumstances are prevalent, this measure is likely to be less meaningful. If the percentage of such situations remains fairly stable from year to year, the changes in the values for the measure would probably still be meaningful to track success in handling calls that represent situations in which deterrence of violence was possible.

The National Commission on Productivity's Advisory Group on Productivity in Law Enforcement suggested a somewhat simpler variation of this measure: "percentage of noisy disturbance calls for which no further attention is required for the remainder of the patrol tour."[25]

Data Collection. Special procedures would be needed to keep track of "family quarrel situations reported to the police." Each dispatcher might log such calls; the frequency of calls to the same address would subsequently be tallied. Records of the initial calls would also have to be checked to determine if arrests had been made. Calls discovered on arrival of police officers to involve felonies (thus making arrest more likely) should be grouped separately.

Special Validity Considerations. These procedures have not been tested, but several police chiefs

have suggested that this category of calls merits close examination. Until satisfactory testing has been done and the meaningfulness of the resulting data examined, this measure should be considered experimental.

Measures of Apprehension Success (Measures 9-14)

Measure 9: Percentage of reported crimes cleared, by type of crime and whether cleared by arrest or by "exception."

This measure is the clearance rate, the traditional measure of apprehension effectiveness. This is the percentage of crimes for which at least one suspect has been arrested and charged, or for which an "exceptional clearance" has been made.[26] The number of exceptional clearances should be presented separately. Exceptional clearances may constitute a substantial proportion of total clearances, and they present special measurement problems, including the following: (1) the degree to which police attempt to get already apprehended criminals to admit to other crimes may change over time; (2) difficulties in definitions of exceptional clearance can make for inconsistent application; and (3) the number of exceptional clearances reported by the suspects will vary with their willingness and capability to confess to other crimes.

As is normally done, clearance rates should be presented for each crime category, so that performance on each type of crime can be assessed. Clearance rates on Part II crimes with victims (such as kidnapping) should receive similar treatment.

Clearance rates vary considerably among types of crimes.[27] Consideration of clearance rates by individual crime categories will permit officials to determine if an improvement or degradation in the overall clearance rate was due to a change in the crime mix. For example, if an unusually large number of "hard to solve" crimes are committed in a given year, a decrease in the overall clearance rate might result even though all clearance rates for individual crime categories increased. Case "difficulty" within crime categories ideally should also be

25. See U.S. National Commission on Productivity, *Opportunities for Improving Productivity in Police Services,* (Washington, D.C., 1973), p. 28.

26. "Exceptional clearances," as defined by the FBI Uniform Crime Reporting System, include cases where an arrestee confesses to other crimes, the accused dies, the victim refuses to cooperate in the prosecution, the suspect is transferred to another jurisdiction to face other charges, and so forth. See the complete definition in U.S. Department of Justice, Federal Bureau of Investigation, *Uniform Crime Reporting Handbook.*

27. For example, the nationwide clearance rate for aggravated assault with guns was 63 percent in 1974 versus 18 percent for burglary involving forcible entry. U.S. Department of Justice, Federal Bureau of Investigation, *Crime in the United States: Uniform Reports 1974* (Washington, D.C., November 1975).

considered. Incidents might be classified for any given crime category by the quality of evidence available to the immediately responding police officer.[28]

Unfortunately, as has already been mentioned, clearance rates as currently defined have major validity problems, and the measure provides only a very crude indication of success in "solving" crimes. This is discussed below.

Data Collection. Clearances are reported monthly by type of crime, in most jurisdictions, as part of the FBI Uniform Crime Reporting System. The major problem in data collection is to assure that the FBI definitions are consistently used, especially those for exceptional clearances.

A local government should consider tallying clearances for each particular unit accomplishing clearances, including "assists" (cases in which one unit helps another). If this is done, care must be taken to establish fair ground rules for "assists" to avoid misuse of the data and promotion of unhealthy rivalries.[29] Clearances can also be categorized by how they were made. Some suggested categories are "response to a call of a crime in progress," "preventive patrol," "follow-up investigation by patrol," "follow-up investigation by detectives," and so forth.

Special Validity Considerations. Using clearance rates as indicators of "solution" success poses some major problems:

1. As noted earlier, the validity of an exceptional clearance is sometimes questionable; for instance, arrestees may admit to multiple crimes in exchange for leniency, because they know they are unlikely to be prosecuted for them in the absence of evidence other than their confessions. As has been noted, definitions of exceptional clearances are complex and not always strictly adhered to.

2. Another problem is that clearances as defined by the UCR reflect only the first arrest on a case and give no credit to subsequent arrests. A crime is considered cleared when only one offender is arrested—even when multiple offenders were known to have participated in it. A department that apprehends only one of the offenders involved in a crime thus would have as high a clearance rate as one that arrested all offenders involved in a similar crime. Measure 10 has been included to address this particular problem.

3. A major problem with clearance rates is that the "clearance" is usually counted even if the arrest does not pass preliminary court hearing (regardless of the reason for its being dropped). Most jurisdictions apparently have little systematic feedback from the court system to the police concerning disposition of arrests. A clearances is not removed from the total if the suspect is released. Thus, the clearance rates do not necessarily indicate the percentage of offenders who are successfully brought to justice or even the percentage of crimes that have been "solved." Measures 11 and 12 have been included to address this problem.

4. Usually the clearance rate is computed as the number of clearances in a year, quarter, or month divided by the number of crimes in the same period. Because some time elapses between crime and arrest, some clearances in a given year will relate to crimes committed in the previous year, and some clearances for crimes in the current year will not show up until the next year. If elapsed time is generally short or if crime and clearance rates are constant, this practice presents little problem. If the lag is considerable and crime clearance rates vary, clearance rates computed the usual way will be somewhat different from the actual clearance rates. Local governments should estimate the distribution of times required to clear various types of crimes (see Measure 13) to determine the severity of this problem for their jurisdictions for various types of crimes. This problem is likely to be considerably less consequential than the previous ones.

Measure 10: Percentage of "person-crimes" cleared,
by type of crime.

As noted under Measure 9, the commonly used apprehension measure, the clearance rate, counts a crime as cleared after the first arrest on a case. The extent to which *all* offenders are apprehended can be reflected better by a new measure, the percentage of "person-crimes" cleared. Although this measure may seem strange at first, it is really more natural than the commonly used "clearance" definition.

A "person-crime" is defined as one person committing one crime. One person committing four crimes or four persons committing one crime would each mean four person-crimes have been committed. Each time a person is arrested for a crime or charged with an additional crime, one person-crime would be counted as cleared. Exceptional clearances of

28. Procedures for such categorizations were not attempted in the work reported here. However, there are forthcoming studies that may provide a sound basis for such classifications. David J. Farmer, "Fact versus Fact: A Selective View of Police Research in the United States," *The Police Journal,* April 1976, p. 112.

29. The Sunnyvale, California "ICAM" System records the effectiveness of various units and activities (e.g., fingerprinting) as they contribute to arrests (and therefore clearances). See Sunnyvale, California, Public Safety Department, *Investigation Control and Management System,* by Charles T. Crabtree, 1973.

person-crimes would be handled the same as for FBI crime clearances.[30]

Data Collection. The known number of offenders is usually already recorded on incident reports. An additional space on the incident report form for the estimated number of offenders would expedite tallies. The total count would be compared to the total number of arrests and exceptional clearances for the reporting period. A trial of this procedure for a sample of 100 cases in one city revealed no significant data collection problems. It was found, however, that when a case is subsequently classified as "unfounded," it is necessary to look up the number of person-crimes in the case file to determine how many to subtract from the total number of person-crimes. As information becomes available to indicate that more (or fewer) persons were involved than previously estimated, the tallies id·ally should be revised.

Special Validity Considerations. The chief difficulty is the accuracy of the information on how many offenders were involved in individual crimes. The data are likely to be most accurate for crimes against the person (because the number of offenders is more likely to be known) as distinguished, for example, from burglaries. When the number of offenders is not known, "one" offender (or the historical average number of offenders per crime in the jurisdiction) might be assumed.

Even with this limitation, this measure appears to be more accurate in reflecting apprehension success than the traditional clearance rates. Its importance depends on whether there are a significant number of crimes known to involve multiple offenders.[31]

Measure 11: Percentage of adult arrests that survive preliminary court hearing (or state attorney's investigation) and percentage dropped for police-related reasons, by type of crime.

Many arrests never lead to conviction and others fail to survive even the preliminary court hearing. Thus, arrest and clearance rates may considerably overstate apprehension effectiveness.[32] In addition, an ineffectual arrest may waste much police, prosecution, and judicial time before it is dropped from the system. Also, arrests are restrictions of personal liberty. Without some measure of the quality of arrests, there may be a perverse incentive for officers to make questionable arrests in order to increase arrest totals (which are sometimes improperly used by themselves as productivity indicators) or to achieve a presumed deterrent or fear-inducing effect.

A suggested approach to measuring the effectiveness of arrests is to determine the percentage that pass judicial screening or screening by a state attorney's office.[33] The quality of police performance probably has more influence on whether a case passes screening than it does on the final court disposition, although the latter is also of importance (see Measure 12).

Because of the newness and potential importance of this measure, special effort was made to test the procedures, and a relatively large amount of detail is provided in the discussion of this measure.

For many jurisdictions, the judicial screening that can be used as the test for this measure is the preliminary hearing in a court of limited jurisdic-

---

30. For purposes of this measure, a "crime" should probably be defined by the FBI definition of an incident, rather than as each offense that may take place during an incident. For example, one person committing four offenses during the same incident would count as only one person-crime and *not* four.

31. In a sample of 100 Part I crimes in Nashville in January 1974, thirteen were "against the person" and seventeen offenders were involved. Thus there were 31 percent more person-crimes than crimes for this type of offense. Assuming one offender for each of the other crimes would lead to a count of 104 person-crimes, or 4 percent over the number of crimes. However, this sample is too small for generalizations. A government could make estimates of the number of offenders for various categories of crimes, using samples of cases that it believed had been fully solved—and use these estimates rather than "one" for crimes for which no evidence was available as to the number of offenders.

32. The potential magnitude of this problem is indicated by the findings from our initial tests of the procedure for obtaining these data. In each of the samples, a significant number of arrests did not survive the initial screening. In one city, a sample of sixty consecutive Part I arrests in 1972 found that 48 percent passed the preliminary hearing. A second sample of fifty-two consecutive Part I arrests in 1973 found 38 percent passing preliminary hearing. A sample of 870 misdemeanor arrests in one month in 1974 was also examined. It showed that 21 percent resulted in a guilty verdict; however, 49 percent of the cases resulted in dispositions we classified as "ambiguous." That is to say, for example, the defendant paid a fine, court costs, or forfeited a bond but was not found guilty. In a second city, a sample of seventy-six consecutive felony arrests in 1974 showed that 68 percent passed the state attorney's hearing and another 12 percent were certified for trial as a misdemeanor, for a total of 80 percent receiving further prosecution. Of a sample of twenty-three consecutive misdemeanor arrests, 61 percent passed state attorney's hearings. Note that the results of these two jurisdictions are not directly comparable because the nature of their hearings and tests applied and the composition of the sample of cases were somewhat different.

33. Another approach, suggested by Nashville, is to measure the percentage of arrest reports that are judged of acceptable quality by a panel of two attorneys. Both the quality of the report itself and the quality of the arrest as described by the report are considered. See John F. Schnelle et al., "Evaluation of the Quality of Police Arrests by District Attorney Ratings," *The Police Chief,* January 1977.

tion.[34] "Preliminary" hearings are usually the second hearing in the process of an arrest. The first is usually an advisory hearing held within twenty-four hours after arrest, depending on the state, to set bail or appoint a public defender if necessary. Usually the advisory hearing is not a sufficient test of probable cause, although in some states (such as Tennessee) there is an attempt to make at least a brief screening of the case. Cases not surviving the advisory hearing obviously would not be counted as passing a preliminary hearing.

The preliminary hearing usually includes a presentation of evidence before a judge. Prosecution and defense are present. The basic test of the arrest at the hearing is whether a crime probably took place as charged, and whether there is "probable cause" to assume that the person arrested was one of the offenders. The arrestee may not be "bound over" if the evidence seems insufficient, if legal procedures in making the arrest and preparing the case were not properly followed, or if police and other key witnesses do not appear. Cases also may be dropped because of crowded court dockets and many other reasons having no bearing on police effectiveness.

The measure should be subdivided to indicate the "percentage of arrests dropped for police-related reasons." This would better reflect the police role, and it would also help provide feedback to the police on specific areas for improvement. The overall measure, however, is still of interest (1) because it is less dependent than the subdivided version on value judgments and (2) because it is meaningful as a measure of apprehension effectiveness in relation to the criminal justice system of which the police comprise but one component.

The District of Columbia's police department started using an analogous measure in 1972, namely, "the percentage of arrests that are 'no-papered,' categorized by reason for 'no-papering'" (that is, the case did not pass initial screening by the U.S. Attorney's Office; D.C. has no preliminary court hearing). Police-related reasons included:

> . . . any deficiency in preparation or procedures, attributable to (their) personnel, which is primarily responsible for the unsatisfactory

disposition of the case. Included for each are . . . improper recovery of evidence, evidence mishandled, unintelligible reports, (improper) search and seizure, and similar matters which by appropriate training and instruction ought to be correctable.[35]

This process of reviewing "no-papered" cases was considered responsible for a subsequent reduction in the number of such cases.

Jurisdictions with no preliminary hearings (such as in the state of Florida) sometimes substitute investigations by the state attorney's office which perform a similar function, with one important difference: The prosecution's investigation purposely considers the likelihood of successful prosecution, and not just the likelihood that a crime took place and that probable cause existed for making the arrest. Thus, cases may be dropped that would have survived a preliminary hearing. Nevertheless, the "percentage that pass the state attorney's hearing," and the "percentage that do not pass for police-related reasons" seem satisfactory arrest effectiveness measures.

Measurement data for felony arrests should be separated from misdemeanor arrest data. Misdemeanor arrests are often processed differently from felonies. Preliminary hearings usually are not held when the defendants waive their rights to jury trials. Instead, cases proceed directly to trial by a judge. The arrest effectiveness measure for misdemeanors, therefore, might be "the percentage that pass a preliminary hearing (or state attorney's investigation) or that are found 'guilty' at trial, or that are turned over to another court for further prosecution." This is a somewhat stricter test than that for felonies because a trial requires tighter standards of proof than does a hearing. It seems desirable also to provide arrest "survival" rates by the major category of offenses for both felonies and misdemeanors in order to direct attention to specific categories with low survival rates.[36]

"Survival" of an arrest should be defined as continued legal processing of at least one charge. Up to

---

34. This measure was also recommended by the 1973 National Commission on Productivity's Advisory Group on Productivity in Law Enforcement. See *Opportunities for Improving Productivity in Police Services* (Washington, D.C.: National Commission on Productivity, 1973), and the earlier Urban Institute report for the National Commission on Productivity, *The Challenge of Productivity Diversity: Improving Local Government Productivity Measurement and Evaluation, Part III: Measuring Police-Crime Control Productivity* (National Technical Information Service, June 1972).

35. See Geoffrey Alprin, "D.C.'s Case Review Section Studies: The 'No-Paper' Phenomenon," *The Police Chief*, April 1973, p. 39. Note that other governments may choose to define "police-related" reasons more broadly to include cases dropped because witnesses were not willing to testify.

36. It may also be useful to distinguish survival rates for arrests made (a) by an officer who either observes a crime in progress or who otherwise responds to a crime call; (b) after a warrant has been issued at the request of the police or prosecution; (c) in response to a warrant obtained by a citizen. In one sample of arrests, we found striking differences among these categories in percentages of arrests surviving hearings.

this point we have referred loosely to preliminary hearings for arrests. Actually, hearings are held for specific charges and not for arrests. One individual may be arrested on several charges which may be heard either at the same time or at separate hearings. Several individuals may be arrested for the same crime and the charges against them heard simultaneously or separately. The main intent of the proposed measure is to determine whether individuals are arrested needlessly. Thus, attention should focus on the percentage of arrests for which at least one charge survives preliminary hearing. If any one charge survives, the arrest could be considered of satisfactory quality.

Juvenile arrests will probably need to be excluded from the measure. In most jurisdictions, juvenile arrests are handled both separately and differently from adult arrests for most noncapital offenses. Based on preliminary investigations in St. Petersburg and Nashville, which have quite different laws and procedures for processing arrests, it would appear that a sound measure of the quality of juvenile arrests cannot be obtained from existing procedures. The processing of a juvenile arrest often focuses on what is best for the juvenile rather than on the validity of the charges. In one jurisdiction examined, the preliminary processing and decision for a juvenile arrest are made by social workers rather than the courts. These case reviewers are not likely to welcome the task of evaluating the quality of police arrests, and they are not trained to make such judgments. Also, juvenile records are held in much greater confidence than adult arrest records—a fact that could make both initial data collection and subsequent audits more difficult. This exclusion of juvenile arrests leaves a major gap in the effectiveness measures.

Does the suggested measure really reflect the quality of the arrest? Only in part. It reflects both the quality of the arrest itself *and* the follow-up processing of the arrest and associated investigation for additional evidence and witnesses. It is conceivable that the arrest itself might have been made on insufficient grounds even though subsequent investigation turned up supporting evidence. The measure also does not reflect "quality" aspects such as whether the amount of force used was appropriate or whether the officer was courteous; nor does it reflect arrests that were not made when they should have been. Conversely, arrests for good cause may be disposed of improperly by prosecution or courts. Despite these difficulties in reflecting purely police effects, this measure should represent the effectiveness of apprehensions more accurately than do clearance rates, and give insights into how to improve arrest procedures and processing.

Data Collection. The principal data collection problem is to establish a procedure for police to receive regularly, or have access to, court disposition data. As a regular procedure, few police departments obtain information on the disposition of arrests, although individual police officers on individual cases of interest may follow them closely. It may well be that police departments will find disposition information valuable not only for providing data for Measures 11 and 12 but also for other purposes.

Data on dispositions of preliminary hearings and state attorney's investigations are usually available in a centralized source, either a court docket book or a computer file. When different courts handle different types of cases, two or more sources may be needed. The number of arrests corresponding to the dispositions for a particular time period can be obtained from either arrest records or booking entries—or from the court records themselves, if the number of arrests dropped out prior to preliminary hearing is very small.

Some of the major procedural findings from the tests undertaken in two cities are presented below.

1. Each jurisdiction will need to develop definitions and ground rules for classifying specific arrest dispositions to determine if each type of disposition should be counted as one that successfully survived the preliminary court prosecution test or one that did not.[37] Such definitions and ground rules need to be adhered to so that the measurement findings will be fully comparable from one time period to another.

2. In general, the number of arrests made is not equivalent to the number of preliminary hearing dispositions, because cases may be dropped before the hearing for a variety of reasons. Each government should make at least an initial examination to see if a significant number of cases are being dropped prior to the hearing. If not, court (or prosecution office) disposition data can be used to obtain the number of arrests as well as to obtain disposition data.[38] If there are a significant number of arrests dropped before the preliminary hearing, the jurisdiction should use the arrest records or booking re-

37. For example, we categorized those misdemeanor arrests with guilty dispositions as "successful" arrests; those involving dismissal by the judge, withdrawal by prosecution, or a verdict of not guilty as "unsuccessful" arrests; those involving forfeit of bond, not-guilty plea coupled with paid fine, dismissal on (court) costs, capias warrant, or referral to another jurisdiction as "ambiguous" arrests.

38. To be precise, the measure would be the percentage of cases heard (arrests) that survive the hearing.

ports for calculating the number of arrests. In a sample of 112 arrest reports in one city, 3 were found to result in no bookings and 2 others could not be traced to a disposition (a total of 5 percent of the arrests). Of 79 felony arrests in a second city, 1 suspect escaped, 3 had charges dropped, and 1 case could not be tracked—6 percent of the arrests. The effect of dropouts on the measure thus was quite small. If these rates for dropouts prior to court disposition are representative, they can be ignored, and the added work of tallying arrest records or number of bookings can be avoided.

3. Similarly, jurisdictions probably can ignore the lapse between the time of arrest and the preliminary hearing. In the cases sampled in two cities, the lapse was small (on the order of one to seven days for the vast majority of the cases). Thus, the number of arrests surviving court test in a period (year, quarter, or even month) could be divided by the number of arrests booked in that period; or the number surviving could be divided by the number of cases heard, with both figures coming from the court disposition. It is recommended, however, that each government initially check the time lag to ascertain if there are many cases involving significant delays, and if so, whether they are uniformly distributed.

4. Care must be taken (a) to avoid recording each charge as a separate arrest and (b) to see whether each arrest resulted in at least one charge that survived the hearing. Even if data are recorded manually and the charges are not recorded consecutively, it seems feasible to attempt to relate charges to an arrest.

5. Felony arrests are frequently downgraded to misdemeanors either before or during preliminary hearings. In our sample of felony arrests in one test city, 11 percent were downgraded to misdemeanors. Care should be taken that these arrests are neither unintentionally recorded twice (once as felonies, once as misdemeanors) nor completely neglected. A charge reduced to a misdemeanor may be recorded as one type of disposition of a felony arrest; alternatively, the arrest may be considered a misdemeanor arrest that was incorrectly labeled. In the latter case, it would be counted with misdemeanors, and subtracted from felonies. It is advisable to choose one approach and stay with it.

6. A major data collection problem involves persuading the courts or the state attorney's office to agree to specify reasons for dropping cases so that the percentage of arrests dropped for each major reason can be measured. It is often difficult to determine if the reason was "police related." Also, it may be embarrassing to admit that cases are dropped for

reasons such as crowded court calendars. Perhaps the best way to resolve this problem is to have representatives of the attorneys, judges, and police attempt to reach a consensus on how to classify reasons for dropping cases. This will probably not be accomplished easily. As mentioned earlier, it has been done in the District of Columbia. The key is to separate categories that involve a significant element of police responsibility from those over which the police have little or no control.

Special Validity Considerations. The principal problems are as follows: First, parts of the criminal justice system other than police also have a role in the outcome for this measure—thus, this measure covers somewhat more than police apprehension effectiveness. And second, there are numerous troublesome data collection details, such as developing and adhering to category definitions, that can cause the data collected to be inaccurate. Thus, periodic, independent checking of the tallies seems particularly advisable for this measure.

Yet this measure appears to have some significant validity advantages over traditional "solution" measures such as clearance rates. If a jurisdiction finds that a significant percentage of arrests do not survive the preliminary hearing, as was the case in the two test cities, the validity of clearance rates as indicators of satisfactorily solving crimes would be in considerable question.

Measure 12: Percentage of adult arrests resulting in conviction (or treatment) (a) on at least one charge, (b) on the highest initial charge, by type of crime.

The ultimate test of the effectiveness of an arrest and its associated police work is whether the arrest leads to conviction or treatment of those arrested.[39] The percentage of arrests leading to conviction or treatment more closely reflects the ultimate effectiveness of the arrest than does the previous measure ("percentage of arrests passing preliminary hearings")—but it also involves to a greater extent the work of the prosecutor's office and court system and to a somewhat lesser extent the role of the

39. This is not to say that it is in the best interest of society to convict every person arrested (some of those arrested inevitably will be innocent), and some arrests that the police officer knows to be on shaky evidence nevertheless can have a beneficial effect on guilty parties in discouraging future criminal activity. Nor do we mean to imply that conviction and subsequent disposition in corrections are always correct and effective. However, ideally only the guilty would be arrested, and all those arrested would be convicted (or at least be provided treatment in lieu of conviction).

police. An arrest may stand the test of probable cause, which is adequate for preliminary hearing, but the evidence may not be strong enough to withstand the test of reasonable doubt at trial. The courts, prosecution, judge, and jury all have a major say in whether an arrest results in a conviction. Given the same evidence and quality of police work, different judges and juries may arrive at different conclusions.

Nevertheless, the quality of evidence obtained by the police, the proper legal handling of the arrested person, the competence of the police in giving court testimony, police lab work, and other factors are all important contributions to the likelihood of conviction and should be considered part of apprehension effectiveness.

Conviction may be for the original charge, a lower charge, or, less frequently, a higher charge. Sometimes a reduced charge results from plea bargaining. The strength of the case prepared by the police (and later the prosecutor's office) probably influences the extent of plea bargaining, but many other factors are also involved that are not controllable by the police (such as court workload or failure of prosecution witnesses to appear). Various forms of the measure may be used, including the "percentage of arrests resulting in conviction for some charge," the "percentage resulting in conviction for the highest original charge," and "the percentage of charges that result in conviction." Each of these might be computed as successively more stringent tests of arrest effectiveness. Changes in these quantities provide somewhat ambiguous information on police effectiveness, but they should be interpreted as signals of possible problems or evidence of success in improving arrest and investigation procedures.

Conviction rates should be reported separately for adult felonies and misdemeanors and by specific type of crime, for the same reasons as noted in the previous measure.

In some situations the outcome of a trial may not actually be a finding of guilt but will imply strong evidence of guilt. For example, in 4 percent of the misdemeanor cases we examined in one month in one city, not-guilty pleas were accepted and fines imposed. Such disposition may be made when a judge or jury feels it is warranted to expedite the case or to protect the record of the person arrested. When such dispositions occur, the measure should probably be computed with such outcomes distinguished separately. Whether these outcomes should be counted with the "guilty" outcomes for assessing quality of arrest is a judgment that each jurisdiction will need to make.

Data Collection. Prosecuting attorney's offices and courts often compile statistics for their own use on the percentage of cases resulting in various dispositions. These data may not be fed back to the police, may include results for several local jurisdictions using the same court mixed together, and are rarely categorized according to percentage of arrests resulting in each disposition. As with the preceding measure, the largest data problem is to establish regular reporting of court data to the police, or to get the prosecutor or courts to make the necessary computations. As states develop reliable offender-based transaction information systems, the data collection problems may be alleviated considerably.

A significant number of arrests may drop out of prosecution subsequent to the preliminary hearing but before the trial. This may result from 'nol prossing' or any of the number of legal options that, in essence, put the case into limbo from which it may be recalled at a later time. Thus it is not possible to obtain the overall percentage of arrests resulting in conviction by simply multiplying the "percentage of those cases that were tried that resulted in conviction or treatment" by the "percentage of arrestees that passed preliminary hearing."

The key technical data collection problem results from long delays between felony arrests and trial, which make it difficult to link arrests to dispositions. Unlike the preliminary hearings, these delays may run into many months for felonies (although an increasing number of states are passing "speedy trial" legislation that requires trial within a fixed period after arrest). Usually misdemeanors are disposed of more rapidly, because the preliminary hearing is often waived and the case goes directly to trial before a judge.

To develop an approximate measure that partially circumvents this problem, the percentage of arrests resulting in conviction might be computed using the convictions for the current time period divided by the arrests for some earlier period. For example, if felony trials usually take place between three and six months after arrest, then the convictions in one quarter might be divided by the arrests from the quarter ending three months earlier. Though there will still be some "edge effects," the resulting statistic may be a more reliable indicator than using convictions and arrests for the same month (or than just considering arrests regardless of their outcome). The reliability will depend on how sharply the arrest rate is changing, whether it varies from season to season, how the times between arrest and trial are distributed, and whether the measure is computed annually or more frequently.

Measure 13: Percentage of cases cleared in less than "x" days (with "x" selected separately for each crime category).

Prompt justice is a goal of our society, not just on ethical grounds, but also for the practical reason that as the time lessens between crime and apprehension, the offender learns his "lesson" more immediately and has less chance to commit additional crimes. Speedy apprehension also improves the chances of finding witnesses with reliable memories. In the absence of professional standards, the value of "x" would be a locally chosen target. Different targets should be considered for different kinds of crimes.

The time to apprehend is not a function of police activity alone. Local laws may have built-in delays for obtaining warrants, or delays may be caused by prosecutors' investigations. Hence, local constraints should be considered in interpreting the data.

The measure could be expressed either as (a) percentages of all reported incidents, or (b) percentages of cleared crimes only. The former seems to provide a more comprehensive perspective.[40]

Data Collection. This measure requires linking the date of each arrest and clearance to the date of the crime. When both are recorded on the same form, as is the case in some jurisdictions, the computation is easy—even easier if the incident report data is computerized. When arrests are not recorded on incident reports, the manual linking of arrest to crime must be done to record a clearance anyway, and the apprehension time could be computed at that time.

A test of computing apprehension times, based on a sample of forty-five Part I crimes in one city, showed that the procedure, using existing records, seemed feasible, although it was slightly cumbersome.[41] Explicitly recording the dates of the crime and apprehension, and/or calculating apprehension times by computer would simplify the procedure.

Measure 14: Percentage of stolen property that is subsequently recovered: (a) vehicles, (b)

vehicle value, and (c) other property value.

Part of the apprehension objective is recovery of stolen property, to help reduce losses from crime.[42] Since property may be recovered without apprehension of the offenders and vice versa, both need to be measured for a full picture of apprehension effectiveness.

Because search and recovery methods involving stolen vehicles are quite different from those relating to most other stolen property—and the recovery rates are often quite different—we suggest that vehicle recovery be measured separately from the recovery of other property. Police attempt to recover all stolen vehicles regardless of value, so the "percentage of vehicles recovered" might be reported rather than, or in addition to, the "percentage of vehicle value recovered." This statistic also is likely to be more reliable than the percentage of dollars recovered because of the inherent problems in valuation.

Because stolen vehicles are often returned damaged, the value of recovered cars preferably should be assessed as the "value when stolen" reduced by the "estimated cost of damages." Year-to-year comparisons should be made in terms of dollars adjusted for changes in price levels.[43]

Data Collection. Many departments already keep records of the number and percentage of vehicles recovered. Issues relating to collecting data on property dollar losses were discussed under Measure 5. Total value of recovered property of all types is also sometimes reported, though it is not usually stated as a percentage of property stolen. Damages to recovered property, especially vehicles, are often noted on reports but seldom deducted from value when stolen.

Value of stolen property may be either exaggerated or underplayed at the time of loss because of insurance claims or estimation errors or other reasons. Even if the absolute loss and absolute recovery value are inflated or deflated, however, using the same values for recovery as were listed for the loss will improve the accuracy of the "percentage recovered." This matching of values is somewhat easier to do for autos, expensive jewelry, and other types of readily identifiable property than for other stolen

---

40. We considered another variation, "average number of days until an arrest is made," but found it less satisfactory. It has these problems: (a) It is not clear how many days should be included for crimes for which an arrest is never made, and (b) some crimes will be cleared after long periods of time, and, although perhaps reflecting great police persistence, might distort the statistic.

41. U.S. National Commission on Productivity, *The Challenge of Productivity Diversity,* p. A-10. The test also showed that for the sample, the distribution of apprehension times was extremely skewed: the median time to clear was one day; the average was thirty-nine days. This indicates the likelihood that most arrests that are made will occur soon after the crime.

42. Large indirect losses may include doctor's bills for victims, repair of damaged goods, and reduced economic activity through fear of crime.

43. Some communities may want to measure not only the amount of property recovered but also the amount that is actually returned to the victim.

items. To improve consistency in valuations, book values for new and used items should be used to estimate values for recovered property for which the value was not listed at the time of loss. Police do not now usually record estimates of the value of recovered property, so instituting such record keeping may be the greatest change required to implement this measure. Nevertheless, this measure uses existing data for the most part, and the added cost of collection should be low.

Procedures for computing the net property recovered—value at time stolen less damages found upon recovery—were not tested by us.

Special Validity Issues. Property recovered in one period may be from crimes in earlier periods. Similarly, when the measure is computed, "property recovered in one's own jurisdiction from crimes committed in others" may not offset "property recovered in other jurisdictions from crimes in one's own." Instead of going to great lengths to adjust for special calculation problems—as when an important fencing operation is broken or when one jurisdiction is a particularly good dumping ground for stolen cars—it should suffice simply to note any large recoveries from previous periods or other jurisdictions. If these problems involve significant dollar values and cannot be corrected for, the measure would be of limited value as a gauge of the jurisdiction's police performance on property recovery.

Measures of Police Responsiveness and Citizen Satisfaction (Measures 15-22)

Measure 15: Percentage of emergency or high-priority calls responded to within "x" minutes and percentage of non-emergency calls responded to within "y" minutes.

Promptness in responding to calls for assistance is a direct service objective as well as a factor contributing to prevention and apprehension effectiveness. Citizens generally want local government to respond quickly to calls for service; this particularly applies to police services—and not just to crime calls. The value of reducing response times is by no means fully clear but for emergency calls there is much professional opinion, supported by some evidence, that for at least the first few minutes, quicker response time is associated with higher clearance rates.[44] Response time may be defined as the "time

from receipt of a call by the police to the time the first unit arrives at the scene.[45]

Response times should be reported separately for calls of different priorities as follows: "emergency calls," used particularly for crimes in progress, critical medical problems, and need for immediate assistance by police officers; and "low priority" calls such as those to investigate crimes that occurred some time ago or calls for trivial complaints. (An intermediate category might also be used: "high priority" calls, such as for crimes that just occurred.) The bulk of calls are likely to be in the "low priority" class, but responsiveness to them should not be ignored, since they are likely to be important to those requesting the assistance. Values for "x" and "y," for example, might be three minutes for emergency calls and twenty minutes for nonemergency calls. Such values would be locally established.[46]

In addition to measuring the percentage of calls responded to in less than "x" minutes, the mean, median, and range of response times are also useful indicators of response time.[47] The mean (or average) response time should not be used alone because it can be quite misleading; a few extremely long response times can sharply affect the average.

Data Collection. The time when a call is received and the time when police are dispatched are recorded by many police departments, frequently on a punched card run through a time clock in the dispatch (communications) office. Somewhat less frequently, the time of arrival at the scene, radioed in by the officers responding, may be recorded. Some jurisdictions do not collect this information because they want to avoid (1) delaying the start of "service" at the scene or (2) clogging the air waves. As communication systems improve, however, more departments are collecting this information, because it is vital for monitoring operations and designing patrol sectors.

44. See, for example, "Task Force Report, Science and Technology: A Report to the President's Commission on Law Enforcement and Administration of Justice," 1967, U.S. Government Printing Office, and Deborah K. Bertram and Alexander Vargo, "Response Time Analysis Study: Preliminary Findings on Robbery in Kansas City," *The Police Chief*, May 1976.

45. It would be preferable to note the "time from the moment the phone starts ringing to the time service is 'applied' at the scene" (which may be several minutes after arrival of the police unit at a multistory building and in other situations). Few governments, however, are likely to consider this additional information worth the added effort it involves. Jurisdictions that should consider this refinement are those in which telephone lines to the department's emergency number are frequently overloaded, or those that have many calls from high-rise office or apartment buildings in which particular offices or apartments are hard to locate.

46. Recently, some police departments have begun trial of procedures in which certain kinds of nonemergency calls are responded to by telephone rather than in person. In such cases, the meaning of "response time" may need to be redefined.

47. The cumulative frequency distribution for response times should probably also be examined. It would show the percentage of calls responded to in less than "x" minutes for various values of "x" and not just for the single value used in the measure.

Because the computation of response times has been used on a regular basis by many police departments, further testing was not undertaken in this project.

Special Validity Issues. The accuracy of response time data depends on the diligence with which the dispatcher's office and the officers in the field report promptly and accurately. An appropriate definition for response time should be established and adhered to. To the extent that arrival times are called in prior to the officers' actual arrival at the scene, the data will not reflect the full intent of the measure.

Measure 16: Percentage of (a) citizens, (b) businesses who feel police come fast enough when called.

Citizen perceptions of the adequacy of response times is another aspect of the results of police services. Citizen satisfaction with the service rendered is likely to be a major service objective, and perceived speed of police response to citizens' calls is likely to be a prime component determining that satisfaction. It can be argued that the more "objective" measure, Measure 15, is superior for measuring promptness of response and, thus, that Measure 16 is secondary. However, if citizen satisfaction is considered a principal issue in nonemergency calls, this measure assumes greater importance.

Citizen perceptions of response time should be reported separately for those who have called for assistance (or at least been present when someone else has called) and for the general public—in order to distinguish firsthand experience from other types.

Data Collection. Perceptions of response times of citizens who have called for service can probably best be obtained by using a survey of a scientifically drawn sample of those who called for service. A similar approach is to include questions on perceived speed of response as part of a municipality's general citizen survey dealing with police issues only or with various government services.

The general citizen survey has the disadvantage that only a portion of the respondents will have had firsthand contact with police during the period of interest; for example, 39 percent of the respondents to the 1974 Nashville survey and 35 percent of the respondents to the 1973 St. Petersburg survey reported having had contact with the police over the previous twelve months. (These figures include persons stopped by police for traffic violations.)

No test of a survey of only those who had requested police services was undertaken in this ef-

fort. (Such a survey is discussed in more detail under Measure 21.) Nor was a question on police response time included in the Nashville citizen survey (see Appendix 1). But relevant questions for this measure were included in the tests of the multiple-service, general citizen survey in St. Petersburg using the question "Would you rate the speed in responding to calls of the St. Petersburg Police: Excellent, Good, Fair, or Poor?" Such a question could be used in a survey of those who had called for service as well as in a general citizen survey. With a general citizen survey, a question such as Number 30 in Appendix 1 would be appropriate to permit distinguishing the responses of those who had had direct contact with police from the responses of those who had not. A similar question for surveys of businesses is noted in Appendix 2, Question 20.

The general citizen survey has one advantage over surveys of only those who have called for services: not all calls for service result in an incident report. Thus, the general citizen survey may include some of these callers. This survey procedure is discussed at greater length in Chapter 14.

The survey of callers ("complainant survey") is discussed in more detail under Measure 21.

Measure 17: Percentage of (a) citizens, (b) businesspersons feeling safe (or unsafe) walking in their neighborhoods at night.

An important police objective is to help establish and maintain an atmosphere of security for residents, the business community, and visitors.

Apparent risk and true risk are not necessarily the same. It seems desirable to measure the perceptions of citizens as well as actual crime rates.

Feelings of security will not necessarily change when *true* risks change. For example, the reporting of crime in the mass media and the actions of civic leaders can affect citizens' perceptions. The importance of providing data for various major citizen groups, in addition to jurisdictionwide totals, is well illustrated by this measure. Feeling of security seems to vary considerably by age groups, sex, and race.[48]

Data Collection. Data on citizens' feeling of security can be obtained using general citizen surveys

---

48. For example, the percentage of both white and nonwhite females not feeling safe at night was 20 percentage points higher than for males in the 1973 St. Petersburg survey and in both the 1974 and 1975 Nashville citizen surveys. The elderly also had significantly high percentages not feeling safe—over 50 percent in all three surveys. Thus, jurisdictionwide percentages can hide significant variations among major citizen groups.

and surveys of businesses. This can be the same survey usable for obtaining data on other measures.

Question 28 of Appendix 1 might be used for residents. Questions regarding areas of the city into which the citizen would like to go but does not for fear of crime (Questions 29 and 29a of Appendix 1) can help measure the atmosphere of security and also suggest specific areas of the community where the problems are worst. An illustrative question that might be used for businesses is presented in Appendix 2 (Question 11).[49]

Measure 18: Percentage of (a) citizens, (b) businesses that feel police are generally fair in dealing with them.

Measure 19: Percentage of (a) citizens, (b) businesses rating police as generally courteous in dealing with them.

The fairness and courtesy with which police services are delivered are of concern to citizens and businesspersons. While response time, clearance rates, and the like can be measured best by more objective data, fairness and courtesy seem to be measured best by obtaining direct citizen feedback on them.

Fairness has several aspects, including evenhandedness in dealing with different clientele groups and individuals, respect for civil rights, use of reasonable force in apprehension, and neither overzealousness nor underenforcement of the law. Each of these aspects may be separately addressed, but considering them as a group—at least at first—appears likely to suffice. If problems develop, supplemental questions could be added to the same or later surveys. An alternative measure is "the number of complaints reported regarding police fairness," but the probable lack of reporting of complaints makes it difficult to know how representative the available figures are.

Courtesy is related to fairness, but, as noted above, one can be fair but not courteous and vice versa. Whether citizens can distinguish between these two qualities remains open to question (as noted below). It may be sufficient to include only one or the other measure, but at present both are recommended.

---

49. A question of the respondent's feeling of security during the day might be considered as an additional measure. Fear during the day would be an even stronger signal of lack of a feeling of security. Question 11 of Appendix 2 illustrates such a question, for businesses.

Data Collection. The general citizen survey can be used to obtain data on citizen perceptions of fairness and courtesy. Examples of questions that have been used are presented in Appendix 1 (Questions 38 and 39). On both the 1973 St. Petersburg and 1974 Nashville surveys responses to these two questions were very similar; still, we are not confident that respondents can distinguish between the attributes of fairness and courtesy as defined in the questions used. If a government wishes to obtain information on these attributes, it is recommended that brief definitions of the two terms be provided to the respondents. Questions regarding the number and possibly the nature of contacts with the police should also be included so that perceptions of persons who have had firsthand experience can be reported separately from the general public's perceptions.[50] (See Question 30 of Appendix 1.)

As discussed under Measure 16 and later under Measure 21, an alternate data collection procedure (untested in this effort) is to survey a sample of those who have called the police department for service (rather than the general public).

Illustrative questions on fairness and courtesy applicable to surveys of businesses are presented in Apppendix 2 (Questions 21 and 22).

Measure 20: Number of reported incidents or complaints of police misbehavior, and the number resulting in judgment against the government employee, by type of complaint (civil charge, criminal charge, other service complaints).

Honesty is a difficult quality to address. The number of citizens likely to have firsthand information regarding police honesty is far smaller than the

---

50. Using the 1973 St. Petersburg survey, we compared the responses of those who indicated that they had had at least one direct contact in the past twelve months with the St. Petersburg police with the responses of those who reported having had no contacts. We did this for the questions that asked for an overall rating of the police and for a rating of their fairness. On neither question was there substantial difference between the ratings. For the overall rating, of those who provided a rating, 75 percent of those with prior contacts gave a rating of either excellent or good, as compared to 80 percent for those without prior contact. On fairness, 85 percent of those with prior contacts and 82 percent of those without prior contacts in the past twelve months gave a rating of "fair" rather than "not fair" or "varies." These suggest that it may not be necessary to distinguish those with contacts from those without for the purposes of these questions. However, the limited evidence presented here is far from conclusive, and intuitively it appears likely that at least under some circumstances there would be significant differences. As would be expected, the number of "don't knows" was considerably higher for those with no prior contact (21 percent versus 5 percent on the overall rating question and 23 percent versus 8 percent for the fairness question).

number likely to be informed on other aspects of police service qualities. It is also questionable whether respondents with firsthand information will be candid about police honesty because of the sensitivity of the issue and potential criminal liability. Questions on police honesty can be included in general citizen surveys, but they seem intrinsically less reliable for use in measures of honesty than do questions on fairness and courtesy.

No satisfactory approach to measuring corruption, malfeasance, and negligence was identified in this project. Yet some, even very crude, measure should be used to indicate the seriousness of the community's concern about this issue, such as the "number of reported incidents or complaints of police misbehavior." Both "the total number of complaints" and "the total number of complaints that have not been invalidated" (as by police internal investigation) probably should be included.

Data Collection. Data on complaints are already routinely collected in some cities.

Special Validity Considerations. As indicated earlier, this measure is far from satisfactory. Clearly, not all incidents will be reported. Incidents invalidated by police internal investigations and police review boards will be subject to question by outsiders. More complaints are likely to be made during periods when police misbehavior receives much publicity than during periods when the level of honesty is no better (and possibly even worse) but when there is little attention to the issue. At best this measure can be considered a very crude indicator.

Measure 21: Percentage of persons requesting assistance for other than serious crimes who are satisfied (or dissatisfied) with police handling of their problems, categorized by reason for dissatisfaction and by type of call.

Most calls for service in most jurisdictions do not involve serious crimes.[51] Yet, except for Measure 8, which focuses on domestic quarrels, and Measures 15, 16, 18, and 19, which deal with particular aspects of service quality (speed, fairness, and courtesy), most previous measures have tended to focus on matters related to serious crime. This

51. For example, of 73,000 calls for service (other than for traffic accidents) received by the St. Petersburg police in 1970, almost 45,000 were for complaints about animals, noise, other disturbances, disorderly conduct, vagrancy, trespassing, and a host of other miscellaneous problems.

measure attempts to provide an indication of overall satisfaction with police services received by those who called for help on nonserious crime matters.

Separate measures could be used for each type of minor complaint. For example, in some communities stray dogs may be a major problem, and measures dealing with the number of animal bites from dogs on the loose might be desired. However, the large number of different types of miscellaneous complaints appears to preclude a separate measure tailored to each, at least for regular measurement.

The approach suggested here is to consider together all miscellaneous calls for service, and to evaluate the effectiveness of the police in handling them on the basis of the satisfaction of those making the calls. In other words, did the police, in the opinion of citizens who called for assistance, help remedy the situation for which they were called or otherwise effectively supply the service desired, or refer the caller to the appropriate agency if the matter was outside police jurisdiction?

Data Collection. A survey of a scientifically drawn sample of those calling, as discussed under Measure 16, can be used to obtain caller satisfaction levels. Data for Measures 16, 18, and 19 would be obtained at the same time. Reasons for any reported dissatisfaction, such as delays in responding or discourtesy, would be requested. This would help identify how to improve service and give some indication of the validity and seriousness of the reported problem. Results could be tallied separately for calls responded to in person or by telephone only, to evaluate the relative effectiveness of the two modes.

The general citizen survey represents another potential procedure for data collection. But the small samples involved for a general citizen survey (500 to 1,000 households) would yield even smaller samples of complainants, and it is not recommended for this measure. As noted earlier, about 35 percent of respondents to the 1974 Nashville survey and 39 percent in the 1973 St. Petersburg survey reported having had contacts with the police (these included contacts on traffic matters). The citizen survey may be adequate to obtain a general idea of overall complainant satisfaction, but is probably inadequate for reporting results by type of call.

A survey of persons who had requested services (complainants) could be made using either (a) a sample of complainants (if properly drawn to avoid biases), probably surveyed by telephone; or (b) all complainants, reached with a short questionnaire sent by mail. Note that no such survey was tested in this project; a local government would need to develop and test the procedures.[52]

The complainant survey could be based on a sample drawn from incident reports chosen at random. Although incident reports are not usually separated by type of crime, the percentage of miscellaneous calls for service or calls for minor crimes is large enough that a random sample could be drawn from the total set, and those not fitting into this miscellaneous category rejected.

Ten minutes are probably enough to obtain the data necessary from each person interviewed. Since the survey would involve only complainants who had called the police department, addresses for a mail survey or phone numbers for a telephone survey will usually be available from the original incident reports. Naturally, the success of this procedure depends on the availability of correct addresses or telephone numbers for at least most of the persons who have called the police department; otherwise, the sample of responses may be biased. Therefore it may be necessary to have department personnel exercise more care in recording callers' names, addresses, and telephone numbers than they are currently required to do.

A mail survey will be less expensive than a telephone survey but its relatively low response rates may cause considerable question as to the representativeness of the responses.[53] Response rates can be increased by second and even third mailings or perhaps by the use of telephone interviews for nonrespondents.

The telephone survey, if done by an outside professional survey firm, is likely to cost $10 per interview (1975 prices). The out-of-pocket expense can be reduced considerably by the use of government personnel for the interviewing. However, to avoid influencing respondents who might fear retaliation for any unfavorable responses, interviewers should not come from within the police department; similarly,

if a mail survey is used, questionnaires should not be mailed back to the police department.

For either type of survey, professional and technical assistance should be used to minimize possibilities of bias.

Measure 22: Percentage of (a) citizens, (b) businesses rating police performance as excellent or good (or fair or poor) by reason for satisfaction (or dissatisfaction).

An overall measure of citizen satisfaction with police services is desirable to provide insight into the composite perception of the citizens about police services.

Data Collection. The general population survey (for household responses) and survey of businesses (for business responses) appear to be the primary sources of data. As for other perception questions, citizen ratings should be reported separately for those with firsthand contact with the police, by type of contact, as opposed to those from citizens with no contact during the period covered by the survey.[54] Categories for "types of contact" could include callers for assistance, witnesses, persons stopped for traffic violations, and persons stopped for other reasons by the police.

As for previous measures reflecting citizen perceptions, a general multiservice citizen survey and, for citizens who have called for assistance, the complainant survey (see Measure 21) can be used to obtain the data. A question such as Number 41 of Appendix 1 could be used for residents; for businesses, Question 23 of Appendix 2.

Measures of Performance on Vice, Drugs, and Similar Offenses (Measures 23-26)

Measuring police effectiveness in controlling crimes against public morals and crimes relating to drugs (the so-called "victimless" crimes) poses special difficulties. The objectives of the laws concerning vice crimes are ill-defined and continually changing with public attitudes. Also, most vice crimes are not reported to the police, and there are no data on the incidence of such offenses equivalent to reported crime data. (Incidents are counted when arrests are made.) Thus even the approximate total incidence of such events is seldom known and we know of no

52. Some police departments have surveyed citizens who have called for services. The sheriff's department of Yuba County, California (population 45,000) used a ten-question survey of persons who called and received service. It included questions on adequacy of response time, fairness, friendliness, concern, courtesy, helpfulness, and overall satisfactoriness of the response. The police department of Albion, Michigan (population 12,500) reported on its use in L. R. Disser and Roland M. Kissinger, "Inspection: A Management Tool," *The Police Chief*, August 1975. For a survey mailed to a sample of persons who had been victims, witnesses, arrestees, or traffic violators, it noted a 46 percent return rate to a mail questionnaire (with no follow-ups apparently attempted).

53. In St. Petersburg, a police department mail survey on another subject to a small sample of all citizens obtained a 50-percent response. Because of the question of representativeness, the resulting information could be used only as a rough indicator for the whole city.

54. See note 50 above for some findings of the differences in responses for those who have had at least one contact with the local police over the past twelve months as contrasted with the responses of those who have not had any contacts. These findings indicate that there may be a surprising similarity in perceptions between these two groups.

appropriate procedure for obtaining such information.

Measures 23 through 26 in Exhibit 6-1 should be considered as a group. Together they may help provide an overall indication of effectiveness in controlling vice crimes, although, with the possible exception of the quality/effectiveness of arrest measure, they are not satisfactory if taken individually. This is a specialized area of crime control, and because no special testing was undertaken on these measures during our project, they are not discussed further in this book.

Summary of Suggested Additions to Incident Reports

Some additions to the information generally collected on incident reports have been suggested in the previous sections. These additions are summarized below; the need for them is cited in the discussion of the individual measures.

1. *Type of victim:* Resident,[55] nonresident, business, or other (for example, institutions).—For Measure 1.
2. *Number of casualties, by cause:* Number of injuries or deaths *to* (a) crime victims, (b) bystanders, (c) suspects, and (d) police associated with the particular crime. It would also be useful to indicate whether the casualty was inflicted *by* (a) crime victims, (b) bystanders, (c) suspects, (d) police, or (e) accidents not caused directly by a person, such as a fall.—For Measure 4.
3. *Type of location:* Outdoors, by type of place (such as public street, alley, park, transit vehicle, transit stop), or indoors by type of place (highrise, single family or multifamily houses, store, school, and the like).—For Measure 6.
4. *Visibility to patrol:* Whether the crime occurred in a place that could be seen by routine car or foot patrol. It may be stated as "yes," "probably yes," "probably not," or "no."—For Measure 6.
5. *Number of offenders:* The probable number of participants in the crime.—For Measure 10.
6. *Disposition of arrests* (from court or state attorney's records).—For Measures 11 and 12.
7. *Response-time information:* The time each call for assistance is received and the time the first police unit arrived at the scene.—For Measure 15.

55. A resident may be defined as someone residing in the jurisdiction more than "x" months per year, with "x" a locally defined standard.

Costs and Staffing Requirements

The principal additional costs for use of the procedures discussed in this chapter are for the following:

1. General citizen survey, to obtain data on household victimization, feeling of security, and citizen attitudes to such aspects of police performance as speed of response, fairness, and courteousness (for Measures 2, 3, 16 to 19, 22, and 24).
2. A survey of businesses to obtain the same data as in (1) but from the business community's perspective (for Measures 2, 3, 16 to 19, and 22).
3. Data from the courts or prosecutor's office on disposition of arrests (for Measures 11 and 12).
4. A survey of persons who have called for assistance to obtain their perceptions as to the helpfulness, speed of response, fairness, and courteousness of the service (for Measures 16, 18, 19, 21, and 22).

General Citizen Survey

Costs are likely to run $10 to $15 (1976 prices) per interview (for about a ten- to fifteen-minute interview). The lower estimate would tend to be for surveys by telephone; the higher one for at-home interviews. For annual samples of 300 (small jurisdictions) to 1,000 households (large jurisdictions), this would mean $3,000 to $15,000. These costs can be much higher if more detailed, elaborate, and larger surveys are undertaken. If these crime questions are included as part of a multiservice survey, the costs (as in St. Petersburg and Nashville) can be spread over a number of government services. The general citizen survey is further discussed in Chapter 14.

Survey of Businesses

Few direct cost data for business surveys are available. Business respondents may be more difficult to reach and interview by telephone or in person. With proper groundwork in obtaining the business community's cooperation, however (see Chapter 15), a mail survey might achieve a reasonably high business response rate, so the cost could be lower than that for the general population survey. Without such groundwork, the costs would probably be about the same.

Survey of Persons Who Have Called for Service

A telephone or mail survey, if adequately followed up to obtain a reasonable response rate and if undertaken by current government personnel (perhaps those from the government's "service and information" office), could require little out-of-pocket expense. The length of the interview should be held to a maximum of five to ten minutes. An annual sample of 100 to 500 callers would probably cost well under $10 per interview, even if done by an outside organization.

Disposition-of-Arrest Data

Costs will depend on the number of different courts, the number of cases, and the extent to which police and court cases are computerized and linked to a common data base. In our tests in two cities, a junior city employee required two or three days to record manually data on preliminary hearing dispositions from court docket books for 900 cases for Measure

11. The additional cost should be lower for Measure 12—concerning final disposition—because the basic arrest information will already have been collected for Measure 11 and court dispositions are usually tabulated by courts or prosecutors' offices.

Analysis Costs

Although basic tabulations are included in these estimates, the time and costs for analyzing the data are not. Analysis is an important step after the data have been collected. In many jurisdictions, analysis capability already exists. Governments without such capability should consider acquiring it; analysis of effectiveness measurement data would be but one activity for a full-time analyst.

This chapter differs somewhat from others in this volume. Some of the principal measures related to fire protection first described in our initial report received additional testing and refinement by nine fire departments in a separate project undertaken jointly in 1974-75 by The Urban Institute and the National Fire Protection Association (NFPA) under the sponsorship of the National Science Foundation. The St. Petersburg Fire Department was the one department that participated in both this special study and the multiservice project that provided the major testing for many of the other service areas discussed in this book.[1] This chapter summarizes the principal findings and recommendations from the 1974-75 project. For more specific information on the findings and procedures, the reader should examine directly the reports from that effort.[2]

1. The other eight fire departments participating in the project were Charlotte, North Carolina; Dallas, Texas; Fairfax County, Virginia; Lynn, Massachusetts; Newark, New Jersey; Portland, Maine; San Diego, California; and Seattle, Washington. Nashville participated in the multiservice study but not in the subsequent study devoted entirely to fire protection.

2. See Philip S. Schaenman, John R. Hall, Jr., Al Schainblatt, Joe Swartz, and Michael Karter, *Procedures for Improving the Measurement of Local Fire Protection Effectiveness*, (Boston, Mass.: The Urban Institute and National Fire Protection Association, 1977), and the three supplementary technical working papers: "Supplemental Technical Report: Supplemental Field Incident Report—Forms and Associated Notes"; John R. Hall, Jr., "Supplemental Technical Report: Measuring the Effectiveness of Fire Inspections"; and John R. Hall, Jr. and Michael Karter, "Supplemental Technical Report: Fire Rates vs. Community Characteristics" (Washington, D.C.: The Urban Institute, April 1976). In addition, an earlier study by The Urban Institute and NFPA provided an initial consideration of fire-protection performance measures, including some that did not receive further testing in the subsequent projects. See Schaenman and Swartz, *Measuring Fire Protection Productivity in Local Government*, (Boston, Mass.: National Fire Protection Association, October 1974).

Fire departments have a long tradition of monitoring the outcomes of the fire protection system. Annual reporting of fire rates, fire losses, fire deaths and injuries, and even response times are commonplace. In many communities, detailed records have been kept on every fire call and every commercial inspection for decades. Nevertheless, important information gaps remain, even in departments with advanced data systems.

Major Improvements Needed and Summary of Recommended Procedures

A full set of suggested fire protection effectiveness measures is presented in Exhibit 7-1. It includes measures of overall service outcomes and of the two principal subfunctions: prevention and suppression. (Suppression measures are presented first because the larger portion of the research effort went into development of those measures, but prevention measures are at least as important.) This chapter discusses only those measures that are deemed most important or those that would require significant changes in data collection procedures.

The following needs for improved measures of fire service performance appear to be of highest priority. Each is discussed further in later sections:

1. Particularly with respect to fires in buildings, fire departments should consider regularly measur-

Exhibit 7-1
SUMMARY OF PRINCIPAL EFFECTIVENESS MEASURES FOR FIRE PROTECTION SERVICE

OVERALL OBJECTIVE: To minimize losses to persons and property by helping to prevent fires from occurring and to suppress losses from fires that occur.

OBJECTIVE	QUALITY CHARACTERISTIC	SPECIFIC MEASURE	DATA COLLECTION PROCEDURE
Overall Loss Minimization	Civilian casualties	1. Number and rate of civilian injuries and deaths per 100,000 population.	Data generally available today, though not always expressed as rates.[1]
	Firefighter casualties	2. Number of firefighter injuries and deaths per 100 employees.	Data generally available today. The data should be classified by circumstance, e.g., casualties at fires, en route to fire calls, in other traffic accidents, in training, at nonfire rescues, etc.
	Property loss	3. Direct dollar loss from fires per $1,000 property served.	Insurance company or fire department estimates.
Suppression	Fire-fighting effectiveness—dollar loss	4. Average direct dollar loss per fire, for fires not out on arrival, by size on arrival and type of occupancy.	Necessary data (except size on arrival) generally available.
	Fire-fighting effectiveness—spread	5. Percentage of fires (not out on arrival of first fire unit) in which spread after arrival is limited to "x" square feet (or "y" percent, or one step of the extent-of-flame scale),[2] by size on arrival and type of occupancy.	Spread after arrival is the difference between the extent of fire damage on arrival of first unit and at extinguishment, as estimated by fire officer at scene. Note that this measure is *not* the overall extent of damage.
	Fire-fighting effectiveness—time	6. Time to control or confirm spread has stopped,[3] by size on arrival and type of occupancy.	Data could be recorded by fire officer at the scene, or taken from dispatcher records.
	Speed of providing service	7. Percentage of response times that are less (or more) than "x" minutes. 8. Average response time, by type of fire.	Response time would be defined as "time elapsed from time fire is reported to the fire department to time of arrival of first unit at scene." This data is often available from fire department's dispatching center.[4]
	Rescue effectiveness	9. Number of "saves" versus number of casualties.	Data collected by fire officers at the scene. Data should be reported separately by risk to victim and type of rescue action.
Prevention	Reported fire incidence rate	10. Number of reported fires per 1,000 population, total and by type of residential occupancy.[5]	Data generally available.
	Reported building fire incidence rate	11. Number of building fires per 1,000 occupancies, by selected occupancy types (e.g., single-family dwellings, duplexes, apartments, mobile homes, small stores) and by fire size.	Number of occupancies by type may be estimated from planning department data (for residences) or from pre-fire inspection records for commercial/industrial occupancies. Fire size estimated by fire officer at scene.
	Reported plus unreported building fire incidence rate	12. Number of unreported plus reported building fires per 1,000 households (or businesses), by type of occupancy.	Survey of a representative sample of citizens and fire incident reports. Reasons for underreporting would also be solicited.
	Preventability of fires	13. Percentage and rate of fires that are relatively preventable by inspection or education.	Intended for internal fire department analysis based on judgments as to the relative preventability or various types of fires.[6]
	Pre-fire inspection effectiveness	14. Rate of fires in inspected versus uninspected (or frequently inspected versus infrequently inspected)[7] occupancies, by type of occupancy and risk class.	Data obtained by linking fire incident reports to fire inspection files (probably feasible manually in most jurisdictions under 1 million population).
	Apprehension effectiveness for fire-related crimes	15. Clearance and conviction rates for arson, incendiarism, false alarms, and code violations.	Data obtained by linking fire incident and fire inspection data to police department arrest records and to court records on case dispositions.

(Exhibit continued on next page)

Exhibit 7-1 continued

OBJECTIVE	QUALITY CHARACTERISTIC	SPECIFIC MEASURE	DATA COLLECTION PROCEDURE
Overall	Deterrence effectiveness for fire-related crimes	16. Number of (a) incendiary and suspicious origin fires per 1,000 population, (b) false alarms per 1,000 population.	Data generally available.
	Detection-response effectiveness	17. Distribution of sizes of fires at arrival.	Sizes are estimated by fire officer at scene.
	Citizen satisfaction	18. Percentage of population rating fire protection service as satisfactory.	Survey of a representative sample of citizens. Data should be reported separately for persons with firsthand contact with fire department. Reasons for dissatisfaction also might be solicited. Separate surveys might be used for businesses and households.

1. To take the work force and visitor population into account, casualty rates per 1,000 average daily population—including residents, workers, and visitors—might also be considered.

2. It may be useful to report the "spread after arrival" in three parts: the spread in flame damage; the spread in total fire damage (including smoke and heat); and the spread in total damage from fire and fire fighting. Although data on the amount of damage from fire fighting for a particular fire are hard to evaluate without knowing a great deal about the fire, cumulative data on fire-fighting damage might give some clues to performance over time. Measures other than of flame damage have not been tested for reliability, however.

3. Other useful versions of this measure are the mean and median times to control—also by size of fire and occupancy type.

4. To be of most use, the data would also be collected so as to permit classification by the major components of response time: time from call to dispatch; time from dispatch to arrival; and time from arrival to putting water (or other extinguishing substances) on the fire.

5. The term "occupancy" refers to a piece of property in terms of its use. For example, the following might be considered separate occupancy types: detached houses containing only one household, duplexes, apartments, sheds, drug stores, warehouses and blocks of offices with a single owner. There may be more than one occupancy in a particular building and some occupancies—for example, phone booths, garbage dumps, and piers—are not buildings at all. Analysis of fire effectiveness data by occupancy type is useful because it compares experience among places with the same kinds of materials present and the same kinds of activities going on.

6. For example, fires started by inflammables stored near ignition source, or in buildings with fire-code violations relevant to the fire start, would be "highly preventable." Fires started by hidden equipment defects not common to that equipment would be relatively "unpreventable." Fires might also be classified by the government action needed to aid in preventing, for example, the "percentage of fires for which an inspection a week before the fire would have detected a hazard," or the "percentage of fires in which building code change would have removed the cause."

7. For categories in which almost all occupancies are inspected, as is usually the case for commercial occupancies, it may not be possible to clearly separate those frequently inspected from those not, within a given risk class. In that case, statistics on times since last inspection for fires and for buildings in general may be used to determine how much the likelihood of fire increases (if it does) as the time since last inspection increases. (If inspections are effective, there should probably be fewer fires in more recently inspected occupancies.)

ing three dimensions: fire size on arrival, fire spread after arrival, and time to control (for Measures 5, 6, and 17), in addition to direct dollar loss. The procedures employed should be field-tested for reliability and sensitivity before full-scale implementation.

Existing measures of fire suppression performance at the scene—chiefly dollar loss and casualty figures—are inadequate. This is because they often reflect what happens before fire suppression forces arrive more than what happens after, and they give extra weight to losses of expensive goods that may be no easier or no more important to save than are their less expensive counterparts. A measure of the "amount of spread after arrival of the fire department" has been developed and tested in nine communities. The "time to control"—another measure of fire suppression performance—has also been tested. As with most other measures, these will reflect a number of factors that are relatively uncontrollable by the fire department—or at least by the fire suppression forces at the scene. For instance, both measures are greatly influenced by the size of the fire at arrival. The larger the fire at ar-

rival, the harder it will be to control and thus, in general, the larger the amount of spread after arrival (Measure 5) and the greater the time to control is likely to be (Measure 6). Therefore, it is strongly recommended that data for these two measures be grouped by "size of fire at arrival." Data on fire size at arrival can be obtained as part of the procedure for estimating fire spread after arrival.

2. There has been no satisfactory method available to separate the impact of some major fire prevention programs, such as pre-fire inspections, from the effects of other factors that also influence overall prevention measures like the fire rate and the fire-loss rate. Hence it has been hard to know whether the greatly increased resources being sought for certain prevention programs would really reduce the fire rate. A procedure for communities to use in examining periodically the probable effectiveness of fire inspection programs has been developed and given initial testing. It is recommended that communities regularly collect data on "the percentage and rate of fires deemed relatively preventable by inspection" (Measure 13) and consider use of other measures of inspec-

tion effectiveness for one-time analyses in areas where the rate of apparently preventable fires seems high (Measure 14).

3. "Failures" of prevention or rescue—that is, deaths and injuries—are recorded, but corresponding successes—such as "saves" at scenes of fires—are not. Although "saves" may also be prevention failures in the sense that prevention has failed if a save is necessary, "saves" are nontheless a major, positive product of fire suppression and rescue efforts. Four cities tested the feasibility of procedures for obtaining data on the number of saves (Measure 9). The principal problems are in defining saves and in developing rigorous, consistent procedures to count different kinds of saves. While continuing to regard the measure as experimental, local governments may want to collect such data regularly.

4. For fire incidence measures (such as Measures 10 and 11), three improvements are suggested: (a) Count very small, no-casualty fires separately from larger, more serious fires. The measure of more serious fires will be less sensitive to variations in the rate of underreporting than the overall measure, because the reported number of small fires is particularly sensitive to reporting fluctuations over time and among areas within a community. (b) Provide clear definitions of fires and cause categories and make periodic checks to see that they are being consistently and properly used. (c) Relate fire rates in various major areas of the community to physical or demographic characteristics of those areas demonstrably associated with incidence of fire (so that actual fire rates can be compared to "expected" fire rates for each of the various areas). All these adjustments will make the interpretation of fire rates as indicators of relative effectiveness more valid.

5. Review of data in several communities and conversations with many fire officers indicate that the reliability of several types of existing fire data is questionable. In addition to the checks on definitions of "fire," "building fire," and "fire cause," noted in 4b above, the following are suggested here: (a) Line officers should be trained and periodically retrained if necessary on how to fill out basic fire incident reports and inspection records. (b) All data on incident reports and inspection records should be screened to see if they appear reasonable; a random sample of reports should occasionally be checked in depth. (c) To provide motivation for accuracy, line officers should receive feedback on how the data they collect are being used, and on common errors being made.

6. Citizen satisfaction is becoming a major concern of government officials. However, unlike most other basic municipal services, the fire department has firsthand contact with only a very small proportion of the citizens of a community in any single year, unless it has broad-scale prevention programs such as homes inspections. Hence, except in communities with such programs, a meaningful assessment of citizen satisfaction with the fire department, based on the opinions of persons who have had contact with the department, probably cannot be obtained efficiently from a general citizen survey of the kind suggested in this report for use by other government services. Other approaches to this measure (Measure 18), such as a follow-up survey of persons who had contacted the fire department, are possible but were not tested in our project.

Individual Fire Protection Measures

This chapter does not individually discuss each measure shown in Exhibit 7-1. It is organized in terms of groups of measures that use the same data collection procedure. The order of discussion roughly parallels the order of presentation of the measures in Exhibit 7-1.

Improved Measures of Fire Suppression Performance[3] (Measures 4-6 and 9)

Fire Spread After Arrival (Measure 5). Firefighting effectiveness is not adequately quantifiable in terms of dollar loss and casualties, partly because much loss and many casualties occur before arrival of the first unit. A measure more closely tied to fire department actions at the scene is the spread of flame damage *after* arrival. "Spread" can be measured in terms of the difference between the area the fire was confined to on arrival and the area it was confined to at extinguishment. These areas can each be described in terms of approximate square feet or in terms of grosser scales indicating the number of rooms, floors, or buildings involved, or in terms of the familiar NFPA 901 "extent of flame damage" scale indicating whether the flame damage was confined to area, room, floor, or building of origin. Whichever scale is used, the important point is that

3. This section also discusses Measures 3 and 17 which use the same procedures as Measures 4 and 5, respectively.

it be used to describe damage *both* at arrival and at extinguishment. The fire officer in charge at the scene would collect the basic raw data by direct observation and discussions with the fire fighters who first saw the fire. Approximate dimensions of the fire at arrival and extinguishment would be paced off or estimated by sight ("eyeballed") *after* extinguishment.

A slightly modified version of the form tested is shown in Exhibit 7-2. A simplified version consisting only of Items 1-6 and 11 could be substituted, at least until a department gains confidence that the basic size and spread information being collected is meaningful. The department could then decide whether the additional information in Items 7-10 would be useful in explaining trends and patterns in fire size and spread.

The key to the feasibility of this procedure is how reliably the size of the fire, especially the size at arrival, can be estimated in spite of smoke and the pressures which accompany any fire emergency. Great precision is neither possible nor necessary. To obtain at least a rough idea of the reliability attainable for fire size and spread estimates, the procedure

was tested in more than 600 building fires in eight communities over a period of several months. For each fire, two officers—typically a battalion chief and the first-in engine company officer—independently estimated fire sizes and fire spread. For some fires, their estimates of size at extinguishment were also compared to estimates by investigators or project researchers. In about one-quarter of the fires in the city reporting the most fires, the battalion chiefs' written estimates of fire size and the resulting estimates of fire spread differed substantially from the first-in officers' estimates.[4] But there was no consistent difference in the way that chiefs and other officers made their estimates, and so the distributions of fire sizes and fire spreads based on the chiefs' estimates were quite similar to the distributions based on the first-in officers' estimates. In other words, there was a considerable cancellation of the differences when a large number of fires were considered: At one fire the battalion chief might

4. More precisely, 25 percent of the cases had disagreement as to whether fires were in the same gross size range. See Schaenman et al., *Procedures for Improving the Measurement of Local Fire Protection Effectiveness*, Chapter 1.

Exhibit 7-2
FORM FOR COLLECTING FIRE SPREAD DATA

| Incident No.: _____ | | Filled out by:_____ |
| | | Company No.: _____ |

PART A—SUPPLEMENTAL FIELD INCIDENT REPORT (SFIR)
(To be filled out for building fires only)

	BY TIME OF ARRIVAL	BY TIME OF EXTINGUISHMENT
1. Check (✔) whether fire was confined to:		
Small area (less than 25 percent) of a single room	_____	_____
Room of origin	_____	_____
Floor of origin; two or more rooms involved	_____	_____
If this line is checked:		
How many rooms on the floor of origin were involved?	_____	_____
How many total rooms are there on the floor of origin?	_____	_____
Building of origin; two or more floors involved	_____	_____
If this line is checked:		
How many floors in the building of origin were involved?	_____	_____
How many total floors are there in the building of origin?	_____	_____
Extended to more than one building	_____	_____
If this line is checked:		
How many buildings were involved?	_____	_____

(If fire originated outside a building, treat the floor first involved as the floor or origin. Write "N.A." in the first column if no building was involved at the time of arrival.)

2. Enter: (a) Square feet (horizontal plan area) burned and/or burning, all floors except attics, in all buildings.

	_____	_____

         (b) TOTAL *square feet* (horizontal plan area) (unburned and burned), all floors except attics in all buildings. _____

(Exhibit continued on next page)

Exhibit 7-2 continued

3. Enter square feet of *attic* (horizontal plan area), burned and/or burning, in all buildings. _____ _____

4. Enter percentage of *roof* burned and/or burning. (If more than one building) was involved, write "N.A.".)

	Time	*Date*
5. Time at which your unit arrived?	_____	_____
6. Time at which spread of fire was confirmed to have stopped?	_____	_____

REMARKS (including any problems in recording above data):

PART B — CONDITIONS FACED BY FIRE FIGHTERS

7. *Building construction*
   a. *Interior finish:* (Answer *either* (1) or (2), *but not both*)
      (1) If interior finish was *involved,* was the spread of flame stopped in any direction because part or all of the interior finish was noncombustible or fire resistant?
          Yes ☐   No ☐
      (2) If interior finish *was not involved,* were any of the exposed wall, floor, or ceiling surfaces (excluding trim) in the fire-involved portion combustible?
          Yes ☐   No ☐
   b. *Structure near the fire area:* (Check one.)
      ☐ Fire-resistant or noncombustible structure   ☐ Mixed structure   ☐ Combustible structure
   c. *Exterior walls near the fire area:* (Check one.)
      ☐ Noncombustible walls   ☐ Mixed walls   ☐ Combustible walls
   d. *Roof:* (Check one.)
      ☐ Wood shingle roof   ☐ Combustible roof (other than wood shingle)
      ☐ Fire-resistant or noncombustible roof   ☐ Mixed roof

8. *Contents:* (Check one.)
   Were flammable liquids or other high-volatility or explosive contents present in fire-involved portions of the building?
      ☐ Yes, burned
      ☐ Yes, did not burn
      ☐ No, not present

9. What effect did private fire defenses have? (Check all appropriate boxes.)	Helped limit spread *after* arrival of first unit	Present but not used or not effective *after* arrival of first unit	Not present
a. Automatic sprinklers	☐	☐	☐
b. Standpipe system	☐	☐	☐
c. Other (Specify devices ONLY IF USED)	☐	☐	☐

_____
_____
_____

10. Weather conditions at fire scene: (Check one box in line a and one box in line b.)
    a. ☐ Fog   ☐ Light rain or mist   ☐ Heavy rain   ☐ Hail, sleet, or snow   ☐ No precipitation
    b. ☐ Light or no wind   ☐ Moderate or heavy wind

11. Did any of the following have an influence on the spread of fire *after* arrival or the time to stop spread? (Check one answer for each line. If Column 1 or 2 is checked, write in problem or circumstances encountered.)	Unusual problems on this factor contributed to spread after arrival or time to stop spread	Unusually favorable circumstances on this factor helped to limit spread after arrival or reduce time to stop spread	Factor not present *or* no clear effect on spread after arrival or time to stop spread

(Exhibit continued on next page)

a. Lack of or failure of fire barriers (e.g., open stair or elevator shaft, lack of fire wall, undivided attic, fire entered ducts or other concealed spaces) _____ ☐ N.A. ☐

b. Fire door propped open_____ ☐ N.A. ☐

c. Preexisting roof venting vented the fire _____ ☐ ☐ ☐

d. Weather effects on fuel (e.g., low humidity, long wet or dry spell prior to fire) _____ ☐ ☐ ☐

e. Weather effects on fire or firefighting (e.g., high or low winds, severe storm during fire fighting, icy conditions) _____ ☐ ☐ ☐

f. Poor or blocked access to water supply (e.g., poor spacing of hydrants, obstructions from illegally parked vehicles or crowds) _____ ☐ N.A. ☐

g. Inadequate water supply (e.g., adequacy of water flow) _____ ☐ N.A. ☐

h. Poor housekeeping or poor handling of normal-fuel-load contents (e.g., poor stock subdivision, high piled stock) _____ ☐ N.A. ☐

i. Influence of highly volatile or explosive contents on the fire _____ ☐ N.A. ☐

j. Unusually flammable interior finish _____ ☐ N.A. ☐

k. Unusually flammable contents (excluding high volatility contents) (e.g., extremely dried-out contents) _____ ☐ N.A. ☐

l. Unusually flammable roof, structure, exterior walls _____ ☐ N.A. ☐

m. Fire rescue/life support activities delayed start of fire fighter's activities in limiting spread after arrival _____ ☐ N.A. ☐

n. Access of men or water to fire-involved areas was blocked _____ ☐ N.A. ☐

o. Unusually dense smoke, extreme heat or unusual danger, given size of fire, reduced fire-fighting effectiveness _____ ☐ N.A. ☐

p. Other _____ ☐ ☐ ☐

Remarks:
_____

Note: The principal modifications in this form, relative to the two versions tested, are these: only one test form separated attic area burned from other square footage burned; neither version asked for the *percentage* of roof involved; a tested item asking whether contents, finish, structure, exterior walls, or grounds were involved at arrival and extinguishment is not included here; and in the test version, separate questions were used to determine the level of involvement (e.g., room versus floor versus building) and the number of involved rooms, floors, and buildings.

have the higher estimate of size (or spread); at another fire, the first-in officer might have the higher estimate.[5]

Whether the reliability and precision obtained in practice will be good enough to indicate the impacts of policy changes is hard to say; it will depend on the minimum amount of fire spread (and fire size) that would be considered significant for a particular type of decision. Reliability might be improved beyond that obtained in these initial trials by better instruction on definitions and more training on how to estimate fire sizes. It should be noted, too, that this same kind of reliability problem exists when policy changes are assessed using fire rates, dollar loss, fire causes, and other currently collected data.

In general, any analysis of a certain category of fire incidents—for example, those fires in a particular type of occupancy and area of community and within a certain range of fire size on arrival—should be based on a sample of at least 30 incidents, and preferably 50 to 100 incidents, in each group analyzed. This will permit medium-size differences in results over time or between categories (that is, differences of about 20 to 40 percent in the percentage of fires that spread or in the average amount of spread) to be detected with adequate statistical confidence. In some communities it may take more than one year to accumulate that many incidents.

Data on fire spread after arrival, coupled with data on the kinds of fire situations encountered, could be used to monitor trends in suppression effectiveness or to identify problem areas by district and by occupancy type. Similarly, they could be used in evaluation studies. For example, they could be used to help determine how well different crew sizes or different types of equipment suppress various kinds of fires. A typical question that might be addressed is the following: If during one year about 95 percent of the fires that were confined to room of origin on arrival did not spread beyond the room of origin, what would the spread-after-arrival data show the next year after the number of fire fighters per company had been increased or decreased?

Perceived reasons for spread (as illustrated by Item 11 in Exhibit 7-2) should also be reported by fire officers at the scene. This can help identify (or confirm) problems most frequently encountered in fire fighting in the jurisdiction. Problems such as improperly stored volatile contents, unusually com-

bustible structure, poor housekeeping, and inadequate built-in fire barriers are probably widespread; the purpose here is to document the problems most prevalent in a particular jurisdiction. Such information can be used as evidence of need to change building codes, to improve certain aspects of inspections, to warn and train fire fighters for hazards frequently encountered, and to monitor the effectiveness of corrective actions.

Because of the relationship between size of fire at arrival and fire spread, data on fire spread should be categorized by size of fire at arrival. A hypothetical example of how the findings for this measure would be presented is shown in Exhibit 7-3. Exhibit 7-4 shows illustrative data obtained from the initial tests in nine municipalities. (Because the data in Exhibit 7-4 reflect a short time period and often involved only a few fire companies in each community, they should not be regarded as descriptive of those communities.)

Fire Size at Arrival (Measure 17). Note that fire size at arrival can be used by itself to help indicate how well detection and private suppression systems are working. For example, smoke detectors should permit detection of fires when they are smaller, and built-in fire suppression devices like sprinklers should keep fires relatively small longer. Hence the effectiveness of these devices should be reflected in the size of fires at arrival.[6]

Time to Control (Measure 6). Time to control can be defined as the time from the arrival of fire apparatus at a fire to the time when fire fighters confirm that the fire has been contained and spread stopped, though the fire may not necessarily have been extinguished.[7] The measure might be expressed in a number of variations such as the median time, aver-

---

5. Accuracy might be better in practice than we found it to be in a test, because in practice the two officers could collaborate or use the judgment of the one with the better view of the fire on arrival. This was not allowed in the test because two *independent* estimates of fire size were required.

6. In addition to their use in measuring effectiveness, data on fire size at arrival can also be used to guide other decisions. For example, the distribution of fires by size, district, and occupancy type could help in making or justifying decisions on crew size per company and on numbers and types of companies to send for first responses in each area of the community. Another example: a decision on whether minipumpers should be used might be preceded by an analysis of the relative frequency of fires of sizes that could, and could not, be contained by minipumper, by area of the city and type of building occupancy. Fire size at extinguishment is probably a good proxy measure for smoke detector and sprinkler effectiveness if the city's fire suppression techniques and force size do not change much from one year to another. The higher the proportion of fires that are still small when detected, the higher the proportion of fires for which spread could be easily and quickly stopped. As a result, there would be fewer fires that would be large at extinguishment.

7. "Time to extinguishment" and "time to apply water on the fire" are other measures already used in several cities. See Schaenman et al., *Procedures for Improving the Measurement of Local Fire Protection Effectiveness,* Chapter 1.

Exhibit 7-3

ILLUSTRATION OF HOW TO PRESENT DATA ON FIRE SPREAD

FIRE SIZE AT ARRIVAL	PERCENTAGE OF TOTAL FIRES HAVING THAT FIRE SIZE ON ARRIVAL OF FIRST UNIT		PERCENTAGE OF FIRES (OF THAT SIZE) THAT SPREAD AT LEAST 10 SQ. FT. AFTER ARRIVAL OF FIRST UNIT	
	1976	1977	1976	1977
Up to 50 sq. ft.	60	30	5	0
51-250 sq. ft.	34	45	30	25
251 sq. ft. and up	6	25	80	75
All fires	100	100	18	30

Note that in this illustration, the *overall* percentage of fires with at least 10 sq. ft. of spread has increased from 18 to 30 percent, but that the percentages for each category of fire size have decreased (e.g., 5 to 0 percent, 30 to 25 percent, etc.). The change in the percentage of all fires that spread reflects the increased proportion of fires that were large at arrival, which more than made up for the reduction in the percentage of fires on each given size that spread. That is, fires spread more after arrival in 1977 because they were bigger on arrival.

age time, or percentage of fires with control time greater than a given value. Data can be collected by having the officer in charge radio the dispatcher upon arrival at the scene, and again when control is confirmed. The times are then obtained from the dispatcher after the reporting officer returns to the station house. Reporting of control time is greatly facilitated when the officer in charge has a portable radio.

The necessary raw data for estimating control times are already reported in many departments, often under other names such as "knock-down" or "tap-out" time. But the data generally are not summarized for the purpose of periodic reporting, and definition of "control" is not always consistent from officer to officer.

Estimation of time to control for large fires may be subject to considerable uncertainty because of the difficulty in judging precisely when control is achieved; yet summary, perhaps annual, statistics on time to control still seem likely to show how fire burn times are being reduced (or not reduced) resulting in more (or less) damage averted. The reliability of this measure was not tested because no way could be devised to check it without disrupting dispatch and command routines in the test communities.

To illustrate the type of information obtained, it was estimated that in one city, for a five-month period in 1975,

- 66 percent of fires were controlled in 0 to 5 minutes;
- 17 percent of fires were controlled in 6 to 10 minutes;
- 12 percent of fires were controlled in 11 to 20 minutes; and
- 5 percent of fires took more than 20 minutes to control.

Exhibit 7-4

ILLUSTRATIVE FINDINGS OF FIRE SIZE AT ARRIVAL AND SPREAD AFTER ARRIVAL

(Communities listed in order of average size of arrival)

COMMUNITY	SAMPLE SIZE[1]	AVERAGE SIZE AT ARRIVAL (SQ. FT.)	MEDIAN SIZE AT ARRIVAL (SQ. FT.)	PERCENTAGE OF FIRES GREATER THAN 1,000 SQ. FT. AT ARRIVAL	PERCENTAGE OF FIRES GREATER THAN 250 SQ. FT. AT ARRIVAL	PERCENTAGE OF FIRES LARGER THAN A ROOM AT ARRIVAL	PERCENTAGE OF FIRES THAT SPREAD MORE THAN 50 SQ. FT.
Seattle, Washington	44	213	39	2	22	30	2
Fairfax County, Virginia	70	304	40	7	19	26	6
San Diego, California	60	307	120	3	34	25	7
Charlotte, North Carolina	32	343	170	9	34	52	16
St. Petersburg, Florida	55	408	50	11	33	41	15
Dallas, Texas	552	423	60	10	25	40	12
Lynn, Massachusetts	69	463	200	12	31	61	21
Newark, New Jersey	105	693	180	18	41	54	29
Portland, Maine	31	1493	600	31	62	61	25

1. This is the number of fires used to compute the average and median fire size at arrival. Sample sizes for other measures vary slightly. Out-on-arrival fires are excluded.

Note: The data in Exhibit 7-4 reflect a short time period and often came from only a few fire companies in the community, so they may *not* be representative of those communities.

Fire size at arrival has a strong effect on time to control. Average control times increased sharply with fire size at arrival. For example, the average size of fires controlled within 1 minute was 30 sq. ft.; in 5 to 10 minutes, 500 sq. ft.; in 20 to 30 minutes, 1,000 sq. ft.; and fires taking more than 30 minutes, 3,800 sq. ft. (These data were based on a sample of about 500 fires.) Therefore, time-to-control data should be grouped by "fire size at arrival."

To maintain the quality of the data, fire departments planning to use time-to-control data should consider at least some spot checks of time to control, possibly by having senior officers attend a sample of fires and compare notes concerning the reported time. In addition, follow-ups should be undertaken on any reports that appear unusual. Fires out on arrival should be reported separately from others, regardless of the time taken to confirm that the fire was out.

Staffing Requirements for Fire Spread and Time-to-Control Measurement Procedure. Typically, data collection for fire size, fire spread, and time to control requires an extra 1 to 10 minutes at the scene (depending on the size of the fire) and 5 to 10 minutes of paperwork per building fire, if all data elements in Exhibit 7-2 are collected. Other costs include:

- Initial training (line officers)
   3 to 4 hours per officer with reporting responsibilities
- Initial training (instructors and staff)
   2 to 4 person-weeks for development of procedures and training of fire suppression personnel; 2 to 4 weeks of field checks of first Supplemental Field Incident Reports (SFIR) filled out by trained officers
- Periodic audits and retraining
   15 to 30 minutes per month per officer; 2 to 4 person-weeks per year for field checks of a sample of the data to check accuracy
- Data compilation and analysis
   3 to 6 person-weeks per 1,000 building fires per year

Measuring Saves at Fire Scene (Measure 9). "Saves" data may help provide proper credit to the fire department for a major outcome of its service.

Data would be collected as part of incident reports by the officers in charge at the fire, based on their personal observations and debriefing of fire fighters, and possibly victims or witnesses if necessary. "Saves" should be reported in terms of the danger posed by the fire to the person "saved" (for example, the person's location in relation to the fire), and the degree of the person's need for assistance (for example, unconscious, invalid, healthy but trapped, and so forth). Thus, a warning to a healthy person able to evacuate a floor below a fire would not be treated the same as the rescue of an unconscious victim from a burning room. This practice should help provide a clearer description of outcomes, reduce perverse reporting incentives, and improve credibility with the public. A sample "Fire Saves Report" is presented in Exhibit 7-5.

These procedures received brief feasibility tests in four cities. The procedure appears to be workable enough to warrant further testing for reliability and usefulness in other communities over longer periods of time. The main problem is the difficulty of making sure the "count" of saves is reasonably accurate— that is, recorded by proper category with none missed and no overreporting.[8] Potential uses of the data include identification of necessary changes in building or fire codes; these might be indicated if a particular class of structures had frequent incidents requiring saves.

Thus it is recommended that, to supplement the currently collected data on fire injuries and deaths, fire departments consider collecting data on "saves" made by fire fighters (and others) at a fire scene.

Improving Fire Loss Estimates (for Measures 3 and 4) to Improve Reliability of Fire Service Effectiveness Data. Given the importance of fire loss in indicating the success of fire protection, fire departments should try to improve the often-questioned accuracy of these data by providing simpler, documented procedures and rules of thumb to be used in the most common situations, and by providing training in the use of these procedures. Having more consistent estimates within a department would be a major step forward.

No single method of estimating loss that can be recommended with confidence emerged from this project; procedures for estimating losses need additional testing for reliability. One of the more promising approaches uses standardized estimates of current cost per square foot for different types of construction and different occupancies. Mountain View and San Jose, California, are two cities that have developed and used this approach. This method would be easier to use if square-foot estimates of fire sizes were collected at fires. (Note that these esti-

8. Saves are particularly difficult to count at high-rise building fires because they involve a great many people, most of whom will usually require little assistance.

Exhibit 7-5
119

SUGGESTED FIRE SAVES REPORT
(With Illustrative Data From 17 Fires)

Part 1–Number and Type of Saves

RISK (FIRE HAZARD) / NEED (VICTIM MOBILITY) / FIRE DEPT. ACTION	UNABLE TO WALK UNCONSCIOUS (CARRIED)	UNABLE TO WALK OTHER (CARRIED)	CAN WALK ONLY WITH ASSISTANCE (AIDED)	CAN WALK PINNED/TRAPPED (RELEASED)	CAN WALK PATH BLOCKED (PROVIDED PATH)	CAN WALK UNAWARE OF FIRE (DIRECTED)	TOTALS
1. Fire in room	1	1	2		1		5
2. Fire on same floor a. Smoke/heat hazard in room			1		10	9	20
b. No smoke/heat hazard in room						2	2
3. Fire on next floor below a. Smoke/heat hazard in room	1				24	2	27
b. No smoke/heat hazard in room					2	2	4
4. Fire more than one floor below a. Smoke/heat hazard in room				3	13	7	23
b. No smoke/heat hazard in room					2		2
5. Within danger zone of hazardous materials fire						1	1
6. Below fire floor of structurally unsafe building							
TOTALS	2	1	3	3	52	23	84

Part 2–Description of Saves[1]

1. Briefly describe why rescue(s) conducted?[2]
   1. Occupant asleep in apartment of origin (1)
   2. Unconscious from products of combustion in room of origin (1)
   3. Smoke in room with victim (6)
   4. Intoxicated in room of origin (2)
   5. Path blocked by heat and smoke (4)
   6. Fear/panic from smoke (2)

2. Who brought about the actual rescue(s)?[3]
   Police _____ Fire Dept. ___14___ Private citizen(s) ___3_____
   Utility company _____ Other (Specify) _____

3. How rescue(s) conducted?
   Aerial ladder ___1___ Interior stairway ___9___
   Exterior stairway ___2___ Fire escape _____ Life net _____
   Other (Specify) back door (1), hallway to safe area (1), ground ladders (4)

4. What was the physical condition of those rescued?
   a. Panic stricken___9___ Dazed, apparently in shock ___5___ Alert ___10___
   b. Conscious ___21___ Unconscious ___2___ Crippled ___2___

5. How many were in structure at the time of the incident?
   Number: 2 (in each of 3 incidents), 3, 18, 38, 70, (2 incidents), 100 (2 incidents), 140 (2 incidents), unknown (5 incidents)
   How estimated: owner/manager (6), physical search (2), guessed (2), pooled fire department estimate (1), newspaper account (1)

6. What support equipment was used?
   a. Masks: Were used ___9___ Were not used _____
   b. Protective stream(s): Were used ___3___ Were not used _____

1. Would normally be on the back of Part 1. On each item, you may check more than one if applicable. Illustrative data from 17 fires.
2. Answers to this question are not precoded entries. An unused form would provide blank spaces for the fire officer to use in entering answers in narrative form.
3. The items following questions 2 through 6 *are* precoded entries.

mates of fire size are obtained as part of the fire-spread measurement procedures discussed for Measure 5.)

In calculating loss rates per $1,000 property served, the dollar value of the property served can be estimated from assessed property values available from the assessor's office. (Rough estimates of the value of *nontaxed* property probably should be added to the denominator to obtain a consistent measurement.) Because individual major fires could dominate the amount, the measure might be calculated both with and without such fires. Constant dollars should be used in comparing loss rates from one year to the next. Note that direct dollar loss does not include lost wages, lost taxes to the community, medical expenses, and many other costs that should be considered when evaluating the total magnitude of the fire problem. A measure of total losses—direct and indirect—therefore might also be considered.

Improved Measures of Fire Prevention Performance (Measures 10-14)

Impacts of Inspections on Fire Rates (Measures 13-14). One approach to measuring effectiveness of inspection programs is to consider the "*number* of fires that are relatively preventable by inspection, per 1,000 occupancies" (or 1,000 households, for a residential inspection program). Changes in this measure over time may indicate a change in inspection impact, because the rate of relatively "preventable" fires would presumably decrease or remain stable if an inspection program is effective.

The "*percentage* of fires deemed relatively preventable by inspection" (Measure 13)[9] might be used to indicate whether reduction in fire rates can best be achieved via improved education programs, as opposed to more frequent inspections of the type now employed. If most fires *do not* seem preventable by inspection, further improvements in inspection techniques cannot be expected to reduce the fire rate significantly. If a substantial proportion of fires *are* deemed relatively preventable by inspection, communities should consider using the methods described below to measure the effectiveness of inspections in reducing fires. Such measurement can help to determine whether commercial inspections should be made more frequently and whether household inspections should be extended to more households or made more frequently.

The ability to identify "relatively preventable" fires depends on the fire-cause categories used and the reliability of identifying and recording those causes. Identifying "preventable" fires from incident data would be easier if fire-cause categories were defined with that purpose in mind. For example, rather than reporting only that a mechanical defect caused a fire, as is typically done, it would be useful to know whether the defect was one that could be seen or otherwise easily identified during an inspection. For a fire on a stove, was it due to a visible accumulation of grease or to a more spontaneous careless action?

Residental inspection programs, in which thousands of residences are inspected annually and other thousands are not, can be evaluated by comparing the rate of fires in the inspected properties to the rate in the uninspected properties (Measure 14). The general procedure is as follows:[10]

Take a list of all residences contacted (whether residences were inspected, residents were not home, or residents refused inspection) during one year's operation of the residential inspection program. For each residence, find out whether one or more fires occurred there within a year of the contact. Compare the rate of fires in inspected residences to the rate of fires in the other residences contacted—those whose occupants had not been home for inspection, or had refused inspection.

A major concern with this procedure is that the "comparison" group—the households that are not inspected—may differ in their propensity to have fires from the households that were inspected. It is possible that households not available for inspection, in some cases because units are unoccupied, are inherently high-risk areas for fires. To check on this possibility, compare the fire rate in the inspected households for a few years *before* they were inspected to the fire rate in the households in which residents were not home when called on for inspections for the same number of years before they received those calls. If the fire rates are about the same, the concern can be ignored; if not, the test results may have to be considered inconclusive.

Unless inspections cut down substantially on incidence of fires, communities with smaller numbers of homes contacted may have difficulty obtaining statistically significant results for any single year. Such communities might undertake the analysis every few years. In the experiments, one to

9. The procedures developed were designed to identify fires preventable by inspection. Fires preventable by education are currently identified primarily as those fires not judged preventable by inspection, but further refinement will be necessary.

10. For details of this procedure, see Schaenman et al., *Procedures for Improving the Measurement,* Chapter 5; and Hall, "Supplemental Technical Report: Measuring the Effectiveness of Fire Inspections."

Exhibit 7-6

EXAMPLE OF FIRE INSPECTION EFFECTIVENESS ESTIMATION IN A CASE WHERE DATA SHOW SIZABLE INSPECTION IMPACT ON FIRE RATES

Suppose there are only 10 buildings subject to inspection in the community. Their inspection histories for a year might look like the chart below.

BUILDING NUMBER	JAN	FEB	MAR	APR	MAY	JUN	JUL	AUG	SEP	OCT	NOV	DEC
					NUMBER OF MONTHS SINCE LAST INSPECTION							
1	8	(9)[a]	10	0[b]	1	2	3	4	5	6	7	8
2	3	4	5	6	7	(8)	0	1	2	3	4	5
3	2	3	4	5	6	7	8	9	10	11	12	(13)
4	6	0	1	2	3	4	5	6	0	1	2	0[b]
5	5	6	7	0	1	2	3	4	5	6	7	0
6	10	11	(12)	0	1	2	3	4	5	6	7	8
7	(9)	0	1	2	3	4	5	6	7	8	0	1
8	1	2	3	4	5	6	0	1	2	3	4	5
9	7	8	9	10	11	12	13	14	(15)	0	1	2
10	3	4	0	1	2	3	4	0	1	2	3	4

a. A circled entry indicates that building had a fire in that month. For example, Building No. 1 had a fire in February and at that time Building No. 1 had not been inspected for nine months.

b. A "0" entry means that building was inspected in that month. Note that the inspection frequency varies considerably among the ten buildings, and in some cases (such as Building No. 4) the inspection frequency varies for the same building.

NUMBER OF MONTHS SINCE LAST INSPECTION	NUMBER OF ENTRIES SHOWING THAT MANY MONTHS SINCE LAST INSPECTION	NUMBER OF FIRES IN BUILDINGS THAT MANY MONTHS FROM LAST INSPECTION	INCIDENCE OF FIRE IN BUILDINGS THAT FAR FROM LAST INSPECTION
0-2	40	0	0 = 0/40
3-5	37	0	0 = 0/37
6-8	24	1	.05 = 1/24
9-11	11	2	.18 = 2/11
12-15	7	3	.43 = 3/7
All entries	120	6	.05 = 6/120

The fire incidence ratios shown in the last column indicate that a considerable increase in fire incidence occurs when buildings have gone without inspections for a long time. Of all fires, for example, 83 percent (5 of the 6) occur in buildings that have gone at least nine months without an inspection, but buildings are in that position only 15 percent of the time (18 of the 120 entries). In practice, the exact fire incidence likelihood numbers will not be known because data on all months will be collected for only a random sample of buildings in the program; however, the percentage increases in the ratios computed will be the same as the percentage increases in the underlying fire incidence values. Also in practice, some adjustments have to be made to reflect the possibility that, when a fire and an inspection in the same building occur in the same month, the fire may have preceded the inspection and thus not have been affected by it.

two person-days of effort proved sufficient for the necessary data collection in places where residential inspection contact records are grouped by street and residences that have had fire calls are listed by address. If these conditions do not hold, particularly the latter condition, more effort would be required.

A different procedure will be needed for residential inspection programs in communities where al-most all residences are inspected, and for commercial inspection programs in which all or almost all occupancies of a kind are inspected at least every two years. This is because there is no comparison group of uninspected similar occupancies. Instead, it is necessary to compare the fire rate for recently-inspected buildings to the rate for those not recently inspected. If the fire rate for recently-inspected buildings is less than for those not recently inspected but of a similar type, this would suggest that a policy of more frequent inspections would make a difference. The general procedure is as follows:[11]

Match the records of all fires during the period of study to the inspection files and determine what percentage of fires occurred in buildings that had had their last inspection "x" months ago, for all "x" up to two years. Draw a random sample of inspection files (assuming one file per establishment) and use their inspection histories during the period being studied to determine what percentage of time a building spends, on the average, in the position of having had its last inspection "x" months ago, again for all "x" up to two years. If the two distributions look about the same, it means that a recent inspection offers no more protection than an old one. If the two distributions do not look the same, the ratios of corresponding percentages can be used to see how much the likelihood of fire rises as the time since last inspection gets larger. An example of such an analysis and its product is shown in Exhibit 7-6.

About ten to fifteen employee-days are needed to draw the necessary data from inspection files A community wanting to use the procedure should have reasonably complete files on inspections for several years previous (a period considerably longer than the time between inspections is needed), preferably in a centralized location or on a computer. If a community does not have complete files going back some years, it can begin keeping files and use the procedure in the future. The reliability of the inspection file data on addresses of fires and inspected buildings must be sufficient to permit matching of almost all fires to corresponding inspection files.

Even if the chances of a fire do not rise as a building's last inspection gets more remote, the chance of a fire may still be lower just because there is an inspection program. The knowledge that inspections are conducted periodically may produce a continuing level of fire prevention awareness, and corresponding actions. This on-going effect can be estimated by comparing fire rates before and after a program is initiated if records go back that far, or by comparing communities with and without inspection programs if comparable cities can be identified. This procedure seems useful for evaluating new citywide residential inspection programs, but it is not likely to be applicable to most commercial inspection programs because most communities have

inspected commercial buildings regularly for years.

In summary, it is recommended that communities consider identifying fires in terms of their "relative preventability by inspection" (Measure 7). The procedures for comparing fire rates by level of inspection (Measure 8) are more complex and may not be useful if the percentage of fires with relatively preventable causes is low. Larger communities should consider using Measure 8, but they may want to use it only every few years, not annually. Communities should not expect these measures to provide quick feedback on the results of changes in inspection policy; at least a year's experience is needed to pick up even very large changes.

Suggestions on Fire Rate Measures (Measures 10-12). The fire rate is, of course, a major outcome measure, one which reflects the effectiveness of fire prevention activities, private as well as public, and other factors that are relatively uncontrollable by a fire department or a local government. Three suggestions on improving the meaningfulness of fire rate information are as follows:

1. *Reporting of minor fires.* A problem in interpreting fire rates is that they may appear to change significantly from year to year because of changes in the percentage of very small fires that are reported. The 1974 National Household Fire Survey conducted by the National Bureau of Standards and U.S.Census Bureau found that about nine out of ten household fires were not reported. Surveys conducted by Nashville and The Urban Institute in 1974 and 1975 found that about half were not reported.[12] (This information could be used to produce Measure 12; see Questions 43 and 43a in Appendix 1.) If, for example, the percentage of small household fires that were reported increased from one year to the next by ten percentage points (which might occur after a new fire prevention program calls attention to the fire problem), the number of *reported* fires could increase by from 10 percent to as much as 90 percent, even though the actual number of fires had not changed at all! (Whether changes as large as ten percentage points in underreporting of fires occur remains to be seen. Reported fire rates did in fact fluctuate by that much and more from year to year in many cities during the 1960s, but the prime reason for those fluctuations could have been factors other than underreporting.)

---

11. The specific procedure for undertaking analysis is presented in Schaenman et al., *Procedures for Improving the Measurement,* Chapter 5; and Hall, "Supplemental Technical Report: Measuring the Effectiveness of Fire Inspections."

12. The most likely explanation for the widely differing results is that whereas the census survey asked many questions probing for various types of fires, the Nashville survey just asked one general question.

It is recommended that communities consider reducing the interpretation problem by reporting separately, and focusing on, those fires considered other than minor. "Other than minor" might be defined as those fires over a specified size at arrival or extinguishment, those with more than a specified amount of dollar loss, and those with casualties. Other definitions could be oriented to the response made, such as "fires that required one or more hoses."

2. *Consistent definition of fires and causes.* There is some evidence that fire officers in a community are not always consistent in their characterizations of fire, mainly because some situations do not easily fit into local category definitions. Periodic checks within a department are needed to see that local definitions are understood and followed.

3. *Community characteristics related to fire rates.* Many community characteristics are associated with differences in fire rates but are largely uncontrollable by fire departments.

This project examined the relationship between population and building characteristics, on the one hand, and reported fire rates, on the other, for census tracts in five communities. Fire data from the early 1970s were used, along with U.S. Census data on seventeen community characteristics.[13] Perhaps the most striking result was that at least one-third, and often two-thirds, of the tract-to-tract variation in fire rates could be explained by one to three of the seventeen variables in each community. The particular factors that best explained the variations differed from one community to another.

Of those factors considered, the extent of undereducation, the extent of poverty, and the extent of parental presence (defined as children living in households with both parents present) explained the greatest portions of the fire-rate variations. (These

factors were also highly correlated with each other and sometimes with others; many tracts with problems in one area tend to have problems in others as well.) Other variables strongly related to the incidence of fires included the extent of homeownership, the racial composition, and the extent of crowding in dwelling units. In two communities, the percentage of housing units located in old buildings was strongly correlated with fire rates, but in others it was weakly correlated. The percentage of new residents, the rate of unemployment, the percentage of aged persons, and the percentage of housing units located in multihousehold structures were poorly correlated with fire rates in all communities.

Analysts of fire rates should identify and consider community characteristics relevant to fire prevention in order to help distinguish the changes in fire rates due to prevention activities from changes attributable to other factors. For example, areas that lack the characteristics associated with high fire rates might be given more demanding targets for prevention programs (that is, they might be expected to achieve lower fire rates) than those areas with characteristics associated with high fire rates.

The analysis would indicate what fire rate would be "expected" in each census tract based on its characteristics; these projections could subsequently be compared against actual rates to identify which tracts had rates that were higher or lower than expected. The comparisons would give an approximate picture of performance in the light of conditions faced. Use of the procedure in some communities might be hampered by the lack of current socioeconomic data by census tract, and the absence of data for many characteristics of interest (such as pride in one's community). Communities with data on fire rates by census tract should try to identify the characteristics that best explain their own intertract variations. This information might be used to help target and shape fire prevention programs, as by preparing special prevention education programs directed toward undereducated adults in areas where that characteristic was important. (Note, however, that a characteristic with a high correlation to the fire rate may not be a "cause" but only a factor somehow associated with true causes. Moreover, the example used above assumes that undereducated adults also have less fire prevention education than other adults, and that it is their lack of fire prevention education—rather than their lack of general education—that results in more fires.) The results also might help guide local government programs aimed at reducing the underlying causes of fires.

13. The characteristics considered (not necessarily ideal ones but rather those considered potentially influential for which data were relatively available) were as follows: percentage of persons under the poverty line; percentage of persons with less than eight years' schooling; percentage of children not living with both parents; percentage of persons with high school educations; percentage of housing units vacant; percentage of housing units owner-occupied; percentage of blacks with less than eight years' schooling; percentage of blacks below poverty line; percentage of blacks; percentage of housing units in pre-1940 structures; percentage of families with incomes over $15,000 a year; percentage of housing units with 1.01 or more persons per room; percentage of housing units in multihousehold structures; percentage of population over age 65; percentage of adult males unemployed; percentage of persons living in same place as five years before; and whether the census tract had had a large change in its percentage of blacks between 1960 and 1970.

Improved Measures of Overall Citizen Satisfaction (Measure 18)

A rating by citizens with firsthand knowledge of a community's fire services as to their perception of the quality of the service would be useful. In most communities, however, the majority of citizens have no firsthand contact with the fire department during a given year and no other valid source of knowledge about its services. Those who have had some personal contact—from fires, prevention inspection, prevention education lectures, or literature—can be identified as part of a general survey of citizens or businesses (the same surveys discussed in other chapters as measurement procedures for other local government services) and asked to rate their fire protection services.

This procedure has been used in Nashville as part of its annual multiservice surveys. In the 1974 Nashville survey about 13 percent of the respondents (129 of about 1,000) indicated that they had had some firsthand contact with the fire department and gave an opinion on its overall quality. In the 1975 survey, about 12 percent (116 of about 1,000) had had firsthand contact.

A question such as Number 45 in Appendix 1 could be used to obtain these data (using Question 44 to identify those with some firsthand contact). In the 1974 survey, 71 percent of citizens with firsthand contact who responded rated services as good or excellent rather than fair or poor. In the 1975 survey this figure climbed to 83 percent. Reasons for dissatisfaction can also be solicited, but this was not done in the survey illustrated in Appendix 1. Data can be disaggregated by area of the city and other groupings to identify specific problem areas. Changes in the level of satisfaction over time may indicate successes or problems in community relations.

If the community is already conducting a regular survey of its citizens, there will be little added expense and effort to include questions on fire services. An alternative procedure—probably more precise but not tested on this project—would be to survey a sample of persons drawn directly from those who have had contact with the fire department.

Chapter 8

General Transportation Services[1]

Effectiveness measures for local transportation services should address a municipality's public transit system and general transportation services. It seems appropriate to separate discussion of general transportation measures from that of mass transit measures because of the usual separation of responsibilities for these two areas as well as the desirability of examining transit performance by itself. Hence this chapter will focus on measures for such transportation concerns as street maintenance, traffic control and safety, pedestrian safety, accessibility, and environmental quality. The next chapter discusses public "mass" transit. The general approach taken for both general transportation and mass transit are described here. This study did not cover air and water transportation or inter-city transportation.

Local Transportation Objectives and Measurement Approaches

To develop a set of effectiveness measures, it is assumed that the objective of a jurisdiction's transportation services is as follows:

To provide access to desired destinations such as employment, shopping, and com-

munity services or other facilities in a quick, convenient, safe, and comfortable manner for all population groups in the community with a minimum of harmful effects on the environment.

Although this discussion focuses on the movement of people, some of the measures and data collection procedures could be easily adapted to assessing the movement of goods as well. Examples are the measures of travel times and safety.

1. A number of transportation characteristics merit attention for annual monitoring. Measures for each of the following characteristics are recommended for both general transportation services and public transit:

- Accessibility of citizens to their desired destinations
- Rapid movement
- Safety
- Comfort
- Convenience
- Air and noise pollution levels
- Overall citizen satisfaction with local transportation services.

Although such extensive measuring can produce a plethora of information to be considered by public officials, each characteristic appears important to the public. Upper-level managers could reduce the demands on their time by regularly

---

1. Many of the measures and measurement procedures discussed here were initially presented in an earlier report by Richard E. Winnie and Harry P. Hatry, *Measuring the Effectiveness of Local Government Services: Transportation* (Washington, D.C.: The Urban Institute, 1972).

examining only those measures that reflect problems or significant change. Staff members could use preselected thresholds or control ranges in selecting measures for scrutiny. The measures suggested for regular monitoring by local governments are presented in Exhibit 8-1 of this chapter for general transportation and Exhibit 9-1 of the next chapter for mass transit.

2. A major new measurement approach proposed here is the use of an annual survey of citizens within the jurisdiction to obtain their opinions of local transportation services. The survey approach seems particularly useful for governments to obtain feedback on citizen perceptions of the following:

• The overall ability of citizens to get where they want to go, such as to work, recreation areas, and shopping centers;

• The "rideability" of streets in their neighborhoods;
• Parking convenience, visibility of street signs and signals, level of traffic noise in citizens' neighborhoods, and adequacy of sidewalks and street lighting near their residences; and
• The transit service's convenience, reliability, comfort, speed, and general acceptability.

3. Data should be collected regularly on travel times between representative origins and destinations within the community, and on the severity and duration of automobile and other congestion in the most crowded areas. Local governments seldom monitor these characteristics, possibly because of the many technical problems involved in obtaining reliable information at a reasonable cost. However, even small annual samples of travel-time-related information can be valuable to public officials who want to com-

Exhibit 8-1
EFFECTIVENESS MEASURES FOR GENERAL TRANSPORTATION SERVICES
(Vehicular and Pedestrian)

OBJECTIVE: To provide access to desired destinations such as employment, shopping, and community services or other facilities in a quick, convenient, safe, and comfortable manner for all population groups in the community with a minimum of harmful effects on the environment.

OBJECTIVE	QUALITY CHARACTERISTICS	SPECIFIC MEASURES	DATA SOURCES
Vehicular Travel Accessibility	Accessibility	1. Percentage of citizens rating their ability to get where they want to go in a reasonable time as satisfactory.[1]	General citizen survey
Rapid Movement	Travel times	2. Average peak and off-peak travel times between key, or representative, origins and destinations.	Timed runs on selected routes
	Severity of congestion	3. Ratio of peak travel time to a "base" travel time between selected pairs of points.	Timed runs on selected routes
	Duration of congestion	4. Length of time that peak travel times exceed "x" percent of the "base" travel time.	Timed runs on selected routes
Safety	Frequency of accidents	5. Number of reported traffic accidents and the rate per 1,000 population.	Police accident reports
	Casualties from accidents	6. Number of deaths and injuries from traffic accidents, and rates per 1,000 population.	Police accident reports
	Property losses from accidents	7. Dollar property loss from traffic accidents and dollar loss per 1,000 population.	Police accident reports
	Preventability of accidents	8. Rate of accidents involving a contributing factor that can be influenced by a local government agency.	Police accident reports
	Feeling of security in driving—driver perceptions	9. Percentage of drivers who feel driving conditions are generally safe (or unsafe) (a) in the community, (b) in their own neighborhoods.	General citizen survey

Exhibit 8-1 continued

127

OBJECTIVE	QUALITY CHARACTERISTICS	SPECIFIC MEASURES	DATA SOURCES
Comfort	Street rideability (surface condition)	10. Percentage of streets with rideability (street surface conditions) rated as satisfactory.	Roughness-measuring instrument or trained observer ratings
	Street surface condition—citizen ratings	11. Percentage of (a) citizens, (b) businesses rating street rideability as satisfactory.	(a) General citizen survey (b) Survey of businesses
Convenience	Parking convenience—driver perception	12. Percentage of (a) drivers, (b) businesses who feel that finding a parking space is a problem, by area of the community.	(a) General citizen survey (b) Survey of businesses
	Visibility and condition of traffic control and street name signs	13. Percentage of streets with one or more traffic control signs, traffic signals, street pavement markings, or street name signs that are missing, blocked, or in otherwise unsatisfactory condition.	Trained observer ratings
		14. Percentage of citizens rating the understandability, visibility, and overall adequacy of traffic signs, traffic controls, street pavement markings, and street name signs as satisfactory.	Citizen survey
	Inconvenience because of lane blockages	15. Percentage of (a) drivers, (b) businesses that feel inconvenienced by blocked lanes.	(a) General citizen survey (b) Survey of businesses
Environmental Quality	Air pollution	16. Air pollutant levels attributable to transportation sources; number of days air pollution exceed "hazardous" threshold; and number of persons possibly exposed to hazardous levels.	Air samples and pollutant dispersion models
	Noise pollution	17. Percentage of street miles with traffic noise above "x" decibels, by residential (or nonresidential) area and type of street.	Noise-monitoring equipment, or estimates based on HUD noise assessment guide
		18. Percentage of citizens stating that they are bothered by traffic noise in their neighborhood.	General citizen survey
Pedestrian Travel Convenience/Safety	Sidewalk "walkability" (surface condition)	19. Percentage of blocks with sidewalks in satisfactory condition.	Trained observer rating
	Sidewalk availability and walkability	20. Percentage of citizens satisfied with the adequacy and condition of sidewalks in their neighborhoods.	General citizen survey
	Adequacy of street lighting	21. Percentage of citizens who feel street lighting in their neighborhood is insufficient.	General citizen survey

1. Measures calling for "satisfactory" ratings may use the term "unsatisfactory" when officials believe that emphasis would be more meaningful.

pare travel times among various parts of the community and over certain periods.

4. It is suggested that road rideability conditions be regularly sampled in various sections of the community either by a mechanical device such as a "roughometer" or by trained observers using a combination of photographic and verbal rating scales. If a trained observer approach is used, other conditions such as visibility of street signs and signals and sidewalk conditions can be rated simultaneously at little added cost. (In addition, ratings of street cleanliness, as discussed in Chapter 2, could also be obtained simultaneously, further increasing the value of the trained observer procedure.)

5. For these measures it is important to group the data to determine levels of service (a) for persons with ready access to cars and those without, especially the aged and handicapped, and (b) for different residential areas. For most of these procedures, such data groupings are easy to make.

One deficiency in these sets of measures is that they do not measure the effects of transportation on other important concerns such as employment and property values. These secondary impacts of transportation are outside the scope of this report because they are inappropriate for regular monitoring. Special in-depth evaluations are needed to measure these impacts.

Individual Measures for General Transportation

The remainder of this chapter discusses vehicular and pedestrian transportation measures—those shown in Exhibit 8-1.

Measure of Overall Accessibility, All Modes (Measure 1)

Measure 1: Percentage of citizens rating their ability to get where they want to go in the jurisdiction in a reasonable time as satisfactory (or unsatisfactory).

This measure attempts to provide an overall assessment of citizen perceptions of the transportation system's accessibility, considering all modes jointly (that is, automobile, bus, rail, and walking). Although the next chapter presents a separate measure of accessibility to public transit services (based on the proximity of residents to transit stops), this latter measure does not indicate whether citizens *perceive* themselves as being able to get to where they want to go, nor does it consider all modes of local transportation.

Data Collection. Data on this measure would be obtained by the general population survey already recommended for other government service areas discussed in other chapters. Covering a number of services in this survey will make the approach both more useful and economically more feasible, as costs would be divided among several service areas. The citizen survey procedure is discussed at length in Chapter 14. To obtain data for Measure 1, this question could be included in the survey:

> In general, how would you rate your ability to get to where you want to go in (name of city or county) in a reasonable amount of time, considering all forms of transportation, including automobiles, buses, and walking: excellent, good, fair, or poor?

In addition, respondents might be asked about their ability to get to specific types of destinations such as work opportunities, recreation sites, and shopping areas.[2] When respondents give negative responses

(for example, "fair" or "poor") to any of these questions, it would be useful to ask them to identify reasons for dissatisfaction.

Questions such as these were not included in either the St. Petersburg or Nashville surveys.[3] Thus, a question such as that suggested above should undergo careful pretesting to minimize ambiguity. The additional, probing questions to identify reasons for dissatisfaction probably should be included at least in the initial tests of the question to help identify possible ambiguities.

Measures of Rapid Movement (Measures 2-4)

Measure 2: Average peak and off-peak travel times between key or representative origins and destinations.

This measure indicates the combined effect of such factors as traffic volumes, speed limits, traffic control devices, and directness of available routes on the time required to travel by automobile vehicles within the community. Travel times for this measure would be determined by annual monitoring of perhaps fifteen to thirty "typical" trips within the community. The average time would be reported separately for each trip or class of trips. A summary form of this measure can be obtained by calculating the average percentage change from year to year for all trips.

The calculation of travel times is a familiar activity for many local government transportation agencies. Few, however, regularly make measurements to provide annual comparisons along key routes. Often what measurement is undertaken appears aimed at use in maps that depict equal travel-time contours for trips from the central business district in metropolitan areas.

A key problem in this measure is selecting the "typical" trips. Types of trips to consider for regular measurement include:

1. Those from residential areas to destinations such as the central business district, large shopping centers, employment centers, medical centers, and major recreation sites;
2. Business or commercially oriented trips such as those between commercial districts or between important local cargo depots and points in busi-

---

2. For example, a question such as the following might be included: For each of the following destinations, please tell me whether, over the past twelve months, it was usually easy, sometimes troublesome, or often troublesome to get to the following locations by some means of transportation—car, bus, or walking: (a) your place of work; (b) stores where you do your weekly shopping; (c) recreation areas within the city (or county); and (d) hospital or medical facilities.

3. However, the state governments of North Carolina and Wisconsin have included questions similar to those presented above in their initial tests of a citizen survey. For a discussion of measurement procedures similar to those discussed in this chapter but for state governments, see Greiner, et al., "Monitoring the Effectiveness of State Transportation Services" (Washington, D.C., U.S. Department of Transportation and The Urban Institute, forthcoming).

ness or manufacturing districts (to monitor times for goods shipments);

3. Trips with special social value, such as from neighborhoods with high unemployment to industrial districts; and

4. Trips to and from areas of likely future residential or commercial development.

Selected trips should probably include both cross-community and radial trips from the central business district.

Origins and destinations should be carefully chosen to minimize the number of origin-destination pairs to be measured. For example, St. Petersburg's trial of this procedure for mass transit travel (see next chapter) showed that some of the selected points simultaneously represented residential areas and medical centers or residential areas and shopping areas. The more paths used, the greater the coverage of the measure, but also the greater the costs of data collection and analysis.

Whenever possible, the paths selected for general transportation travel time measurements should also be usable for measuring transit travel times so that auto and transit travel times can be compared. St. Petersburg identified ten residential area origins and twelve commercial-medical-entertainment destinations. These identifications defined 120 (10 × 12) paths for which transit travel times were calculated. (The nearest transit stop was identified for each selected origin and destination.)

Data Collection. For each path included, an average travel time should be computed from the results of a number of runs made on the prescribed route. Drivers should attempt to move at the "average" speed of the traffic, keeping within posted speed limits. Separate measurements should probably be made for (1) peak-hour trips between residential and employment centers, (2) off-peak trips within the business district, and (3) off-peak trips between residential and commercial or recreation areas.

Several runs, preferably at least six,[4] should be made under similar driving conditions (for example, peak periods or off-peak periods) to provide a basis for computing the averages. If there is a wide variation among the times, additional runs would be advisable.[5] Runs should not be made in inclement weather. Runs during which other unusual traffic

conditions are encountered (for instance, a traffic accident or stalled car) should not be counted. The average of a small number of timed runs could be severely distorted by such disruptions.

This procedure is a variation of the somewhat more common approach mentioned previously, of measuring travel times for a number of radial routes emanating from the central business district of a metropolitan area, in order to provide maps showing equal-time contours.[6]

Data could be collected either by regular employees or temporary staff such as summer interns hired specifically for the task, or by street repair crews and supervisory employees who regularly travel throughout the city. The latter may be able to adjust some of their trips to include a specified path to record off-peak travel times. Alternatively, city employees could record data on routes that lie generally within their normal travel patterns. For example, office employees might gather data on rush-hour trips. In all cases, however, the employees would need to be adequately instructed, and a sample of such runs should be checked to ensure that correct procedures are being followed. If these problems can be surmounted, costs might be reduced and more frequent measurements might be possible throughout the year.

Approximately thirty-five employee-days of efforts would probably be required to make six runs over each of thirty routes during peak travel periods in a large city or county area. Fewer or additional routes or repetitions would alter the required effort proportionately.

Special Validity Considerations. 1. There are drawbacks in using the same routes each year so that trends can be identified. Conditions may change from year to year, making the selected routes no longer "typical." Thus, it may be necessary to revise some of the route selections from time to time, with a resulting loss in comparability.

2. A second potential problem is that government agencies might give special attention to the

---

4. This is the number often used by ad hoc transportation travel-time studies.

5. A procedure for determining when additional runs are needed is described in "1975 Metro Area Travel Times—Auto and Transit" (Washington, D.C.: Metropolitan Washington Council of Governments, April 1, 1976), p. 42.

6. For more details on travel-time estimation procedures, see, for example, "1975 Metro Area Travel Times." This study used six runs on each of nine routes, with each route divided into a number of sections and travel times calculated for each section. The runs were made on different days and always during the peak period (5:00-5:30 p.m.). More details on the procedures are included in the report. Other good descriptions of procedures for conducting travel time runs in urban areas are reported in "Driving Time Studies: A Procedure Guide," Stock No. 3253 (American Automobile Association, Traffic Engineering Division, June 1963), and "1973 Travel Time Inventory and Analysis" (Spokane, Wash.: Transportation Study Division, Spokane Regional Planning Conference, March, 1974).

particular routes included in the measurements, at the expense of those paths not included. Again, annual review of the selected trips seems desirable and changes should be made where appropriate.

3. The small number of travel-time runs likely to be economically feasible for each route limits the representativeness of the results in terms of estimating conditions for the entire year. Also limited is the accuracy of the averages calculated for each route. Ideally, the routes should be covered at various times of the year. In addition, a large number of runs should be made to increase both the accuracy of the travel time estimates and the likelihood that the averages calculated are representative of conditions throughout the year.[7]

Measure 3: *Ratio of peak travel time to a "base" travel time between selected pairs of points.*

Measure 4: *Length of time that peak travel times exceed "x" percent of the "base" travel time.*

These two measures are intended to indicate the severity and duration of congestion at peak travel times, both of which have potential importance to citizens. For example, changes such as staggered work hours may decrease the severity of peak congestion but spread the rush hour over a longer time. Such measures are most practical if applied to the most heavily traveled arterials. Data for several arterials presented together would help provide a picture of overall congestion in the community.

"Congestion" can be defined for this measure as a condition where the travel time between two points on an arterial route exceeds a "base time" by some minimum, such as 25 percent. This base time could be either actual travel time measurements at off-peak hours or a standard such as the number of minutes needed to travel between two points at the legal speed limit. The "severity" of congestion would be the ratio of the maximum travel time to base time (for example, 35 percent greater than the "base time"). The "duration" of congestion would be the length of time that travel times exceed the threshold percentage, for example, one hour at 25 percent or more over the base.

Data Collection. The first steps in data collection are selecting the arterials of interest and identifying points on these arterials between which congestion is to be measured (for example, one-half to three miles apart). Travel times between these two points might be measured during peak traffic flow periods on each of at least three and preferably more, weekdays. William P. Walker has reported on the number of such observations needed for various levels of precision.[8] If the worst congestion on a road occurs on weekends (roads leading to beaches, for instance), then Saturdays and Sundays should be used rather than weekdays.

Two observers, one stationed at each measurement point, can record the times and license numbers of vehicles as they pass; a two-way radio link might help with this identification process. The vehicles could be (1) city vehicles driven on the route especially for the measurement and circling back to the start for subsequent measurements; (2) buses, if the measurement points lie along a bus route segment with frequent service (but not "bus-only" lanes) and no bus stops on that segment; or (3) private vehicles traveling the route.

No field testing of these measures was conducted during this project. Note that Measure 3 should be considerably less expensive than Measure 4 because it requires estimates at only two points in time per route.

Special Validity Considerations. Measures 3 and 4 are affected by the same concerns regarding number and timing, as described under Measure 2. An additional concern is the length of the "peak period" in smaller cities and counties. The latter may be so short as to preclude obtaining enough observations to define its duration accurately. Of course, if the peak period is very short, a government may not feel it is worthwhile to use congestion measures, or at the very least, the precision advisable for larger jurisdictions would not be required.

Measures of Safety (Measures 5-9)

Measure 5: *Number of reported traffic accidents and the rate per 1,000 population.*

Measure 6: *Number of deaths and number of injuries from traffic accidents and the rate per 1,000 population.*

7. Walker reports that on congested, signalized, two-lane urban streets, forty test car runs would be needed to obtain travel-time estimates with a maximum error of 5 percent and a 95-percent degree of confidence. For a maximum error of 10 percent, ten test runs would be necessary. William P. Walker, "Speed and Travel Time Measurement in Urban Areas," *Traffic Speed and Volume Measurements,* Highway Research Bulletin 156 (Washington, D.C., 1956), p. 30.

8. For instance, using license-plate-matching techniques on congested, signalized urban streets, at least 36 observations would be needed for a two-lane facility and 102 for a multilane facility in order to achieve an estimation error of no more than 5 percent and a 95-percent confidence level. See Walker, "Speed and Travel Time," p. 29.

*Measure 7:   Dollar property loss from traffic acci-
                    dents and dollar loss per 1,000 popula-
                    tion.*

Accident rates (Measure 5) provide an indicator of frequency of problems, whereas casualty rates and dollar value of property damage (Measures 6 and 7) are indicators of the severity of the incidents.

Rates of traffic accidents, deaths and injuries, and property loss are commonly used as measures of a transportation system's safety. These rates reflect traffic control efforts and road network design, as well as conditions substantially beyond local government transportation agencies, including the design and condition of private vehicles and the quality of driver education. Accident, injury, and property damage information should be categorized by mode of transportation (for example, automobile, bus, pedestrian, or rail) as well as in summary form.

Because of the existing prevalence of basic accident tabulations, no special effort was undertaken in this project to identify and test possible improvements. However, the following section does provide a few suggestions in that area to ensure validity and meaningful analysis. (In addition, Measures 8 and 9 suggest two somewhat new measurement approaches, for which initial investigations were made.)

Data Collection. The number of traffic accidents is reported almost universally, but not all communities compute accident rates. The rates in Measures 5, 6, and 7 are computed by dividing the number of accidents, deaths and injuries, or dollar loss, respectively, by estimates of current population, which are usually available from local planning departments.

The city's residential population is commonly used as the denominator for these measures. That normalization provides a useful overall indicator, especially for comparisons over time and with other communities, or for comparisons among various residential areas of the jurisdictions. However, residential population does not reflect the effects of non-residential (that is, visitor and business) traffic on a community.

To allow for this problem, the estimated nonresident (daytime) population could be included in the denominator. Or, the number of accidents, deaths, and injuries of resident drivers per 1,000 residents could be stated as separate measures. Accident reports usually include addresses of the drivers involved, thus allowing computation of accident rates separately for residents and nonresidents.

Two other denominators might be considered in computing the rates in Measures 5 and 6. First, the number of accidents or deaths and injuries per 1,000 vehicle-miles driven would reflect safety in terms of vehicle usage. Second, the number of accidents or deaths and injuries per 1,000 passenger-miles could be used to compare the relative safety of various transportation modes. Both vehicle-miles driven and passenger-miles are difficult to estimate accurately. Rough estimates of the former could be based on areawide gasoline consumption.

The numerator of Measure 5, number of reported accidents, currently is tabulated by most cities, but this figure is likely to be underestimated because not all accidents are reported to the police. Citizen surveys or possibly insurance company records could be used to determine the degree of nonreporting and thus provide a more accurate estimate of total accidents.

An issue pertaining to Measure 6 is the type of injury that can be counted in this measure. The state of Florida has categorized injuries into three classes, based on what is visible at the scene:

1. Physical signs of injury such as bleeding wounds, a distorted limb, or a victim who had to be carried from the scene;
2. Other visible injuries such as bruises, abrasions, swelling, or limping;
3. No visible injuries, but complaint of pain or momentary unconsciousness.

For purposes of Measure 6, at least categories (1) and (2) should be included. Whatever the definition chosen by a community it should be made clear to those compiling the tabulations and used consistently.

The numerator of Measure 7 is the total dollar amount of property loss from traffic accidents. Police accident reports generally indicate property damage, but dollar estimates of damage are infrequently made. Police officers generally lack training for making damage estimates; furthermore, estimating damages might interfere with essential police duties at accident scenes.

Several methods for gathering accident cost data are available, including the following:

1. Professional appraisers can be used to estimate damages at the scene of a sample of accidents.
2. A follow-up survey of victims of a sample of accidents can attempt to ascertain the costs of repairing property damage.
3. Summary data on the cost of all or a sample of accidents can be obtained from insurance com-

panies, provided such data are not confidential. However, this procedure would not pick up costs of accidents involving uninsured drivers.

When data from Measure 7 are compared over time, they should be expressed in constant dollars (adjusted for price changes) or plotted against changes in indices for automobile prices and repair costs.

Measure 8:   *Rate of accidents involving a contributing factor that can be influenced by a local government agency.*

Many local government activities affect accident rates to some extent. These activities include police traffic control and law enforcement, street engineering and repair, traffic signing and signaling, and street lighting. This measure attempts to separate accidents involving contributing factors that could be affected by local government from those that would not.

Data Collection. Many communities routinely record data regarding conditions at the time of the accident. For example, Nashville police accident reports contain a check list of possible contributing factors, such as apparent traffic violations, physical condition of the driver, obstructions to vision, unreasonably high speed limit, absence of traffic control, pavement defects, little advance warning of intersection, and rough shoulders. The Florida state accident form lists items such as road defects, driver traffic violations, and "physical conditions." Lists such as these would provide a starting point for gathering data for this measure, although additions and reorganization would probably be necessary. Exhibit 8-2 illustrates one such categorization.

Reporting forms and data displays should describe relevant conditions as "possible contributing factors" rather than "causes." Rarely is it possible to identify actual causes with certainty during the cursory investigation a police officer conducts at an accident scene.

A review of completed accident reports in the two test cities showed that many contained incomplete information. Officers should be instructed on the proper preparation, intended use, and importance of reports. Sample accident reports should be reviewed periodically to ensure that they are being filled out properly.

The procedure suggested for this measure is quite similar to those already being used by many communities, including St. Petersburg and Nashville, as described above. Most communities would need to make some changes in existing acci-

Exhibit 8-2
FACTORS CONTRIBUTING TO ACCIDENTS AND RELATED TO LOCAL GOVERNMENT FUNCTIONS

CONTRIBUTING FACTOR	TYPICAL AGENCY WITH PRIME RESPONSIBILITY
a. Street surface condition, by type (e.g., pothole, severe bump) b. Ice or snow on road	Streets
c. Traffic control (signal, sign, or pavement marking) malfunction, missing, not visible, confusing; by type of control and type of problem. d. Traffic control lacking where needed (in judgment of police officer reporting)	Traffic
e. View obstruction (e.g., buildings, hedges)	Parks (possibly streets)
f. Driver under influence of alcohol or drugs g. Moving violation, by type of violation h. Vehicle malfunction or defect in violation of the law (e.g., no lights)	Police
i. Other vehicle malfunction or defect j. Driver's health or physical condition (other than alcohol or drugs)	Not usually local government responsibility, but probably of concern to other levels of government[1]
k. Other (specify government-related factors)	Various agencies

1. Local governments may use these data to help inform state governments of problem areas that are usually state responsibilities, such as vehicle inspections and driver licensing (including testing). Alternatively, the localities might pass special ordinances for such testing themselves.

dent reports, particularly in the manner of summarizing and reporting data to relevant government departments on a regular basis. In communities where accident report data are computerized, periodic tallies of the number of accidents involving various factors could be accomplished at a small incremental cost. Otherwise, manual tallies might be made for at least a sample of accidents.

Measure 9:   *Percentage of drivers who feel that driving conditions are generally safe (or unsafe) (a) in the community, (b) in their own neighborhoods.*

Driver perceptions of conditions as unsafe may make travel unpleasant or even unhealthful for them. When such perceptions are intense, they may cause persons to avoid driving on particular roads, or even at all.

A local government's potential influence on driver perceptions of safety may be quite limited, but those feelings probably can be somewhat influenced by clear and ample traffic control, nighttime markings, shoulders, railings, and the like; police enforcement of traffic laws; driver education programs; and safety campaigns that encourage courteous, careful driving behavior. The proposed measure would be useful primarily to gauge the "feeling" of security; it may or may not be correlated with the actual extent of driver safety.

Data Collection. Data for this measure would be gathered from the multiservice citizen surveys, although the ones conducted during this project did not include a question for this measure. The following query might be included:

> How safe from traffic accidents do you generally feel while driving in your neighborhood: very safe; somewhat safe; somewhat unsafe; very unsafe?

A follow-up question might identify the sources of perceived danger, such as defective road surfaces, seemingly narrow lanes, confusing traffic control devices, actions of other drivers, inadequate pavement marking at night, or other factors. A very limited pretest of these questions indicated that the latter question might be used as a separate measure in the form of "percentage of respondents who cite (specific problem areas)."

Although not included in the list of measures, the " ercentage of citizens who feel there is relatively low (or high) danger to pedestrians (especially children or the elderly) from traffic in their neighborhood" also might be obtained through the citizen survey, although such a question was not included in the Nashville or St. Petersburg surveys.

Measures of Comfort (Measures 10 and 11)

Road maintenance is a major activity of local transportation. These two measures are of particular importance because they attempt to provide indicators of that activity.

Measure 10 uses an "objective" approach to measuring road conditions that appear directly related to comfort or "rideability" for users of the roads. Measure 11 uses a subjective approach by obtaining ratings from citizens on their perceptions of road conditions.

Measure 10: Percentage of streets with rideability (street surface conditions) rated as satisfactory (or unsatisfactory).

The construction and maintenance of street surfaces affect the comfort, and, at some point, the safety and time involved in local travel.[9] The con-

cern here is with the rideability for road users, whether they are in automobiles or buses.

Local street maintenance agencies regularly examine road conditions to rate the surface conditions of streets from an engineering viewpoint. They then determine priorities for maintenance and repair programs, such as resurfacing, before rideability becomes a problem. This is essentially preventive maintenance. Desirable as this latter measurement is, it is not an "outcome" measurement, which is the subject of this report. Here the concern is with measuring current rideability—the quality of the "ride," given existing road conditions.

Measure 10 (and Measure 11) can be used to help assess the success of preventive street maintenance programs. Potholes or other conditions of road bumpiness may be considered by a street maintenance agency as superficial blemishes on a road, but rideability-bumpiness is of direct concern to citizens using the roads.

Data Collection. Basically, there are two approaches for obtaining "objective" assessments of street rideability: (1) using mechanical roughness-measuring devices, and (2) having "trained observers" make visual ratings.

Mechanical Devices for Measuring Roughness. Several mechanical devices exist for measuring road surface conditions. These include the Bureau of Public Roads (BPR) "roughometer," the Portland Cement Association (PCA) Roadmeter, and the Mays Ride Meter (developed by the Texas Highway Department and sold commercially by Reinhart Company of Austin, Texas). The BPR roughometer is mounted on a trailer and towed along the streets at about 20 mph. Both the PCA Roadmeter and the Mays Meter are mounted inside a test car, connected to the suspension, and can be used at speeds up to 50 mph.

These devices were developed primarily for measuring the smoothness of newly constructed roads and high speed roads, but they can be used for city streets as well. All require technicians for calibrating and operating the equipment.

In 1972, The Urban Institute used a BPR roughometer to compare road surface conditions in several neighborhoods of Fairfax County, Virginia.[10] The operating cost of this device was $200 per day, including labor and rental. Several state highway departments have purchased or built

---

9. A moderate level of street pavement disrepair is not likely to affect safety or travel time significantly because of the low speed limits in most jurisdictions, but extreme conditions cause damage to vehicles.

10. Andrew J. Boots, III, et al., *Inequality in Local Government Services: A Case Study of Neighborhood Roads* (Washington, D.C.: The Urban Institute, 1972).

roughometers for their own use. Ohio uses a Wisconsin Road Meter (a version of the PCA model) for making roughness measurements on state highways. The device was purchased in 1972 for about $1,600 from a commercial source; it was modified by department personnel at an additional cost of about $400.

In 1966, Minnesota's Department of Highways built its own PCA Roadmeters for about $375 each; each costs about $25 per year to maintain. Similar roughness "meters" are owned and operated by many other state governments. They could be borrowed or rented by local governments wanting to make periodic effectiveness measurements but not wanting to build their own devices.[11]

To relate the results obtained from such devices to citizen perceptions of discomfort, a bumpiness scale should be developed from the mechanical readings. This can be done by correlating data gathered mechanically with ratings of road bumpiness made by a panel of blindfolded citizens riding over the same streets.[12]

Trained Observer Ratings. When instruments for measuring roughness are not available or are considered too expensive or unwieldy, it is possible to obtain at least a general indication of street surface conditions by having trained observers rate the streets, using preestablished visual ratings or "seat-of-the-pants" bumpiness ratings made from cars.

These measurements can be made by a driver or passenger in a car cruising at a fixed speed. Ratings of street surface conditions can be made along with those for street litter (see Chapter 2), conditions of street signs (Measure 13), pavement markings (Measure 14), and sidewalks (Measure 24). Nashville tested this approach by relying primarily on visual ratings, but bumpiness during the ride was also used to detect road roughness not easily visible and to help rate severity. Bumpiness ratings are influenced by the vehicle's suspension system, so the same type of vehicles preferably should be used for all test runs.

Visual ratings should normally be from the center line of the street to the right curb, because it is hard to observe both sides of the street simultaneously and because the observer has not experienced the quality of the ride on the other side.

The visual ratings should be based on a scale described both photographically and verbally. The intent here is to reduce the subjectivity of the ratings so that different inspectors using the rating guidelines would give the same rating to given street conditions.

Photographs should be developed that show various levels of "rideability." Exhibit 8-3 shows photographs representing the four levels of ratings used in Nashville to help trained observers standardize their field observations. However, it was difficult to find a satisfactory picture of a "4" (worst) condition because of the difficulty in distinguishing pothole depths in photographs.

Exhibit 8-4 gives definitions of the four condition levels tested in Nashville, based on a scale of 1 to 4.[13] It proved desirable to provide for conditions that fall between two levels by using the half-level ratings, such as 1.5. Numbers on the four-point scale describe certain conditions and are not part of a continuous, equal-interval rating scale. Therefore, the results actually should be presented as "the percentage of streets within each level" or "the percentage of streets that are worse than some level (such as 2.5)" rather than as "average" ratings.[14] Rideability ratings should be made at least once a year, and preferably more frequently to help reduce seasonal distortions in the measurement; the timing will depend on the local climate and the street maintenance schedule. Communities that experience cold winters might record conditions at the time of year when the worst street conditions are present (for example, after thawing) and at the "best" time of the year (for instance, the dry season or immediately

11. Recently, a team from Indiana University developed a new measuring instrument, the Residential Street Roughness Indicator, expressly for rating the smoothness of residential streets. This device was designed to be easily constructed and inexpensive enough for a local government to build by itself or purchase at a low price (an estimated $1,000 to $1,500). The device has multiple tracks, which permit more street surface to be measured than is possible with some of the other devices described above. However, the instrument must be towed at 3 mph and requires a crew of three to operate.

A sample of seventy blocks can be rated in two days, based on tests in Indianapolis by the Indiana team using this device. See Richard Rich, "The Development of Residential Street Roughness Indicator as a Mode of Measurement for the Survey of Municipal Services," Research Report No. 6 (Bloomington: Indiana University, Department of Political Science, n.d.).

12. For a description of the development of such a scale see Boots et al., *Inequality in Local Government Services.*

13. Both the Indiana University project and a more recent Oklahoma State University project have been developing visual rating scales under efforts sponsored by the National Science Foundation. The Oklahoma study is developing a procedure for using citizen volunteers to rate the street conditions. See Elinor Ostrom and Roger B. Parks, "Measuring Urban Services: A Multi-Mode Approach," a portfolio by the Workshop on Political Theory and Policy Analysis, Department of Political Science (Bloomington: Indiana University, 1975), and Earl Ferguson, *Final Report on National Science Foundation Grant No. GR-43107* (Stillwater: Department of Industrial Engineering, Oklahoma State University, September 1975).

14. "Average" ratings are not technically correct; however, it is tempting to use averages, and no great distortion seems likely to occur from them. Nevertheless, the forms listed above would appear to be more informative. See our discussion of this point in regard to the litter condition rating scale in Chapter 2.

Exhibit 8-3
EXAMPLES OF STREET RIDEABILITY CONDITIONS

Condition 1
Smooth

Condition 2
Slightly Bumpy

Condition 3
Considerably Bumpy

Condition 4
Potential Safety Hazard of Cause of Severe Jolt[1]

1. Unfortunately we found no good example of a "4" condition that was photographically clear. But because condition 4 is the only rating that is physically measurable, no photo is really needed.

Exhibit 8-4
RATING SCALE FOR STREET RIDEABILITY
(Visual rating made from an automobile)

CONDITION	DESCRIPTION
1.	*Smooth* a. No noticeable defects. This could be split off as a separate "perfect rating" category if desired; <div align="center">or</div>b. One or two minor defects, such as a small open crack, minor bump, small hole less than 2 inches across; or cracked surface with no perceived bumpiness (e.g. Condition 1 on the photographic exhibit).[1]
2.	*Slightly bumpy* a. Several minor defects or small potholes, but none severe; <div align="center">or</div>b. A sizable single bump or many minor bumps; <div align="center">or</div>c. Gravel or dirt road in good condition.[2]
3.	*Considerably bumpy* Much of the street is broken up or has easily visible bumps, but no single safety hazard (as defined below) is present.
4.	*Potential safety hazard or cause of severe jolt* One or more large potholes, "steps," or other major defects 3½ inches high or deep.[1] (This category could be divided into parts to distinguish streets with only one hazard from those with more than one.) Types of hazards should be noted.

1. Subjective, somewhat arbitrary, dimensions based on judgment of The Urban Institute and Nashville researchers after experimentally driving over holes of various sizes. Others might choose different criteria.

2. Unpaved roads and roads with rough surfacing for aesthetic reasons (such as bricks or cobblestones) might be rated along with other types of roads using this rating scale with 2c included. Alternatively, such roads might be rated apart from paved roads, using the scale from 1 to 4 with 2c deleted. The percentage of roads that are unpaved and the "percentage by special surfacing type" might also be reported as a separate measure.

after the conclusion of repair programs for the year). If ratings are not spread out throughout the year, they should be made at about the same time(s) each year to avoid seasonal distortions.

The number of streets to be rated depends upon the number of levels on the rating scale, the desired range of accuracy, the variation in street surface conditions within the city, and the resources to be devoted to ratings. In the first trial of its rating method, Nashville used trained observers to rate 500 streets, a random sample of fifty streets in each of ten areas in Davidson County. Rating perhaps 100 streets per area would provide more precise findings and is suggested for other communities.[15] Based on the Nashville trials, about 100 streets could be rated twice per year with approximately twenty-five person-days of effort.[16]

15. See Louis Blair and Alfred I. Schwartz, *How Clean Is Our City?* (Washington, D.C.: The Urban Institute, 1972), Appendix B, pp. 65-67, for a brief discussion of sample sizes and significance tests.

16. A more extensive discussion of costs, along with cost estimates for a somewhat larger scale inspection program, is presented in Chapter 13.

In communities where public works departments visually rate streets at regular intervals for engineering purposes, the rideability ratings probably could be added readily, thus providing these data on a potentially large sample of streets at small additional cost. A problem with this is that having the same persons responsibile for maintaining the streets also do the rating might affect the objectivity and the credibility of the results. However, with reasonable quality control checks on the inspections, this problem can be reduced.

The greatest difficulty in making ratings seems to lie between the 1.0 and 2.0 levels of the scale in Exhibit 8-4. A possible reason is that in distinguishing between these two levels of fairly good road conditions, an observer may overlook a defect that would make the road a 2.0 rather than a 1.0.

The accuracy of the visual rating system remains to be determined fully. Based on results of initial tests, however, it appears that a high degree of consistency among observers can be obtained with proper initial training and periodic replications of a sample of ratings by a second "judge."

Whether ratings on these measures are undertaken separately or simultaneously, the following points are important for proper use of the procedure:

1. The rating scale for each measure should be pretested in each municipality prior to its use, to assure that persons with proper training will give reliable ratings. Some of these procedures are discussed in Chapter 13—for example, the requirement that 75 percent of the ratings by a new inspector be in exact agreement with, and that 90 percent be within one-half grade of, the ratings by an independent judge. If the municipality uses the particular rating scales included in this report, it is advisable to test them for local conditions prior to use.

2. Past experience with trained observer ratings, especially in our studies on street cleanliness ratings, indicates the importance of providing adequate training in the use of the rating scales. This means both initial training for new observers and refresher training at suggested six-month intervals for experienced inspectors. There is a tendency for raters to deviate from the scales without periodic refresher training. Initial training requires approximately two to three days; probably two half-day sessions are enough for refresher training.

3. A fraction (10 to 25 percent) of the ratings made by each trained observer on each measure should be replicated by an independent judge. If significant deivations between ratings occur, refresher training or other action is needed.

4. If, in order to keep down measurement costs, only a sample of the streets are rated periodically rather than all streets in the jurisdiction, proper sampling techniques must be used to assure that the sample is reasonably representative. This is basic good practice and, along with the rating replications, will help yield proper ratings and give credible results.

5. To keep trained observer ratings useful for comparing conditions over time (an important use for systematic measurement procedures), the rating scales and key procedures should be kept stable. Changes in those scales and procedures may affect the comparability of findings and degrade the usefulness of the rating effort. Careful pretesting of the procedures, as suggested in (1) above, will help avoid the need for subsequent revisions.

More details on trained observer procedures are presented in Chapter 13 and Appendix 13.

Comparison of Trained Observer and Mechanical Device Ratings. Studies by Indiana University indicated that ratings by trained observers using a four-level scale were highly correlated with those gathered on the same roads by mechanical devices.[17] Mechanical roughness measurement devices have two important advantages over ratings by trained observers: (1) Their measurements generally are more reliable, if the equipment is suitably calibrated and working properly; and (2) some devices, such as the Mays Meter, produce a printed record of each road's bumpiness, which allows management to identify specific areas needing attention. However, these readings include only the portion of the roadway touched by the wheels of the device or test vehicle, and may miss bumps or hazards, especially those near curbs. In addition, operating costs for some devices (notably, the BPR roughometer) may be higher than for trained observer measurements. However, with the advent of devices such as the PCA Roadmeter, which can be constructed for as little as $400 and operated by one technician at speeds up to 50 mph, mechanical roughness measurements appear feasible for local governments. If a reliable, low-cost mechanical device such as a PCA Roadmeter or a Mays Meter is available, possibly on loan from a state highway department, the use of a mechanical device is warranted. Otherwise, the trained observer approach seems adequate, provided suitable training and periodic replications are assured. Some state highway departments have decided that mechanical measurements are the most

economical approach to meet their needs, but somewhat different conditions, such as higher speeds, exist in the areas under state jurisidiction.

Measure 11: Percentage of (a)citizens, (b) businesses rating street rideability conditions as satisfactory (or unsatisfactory).

In addition to safety, another key concern is whether the users of a jurisdiction's roads find them comfortable to ride on. Whether or not citizen or business ratings are "accurate" in a technical sense, the public's perceptions are likely to be important to many officials. Individuals will differ in their sensitivity to road problems, but the resulting data on the distribution of ratings should be useful for assessment purposes, especially when compared across major areas of the community and from one time period to another.

Citizen perceptions may include factors beyond those considered in trained observer or mechanical ratings and can add a dimension to those ratings by, in effect, "weighting" or "summing" various quality characteristics.

Data Collection. The general citizen survey suggested for Measure 1 and for a number of other measures throughout this report can be used to obtain data on the citizen's perspective. Question 9 in Appendix 1 could be used in that survey, since it asks respondents about conditions on streets in their neighborhoods. Additionally or alternatively, respondents might be asked to rate streets in the community as a whole. However, citizens are likely to be most familiar with a more limited area, such as conditions in their neighborhoods.

Although not included in the questionnaire in Appendix 1, the reasons for negative responses should be pursued with probing questions to identify better the particular nature of respondents' problems and perhaps their location. Finally, the views of businesspersons on street conditions in their areas can be obtained from a question in a survey of businesses, such as Number 4 in Appendix 2.

Mechanical Ratings of Street Conditions Compared to Citizen Perceptions. In the Indiana University research described above, comparisons of citizen perceptions of street roughness and mechanical ratings of that roughness showed a fairly strong correlation.[18] The comparison of trained observer and

17. Susan Carroll, "An Analysis of the Relationship Between Citizen Perceptions and Unobtrusive Measures of Street Conditions," Technical Report M-10, Workshop on Political Theory and Policy Analysis (Bloomington: Indiana University, 1975).

18. Elinor Ostrom, "Multi Modal Approaches to Measurement of Government Productivity," Workshop on Political Theory and Policy Analysis (Bloomington: Indiana University, 1975), p. 11. Some variation was noted for certain population groups; those persons with more than a high school diploma, those over 45, those who have lived on a block more than five years, and those living on medium to short blocks tended to give ratings more "consistent with mechanical ratings."

citizen survey ratings we undertook indicates some relationship but not enough, in our judgment, to suggest that the use of one adequately reflects the other. (See Exhibit 8-5 for an illustration of that relationship, based on Nashville data.)

In our experience, street maintenance officials believe themselves considerably more capable of identifying road rideability than are citizens providing aggregate impressions. From a technical viewpoint, this seems correct. Nevertheless, citizen perceptions of road rideability, even if they are not in agreement with the more technical measurements such as those in Measure 10, are likely to be of major concern to public officials.

The best approach suggested by the evidence to date seems to be to use the mechanical device ratings or trained observer ratings, based on a combination of photographs and verbal definitions to obtain reasonable rating reliability. Where the local government undertakes citizen surveys, questions on neighborhood road conditions should be included to obtain citizen perspectives.

Measures of Convenience (Measures 12-18)

Measure 12: Percentage of (a) drivers, (b) businesspersons who feel that finding a parking space is usually (or sometimes or infrequently) a problem, by area of the community.

No satisfactory "objective" measure of parking space availability emerged in this effort. It is true that the supply of on- and off-street parking spaces can be inventoried, and the "percentage of capacity used" can be obtained. However, it is difficult to develop an estimate of demand for parking spaces that can be compared to the number of spaces available and is appropriate for regular monitoring. It is even more difficult to formulate a measure that can encompass specific convenience characteristics such as location, price, security, and shelter from weather. Considering utilization rates for available parking facilities also means dealing with ambiguities. For example, underutilization of available parking could indicate that there is either sufficient parking in the area or possibly that such parking is unsuitable for citizens' needs.

Citizen perceptions of the overall convenience of existing parking, although probably not so "objective" as transportation officials might like, provide important input. The general citizen survey, if undertaken regularly, provides a convenient way for a municipality to obtain these data. A question such as Number 3 in Appendix 1 might be used. Because

Exhibit 8-5

COMPARISON OF TRAINED OBSERVER AND CITIZEN SURVEY RATINGS ON ROAD SURFACE CONDITIONS

NEIGHBORHOOD	TRAINED OBSERVER PERCENTAGE OF STREETS RATED 3 OR 4		CITIZEN SURVEY: PERCENTAGE RATING CONDITIONS OR STREETS AS HAVING "MANY BAD SPOTS"	
	1974	1975	1974	1975
1	16.0	11.0	71	50
2	6.1	8.0	34	28
3	0	6.7	21	41
4	8.0	6.7	29	47
5	0	4.7	27	33
6	8.0	4.0	26	29
7	8.1	13.0	31	33
8	4.0	8.0	33	34
9	2.0	1.3	16	25
10	12.0	7.3	29	35
Countywide	6.5	7.1	29	36

Source: The citizen survey data are from the Nashville citizen surveys in 1974 and 1975, using Question 9 of Appendix 1: "How would you rate the condition of street and road surfaces in your neighborhood? Are they in good condition all over, mostly good but a few bad spots here and there, or are there many bad spots?" For the trained observer ratings, about 50 were made in each Nashville neighborhood in 1974; 150 were made in each neighborhood in 1975. Note that the respondents in the citizen surveys undoubtedly used a somewhat more narrow geographical definition for "neighborhood" than was used for the trained observer tallies.

The correlation coefficient between 1974 trained observer and citizen survey ratings was .74, indicating that about 55 percent of the variation in citizen survey ratings could be explained by trained observer ratings. However, much of this correlation appears to be the result of the extreme ratings given to Neighborhood 1. A Spearman's rank correlation test, which reduces the disproportionate influence of such extreme points, found that 28 to 39 percent of the variance could be explained.

customer parking convenience is of special interest to businesses, the local government undertaking a periodic survey of businesses could include a question on parking. An example is Question 9 in Appendix 2.

Measure 13: Percentage of streets with one or more traffic control signs, traffic signals, street pavement markings, or street name signs that are missing, blocked, or in otherwise unsatisfactory condition.

The principal effect of obscured or missing signs is likely to be inconvenience, but such defects can also cause danger and travel delays.

Traffic signs and signals fall into two categories: regulatory and advisory. Regulatory signs control or limit driver actions in ways enforceable by legal penalties. These include traffic lights and signs indicating the following: stop, yield, one way, do not enter, no left turn, or parking and speed limits. Advisory signs are intended to provide information to the driver designating exits, route numbers, school or bicycle crossings, the location of specific facilities, and street names.

Four important characteristics of traffic and street signs are likely to be important:

Visibility:
Positioning, lack of obstruction or defacement, size of lettering, and cleanliness. Ideally, the factors of day, night, and poor weather visibility should all be considered.

Understandability:
Clarity and lack of ambiguity in the message.

Sufficiency:
Whether the number of signs is adequate to (1) keep drivers advised of regulations and hazards, and (2) make it convenient for them to get around.

Oversigning:
The extent to which the number of regulatory signs makes it difficult to drive about conveniently. Too many signs can be confusing and may dull the impact of important signs, as well as being aesthetically unpleasant.

To identify specific problems, ratings could be separated into four subjects: traffic control signs, traffic signals, street name signs, and street markings.

Data Collection. Based on initial test results in Nashville, the use of trained observers appears to be a feasible procedure for making standardized ratings of the visibility and understandability of traffic control and street name signs.[19] These ratings can be made concurrently with ratings of other street characteristics such as road rideability (Measure 10) and street cleanliness (see Chapter 2). Chapter 13 not only sets forth procedures for rating several types of street conditions simultaneously, but also suggests rating scales for stop, yield, and street name signs. These scales were used to rate 500 randomly selected streets in Nashville in an initial test of that city's rating procedures.

The ratings for this measure can be made by either the driver or a rider from a car driven slowly down the block. The car should be stopped short of intersections to allow time for the rater to note the condition of street name signs, traffic lights, if any, and other equipment.

Both a written rating scale and photographs illustrating the various conditions corresponding to

each level on the scales should be employed. An illustrative written rating scale is provided in Appendix 13. Illustrative photographs used in rating stop signs and street name signs are shown in Exhibits 8-6 and 8-7.

Space does not permit a presentation here of the specific procedures and detailed findings of the trials in Nashville. Of 165 sign ratings there, 84 percent were identical between judge and rater, and all were within one level of each other. This indicates that a reasonable level of reliability can be achieved. The principal problem found was with signs being missed by raters rather than with disagreements over the ratings of particular signs.

Adequate training and retraining are needed. In the area with the lowest consistency between the judge's and the prime observer's ratings, retraining produced a noticeable improvement. As already discussed under Measure 11 and the trained observer street cleanliness ratings in Chapter 2, part of the ratings must be replicated, with retraining undertaken when the replications indicate significant differences in ratings.

In developing an initial trained observer rating system for signs, it seemed too complicated to have the observers rate streets as to (1) the need for signs not already present, (2) the sufficiency of signs for directing drivers to various destinations, or (3) whether there were too many signs altogether. These additional conditions can be reflected, at least grossly, by surveys of citizens' perceptions of the adequacy of signs. (See discussion of the next measure.)

Night and bad weather ratings. Separate trained observer systems for night ratings and bad weather ratings were not tested here. They seem desirable, however, and can be developed using a photographic rating scale similar in concept to those already discussed for daytime ratings.

An alternative approach is to use the Highway Sign Inspection Guide developed by the 3-M Company. Pieces of reflectorized material, chosen because the degree of their reflectivity is considered desirable for important signs, are held next to a sample of existing signs at night. The brightness of the test material is compared to that of the sign sample being tested. These ratings can be done using a flashlight at close range or headlights from a distance. A panel of citizens might be used to make the initial selection of materials considered bright enough. Alternatively, subjective ratings by trained observers or from citizens on citizen surveys can be used.

---

19. For traffic signals, those conducting the rating could use the frequency of repairs and related downtime, at least as measured from the time the first report of the problem was received. These are viewed in this report as being primarily internal measures of performance and are not discussed further.

Exhibit 8-6
EXAMPLES OF STOP SIGN CONDITIONS 2 AND 3

(Note: Condition 1 is a "perfect" sign and not illustrated here)

Condition 2

Condition 2

Condition 3

Condition 3

Exhibit 8-7
EXAMPLES OF STREET NAME SIGN CONDITIONS 1, 2, AND 3

Condition 1

Condition 2

Condition 3

Condition 3

Rating pavement markings at night and in the rain, using similar principles, though not tested in this project, might also be considered by local governments.

Measure 14: Percentage of citizens rating the understandability, visibility, and overall adequacy of traffic signs, traffic controls, street pavement markings, and street name signs as satisfactory (or unsatisfactory).

Citizen perceptions directly indicate "user" views as to the satisfactoriness of signs and signals.

Data Collection. A survey of drivers, obtained either by the general citizen survey, or perhaps by a special driver survey, could be used to gather data on this measure.

Questions in Appendix 1 such as Questions 5 and 5a (on traffic signs) and Question 7 (on street name signs) can be used to obtain these data. Questions 5 and 7 measure the adequacy of both traffic and street name signs in terms of the rating "easy to see and understand quickly." Question 5a illustrates how, when a problem is indicated in a response, an attempt can be made to identify the specific nature of that problem (for example, blocked view, missing signs, or signs too small). Similarly, Question 4 provides data on the visibility to citizens of pavement markings such as center lines.

Note that these questions are asked only of those citizen survey respondents who indicated in a previous question that they had driven an automobile in the jurisdiction during the past twelve months.

In general, survey responses in the Nashville trials were consistent with trained observer ratings. For example, both types of ratings showed street name signs to be a greater problem than were other types of signs. Citizen ratings showed no large variations among areas of the city, but large area variations appeared in the trained observer ratings. Part of this difference may stem from the fact that survey questions stressed the visibility and understanding of existing signs rather than whether the signs were missing; trained observer ratings also considered missing signs.

The Nashville and St. Petersburg results indicated more problems with the adequacy of street signs and markings than were anticipated. For example, in Nashville in 1974, 31 percent of the driver-respondents indicated that traffic signs were "sometimes" or "often" difficult to see or understand. The most frequently mentioned problem with traffic

signs, cited by a third of that 31 percent, involved signs blocked from view. Another example was that 35 percent of the drivers found pavement markings hard to see "fairly often" or "very often." However, the largest problem category was in street name signs; 43 percent found them "sometimes" or "often" hard to see or understand. These initial results suggest that the conditions indicated are reasonably prevalent, and that a procedure for tracking progress in their reduction is likely to be needed.

Measure 15: Percentage of (a) drivers, (b) businesses who feel frequently (or infrequently) inconvenienced by blocked lanes.

Blocked lanes are, of course, inconveniences to street users and can be a safety hazard as well as source of irritation. Although records of government public works projects could be used to monitor the frequency and magnitude of such disruptions, Measure 15 provides more subjective information on the extent of citizen feelings about being inconvenienced.

A blocked lane may be defined as one in which drivers are forced to divert at least partly out of the lane to avoid an obstruction. Blocked lanes may be caused by construction or major repairs either in the street or immediately adjacent to the street. Street lanes also may be blocked by vehicles that are double-parked.

Data Collection. Trained observers could obtain data on blockages along with information on other street characteristics. In the trained observer test in Nashville, however, only two or three of the random sample of 500 streets were found to have a blocked lane. For many communities such as this, it probably is not worthwhile to exert effort on monitoring such obstructions, at least not on a regular, on-going basis. Still, in places where problems are suspected and where governments are undertaking a regular citizen survey, a question could be included to obtain respondent ratings of this problem.

The issue of blocked lanes was not considered sufficiently important to include in the Nashville citizen survey, but the following question was included in the St. Petersburg survey: "Have you, yourself, been inconvenienced by street lanes blocked by construction in the last twelve months?" This could have been followed up by questions as to where and what type of lane blockage seemed to cause any problems reported.

In response to the above question in 1973, 15 percent of the drivers surveyed stated that they encountered lane blockages fairly often or very often, and another 22 percent stated "once in awhile." A total of slightly more than one-third of the respondents were inconvenienced at some time during the previous twelve months. Almost half of the St. Petersburg drivers surveyed in the central and northern parts of the city, which were areas with the most construction, felt they were inconvenienced at least occasionally by blocked lanes, whereas only about a quarter of the citizens in the southern two areas felt there was a blockage problem. These data are certainly not conclusive but do suggest that the problem is sufficiently prevalent in some jurisdictions to warrant inclusion of Measure 15.

An illustrative question on street and sidewalk blockages for use in a survey of businesses is shown in Question 6 of Appendix 2.

Measures of Environmental Quality (Measures 16-18)

Air and noise pollution are generally considered important potential problems for transportation systems. Thus regular monitoring of air quality and noise levels by jurisdictions with actual or incipient pollution problems seems very desirable. It was beyond the scope of this effort to examine this highly specialized area, but a few suggestions appear below. For the most part, these are general air and noise pollution measures; whenever possible, efforts should be made to relate them to transportation sources.

Measure 16: Air-pollutant levels attributable to transportation sources; number of days air pollution exceeded "hazardous" threshold; and number of persons possibly exposed to hazardous levels.

Air pollutants of potential concern include hydrocarbons, nitrogen oxides, ozone, and carbon monoxide. The last is primarily a vehicle-related pollutant. The other three types of gases are generated by both vehicles and other sources, and separating out the contributions from transportation alone is a problem. To minimize the influence of nontransportation sources, these measurements should probably focus on geographical areas likely to be most affected by vehicle emissions.

Pollutant levels can be expressed in terms of the following:

1. The average levels of various pollutants in the air at various times of the year, distinguished if possible as to the approximate amount generated by transportation sources;
2. The number of days when various pollutants exceed designated "hazardous" thresholds; and

3. The number of persons exposed to hazardous levels of pollutants.[20]

Data Collection. Local governments have been steadily improving the number and precision of air pollution measurements, using both stationary and mobile monitoring stations. The latter might be especially useful for measuring along heavily traveled arterials. It would also be desirable to calculate the number of persons exposed to air pollution. Maps showing the distribution of various levels of pollution over a geographical area could be overlaid on a population density map to estimate the number of persons affected by various pollution levels. Few communities now make enough measurements to develop directly such overlays.

Rather than using actual measurements, some communities employ pollution dispersion models based on such factors as traffic counts, the local mix of automobiles of various ages, and meteorological conditions that can be used to make estimates of pollution contours, and the population affected. The U.S. Environmental Protection Agency has been experimenting with several models, but the reliability of their estimates, especially in terms of providing sufficient detail for developing contour maps, is still under study.

Although it has not been included as a measure here, governments with a regular citizen survey might want to obtain the following information:

> Percentage of citizens who state that they are bothered by polluted air in their neighborhoods frequently, occasionally, or rarely.

Citizen perceptions of the severity of pollution in their neighborhoods reflect the aesthetically objectionable aspects of pollution, such as visible smoke, haze, and bad odors. In view of the inadequacy of air pollution measurement systems and models, these citizen perceptions are useful in obtaining information on pollution. But citizens are not likely to be able to distinguish transportation-caused pollution from other causes; not can they identify the extent to which individual transportation modes are responsible.

---

20. These thresholds can be federal, state, or locally defined standards. Considerable national research is underway to define levels that are hazardous to humans. A new air pollution index, Pollutants Standards Index, has been developed by the federal government. It provides a procedure for gauging air quality on a scale from 0 to 500, based on the levels of carbon monoxide, oxidants, particulates, sulfur dioxide, and nitrogen dioxide in the air. The scale will permit interpretations meaningful to the general public: "good" air will fall in the 0-50 range; "moderate" air, 50-100; "unhealthful," 100-200; "very unhealthful," 200-300; and "hazardous," above 300.

The general citizen survey in St. Petersburg in 1973 included the following questions: "Are you ever bothered by polluted air in this neighborhood?" If so, respondents were then asked to indicate whether they were bothered almost daily, at least once a week, or less than once a week. No air pollution question was included in the Nashville survey.

Measure 17: Percentage of street miles with traffic noise above "x" decibels, by residential (or nonresidential) areas and by type of street.

Measure 18: Percentage of citizens stating that they are bothered by traffic noise in their neighborhoods frequently, occasionally, or rarely.

These measures are intended to be complementary. The first provides "objective" measurements of the amount of noise, while the second offers citizens' perceptions of the extent to which citizens felt bothered by noise.

Data Collection. Noise levels can be physically measured with such monitoring equipment as an "A-weighted" noise meter used at selected points along a sample of city streets. These streets might be selected to indicate the different conditions in business and residential areas and along some of the most heavily traveled arterials with an adjacent residential or work population. Depending on the nature of local traffic conditions, physical measurements might be made at various times of the day, days of the week, and seasons of the year in order to reflect noise fluctuations.[21] To adapt this method for gathering measurement data on different areas of a city, it would probably be desirable to designate measurement points at a standard distance from the roadway and certain height above the ground (for example, five and one-half feet).

An alternative to physical measurement is to estimate noise based on traffic volume and other factors by a method described in the Department of Housing and Urban Development Noise Assessment Guidelines.[22] Although developed to assess alter-

nate sites for proposed public housing, this method seems applicable to regular monitoring of noise levels. Its estimates are based on the volume and composition of traffic on selected streets, and on the existence of barriers between the observation point and roadway. The noise level is estimated by using a series of nomographs and charts. Although these noise assessment guidelines have been tested, the application suggested here has not.

For Measure 18, Questions 8 and 8a in Appendix 1 can be used. The first provides information on the percentage of respondents bothered by traffic or construction noise with various frequencies over the previous twelve months. Question 8a attempts to obtain from the respondents information on the perceived major cause of the noise; this is an effort to distinguish various transportation modes from other causes.

The surveys in Nashville and St. Petersburg indicated that citizens were willing to distinguish types of noise that bothered them, but no measurements of actual noise levels were made that could have been compared to survey results.

Measures of Pedestrian Travel (Measures 19-21)

Measure 19: Percentage of blocks with sidewalks in satisfactory (or unsatisfactory) condition.

Measure 20: Percentage of citizens satisfied (or dissatisfied) with the adequacy and condition of the sidewalks in their neighborhoods.

Measure 21: Percentage of citizens who feel street lighting in their neighborhoods is insufficient, about right, or too bright.

Pedestrians also have concerns relating to local government transportation services. In addition to safety from traffic accidents (see Measures 5 and 6), the adequcy of sidewalks (Measures 19 and 20) and of street lighting (Measure 21) are also of concern.

Measure 19 is an "objective" rating of sidewalk conditions, using the trained observer procedure already discussed in terms of road conditions, the condition of signs and signals, and street cleanliness. An illustrative scale for rating sidewalks as to their convenience for pedestrians is included in Appendix 13. For further discussion of the procedures, see Chapter 13.

The results of the initial trials in Nashville indicated that the reliability of sidewalk ratings by the trained observers was about as good as trained

21. Much literature exists on techniques of noise measurement and on the correspondence of noise levels to human perceptions. For example, see T. J. Schultz, "Noise Assessment Guidelines—Technical Background," prepared for the Department of Housing and Urban Development by Bolt, Beranek, and Newman (Washington, D.C.: U.S. Government Printing Office, 1972).

22. T. J. Schultz and Nancy M. McMann, *Noise Assessment Guidelines,* prepared for U.S. Department of Housing and Urban Development by Bolt, Beranek, and Newman (Washington, D.C.: U.S. Government Printing Office, 1971).

observer ratings of other matters. Of twenty-five blocks rated by two observers, twenty pairs of ratings (that is, 80 percent) were identical, and four pairs were in disagreement by only one level. The ratings on one block were two levels apart; a hazard in an otherwise good sidewalk was missed by one observer.

For Measure 20, data can be obtained from the general citizen survey shown in Appendix 1 using Questions 11 ("Are there enough sidewalks in the neighborhood?") and 12 ("Are the sidewalks in the neighborhood in good condition?"). These questions were used in both the Nashville and St. Petersburg surveys. A question similar to Number 5 in Appendix 2 might be used in a survey of businesses to rate the condition of sidewalks in front of their establishments.

The results of the initial trials in both test cities indicated that significant proportions of citizens were not satisfied with present sidewalk conditions. About 60 percent of Nashville respondents and 50 percent of those in St. Petersburg reported there were too few sidewalks.

The results from the citizen survey (Measure 20) and from the trained observer ratings (Measure 19) were generally consistent. Together they indicated a significant percentage of sidewalks with poor walkability. For example, in two areas of Nashville with substantial numbers of sidewalks, almost one-quarter of the citizens (half of those who said they had sidewalks in their neighborhood) said those sidewalks were not generally in good condition. The trained observers found that from one-quarter to one-third of the sidewalks in those two areas posed potential safety hazards to walking (condition 3 on the trained observer scale in Appendix 13). Another quarter to one-third of sidewalks were rated as presenting some walking discomfort (condition 2).

For Measure 21, the adequacy of street lighting, data can also be obtained from the general citizen survey using Question 10 of Appendix 1. The trials in both test cities indicated that significant percentages of citizens were not fully satisfied. In Nashville, 39 percent rated lighting "too low," 1 percent "too bright," and 57 percent "about right." In St. Petersburg, the corresponding figures were 27, 1, and 71 percent.

Another approach to assess street lighting would be to measure the amount of light with a photoelectric meter. Preliminary work by Indiana University has indicated some but not very good correlation between citizen perceptions and physical readings.[23] If a citizen survey is undertaken on a regular basis, that approach seems to offer a better way to measure citizen satisfaction with street lighting.

23. See Vernon Green, "An Analysis of the Relationship Between Citizen Perceptions and Physical Measures of Street Lighting," Workshop in Political Theory and Policy Analysis, Research Report No. 7 (Bloomington: Indiana University Department of Political Science, n.d.).

This chapter discusses effectiveness measures and data collection procedures for public mass transit, both bus and rail. A general statement of transportation objectives and a summary of the principal measurement approaches proposed, applicable jointly to public mass transit and other local government transportation procedures, has been presented at the beginning of the previous chapter. In addition, the previous chapter also presented measures jointly applicable to public mass transit and other transportation services: a measure of the overall accessibility of citizens to places they want to go (General Transportation Measure 1 of the previous chapter); overall air and noise pollution effects (General Transportation Measures 16-18); and overall safety (General Transportation Measures 5-9).

It is beyond the scope of this report to examine all of the complex factors comprising citizen satisfaction with, and preferences for, public transit as distinguished from automobiles.

Individual Transit Measures

The measures discussed in this chapter are shown in Exhibit 9-1. Some appear relevant to other forms of public transportation—such as taxis and dial-a-rides—that were not considered in this work.

For government officials primarily concerned with a general picture of transit services in their jurisdictions, the overall measures of citizen satisfaction (Measures 17-19) may be sufficient. The other measures discussed here permit an examination of many of the major components likely to affect this satisfaction.

Rapid Movement (Measures 1-3)

Measure 1: Travel times between selected key origins and destinations.

Travel times represent one factor influencing citizens' use of and satisfaction with mass transit. Especially important is the comparison of transit travel times with private auto travel times. To emphasize this comparison, transit times can be expressed both in minutes and as a percentage of auto travel times for the same trip.

Most of the discussion of travel times covered under General Transportation Measures 1-4 also applies here. Selected origin-destination pairs for which travel times would be estimated preferably should be the same as, or a subset of, those used to assess vehicular transportation in general (see General Transportation Measure 2).

The emphasis of Public Transit Measure 1 is on area-to-area rather than door-to-door travel times. Thus in-vehicle times from one transit stop to another would be used. The accessibility (walking distance and time) of transit stops to residences is discussed in Measures 4 and 5.

Travel times should be of particular interest for year-to-year comparisons of the same trips and for measuring the combined effects of changes in (1) road network and traffic controls, (2) transit vehicle routing, and (3) special expediting features such as transit-only lanes, transit-controlled traffic signals, and changes in types of community activities.

Exhibit 9-1
EFFECTIVENESS MEASURES FOR PUBLIC MASS TRANSIT

OVERALL OBJECTIVE: To provide access to desired destinations in a quick, convenient, safe, and comfortable manner with minimum harmful effects on the environment.

OBJECTIVE	QUALITY CHARACTERISTICS	SPECIFIC MEASURE	DATA SOURCES
Rapid Movement	Travel times	1. Travel times between selected key origins and destinations.	Transit schedules and test runs
	User satisfaction	2. Percentage of users who rate travel times as satisfactory.[1]	General citizen or user survey
	Nonuser dissatisfaction	3. Percentage of nonusers who state that travel time is a reason for nonuse.	General citizen survey
Convenience/ Reliability	Accessibility of service	4. Percentage of (a) residents, (b) work force within "x" feet of a transit stop.	Calculations based on maps of transit stops and population distribution
	Reliability (dependability)	5. Percentage of runs that (a) are missed altogether, (b) vary from schedules by more than "x" minutes.	Transit inspector or other independent trained observer for a sample of runs
	User satisfaction	6. Percentage of users who rate factors related to convenience and reliability as satisfactory.	General citizen or user survey
	Nonuser dissatisfaction	7. Percentage of nonusers who state that factors related to convenience or reliability of transit are reasons for nonuse, tabulated by factors cited.	General citizen survey
Comfort	User satisfaction	8. Percentage of users who rate factors related to riding comfort as satisfactory.	General citizen or user survey
	Nonuser dissatisfaction	9. Percentage of nonusers who give factors related to riding comfort as reasons for nonuse, tabulated by reason.	General citizen or user survey
Safety	Frequency of traffic accidents	10. Number of accidents per 1,000 vehicle-miles driven.	Accident reports
	Casualties from traffic accidents	11. Number of (a) deaths, (b) injuries per 1,000 passenger-trips and per 1,000 passenger-miles.	Accident reports
	Property loss from accidents and crimes	12. Dollar loss from (a) accidents, (b) vandalism and other crimes, per 1,000 vehicle-miles driven.	Accident and crime accident reports
	Crime rate	13. Number of crimes committed against persons (a) on-board (b) at stops, per 1,000 passenger-trips.	Crime incident reports; victimization surveys
Environmental Quality	Air pollution	14. Percentage of transit vehicles that do not comply with local air pollution standards (or, preferably, the percentage of vehicle-days of noncompliance).	Periodic testing of vehicles
	Noise pollution	15. Percentage of transit vehicles that do not comply with local noise standards (or, preferably, the percentage of vehicle-days of noncompliance).	Periodic testing of vehicles using noise meters
Overall citizen satisfaction/ Usefulness	Usage	16. Total and per capita number of passenger trips.	Fares collected
	Usage	17. Percentage of population using service more than "x" times per month.	General citizen or user survey
	Mode choice	18. Percentage of all motor vehicle passenger-trips made by transit.	Origin-destination surveys
	Citizen satisfaction	19. Percentage of citizens who rate transit service as satisfactory, tallied by extent of transit use.	General citizen or user survey

1. "Satisfactory" ratings may be changed to "unsatisfactory" when that appears more meaningful to local officials.

Data Collection. If found to be reliable, transit schedules can be used to estimate travel times for selected origins and destinations. Reliability can be checked internally by the transit department, using driver- or inspector-derived data on starting, mid-route, and end times for a sample of runs. Schedules can also be checked independently by trained observers riding a sample of runs. Volunteers from among city employees who normally ride the bus might be used as a third source for validation.

For trips requiring transfers, the waiting time between legs of the trip should be included in the trip time. Working from transit schedules, the scheduled arrival time of the next available vehicle reaching a midway transfer point would be used to compute the time for the final part(s) of the trip.[1] When there is a choice of routes, the one yielding the shortest travel time should be used, though this may not be the shortest trip in length.

Most stops are not listed on transit schedules. When an origin or destination point is not shown on a schedule, the time of arrival at the selected stop can be estimated from arrival times at the closest up-route and down-route stops appearing on the schedule.

The procedure described above was used in an initial trial by the St. Petersburg Transit Department, and required two person-days of effort. A summer intern, guided by a transportation analyst, worked from bus schedules to estimate travel times between 120 origin-destination pairs. The transit department felt the schedules were reasonably reliable, based on their own internal checks. The selected pairs were origin-destination connections of ten residential areas or origins and twelve business, shopping, or hospital areas (destinations) chosen in coordination with the traffic department.

Each trip was computed from the same starting time each day. Other jurisdictions may wish to compute different types of trips for different times of day—for example, residential to shopping areas at off-peak times and residential to work areas at peak times.

As a byproduct, the analysis of travel times revealed some scheduling problems, such as long waits to make certain transfers.

Measure 2:   Percentage of users who rate travel times as satisfactory (or unsatisfactory).

1. The inconvenience of transferring is reflected in Measure 6, and the overall effect of transferring convenience and travel time should be reflected in Measure 19, overall citizen satisfaction.

Measure 3:   Percentage of nonusers who state that travel time is a reason for nonuse.

Although Measure 1 provided an "objective" measure of travel times, another important gauge is the perceived satisfaction level of users and potential users in terms of travel times. Measure 2 provides information on user ratings, and Measure 3 focuses on travel times as a reason for nonuse.

Data Collection. General citizen surveys can be used to collect data on both of these measures. Alternatively, for Measure 2, a survey of transit riders could be used.[2]

A question such as Number 15c in Appendix 1 can be used to obtain the data for Measure 2. Although Questions 18 and 19 in the same appendix could be used for Measure 3, we suggest instead a question worded as follows: "Which, if any, of the following are reasons you did not ride city buses more often? (1) service not frequent enough, (2) bus stop too far from home, (3) bus takes too long, (4) too many transfers required, (5) buses don't run on schedule, (6) fares are too high, (7) waiting conditions at bus stops are poor (no shelters or benches; areas muddy or dusty), (8) danger of crime at bus stop, (9) can't find out when and where buses run, or (10) prefer to go by automobile (or bike).[3] This ques-

2. We did not test such a procedure, but occasional on-board surveys are undertaken by many transit systems and others. If the local government undertakes a general citizen survey, as was done in St. Petersburg and Nashville, questions on transit can be asked at a low added cost. However, because many respondents may not have used the transit system, ratings for Measure 6 obtained from a general citizen survey might have to be based on small sample sizes. For example, in the Nashville 1974 and 1975 citizen surveys, only about 23 percent of the respondents had used the area's bus service in the previous twelve months; thus, about 230 of 1,000 respondents were able to provide ratings for transit from a user's perspective. In St. Petersburg, where a smaller total sample was run, about 31 percent of the respondents had used the city bus service at least once during the previous year; however, ratings were asked only of those who had used them at least once a month, or 133 of the 627 persons interviewed.

3. The wording shown in Questions 18 and 19 in Appendix 1 is not recommended because the response "prefer to go by automobile" was permitted as a preference *to the exclusion of other responses.* The initial trials in Nashville indicated that this response predominates when it is permitted in this way. This response appears to hide the many reasons *why* the respondents prefer to go by automobile. The suggested wording (used in the St. Petersburg survey) asks respondents to rate each option *separately* or, if "prefer to go by automobile" is included, to ask respondents to indicate why they prefer the automobile. In the 1973 and 1974 St. Petersburg surveys, 85 to 90 percent of respondents indicated preference for automobile but the response "bus trip takes too long" was rated by about 20 percent of the respondents as a reason for nonuse. ("Takes too long" was the single highest reason among those respondents were asked about; the other reasons explored were very similar to those listed under Questions 18a and 19a of Appendix 1.) Questions 18 and 19 have since been dropped from the Nashville surveys.

tion would be further strengthened if respondents were asked to indicate whether each reason was "a *major* reason" or "a *minor* reason."

The number of "bus takes too long" responses to the question just cited would yield the data for Measure 3. Other measures such as 7 and 9 use data from other responses to the same question.

Governments also should probably compare the relative importance of the various reasons for nonuse of the public transit service. However, since in-depth questions of respondents is not undertaken in these surveys, the reasons given for nonuse should be considered only as rough indications of problems.

The findings in both Nashville and St. Petersburg suggest that transit services have trouble helping citizens "to get where you want to go in a reasonable amount of time." These findings indicate the desirability of including a time gauge such as Measure 2 in a rating effort. In Nashville, the 1974 survey found 43 percent of transit users rating this factor as "fair" or "poor" (rather than "good" or "excellent"). In 1975, after considerable local attention to transit conditions, that figure dropped to 26 percent. In St. Petersburg in 1973, 26 percent of nonusers rated transit travel times only fair or good.

One minor problem is in defining the term "nonuser." The definition appears to be chiefly a matter of judgment and the individual jurisdiction's preference. Nashville defined a "nonuser" as a respondent who did not use the buses at all in the previous twelve months. St. Petersburg also used the previous twelve months as a reference interval, but for Measure 3 included as nonusers those who had used city buses less than once a month (about an additional 10 percent of the respondents). Similarly, St. Petersburg asked for user ratings under Measure 2 only from those who had used buses at least once a month during the previous twelve months.

Convenience—Reliability (Measures 4-7)

These measures cover four aspects of the convenience and reliability of transit services. Measure 4 focuses on the proximity of transit stops to the population; it includes a variation that reflects transfer frequencies, the assumption being that transfers can be a major inconvenience. Reliability, or dependability, is often considered a major concern for transit users, and that is the focus of Measure 5. Although Measures 4 and 5 can be considered "objective," ultimately it is the users' and potential users' viewpoints on convenience that are important. User ratings of convenience are sought by Measure 6, while nonuser ratings of inconvenience as a reason for nonuse are the focus of Measure 7.

Measure 4:   Percentage of (a) residents, (b) work force within "x" feet of a transit stop.

Variation A: Percentage of residents within "x" feet of a transit stop from which they can travel to within "y" feet of key destinations in less than "z" minutes.

Variation B: Percentage of residents within "x" feet of a transit stop from which they can travel to within "y" feet of key community destinations with one transfer or less.

This measure attempts to gauge the degree to which public transit is physically convenient to the population. But the proximity of citizens' residences to transit stops does not mean that transit vehicles go where citizens want to go within a reasonable time; thus Variation A is included. Also, because the need to transfer is likely to be a special inconvenience, Variation B is included.

Data Collection. Measure 4 can be estimated by using a map of transit stops overlaid on a population density map, which can be obtained from U.S. Bureau of Census data and updated by city or county planning department estimates. A circle can be drawn around each stop, with a radius equal to one-fourth or one-eighth of a mile, or whatever walking distance is chosen as the criterion for "x" in the measure.[4] The population within the circles is then estimated.

A simplified procedure, tried in St. Petersburg, can be used as an approximation for areas of the community in which stops are close together and circles overlap. All persons residing within a quarter mile (or whatever value is chosen for "x") of the transit line would be counted as near a stop.

Some communities do not have maps of every transit stop for buses. Such maps must be prepared as a first step in the data collection procedure, unless the stops are close enough together that the approximation described above can be used.

When possible, barriers in citizens' paths to bus stops (such as freeways, streams, or railroads) should be considered, and not just the straight-line distance; this consideration will, however, complicate the computation.

In the St. Petersburg experiment, Measure 4 took two person-days to compute, with Variation A requiring an additional person-day. The computa-

---

4. Lower values of "x" (that is, shorter walking distances) can be used as criteria for areas where the elderly are concentrated.

tions were made by a summer intern in the transit department.

About 90 percent of St. Petersburg's population was estimated to be within one-fourth of a mile of a transit route (Measure 4). And 70 percent of the city's residents could get to each of the twelve selected key destinations with a walk of less than one-fourth mile at each end (Variation A). These findings meant that 20 percent more citizens had access to a stop than could get to the selected destinations within the time limit set. Thus, Variation A seems to add a potentially important dimension to the measurement of service accessibility.

The computations for the St. Petersburg transit system were made immediately after a major change in the design of routes for the entire system. The measure seems particularly useful for determining the before-and-after conditions of that type of change.

The accuracy of Measure 4 is limited primarily by the accuracy of population estimates by block or area of the city. The validity of Variation A also is limited by these population estimates, and by a city's ability to select an adequately representative set of destinations.

For Variation B, the procedure would be very similar to that in Variation A, except that instead of computing travel times, one would count the number of transfers for each origin destination-pair. The measure would require little additional time to obtain—perhaps half a day of staff time.

An option in this process is to calculate Variation A allowing only one transfer per trip.

Measure 5:   *Percentage of runs that (a) are missed altogether, (b) vary from schedules by more than "x" minutes.*

A particularly important aspect of convenience in transit service is dependability, which enables transit users to avoid excessive waiting and generally to arrive as scheduled.

Transit officials obviously do not have complete control over punctuality and reliability. Variations in weather, traffic conditions, accidents, the number of passengers, and driver illnesses can play a major role. However, punctuality and reliability also are affected by other factors that transit managers do control. These include vehicle maintenance, proper scheduling, safe driving, and management of substitute drivers and buses.

Runs that are missed altogether, that is, dropped from the schedule without advance notice, might be reported separately from the percentage that are early or late. On routes with relatively infrequent service, missed runs represent potentially greater inconvenience to riders than do early or late arrivals. Typically, missed runs will comprise a much smaller number than early or late runs, so these particularly inconveniencing incidents might be lost in the overall statistics if they are not reported separately.

Data Collection. The raw data for Measure 5(a) are usually collected routinely by transit dispatchers or inspectors, although normally they may not be summarized.

Data collection for Measure 5(b) could consist of sampling arrival times at one or more mid-route points and the route terminus for a sample of runs. These times would then be compared with route schedules to obtain data for the measure. Times might be gathered by vehicle drivers,[5] trained observers stationed at measurement points, or volunteers who normally ride buses. Data should be collected on several days, preferably throughout the year.

Probably the main data collection difficulty is in choosing a representative sample of runs and measurement points along each run. The sample runs monitored for Measure 5 might be the same set used to compute travel times in Measure 2, or a random sample of runs might be selected, perhaps with extra weighting given to those runs carrying a heavier passenger load.

These procedures were not tested during the project period.

Measure 6:   *Percentage of users who rate factors related to convenience and reliability as satisfactory (or unsatisfactory).*

Convenience and reliability are basically subjective qualities. Both this measure and the next one are based on citizen perceptions. The first focuses on the views of citizens who have used the service over some past length of time such as twelve months, while Measure 7 focuses on nonusers.

Convenience- and reliability-related factors that users can be asked to rate in terms of satisfaction include: frequency and reliability of service, ability to obtain schedule and route information, ability to reach desired destinations without transferring, closeness of bus stops, and waiting conditions at bus stops.

Data Collection. Data can be obtained through the same general citizen survey used for other

---

5. Drivers can collect data on a much larger sample of runs and points along runs than trained observers can, but self-reporting has the inherent problems of bias and possible interference with driver duties.

measures or by a special survey of transit users, as discussed under Measure 2. Questions such as Numbers 15 a, b, d, f, and g in Appendix 1 can be used to obtain the data. Respondents could be asked for an overall rating of "convenience and reliability," but because the terms can be interpreted in many different ways, it is suggested that the various components be rated individually. This will also provide more information to help determine needed government actions.

Measure 7: Percentage of nonusers who state that factors related to convenience or reliability of transit are reasons for nonuse, tabulated by factor cited.

Persons identified in a general citizen survey as not using transit services can be asked about their reasons for nonuse. Such information may suggest problem areas; however—as we have cautioned earlier—correcting a problem cited frequently as a reason for nonuse may not lead to significantly increased use.

Data Collection. Data can be obtained through the same general citizen survey used for other measures. As discussed under Measure 3, the kind of question used in St. Petersburg seems advisable: "Which, if any, of the following are reasons you do *not* ride city buses . . .?" Respondents also can be asked to indicate major or minor reasons. For Measure 7, respondents would be asked about the following: (1) service not frequent enough, (2) bus stop not close enough to home, (3) too many transfers required, (4) buses don't run on schedule, (5) can't find out when and where the buses run.[6]

The reasons given most often by nonusers in the 1973 St. Petersburg survey were: "takes too long to go by bus" (data for Measure 3), 20 percent; "too many transfers required," 13 percent; and "service not frequent enough," 12 percent. For each of items (2), (4), and (5), about 6 to 7 percent of the nonusers gave these as reasons for nonuse.

Reasonableness tests applied to the data seem to support the general validity of the findings. For example, the northwest area of Nashville was essentially without transit service. Some 76 percent of the commuter nonusers and 73 percent of other nonusers residing in the northwest area mentioned lack of access to services as one of the three most important reasons they did not use transit services. These

figures compare with an overall citywide total of about 25 percent of each group of nonusers.

Comfort (Measures 8-9)

Measure 8: Percentage of users who rate factors related to riding comfort as satisfactory (or unsatisfactory).

Measure 9: Percentage of nonusers who give factors related to riding comfort as reasons for nonuse, tabulated by reason.

Comfort is clearly a concern to both users and potential users of transit services. These measures include such aspects as crowding (including having to stand), temperature, noise, odors, cleanliness, smoothness of ride, seat comfort, and possibly driver helpfulness and courtesy. Both on-board and waiting conditions at stops are relevant.

Measure 8 provides users' ratings of public transit services as to their perceived satisfaction with the various aspects of comfort. Measure 9 indicates the percentage of nonusers who cited the lack of certain aspects of rider comfort as a reason for their nonuse.

Also considered in this project were "objective" measures such as (1) those reflecting the frequency with which riders had to stand during some portion of the runs; (2) trained observer ratings of on-board conditions such as cleanliness, noise, and smoothness of ride; and (3) tallies of the percentage of transit stops where there were no benches or shelters.

On balance, the direct feedback from citizens appears more meaningful and comprehensive; including the "objective" measures seems to constitute "overkill." Nonetheless, the more objective measures may be attractive to some jurisdictions.

Data Collection. The general citizen survey (Appendix 1) can be used to obtain the data for both these measures. For Measure 8, questions such as the following can be used: Questions 15e (driver helpfulness and courtesy), 15h (waiting conditions at bus stops), 16a (vehicle temperature), 16b (on-board odors and cleanliness), and 16c (smoothness of ride). Not provided for in Appendix 1 are ratings of on-board crowding, seat comfort, and noise, but these could readily be added.

For Measure 9, as for Measures 3 and 7, nonusers could be asked to indicate "Which if any of the following are reasons you did not ride city buses. . .?" Various comfort reasons such as those listed above can be addressed. In the 1973 St. Petersburg survey, for example, "Poor waiting conditions at bus stops

---

6. This list is based on Question 5 of the 1973 St. Petersburg survey. The full questionnaire is included in our initial report. The wording above is preferred to the wording in Questions 18 and 19 of Appendix 1.

"(no benches or shelter)" was indicated by 13 percent of the nonusers interviewed. That rating was about as high as or higher than most of the various convenience factors (see Measure 7).

In both the St. Petersburg and Nashville surveys, users gave generally good marks to the various comfort factors. One exception was "waiting conditions at bus stops." In Nashville, both the 1974 and 1975 surveys showed 24 percent rating them as "poor" and another 34 percent (1974) or 24 percent (1975), "fair." (St. Petersburg did not include this item in its user rating questions.)

Safety (Measures 10-13)

Measure 10: Number of accidents involving transit vehicles per 1,000 vehicle-miles driven.

Measure 11: Number of (a) deaths and (b) injuries per 1,000 passenger trips and per 1,000 passenger miles.

Measure 12: Dollar loss from (a) accidents, (b) vandalism and other crimes, per 1,000 passenger-miles.

Measure 13: Number of crimes committed against persons (a) on-board, (b) at stops, per 1,000 passenger-trips.

Measures 10-12 are the rates of accidents, dollar property losses, and deaths and injuries, respectively, which indicate the safety of transit operation. Most of the discussion under General Transportation safety Measures 5 to 7 also applies here. However, somewhat different bases or denominators are suggested for transit vehicles. Public Transit Measures 10 and 12 call for the number of accidents and dollar loss per 1,000 vehicle-miles driven, and reflect safety from the viewpoint of the reliability of the vehicle-driver system. Public Transit Measure 11 considers safety from the viewpoint of the rider; it is stated as a rate per 1,000 passenger-trips or passenger-miles.

In general, these tallies should reflect all incidents involving a transit vehicle—even though other modes of transportation may also be involved.

Losses from vandalism and other crimes, included in Measure 12, often are significant in public transit, and should be measured to indicate the intensity of the problem and the government's effectiveness in preventing these crimes.

Measure 13 is included to reflect the occasional problem of crimes involving transit vehicles and passengers. These crimes may deter usage, especially at night or in certain areas. Procedures requiring drivers not to carry cash on buses may reduce some types of crime, such as robbery.

Data Collection. Data on vehicle-miles traveled, the number of passenger-trips[7] and estimates of passenger-miles traveled are already routinely available in most transit agencies. Also routinely collected are data on the number of accidents (Measure 10), the number of deaths and injuries (Measure 11), and the cost of repairing damage due to accidents and vandalism (Measure 12).

For Measure 13, crimes against the transit service itself (for example, robberies or assaults against the driver, refusal to pay the correct fare, and disorderly behavior) might be tabulated separately from those committed against riders. Data for Measure 13 might be obtained either from driver reports or police department records. It is important to note that current recording methods in most police departments do not allow simple identification of on-board crimes; some changes in recording procedures of the police or transit agency might be needed to facilitate data collection.

An additional approach would be to obtain ratings from respondents to the general citizen survey as to their "feeling of security" about transit services, with respect to both crime and accidents. For example, the percentage of respondents indicating that a reason for nonuse of public transit was "danger of crime at bus stop" (see discussion under Measure 3) could be used as an additional measure.

Environmental Quality (Measures 14 and 15)

Measure 14: Percentage of transit vehicles that do not comply with local air pollution standards (or, preferably, the percentage of vehicle-days of noncompliance).

Measure 15: Percentage of transit vehicles that do not comply with local noise standards (or, preferably, the percentage of vehicle-days of noncompliance).

General Transportation Measures 16-18 provide estimates of air and noise pollution levels from all sources, along with rough estimates of amounts resulting from individual modes. These measures would help indicate changes in overall pollution levels that occur after changes in the mix of transportation modes.

7. This is usually estimated by dividing total fares collected by the average fare charged, rather than by actual on-board counts.

It also seems desirable to monitor the pollution generated by each mass transit vehicle, especially pollution that is visible, smelly, and likely to offend motorists and pedestrians. Air and noise emission levels from each vehicle can then be compared to preselected standards in order to provide tallies of the percentage of vehicles that do not meet the air (Public Transit Measure 14) or noise (Measure 15) emission standards. If such measurements are taken often enough, estimates of the number and percentage of vehicle-days of noncompliance can be obtained.

Data Collection. Neither air nor noise pollution measurements were tested in our effort. However, some tentative suggestions for data collection follow. For air pollution, the exhaust from transit vehicles might be rated for its "blackness" or opacity. This could be done by using trained observers and a smoke density rating scale similar to the Ringlemann Charts, which rate emissions from smoke stacks. Even simpler, the observer could note on a possible four-part scale whether there is an extreme amount of obnoxious exhaust smoke, a considerable amount, a small amount, or none at all. This scale might be based on a photographic rating guide, showing the various exhaust conditions.

Conditions could be tested with vehicle engines at idling, accelerating, and cruising speeds, since conditions (especially the amount of visible smoke) may vary with these changes. Devices exist for making pollution measurements directly from vehicle exhausts; at least one local government, the city of Chicago, is already using them. Transit vehicles might be tested with such devices at least once a year to see if they are within local and federal standards.

With regard to noise, sound generated by transit vehicles while idling, while accelerating from "0" to some specified miles per hour, and while operating at cruising speed could be measured and compared to locally set standards for tolerable levels. The location of sound meters in the test is a matter for expert judgment. Consideration might be given to choosing meter placements that will correspond to a typical distance between pedestrians on the sidewalk and a bus on the street. Calibrating noise meter levels by using a panel of citizens to distinguish degrees of unpleasantness in transit noise remains to be tried.

Overall Citizen Satisfaction (Measures 16-19)

Measure 16: Total and per capita number of passenger-trips.

Measure 17: Percentage of population using service more than "x" times per month.

Measure 18: Percentage of all motor vehicle passenger-trips made by transit.

Measure 19: Percentage of citizens who rate transit service as satisfactory (or unsatisfactory), tallied by extent of transit use.

Overall citizen satisfaction is perhaps the most important issue in measuring transit effectiveness. Two basic types of measures seem appropriate: (1) the degree to which the service is actually used (Measures 16-18), and (2) citizen perceptions of the adequacy of that service (Measure 19).

Usage is commonly used as a gauge of transit performance.[8] Most local government officials will probably continue to measure performance by usage as long as public transit is considered a way to reduce both congestion and air and noise pollution. It can be argued that many users, such as the poor and the elderly, are captive audiences, however, and that usage alone is not a good indicator of satisfaction.

Measure 16, the number of passenger-trips, is the traditional measure. Measure 17, the percentage of the population who have used the transit service (that is, the number of different users), is not now in general use, because of the lack of data for it. Measure 18 is a direct attempt to measure the proportion of motor vehicle trips made by the transit service; this can be considered an effectiveness measure if one assumes that it is important to shift vehicle trips from the automobile to transit vehicles. Measure 19, like Measure 17, is not currently in general use; it provides ratings of citizens' overall levels of satisfaction with transit service.

Transit measures described earlier addressed citizen perceptions of individual service qualities. Measure 19 attempts to measure overall satisfaction. In effect, this measure provides an integrated rating of all elements. A respondent might rate individual elements as poor but service overall as satisfactory, and vice versa.

Measure 19 will provide more insights if the information is disaggregated by the extent of transit usage (for example, transit used at least weekly, less than weekly, rarely, or not at all). A typical question might be: Do regular riders rate the overall service

---

8. Of course, the revenues obtained are critical to government officials, especially as compared to expenditures. (Even for private transit systems, governments commonly have to make up the deficits.) However, these measures are not measures of "effectiveness" as defined here, and therefore are outside the scope of this report.

higher (or lower) than do those who rarely use the transit system?

Data Collection. Data on the number of passenger trips made by transit (Measure 16) usually are available in most jurisdictions. The data are often approximations based on total fares divided by the average fare, and may not include passengers who ride free of charge.

Data for Measure 18, the percentage of trips made by different modes, probably requires origin-

Exhibit 9-2

TRANSPORTATION MEASURES CALLING FOR DATA FROM THE GENERAL CITIZEN SURVEY

QUALITY CHARACTERISTIC	MEASURE NUMBER	ILLUSTRATIVE QUESTION FOR OBTAINING THE DATA (APPENDIX 1)
General Transportation	*Exhibit 8-1*	
Accessibility	1	—*
Safety: Feeling of security in driving	9	—*
Street rideability conditions	11	9
Parking convenience	12	3
Visibility of traffic signs and signals	14	4, 5, 7
Inconveniences because of lane blockages	15	—*
Noise pollution	18	8
Sidewalk conditions	20	11, 12
Adequacy of street lighting	21	10
Public Transit	*Exhibit 9-1*	
Satisfactory travel times—users	2	15c
Satisfactory travel times-nonusers	3	18, 19**
Convenience—users	6	15a, b, d, f, g
Convenience—nonusers	7	18, 19**
Comfort—users	8	15e, h, 16
Comfort—nonusers	9	18, 19**
Use by different households	17	13, 14
Overall citizen satisfaction with transit services	19	20

*Appropriate questions for these measures were not included in the Nashville citizen survey, the questionnaire for which is reproduced in Appendix 1. However, illustrative questions are contained in the text.

**Because of problems caused by the inclusion of the response option "prefer to go by automobile," we do not recommend the wording used in these particular questions in Appendix 1. See the text for the suggested alternative wording.

destination studies (that is, citizen surveys in which household trips are analyzed). General citizen surveys can be used to collect data for Measures 17 and 19.

For data on the percentage of the population using transit services with various frequencies (Measure 17), questions such as Numbers 13 (usage by respondent) and 14 (usage by others in the respondent's household) can be used. Answers to the latter question will probably be less accurate because the respondent is asked to answer for other members of the household. A local government might want to interview each member of the household above a certain age, but this practice raises the survey cost.

For further insights, usage information might be grouped by the number of cars in the household, using a question such as Number 68 in Appendix 1.[9]

For Measure 19, a question such as Number 20 in Appendix 1 can be employed to obtain the citizens' overall ratings of satisfaction with local transit service.[10] Cross-tabulation of these data for Measure 19, by amount of usage and by access to private autos, can provide insights into how satisfactory the service is for persons with various levels of usage and degrees of dependency on it.[11] Question 13 (fre-

9. For the 1973 St. Petersburg survey data, we cross-tabulated the frequency of transit usage by the number of cars in the household. As expected, households with cars used transit service much less than households without cars, and the more cars owned by the household, the less the transit usage. For example, 71 percent of respondents in households with one car reported that they had not used public transit in the past twelve months; 88 percent of respondents in households with more than one car had not used it; but only 29 percent of those in households without cars had not used it.

10. In St. Petersburg's 1973 survey, 48 percent rated the bus service as either "excellent" or "good"; 22 percent rated it "fair" or "poor"; and 30 percent (mostly nonusers of the transit service) said "don't know." For the 1974 Nashville survey, the figures were 28 percent, 51 percent, and 22 percent respectively. These figures improved to 38 percent, 37 percent, and 25 percent in the 1975 Nashville survey (probably resulting from substantial efforts to improve the transit service).

11. For the 1973 St. Petersburg data, we cross-tabulated the overall rating of the bus service against the amount of public transportation use. Some 68 percent of all survey respondents reported that they had not used the transit service at all during the past twelve months, and 32 percent had used it at least sometimes. Of the latter group, 69 percent rated the service available to their household as "good" or "excellent," overall. Some 38 percent of those not using the service at all rated it "excellent" or "good"; that is, many nonusers thought the available service was good, but still did not use it. Whether their opinions were based on the experience of other members of the household, personal experience in the past, overall knowledge of service schedules, perceptions gained in other ways, or even on mere guesses, was not clear. As expected, a substantial number, 42 percent of those that had not used the transit service at all, said "don't know" rather than giving the service an overall rating. By comparison, only 11 percent of those that reported using the service less than once per month, 2 percent of those using transit less than once per week, and *none* of those using the service more than once per week said "don't know."

quency of riding buses) and Question 68 (number of automobiles in the household) in Appendix 1 could be used for these cross-tabulations.

Some Notes on the General Citizen Survey Procedure

A number of measures in this chapter and the preceding one call for data obtained from a survey of a representative sample of households in the community—nine of the twenty-one general transportation measures and eight of the nineteen public transit measures. Such a general citizen survey is discussed at length in Chapter 14. Exhibit 9-2 identifies the transportation measures that use data obtained from citizen surveys.

A principal obstacle to the use of citizen surveys on an annual basis is the potential cost. In other chapters, the citizen survey has been recommended as a procedure for obtaining feedback on many other local government services. Performance information on those other services and on transportation could be obtained in the same citizen survey. Thus the cost of the survey could be allocated among a number of services so that no individual one would face too large a financial burden. In addition, as discussed in Chapter 14, various "bargain basement" approaches seem possible in order to make the survey reasonably practical without unduly sacrificing precision or accuracy.

Chapter 10

Water Supply

The principal goals in water supply are prevention of waterborne disease and assurance of a supply adequate to meet demand. The traditional health concerns related to water were bacterial epidemics, such as cholera and typhoid, which modern water treatment methods can now prevent. More recent health concerns include a range of chemicals and organic poisons that enter the water from both industrial discharges and some natural sources. Viruses also cause worry, but no adequate procedures for their regular measurement or treatment now exist. In addition, a number of other properties of water are important because they may affect the water's suitability for drinking, bathing, washing, and cooking.

Local jurisdictions, therefore, will be concerned either explicitly or implicitly with health hazards, flow adequacy, and a wide range of water characteristics affecting citizens. They will treat these problems through purification, softening, fluoridation, taste and odor control, and the installation and maintenance of pipe and pumping capacity.

Some localities assume responsibility only for water they supply, leaving other water supplies to the supervision of state health departments; other localities take responsibility for all water their residents consume. The mix of public and private operations varies widely.

Water Supply Objectives

The following overall general statement of water supply objectives has been used in formulating the list of measures of effectiveness:

To provide an adequate supply of water that is free of health hazards, aesthetically acceptable, and of adequate quality for household, commercial, and industrial use. To provide prompt, courteous, reliable service and to minimize injuries and damage associated with the system.

Principal Measures and Measurement Procedures for Water Supply

Because of federal and state requirements, local governments already undertake extensive monitoring of various characteristics of the water supply. As of the summer of 1977, in fact, most tests of the water supply's freedom from health hazards will be federally mandated under the Safe Drinking Water Act of 1974. Most of the current and proposed testing requires considerable expertise in biological chemical processes; it is beyond the scope of this report to examine and evaluate these technical procedures.

Nonetheless, it remains the responsibility of government officials to protect the public welfare and to provide for adequate monitoring so that public officials can be alerted to potential major problems.

Our principal recommendations follow. A full set of measures is provided in Exhibit 10-1.

1. A principal concern regarding the water supply is that it be as free as possible of health hazards. As

Exhibit 10-1
MEASURES OF EFFECTIVENESS FOR WATER SUPPLY SERVICE

OVERALL OBJECTIVE: To provide an adequate supply of water that is free of health hazards, aesthetically acceptable, and of adequate quality for household, commercial, and industrial use. To provide prompt, courteous, reliable service and to minimize injuries and damage associated with the system.

OBJECTIVE	QUALITY CHARACTERISTIC	SPECIFIC MEASURE	DATA COLLECTION PROCEDURE
Health Hazards	Presence of substances linked to health risks	1. Number of presumed days per year that one or more water quality characteristics were below standard.[1]	Regular testing done by a qualified chemist using standard tests such as those of the American Public Health Association
	Evidence of waterborne diseases	2. Number of confirmed cases, if any, of waterborne disease among city population, with those due to public water supply separated from those due to other water supplies.	Reports from county and state public health departments
Aesthetic Quality	Presence of substances with adverse effects on appearance, taste, or odor	3. Number of presumed days that one or more aesthetic characteristics were below standard (testing for such qualities as turbidity, color, and chemicals like chlorides or sulfates that affect taste and appearance.	Regular testing by a qualified chemist
	Citizen perception of water quality	4. Percentage of persons who rate their drinking water as satisfactory (or unsatisfactory) in appearance, taste, and odor.	General citizen survey
	Rate of validated complaints about water aesthetics	5. Number of validated citizen complaints per 1,000 customers about drinking water appearance, taste, or odor, by type of complaint.	Tallies of reported complaints
Household Use Quality	Levels of water characteristics with effects on household use	6. Number of presumed days that one or more of the following characteristics failed to meet its standard(s): hardness and pH (cleaning effectiveness), and iron and manganese (staining).	Regular testing by a qualified chemist, using guidelines from sources such as the American Water Works Association. (Optional additional tests for alkalinity and corrosion)
Flow Adequacy	Restrictions on household or commercial usage	7. Number of days of restrictions on household and business water use, by type of restriction.	City and department records
	Citizen perceptions of flow problems	8. Percentage of (a) households, (b) businesses reporting problems with water pressure or flow, by type of problem.	(a) General citizen survey; (b) business community survey
	Rate of validated complaints about flow or pressure	9. Number of valid complaints about water flow per 1,000 clients, excluding complaints on matters shown to be private responsibility.	Tallies of reported complaints
	General flow adequacy	10. Percentage of fire hydrants surveyed that meet static water pressure standard of, for example, 40 pounds per square inch.	Annual inspections of the fire hydrants to assure their operational readiness for firefighting

(Exhibit continued on next page)

Exhibit 10-1 continued

OBJECTIVE	QUALITY CHARACTERISTIC	SPECIFIC MEASURE	DATA COLLECTION PROCEDURE
Service Adequacy and Responsiveness	Rate of validated complaints	11. Total number of valid complaints and requests for nonroutine service (not shown to be private responsibility) per 1,000 clients, by type of complaint (including billing overcharge, water quality, broken or leaking pipe or meter).	Tallies of reported complaints
	Citizen perception of adequacy of response to calls	12. Percentage of persons complaining or requesting service who were satisfied (or dissatisfied) with the handling of their complaints or requests by type of complaint.	Survey of a sample of persons complaining or requesting service
	Speed of response	13. Percentage of valid complaints and requests that are effectively responded to within an allowed period of time, overall and for each class of requests.	Revised forms for recording citizen calls and actions taken in response to calls

1. "Below standard" in terms of water quality usually means that pollutants are found to exceed certain limits.

already noted, much regular testing is required to meet national and state standards for various water characteristics. For regular performance measurement purposes, these tests will suffice if they are comprehensive and their results, particularly when deficiencies are found, are reported in a form comprehensible to top officials and the public. A community should use an explicit, nontechnical measure such as "the number of presumed days per year that the water quality failed to meet its standard" (see the discussion of Measure 1, particularly in Exhibit 10-2, for details). The measure takes into account the fact that most communities do not perform daily water tests.

A specific check list of water quality characteristics (that is, the various potential contaminants) should be identified and a health-related standard specified for each characteristic. As evidence on new contaminants permits identification of appropriate standards, these new contaminants should be quickly added to the list of those to be monitored. Complete agreement on appropriate standards will be rare, because evidence on effects of various contaminants is often spotty. Moreover, considerable variation exists in individual sensitivities to contaminants and in individual daily water consumption, which determines consumers' daily exposure to contaminants. Hence, a number of competing bases for set-

ting standards may be available. In selecting a standard, national standards can often be adapted for local government use. Once the biological or chemical test is made and the technical measure is determined, the additional resources required to compute this form of measure are nominal.

2. The second principal concern is that the supply of water be sufficient to serve the demand. To assess this, a measure of "the number of days of restrictions on household (or business) water use" is suggested. These would include such restrictions on the public as restrictions on watering lawns in summer or restrictions resulting from broken water mains or water shortages.

3. Missing from the effectiveness information available in most communities is regular feedback from the population as to their perceptions of the qualities of the water—its appearance, taste, odor, and flow (pressure). If the community undertakes an annual multiservice survey using a representative sample of households (as suggested in other chapters of this report), this information could be readily obtained at slight additional cost. This procedure has been used in St. Petersburg and Nashville.

4. The adequacy of the local government's responses to citizens' complaints and requests for service relating to the water supply is seldom assessed by communities. A survey of a sample of persons

who have complained or requested service could be undertaken. Each household surveyed could be asked whether the agency's response was generally satisfactory and whether the service was provided courteously and promptly. Billing problems, which constitute a large share of all complaints, should probably be distinguished from service complaints.

These surveys require some additional staff effort and resources. Illustrative questionnaires that might be used for such surveys are provided in Appendix 9. Neither the survey questionnaires nor the procedures for computing measures from the survey results, however, have been field tested. Some testing will be required before a government implements the procedure.

Individual Measures

The following discussion of proposed measures is organized under five headings—health protection (Measures 1 and 2), aesthetic quality (Measures 3-5), household use quality (Measure 6), flow adequacy (Measures 5-10), and service adequacy and responsiveness (Measures 11-13).

Health Protection (Measures 1-2)

Measure 1: Number of presumed days per year that one or more water quality characteristics were below standard.

Measure 2: Number of confirmed cases, if any, of waterborne disease among city population, with those due to public water supply separated from those due to other water supplies.

These two measures attempt to assess the actual impact on health (Measure 2) and the potential impact on health (Measure 1) of the public water supply and, to a lesser extent, of other water supplies serving the area. Measure 2 covers actual reported incidents of illness attributed to the water supply. Because it reflects the actual impact on citizens, it would be the best primary measure of health hazards except for the fact that many dangerous contaminants cause ill effects only after years of exposure. This means that a water department rated solely on incidence of disease could appear effective during long periods when it was actually endangering the future health of its citizens. Moreover, by the time disease effects began to appear, it might be too late to do anything to help those citizens who had

consumed city water for many years. Therefore, Measure 1, which measures the presence of substances related to health risks, is likely, in practice, to be a more sensitive measure than Measure 2 and is treated here as the primary measure.

For Measure 1, the tests that should be made regularly include those for the following: total coliform, carbon chloroform extract, lead, barium, cadmium, hexavalent chromium, selenium, silver, arsenic, cyanide, zinc, gross beta activity, radium, strontium, fluoride, nitrate, sodium, and possibly residual chlorine.[1] Tests for other pollutants should be added if new problems are suspected or as standards suitable for regular measurement become available.[2] The "number of days" referred to in Measure 1 is obtained by counting the number of days between the first test of the characteristic that shows it failing to meet its standard (or the start of year, if the characteristic ended the previous year over standard) and the first subsequent test showing that the characteristic is within standard (or the current date, if the characteristic has not yet been brought within standard). A water quality characteristic is "below standard," it should be stressed, when pollutants *exceed* certain prescribed limits.

The procedures to measure the contamination levels used in Measure 1 are well-established, well-tested practices given in the APHA's *Standard Methods for the Examination of Water and Wastewater*. But the particular form of the measure used here—based on the number of days after tests revealed problems until inspections showed these problems were corrected—is new and not known to have been tested anywhere. The reasons for this form are (1) to convert the technical measures of water quality into a form understandable to officials (and the public), (2) to reflect, at least to some extent, the *duration* of exposure to potentially hazardous water,[3] and (3) to reflect the speed of the local government's response to problems after they are detected. Exhibit 10-2 gives an example of the calculation of this measure. Note that when testing first shows a violation of the standard, the entire period of time since the last test that showed no violation

1. This list was the one recommended by the U.S. Public Health Service (PHS) as of 1974. Some changes may have been made in the list since then and communities should contact the PHS to obtain the latest list. For example, in 1974 standards for asbestos were first being considered, and a proposal to drop the carbon chloroform extract test—a general test of organic contamination—was under study.

2. A brief discussion of these contaminants is contained in Appendix 10.

3. The magnitude of hazard should be reported as supporting information, possibly in the form of the average test reading during any continuous period when a standard is not being met, expressed as a percentage of the standard.

Exhibit 10-2

SAMPLE CALCULATION OF "NUMBER OF PRESUMED DAYS THAT ONE OR MORE WATER CHARACTERISTICS WERE BELOW STANDARD" (MEASURE 1)[1]

During January all tests except those for lead and iron were within standards.

(a) Test on Lead in Water

January

Date	1	2	3	4	5	6	7	8	9	10	11	12	13	14	15	16	17
Testing reading	.01						.06	.06	.04						.02		
Did test show satisfactory conditions?	Yes						No	No	Yes						Yes		
Cumulative number of violation days							1	2									

Scenario: Normally, testing is performed weekly with a standard of 0.05 milligram per liter (mg/l). The test on January 7 showed a violation. Steps were taken to detect and cure the problem; at the same time, the testing schedule was accelerated to monitor the success of corrective actions. The test on January 8 still showed a violation, but the test on January 9 showed that the standard was again being met. The days on which the last test showed a violation were January 7 and 8, leading to a count of two days of violations.

(b) Test on Iron in Water

January

Date	1	2	3	4	5	6	7	8	9	10	11	12	13	14	15	16	17
Test reading	.1							.4							.2		
Did test show satisfactory conditions?	Yes							No							Yes		
Cumulative number of violation days									1	2	3	4	5	6	7		

Scenario: Normally, testing is performed weekly with a standard of 0.3 mg/l. The test on January 8 showed a violation. Steps were taken to detect the cause of the problem, but testing was not accelerated because this is a characteristic related only to household use, and hence not of critical concern. (This judgment is assumed only for purposes of this example; it is not recommended as a policy.) The next regular test was on January 15. It showed no violation. The days on which the last test showed violations were January 8 to 14, leading to a count of seven days of presumed violations.

(c) Combined Measure

For the combined set of water characteristics, there were eight days (January 7 to 14) when at least one characteristic showed a violation of its last satisfactory test. (On one of those two days, two characteristics were in violation.)

[1]This example also applies to Measures 3 and 6.

becomes suspect, in as much as the violation may have begun at any time in that period. By the same token, referring to test (b) in Exhibit 10-2, it is not known that the violation persisted every day from January 8 until the next test on January 15—but that is the presumption which it seems reasonable and useful to make.

In the form of the measure presented here, only the time *following* observation of a violation of standard is counted. Measure 1 thus reflects fairly accurately the speed of response to a problem once it has been identified, but it is likely to understate the actual duration of the problem. As an alternative, a government might prefer to count as *not* meeting standard all days back to the time the last test showed the characteristic to be meeting its standard. Or, it might split the difference. These two alternatives would reflect both the government's speed in responding to known problems and its speed in discovering problems; hence, they would probably create an incentive for more frequent testing to assure that long delays in discovering violations could not possibly occur.

The reason it is recommended here that violations be counted back only to the time the first test shows a violation is that some local governments have quite valid rationales for testing for chemicals only once a year, or even less often. If the public water supply has a well-protected, deep, groundwater source, safe from any risk of industrial pollution and located in an area where the local rock strata are not the kind that might lead to natural pollution, infrequent testing could be justified. This was the case in one of our test cities—St. Petersburg, Florida—and its officials did test infrequently. If a city that tests infrequently were to use a measure that penalized the city for some or all of the days from a first unsatisfactory test back to the last satisfactory test (in addition to the days between the unsatisfactory test and the next satisfactory test, which all forms of the measure include), then the only possible values for the measures would indicate "no problem" or "large problem." The setting of targets would then become a fairly meaningless exercise, because the delayed discovery periods would dominate the values of the measures, overshadowing any progress made in quickly correcting discovered violations.

Conversely, using the measures in the form recommended can create incentives to do too little testing or to tamper with the scheduling of the tests, even in communities where frequent testing is desirable. For example, a city that is downstream of a facility from which large amounts of pollutants are occasionally spilled might try to schedule its tests around those spills—postponing some tests if necessary—so as to conceal transitory problems. If testing for all pollutants is done at least once every two to three years at prespecified times the risks may not be too great, but generally annual or semiannual testing is recommended. All these tests except those covering organic contamination (coliform and carbon chloroform extract) are based on levels that produce *long-term* problems, and the standards include large safety margins. The coliform test is the one test for which the public health service standards also specify a strict minimum frequency of measurement according to population served. As long as inspection schedules match those called for by the standards, the population should be protected.

Whenever Measure 1 exceeds zero, information should be provided as to the substance(s) that exceeded standards, the dates of tests showing the violations, and the actions taken in response.[4] Breakouts of this measure by individual treatment plants are likely to be quite useful.

What standards should be used for each contaminant and how frequently should testing be done? These questions involve complex technical judgments about short- and long-term effects of different substances; they also involve judgments as to the degree of natural protection of the water source, how much risk is acceptable, and the financial costs of reducing the risk. An adequate review of these issues is beyond the scope of this report, but Appendix 10 presents a brief discussion of them.

For Measure 2, the "number of confirmed cases of waterborne disease" will normally be collected routinely by county health departments, which must supply such information to the National Center for Disease Control. The city or county can obtain reports on any incidents from the local health department. Health incidents are likely to be extremely rare or nonexistent for most local governments; not only were no such incidents or complaints identified in either St. Petersburg or Nashville in the 1973-74 period of study but none was recalled as having occurred in the past.[5] The measure should be retained, however, to monitor the major *potential* problem in water supply. No special expense seems required other than for the small amount of time necessary for an analyst to check periodically with the health department.

The cost of the measurements required by Measure 1 will be fairly low provided that testing is already being undertaken. These tests are desirable for the protection of the community even if a formal measurement reporting system as discussed here is not used. Therefore, no extensive attempts to

4. Furthermore, a list of substances that have not been tested at all in the previous twelve months should be provided, with the date of the last test and the scheduled date of the next test; this will provide a rough check to assure that some regular testing schedule is followed. Finally, dates and results (approval or disapproval) of any EPA tests of the water at interstate carrier sites (such as airports or bus terminals) should be reported.

5. A study of disease outbreaks attributed to drinking water between 1961 and 1970 found 128 cases nationwide, of which 34 came from public water supplies. See "Safe Drinking Water Act—1973," Hearings before the Subcommittee on Public Health and Environment of the Committee on Interstate and Foreign Commerce, U.S. House of Representatives, 93rd Congress, March 8-9, 1973, pp. 88-110. Infections encountered included hepatitis, typhoid, dysentery, gastroenteritis, amebiasis, shigellosis, salmonellosis, and giardiasis. (No cholera episodes were reported.) In addition, incidents of poisoning from pesticides, selenium, arsenic, hexavalent chromium, and antifreeze were reported. Almost all incidents involved improper cross-connections or other problems in the distribution system; very few incidents could have been detected at the treatment plant.

analyze testing costs were made in this project.[6]

In summary, each community needs to pay careful, regular attention to the design of its water-testing program—the choice of potential contaminants to cover, the specific standards established for each, and the frequency of testing. The proper bases for these decisions are technical information not discussed in this report. The concern here is with how best to report results to enable officials (and the public) to monitor potential health problems and progress in alleviating any that appear.

Aesthetic Quality (Measures 3-5)

Measure 3: *Number of presumed days that one or more aesthetic characteristics were below standard (testing for such qualities as turbidity, color, and chemicals like chlorides or sulfates that affect taste and appearance).*

Measure 4: *Percentage of persons who rate their drinking water as satisfactory in appearance, taste, and odor.*

Measure 5: *Number of validated citizen complaints per 1,000 customers about drinking water appearance, taste, or odor, by type of complaint.*

These measures provide three different perspectives on the aesthetic quality of the public drinking water supply. Measure 3 covers the number of days that the last test of some quality characteristic related to appearance, taste, or odor violated its standards—in a way similar to Measure 1. (The procedure illustrated in Exhibit 10-2 applies here as well.) It covers "objective" information related to aesthetic quality (although the standards are often based on taste/odor thresholds and thus are some-

what subjective). Measures 4 and 5 cover the subjective impressions of citizens. Measure 4 provides representative, communitywide data from a citizen sample, whereas Measure 5 reflects tabulation of the rate of episodes that citizens deemed serious enough to report. Measures 4 and 5 cover somewhat the same characteristics, but there are important differences in the readings obtained from solicited opinions and unsolicited complaints.

The procedures for collecting the data for Measure 3 are, like those in Measure 1, well established, well tested, and available in the APHA's *Standard Methods.*[7] The arguments in favor of the "number of days" measure are the same as for the components of Measure 1, except that here the impact of violations is likely to be short term. Fairly frequent measurement of at least the four basic factors of turbidity (reduction in light intensity), color (as it deviates from normal water color), taste, and odor appears to be warranted. If these tests are made, additional tests for specific dissolved minerals that contribute to taste and appearance problems can be undertaken less often, since grave problems with any of these dissolved materials will show up as taste, odor, or appearance problems as well.[8] Neither test city has tried recording these data in "number of days" form, but neither city has had recent violations.

The U.S. Public Health Service has standards for odors, turbidity, and color; the standards for odor should help assure the absence of objectionable tastes as well.[9] Measurement of temperature is not

---

6. An Environmental Protection Agency estimate of the cost of doing the tests in their labs once requisite water samples are in hand indicated that the tests for most pollutants can be performed in about 2.5 employee-days at a cost for labor and materials of about $200 (1973 prices) or about $270 in 1976 prices. The most expensive test is carbon chloroform extract (about one employee-day, or about $52 at 1973 prices); most others involve about one employee-hour or less. (Based on information from James E. Warren, Water Supply Division, Office of Air and Water Programs, U.S. Environmental Protection Agency, July 19, 1973.) For the semiannual testing program recommended by the Public Health Service, the cost would be about five employee-days and about $400 per year (1973 prices) or about $540 in 1976 prices. Some local governments, such as those served by rivers subject to industrial pollution, will want to perform measurements far more often—weekly or daily—and the costs will rise accordingly. The test city of Nashville, which is downstream from a few industrial effluent sources, performs most tests daily.

7. The specific tests that appear relevant for Measure 3 are for turbidity (appearance), color (appearance), odor, taste, chlorides (taste), sulfates (taste), copper (taste), and methylene-blue-active substances (taste and appearance). Tests for aluminum (appearance) and uranyl ion (taste, appearance) might also be included.

8. The more variability a particular measure shows—whether it violates a standard or not—the more frequently it needs to be measured to assure that the maximum remains below an acceptable level.

9. The generally accepted practice in treatment of water for aesthetic purposes is to use the natural condition of the water as a standard. It is known that most natural water has some taste, turbidity, and color, but not such as to cause concern. Of the substances that should be monitored, sulfates and chlorides, or mineral salts, account for the taste of mineral waters. The U.S. Public Health Service's recommended limit of 250 milligrams per liter (mg/l) for each of those groups of substances is intended to insure that the water will have no foul taste or laxative effect, either for area newcomers or for long-time residents.

Similarly, methylene-blue-active substances (MBAS), the water-surface-tension-breaking agents used in detergents, are known sources of foaming and foul taste in water. The suggested limit of 0.5 mg/l is set below the point at which taste effects increase sharply with the concentration of the substance. The limit for copper of 1.0 mg/l is set at its taste threshold. For both these substances, the American Water Works Association goals are more restrictive (.01 mg/l for MBAS substances and 0.2 mg/l for copper) and, therefore, more likely to assure that even the most sensitive persons in the community have no problems.

included in Measure 3, even though the temperature of the water supply is important to its aesthetic quality. Our reason is that the temperature is likely to be virtually uncontrollable by the city. The cost of lowering the temperature for the quantities of water involved in a municipal water supply operation would be quite high, especially relative to the benefits to be derived. Only in rare instances in which placement of pipes leads to exposure to direct sunlight can the temperature be changed at an acceptable cost. Temperature is, nonetheless, included under Measure 4.

Problems can, of course, arise anywhere along the water distribution system—from its original source, through the public distribution system, and in the private distribution components, such as pipes in private homes and buildings. For this reason, tests at various points in the distribution system are desirable to identify the locations of problems. A question arises as to whether such tests should be made in private households, where public responsibility is less clear and public access cannot be commanded. To provide a partial test of the water supply as it reaches the public, one public agency has suggested testing at such readily accessible locations as gas stations.

For Measure 4, the data are obtained from a survey of a representative sample of the citizens of the community. Questions 55, 55a, and 55b of Appendix 1 can be used to obtain the data for this measure. Such a survey is likely to be impractical if limited to questions on water quality. If a government undertakes a survey covering a number of government services, as suggested throughout this report, however, the additional cost of questions on water supply issues should be quite small. The citizen survey procedure is discussed at greater length in Chapter 14.

Question 55 attempts to rate the overall satisfactoriness of the water supply in terms of taste, odor, appearance, and temperature. Question 55a asks those respondents who were *not* satisfied to identify the specific water characteristic(s) to which they objected. Question 55b asks about the frequency of the problem identified in Question 55a. The wording of these questions remains imperfect. For example, information as to the *degree* of dissatisfaction with each particular problem is not requested. In addition, these questions refer only to the quality of drinking water, not the adequacy of the water for other household uses. (Questions with regard to the latter were omitted because respondents were believed to be less able to separate problems in the water itself from problems caused by

other factors such as the choice or amount of detergent. In both Nashville and St. Petersburg, constraints on the overall length of the survey also prevented more extensive questioning.)

As is likely in most communities, a large percentage of respondents in both cities indicated satisfaction with their water. (In Nashville 8 percent and 10 percent of the respondents rated their drinking water as unsatisfactory in 1974 and 1975, respectively. In St. Petersburg, where a slightly different question asking about any complaints was used, just under 20 percent of those interviewed in the 1973, 1974, and 1975 surveys indicated complaints with the taste, odor, or appearance of their drinking water.)

Question 55a, or some similar question, is desirable to try to identify the specific reason for dissatisfaction, so that officials can better determine possible problems and corrective action. The primary cause for dissatisfaction cited in both cities was the taste of the water. Many taste complaints are attributable to the chlorine used to disinfect the water, particularly at dead ends of the distribution system where the chlorine may separate from the water, and to dissolved material dislodged by construction activity. These were, in fact, the principal causes of aesthetic problems in complaints filed in both test cities.

Because citizens may become accustomed to the taste of their water and thus insensitive to it, cross-community comparisons of survey results are risky. Nevertheless, even desensitized persons may detect significant adverse changes. For Measure 4, it may be particularly informative to compare the responses for citizens who have recently come to the community to those of longer-term residents. Question 1 of Appendix 1 could be used as a basis for cross-tabulating the responses to Questions 55 and 55a.

For Measure 5, the number of validated complaints about the drinking water can be obtained by tallying complaints reported by citizens. Although most jurisdictions have procedures for the processing of complaints, tallies by type to provide a record of the trends in complaints are less common. As discussed elsewhere in this report, complaints cannot necessarily be considered representative of the level of concern in the population because of the limited conditions under which citizens will complain. (This is why Measure 4 is needed; proper sampling procedures can provide representative information.) Reported complaints do, however, provide convenient data for tracking major drinking-water problems of concern to a segment of the population.

Levels of Water Qualities with Effects on Household Use (Measure 6)

Measure 6: *Number of presumed days that one or more of the following characteristics failed to meet its standard(s): hardness and pH (cleaning effectiveness), and iron and manganese (staining).*

Measure 6 covers the quality of the water for household uses other than drinking. The arguments in favor of using the "presumed days of unsatisfactory quality" form of the measure are essentially the same as those indicated for Measures 1 and 3, that is, the need to present test results in a manner understandable to public officials and to focus on problem areas needing attention. Fairly frequent testing of these qualities is probably warranted, especially if the water is softened. These tests can be completed in about one employee-hour,[10] so the cost is minimal.

Procedures for the four tests that appear appropriate are provided in the APHA's *Standard Methods.*[11] Neither of the two cooperating cities has tested the use of the "number of days" form for the measure, but both currently measure the qualities regularly. The procedure for translating the results of these tests into Measure 6 is illustrated in Exhibit 10-2 although the procedure was actually applied to Measure 1. The additional cost for these tallies should be quite small.

Flow Adequacy (Measures 7-10)

Measure 7: *Number of days of restrictions on household and business water use, by type of restriction.*

Measure 8: *Percentage of (a) households, (b) businesses reporting problems with water pressure or flow, by type of problem.*

Measure 9: *Number of valid complaints about water flow per 1,000 clients, excluding complaints on matters shown to be private responsibility.*

Measure 10: *Percentage of fire hydrants surveyed that meet static water pressure standard of, for example, 40 pounds per square inch.*

These measures provide four different perspectives on the question of the adequacy of water supply

10. Based on information from James E. Warren, Water Supply Division, Office of Air and Water Programs, U.S. Environmental Protection Agency, July 19, 1973.

flow and pressure. Measure 7 permits tracking of a major impact of inadequate flow—restrictions on households or businesses in their water use. It should be noted, however, that these restrictions usually are not set by the water department; furthermore, they generally reflect problems of access to supply that the water department cannot solve on its own. Restrictions seldom occur in most communities, but flow problems may show up in less dramatic ways—for example, in flow or pressure problems in households and businesses. Measure 8 provides information on the water flow problems as perceived by a representative sample of households, and possibly businesses. Measure 9 uses tallies of reported citizen complaints on water flow problems. Although data on reported complaints (unlike the information collected for Measure 8) cannot be as-

11. Tests for iron and manganese (as well as for hardness and pH) are included here because their PHS-suggested limits (0.3 mg/l for iron and 0.05 mg/l for manganese) are based on the concentration required to stain laundry. The American Water Works Association limits for both are stricter: 0.05 mg/l for iron and 0.01 mg/l for manganese. Both substances may also have taste effects in larger concentrations.

Hardness is a measure of the propensity of water to form deposits on clothes washed in carbonate-based detergents (as opposed to phosphate-based detergents). The carbonate combines with calcium or magnesium to form deposits that precipitate onto clothes during the spin cycle. Hardness is a measure of calcium, magnesium, and other minerals available for precipitation. It is expressed in terms of calcium carbonate equivalents, as calcium carbonate is by far the most common precipitate. From the standpoint of cleaning, then, the softer the water is, the better it is.

This simple relationship has been complicated in recent years by the discovery that soft water and heart disease are strongly correlated. No one yet knows whether the cause of the correlation is the softness itself or one or more of the many related conditions of the water.

For policy purposes, there is the problex that the range of acceptably hard water for cleaning (about 80 to 100 mg/l of calcium carbonate equivalent) is well within the range of softness that is correlated to heart disease (up to about 200 mg/l). Local governments do not now take steps to harden naturally soft water, and no organization has recommended that they should. Hence, the standard for hardness can be set in terms of an upper bound only. There are no generally accepted upper bounds, but by combining various sources, a value of 120 mg/l can be selected as a reasonable limit. If a lower bound is later deemed to be desirable, a value of about 80 mg/l is a reasonable limit, based on a variety of published sources.

For pH, which measures hydrogen ion activity, there is again a correlation with alkalinity and acidity. Many different ranges of acceptable pH levels exist and there appears to be no basis to choose among them. Scores of chemical processes are affected by pH, but their sensitivities to changes are quite different. A pH of 7.0 is neutral and so all ranges of acceptability are built around 7.0. (Measures of pH are expressed without units.) There is no generally accepted recommended range, but combining the recommendations of several sources leads to a possible range of 6.5 to 8.3. The prevailing practice in most local jurisdictions is to try to keep the pH fairly close to the natural level, whatever that may be, to avoid excessive costs and injury to local fish life. Hence, pH monitoring is employed only to assure that industrial wastes do not produce any sizable shifts.

sumed to be representative of problems occurring throughout the community, this information is readily available and likely to provide a rough indication of major flow problems of concern to at least a portion of the population. Measure 10 uses measurements of water pressure at fire hydrants to provide an indication of the adequacy of flow at a number of fixed points in the distribution system. (Since fire fighting is an important use for the water supply of every jurisdiction, this measure directly reflects the operational readiness of fire hydrants for fire fighting.)[12]

Measure 7 is intended to tally incidents of water restrictions; each incident is weighted by its duration but not by the number of households and businesses affected, because that information does not appear to be generally available at reasonable cost.[13] It would include bans on watering lawns and outages due to broken water mains. The number of such incidents seems likely to be small in most communities; yet, in the Nashville 1974 and 1975 citizen surveys, about 10 percent of those interviewed indicated that they had been without water for at least one hour at least once over the preceding year (see Measure 8). Nashville reported no restrictions on water usage in recent years, but St. Petersburg, the other test city, had experienced a ban on watering lawns. There the "number of days" measure was not used, but the information that could be used to construct it was recorded separately—the fact that a ban had existed and the date it had gone into force. In any local government, the cost of recording this measure is likely to be quite small.

Changes in the annual rainfall should be taken into account in interpreting the occurrence of restrictions. Restrictions may reflect unusual weather rather than failure of an operating component of the municipal water supply system.

Measure 8 is important because interrupted or reduced water flow can be a considerable irritant for households and businesses. The frequency of such interruptions in service as perceived by users is a major indication of flow adequacy. A survey of a sample of households and businesses can be used to provide statistically reliable estimates of the perceived prevalence of these problems. Data for this

measure would be obtained from the same citizen survey used for Measure 4. Questions such as 56, 56a, and 57 of Appendix 1 can be used to obtain this information from a representative sample of households. For businesses, questions such as 37, 37a, and 37b of Appendix 2 can be used. (The citizen and business surveys are discussed further in Chapters 14 and 15, respectively.)

Although water pressure and flow are probably as important to citizens as water aesthetics (see Measure 4), they are harder to measure accurately because inadequacies in pressure or flow can take many forms, ranging from chronic low pressure to occasional short-term stoppages. The survey questions ask about the existence of any problem during the past year (the assumed interval between surveys), then about the nature of the problem, and finally about the frequency of its occurrence. Tallies by type of problem are particularly important here. Many, if not most, pressure and flow problems originate in deficiencies in private plumbing or in demands upon the system for several simultaneous heavy uses. Identification of the types of problems encountered is intended to provide at least some evidence of whether the responsibility for the problems is public or private. The check list provided in Question 56a (Appendix 1) probably can be improved by the use of more probing questions about the nature of problems to pinpoint sources. The cost of collecting this measure will be a part of the cost of the survey.

Both St. Petersburg and Nashville have used questions such as these in their citizens' surveys. The Nashville survey's Question 56a as to the nature of the problem was added because surveyors suspected that many complaints cited in the first St. Petersburg survey stemmed from private sources—such as household plumbing—and therefore were not the responsibility of the city.[14] Certain kinds of problem descriptions are more likely than others to reflect public system inadequacies.

Measure 9, the number of complaints (as discussed under Measure 5), may be of limited value in reflecting the perceptions of all citizens, but data for it are usually readily available and it is worth tracking for that reason. Usually complaints about flow or pressure adequacy can be easily tallied to provide a

12. A number of other, more detailed standards on flow are required by the American Insurance Association, which rates cities for fire insurance purposes. Some of these other standards could also be incorporated into regular measures of effectiveness.

13. If a jurisdiction believes reasonably accurate estimates of the number of households and businesses affected could be obtained without excessive costs, such figures could also be used to weight each incident in terms of the scope of the restriction (that is, an outage affecting fifty families would be more severe than a similar outage affecting ten).

14. For the Nashville 1974 and 1975 surveys and St. Petersburg 1973, 1974, and 1975 surveys, the range of those reporting flow problems was 6 to 17 percent. The problem cited most frequently by the Nashville respondents in both surveys was that pressure was "always too low." In the Nashville surveys, 11 percent of all respondents in each year indicated that they had been without water for at least one hour at least once during the previous year.

gross indicator of major problems for at least the "vocal" citizens.

The information for Measure 10 is based on regular (at least annual) inspections of fire hydrants already performed by most local governments in order to maintain their fire insurance ratings. Thus the additional cost of this measurement is likely to be very small. Fire-hydrant water pressure is both relevant to fire-fighting usage and indicative of the pressure provided nearby homes and other buildings.

Different goals or standards of pressure can be set for different water uses. A pressure commonly used for fire-fighting purposes, which places the highest demand on flow, is 40 pounds per square inch (psi). For domestic purposes, a lower standard such as 30 psi might be appropriate. Below 30 psi, some machinery requiring water, such as washing machines and dishwashers, may not receive the pressure they require.[15] At pressures below 20 psi, there is danger of backwashing—that is, water moving opposite to the intended flow in places—and associated water contamination. A standard somewhere between 30 and 40 psi will be in accordance with established practices.

The two test cities both perform these fire-hydrant inspections and tally the results, but they have preferred to present the data in terms of average, minimum, and maximum readings rather than the percentage failing to meet a given standard. St. Petersburg, which had a goal of at least 40 psi for its hydrants, was meeting it in most areas, but it was not reporting the number or percentage of hydrants that fell short. Nashville had no precise goals. Because its terrain is hillier and its population more scattered than those of St. Petersburg, a goal of 40 psi would be harder for Nashville to meet. Nashville officials said pressures stayed above 35 psi and that the lower pressures were confined to outlying areas that had not expressed a willingness to pay the cost of obtaining higher pressure.

The Insurance Service Office of the American Insurance Association periodically rates each city's water system for fire-fighting purposes. These ratings are infrequent, however, and some simple, annual measurements by every city are needed to supple-

15. The 40 psi *static* pressure is a commonly used, simple reference standard that approximates the more elaborate standards for required flow over a particular duration as stated in the American Insurance Association's grading schedule for urban water supplies.

For non-fire-fighting needs, AWWA uses a reference of 30 psi *residual* pressure at the point of use, to be monitored by meters near the points of use. See *Willing Water* (American Water Works Association, Inc., New York: May 1971).

ment this more comprehensive rating. The use of fire hydrants as test points, rather than some sample of household taps or a sample of points leading up to households but short of the private property line, is recommended for two reasons. First, measurement at the tap would present serious access and measurement procedure problems and, more seriously, would confuse public and private responsibility. Second, measurement at points just outside the property line would be fairly difficult to do and would cost more than the hydrant test which will have to be done anyway for fire insurance purposes.

Service Adequacy and Responsiveness (Measures 11-13)

Measure 11. Total number of valid complaints and requests for nonroutine service (not shown to be private responsibility) per 1,000 clients, by type of complaint (including billing overcharge, water quality, broken or leaking pipe or meter).

Measure 12: Percentage of persons complaining or requesting service who were satisfied (or dissatisfied) with the handling of their complaints or requests, by type of complaint (for example, billing complaints).

Measure 13: Percentage of valid complaints and requests that are effectively responded to within an allowed period of time, overall and for each class of requests.

These three measures cover three aspects of adequacy and responsiveness of water supply service, with "service" used in the limited sense of government maintenance of the system and response to customers' requests. Measure 11, the rate of valid complaints per 1,000 customers, is a measure of service effectiveness in preventing problems. Measure 12 reflects the citizens' own perceptions of how well the government responds to their requests. Measure 13 provides information on the government's response time in resolving requests for assistance, an aspect of service quality that lends itself to the collection of "objective" information.

Measure 11, the rate of valid complaints, can be used to track problems of at least the vocal segment of water supply customers, as discussed with regard to Measure 5 (complaints on drinking water quality) and Measure 9 (complaints on water pressure and flow). However, reported complaints cannot be considered to represent reliably the views of all water customers. The rate of unreported complaints is likely to vary markedly over time and from place to place within the city. Yet, when reported complaints are tallied by subject, they do permit the government to identify patterns of problem areas that need more attention.

Although most governments have some provision for handling citizen complaints, few actually tally complaints as a monitor of performance. Tallying is complicated by the fact that complaints may be reported to a variety of places, such as the chief executive's office, the council, or the water supply agency. It is unlikely that procedures will be in place to bring all complaints together and to tabulate the valid ones. In St. Petersburg, a centralized service and information agency brought together many of the water supply complaints originating outside the water supply agency, but it had less success in tabulating complaints that did not pass through the centralized agency en route to the water agency. Nashville officials prepare a detailed list of all complaints by type, with all actions taken to validate and correct them. They do not total complaints by categories, but their list contains the information needed to make those calculations. Hence, although the measures were not fully tested in either city, the components of the procedures were in place and the crucial classification problems, in particular, had been resolved to some extent. A more extensive discussion of the processing and tallying of complaint data is presented in Chapter 11.

The measure is expressed as a rate per 1,000 customers to permit fairer comparisons over time, on the assumption that the number of complaints is proportional to the number of customers. Use of the rate is important chiefly to jurisdictions with significantly changing populations. Rates are also needed in making comparisons with regard to numbers of complaints from various segments of the population (such as those living in different neighborhoods)—to reflect different numbers of customers in each population segment.

Measure 12 gives an important type of feedback on the quality of government response to a citizen complaint (or request for routine service)[16]—the degree of complainant satisfaction with the government response. Citizen surveys of the whole population probably cannot provide this information because there are usually too few respondents who

have reported complaints in the past year.[17] Thus, it appears appropriate to ask customers who have received such service to rate it. Several aspects are relevant. In addition to a rating for an overall level of satisfaction, ratings can be obtained on specific aspects of quality, such as the promptness and courtesy of government employees.

The procedure suggested here is to survey a sample of persons who have actually called the government for water supply service. A series of questions such as those shown in Appendix 9 could be used. The questions were designed to obtain ratings on the convenience, promptness, courtesy, and satisfactoriness of the response to the complaint or request. Concerns over billing are also encompassed in the questions in Appendix 9. For Measure 12, responses to Questions 13 or 14 of Appendix 9 would suffice. The other questions focus on more specific aspects of the service quality.

This procedure has not been field tested. A government wanting to obtain such regular feedback from its clients should develop a questionnaire and fully test it for clarity and coverage of major types of complaints before using it to measure performance.

Telephone interviews should not require more than five to ten minutes each; they are recommended to assure an adequate return rate. Mail surveys have poor return rates, which make it difficult to assure that the final sample is representative of the population being surveyed. Personal interviews are much more expensive and probably unwarranted for a brief, narrowly focused survey like this.

Telephone interviews are sufficiently expensive that a government will probably want to interview only a random sample of complainants. Mail surveys cost relatively little, so forms could be sent to each complainant, possibly just after the department finishes responding to the complaint. If a mail survey is used, a shorter version of the survey in Appendix 9 would be necessary. If nonrespondents are contacted a second time and the overall response rate rises to 50 percent or better, the mail survey could prove adequate. (Telephone follow-ups of nonrespondents could also be undertaken to increase the response rate or at least to determine whether those not answering by mail appeared to have similar viewpoints to those who did.)

The required sample size will depend principally upon four factors: (1) the number of neighborhoods into which the jurisdiction is divided and

16. Some governments may choose to separate "complaints" from other "requests" (such as new hookups). See Chapter 11 for discussion of this distinction.

17. For example, a survey that samples one or two persons per 1,000 population in a city that receives a few thousand complaints a year is likely to reach fewer than ten persons who have complained in the past year. This is even more true of certain types of complaints, since most complaints will concern billing.

for which comparisons and results are desired; (2) the desired confidence level (which is a percentage such as 95 percent that measures the probability that the sample would show no significant difference in the answers given by two groups if there really were no difference in the attitudes or experiences of those groups when all their members were taken into account); (3) the degree of dissatisfaction in a group (or between groups) which the survey must show before management thinks it necessary to modify operations to reduce that dissatisfaction (or reduce the difference in dissatisfaction levels between groups); and (4) the total number of complaints or requests received. This issue and others related to client surveys, as well as general citizen surveys, are discussed further in Chapter 14.

Interviews could be spread out over the year or scheduled at one time during the year. Because households should be surveyed as soon as possible after "completion" of the service, spreading interviews over the year is preferable. If surveying is done only once a year for those served during the past year, some respondents might have trouble recalling how they felt at the time of their complaint.

Measure 13, the time it takes to respond to and complete requests for service, is important to those requesting service—whether the call is an emergency or not. Measure 12 takes care of this problem to some extent, in that ratings of overall satisfaction as perceived by customers are likely to reflect response time. In addition, the survey procedure can be used to provide customers' ratings on promptness; a question such as number 11 of Appendix 9 can be asked of those surveyed to provide this rating.

More "factual" data can be obtained by keeping records of response times. This is likely to require some revision of the forms for recording customer calls and actions taken in response to them. It is hard to know how much precision and accuracy in this information are necessary. Just when a request for service has been effectively resolved can be difficult to determine and subject to different operational interpretations. (This issue is discussed further in Chapter 11.) Response times should be broken down by whether the calls were emergencies or nonemergencies and probably by nature of the complaint or request.

No testing of this measure has been undertaken in this work. The reliability problems noted above would need careful attention. The costs are likely to be small unless a major effort is needed to determine when a service call has been resolved. Some start-up costs will occur as forms are revised.

Developing Measurement Data for Major Client Groups

Although the water supply tends to be "equally" provided to all parts of a local jurisdiction, certain localized geographical conditions can affect the water quality at the receiving end, and different groups may have slightly differing tastes. Thus, as with most other local government services, some disaggregation of the measurement data by major client groupings seems desirable—at least for some of the measures.

For almost all measures, computation of values for each geographical area of the community would permit potentially useful comparisons of service levels. Groupings by age, race, sex, and income group can be made only when such data are commonly available, as for the measures involving interviews with citizens (see Measures 4, 8, and 12). Differences in values among these groups will usually reflect either (1) residential patterns combined with varying levels of service to different areas or (2) differences in sensitivity that the city cannot control and may not feel it necessary to consider. Two exceptions are the acceptability of water for household uses—in this instance, women may be more knowledgeable than men—and adequacy of responses to complaints. In the latter case, however, demographic characteristics are not likely to be available.

Costs and Staffing Requirements

The major costs involved are those associated with the periodic testing of the various water characteristics (for Measures 1, 3, and 6), but such testing should be undertaken whether or not effectiveness measurement is undertaken. The other sources of potentially large costs are the general citizen survey (for Measures 4 and 8) and the survey of complainants and persons who have requested service (Measure 12). A general citizen survey will probably be undertaken only if several government services are included, in which case it would cost little more to obtain data for Measures 4 and 8. The client survey is likely to be the largest single added cost for the measures presented here. A telephone survey of perhaps 200 clients annually would cost about $1,600 (based on the estimate of $3 to $5 per telephone interview in Chapter 2, which involved a similar situation for interviewing plus equal amounts for tabulation and tallying and for analysis). Even this cost could be reduced as an out-of-pocket expense if a government has persons available who could do the interviewing during their normal working hours. Some minimum professional survey assistance is needed to assure that reasonably sound technical procedures are used in these surveys and that interviewers are trained properly.

Overall, with the qualifications noted above, the annual data collection costs for the most important measures (1 through 4, 6, 8, 12, and 13) are estimated at about $5,000 to $10,000 (1976 prices). Preparation of the other measures (5, 7, 9, 10, and 11) may add another $2,000 to $5,000 annually. These figures do not include time for data analysis, which is important but often neglected.

Chapter 11

Handling Citizen Complaints and Requests[1]

At one time or another, nearly every household has occasion to contact its local government. It may be

- *To complain about poor government service*—a missed trash collection, potholes, inadequate street lighting, or some other condition requiring corrective action;

- *To seek service or assistance*—a special pickup of bulk refuse; needed health and social services; or intervention in some situation the government might be able to influence, for instance, a tenant-landlord dispute or a consumer problem;

- *To seek information*—to find out about waste collection policies, to determine the impact of a new tax provision, or to learn about a specific government program or facility; or

- *To offer a suggestion or comment*—an idea for improving a particular service, a word of praise or appreciation, or an opinion on a government issue or action.

Complaints, requests, and suggestions like these constitute an important part of the day-to-day communication between local governments and the public. Increasingly, local governments are encouraging citizens to contact public agencies and officials directly with their complaints and concerns so that they can be dealt with quickly and constructively. Yet few governments systematically report on these communications and how they were handled. Al-

most no jurisdictions check on the citizen's satisfaction with the government's response to a particular complaint or request.

Jurisdictions differ in their approaches to handling citizen complaints and requests. Most local governments leave it to individual departments to process those items they receive. Some governments also provide special centralized facilities such as service and information offices, multiservice centers, "little city halls," or ombudsman offices for receiving, referring, and—if possible—resolving citizen complaints and requests. The effectiveness measures identified in this chapter appear applicable whether complaints and requests are handled by individual functional agencies or a central office.

Principal Measures and Measurement Procedures

For purposes of effectiveness measurement, it is recommended that citizen requests for services and information be distinguished from complaints. For the convenience of the reader, complaint measure numbers are preceded by a "C," request measure numbers by an "R."

Ten major effectiveness measures are suggested for assessing the handling of citizen complaints. (These measures are all listed in Exhibit 11-2.) The complaint measures address (1) the satisfactoriness of the jurisdiction's responses to complaints from the perspectives of both the local government and the

---

1. This chapter excludes citizen reports of crimes. The handling of complaints pertaining to crime is discussed in Chapter 6.

complainants (Measures C1 and C2); (2) the quality of the treatment received from government complaint-processing personnel as reflected in response time, courtesy, helpfulness, and fairness (Measures C3-C5); (3) the willingness and ability of citizens to make their complaints known to government officials as indicated by the number of legitimate complaints *not* reported to city officials and the ratio of reported to unreported items (Measures C6 and C7); and (4) the degree to which the overall need for citizen complaints is reduced, as indicated, for instance, by the combined annual incidence of justifiable reported *and* unreported complaints (Measures C8-C10).[2] Unreported complaints can be identified with the help of a general citizen survey.

The six measures proposed for assessing the handling of citizen requests are similar to the first six for assessing complaints. That is, they attempt to measure from various perspectives the satisfactoriness of the government's responses to requests for service and information (Measures R1 and R2), the speed and quality of the treatment received (Measures R3-R5), and the extent to which the public is inhibited from making such requests (Measure R6). (These measures are all listed in Exhibit 11-5.)

To support these complaint and request measures, the following measurement procedures are suggested for regular usage at least once a year:

1. A "user" survey—that is, a survey of citizens who have reported complaints or made requests for services—can be undertaken on a recurring basis. At some specified interval after the citizen's initial complaint or request, the government would ask all or a sample of citizens who had contacted it to rate the extent to which they were satisfied with the resolution of their complaints or requests and to evaluate various aspects of the service received. These include the government's response time, the courtesy and helpfulness of government personnel, the fairness of the treatment received, and the absence of bureaucratic red tape or "run-around."

   Such a survey could be conducted by telephone or by mail. Tallies made from the re-

sponses received would provide the appropriate performance measures (for instance, "the proportion of respondents satisfied with the resolution of their complaints," "the proportion experiencing 'run-arounds' or red tape," and so forth). Much of the work connected with the user survey (including both conducting the interviews and preparing the tallies) could probably be done by personnel from the local government's complaint/request office at little additional cost to the community.

2. A general citizen survey regularly can be used to canvass a random sample of citizens concerning their unreported complaints and their reasons for not reporting complaints and requests. This would provide data to help estimate the extent to which the local government's handling of complaints or requests encouraged and facilitated citizen reporting of legitimate matters. Estimates of both the number and percentage of previously unreported complaints and the percentage of persons inhibited from filing requests would be obtained.

   Such a general citizen survey would probably be too expensive for a local government if used only for assessing the handling of complaints and requests. However, if (as is recommended here) the government regularly undertakes a survey covering a group of government services, questions on topics such as the extent of and reasons for unreported complaints could be added to the general survey without significant additional cost.

   The main problem with using survey data as a source of information on unreported complaints is that of establishing whether the complaints elicited are really of concern to and within the jurisdiction of the government. Our initial examination indicates that some of the unreported complaints identified by the respondents are likely to be invalid or outside the government's jurisdiction. However, this tendency to exaggerate the number of unreported complaints is probably partly offset by the respondents' memory limitations. The problem of overcounting can also be alleviated to some extent, although at added expense, by screening the survey responses to eliminate clearly unjustifiable complaints. In any case, if used with proper caution, such estimates are probably meaningful for comparing data from one time period to the next.

3. Data on the incidence of unreported complaints (obtained from the general citizen survey) can be used to estimate the "total" incidence of justifi-

---

2. Note that in assessing the degree to which the need for citizen complaints is reduced, it is important to ensure that the government is not held responsible for frivolous matters or problems outside its jurisdiction. Moreover, the presence of such assessments must not tempt government officials to discourage citizens from reporting legitimate complaints in order to make the "need" for complaints appear to be falling. The latter possibility is reduced by monitoring citizen willingness and ability to make their complaints known (Measures C6 and C7). The former concern is addressed by focusing, whenever possible, on "justifiable" complaints. A suggested definition of a "justifiable complaint" appears in Exhibit 11-1.

able citizen complaints—whether or not reported to the government. The estimate of the total number of complaints would be obtained by adding the number of previously unreported complaints to the number of reported complaints. Changes in this figure from year to year would indicate whether the "need to complain"—that is, the total number of perceived problems within the government's jurisdiction—had increased or decreased. This would provide an indication of the degree to which problems (that is, justifiable citizen complaints) have been prevented. The validity of the number of unreported complaints would again be in question, but if the estimates are used with caution, they would appear to provide a better indication of the total number of problems existing in the local government than would be obtained by relying solely on reported complaints.

4. Existing records on complaints and requests can be used to get data for such measures as the number of justifiable complaints that are reported, the median response time, the percentage of excessive delays, and the satisfactoriness of the responses received (as viewed from the perspective of the local government). Regular preparation of such measures may require some relatively inexpensive modification of the forms, reporting requirements, and filing procedures used by the various offices.

The foregoing measurement procedures indicate the importance of having government personnel agree on (1) specific practical definitions of complaints as distinguished from requests for services and (2) the conditions under which a complaint should be considered justifiable. The formulation of and adherence to such definitions and ground rules for tallying complaints are especially important for jurisdictions that do not handle complaints or requests on a centralized basis. Exhibit 11-1 presents illustrative definitions for such items as "complaints," "requests for services and information," and "justifiable complaints."[3] Governments may also find it useful to categorize this information by the *type* of complaint or request. Exhibit 11-1 contains an illustrative listing of useful types.

In the following sections, specific measures and related data collection procedures are discussed, first for complaints and then for requests for service and information.

3. An operational definition of a "satisfactory response" (from the city's perspective) is suggested in the discussion of Measure C1; see also Exhibit 11-3.

The Handling of Citizen Complaints

The complaint-handling operation is usually concerned with three fairly distinct objectives:

1. **To provide an effective mechanism for responding to and—if technically and legally possible—properly resolving reported complaints with speed, fairness, and courtesy to the mutual satisfaction of the government and the complainant. This includes providing equitable treatment of citizens making complaints.**

2. **To encourage and facilitate the reporting of legitimate citizen complaints. This objective implies that the government needs to have an accessible system that permits citizens to conveniently make their complaints known to the proper government officials.**

3. **To reduce or prevent the occurrence of circumstances that lead to justifiable citizen complaints, whether or not they are reported to government officials. (Although this is an important objective for the government as a whole and for individual operating agencies, it may not be considered a specific responsibility of a central office for receiving complaints.)**

A government's approach to handling complaints will reflect its priorities among these objectives. Some governments may be especially interested in encouraging citizens to speak out, for instance, by providing central referral facilities, mobile complaint centers, and other "outreach" programs. These jurisdictions may therefore be primarily concerned with measuring accessibility. Local governments with an ombudsman may be especially anxious to ensure proper treatment for all complainants and to prevent future recurrences of the problems reported. In most cases, the local government will be concerned only with processing "justifiable" complaints, those in which the reported conditions (1) do, in fact, appear to exist and (2) lie within the jurisdiction and responsibility of the local government to correct (see Exhibit 11-1).

Effectiveness measures for the foregoing objectives are summarized in Exhibit 11-2. The measures should reflect performance over a specific timespan, such as a year. Attention should be given not only to the absolute numbers involved but also to the changes in these measures over the period of interest.

Exhibit 11-1
SUGGESTED DEFINITIONS AND POLICIES FOR DISTINGUISHING COMPLAINTS AND REQUESTS[1]

Basic Definitions

Request for Information—A request explicitly seeking intelligence or data in symbolic form (for example, in terms of spoken or written words, pictures, maps, etc.). If the information is not readily available (for example, if data must be developed), the provision of that data should probably be interpreted as a service.

Request for Service—A request which potentially involves action or activity on the part of city personnel (other than the provision of readily available information) but which does not reflect any evidence of dissatisfaction on the part of the requester.

Complaint—An expression of annoyance, an indication that something is wrong or unsatisfactory. The presence of explicit or implicit dissatisfaction (and a consequent need for corrective action) distinguishes a "complaint" from a "request for service or information."

Justifiable Complaint—A situation in which both (1) the reported unsatisfactory condition does, in fact, appear to exist, and (2) the matter is within the jurisdiction of the local government (that is, the government has legal authority for correcting the problem). It is not recommended that the assessment of justifiability include considerations of government fault with regard to the presence of a problem, the degree to which the complainant blames the government, or the availability of a government capability to remedy the problem. For purposes of measurement, some governments may also wish to classify as "unjustifiable" those complaints that are vague, unfocused, unrealistic (in the immediate future), or only indirectly relevant to the complainant.

A Policy for Handling Ambiguous Items

If an item exhibits characteristics of both complaints and requests, it should preferably be classified as a complaint.[2] Officials should establish clear policies for classifying the most common types of ambiguous items. Examples include requests for repairs or maintenance of existing municipal facilities (such as notification of the location of a pothole or a malfunctioning traffic light), requests for inspections, requests that city officials intervene as a third party (for instance, to force a property owner to clean his lot), and long-range requests (such as those seeking creation of a new park or installation of storm sewers).

Useful Ways to Characterize the Type of Complaint or Request

"Type" refers here to any useful property of complaints or requests by which such citizen communications can be classified and analyzed. Potentially useful classifications include groupings in terms of

- the agency initially contacted
- the agency ultimately responsible for handling the matter
- the detailed subject of the complaint or request (see below)
- the source of the complaint or request (government employees versus other citizens)
- the neighborhood in which the complainant or requester lives
- the urgency of the matter (how soon a response is needed)

Illustrative categories for classifying the subjects of complaints or requests include storm drainage, streets and sidewalks, general transportation, economic needs and resources, protection from physical and economic harm, housing and shelter, solid and liquid waste removal/disposal, water supply and service, environmental quality and protection, health needs, social needs and problems, citizen participation, cultural and aesthetic needs, education, and miscellaneous/general items. Each of these could, in turn, be divided into various subcategories.

---

1. No matter how carefully these terms and policies are defined, there will always be borderline cases for which classification will be highly subjective. It is hoped, however, that the procedures suggested will minimize the need for such judgments.

2. Such a strategy will ensure that these items are included in Measures C7–C10, which, unlike any of the measures associated with requests, depend on an accurate tally of the *number* of items reported.

Measures of the Satisfactoriness and Quality of Complaint Resolution (Measures C1–C5)

Measure C1: Percentage of justifiable complaints, by type,[4] that were satisfactorily (or unsatisfactorily) resolved, as determined by government personnel.

Measure C2: Percentage of complaints, by type, that were satisfactorily (or unsatisfactorily) resolved, as judged by complainants.

These two measures focus on the final disposition or outcome of citizen complaints. As citizens and

4. For examples of some potentially useful ways to distinguish various "types" of complaints, see Exhibit 11-1.

government personnel may differ in their assessments of what constitutes a satisfactory outcome, it seems useful to collect and present data from both perspectives.

Data for Measure C1 can be derived from existing government records if those records describe the nature and disposition of the complaints received. If they do not record dispositions or give adequate information for assessing the justifiability of the complaint, the government would need to modify its record keeping to collect these data. "Satisfactory resolution" must be defined with care. An approach for making such judgments is illustrated in Exhibit 11-3. Under the procedure given in this exhibit, complaints are considered to have been resolved

Exhibit 11-2
MEASURES OF EFFECTIVENESS FOR HANDLING CITIZEN COMPLAINTS

OBJECTIVES:
1. To provide an effective mechanism for responding to and, if technically and legally possible, properly resolving reported complaints with speed, fairness, and courtesy to the mutual satisfaction of the government and the complainant.
2. To encourage and facilitate the reporting of legitimate citizen complaints.
3. To reduce or prevent the occurrence of circumstances that lead to justifiable citizen complaints, whether or not they are reported to government officials.

OBJECTIVE OR QUALITY CHARACTERISTIC ADDRESSED	SPECIFIC COMPLAINT MEASURE	DATA COLLECTION SOURCES OR PROCEDURE
Satisfactory Reponse to, and Resolution of Complaints	C1. *Government's perspective:* percentage of justifiable complaints, by type,[1] that were satisfactorily (or unsatisfactorily) resolved, as determined by government personnel.[2]	Agency complaint records
	C2. *Complainant's perspective:* percentage of complaints, by type, that were judged by the complainant as being satisfactorily (or unsatisfactorily) resolved.	Either (a) a follow-up survey of past complainants or (b) a general citizen survey
Speedy Resolution of Complaints	C3. Median response time for resolution of justifiable complaints, by type of complaint.	Agency records
	C4. Number and percentage of excessively delayed responses (those in which the response time exceeds, perhaps, 30 days), by type of complaint.	Agency records
Quality of Treatment of Complainants (Speed, Courtesy, Fairness, etc.)	C5. Percentage of complainants satisfied (or dissatisfied) with the following aspects of their treatment by complaint-processing personnel: (a) Speed and timeliness of response, (b) Absence of red tape, "run-around," and similar bureaucratic inconveniences or complexities, (c) Courtesy, helpfulness, and general attitude of government personnel, and (d) Fairness of treatment.	"Client" survey or general citizen survey
Willingness and Ability of Citizens to Make Their Complaints Known to the Government	C6. Number of *unreported* complaints, expressed as (a) Jurisdiction total, (b) Overall rate per 10,000 adults, (c) Total for each type of complaint, and (d) Rate per 10,000 adults by reason for not having reported the complaint.	General citizen survey
	C7. Proportion of citizen complaints reported: (a) Jurisdiction total, and (b) Total for each type of complaint.	Data collected for Measures C6 and C8
Reduction or Prevention of Justifiable Citizen Complaints	C8. Number of justifiable complaints received by the jurisdiction, expressed as (a) Jurisdiction total, (b) Overall rate per 10,000 adults, (c) Total for each type of complaint, and (d) Rate per 10,000 adults for each type.[3]	Agency records or general citizen survey for number of justifiable complaints; planning department for population data
	C9. Total number and rate of citizen complaints, including both reported and unreported complaints, expressed as (a) Jurisdiction total, (b) Rate per 10,000 adults, (c) Total for each type, and (d) Rate per 10,000 adults for each type.[3]	Data collected for Measures C6 and C8
	C10. Number of different *complainants* per 10,000 adults: (a) Persons reporting complaints, per 10,000 adults, (b) Persons with unreported complaints, per 10,000 adults, and (c) Persons with reported *or* unreported complaints, per 10,000 adults.	Agency or central office complaint files, and a general citizen survey

1. Throughout this exhibit, "type" of complaint refers to the complaint classifications selected by the local government as being useful. Classifications might be by agency responsible for the problem or its resolution, by type of problem, or by degree of urgency (see Exhibit 11-1 for other potential groupings).

2. "Satisfactorily resolved" is defined to include those cases where corrections were completed and those cases where an adequate reason exists (and was given to the complainant) as to why no help was possible.

3. Certain types of complaints can also be displayed as a rate per 10,000 *customers* (e.g., sanitation complaints per 10,000 garbage accounts) or per 10,000 *exposures* (e.g., water bill complaints per 10,000 bills issued).

Exhibit 11-3

ASSESSMENT OF "SATISFACTORY RESOLUTION" OF COMPLAINTS BY GOVERNMENT PERSONNEL: A SCHEMATIC REPRESENTATION

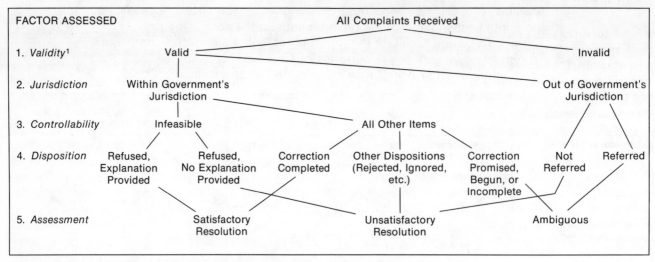

1. A complaint is defined as "valid" if the reported situation does appear to exist.

satisfactorily from the standpoint of the local government if correction has been completed *or* if resolution was impossible but an adequate explanation of the reason was provided to the complainant. The outcomes of complaints for which action is pending or is in process could be considered ambiguous and recorded separately in the outcome measurement tallies.

It is just as important to measure the complainants' own satisfaction with the handling of their complaints (Measure C2). Data for this measure can be obtained as part of a general citizen survey using, for example, Question 1e of Appendix 11. However, the number of respondents who have complained will probably be too small (less than 100) to allow comparison of responses between population subgroups or to determine how well a particular department has resolved the complaints directed toward it.

A better way to collect data on complainant satisfaction is to conduct a follow-up survey of a sample of the persons who have registered justifiable complaints. An illustration of such a survey is presented in Appendix 12. Questions 5 through 5d in that appendix would provide the data needed for this measure. Questions 5b, 5c, and 5d in Appendix 12 are designed to elicit reasons for dissatisfaction with the government's response. This makes it possible to track the number and proportion of dissatisfied complainants, classified according to the reasons for dissatisfaction. Such data could provide clues to government officials as to possible corrective actions.

The validity of the information obtained from a complainant survey depends on the willingness of the complainants to respond completely and accurately, and on the quality of the survey process. Note that the comparability between Measures C1 and C2 could be improved by screening out unjustifiable complaints when determining Measure C2.

Exhibit 11-4 presents the results for several recent assessments of satisfaction among citizen complainants with municipal complaint-processing efforts.

Measure C3: Median response time for resolution of justifiable complaints, by type of complaint.

Measure C4: Number and percentage of excessively delayed responses (those in which the response time exceeds, perhaps, 30 days), by type of complaint.

These measures provide two perspectives on the time it takes the government to resolve a complaint. The median response time (Measure C3) indicates the typical time required for processing a complaint.[5] Specifically, it is the length of time within

5. Other ways to present response-time data include using (a) the average response time, (b) the time until "x" percent of all complaints are resolved (where "x" is selected by the jurisdiction, perhaps 75 percent or 90 percent), and (c) the actual frequency distribution for the various response times (for example, the percentage of complaints resolved within various time periods). Note that *citizen* ratings of the timeliness of the government's response also may be considered an important measure; this is discussed as part of the quality of treatment, Measure C5.

which half of all the complaints received were handled, from receipt of the complaint to final disposition. Information for this measure can usually be obtained from government records on the disposition of each complaint. Local governments may find it useful to establish performance targets regarding median response times, as New York City has done.[6]

Measure C4 focuses on preselected performance criteria defining "excessive" response times. Different time periods might be used for different types of complaints. It might be possible to maintain a running tally of excessively delayed complaints in conjunction with a "tickler" file of pending complaints (used to identify agencies that need prodding).

Measure C3 and C4 ideally should be reported separately for different types of complaints. For instance, an agency is likely to find it useful to compute these response-time measures for (1) each department receiving complaints, (2) each major complaint topic, and (3) complaints of differing urgency.[7] One city has used the following approach for classifying the urgency of street maintenance complaints:

6. Citizen Feedback Unit, "Guidelines for the Establishment and Monitoring of Service and Complaint Response Standards" (City of New York: Office of the Mayor, June 1972).

7. See Exhibit 11-1 for other potentially useful ways to differentiate complaints by kind.

- Priority 1—Emergency, requiring immediate attention even if after hours and demanding interruption of any lower-priority activities;
- Priority 2—Serious, requiring attention within twenty-four hours even if overtime is necessary but without interrupting a job in progress;
- Priority 3—Nonurgent, not requiring attention within twenty-four hours.[8]

Two problems can affect the accuracy of Measures C3 and C4. One is the difficulty of deciding when a complaint has finally been disposed of, especially when a citizen repeatedly contacts the municipality about a given item. In such cases the government might distinguish separate response times for each new contact made by the citizen (measured from the time of the contact to the next government response) and for the total length of time required for the overall disposition of the matter. The other problem involves a department's reporting a complaint as being completed when it has only been scheduled for action. The government should distin-

8. "Street Maintenance Priority System," *Kansas City, Missouri Management Analysis Procedures Manual* (Kansas City, Mo.: Streets Division, Department of Public Works, n.d.), p. IX-D-8.

Exhibit 11-4

RECENT RESULTS ON CITIZEN SATISFACTION WITH MUNICIPAL COMPLAINT-PROCESSING EFFORTS

JURISDICTION	PERCENTAGE SATISFIED	DATE OF SURVEY	TYPE OF SURVEY
Dallas, Texas	59	1974	General population
Dayton, Ohio (Ombudsman)	40	1971	General population
Falls Church, Virginia	42	1974	General population
Forest Heights, Maryland	59	1974	General population
King County, Washington (Ombudsman)	55	1972	Complainants
Nashville, Tennessee		1974	General population
	49		—Most important complaint or request
	39		—Second most important
	30		—Third most important
New York City	44	1971	Complainants
		1972	General population
	31		—Most important problem
	32		—Second most important
Palo Alto, California	60	1974	General population
Randolph Township, New Jersey	55	1974	General population
Seattle, Washington (Ombudsman)	50	1972	Complainants
St. Petersburg, Florida	42	1973	General population
	80[1]	1974	Complainants
	44	1974	General population
	43	1975	General population
Nationwide (Harris Survey)	39	1973	General population

1. The high rate of satisfaction indicated by St. Petersburg's complainant survey, as compared to the rate indicated by its general citizen survey, may have been due to the following factors: (1) only complaints perceived as justifiable were retained in the complaint records that formed the basis for drawing the sample for the complainant survey; and (2) the complainant survey actually included numerous persons who had only made requests for service (city complaint records did not distinguish complaints from service requests).

guish items that are "in progress" from those that have been "resolved"; only items which have been "resolved" should be used in preparing these measures.

Measure C5: *Quality of treatment: percentage of complainants satisfied (or dissatisfied) with the following aspects of their treatment by complaint-processing personnel:*
   (a) *Speed and timeliness of response,*
   (b) *Absence of red tape, "run-around," and similar bureaucratic inconveniences or complexities,*
   (c) *Courtesy, helpfulness, and general attitude of government personnel, and*
   (d) *Fairness of treatment.*

This measure (actually a group of measures) is designed to track various aspects of the quality of the service provided other than the satisfactoriness of the disposition of the complaint. It addresses such service characteristics as speed and timeliness, absence of red tape or evasiveness, attitudes of government employees (courtesy, helpfulness, and concern), and fairness (the extent to which the complainant feels that city employees were biased toward the city's position or that other complainants have received better treatment).

The principal approach for obtaining these data is to survey complainants, as already discussed under Measure C2. Questions 7 through 11 on the complainant survey in Appendix 12 could be used to obtain this information. A general citizen survey could also be used, as illustrated by the response options to Question 1e of Appendix 11. As noted earlier, however, the potential disadvantage of using a general citizen survey is that only a relatively small number of citizens who have used the government's complaint services are likely to be included in any given general citizen survey. Thus, too few ratings may be received to provide the government with a representative, statistically reliable sample for assessing these qualities.

Measures of the Extent to Which the Reporting of Legitimate Citizen Complaints Is Encouraged and Facilitated (Measures C6 and C7)

Two measures are presented as indicators of the extent of citizen willingness and ability to make their complaints known to the government. The first is an estimate of the *number* of unreported complaints;

the second is the *percentage* of total complaints reported. Neither measure is currently collected by most local governments, and both require data from a general citizen survey.[9]

Measure C6: *Number of unreported complaints, expressed as (a) jurisdiction total, (b) overall rate per 10,000 adults, (c) total for each type of complaint, and (d) rate per 10,000 adults by reason for not having reported the complaint.*

This measure can provide an indication of the inaccessibility of the complaint-processing operation and the extent to which citizens feel that the government will not or cannot resolve their complaints. Data would be collected by using a general citizen survey question similar to Question 3a in Appendix 11. A brief description of each previously unreported complaint would also be obtained from the respondent to permit an assessment of its justifiability. (Question 3b in Appendix 11 illustrates such an approach.)

An important purpose of this measure is to identify *why* people have not reported their complaints. Some possible reasons are shown in the response options to Question 3 in Appendix 11. Figures on the number or percentage of persons who, for specific reasons, failed to report legitimate complaints can be used by a government to help identify what might be done to reduce the barriers to reporting complaints.

There are two main problems with this measure and the proposed data collection procedure. First, because of the relatively small sample sizes expected to be associated with a general citizen survey, the survey probably will provide only a rough estimate of the number of persons who have had specific reasons (such as not knowing where to complain) for not reporting their complaints. Second, respondents indicating unreported complaints may actually be

9. Some governments may prefer a more direct assessment of the degree to which citizens are aware of the proper place to lodge their complaints and the degree to which misdirected complaints subject the citizen to a "run-around." For example, tallies of "the proportion of reported complaints that were initially directed by the citizen to the wrong agency" would provide an indication of the effectiveness of municipal efforts to publicize complaint-processing channels. (Analyses of complaints communicated directly to certain agencies in New York City and St. Petersburg indicated that as many as 30 percent of the complaints and requests received were misdirected.) A possible direct measure of the degree to which citizens have avoided experiencing a "run-around" is "the number and percentage of justifiable reported complaints handled with no intra-governmental referral of the complainant." Each of the foregoing measures could be prepared from government complaint rekords if provision were made for recording each referral as part of those records.

referring to unjustifiable complaints (perhaps a problem outside the jurisdiction of the government) or to items that would more correctly be classified as requests for service. Inclusion of such items could cause the number of unreported complaints to be overstated significantly.

To alleviate the latter problem, the questionnaire should provide an opportunity for respondents to describe the nature of their previously unreported complaint(s) (see Question 3b in Appendix 11). Such complaints can then be screened for justifiability before preparing Measure C6. Examination of the results of the 1973 St. Petersburg survey indicated that of 232 unreported complaints, 86 percent appeared to be valid and 9 percent did not (validity could not be established for 5 percent). But 18 percent of the valid complaints appeared to be outside the city's jurisdiction, so of the overall total of 232 unreported complaints, at least 24 percent were not justifiable. In addition, 31 percent of the remaining justifiable complaints cited no specific city problem or objectionable action; many, for instance, indicated a general dislike of certain city policies. Under some definitions of "justifiability" (see Exhibit 11-1), general complaints like these, which are unspecific or unrealistic, or for which action is either not required or impossible, might be classed as "unjustified" for measurement purposes.

Conversely, because memories are short, respondents probably tend to understate the number of complaints they have had but failed to report. If a government focuses more on changes in the number and percentage of unreported complaints (from one time period to another) rather than on the absolute number, there is less likelihood of its being misled by tendencies to understate or overstate the number of unreported complaints.

Measure C7: *Proportion of citizen complaints reported: (a) jurisdiction total and (b) total for each type of complaint.*

The ratio of the number of complaints that *are* reported to the sum of those reported *plus* the estimated number of unreported complaints (as obtained in Measure C6) indicates the willingness of citizens to use the complaint-processing mechanism (and by implication, indicates the accessibility of that mechanism).

Data on the number of reported complaints could probably be obtained either from government records or from a general citizen survey (see Question 1a of Appendix 11). The pros and cons of each procedure are discussed later in connection with Measure C8. However, for estimating the *proportion*

reported, the results of the general citizen survey may be all that is needed. For instance, Questions 1a and 3a in Appendix 11 could be used to determine the numbers of reported and unreported complaints among the persons surveyed; the appropriate ratio can then be computed directly from these two quantities.[10] Measure C7 would probably be more meaningful if both the reported and unreported complaints identified in the survey were screened for justifiability.

Breakouts of Measure C7 by type of complaint will indicate the degree to which some types of complaints are escaping the attention of government officials or cases in which, because of underreporting, reported complaints are unlikely to indicate the full scope of citizen dissatisfaction. Breakdowns by population subgroups (discussed later) might identify special problems concerning the inaccessibility of the complaint-receiving mechanism or the unwillingness of certain segments of the population to register complaints.

To illustrate the data obtainable for this measure, the following estimates were derived from recent citizen surveys in three cities:

	St. Petersburg (1973)	Nashville (1974)	Palo Alto (1974)
Percentage of complaints reported[11]	29	54	N.A.
Percentage of *persons* with complaints who claim to have reported all of them[12]	33	43	51

The second measure, "proportion of persons with complaints who claim to have reported all of them," is an alternate form of Measure C7. Since this form depends only on whether a respondent had *any* unreported complaints, it reduces the effects of respondent memory limitations regarding the *number* of reported and unreported complaints. Data for this alternate form would be obtained from the general citizen survey (Questions 1 and 3 of Appendix 11). The alternate form of Measure C7 can then be computed as the number of "yes" responses to Question 1

10. This provides a means for preparing Measure C7 when no central records are kept of the complaints received by each agency.

11. The survey questions used were similar to Questions 1a and 3 in Appendix 11. Since Question 3a (Appendix 12) was not included in these surveys, it was assumed for estimation purposes that citizens with unreported complaints had only one such complaint.

12. The survey questions used as the basis for this measure were similar to Questions 1 and 3 in Appendix 11.

divided by the sum of the "yes" responses to Questions 1 *and* 3, Appendix 11.

Measures of the Overall Level of Complaints (Measures C8-C10)

The objective of these measures is to reflect the desire of governments to reduce or prevent the occurrence of circumstances leading to justifiable citizen complaints, reported or unreported. A jurisdiction may consider this as an overall objective rather than a specific responsibility of a central complaint-receiving agency.

It is generally not possible to measure the number of problems prevented. What is measurable, however, is the number of complaints that have *not* been averted. The three measures presented here focus on various aspects of the number of complaints which *do* occur.[13] Measure C8 is one commonly found in local governments, namely, the number of reported justifiable complaints. A better estimate of the total number of citizen complaints that occur would appear to be one that incorporates unreported complaints. Measure C9 includes such incidents as estimated by a general population survey. Finally, because complaints may come largely from a select segment of the population that complains frequently, a government may want an estimate of the number of different complainants as well as of the total number of complaints. Measure C10 tries to provide such an estimate.

Measure C8: Number of justifiable complaints received by the jurisdiction, expressed as (a) jurisdiction total, (b) overall rate per 10,000 adults, (c) total for each type of complaint, and (d) rate per 10,000 adults for each type.[14]

This measure reflects the level of expressed citizen dissatisfaction. A justifiable complaint, as defined earlier, is one in which the reported condition existed and was within the jurisdiction and responsibility of the government to correct. Because

---

13. These measures address only indirectly another aspect of Objective 3—the degree to which complaints serve as a positive force to improve service. A more direct way to address this concern would be to determine the "percentage of justifiable complaints that have led to lasting beneficial changes in government services or policies." This appears more appropriate for a special study, however, than for the regular performance monitoring upon which this report concentrates.

14. The rate of reported complaints can also be used to assess the effectiveness of specific municipal services such as solid waste collection.

records of complaints are frequently kept by government departments, data for this measure are often readily available. The "type" of complaint here refers to any or all of the complaint classifications the local government selects as being useful, such as the agency responsible for the problem or its resolution, the type of problem, or the urgency of the matter. For some types of complaints, it may be more appropriate to calculate complaint rates relative to the number of potential sources of a complaint (for instance, sanitation complaints per 10,000 households served or water bill complaints per 10,000 bills issued).

Certain factors will affect the accuracy of this measure. Complaints are usually received by a number of different government officials or agencies. A complaint about a missed refuse collection, for example, might be made to the mayor, a city council member, the chief administrator's office, the sanitation department, or to several of these offices. Complaints may be lost or counted more than once. Some matters (a missed refuse collection is a good example) may be referred to a government unit for immediate action without being recorded. And some departments may not keep good records on the number of complaints received, especially if complaints are perceived as indicators of poor performance.

There is also a definition problem. To make a department's record on justifiable complaints look somewhat better, some departments may tend to liberally classify citizen complaints as unjustifiable (that is, as not within the responsibility of the department to correct) or as not being complaints at all (instead, they may be deemed to be requests for service). A set of specific definitions, perhaps based on those in Exhibit 11-1, should be established and applied consistently.

Some of the record-keeping inaccuracies might be overcome by estimating the number of reported complaints from the responses to an appropriate general citizen survey question such as Number 1a of Appendix 11. However, there are certain problems with this procedure too (including respondent memories and sampling errors), as discussed later in this chapter in the section on the general citizen survey.

Figures from the two sources can be hard to reconcile. In St. Petersburg, estimates extrapolated from 1973 survey findings indicated that about 57,000 complaints had been reported over the previous twelve months, whereas estimates based on available city records showed no more than 35,000 complaints.[15] Because government records at present are likely to have greater credibility than complaints reported in a survey, the former may be preferable for preparing Measure C8.

This measure does not include unreported complaints. Thus, changes in the value of Measure C8 could stem from changes in the accessibility of the complaint system, among other things, rather than from any change in the number of complaint-provoking incidents. For example, improvements in handling complaints may lead to more reported complaints because citizens feel that the government has become more responsive. To alleviate these ambiguities, Measure C9 is presented.

Measure C9: Total number and rate of citizen complaints, including both reported and unreported complaints, expressed as (a) jurisdiction total, (b) rate per 10,000 adults, (c) total for each type, and (d) rate per 10,000 adults for each type.

A comprehensive picture of citizen problems and dissatisfaction cannot be obtained by looking only at reported complaints (Measure C8). Findings in St. Petersburg and Nashville indicate that sometimes more than half of the complaints are not reported (see Measure C7). Thus, a more thorough-going assessment of the level of citizen problems and dissatisfaction—and changes in that level over time—can be obtained by looking at the sum of reported and unreported complaints.

The estimated number of unreported complaints can be obtained as discussed under Measure C6, and the number of reported complaints as discussed under Measure C8. Thus, Measure C9 will be subject to the potential accuracy problems discussed in connection with each of those measures. However, if the focus is on tracking relative changes over time rather than the absolute number of reported plus unreported complaints, Measure C9 should be useful. Such changes should reflect both the long-range effectiveness of complaint-processing activities and the overall effectiveness of government services in preventing the causes of citizen complaints. The values of Measure C9 will also, inevitably, reflect the influence of external factors such as the emergence of new problems, changes in citizen expectations, and similar influences which the local government may not be able to control entirely. Whenever possible, such factors should be identified and their likely effects should be noted in reporting and interpreting this (and any other) measure.

As with Measures C6, C7, and C8, the accuracy of Measure C9 will be enhanced if respondents to the citizen survey are asked to describe briefly their reported or unreported complaints, and if these descriptions are subsequently screened to delete clearly unjustifiable items. The use of complaint rates per 10,000 adults, exposures, or clients will help produce "fairer" comparisons between different years or client groups (for example, in situations in which the sizes of the populations are likely to differ significantly). Rates for individual types of complaints can be calculated if the data on unreported complaints obtained in the general citizen survey provide enough detail to categorize them by type.

Measure C10: Number of different complainants per 10,000 adults: (a) persons reporting complaints, per 10,000 adults, (b) persons with unreported complaints, per 10,000 adults, and (c) persons with reported or unreported complaints, per 10,000 adults.

In contrast to previous measures that focus on the number of complaints, this measure indicates the number of *different persons* who have complained. The 1973-74 surveys in Nashville and St. Petersburg indicated that there were approximately one and one-half reported complaints per person complaining.[16]

Measure C10 can be used to provide a supplementary perspective—or even an alternative—to Measures C6, C8, and C9. Indeed, Measure C10 may be more accurate than these measures, as it avoids the need to obtain details on the *number* of reported or unreported complaints from persons with more than one complaint. Measure C10 will also help to compensate for the presence of chronic complainers.[17] Unlike Measures C6, C8, and C9, however, it provides less information about the frequency with which problems are being encountered. The latter information can be quite useful to a gov-

15. The discrepancy in the case of St. Petersburg may have arisen from several factors. Extrapolations based on the citizen survey did not exclude unjustifiable complaints; tallies based on city records generally did exclude such items. Also, St. Petersburg's central file of complaint records did not include complaints made directly to certain high-visibility departments such as water or licenses and inspections; such complaints would have been reported in the general citizen survey.

16. In St. Petersburg, there were approximately 177 reported complaints for the 113 complaining respondents; in Nashville, the survey indicated about 398 reported complaints among 251 complainants.
17. Note that Measure C8 addresses *all* justifiable complaints, whether by one person or many.

ernment for tracking progress in the prevention of complaint-provoking situations.

The data for this measure can be collected from the general citizen survey using Questions 1 and 3 of Appendix 11. Alternatively, estimates of the number of different people who have *reported* complaints can be made by analyzing complaint records from the past year, if they show the names of complainants.[18] One way to do this would be to keep an alphabetical file of complaints by complainant and divide the total number of complaints received in a year by the number of names in the file. Anonymous complaints should be filed separately and not included in the computation; the errors introduced by their exclusion should be small. The accuracy of Measure C10 can, of course, be improved by screening out unjustifiable complaints, as described in conjunction with other complaint measures.

The Handling of Citizen Requests for Services and Information

The processing of citizen requests for services and information generally addresses the following overall objective:

> **To provide a convenient and effective mechanism for receiving, responding to, and, when technically and legally possible, properly fulfilling citizen requests for service and information with speed, fairness, and courtesy, to the mutual satisfaction of the government and the citizen.**

This objective is similar to those suggested in connection with citizen complaints except that the volume of requests (and its increase or decrease) is not considered to be an aspect of request-processing effectiveness.[19]

The relevant effectiveness measures for handling requests are summarized in Exhibit 11-5. Although the following discussion is primarily in terms of requests for services, the measures can also be used for examining the handling of requests for information. It is recommended that measures for

18. Complainants, however, should not be *required* to provide their names; introducing such a requirement could discourage citizens from reporting legitimate complaints to government officials.

19. Although the volume of requests for service and information is clearly important for planning and budgeting, neither increasing nor decreasing the volume of those requests appears to represent an explicit government objective.

these two major classes of requests be displayed separately because the two activities have significant operational differences, including the volumes handled, the response times involved, the variety of response options available, the effort required, and the completeness of the records maintained.

Request Measures R1-R5 correspond to Complaint Measures C1-C5. Since much of the discussion of those complaint measures and the associated data collection procedures applies to the measures presented here, it will not be repeated. See the discussions of the corresponding complaint measures for more detailed information.

One important general difference between complaint and request measures is that the latter depend on an analysis of *all* types of citizen requests—not just those considered justifiable. The given objective implies good treatment for *all* citizen communications, even those that seem irrelevant or unjustifiable. Because good treatment includes appropriate referrals for matters beyond the government's jurisdiction and thorough explanations even when unreasonable requests must be refused, it is desirable to report on the disposition of all requests. If the volume becomes unmanageable, however, effectiveness information should be obtained for only a sample of request records, or the measurements should be limited to certain types of requests of special significance.

Measure R1: Percentage of requests for (i) service, (ii) information that were (or were not) satisfactorily disposed of, as judged by government personnel—by type of request and, when appropriate, by type of unsatisfactory response.

A practical procedure for defining requests disposed of satisfactorily from the standpoint of the government would be to include only those cases in which the original request was fulfilled or, if fulfillment was infeasible, an "approved" reason was given. Such reasons might include the following: government regulations or ordinances prohibit complying with the request; circumstances make the requester ineligible to receive the service; or the service has already been scheduled for delivery at a future date (as in the case of major road improvements or other planned facilities). Requests that were (1) still pending or (2) referred to other organizations because of the government's lack of jurisdiction in the matter would be considered ambiguous; all other dispositions might be assumed to be unsatisfactory.

It will probably also be helpful to report the results for Measure R1 separately for different types of

Exhibit 11-5

SUGGESTED OBJECTIVES AND MEASURES OF EFFECTIVENESS FOR HANDLING CITIZEN REQUESTS FOR SERVICES AND INFORMATION

OBJECTIVE: To provide a convenient and effective mechanism for receiving, responding to, and, when technically and legally possible, properly fulfilling citizen requests for service and information with speed, fairness, and courtesy to the mutual satisfaction of the government and the citizen.

OBJECTIVE OR QUALITY CHARACTERISTIC ADDRESSED	SPECIFIC REQUEST MEASURE	DATA COLLECTION SOURCES OR PROCEDURE
Satisfactory Response to, and Fulfillment of, Requests for Service and Information	R1. *Government's perspective:* percentage of (i) Requests for service (ii) Requests for information that were (or were not) satisfactorily disposed of, as judged by government personnel—by type of request[1] and, when appropriate, by type of unsatisfactory response.	Government records of citizen requests, perhaps incorporating some modifications
	R2. *Citizen's perspective:* percentage of (i) Requests for service (ii) Requests for information that were (or were not) satisfactorily disposed of, as judged by requesters—by type of request and, when appropriate, by major reasons for dissatisfaction.	A survey of requesters (Questions 5a, 5b, 5c, and 5d of Appendix 12) or, less desirably, a general citizen survey (see Appendix 11, Question 2d—especially responses 2, 3, 4, and 8)
Speedy Disposition of Requests for Service and Information	R3. Median response time for each type of service and information request received.	Government records
	R4. Number and percentage of (a) Requests for service received during the past year for which the response time exceeded, perhaps, 14 days (b) Requests for information received during the past year for which the response time exceeded, perhaps, 1 day (grouped or identified by type of request).	Government records
Quality Treatment of Persons Requesting Service or Information	R5. Percentages of persons who have requested (i) Service (ii) Information who rate the following aspects of their treatment as satisfactory (or unsatisfactory): (a) Speed and timeliness of response, (b) Absence of red tape, "run-around," and similar bureaucratic inconveniences or complexities,[2] (c) Fairness of treatment, (d) Courtesy, helpfulness, and general attitude of government personnel.	Citizen survey (Appendix 11, Question 2d, especially responses 5 through 7) or survey of requesters (Appendix 12, Questions 7 through 11)
Convenient and Effective Intake of Citizen Requests	R6. Percentage of population inhibited from filing requests for service or information, grouped by the reasons for not filing.	Citizen survey (see Appendix 11, Question 4)

1. "Type of request" should probably incorporate the following basic breakdown: (1) requests for municipal services, (2) requests for other forms of assistance, (3) inquiries concerning local government matters, and (4) general inquiries. Other distinctions might also be of interest, including the agency receiving or responsible for handling the request, the specific nature of the request, and the urgency of the matter.

2. Some jurisdictions may prefer a less subjective assessment of the degree of "run-around," for example, by an analysis of statistics on referrals or misdirected requests. Potential criteria of this type are discussed in the notes to Measures C6 and C7.

requests, for example, according to the nature of the request, the department responsible, and the urgency of the matter (see Exhibit 11-1). The following breakdown appears to be useful for isolating requests the government would be unlikely to be able to respond to routinely (see groups 2 and 4 below):

1—Requests for municipal
services
2—Requests for other   } Service requests
forms of assistance

3—Inquiries concerning
local government matters   } Information requests
4—General inquiries

To help the government identify what remedial efforts are needed, requests not responded to satisfactorily might be grouped by the kind of unsatisfactory response: refusals without adequate explanations or referrals, promises made and ignored, or incorrect responses (provision of the wrong service, erroneous or out-of-date information, or faulty/ineffective service).

The accuracy of this measure depends largely on the extent to which the request and its outcome are documented. When the accuracy of the recorded information is in doubt (or records of requests are not maintained), the government may want to flag a sample of requests as they come in and follow them up using other government records and interviews with both the requesters and the government personnel who handled the matters.

Measure R2: Percentage of requests for (i) service, (ii) information that were (or were not) satisfactorily disposed of, as judged by requesters—by type of request and, when appropriate, by major reasons for dissatisfaction.

Data for Measure R2 can best be obtained by a special survey of requesters, using a question such as Number 5a in Appendix 12.[20] Obtaining the names and telephone numbers of requesters for such a follow-up may, however, pose complications. If, on the other hand, the government undertakes a general citizen survey, citizen satisfaction with the responses to their requests for services or information could be measured using a question such as Number 2d of Appendix 11. However, as discussed previously in connection with the complaint measures, only a small portion of those sampled in such a survey are likely to have requested services or information in

the previous twelve months. The small number of requesters expected to be encountered will limit the possibility of comparing responses by type of request, client group, or reason for dissatisfaction. Jurisdictions may want to experiment with both data collection approaches to determine which is more practical for their own circumstances.

When surveying requesters, the government probably should also identify the reasons for the citizens' dissatisfaction, if any, with the handling of their requests by including questions such as Numbers 5b, 5c, or 5d from Appendix 12 or Question 2d from Appendix 11. This information could enable officials to identify correctable problems.

A similar approach, but one that also attempts to obtain information on reasons for requester *satisfaction,* was used in a study by the Bureau of Applied Social Research at Columbia University.[21] Responses were classified under one of the following categories:

> Reasons for satisfaction:
> Problem solved
> Problem not solved but tried
> Treated well and sympathetically
> Other
> Reasons for dissatisfaction:
> Nothing solved (no blame implied)
> Nothing solved (blame implied)
> Something done but not enough
> Other

Measure R3: Median response time for each type of service and information request received.

The median response time indicates the interval likely to be required for processing a request, from initial receipt to final fulfillment or other disposition. Median response times should be broken down by type of request (such as the urgency or nature of the request) and by agency responsible. As discussed under Measure C3, the primary data collection procedure would be the analysis of government records.

Measure R4: Number and percentage of (a) requests for service received during the past year for which the response time exceeded, perhaps, 14 days, (b) requests for information received during the past year for which the response time exceeded, perhaps, 1 day (grouped or identified by type of request).

---

20. Note that the illustrative questionnaire in Appendix 12 is intended for use by citizens who have requested service or information as well as by those who have reported a complaint.

21. Bureau of Applied Social Research, "New York Neighborhood Study: Public Survey with Marginals" (New York: Columbia University, June 1972).

The determination of what constitutes an "excessive" response time will depend on the nature of the request for service or for information—fourteen days may be appropriate for some services, one day for some information requests. The same records used to collect information for Measure R3 can also be used as the basis for calculating this measure.

Measure R5: Quality of treatment: percentages of persons who have requested (i) service or (ii) information who rate the following aspects of their treatment as satisfactory (or unsatisfactory):
  (a) Speed and timeliness of response,
  (b) Absence of red tape, "run-around," and similar bureaucratic inconveniences or complexities,
  (c) Fairness of treatment,
  (d) Courtesy, helpfulness, and general attitude of government personnel.

This measure is designed to obtain information on various attributes (other than the actual disposition of the request) associated with the quality of the government's request-handling process as perceived by the requester, including the timeliness of the process, the absence of red tape or run-around, and the fairness, courtesy, helpfulness, and attitude of the government personnel with whom the requester has dealt. As discussed under Measure C5, Questions 7 through 11 of Appendix 12 can be used to collect the data in a survey of requesters; if a general citizen survey is undertaken, Question 2d of Appendix 11 could be used.

Measure R6: Percentage of population inhibited from filing requests for service or information, grouped by reasons for not filing.

This measure attempts to provide information on the accessibility of the request system and reasons for inaccessibility, some of which the government may be able to improve or correct. The best method of data collection for this measure appears to be the general citizen survey; Question 4 from Appendix 11 can be used. In Nashville, 90 percent of the respondents to a 1974 survey reported no reluctance or other impediment to making a request. If this experience is typical of other cities, the general citizen survey might not identify enough respondents who *had* encountered barriers in filing requests to be able to obtain accurate statistics on the nature of the barriers that did exist. (Of course, if only a small proportion of respondents reported feeling inhibited from making requests, this result would indicate that little needed to be done. In such a situa-

tion, the absence of accurate statistics on specific barriers to filing requests would be correspondingly less important.)

Special Data Collection Considerations

The suggested measures of effectiveness for the handling of citizen complaints and requests for services and information require data from three major sources: (1) from a general survey of (adult) citizens, (2) from a survey of a sample of persons who have complained or requested services or information, and (3) from government records of the complaints and requests processed. Readers are referred to Chapter 14 for a more extensive discussion of the procedures and problems associated with undertaking a general citizen survey. This chapter discusses some additional considerations especially pertinent to the examination of complaint and request handling.

The General Citizen Survey

Nine of the sixteen measures proposed in this chapter rely on at least some data from a general citizen survey. Indeed, a general citizen survey appears to be the only practical way to obtain certain kinds of information such as the incidence of unreported complaints or reasons for not reporting complaints or requests for services.

Appendix 11 presents an illustrative set of questions for obtaining effectiveness information on the handling of citizen complaints and requests for services and information, using a multiservice citizen survey. It is based on a synthesis of survey questions and experiences in St. Petersburg, Nashville, and Palo Alto and thus reflects the best aspects of each of those survey efforts.[22] The specific measures addressed by each question are noted in the left margin.

Questions asking the respondent to briefly describe the complaint (such as Question 1b in Appendix 11) do complicate the coding and analysis of the data. Yet they provide information for at least a rough verification of whether the complaints are jus-

22. The questions actually used in the Nashville citizen survey are given in Appendix 1 (see Questions 58-63); those used in St. Petersburg are provided in our earlier report, *Measuring the Effectiveness of Basic Municipal Services: Initial Report* (Washington, D.C.: The Urban Institute and the International City Management Association, February 1974).

tifiable; the information can also be used to provide a useful breakdown of the nature of the complaints. Questions such as 1c and 2b provide data for determining where citizens tend to take their complaints or requests and, when cross-tabulated with the responses to other questions, also permit limited analysis of the performance of each office.

Citizens may be dissatisfied if told that the city has no authority to handle their concerns. Questions 1d and 2c provide information to check for just such a situation. Cross-tabulations of these questions with the corresponding questions on citizen satisfaction (1e and 2d) can indicate if dissatisfaction is related to whether or not a problem is within the city's jurisdiction.

One problem that this research was not able to explore is how long citizens can accurately remember complaints or requests. For instance, will persons tend to remember only complaints and requests from the last several months, thus underestimating the number of items in a twelve-month period? Further research is called for. One way to alleviate this problem would be to reduce the recall period to six months or even three months and to conduct surveys more frequently. However, if the interviews are conducted only once a year (a less expensive procedure), then data based on only a three- or six-month recall period would probably have to be projected to a twelve-month interval, and seasonal effects would then have to be considered, as discussed below. Another approach is to focus on the number of persons who complain rather than the number of complaints (that is, on Measure C10 rather than Measures C6, C8, and C9), since data resulting from a focus on complainants would probably be less affected by memory lapses. It is important to keep the same time period, whatever it is, from survey to survey so that changes will be attributable to different conditions rather than to variations in how much respondent memories are taxed.

Other special issues in implementing a general citizen survey for collecting data on the handling of citizen complaints and requests are discussed below.

Timing of the survey. Seasonal changes and other external events can affect the number of citizen complaints and requests. A government should be alert for such events just before or during the administration of a survey, and it should interpret the survey results accordingly. On the basis of an analysis of factors likely to influence the incidence of citizen complaints and requests (and the timing of those factors), our judgment is that either spring or fall is probably the best time for a survey.

Special interviewer instructions. Our tests indicate that interviewers should be given special instructions regarding the survey questions pertaining to citizen complaints and requests. For instance, they should be informed of:

1. How to count distinct problems or matters (see Question 1a, Appendix 11). Repeated calls on the same item should not be counted as separate problems. For example, three calls to rectify a single missed trash collection obviously equal one situation, but three calls to rectify three separate missed trash collections should be counted as three situations. One call to report three separate problems (noise, water bill, missed collection) equals three situations.
2. Which offices or organizations are and are not part of the city government.
3. When multiple responses (such as several reasons for dissatisfaction) may be recorded.
4. How to define in detail each of the response options. For instance, in Question 2d (Appendix 11), how to distinguish "took too long" from "had to keep pressuring them to get results."[23]

Additional explanatory data. Information on citizen alienation, participation, and general attitudes toward local services—data that may also be obtained by a general citizen survey—can help in interpreting responses by complainants. Some appropriate questions are shown in Exhibit 11-6. Such questions assess certain elements of citizen feedback not covered by the flow of complaints and requests. They also can form the basis for cross-tabulations designed to identify some of the factors influencing survey results. For instance, in St. Petersburg it was found that respondents who did not feel "alienated" were almost twice as likely to be satisfied with the city's response to a complaint as those respondents who felt alienated.[24]

Question 4 in Exhibit 11-6 is important where local officials are particularly concerned about respondents with a "generally negative" attitude toward government. Using this question, analysts might want to try to distinguish citizens whose

23. The latter emphasizes active pressure exercised by the citizen—repeated letters or calls, use of influence, and the like. "Took too long" refers to the waiting period, whether or not pressure was applied.

24. The actual ratio of the likelihoods for the two groups was 1.9, statistically significant at a 95-percent confidence level. "Alienated" respondents were defined as those who answered "yes" to a question identical to Number 1 in Exhibit 11-6. Related results indicated that alienation had little correlation with either the likelihood of registering a complaint or the presence of unreported complaints. However, among respondents *with* unreported complaints, alienated persons were more likely to feel that it would have done no good to complain than were those who apparently were not alienated.

Exhibit 11-6
SUPPLEMENTARY CITIZEN SURVEY
QUESTIONS ON CITIZEN ALIENATION,
PARTICIPATION, AND OVERALL ATTITUDE
TOWARD GOVERNMENT SERVICES[1]

1. Do you feel you could have a say about the way the city government is running things if you wanted to?	1( )	Yes
	2( )	No
	3( )	Don't know
2. During the past year, have you or any members of your household attended any meeting or hearing of the city council or any other city government body?	1( )	Yes
	2( )	No
	3( )	Don't know
3. (IF YES, ASK) Do you feel that your attendance at these meetings or hearings was time well spent?	1( )	Yes
	2( )	No
	3( )	Don't know
4. In general, do you feel the city government is doing an excellent, good, fair, or poor job in meeting the needs of you and your family?	1( )	Excellent
	2( )	Good
	3( )	Fair
	4( )	Poor
	5( )	Don't know

1. For additional examples, see Questions 64 and 65 of the 1974 Nashville questionnaire presented in Appendix 1.

negative attitudes are focused upon political concerns from persons who are generally dissatisfied with public services.

Analyzing and presenting the survey findings. This step is vital if municipal operations are to benefit from the survey process. The government should plan in advance to conduct the supplementary cross-tabulations needed to make full use of the information obtained (for instance, to analyze citizen satisfaction in terms of the department initially contacted or previous citizen participation).[25] An analyst should be available to review, classify, and encode the various open-ended responses according to the definitions and distinctions agreed upon by government officials. Information on survey results from other jurisdictions can also be helpful in interpreting the data (see, for instance, Exhibit 11-4).

Survey of Complainants and Requesters of Services

The complainant-requester survey could be administered by telephoning a randomly selected sample of persons who had contacted the government to complain or to request service or information, if the telephone numbers of such persons are available. Alternatively, a mail questionnaire could be sent out to all (or a sample of) clients. As noted earlier, a "client" survey such as this can be especially useful for obtaining a variety of information on government services provided to special segments of the population, including satisfaction with the gov-

ernment's responses, ratings of various aspects of the quality of the service, and client characteristics. If a government wants to use such a survey to identify operating conditions needing correction, frequent polls (monthly, if possible) of complainants and/or requesters would be needed.

The client survey can be administered at low cost. The first use of a telephone survey covering about 750 "clients" in the course of a year would cost about $3,100 at 1976 prices. It could be repeated for perhaps less than three-quarters of that cost. If existing government personnel have enough slack time to serve as interviewers (a total of about 250 employee-hours would be required), the survey could be conducted without significant additional outlays.

The data from a client survey may be subject to subtle biases that a general citizen survey avoids. Records on complainants or requesters (from which the sample is drawn) may not include complaints or requests from all the departments that have actually received them. Those records that *are* available may reflect various degrees of screening by government personnel who perhaps chose not to record what they viewed as "unjustifiable" requests. Sometimes numerous anonymous complaints or requests may be encountered. Systematic biases such as these should be identified and corrected, if possible.

An example of a client survey is presented in Appendix 12. Portions were adapted from a survey designed and implemented by the city of St. Petersburg for its Services and Information Center. Questions 6, 7, 10, and 12 and Questions 3, 3a, and 5 (using slightly altered wordings) have been successfully used in St. Petersburg.[26] Question 11 has been tested successfully by the Seattle-King County Office of the Ombudsman. However, the other questions in Appendix 12 have not been tested. Governments contemplating their use should carefully pretest them to identify ambiguities in the wording. Note that at the end of the interview, the government should ask demographic questions similar to those on a general citizen survey in order to be able to cross-tabulate the results by population subgroups.

Some additional considerations in implementing a client survey are discussed in the following sections.

Sample selection.[27] The sample should be drawn

25. Any of a number of computerized statistical routines could be used, including the Statistical Package for the Social Sciences (SPSS) or the multiple cross-tab program developed by The Urban Institute for the analysis of citizen survey data. The latter program is available at cost from The Urban Institute.

26. "Successful" means that there were no significant percentages of "don't know" or "no response" replies and that interviewers did not identify any ambiguities during their interviews.

27. Techniques for determining sample sizes based upon detailed statistical considerations are given in most introductory texts on survey techniques and statistical analysis. See, for instance, Leslie Kish, *Survey Sampling* (New York: John Wiley and Sons, 1965).

from a listing of all, or virtually all, of the persons who have made complaints or requested services or information in the time period of concern. Enough names should be drawn to obtain at least 50 to 100 responses for each category of concern—50 to 100 incidents involving each department whose effectiveness is of special interest, 50 to 100 persons complaining about specific important problems for which the government wants detailed information, and so forth. Separate samples should be drawn for complaints, requests for service, and requests for information (if each is to be examined). One option is to sample requests and complaints in each department by using the relevant department files. Analysts might begin by concentrating on the departments that handle the largest portions of the city's complaints or requests.

Central complaint or request files may also constitute an adequate listing. But if some departments are not included in those files or if individual departments vary in their thoroughness in reporting complaints to the central office, a sample of central files may not be representative of all citizens who have had contacts with the government. Indeed, reliance on the records of a central complaint-referral office may result in missing persons who have called the appropriate department directly. Perhaps the best way to obtain a fully satisfactory sample will be to design and implement simple, uniform record-keeping procedures for all departments handling complaints or requests. Such procedures, however, must not be so demanding as to interfere with the servicing of the items received.

A related question in drawing the sample is the *age* of the records. Contacting persons about a week after the government has disposed of their complaint or request would appear most desirable. This would give the citizen time to reflect on the results but not to forget. Such a procedure would require spreading the interviews over a number of weeks. To avoid biases related to the timing of the survey, the sample should not be limited to persons who contacted the government during one particular week, but should instead be drawn from citizen contacts throughout the period over which the measure is to be prepared. For example, if annual measurements are sought, the total desired sample size should be estimated and a few interviews conducted, perhaps, during one week each month.

If a few kinds of common complaints tend to crowd out items of special interest to the government, the latter might decide to oversample the less common complaints. However, care must be taken in analyzing the results from such a stratified sample;

they cannot be simply lumped together and averaged to obtain an overall effectiveness measurement.[28]

In view of the complexity of drawing a client sample, sample selection and the establishment of a detailed sampling procedure should probably be done with the help of a person with statistical sampling experience.

Timing. Major concerns in the timing of the client survey include (1) the ultimate use of the data (the information might be needed for an annual set of effectiveness measures keyed to the budget cycle or to provide a monthly indication of developing operational problems) and (2) the availability of necessary personnel. Some governments may elect to conduct an on-going client survey with a few calls every week, as was done in St. Petersburg.[29]

Administering the survey. The survey should probably be conducted by telephone to minimize the costs involved while providing reasonably representative results. Many of the persons who have contacted the government to complain or make requests will have done so by phone, and they may have given their phone numbers to facilitate subsequent contacts. A questionnaire similar to that in Appendix 12 could probably be completed within ten minutes once an acceptable respondent has been reached.

A cheaper but otherwise less satisfactory option is to rely only on a mail survey—for example, by mailing out a version of the questionnaire in Appendix 12, perhaps to *all* clients. Such mailings might be made on a routine basis, for instance, at a predetermined interval after the initial complaint or request has been received. An important potential problem is the low response rate (well below 50 percent) usually associated with mail surveys. This means that substantial questions can be raised about the representativeness of the responses, impairing the credibility of the survey. If a mail survey is used, a second and possibly a third mailing to those clients who have not responded should be undertaken to raise the response rate to a more defensible level.

Anonymity of citizens who make complaints or requests. Follow-up surveys of complainants and re-

---

28. See Kish, *Survey Sampling,* for ways to deal with the results from stratified samples.

29. St. Petersburg used personnel from its central complaint-processing facility, the Service and Information Center. Calls were made by members of the center's staff during periods when the rate of incoming complaints and requests slowed down.

questers require adequate information on the identity of citizens making complaints and requests so that they can be contacted for survey purposes. A significant proportion of anonymous complaints or requests may bias the survey sample in unknown ways. Note that officials responsible for processing complaints in St. Petersburg reported a sharp increase in the number of anonymous complaints over the past few years, an experience shared by other local governments. Anonymous complaints are likely to make it increasingly difficult for municipalities to be sure of the representativeness of client surveys focused on complainants or requesters.

Government Records of Citizen Complaints and Requests

The third important data collection procedure associated with the evaluation of citizen complaint- and request-handling operations is the use of government records. Although complaint and request files in many jurisdictions often contain considerable information, they will probably not include certain kinds of data—especially on dispositions—needed for some of the suggested effectiveness measures. Thus certain modifications are likely to be needed. In general, the following three types of changes may be necessary: revisions in the forms used, revisions in filing procedures, and implementation of certain special data collection procedures. These changes would make possible better description and classification of the requests and complaints handled, tallies of the number of complaints, response-time determinations, and consistent assessments (by government personnel) of the disposition of complaints and requests.

Revisions of Forms and Records. Before a consistent set of forms can be designed, government officials must determine for what purpose each piece of information is to be collected; they also must agree on and formalize the many definitions and distinctions that will be needed. What constitutes a complaint, a request for service, or a request for information? When is a complaint justifiable? How should various types of complaints be defined? What will be accepted as a "satisfactory" disposition? Exhibit 11-1 presents some suggestions for such definitions.

The use of a single form by all government agencies for reporting complaints and requests for services would simplify the paperwork and reduce the burden on personnel for making accurate distinctions between the types of communications re-

ceived. Forms for recording complaints and service requests should contain at least the following information: the citizen's name, address, and telephone number; identification of the matter as a complaint or a request; the general subject; a description of the specific complaint or request; an indication of its urgency; the location of the matter; the government agency receiving the complaint or request; the agency responding to it; a judgment as to the justifiability of a complaint; the jurisdiction of the government in the matter; the disposition of the matter; and the response time.

Local governments maintain few—if any—records on requests for information, perhaps because of the great volume of such requests (about 80 percent of the 135,000 calls received by St. Petersburg's Service and Information Center in 1973 were requests for information). For reporting and evaluating information requests, a simplified form might be used to record the date, the requester's phone number, and the response provided (including an indication of whether a referral was made, an explanation given, or the answer delayed). However, many governments may consider it relatively unimportant to monitor the handling of information requests and therefore may not feel that the special effort required to record the foregoing information would be worthwhile.

Revised Filing Procedures. Alphabetical and tickler files for government complaint and request records will be helpful in gathering data for the proposed measures, as well as for other management purposes. The two files are described as follows:

ONE. Alphabetical files of complaints and service requests.[30] Complaint records should probably be filed alphabetically (by the last name of the complainant).[31] Of course, a high percentage of anonymous complaints will complicate this approach. Care should be taken not to violate client confidentiality; the filing of complaints by the last name of the complainant should be used only to provide a means for conveniently computing the average number of complaints per complainant for Measure C10.

Separate files should be kept for complaints and for service requests. Requests need not be filed alphabetically since no estimates of the number of re-

30. Filing procedures and data retrieval methods will be somewhat different from those described here if the local government's record keeping is computerized.

31. Examples of city offices that have maintained alphabetical files of this type include St. Petersburg's Ombudsman Office, the mayor's office in Nashville, and the Mayor's Office of Information and Complaints in Philadelphia.

quests per requester are needed. New files should be started every fiscal year and retained for at least twelve months after the end of that fiscal year to facilitate annual data analysis. A complete file will probably not be feasible for requests for information because of the large numbers involved; instead, only a random sample of the information requests received might be retained in the files. A random selection procedure can be developed for the available files to select samples of complaints and requests for client surveys.

TWO. Tickler files. Copies of all pending complaints and requests should be filed in a "tickler file" by the date the matter was first reported. When the complaint or request is resolved, a summary of the disposition of the matter should be returned by the various offices involved, at which time the corresponding complaint or request record should be removed from the tickler file.[32] Periodic examinations of these files can serve as a basis for prodding agencies about tardy responses and conveniently preparing Measures C4 and R4 ("items delayed longer than 'x' days").

Special Data Collection Procedures. Running tallies prepared on a daily or weekly basis (and subtotaled monthly) could provide a convenient way to routinely collect the information needed for reporting on measures which require data only from government records (Measures C1, C3, C4, C8, R1, R3, and R4). An important advantage of using running tallies is to make the preparation—and perhaps the use—of the measures a regular activity, rather than the focus of a concentrated effort once or twice a year; the latter is often disruptive and may use personnel inefficiently.

If a high volume of complaints and requests presents a problem for preparing running tallies or storing records, the government might retain only randomly selected samples of the records as required for measurement purposes. Using large enough samples can keep errors due to sampling acceptably small.

The classifications made by government personnel should be monitored periodically to ensure consistency with the definitions that have been established. If deviations are noted, additional (or refined) definitions, guidelines, or training may be necessary.

Miscellaneous Data Collection Considerations

Much information will be generated by the proposed measures, particularly if some are categorized by various complaint and population characteristics. Exhibit 11-7 illustrates a format for summarizing the effectiveness information for complaints and requests.[33] Of greatest importance in analyzing the effectiveness measures are the changes from year to year, rather than the absolute numbers involved. Therefore, the proposed measurements have been designed for periodic—at least annual—reporting.

The suggested measures of effectiveness involve manipulations of a few basic sets of data: citizen survey data, client survey data, and government complaint and request records. Much of this information could easily be computerized. Governments with adequate data-processing facilities should weigh the advantages against the costs of designing a comprehensive package of data collection procedures, data forms, summary information formats (for management review), computerized information files, and computer programs for the preparation and analysis of the measures.[34]

The business community represents a special clientele group whose interests in local government services may require a somewhat different emphasis from that provided by the data collection procedures described above. Although the same general concerns and quality considerations of interest to private citizens regarding the handling of complaints and requests should be of interest to the business community, there are likely to be a few exceptions. For instance, the complaints and requests of the latter group will probably be related to their commercial activities and the impact of the government upon those activities. Moreover, requests for service, such as an inspection, will probably be more common and important for businesses. Questions 40-43 of the business community survey shown in Appendix 2 represent a set of appropriate questions on complaints and requests for a survey of business persons.

The question of who should collect the data for the measures of effectiveness may pose a problem for some governments. If available, an office that handles complaints of *all* types—a central complaint-

---

32. These copies could then be held in special files such as "complaints by type" or "requests by agency responsible" until the appropriate periodic tabulations can be prepared.

33. If the city decides to set annual performance targets, the format of Exhibit 11-7 could be readily adapted to provide a comparison of "actual" versus "targeted" achievements.

34. For instance, computer programs could be written which would calculate the total number of reported complaints, the associated complaint rates, and breakdowns by type of complaint (Measure C8), and which could then check the data on each type of complaint for (1) major changes in level or rate over that of the past year and (2) discrepancies between clientele groups.

Exhibit 11-7

ILLUSTRATIVE FORMAT FOR EXHIBITING MEASURES OF EFFECTIVENESS
FOR COMPLAINT AND REQUEST HANDLING

OBJECTIVES AND MEASURES	CITYWIDE TOTAL			NEIGHBORHOOD AREA (CURRENT YEAR)					
	PRIOR YEAR	CURRENT YEAR	PERCENTAGE CHANGE	CENTRAL	NORTH-EAST	NORTH-WEST	SOUTH-EAST	SOUTH-WEST	

Reduction or prevention of justifiable citizen complaints

Number of justifiable complaints received during the past year (Measure C8), expressed as:

a. City total

b. Total for each type:
   Problem 1
   Problem 2
   • • •

c. Overall rates:
   Per 10,000 adults
   Sanitation complaints per 1,000 garbage accounts
   Utility bill complaints per 1,000 accounts
   • • •

d. Rate per 10,000 adults, for each type:
   • • •

Willingness and ability of citizens to make their complaints known to the government

Total number of reported and unreported complaints during the past year (Measure C9), expressed as:

a. City total

b. Total for each type:
   Problem 1
   Problem 2
   • • •

c. Rate per 10,000 adults

and request-processing facility, or persons on the staff of the mayor or chief administrative officer who are assigned to handle complaints and requests—would be the logical focus for establishing a data collection capability. Governments without such a facility might use another office with a special interest in the management feedback information implicit in citizen complaints and requests (for instance, the budget office).

Another alternative is to have a single person coordinate individual departmental efforts to develop the effectiveness information. Each departmental effort would be somewhat independent, but the use of common formats, definitions, and forms would be extremely important. By combining individual departmental totals and measurement results, a coordinator could provide a fairly comprehensive perspective on the complaints and requests received by the city.

If measurement data are categorized by various population subgroup characteristics, a government will be able to detect whether certain groups appear to be getting better services—or having more problems—than others; such information might indicate a need for service revisions. Data on the location and sex of the complainant or requester will often be available, permitting disaggregation of many of the proposed measures by neighborhood of residence and by sex. Other types of demographic characteristics (such as age group, income group, and race) are likely to be available only for certain measures (those utilizing survey procedures routinely collect such information).

A special case occurs for Measure C7, "the proportion of complaints that are reported." If the necessary data on reported complaints are obtained from government records, information on characteristics such as income or racial group will not usually be available. Breakouts by characteristics such as income or racial group could be made, however, if the alternate data collection procedure for Measure C7—a general citizen survey—is used.

When analyzing effectiveness measures derived by the use of sampling techniques, government personnel will need to consider the statistical confidence associated with the particular sample sizes used.[35] This determines to what degree observed differences might have been due to the "luck" of the sample drawn rather than to real differences in the entire population of interest. Some of these issues are discussed further in the chapter on general citizen surveys.

Costs and Staffing Requirements

Costs will vary according to the volume of complaints and requests, the frequency of conducting client surveys (and the sample sizes chosen), the availability and cost of computer facilities, and the degree of centralization among the complaint- and request-processing operations. Because it is not generally practical for local governments to undertake a general citizen survey solely for the complaint- and request-handling function, it is assumed here that any such survey will cover numerous local services and that the additional cost for including questions on complaints and requests will be minimal.

A part-time general coordinator will probably be needed to supervise the data collection for the complaint and request measures and the computation of the various measures, to deal with departments that have their own units for handling citizen complaints and requests, and to help analyze and interpret the results. This work might take about four employee-days per month; a few additional employee-days will be needed occasionally to prepare quarterly and annual measurement reports.

One or two part-time interviewers should be trained to administer the client survey; normally they could be expected to administer about three surveys per staff-hour. Some evening survey work may be necessary. An outside expert would probably be needed to instruct the interviewers in survey techniques, and an analyst would be required from time to time to handle computer runs, prepare measurements, run cross-tabulations, and the like. Also, a person with knowledge of survey sampling—perhaps the analyst—will be needed to draw the sample of clients to be interviewed. The length of time needed to draw the sample depends largely on the way the records are kept.

Exhibit 11-8 gives an estimate of the cost of implementing and operating a measurement and data collection system for citizen complaints and requests. These estimates may be high; costs could be pared by adhering to tighter schedules or by reducing the sample sizes, the length of the interviews, the analysis of the survey results, or the size of the coordination effort.

35. Additional discussions can be found in Carol Weiss and Harry P. Hatry, *An Introduction to Sample Surveys for Government Managers* (Washington, D.C.: The Urban Institute, March 1971) or any good text on statistics or sampling, e.g., Kish, *Survey Sampling*. Graphs of confidence intervals for estimated proportions (as a function of sample size) are given in Erwin L. Crow, Frances A. Davis, and Margaret W. Maxfield, *Statistics Manual* (New York: Dover Publications, 1960), charts II-IV in the appendix.

Exhibit 11-8

ESTIMATED ANNUAL COSTS OF EFFECTIVENESS MEASUREMENTS FOR COMPLAINT- AND REQUEST-PROCESSING SERVICES (AS OF 1976)

ITEM	START-UP COSTS (EMPLOYEE-DAYS)	YEARLY OPERATING COSTS (EMPLOYEE-DAYS)
General Citizen Survey (complaint and request portion only)		
Prepare survey questions	2	2
Special analyses of complaint and request data		5
Client Survey		
Prepare and test survey questions	10	
Training two interviewers	8	
Draw sample		4
Conduct interviews (750 total)		31
Analyze and present results		20
Government Complaint/Request Records		
Design forms	3	
Print forms	$125	
Prepare daily tallies (1 hour/day)		32
Conduct annual sample of records		3
Miscellaneous		
Specify definitions, classifications	5	
Train staff in using forms, definitions	13	
Coordinate measurement effort		44
Prepare three quarterly sets of (client survey) measures		6
Prepare annual set of effectiveness measures		5
Miscellaneous computer costs		$100
TOTAL	41 employee-days + $125 for new forms	152 employee-days + $100 computer costs

Assumptions

Conduct one general citizen survey per year at no cost to the operating agency.

Three quarterly reports are prepared on client survey results; one annual report on *all* measurements is prepared.

A single sample of complaint files is conducted once per year, just before preparation of the annual set of effectiveness measures (e.g., to measure complaints per complainant).

Coordination will require four employee-days per month plus an additional two employee-days at the end of each of the first three quarters to draw together the client survey results and an employee-week at the end of the fiscal year to prepare the annual set of measures of effectiveness.

Chapter 12

Using Effectiveness Measurement Information

This chapter discusses some specific uses for effectiveness measurement data, ways of reporting such data to facilitate their use, and ways of analyzing the data. Because measuring the effectiveness of basic community services is relatively new, information upon which to base a discussion of these issues is scarce. The preliminary suggestions that follow, however, are based whenever possible on actual experiences of local governments.[1]

Some Uses for the Data

This section presents nine potential uses for effectiveness measurement information: (1) review of progress and trends of government services; (2) resource allocation decisions; (3) budget formulation and justification; (4) in-depth program evaluation and analysis; (5) employee motivation; (6) performance contracting; (7) quality control checks on efficiency measurements; (8) management control; and (9) communication between citizens and government officials.

1. *Review of progress and trends of government services.* If data collection procedures such as de-

scribed in this report are undertaken annually, performance can be reviewed and compared from year to year, permitting identification of problem areas, progress that has been made, and, after several years of data collection, time trends. (Problems identified are likely to require a closer look to determine, first, whether action needs to be taken and if it does, which options appear most suitable.) Progress and time trends can indicate to government officials whether a service is adequate.

2. *Resource allocation decisions.* By identifying problem areas, effectiveness measurement information can help provide guidance to management concerning allocation of resources. Breaking out the measurement data by neighborhood residential areas, and by other important client-group characteristics within the jurisdiction, as suggested throughout this report, will provide information on the specific geographical areas and client groups with major problems or needs. In addition, measures that yield information on *specific* service characteristics (as distinguished from the overall ratings for service areas) can provide operating agency management with information on specific problems. For example, the city of St. Petersburg used information on the "percentage of respondents reporting rat sightings" by geographical area to help guide its rodent-control program. Savannah, Georgia, has used the effectiveness measurement information to help quantify the liveability of the city's approximately twenty geographical planning areas in order "to maintain an acceptable standard of living throughout all areas of the municipality." Savannah's procedures attempt to distinguish high-need

---

1. Some additional information on uses for and interpretation of effectiveness data is provided in Chapter 2 of *Measuring the Effectiveness of Basic Municipal Services: Initial Report.* Another discussion of the early utilization of the effectiveness measurement information in St. Petersburg, Nashville, and other cities is provided in the National Science Foundation-sponsored utilization assessment, "Case Study No. 10: Effectiveness Measurement Methods: Urban Institute" (Research Triangle Park, N.C.: Research Triangle Institute, July 1975).

areas of the community and subsequently to allocate resources in accordance with need.[2]

The use of effectiveness information by local governments to assess community needs is further illustrated by the experience of Birmingham, Alabama. The health and welfare council of that city used the recreation citizen survey (see Chapter 4) to identify recreation needs by geographic area, and then used this information to persuade authorities to fill the gaps.[3] In one case, the council identified one neighborhood's desire to have programs for teenage girls; a nonprofit organization subsequently met that need.

A related issue is equality in the distribution of recreation services. Effectiveness data adds an important ingredient to any review of equality of distribution of services. Past court suits have focused almost entirely on the distribution of inputs such as staffing, equipment, and the number of facilities. The Hawkins-Shaw decision and recent court cases including ones in Washington, D.C., and Fairfax County, Virginia, have considered not only the amount of government resources provided, but also the effectiveness of those resources, such as the quality of facilities and services.[4]

The use of effectiveness measurement information to help with the allocation of resources can be "a significant move away from 'squeaky wheel' decision making."[5]

3. *Budget formulation and justification.* The budget process is clearly an important element in governments' allocation of resources. It should include information from the regular monitoring of service effectiveness. After effectiveness measurement procedures have been tested and appear to yield sufficiently reliable data, effectiveness information can be included as a requirement for budget preparation and justification. This information should help guide initial budget decisions and subsequently permit government officials to provide

better justifications for expenditures to the council and to the public. Jurisdictions with some form of program budgeting, zero-base budgeting, program planning and budgeting system, and the like should find effectiveness information of considerable importance in making rational budget choices.[6] Without regularly available information abut the effectiveness of individual government services, it is hard to see how such budgeting procedures can be truly meaningful.

4. *In-depth program evaluation and program analysis.* Examining the performance of existing programs (program evaluation) and considering various options for future implementation (program analysis) are basic elements of management. Some governments have begun to make provision, sometimes with separate staffs, for undertaking in-depth studies of important program issues. An essential requirement for these studies is detailed information on program effectiveness. This information will be more easily assembled if service-area effectiveness measurement data are collected regularly. Even when special data are needed for particular evaluations or analyses, measures of effectiveness and data collection procedures such as those discussed in this report are likely to be useful for these studies.

Similarly, effectiveness measurement procedures and findings can be used as part of a productivity assessment and analysis program, especially if combined with data on unit costs.

An example of the use of effectiveness measurement procedures for a program evaluation study was the District of Columbia's use of the street cleanliness-rating and citizen survey procedures (see Chapter 2) to evaluate its special 1971 "Operation Clean-Sweep." This intensive, one-time clean-up campaign sought to remove accumulated litter and other solid wastes from public and private property. Several hundred regular and supplemental cleaning personnel combed the city, cleaning all public streets and alleys one area at a time. Residents were encouraged to tackle their own properties and to set out the refuse for collection.

The city undertook an evaluation to determine the program's potential to bring about both short-

2. The Savannah, Georgia, experience is described in International City Management Association, *Improving Effectiveness: Responsive Public Services,* Municipal Innovation Series No. 10, June 1976.

3. For a further discussion of assessing recreation needs, see Michael P. Rogers, "Assessing Public Recreation Needs" (Ann Arbor, Mich.: U.S. Bureau of Outdoor Recreation, November 1974).

4. For examples of such materials used in court cases see Donald M. Fisk and Cynthia A. Lancer, "Equality of Distribution of Recreation Services: A Case Study of Washington, D.C." (Washington, D.C.: The Urban Institute, July 1974) and Andrew J. Boots, Grace Dawson, William Silverman, and Harry P. Hatry, "Inequality in Local Government Services: A Case Study of Neighborhood Roads" (Washington, D.C.: The Urban Institute, 1972).

5. International City Management Association, *Improving Effectiveness,* p. 4.

6. A related measurement approach labeled Total Performance Measurement System (TPMS) has been formulated recently by the federal Joint Financial Management Improvement Program and U.S. General Accounting Office. At this writing, it is being tested in a variety of agencies at the federal, state, and local levels of government. It explicitly calls for client ratings, agency performance data, and employee attitude surveys. Measurement systems such as TPMS will need effectiveness measurement information to provide a meaningful perspective on government performance.

term and lasting improvements in neighborhood cleanliness. The three bases for evaluation were:

a. Changes in cleanliness ratings of streets and alleys. Visual inspections of virtually every street and alley were made the week before and the week after the special collection in each area; results were expressed in terms of average cleanliness ratings and the percentage of blocks with ratings of 2.5 or worse,

grouped for each sanitation district (see Chapter 2 for a description of this procedure).

b. Changes in citizen perceptions of cleanliness as determined by comparing results of a citizen survey taken four months *after* "Clean-Sweep" with those of a citizen survey taken four months previous to the operation.

c. Program costs.

Exhibit 12-1 illustrates the effectiveness information that was obtained.

Exhibit 12-1

ILLUSTRATION OF USE OF EFFECTIVENESS MEASUREMENT PROCEDURES FOR PROGRAM EVALUATIONS: D.C. OPERATION CLEAN-SWEEP

A. Trained Observer Cleanliness Ratings

SERVICE AREA	PERCENTAGE OF STREETS WITH LITTER RATINGS OF 2.5 OR WORSE	
	Before	*After*
1	3	1
2	19	5
3	21	12
4	20	7
5	20	15
6	46	47
7	40	6
8	0	0
9	4	4
TOTAL	19	11

B. Citizen Survey Results

QUESTION	PERCENTAGE OF RESPONSES	
	4 MONTHS BEFORE CLEAN-SWEEP (101 RESPONDENTS)	4 MONTHS AFTER CLEAN-SWEEP (110 RESPONDENTS)
What do you think of the cleanliness of the street on which you live?		
a. Clean	14	13
b. Mostly clean	45	50
c. Fairly dirty	27	24
d. Very dirty	14	13
e. No opinion	0	0
Percent satisfied (a + b)	59 ± 8	63 ± 7
Percent dissatisfied (c + d)	41 ± 8	37 ± 7
Have you noticed any change in the cleanliness of your streets in the last 3 or 4 months?		
a. Very much cleaner		10
b. Somewhat cleaner		28
c. Somewhat dirty	not	3
d. Very much dirtier	applicable	2
e. No change noticed		52
f. Don't know/no opinion		5

Source: Louis Blair and Alfred Schwartz, *How Clean Is Our City?* (Washington, D.C.: The Urban Institute, 1972), and Washington, D.C., data. For discussions of the procedures used, see Chapter 2 in this book and the 1972 publication.

A trend toward auditing government services and programs by performance or results has been growing.[7] The legislative body or the chief executive can sponsor such auditing. Auditing program results is, in effect, program evaluation, the principal distinction probably being the evaluators' independence from the agency responsible for the program. Such auditing depends heavily on the existence of adequate measurements of program effectiveness and quality. Similarly, the increasing concern with "accountability" encompasses outcomes of services as well as financial probity. Measures and data collection procedures such as those discussed in this report seem vital for such auditing and accountability.

5. *Employee motivation.* The availability of effectiveness information is likely to make establishment of performance targets or incentive systems for both management and nonmanagement employees considerably more practical and meaningful. The development of performance incentives in the public sector in the past has been greatly handicapped by the lack of meaningful measures of the effectiveness and quality of services. Governments attempting to focus on objective measures of performance have often had to rely chiefly on measures of input, process, or workload. Unfortunately, reliance on such measures can encourage government employees to overemphasize "quantity" aspects of their job, with resulting deterioration in the overall quality of government services.

Among several recent attempts to apply performance incentives are those of Detroit and Flint, Michigan, which have included in their incentive-bonus formulas for solid waste collectors (a) completion of collection routes on schedule, (b) waste collection efficiency, and (c) selected service quality factors. The city of Orange, California, has tied future wage increases for its police to reductions in certain types of crimes. These efforts represent a very early stage in the development of quality-related incentives.[8] The design of formulas tying earnings to performance can involve complex issues that need careful handling. The point here is that if employees are to be offered incentives to provide better service or to improve efficiency without lowering the quality of service, provision for measuring that quality seems indispensable.

Governments using some version of "management by objectives" should also find measures similar to those discussed in this report useful for inclusion in their lists of objectives, in order to ensure that service quality is explicitly addressed.

Even if performance is not formally tied to employee benefits, providing information to employees about the outcomes of their efforts can prove beneficial. Findings such as those from the citizen surveys can help make government employees more sensitive to citizens' perceptions of the services provided and encourage them to be more responsive to citizens' needs.

6. *Performance contracting.* Governments that contract for major portions of public services, such as solid waste collection, can use effectiveness measures to control the quality of the contractor's performance. This might be done by including minimum quality levels in the contract or even by providing financial incentives for attainment of higher quality levels. Currently, few contracts include such performance standards, partly because the data required are rarely available on a regular basis.

7. *Quality control checks on efficiency measurements.* Governments attempting to assess efficiency and productivity need to consider the quality as well as the quantity of the work performed. Increases in work accomplished per dollar or per employee-hour do not in themselves guarantee real net improvement in performance. Reductions in cost per unit of work accomplished that occur at the expense of quality of the service should not be considered improvements in efficiency or productivity. Measures similar to those identified here are likely to be useful for quality checks. At the very least, effectiveness data should be presented along with the unit-cost data to give public officials a perspective on the relationship between effectiveness and efficiency. This issue is discussed at greater length in Chapter 16.

8. *Management control.* In some cases, the measurement procedures can also be used for management control. The determining factors for this use are the frequency of data collection and timeliness of feedback to managers. When data are collected weekly, monthly, and even quarterly, managers may be able to use the information to reallocate

---

7. A chief element in the initiation of this trend was the issuance by the U.S. General Accounting Office of "Standards for Audit of Governmental Organizations, Programs, Activities, and Functions" (Washington, D.C.: Comptroller General of the United States, 1972).

8. See, for example, John M. Greiner, "Tying City Pay to Performance: Early Reports on Orange, California, and Flint, Michigan" (Washington, D.C.: Labor-Management Relations Service, December 1974); James Neubacher, "Detroit Sanitation Productivity—Everyone Wins," Strengthening Local Government Through Better Labor Relations No. 18 (Washington, D.C.: Labor-Management Relations Service, November 1973); and John M. Greiner, Roger Dahl, Harry P. Hatry, and Annie Millar, *Monetary Incentives and Work Standards for Public Employees,* (Washington, D.C.: The Urban Institute, 1977).

their resources. For example, frequent collection of street cleanliness ratings such as those undertaken in New York City, can permit allocation of crews to increase frequency of coverage in areas of greatest need. Some data, such as crime and arrest clearance rates, are already reported frequently, and can affect resource allocations from month to month. Because of their cost, procedures such as surveys of citizens will probably be undertaken less often, and several weeks may be required for processing, analyzing, and writing up the information for management. As a result, such data often may not be available quickly enough for management control purposes.

9. *Improved communication between citizens and government officials.* There are two aspects to this use for measurement data. First, a number of the measures suggested in this report call for using information obtained directly from citizens—the customers for basic municipal services. Unstructured nonsurvey approaches are likely to yield information unrepresentative of the views of the full population. Proper data collection procedures such as citizen surveys, trained observer ratings, and business surveys can yield information more representative of the community than can other common sources of citizen feedback, such as citizen complaint data, personal observations by individual

managers, or periodic contacts between officials and selected parts of the population.

Second, the availability of effectiveness information can also enhance communication in the other direction—from government officials to citizens. The measures presented in this report focus on service characteristics of direct concern and interest to the citizens of a given jurisdiction. They are more likely to be important to citizens than are typical municipal statistics such as level-of-activity (workload) measures. An example of the use of effectiveness information to inform the public is provided by Nashville, which has presented highlights of the measurements in reports to its citizens.[9]

Reporting Effectiveness Measurement Data

How measurement data are reported can have a major impact on whether and how they are used. The information should be presented in as meaningful, concise, and interesting a fashion as possible.

9. Metropolitan Nashville-Davidson County, "How Well is Metro Doing?" 1974 and 1975 editions.

Exhibit 12-2

ILLUSTRATIVE SUMMARY FORMAT FOR PRESENTATION OF SELECTED EFFECTIVENESS MEASUREMENT DATA: RECREATION SERVICES

MEASURES OF EFFECTIVENESS	REGION (CURRENT YEAR)									TOTAL CITY	
	I	II	III	IV	V	VI	VII	VIII	IX	CURRENT YEAR	PREVIOUS YEAR
1. Percentage of persons who used government facilities fewer than 5 times during the year.	15	25	25	70	10	60	5	70	80	40	50
2. Percentage of persons who used government facilities fewer than 5 times during the year and whose reasons for nonuse were at least partly capable of being affected by government action.	7	20	10	40	2	40	4	50	60	25	30
3. Percentage of persons *not* within 15 minutes driving time of a park.	6	8	10	8	7	21	3	16	22	11	14
4. Total number of severe injuries.	4	0	2	3	1	3	1	4	7	25	32
5. Percentage of persons rating overall recreation opportunities as either "fair" or "poor."	10	7	5	18	14	30	5	12	25	12	12

Note: Space could be provided on the form for listing highlights and important problem areas, and steps planned or already taken to alleviate the problem. See Chapter 4 for discussion of the measures.

Exhibit 12-3
ILLUSTRATIVE SUMMARY FORMAT FOR PRESENTATION OF SELECTED EFFECTIVENESS
MEASUREMENT DATA: SOLID WASTE COLLECTION SERVICES

MEASURES OF EFFECTIVENESS	1976		1977		IMPROVEMENT		NOTES
	INNER CITY	REMAINDER OF CITY	INNER CITY	REMAINDER OF CITY	INNER CITY	REMAINDER OF CITY	
Street cleanliness: Percentage of streets rated 2.5 or worse. (4.0 is very dirty; 1.0 is very clean).	47%	11%	21%	14%	Yes	?	Definite improvement in inner city sample; too small to tell if change in rest of city was significant.
Steet cleanliness: Average street litter rating.	2.8	1.6	2.3	1.8	Yes	No	Rest of city got slightly dirtier; tends to confirm that there was a worsening in actual conditions in remainder of city.
Alley cleanliness: Percentage of alleys rating 2.5 or worse.	54%	14%	34%	21%	Yes	No	Rest of city got dirtier, apparently because special collection items are normally placed in alleys awaiting collection.
Citizen opinions of street cleanliness: Percentage responding "fairly clean" or "very clean."	31%	68%	47%	64%	Yes	?	Improvement in inner city; sample too small to determine if difference in remainder of city is significant. With cleanliness ratings, tends to confirm cleanliness improvements in inner city.
Number of complaints of dirty streets.	57	16	114	46	No	No	More complaints; possibly inner-city residents increasingly feel that if they complain, something will happen.
Offensive odors: Percentage of citizens who had noticed widespread odors.	22%	4%	19%	3%	?	?	Sample too small to detect changes; apparently no change.
Noise: Percentage of citizens complaining of being bothered by noise.	11%	12%	11%	12%	No	No	Most complaints of noise from refuse collection packer operation.

Note: See Chapter 2 for discussion of these measures.

Unclear or overly long reports, especially those heavily dependent on statistics, should be avoided. The following suggestions may help.

1. Reports should emphasize *comparisons* of interest (rather than merely presenting jurisdictionwide totals) such as (a) changes from one year to the next; (b) differences between areas of the community; (c) findings for various clientele groups (different age, sex, income, and racial groupings); and (d) planned performance versus performance achieved. Exhibits 12-2 and 12-3 present two summary formats which highlight comparisons among geographical neighborhoods within the community.

Each format also compares the current year's findings with those of the previous year.

With citizen surveys a special problem arises in how to summarize the voluminous data generated. Those working in this project and the cooperating governments have found the format shown in Exhibit 12-4 to provide a useful, concise summary of the results. For each major question on the survey, the format provides a one-page summary of the findings for each of a number of demographic and geographic breakouts of the data. This compact format eliminates the need for users to pore through pages of printout, while it permits them to identify

Exhibit 12-4
ILLUSTRATIVE FORMAT FOR SUMMARIZING DATA FOR EACH SURVEY QUESTION
(Hypothetical Data)

Question 2: About how often have you ridden on inter-city buses in the past 12 months?

	DAILY	LESS THAN DAILY BUT AT LEAST ONCE A WEEK	LESS THAN ONCE A WEEK BUT AT LEAST ONCE A MONTH	LESS THAN ONCE A MONTH	NOT AT ALL	DON'T KNOW	TOTAL RESPONDING
Number responding	36	49	50	63	429	0	625
Percentage of total responding	5	8	8	10	68	1	100
Respondent class	Percentage of total respondents in class						
(Percentage by responses)							
Sex White male	4	7	7	10	71	1	265
and White female	5	8	8	11	68	0	284
race Nonwhite male	19	11	11	6	53	0	36
Nonwhite female	10	7	10	8	65	0	40
Age: 18-34	5	11	13	13	58	0	272
35-49	3	8	6	8	75	0	125
50-64	8	3	3	5	80	1	105
65 and over	7	4	6	9	74	0	123
Family under $3,000	9	13	12	11	55	0	150
Income: $3,000-4,999	9	10	15	11	55	0	117
$5,000-7,999	5	11	4	10	70	0	100
$8,000-9,999	3	2	7	10	78	0	69
$10,000-15,000	3	6	2	11	78	0	104
over $15,000	1	1	3	7	88	0	85
Region: 1. Central	4	13	12	11	60	0	150
2. Northeast	4	12	13	11	59	1	174
3. Northwest	9	3	6	8	74	0	76
4. Southeast	5	4	3	11	77	0	113
5. Southwest	4	5	5	15	71	0	112

Note: The linked circles illustrate how key findings might be highlighted.

quickly the significant problem areas and instances of unusually high performance.[10] After the citizen survey has been repeated, comparisons of results over time will probably become of considerable importance and interest. A summary format that facilitates comparisons of the current year's findings with those of previous years can be readily prepared.

2. It is very desirable to have staff personnel review the findings and summarize the highlights in an "executive summary" for management and perhaps for the local legislative body. Oral summaries of the major findings may also be desirable for some officials.

3. Reporting to managers using the principle of "management by exception" also seems a good strategy for handling effectiveness measurement data. To define systematically what constitutes an "exception," the government might select certain "control" limits for the magnitude of each measure, the magnitude of differences between population groups, and

10. Typically, survey results are presented on many individual sheets, each of which provides one question tallied for one demographic breakout. The format shown in Exhibit 12-4 can be generated manually by having clerical personnel transfer information from individual computer sheets to the illustrated format. An alternative is to use a computer program to generate the form directly from the data. Most survey firms and local governments do not appear to have such a program. The Urban Institute has developed a FORTRAN computer program for this purpose. Documentation on the program as well as a tape copy can be obtained by governments from the Urban Institute Computer Services Division. See Joseph Gueron and Binyork Ouyang "UI-MCTAB, A Multiple Crosstab Program" (Washington, D.C.: The Urban Institute, August 8, 1974).

the magnitude of changes for a given group from one time period to the next. For example, each of the findings for the various population-group breakouts could be compared to the governmentwide results. Differences exceeding, for example, 20 percent (or, for measures expressed as percentages, perhaps ten percentage points) would then be highlighted.[11] Similarly, after the measurement data have been collected for more than one year, the government might select certain limits for differences from the previous year's results. These might also be 20 percent (or, for measures expressed as percentages, ten percentage points). Any measure found to exceed these limits in the current year would be reported to management. Such "out-of-control" findings might also be highlighted by flagging them on the reports.

Because the findings of citizen surveys may be politically sensitive, upper-level management probably should receive a complete set of these findings. Staffs should flag those results that appear to present unusual problems or to indicate unusually good performance in that period (as illustrated in Exhibit 12-4).

In addition, values for *key* measures, preselected as particularly important to management, should probably be shown regardless of their levels.

4. After enough experience has been accumulated to permit realistic assessments of what achievements are possible, it may be desirable to attempt to develop target values for the various measures. Actual performance would subsequently be compared to the targets. Exhibit 12-5 illustrates such a format. This approach has been used by some local governments, including New York City; the District of Columbia; Charlotte, North Carolina; Fairfax County, Virginia; and Savannah, Georgia. Both Savannah and the District of Columbia used targets for individual geographical areas within the city. Savannah used the citywide average performance level for each measure as the norm for performance in developing targets for each of approximately twenty neighborhoods.[12] The District of Columbia used the ratings for the cleaner areas of the city as targets for the other areas of the city.

The determination of targets can be difficult and complex, particularly for effectiveness measures such as those presented in this report. There are no national standards or comparative data for most of them.[13] We recommend deferring use of targets until some years of experience are gained or until sufficient analysis has been made of the particular service area to give the government some confidence that the targets are reasonable.

5. The "reporting" of effectiveness measurement findings should include feedback from operating agencies regarding the meaning of the findings and what might be done in response to them. Exhibit 12-6 presents an illustrative memo to operating agencies requesting such information; it is adapted from one used by Nashville and St. Petersburg. Although it is specifically directed toward review of citizen survey findings, essentially the same wording can be used in connection with annual reports on all measures for each service area. The memo also suggests that agencies discuss the findings with employees in their organization to help sensitize employees to the needs and interests of their clients.

Analysis of the Data

The previous sections have already suggested some basic analyses of the effectiveness measurement data, such as comparing data among various population groups within the community, comparing findings with those of previous years, and comparing actual performance against targeted performance. Even though the presentation of the basic cross-tabulations can inform government officials on problems, progress, and trends in various aspects of individual service, the data collected can also be subjected to considerably more extensive analysis. A few suggestions for additional, but not highly technical, analysis follow.

1. Many straightforward analyses require rela-

---

11. For findings derived from samples, such as citizen survey data, statistical significance should also be considered; deviations which are likely to result from the "luck of the draw" should be so identified. We do not recommend, however, that *statistical* significance be used as the principal criterion for identifying findings of concern. With relatively large samples, even a difference of, perhaps, three percentage points or less might be statistically significant, but such differences may be of little practical concern for program and policy decisions. Therefore, we recommend that "practical" significance be the primary criterion, with statistical significance used to identify the likelihood that chance caused unusual differences or changes.

12. Savannah used the statistical concept of the standard deviation (from the average rating for the whole city) on a particular measure as the score for each measure. See International City Management Association, *Improving Effectiveness*. Note that the ICMA report indicates that reviewers of the system, as well as Savannah's staff, suggested a simpler approach than the use of the statistical standard deviations.

13. In a few instances, comparative data such as numbers of reported crimes and fires, and crime clearance rates are available. Despite their many problems (see Chapter 6), these can be used to provide some crude targets—for example, a jurisdiction might use the average clearance rates for specific categories of crime for local governments with similar demographic characteristics as "target" values for itself.

Exhibit 12-5

ILLUSTRATIVE FORMAT FOR REPORTING ACTUAL VERSUS TARGETED PERFORMANCE:
SOLID WASTE COLLECTION

MEASURES OF EFFECTIVENESS	ACTUAL VALUE PREVIOUS YEAR (FY 76)	TARGET CURRENT YEAR (FY 77)		QUARTERLY PERFORMANCE			
				1st	2nd	3rd	4th
Percentage of blocks whose appearance is rated unsatisfactory ("fairly dirty" or "very dirty"—2.5 or worse on visual rating scale)	18%	13%	Target	16%	14%	12%	10%
			Actual				
Average block cleanliness rating	2.2	1.8	Target	2.1	1.9	1.7	1.6
			Actual				
Number of fires involving uncollected solid waste	17	12	Target	3	4	3	2
			Actual				
Percentage of households reporting having seen one or more rats during the period of a year	15%	8%	Target	Citizen survey undertaken once, in third quarter		8%	
			Actual				
Percentage of households reporting one or more missed collections during a year	17%	12%	Target	Citizen survey undertaken once, in third quarter		12%	
			Actual				
Percentage of households rating overall neighborhood cleanliness as usually "fairly dirty" or "very dirty"	23%	18%	Target	Citizen survey undertaken once, in third quarter		18%	
			Actual				

Notes: (a) A government may also want to display the cumulative results at the end of each quarter. (b) Space for agency comments on its performance on each measurement would also be desirable. (c) Quarterly targets should be set to reflect seasonal variations. (d) Ideally, estimates of the amount of statistical uncertainty should be provided when appropriate, as with citizen survey data. See Chapter 2 for discussion of the measures.

tively small amounts of analytical time. These include calculations of the percentage change from one time period to another and, after data covering periods of more than two years are available, analysis of the time series for individual measures to indicate longer-term trends. The time-trend lines might also be used to provide projections to which measurements taken after program changes have been made can be compared, thus giving an indication of whether improvements occurred after those program changes.

2. A variety of additional cross-tabulations can be made to provide further insights as to what has happened. For example, citizen survey ratings of neighborhood street cleanliness or street rideability might be compared to more "objective" trained observer measures for these same characteristics. This comparison would help to identify whether lower satisfaction levels were due to a degradation in physical conditions, or instead to an increase in citizens' expectations or to some factor not picked up by the ratings. The latter possibilities would be indicated if citizen satisfaction decreased while the trained observer ratings stayed at about the same level or improved. If appropriate "alienation" questions have been included in the citizen survey,

Exhibit 12-6

ILLUSTRATIVE MEMO TO OPERATING AGENCIES TRANSMITTING DETAILED CITIZEN SURVEY
RESULTS AND REQUESTING AGENCY VIEWS ON THE FINDINGS

MEMORANDUM
To: Operating Agencies
From: (Chief Executive/Chief Administrator)
Subject: Results of Citizen Survey

Attached are the results of the citizen survey conducted in July 1976. During the survey, adults in 600 households were interviewed. The survey procedures were based on modern survey techniques. Hence, although they were based on only a small percentage of the total population, they provide a much more representative cross section of citizen views than can be obtained by other means, such as casual contacts or complaint data. The citizen perceptions and experiences documented here can therefore be considered to be fairly representative of the households in our city.

Citizen feedback is a vital concern to us all. *I would like to have your agency's view as to what you believe are the highlights and implications of these findings for government programs and policies.* Please review these findings carefully, looking particularly at differences in response by neighborhood area, age group, income class, race, and sex.

In your reply please address the following questions:

1. What are the significant findings? For example, what are the apparent problem areas or particular groups or neighborhoods needing attention, and what are the major successes?

2. What might explain the reasons for these problem areas or apparently significant successes? (The answers may not be apparent from the survey; you will probably need to draw on your own insights and other department information.)

3. What actions should be considered to alleviate the problems or to expand the successes?

You may want to take the opportunity to discuss the findings of the survey with employees in your organization both to obtain their suggestions and to provide them with a clearer perspective as to citizen perceptions of the services they are providing.

In addition to providing information that may be of assistance to you in planning your program this year, it is hoped that these citizen survey findings will become a baseline for comparisons with future citizen surveys, which we expect to undertake on an annual basis.

I would like to provide to the city council and the public a summary report in approximately four weeks. This will be based in part on the material you provide. Please forward the results of your review to my office in two weeks. Subsequent discussions will be held as needed to clarify the findings and to consider any actions that seem appropriate.

cross-tabulations can also be used to determine whether a problem indicated by the citizen responses stems largely from citizen alienation with government.[14] Another example: if persons in only one geographic area appear to rate all or most services as poor, special neighborhood needs rather than solely individual service deficiencies might be indicated.

3. Because many factors outside government control can affect the outcomes on the individual service qualities, operating agency personnel should identify major external events that occurred during the relevant period which offer possible explanations for changes observed in service effectiveness. For example, unusually bad weather during the year is likely to affect significantly ratings of such measures as street rideability, street cleanliness, and storm drainage. Of course, this practice could open the door to all sorts of "excuses," but if

analysts examine such explanations objectively, the additional information would probably be useful in interpreting performance.

4. Analyses similar to those undertaken by Savannah can be used to relate the values for measures in particular areas of the community with factors peculiar to such areas and thus help explain differences among neighborhoods. For example, such conditions as age of buildings, level of education, level of income, and stability of families might be found by statistical analysis to be highly correlated with fire-rate differences among neighborhoods.[15] Analysis could then provide a basis for governments to set different performance targets in various neighborhoods. For example, areas with older, more dilapidated buildings would be expected to have more fires than others. The government's

14. See Chapter 11 on the handling of citizen complaints for a discussion of such an analysis.

15. A preliminary examination of this approach is presented in Philip S. Schaenman et al., "Measuring Local Fire Protection Outcomes: Some Potential Improvements" (Washington, D.C.: The Urban Institute and National Fire Protection Association, forthcoming).

eventual aim, of course, would be to improve these basic underlying conditions; after such improvements, target expectations would be adjusted accordingly.

Need for Analytical Resources. To get the most out of the effectiveness information, a government will need to allocate adequate resources for analysis. The shortage of analytical resources in local governments probably has been a prime restriction on the use of performance data. Yet governments undertaking service effectiveness measurement are likely to find that investment in only a small amount of analysis provides large returns. The analytical resources can be used not only to enhance the effectiveness information but also to examine other relevant information, such as cost data and information on program characteristics and external factors.

A Final Cautionary Note

The type of data collection discussed in this report can significantly improve the supply of information relevant to government programs and policies, but unless a determined effort is made to utilize the results, and unless resources are allocated to analyze and use the data, the effort spent in collection will be wasted. If a government has no plans to use the effectiveness measurement information or if it undertakes measurement and subsequently finds—after sufficient trial—that it is not using the results, the measurement effort should be discontinued. It is important to remember, however, that because of the lack of early payoff, the first year or two of a measurement program can be discouraging.

Chapter 13

Trained Observer Rating Procedures

Some of the measures of solid waste collection (Chapter 2) and transportation (Chapter 8) involve the use of trained observers to obtain relatively objective rating data for particular conditions.[1] These measures include street and alley cleanliness; street roughness and pavement conditions; sidewalk pavement conditions; and the visibility and physical condition of stop signs, other traffic control signs (such as yield, one way, do-not-enter), and street name signs. All of these are conditions that can be detected by a driver or rider in an automobile moving at moderate speeds.

Trained observer ratings enable governments to quantify conditions from ratings of either a sample of locations selected in a statistically random manner, or all locations in the community. Comparisons may be made either among different neighborhoods at any given time, or among conditions in the same neighborhood or the whole community at different times, to measure any changes. After appropriate training, different persons acting at different times and using the same photographic guidelines and rating procedures have been able to produce comparable ratings. The photographic guidelines consist of several photos showing typical conditions that identify or define a rating value. Observers compare the actual condition under observation to the photographic guidelines to determine which rating to assign. The ratings can be readily understood by other persons, particularly if shown the photographs and written guidelines used for making the ratings.

If ratings of a number of measures are undertaken simultaneously, the costs of collecting data for each measure are substantially reduced. But if the number of conditions to be measured increases beyond two or three at every inspection point, it is usually necessary to have another observer in the vehicle to share the rating jobs.[2] Costs will, of course, increase substantially if two-person teams are used.

A number of aspects to be considered in making decisions on using trained observers and in implementing and supervising a trained observer program are discussed below.

---

1. Other aspects of the quality of particular services such as exposed refuse or health hazards at sanitary landfills and the cleanliness or state of repair of public recreational facilities can also be rated by trained observers. Such inspections require observations in selected parts of the community and do not lend themselves to ratings made from automobiles as do the measures discussed here. However, many of the procedures for setting up, operating, and monitoring a trained observer program apply regardless of where the inspections are made or which specific observations are to be made.

2. During the initial phases of development of the multiple trained observer rating procedure in Nashville, the driver and the rider each tried to rate five different items. Even when the observers stopped their vehicles at the end of blocks to allow time for completing the ratings, they suffered undue strain, frequently failed to record all data, and produced inconsistent ratings. Traffic in New York City was so congested that it was not considered prudent to have drivers make ratings. In other cities, traffic congestion, even in commercial areas, has not been so great as to prevent drivers from making ratings.

Reliability: Can Independent Observers Consistently Arrive at Same Ratings?

The ratings are made using carefully developed photographic standards and written guidelines that enable observers to assign discrete grades to conditions (generally 1.0, 2.0, 3.0, or 4.0 with intermediate 0.5-point ratings when an observer cannot decide on an integer rating). Experience in the training programs in Nashville, St. Petersburg, and Washington, D.C., showed that in most cases two or more persons rigorously applying the guidelines and standards arrived at the same grade for a scene. Although trainees might initially disagree over a rating, they usually settled on a common rating when they reinspected the scene and applied the guidelines.

There are some factors that can cause observers to rate conditions improperly. These include the following:

- Forgetfulness—observers may inadvertently apply modified guidelines if they fail to refer frequently enough to the standard. Or, observers who have several different conditions to rate at once may forget to record one rating in the process.
- Boredom or fatigue may cause observers to fail to examine all of the characteristics that need to be considered in assigning a rating.
- Excessive speed, visual obstructions, parked vehicles, or traffic, may cause observers to miss conditions.
- Inability to take the strain of driving and rating, or perhaps inability to read maps or to navigate.
- Cheating—that is, falsifying ratings to avoid the rigors of inspection.

How well these problems can be avoided or overcome will depend on the quality of the inspection personnel, the adequacy of the training program, and the comprehensiveness and intensity of the monitoring and supervision. Experience has shown that a high degree of accuracy can be obtained only if the supervisors repeat a sample of ratings made by observers for quality control and discuss any differences the same day the ratings are made.

Exhibit 13-1 shows the agreement achieved between pairs of observers making independent ratings of the same conditions within a few hours of one another for data from Nashville, St. Petersburg, and Washington, D.C.

In Nashville, the 1974 inspection program achieved a much higher degree of accuracy than the 1975 program. In 1974, the first year for the program, supervision was close and inaccuracies were discussed immediately with observers; observers were urged to refer often to the photographic and written guidelines. In 1975, the supervision of observers was loose and differences were not discussed immediately with them; these conditions probably account for the substantial degradation in accuracy. The experience in St. Petersburg, where inaccuracies were discussed with raters, shows substantially higher agreement on street litter ratings. The District of Columbia conducts a tightly supervised operation, in which 10 to 15 percent of the ratings are repeated; any discrepancies are immediately discussed, and observers are retrained, if necessary.

Accuracy rates at least as high as those for St. Petersburg or the District of Columbia can be obtained if supervisory personnel are willing to monitor performance closely through extensive replication, if they make corrections (retraining or replacement) quickly, and if they have some latitide in selecting persons for the inspection task. The performance figures for Nashville are probably typical of those that can be expected with minimal supervision and no freedom to replace inspectors who perform poorly.

Steps in Establishing a Trained Observer Rating System

The following steps are needed to establish an operational trained observer rating system:

1. *Develop and document explicit definitions for the grades for each condition to be measured.*

The heart of the trained observer rating system is a set of guidelines that enables observers to assign a grade or numerical rating to each condition being evaluated. The guidelines should be thorough and clearly documented; all observers should have their own copies so that they can refer to the appropriate sections when making the various ratings. The guidelines will, in general, consist of several photographs of typical scenes with litter (or whatever condition is being rated) and a written description of the conditions which constitute a particular rating. The guidelines should:

- Define the area to be inspected;

Exhibit 13-1
TRAINED OBSERVER RELIABILITY IN THREE CITIES[1]

CONDITION RATED	CITY	YEAR	NUMBER OF INSPECTION POINTS	PERCENTAGE OF RATINGS IN EXACT AGREEMENT	PERCENTAGE OF RATINGS DIFFERING BY NO MORE THAN 1 POINT
Street litter	St. Petersburg	1974	288	82	97
	Washington, D.C.	1975	N.A.[2]	75[3]	95[3]
	Nashville	1975	300	63	99
	Nashville	1974	116	70	100
Yard litter	Nashville	1975	300	65	98
	Nashville	1974	115	70	100
Alley litter	Washington, D.C.	1975	N.A.[2]	75[3]	95[3]
	Nashville	1975	61	56	77
	Nashville	1974	18	67	100
Street rideability	Nashville	1975	300	71	98
	Nashville	1974	116	74	100
Sidewalk pavement	Nashville	1975	48	50	85
	Nashville	1974	25	80	96
Stop signs	Nashville	1975	112	60	81
	Nashville	1974	39	77	100
Other traffic signs	Nashville	1975	97	59	69
	Nashville	1974	24	67	79
Street name signs	Nashville	1975	276	76	93
	Nashville	1974	107	87	100

1. Reliability is based on the percentage of inspections in which two trained observers making independent judgments arrived at the same rating.

2. Several hundred inspection points are checked annually by the supervisors but no logs are kept of the exact number inspected.

3. Estimates of reliability were provided by inspection supervisor; no logs were available.

- Identify the items or conditions that determine the rating to be given;
- Cover the entire range of conditions likely to be encountered;
- Be sufficiently precise and detailed that the trained observer using the guidelines can make accurate ratings with a minimum of guesswork and a high degree of consistency;
- Provide at most four or possibly five major rating points (1.0, 2.0, 3.0, 4.0, and, perhaps, 5.0);
- Cover conditions that are of concern to the particular department. A combined rating that included the cleanliness of the street (responsibility of the sanitation department) and the cleanliness of the front yard (responsibility of zoning for enforcing antilittering ordinance) would be of less value to either department than the separate ratings; and
- Be bound in a looseleaf notebook for easy updating and quick reference during inspection.

Examples of the guidelines based on those developed for Nashville are presented in Appendix 13. Communities that decide to adopt these guidelines should probably modify them to make them conform as closely as possible to their own conditions. Persons who adapt the guidelines will in the process develop a better understanding of the strengths and weaknesses of the system and the way it relates to other effectiveness indicators such as citizen complaints.

A procedure for developing guidelines that has been used in Nashville, Washington, D.C., and St. Petersburg is illustrated in Exhibit 13-2.

2. *Develop and document procedures for selecting inspection locations, directing inspectors, recording data, and transcribing and processing data.*

Inspections based on rating only a sample of blocks require a method for selecting blocks at random. The planning department or some other government agency may have assigned numbers to the blocks or block faces in the jurisdiction, from which a

Exhibit 13-2
SUGGESTED PROCEDURES FOR DEVELOPING TRAINED OBSERVER GUIDELINES

A. *Determine Government Responsibilities and Set Boundaries for Inspections*
The responsibilities and jurisdictional limits of the government and of the individual departments need to be spelled out to assure that the trained observer system is used to rate conditions controllable by the government or particular department. For example, if street cleanliness is being measured and the particular department is responsible for cleaning only from curb to curb, the condition of the sidewalk should not be included in the litter rating. Ordinances and departmental regulations defining specific areas of responsibility should be reviewed.

B. *Document the Full Range of Conditions Throughout the Areas of Responsibility*
Two or three observers need to travel throughout the jurisdiction to photograph and describe the full range of conditions that occur in the areas for which their department is responsible. Individual alleys, for example, should be photographed to illustrate gradations from the cleanest to the dirtiest; different types of litter should be noted. Any difficulties in distinguishing public from private sidewalks or in differentiating between blocks that have more than one alley should be noted, so that procedures can be developed to handle such situations consistently. The observers might take as many as 100 to 200 photographs of littered streets and alleys in a variety of neighborhoods and 25 to 50 photographs to illustrate each of the other problems such as broken sidewalks or street sign problems.

C. *Select Representative Photographs and Develop Measurement Guidelines*
The photographs should be examined to ascertain whether they cover the full range of conditions; if any gaps are discovered, additional photographs must be taken. Five to ten persons not associated with the project should independently review and classify the photographs as representing conditions they judge from excellent to very bad. Each category should contain three to six photographs that are generally agreed upon as representative of that classification. A four-category, or four-point, scale will usually be sufficient for grading photographs of street pavement conditions or litter, although a five-point scale might be appropriate in some jurisdictions with areas that have extremely rough pavement or exceptional amounts of litter. A three-point scale will generally be sufficient for rating street and traffic signs and sidewalk pavement conditions.
Persons responsible for developing the measurements should then review the photographs to confirm that they cover the range of conditions. Additional photographs should be taken if required to distinguish further between the two middle-range categories, in which judgments are most difficult. Definitions to accompany the different photographic groups should also be prepared.

D. *Test the Photographic Categories and Guidelines; Document the Rating Scales*
The photographs and tentative guidelines must be tested to make sure they produce consistent ratings and to determine if additional guidelines or photographs are needed for handling unusual situations. For each measure, several persons should independently make from fifty to sixty ratings at randomly selected locations throughout the community. Because the extreme ratings are easiest to make, particular attention must be paid to the middle categories. The ultimate test of the procedures is whether the raters, working independently and using the guidelines, agree on at least 90 percent of the ratings.
In evaluating the system, the following questions should be asked: (1) Did the ratings agree? If not, were the disagreements caused by errors in judgment, inability of the raters to discriminate among conditions, or inadequate guidelines? (2) Were there conditions that the proposed system could not cover adequately? The system should provide a consistent procedure for rating every situation that arises. (3) Do the guideline definitions make sense? Are they practical in application?
Once a scale has been developed, it should be clearly documented and reproduced in large enough quantities to provide individual sets to each trained observer and to all other persons concerned with the system.

random sample can be selected. If no such numbering exists, it will be necessary to assign numbers to blocks, perhaps numbering the blocks in each census tract. It is preferable to number each block face and each alley, rather than each block (the number of block faces and of alleys is likely to vary substantially from one block to another). This practice ensures that each block face (or alley) has an equal probability of being selected and that ratings of the sample will be statistically representative of the conditions in an entire area.

Good maps are essential for marking the locations for inspection and for laying out routes for inspectors to follow before they go into the field. In Washington, D.C., maps with a scale of approximately 1 in. = 650 ft. were most appropriate for directing inspectors rating all blocks; maps with a scale of 1 in. = 1,400 ft. seemed most appropriate for

a sampling inspection. The maps should be current and should show alleys as well as streets.

Rating data can be entered onto a written form or they can be dictated into a small cassette recorder for later transcription. The recorder facilitates further notations of any unusual conditions or situations requiring immediate attention. In Washington, D.C., the observers not only recorded street and alley cleanliness ratings but also noted all cases of abandoned autos, dead animals, evicted families, illegal dumps, exceptionally littered vacant lots, overflowing public refuse containers, and missed collections; these were reported to appropriate government agencies for prompt attention. But transcribing tapes requires more clerical labor than handling written forms. Moreover, unless observers refer frequently to a check list for the items to be rated, they are apt to forget to record some data at inspection points where more than one condition is being rated.

The data should be transcribed within twenty-four hours so that any unusual conditions—health or fire hazards or other problems noted above—can be handled promptly. This transcription can be done by clerical personnel or by the observers; such work provides a break from the routine of making inspections and seems to encourage trained observers to record ratings in an orderly manner. If automatic data processing is being used, the data would be keypunched or entered onto mark-sense cards. Otherwise, the ratings can be summarized on ledger sheets, giving values of each measure by census tract, service area, or whatever geographic or clientele groupings have been decided upon.

All procedures developed should be carefully documented first, to help the trained observers in their work and, second, to assure that identical or compatible procedures are used for all inspections, thus allowing meaningful comparisons among areas and over long periods of time.

3. *Select and train observers.*

Inspecting is not difficult, but it can be tedious. Candidates must be reliable, capable of sustained motivation, and able to work alone for long periods when necessary. They must read maps well, and be observant of details. Most applicants can learn to make inspections, but those who find the work difficult and distasteful should be replaced with others who enjoy the relatively independent field inspections and find the rating process interesting.

A variety of types of personnel have been used. St. Petersburg used environmental and sanitation inspectors; Nashville used summer interns from a local university; Washington, D.C., used existing sanitation department personnel; and New York City employed ex-drug addicts. A proposed training program and schedule are depicted in Exhibit 13-3.

4. *Set up a procedure for systematically checking the ratings of the trained observers.*

To maintain the reliability of the trained observer system, it is essential that observers understand that a randomly selected portion of their ratings will be checked by a supervisor and that if their ratings are inaccurate or incomplete they will be retrained or replaced. Replication is conducted by the supervisor, who reinspects sample blocks already graded by the observers, without the latters'

Exhibit 13-3

SUGGESTED TRAINING SCHEDULE FOR CANDIDATE TRAINED OBSERVERS[1]

MONDAY:	Trained instructors provide overview of the evaluation system and uses of the information collected. Distribute an inspection manual to each candidate. Verify drivers' permits.
	Discuss litter ratings by visual inspection using photographic standards and written descriptions of conditions to be rated. Introduce maps and map routing. Discuss all items to be observed and recorded. Discuss data recording (using sheets or tape recorders) and explain codes for special items.
	Allow time for candidates to read inspection manual and ask questions.
TUESDAY:	Instructors and candidates visit an inspection area, preferably in one vehicle. Make trial inspections together. After each inspection, discuss ratings in detail so that each candidate understands why the scene has a particular rating. Drive to different areas to rate a variety of conditions. Explain hazards in driving and reporting.
WEDNESDAY:	Candidates travel again to the field in one or two vehicles. Each candidate makes independent ratings on a sample of streets and alleys selected to provide a variety of conditions. Give practice in map reading and navigation. Make reports on the same forms or tape recorders that will be used in regular inspections. Review ratings and discuss any problems. Reinspect any sites where there was substantial disagreement in ratings (off by one or more points). Discuss any problems or ways to handle unusual situations.
THURSDAY:	Candidates make independent inspections under conditions to be used in actual inspections. (If one person per vehicle is to be used for the actual inspections, then use one person per vehicle here.) All candidates rate the same set of streets and alleys. Compare the ratings. Review data-recording procedures.
FRIDAY:	Candidates make more independent inspections. Leaders review performance of each inspector candidate and discuss any problems; review or retrain as necessary. By this time, at least 80 percent of the cleanliness ratings of each candidate should be in *exact* agreement with those of the trainer, who is the master judge. At least 95 percent of the special conditions to be counted (such as health hazards and abandoned autos) should have been noted by each observer.

1. A modified version for periodic retraining of inspectors might consist of the Tuesday and Wednesday sessions only. Approximately six hours each day are needed.

Source: This training schedule is based on the schedule developed for the District of Columbia and described in Operations Analysis Division, Department of Environmental Services, *Supervisor's Manual for Visual Inspection and Report System* (Washington, D.C.: District of Columbia Government, January 1973).

knowing when or where the replications are to be made. The supervisor then compares his ratings with those of the observers and calculates the percentage of agreement. Any inaccuracies should be discussed with observers; the observers and the supervisor should reexamine any scene over which there was a rating disagreement of one or more points. If the rating system is to be valid, observers who cannot maintain specified rating accuracy levels (75 percent of ratings in agreement and 90 percent within one-half grade) must be retrained or replaced.

In addition to the replication procedure, the supervisor might also examine periodically the rating sheets (or listen to the tapes) of the observers and examine the mileage of the vehicles to make sure that observers are keeping to their routes and maintaining orderly notes on the rating information.

Costs of the Trained Observer Program

Costs vary greatly, according to the type and frequency of trained observer ratings and the geographical layout and flow of traffic in the community.

Principal cost elements include the following:

1. *Sample versus continuous inspections.* If a random sample is selected, travel time between points and perhaps some navigation problems will limit inspections to about fifty locations per day under the most favorable conditions. If a continuous inspection program is conducted with ratings made on every block, and there is virtually no extraneous travel time, up to 250 inspection points can be rated in a day by a single inspection team.

2. *Number of conditions to be rated on each block.* If more than two or three conditions are to be rated every time (street cleanliness, street pavement conditions, sidewalk pavement conditions, street signs on each block) two inspectors per vehicle will probably be essential.

3. *Frequency of inspection and total number of locations inspected.*

4. *Inspectors' wages and benefits.* These will probably vary from a minimum of $500 per month for summer interns to $1,000 to $1,200 per month (1976 prices) for full-time, experienced government personnel. Fringe benefits will probably constitute an additional 25 to 30 percent.

5. *Clerical personnel wages.* About one employee-day of clerical personnel support time for transcribing rating data for data processing or for hand analysis, laying out routes, preparing maps, and the like will be required for every two days of observer time; this estimate will be slightly less for multiple measurements. Costs will vary from about $500 to $800 per month.

6. *Supervisory personnel wages.* About one employee-day of supervisory time for training and supervising observers including regularly replicating some of their inspections will be required for every four to six employee-days of inspection time. Supervisory salaries may be as high as $1,300 to $1,500 per month plus benefits.

7. *Vehicle costs.* These can be estimated on the basis of the projected mileage for observers and supervisors.

8. *Data-processing costs.* Several employee-months of computer analyst time will be required to develop programs for processing data and developing fairly elaborate data printouts (tables and maps) to be used in periodic reports. Costs for individual reports should be minimal once the programs have been written.

9. *Report preparation.* Trained observer data will need to be analyzed and interpreted. The cost for this activity is discussed in the pertinent chapters on individual services.

Exhibit 13-4 presents some illustrative cost figures for different trained observer rating operations and analysis of the data in a medium-size city. Multiple ratings produce some shared savings in clerical support and vehicle usage and report preparation. The costs of this routine inspection system appear to be modest when compared to the annual costs of street cleaning, sidewalk maintenance, and sign maintenance.

Exhibit 13-4
ILLUSTRATIVE COST ESTIMATES FOR VARIOUS TRAINED-OBSERVER INSPECTION OPTIONS[1]

(Approximate direct costs for one set of inspections in a medium-size city:
5,000 blocks; 1,500 alleys; 6 service areas)

INSPECTION OPTIONS	INSPECTION FOR STREET AND ALLEY CLEANLINESS ONLY (1-PERSON CREW)		INSPECTION FOR STREET AND ALLEY CLEANLINESS, STREET AND SIDEWALK PAVEMENT CONDITION, STOP SIGNS AND OTHER TRAFFIC SIGNS, STREET NAME SIGNS (2-PERSON CREW)
Sample: 70 blocks and 70 alleys inspected per service area (30 alleys or 40 blocks inspected per day)	Inspector:	24 days = $1,800	48 days = $3,600
	Clerical:	12 days = 600	20 days = 1,000
	Supervisory:	6 days = 500	8 days = 700
	Vehicle:[2]	30 days = 600	32 days = 600
	Analysis and report by supervisor:	20 days = 1,800	40 days = 3,600
	Total direct costs:	$5,300	$9,500
Complete: (200 blocks or 75 alleys inspected per day)	Inspector	45 days = $3,400	90 days = $6,800
	Clerical:	22 days = 1,100	36 days = 1,800
	Supervisory:	9 days = 800	15 days = 1,400
	Vehicle:	54 days = 1,100	60 days = 1,200
	Analysis and report by supervisor:	20 days = 1,800	40 days = 3,600
	Total direct costs:	$8,200	$14,800

1. Estimates to the nearest $100. Costs are based on the highest estimates made in the text, on a twenty work-day month (at typical 1976 wage and price levels), 25-percent fringe benefits. Costs do not include basic set-up costs.
2. Costs estimated at $20 per day per vehicle.

Chapter 14

The Multiservice Citizen Survey

A number of aspects of government service performance are nearly impossible to measure without obtaining direct feedback from citizens. Surveys can provide citizen ratings of various service characteristics; they can indicate the views and perceptions of citizens on such matters as their security from crime, accessibility of particular services, courtesy of government employees, and the responsiveness of those employees to citizen requests. In addition, the citizen survey can yield certain types of factual data that are otherwise very difficult to obtain. Examples of such data include crime vicitimization rates (which permit the estimation of unreported as well as reported crime incidents); household participation rates in such services as recreation, library, and transit (which permit an estimate of the number of *different* persons or households using and not using particular government programs); and the frequency of unreported citizen complaints. Of the measurements suggested for the various government services included in this study, approximately one-third seem best obtained through citizen surveys.

This chapter discusses various procedural issues involved in the multiservice citizen survey and discusses its accuracy. Appendix 1 contains an example of a multiservice questionnaire, the version used by Nashville, with the questions cross-referenced to the specific measures of effectiveness for which each question provides data.[1] In addition, Appendix 14

provides some guidelines for local governments, especially those considering contracting for a citizen survey for the purpose of effectiveness measurement. Detailed survey methodology is not discussed in this report as there are numerous works available on that topic.

Fortunately, modern survey techniques seem to permit governments to obtain generally valid and reliable information at reasonable cost. These techniques make possible the interviewing of a small portion of the population (perhaps only a few hundred households) to obtain rough, but probably adequate, estimates of conditions representative of a community's total population. This sampling procedure helps keep survey costs down. By incorporating questions on a number of municipal services into one survey, additional economies can be achieved. Thus, it appears that the citizen survey is a feasible and appropriate procedure for local governments.

Note that the citizen survey described here is intended to be repeated by the government on a regular basis, usually annually, to permit comparisons from one time period to another. Comparisons can indicate whether progress has been made, whether problems have arisen, and whether changes in government programs or policies seem to have affected service effectiveness and quality. To facili-

---

1. See Chapter 4 of our earlier report, *Measuring the Effectiveness of Basic Municipal Services: Initial Report,* for an overview of the principal characteristics of such a survey, including a discussion of its pros and cons and a copy of the questionnaire used in St. Petersburg. Earlier reports by Kenneth Webb and

Harry P. Hatry, *Obtaining Citizen Feedback* (Washington, D.C.: The Urban Institute, 1973), and Carol H. Weiss and Harry P. Hatry, *An Introduction to Sample Surveys for Government Managers* (Washington, D.C.: The Urban Institute, March 1971) discuss, in greater detail, the uses and procedures for citizen surveys as they pertain to local governments. In addition, there is a wide variety of literature available on various aspects, especially the technical elements, of such surveys. A number of references are listed in the selected bibliography.

tate comparisons, therefore, the majority of the survey questions should remain the same from one time period to the next. Inevitably, some changes will be desired. Questions may be added and some may be deleted from one year to the next, but the overall questionnaire content should remain fairly stable. Even seemingly minor changes in the wording can sometimes elicit substantially different responses.

Annual surveys by the city of Dallas sample 3,400 households in even-numbered years, and 800 in odd-numbered years. Each year a different service has been emphasized with more detailed questions. Such a survey strategy seems well worth considering by other governments.

The citizen surveys described here and throughout this report are not "attitude" surveys. Respondents are not asked to set priorities among services or to express opinions about what they would like. Such questions do not appear appropriate for assessing the effectiveness of government services.

Various Procedural Issues

A number of governments have undertaken citizen surveys on effectiveness measurement of the type discussed here. These include St. Petersburg (initially in the fall of 1973 and subsequently in 1974, 1975, and 1976); Nashville (initially in 1974 and subsequently in 1975 and 1976); Palo Alto, California, in 1974 (using similar procedures, but concentrating on police, recreation, and the handling of complaints and requests for services and information); Randolph Township, New Jersey (1974); Dallas, Texas (initially in 1974); Sunnyvale, California (1974); Washington, North Carolina (1974); Zeeland, Michigan (1976); and Sioux City, Iowa (1976).[2]

This discussion focuses on the experiences of the first three cities in their initial surveys. The sample sizes used were 626, 1,002, and 574, respectively. Each of the three governments employed an outside organization to undertake the in-person, at-home interviews. Out-of-pocket costs averaged approximately $10 to $15 per interview. No extensive development of population lists for the sample was required; each city started by providing the contractor with a draft questionnaire for pretesting, and each

requested from its contractor no analysis other than basic cross-tabulations.

Both St. Petersburg and Palo Alto provided survey reports to their city managers and councils. Nashville has provided the results in a report to the public.[3] Although not all of the specific applications of the information obtained from the survey are known, some of the uses city officials in St. Petersburg have reported are as follows:

- The police department has been using the annual victimization data to improve its understanding of the relationship between reported and unreported crimes. The data were also used to determine where emphasis should be placed in crime prevention programs.
- The city manager and council used the results of the citizen survey when considering water, sewer, and sanitation rate changes.
- The transit department used the results for designing and scheduling new routes.
- The city manager and council used results to determine citizen reaction when establishing a program to assess sidewalk improvement.
- Responses to a question about the frequency of rat sightings in various neighborhoods helped to determine which locations would receive emphasis in the rat control program.
- Responses have directed special attention to parks rated low on cleanliness.

It is important to keep in mind that citizen survey findings provide information for only a part, perhaps one-third, of all effectiveness measures. In general, citizen survey findings alone should not be used to direct government program and policies. Information is needed on other measures (such as those based on government records or on systematic observation by trained observers), on program costs and other program and political information.

Who Should Undertake the Survey?

Because of the many technical aspects of undertaking a citizen survey, it is recommended that governments use an experienced survey firm. Only those governments with substantial in-house capabilities should consider undertaking a survey by themselves. Even governments that have the

2. The Sioux City, Sunnyvale, and Zeeland experiences are described in: International City Management Association, *Using Citizen Surveys: Three Approaches*, Municipal Innovation Series No. 15, February 1977.

3. See St. Petersburg, Office of Management and Budget, *Multi-Service Citizen Survey for the City of St. Petersburg,* 1973, 1974, and 1975 editions; Nashville—Davidson County, Tennessee, Department of Finance, *How Well Is Metro Doing?* 1974 and 1976 editions; and Palo Alto, Finance and Public Works Committee, *Staff Reports to the City Council,* regarding the citizen surveys of May 23, June 6, June 20, and July 11, 1974.

technical capability to handle the surveys on their own may have difficulty in gaining public credibility for the findings if they do not use outside experts.

There are, however, some cost-cutting alternatives for governments, such as hiring outside technical consultants to direct the process while using citizens' groups or government employees to conduct the actual survey. For example, the League of Women Voters helped with the Randolph Township, New Jersey, 1974 citizen survey, and government employees were used by the District of Columbia, St. Petersburg, and Nashville for surveys limited solely to questions on recreation.[4] As long as outside expertise is used to provide adequate training and oversight, the technical quality can be obtained and public credibility maintained. However, in each of the three latter instances, the governments involved found that using employees for interviewing imposed a considerable strain on employee resources. Thus, this option is not suggested for regular use.

Other survey activities that local governments can undertake to reduce out-of-pocket costs include preparation of the list of persons from which the sample will be drawn, various data-processing activities such as preparation of cross-tabulations, and preparation of reports on the findings. Each of these activities was undertaken by at least one of the governments noted above.

What government office should coordinate the activity? It seems clear that because the survey discussed here covers a number of services, a central staff office is appropriate for this task. Such an office was used in all the test cities. However, in some instances, surveys limited to recreation were also undertaken by the local government's recreation agency. Such single-service agency-sponsored survey efforts may be particularly subject to a lack of continuity (see Chapter 4).

Provision for Analysis of Survey Findings

The amount of information yielded by the citizen survey is considerable, but the current scarcity of analytical staff in most municipalities means that government staffs have time and resources to analyze only selected results. This is definitely a drawback in the utility of the citizen survey for local governments. However, local government staffs should examine all findings in order to identify the important results. A penetrating analysis to explore more fully the information provided may have to wait for the strengthening of local government analytical staffs or the use of outside consultants or local university personnel. (See Chapter 12 for some suggestions on data analysis.)

To facilitate reviewing survey results, the use of a multiple cross-tabulation summary form, as shown in Exhibit 12-4 of Chapter 12 is suggested. This form permits users to work with about one-fifth of the paper that is otherwise necessary; it also allows users to spot quickly the major population group differences in responses to individual questions.[5] In addition, standard statistical computer programs such as the Statistical Package for the Social Sciences (SPSS) can be useful for a variety of special data analyses.

Reporting the Results

Chapter 12 provides a number of suggestions for reporting the findings from measurement procedures, including the citizen survey. Here some of those suggestions are repeated and other concerns especially associated with findings from citizen surveys are added:

1. After a survey has been completed, the findings should be presented in a written report for use by government officials, the legislative body, and the public.
2. The results from each question should be presented in a concise, easy-to-interpret format. Exhibit 12-4 in Chapter 12 shows a format found useful not only for analysis by government officials but also as a concise summary for others. In general, for the type of questions recommended in this report (see Appendix 1), the principal form of presentation should express the findings as the

4. Other examples include the town of Washington, North Carolina (population 9,000) which conducted a citizen survey of the type discussed in this report in the fall of 1974. Nearly 300 persons were interviewed, all but about 5 percent in person and the remainder by phone. Interviewers were city planning staff members, supplemented by volunteers from the community, including some civic club members. Free technical assistance was provided by East Carolina University's Regional Development Institute and Department of Political Science. See Larry Mazer and Kenneth Andrews, "A Municipality Surveys Its Citizens," *Popular Government*, 41, 1:29–35 (Summer 1975). A more recent application is the 1976 survey by Zeeland, Michigan, a town of approximately 5,000. Zeeland received technical assistance from Western Michigan University. For interviewers, the city used personnel funded by the Comprehensive Employment and Training Act. About 320 interviews were obtained. See Office of City Superintendent, Zeeland, Michigan, "1976 Multi-Service Citizen Survey."

5. The Urban Institute computer services office has a FORTRAN program that produces this output. A copy of the documentation and the program is available to local governments. See Joseph Gueron and Binyork Ouyang, "A Multiple Crosstab Program" (Washington, D.C.: The Urban Institute, August 8, 1974).

percentage of the sample that gave each response.

3. The specific wording used in the questions asked should be provided in the survey report so that readers can better draw their own conclusions as to the findings.

4. The total number of persons responding to each question also should be identified so that readers can see the basis for the findings (as illustrated in Exhibit 12-4). When specific highlights are singled out that involve quite small sample sizes (such as 100 or less), this fact should be noted. Statistical significance levels for selected findings might be included as footnotes, although this type of information may be unfamiliar to many readers.

Operating Agency Involvement

Involving operating agencies in the entire survey process is crucial. Within operating agencies are the government employees who can if necessary respond most directly to survey findings. We therefore urge local governments to involve individual agencies both in the initial preparation of the questionnaires (especially in reviewing the proposed questions) and in the subsequent review of the survey findings. This advice is more easily given than taken. Three problems have seemed particularly troublesome:

1. *Interest in citizen survey data is mixed.* In the trials that we have reviewed, some agencies (for example, park and recreation departments) were quite interested in obtaining citizen feedback on recreation services. Other agencies, however, were much more skeptical about the utility and meaningfulness of citizen responses. The latter group responded with such remarks as: "Why do we need to ask for citizens' perceptions of road rideability when we are perfectly able to determine it ourselves through government employees?"; "Let sleeping dogs lie"; and "Citizens are not capable of rating our service."

2. *There is great temptation for the central staff coordinating the survey to become impatient.* These staff persons may not want to take the amount of time (often considerable) to keep numerous individual agency personnel informed about the uses and purposes of the survey information.

3. *Agency staff analysis time is either limited or nonexistent.* Part of this problem stems from the absence of analysts within many local government agencies; part stems from the pressure of day-to-day activities, which prevent existing staff from spending much time reviewing survey

data. Almost all agency managers, however, can examine the data relevant to their agencies with considerable insight. Still, the trained analysts can help achieve greater understanding of the responses, particularly through the simultaneous examination of responses to more than one question. The problem of scarcity of analytical staff can be partly alleviated if analysts are available from a central staff to help agency personnel.

It is extremely important to set the right atmosphere during various stages of the citizen survey. If the survey findings are so handled as to focus completely on negatives and on attributing blame, the reactions to them will be defensive, and the survey information may not be used. Therefore, to the extent possible, a constructive atmosphere should be maintained—one that encourages constructive changes and gives credit to successful programs and policies without causing the city or individual agencies to feel continually on the defensive. Exhibit 12-6 in Chapter 12 illustrates the type of request that a central agency coordinating the survey could make to individual operating agencies in requesting their review of the findings.

Role of a City or County Planning Agency

The city or county planning agency is an additional source of assistance to the office coordinating the survey. This agency has certain special knowledge applicable to the citizen survey. The planning agency can be particularly useful in identifying an adequate listing of households from which the sample should be selected. In addition, this agency should be a major source of suggestions for appropriate geographical boundaries for grouping responses by major neighborhood areas within the jurisdiction.

The planning agency may also be a potential source of help for analyzing the data; it often has staff members with analytical skills that other agencies lack. Furthermore, the planning agency probably has a special interest in the use of the survey information. Some of those data should be helpful in preparing capital budgets, master plans, and the like. In both St. Petersburg and Nashville, planning departments provided assistance in determining neighborhood boundaries and in compiling the lists from which the survey sample was drawn.

The Questionnaire

Appendix 1 presents the questionnaire for the Nashville citizen survey undertaken in February and March 1974. The St. Petersburg questionnaire of September and October 1973 was reproduced in our initial report. These two questionnaires are quite similar. (Neither includes any detailed questions on recreation. This omission reflects an effort to limit the length of the interview. The recreation departments in these two cities conducted separate surveys, but other governments may prefer to include recreation questions in a multiservice citizen survey.[6])

The questions on the Nashville and St. Petersburg questionnaires can serve as starting points for other local governments. However, each government inevitably will want to modify the existing questions, delete some, and add others to cover aspects of local concern. Prior to conducting the survey, each local government is urged to have its questions adequately examined and "pretested" to check for possible bias and to ascertain local citizens' interpretation of the wording. The pretesting should identify such problems as (1) long, awkwardly worded, or ambiguous questions, (2) local language usage that requires a special choice of words, (3) confusing or incorrect instructions to interviewers regarding "skip" patterns, (4) redundant questions, (5) wording that may offend or sound foolish to respondents, (6) illogical or awkward sequence of questions, and (7) difficulties encountered by interviewers in recording responses. The pretest also may be used to help establish the response categories for questions that will be asked of respondents in the full survey.

Government Ability to Improve Citizen Satisfaction Levels

Some persons working in operating agencies have expressed considerable concern that they could take little action to improve citizen satisfaction levels for the service characteristics measured. However, each question or topic suggested for a citizen survey in this report (and illustrated in Appendix 1) has been subjected to this test: "Is there at least one government action that realistically could be expected to affect citizen responses?" In a small number of cases, questions were removed because they could not meet this test. (For example, the fire protection questions in the 1974 Nashville survey, shown in Appendix 1, appear to be marginal in value because the local government has limited ability to influence the findings.[7])

6. See Chapter 4 for a discussion of this option.

7. Responses to the survey in Nashville, the only location where these particular questions were tested, indicated that there were few situations in which an unreported fire would be of any significance to the city government. (Only 34 households of 1,002 interviewed reported having had a fire in their homes in the previous twelve months; of these, 19 were not reported, but only 2 for reasons of concern to the government.) This suggests that questions aimed at obtaining information on unreported fires should probably be dropped.

Costs of the Survey

The experience in St. Petersburg, Nashville, and Palo Alto indicate that for a range of 600 to 1,000 interviews, the cost (at 1976 rates) would probably be approximately $10 to $15 per interview. In St. Petersburg, the survey firm's price for 600 at-home interviews in the 1973 and 1974 surveys averaged about $10 per interview. In both Nashville and Palo Alto, the costs averaged $10 to $12 per at-home interview in 1973 and 1974.

These figures cover pretesting, final questionnaire preparation and printing, interviewing, editing, card punching, and initial summary tabulations. Not included are such tasks as developing the initial set of topics for the questionnaire, including the time of central staff or operating agency personnel; any significant development of the list of the population from which the sample is drawn; or any analysis of survey results. The project team and local government personnel worked for many days in determining questionnaire topics and wording. In addition, several days of manual work were required to translate the basic tabulation data to the multiple cross-tabulation summary output format shown in Exhibit 12-4.[8]

The Nashville government, rather than the interviewing firm, undertook the tasks of card punching and tabulating results for its first survey. This required new computer programs, as the city did not have a tabulation program of this type (and most local governments probably will not). These extra steps placed a burden on the staff and led to some minor delays in finding and obtaining usable output data. Such tasks as developing new computer programs should not be undertaken at the last moment.

The out-of-pocket outlay for the survey was approximately $6,000 to $12,000 for the sample sizes mentioned earlier. This does not seem beyond reach of most local governments, even for annual administration.

Falls Church, Virginia, and Randolph Township, New Jersey, two small jurisdictions with populations of about 11,000 and 14,000 respectively, undertook a version of the survey. They were able to keep expenditures below $1,000 for surveys of about 200 and 250 households respectively. They adopted modified versions of the survey questionnaire shown in Appendix 1. Randolph Township used the local chapter of the League of Women Voters for the in-

8. As mentioned in Note 5, this summary output format has since been programmed for automatic data processing. Use of such a program should permit governments to reduce substantially the preparation time for multiple cross-tabulation summaries, which otherwise would have to be done manually.

terviewing, with Rutgers University personnel supervising. Computer processing was done by the community college. Falls Church used the League of Women Voters for interviewing; training and supervising of interviewers were conducted jointly by a city staff member and a consultant from a survey research organization.

Interest by Local Governments

There has not been enough time to obtain much substantive information as to local governments' long-run interest in and use of citizen survey information. Initially, the governments of St. Petersburg, Nashville, and Palo Alto (at least their central staffs) raised few obstacles to testing the survey. A few operating agencies presented some resistance, but in no instance was this resistance so great as to delay significantly the survey activities. However, lack of interest and some uneasiness about survey data (as well as other effectiveness measurements) within some government operating agencies are important problems that probably will inhibit the use of surveys.

Discussions with local officials have indicated considerable local interest in the citizen survey as a way to obtain citizen feedback on the effectiveness of government services. The interest of small governments, such as Randolph Township, New Jersey; Falls Church, Virginia; Zeeland, Michigan; and Washington, North Carolina, as well as much larger ones (Dallas, Sioux City, and Sunnyvale), suggests a wide applicability. The fact that St. Petersburg and Nashville have continued to undertake annual citizen surveys suggests that some other local governments will find the information of sufficient value to collect it regularly.

If such interest continues and is translated into active and regular use of the survey approach, the need for sound survey procedures becomes increasingly important. This issue is the topic of the next section.

Citizen Survey Accuracy Issues

The question of the validity of the specific survey questions is addressed in the various chapters on procedures for measuring the effectiveness of individual service areas. This section discusses validation issues relevant to the survey as a whole. Sources of survey inaccuracy to guard against include the following: (1) problems in obtaining a

sample that represents at least an approximate cross section of the population; (2) inability to obtain or to complete interviews with those included in the sample; (3) problems in wording of questions; (4) knowledgeability of respondents; (5) poor interviewing techniques; (6) respondents' memory lapses or lack of honesty; and (7) various clerical, coding, or tabulation errors in processing the interview results. It is beyond the scope of this report to discuss in depth the many technical issues involved, but here are our own suggestions on some of these issues that merit special attention by local governments. Appendix 14 presents further details on some of these matters.

Obtaining a Representative Interview Sample

Numerous issues are involved here, some of them highly technical. These three are discussed here: (1) who in a particular household should be interviewed; (2) a means to check, though crudely, how well the sample represents various demographic characteristics of the whole population; and (3) problems with the use of "cluster sampling" for this type of survey.

Who Should Be Interviewed in a Particular Household?

To keep costs down, only one adult was interviewed per household in the test cities. On some issues, survey professionals believe it best to interview the housewife, who is considered more knowledgeable than other members of the household with regard to family usage of recreation or library facilities. About such questions as family income, the head of the household—male or female—is likely to be most knowledgeable. On other issues, such as on perception of library accessibility, it seems preferable to obtain responses from a cross section of household members.

In both St. Petersburg and Nashville, the survey firms chose to interview adults so that the total respondents represented a proper proportion of each sex and age category. The omission of children as respondents is a concern, particularly with respect to recreation and library services, but children would probably not be able to answer many of the other questions.

The St. Petersburg and Nashville questionnaires called for respondents to answer only for themselves concerning most questions. For some issues, however, they were asked to respond for all members of the family; examples were crime victimization and reasons for nonuse of libraries.

The St. Petersburg and Nashville procedures seem reasonable, but there is no clear-cut preferred procedure. Each local government should make its choice after considering the specific topics to be included and the kind of information desired.

Check of Demographic Characteristics

A somewhat crude procedure is often used to check the representativeness of the sample in terms of a few demographic characteristics. That procedure involves determining the extent to which the sample appears to have characteristics similar to those of the large population it is supposed to represent. This comparison should be undertaken by the survey firm and the local government—before interviewing if checkable characteristics such as geographical distribution of the sample are available, but in any case, after the findings have been obtained on characteristics of the sample such as age, race, and income distribution.

Significant deviations in the sample might be partly compensated for by weighting the responses of the various population groups so that weights are increased for underrepresented groups—thus yielding a community average that has been made more nearly representative. At the very least, the sensitivity of jurisdictionwide totals to possible undersamplings of some groups should be identified.

As census information on the whole population becomes dated, this comparison will be less useful, unless such bodies as the local planning agency update estimates of population size and of the various characteristics noted above.

Problems with Cluster Sampling

Cluster sampling is a common survey procedure used to save interviewer transportation costs. Interviewers seek a number of completed interviews in the immediate vicinity in each randomly selected location. Because many of the items in the effectiveness measurement questionnaire are aimed at respondents' evaluations of conditions in their own neighborhoods, however, it seems quite possible that the use of cluster sampling may reduce the number of independent observations.

Neither St. Petersburg nor Nashville used cluster sampling (and their survey costs reflect the additional interviewer travel time required by noncluster sampling procedures). Palo Alto did employ cluster sampling, and it might be informative to use Palo Alto data to examine cluster variances for particular survey questions as a rough indication of the magnitude of this problem. Pending the findings of such studies, it is suggested that, whenever practical, local governments avoid the use of cluster sampling.

Inability to Obtain Complete Interviews

At least three problems can arise in this regard. First, persons to be interviewed may not be at home when the interviewer calls. Second, an individual may refuse to be interviewed, and third, a person may terminate the interview before it is completed.

Not-at-homes. The problem here is that those who often are not at home (at least when interviewers call) may be different types of persons with experiences and viewpoints on government services that are quite different from those who are more often at home. Some survey firms, such as the Gallup organization, use at-home interviewing procedures that do not require call-backs when the person is not at home; instead, the interviewer proceeds to the next home. However, these firms establish age and sex quotas so that the resulting sample will be roughly representative of the community age and sex mix. Such a procedure was used by the St. Petersburg survey firm. Other firms require interviewers to make a certain number of call-backs before replacing one household with another. In the 1974 Nashville survey, one call-back was undertaken before the interviewer substituted another household.

Survey firms using few or no call-backs generally try to interview at various times and various days of the week, and they attempt to use "quotas" to obtain adequate representation of the various age and sex groups. In a brief examination of the Nashville citizen survey, to compare responses for those interviewed on the callback interview with those interviewed at home on the first call, we did not detect any important, large-scale differences.[9]

Procedures using call-backs provide "purer" sampling but are more costly. The difference in accuracy levels achieved by these two approaches is not known. If telephone interviews are used, a larger number of call-backs can be undertaken because of the relatively small added costs. (This telephone interview option is discussed below.)

Refusal Rates. Refusal rates are sensitive to the survey procedures used and the quality of the interviewers. Interviewing was undertaken in both St. Petersburg and Nashville by professional organizations with previous experience in survey work. In St.

9. We undertook some limited chi-square testing and also examined the data from a judgmental viewpoint. The test was applied to twenty-four questions chosen to cover a number of service areas. Only two showed a significant difference at the 90-percent level—which one might expect based solely on chance. Neither these nor our observations on other questions indicated a systematic bias toward either better or worse ratings of government service quality or behavior in any service area. However, such limited data and investigation can hardly be considered definitive.

Petersburg only one refusal was recorded, but in Nashville the refusal rate was 12 percent overall (7.5 percent of those who had received a letter in advance, 16.5 percent for those who had not). The Nashville Urban Observatory group, which did the interviewing, attributed refusals to fear of letting strangers into the house. For female interviewers, the refusal rate was 4 percent for persons who had received advance letters and 10 percent for those who had not; for male interviewers, the comparable figures were 11 percent and 24 percent. The Nashville Urban Observatory is considering the idea of using some combination of mail and at-home surveys or telephone and at-home surveys.

Early Terminations. The willingness of a cross section of citizens to complete the interview once it has started was at first a matter of concern, particularly because completion of a questionnaire such as that in Appendix 1 requires about thirty minutes. However, in the project experience, completion rates were very high. In both Nashville and St. Petersburg, at-home interviewing was undertaken. Neither St. Petersburg, with 626 interviews in 1973, nor Nashville, with 1,002 interviews in 1974, had any interviews that were not completed once they were begun. The St. Petersburg survey firm indicated that citizens appeared most interested in the survey. If anything, the chief problem was how to complete the interview tactfully without excessive conversation. To some extent, this finding may reflect the large proportion of elderly persons in St. Petersburg who apparently enjoyed talking to the interviewers.

Telephone Interviewing as an Option

All three local governments mentioned above used at-home, in-person interviews, but the telephone interview has a number of attractive features and has become increasingly respectable to survey professionals in recent years. Telephoning saves interviewer travel time, and a number of call-backs become feasible in order to obtain interviews with those less often at home. Also, this interview method allows greater access in areas where people are reluctant to allow strangers into their homes. Moreover, closer supervision of interviewers becomes possible when the calls are made from a central location.[10]

Telephoning has some potentially important

10. For a recent comparison of in-person versus telephone interviewing using random digit dialing see Alfred J. Tuchfarber and William R. Klecka, *Random Digit Dialing: Lowering the Cost of Victimization Surveys,* (Washington, D.C.: Police Foundation, 1976). The authors' findings lead them to come out strongly in favor of telephone interviewing using random digit dialing both because of cost savings and improved access to various disadvantaged groups of citizens.

problems: It may be difficult to hold the respondent on the phone for interviews as long as thirty minutes; some families do not list their phone numbers (this problem is overcome by using a random digit dialing technique); and some do not have telephones at all. The last may be a particular problem with low-income, highly mobile families. There also is a problem in terms of restrictions on the use of certain types of questions, such as those involving visual material. For example, to solicit information on family income, some survey firms have found it useful to hand respondents a card listing various income ranges and ask them to tell the interviewer the letter corresponding to the proper range. This approach seems to produce better response rates than a direct question about income.

During the at-home interviews in St. Petersburg and Nashville, respondents were asked whether they had a telephone in their home. In St. Petersburg, 90 percent of the families indicated they had a telephone, and in Nashville, 89 percent. (In the latter city, 7 percent would not give their number to the interviewer; in St. Petersburg, 2 percent of the respondents would not.)

Of more concern than the figure of 10 to 11 percent of families without telephones was the distribution by race. In both cities, 8 percent of white respondents compared to 28 percent of nonwhite respondents reported that they did not have telephones. This indicates a potential bias in using a telephone survey. The total proportion of nonwhites interviewed in St. Petersburg was 12 percent of those sampled, and in Nashville, 18 percent of those sampled. The effects on citywide totals in these cases are not likely to be significant, because nonwhites without phones represented roughly only about 5 percent of the total city population. However, in reflecting accurately the perceptions and experiences of nonwhites, an all-telephone survey would face this potentially important problem.

Nashville undertook a very small test of telephone interviewing—seventeen interviews. Only one refusal was reported. All sixteen interviews were completed. This appears to indicate that this kind and length of survey (thirty minutes) can be undertaken by telephone. In fact, if the family has a telephone, it may be easier to obtain an interview by telephone than by other survey techniques; this is particularly true in cities where households tend to be reluctant to allow strangers inside for interviews.

The appropriate direction for these surveys appears to be toward a combination of telephone and at-home interviews, perhaps even with a mailed questionnaire being tried first. However, such combination strategies have as yet received little trial.

Wording of Questions

The Urban Institute staff and the survey firms in Nashville and St. Petersburg attempted to screen survey questions for obvious bias and lack of clarity. In addition, pretesting was undertaken in both cities, and as a result some wording was changed and some questions were reordered. The plausibility of responses to individual questions was considered both for the citywide totals and for various populations subgroups such as age, race, sex, income, and neighborhood groups. As far as could be determined, answers to questions in most cases were within reasonable bounds; that is, the responses were sensible. However, this test is useful only in selected cases, inasmuch as unexpected findings can be legitimate. Some surprises were found in the results, but for the most part, they could be defended as being plausible. Comparisons of results for similar questions asked in both cities also were made. In general, the differences seemed to be consistent with our own impressions and those of staff personnel in Nashville and St. Petersburg with respect to the characteristics of the two cities.

A useful procedure for the initial tests of the questionnaire is to ask respondents a question such as, "Why did you rate that characteristic 'poor' (or 'excellent')?" The responses may indicate that respondents are interpreting questions differently from the way that was intended.

Knowledgeability of Respondents.

Can survey respondents realistically be expected to be knowledgeable about the topics on which information is requested. An important ground rule used in developing the questions to obtain effectiveness measurement data was that individuals should be asked only about events within their own personal experience or the experience of other members of their household. In a sense, these are the events about which the citizen is an "expert." The questionnaires do not include technical questions or expression of opinions requiring knowledge that citizens normally would not be expected to have.

Some operating agency personnel have expressed concern that citizens may not be qualified to answer particular queries. Probably the most notable example of this concern pertains to the question about the condition of roads in one's neighborhood. However, the measure for which the question is used is intended to reflect the "comfort" aspect of streets (see Chapter 8), and not the technical condition of the road. As long as individuals are asked about effects on themselves and their families rather than technical issues, such questions seem to be legitimate candidates for the citizen survey.

Interview Quality

Adequate training and supervision of interviewers are important elements in conducting a quality survey. Major problems can develop if a local government decides to do the interviewing itself with inexperienced interviewers. Regardless of who manages the interviewing, it is important to verify a percentage of the interviews conducted by each interviewer (perhaps 10 percent), to assure that interviews actually were undertaken and were of reasonable quality. This is a common and appropriate practice of survey organizations.

Respondents' Memories and Honesty

Some survey questions ask for information about the frequency of certain events, such as use of transit or library facilities, or crime victimization. The recall period used in these initial surveys has generally been twelve months; this reflects the twelve-month interval expected between surveys and conforms to the normal budgeting-planning cycle for local governments. Yet, this period is somewhat arbitrary and could be reduced. For other survey questions, in which the citizen is asked for a rating of particular survey characteristics, the rating is primarily about current conditions, so the memory problem is of less concern.

The interviews could be spread out, perhaps throughout the year. However, for once-a-year surveys, the question arises as to what time of the year they should be undertaken. Does the optimum time vary significantly among service areas? This question is related to the memory problem, for if citizens could recall events adequately for twelve months, the issue of when to interview would be considerably lessened. There is little conclusive information on this problem, especially as related to the various topics that are the subject of these questionnaires.[11] However, respondent ratings are bound to be influenced by the timing of the interview. Both the season of the year and current events could conceivably

11. Some limited studies of citizen recall abilities have been made, especially on crime and health issues: These studies confirm that recall periods of perhaps six months will be more accurate than periods of one year, but the increase in accuracy does not seem great. See, for example, "Reporting of Hospitalization in the Health Interview Survey," U.S. Department of Health, Education, and Welfare, *Vital and Health Statistics,* series 2, no. 6, July 1965; "Optimum Recall Period for Reporting Persons Injured in Motor Vehicle Accidents," U.S. Department of Health, Education, and Welfare, *Vital and Health Statistics,* series 2, no. 50, April 1972; and "San Jose Methods Test of Known Crime Victims," U.S. Department of Justice, Law Enforcement Assistance Administration, June 1972. To some extent, there appear to be offsetting sources of errors as the recall period is lengthened: On one hand, events are forgotten, but on the other, respondents appear to include in their responses events from prior periods. The latter practice is sometimes referred to as "telescoping."

affect responses. For example, recent announcements of a crime wave could be expected to affect the respondents' feeling of security.

In reviewing individual kinds of service, it is clear that most are affected by seasonal weather conditions. Spring or fall may represent the best compromise for the time of the survey, being "less extreme" seasons and times when it may be easier to find respondents at home. Surveys undertaken only annually should occur at about the same time each year to increase the comparability of findings from one year to the next.

Our initial report made a recommendation that is repeated here: Avoid having survey results come out just before an election, lest the data become a political football—probably with the survey team getting kicked around.

As for the question of honesty of responses to be expected in a citizen survey, this does not appear to be a major cause for concern. The topics included on the questionnaire illustrated in Appendix 1 do not generally appear "threatening" to the respondents or their self-image, except possibly for the questions asking for income and age. Even in these instances, if respondents are asked for approximate ranges, most individuals appear willing to answer to the best of their ability. A small proportion of the respondents may not take the interview seriously, but if the interviewers are of reasonable quality, this should be minimized and the findings are not likely to be significantly distorted.

Survey Issues Needing Further Research

If there is wider and more regular use of citizen surveys by governments, with questions repeated from one year to the next, it will become important to further validate and improve survey procedures. A list of key issues is presented below, both to alert local governments to aspects of citizen surveys that are far from fully resolved, and to encourage more long-term research on them.

Questionnaire Issues

1. How long a memory can the respondent be expected to have in recalling the various types of events? (The recall and seasonality issues.)
2. Should individuals be asked to respond only for themselves or should they also answer for their whole household?
3. What is the maximum appropriate interview length for this subject matter?
4. How valid are respondents' answers to questions about nonuse of services?

5. What rating categories should be used for various types of questions?

Sample Selection and Design Issues

6. How frequently should these surveys be undertaken?
7. Should interviewing be conducted by telephone, by in-person interviews, by mail, by combinations of these techniques?
8. How can the most representative sample be obtained? To what extent is there a need for callbacks of those not responding on initial attempt to contact? Should clusters be used? What list of the population should be used from which the sample will be drawn?
9. Should respondents include juveniles?
10. How can the validity of the survey data be checked?

Implementation Issues

11. How accurate and precise must the results be? How should information on the precision of the findings be presented to government officials?
12. Can local governments handle the large amounts of data coming from the surveys? How can they become more skilled at using these data?
13. Who should be responsible for the various parts of the survey effort?
14. To what extent will public release of the survey results cause major problems for local officials, and how should the release be handled?
15. Under what conditions will citizens become oversurveyed?

Other Uses for the Citizen Survey

Governments may find it tempting to add items to the questionnaire that ask for a variety of information on respondents' attitudes and opinions. It seems reasonable for governments to include a few special questions each year, provided those new queries seek citizen assessment of specific projects or programs. For example, the city of Nashville used Questions 26 and 26a in Appendix 1 to obtain feedback on both the size of the government radio station's listening audience and the reasons others did not listen to the station. A variety of other information on specific government programs also might be sought. For example, Question 46 in Appendix 1 obtains information on the willingness of citizens to allow fire fighters into their homes to check for fire hazards. The purpose of this question is to pretest the probable success of such a program.

Questions asking for citizens' opinions of current issues are particularly susceptible to bias in their wording. If such opinions are sought, special care should be taken to determine that such questions are unbiased and clear and that they request

information about which citizens are likely to be knowledgeable.[12]

12. This problem can be illustrated by the following example. The responses from an opinion question worded "Are you in favor of your government's providing more of service 'x'?" would probably receive a much higher percentage of "yes" responses than one worded "Are you in favor of your government's providing more of service 'x' with the costs paid for by increasing property taxes?" We argue that neither wording is likely to solicit very informed responses. The respondents would be able to give much better informed responses if they were provided estimates of the amount of tax increase and what benefits they would probably gain from the added level of service.

Chapter 15

Surveying the Business Community: A Preliminary Examination

Business establishments located within a jurisdiction are major clients of many services provided by the local government. Many of the effectiveness measures and measurement procedures discussed in the chapters on individual government services also concern the economic or business life of the community. For example, crime and fire data should be categorized by whether the victims are residential or commercial so that crime and fire rates for business establishments can be monitored. An important source of client feedback is the citizen survey, but because it focuses on respondents in their roles as individual citizens or members of households, an additional survey of businesses can be useful in providing a more complete perspective.

Procedures similar to those used for the citizen survey discussed in Chapter 14 can obtain information from a sample of business managers on their perceptions of the quality of individual services; they can also obtain certain factual data that may be unavailable in existing government records, such as crime victimization.

This chapter offers some suggestions for procedures for surveying the business community. Appendix 2 presents an illustrative questionnaire. The questionnaire focuses on questions likely to be of concern to a large number of businesses. The procedure and the survey questionnaire have not been tested in any city, but some preliminary pretesting of the questionnaire was undertaken, and the procedures and questions are similar to those for the citizen survey, which has been used with some frequency.

A local government planning a survey of businesses should first thoroughly review the questionnaire and then arrange for it to be carefully tested.

The preliminary questionnaire in Appendix 2 contains one or more questions on each of the following services:[1]

- Local transportation services, including public transit;
- Crime control;
- Health and sanitation inspections;
- Fire control;
- Sanitation;
- Water supply;
- Wastewater removal and storm drainage, including sewer services;
- City handling of complaints and requests for services and information;
- Consumer affairs.

The questions in the survey are intended to provide data for the measures of service effectiveness identified in the previous chapters. References in the margin of the sample questionnaire relate particular questions to particular measures. To limit the size of the questionnaire (and thus keep down its costs and make it more practical), there has been no attempt to cover all possible service characteristics.

1. Two services, recreation and library services, that are included in the *citizen* survey (see Appendix 1), are not represented in the illustrative questionnaire for businesses. Our initial investigation indicated that these two services would not be of major direct concern to the business community.

(For example, many more detailed questions on the quality of water services could be added for restaurants and laundries, which make considerable use of government water services.) The questionnaire shown in Appendix 2 is estimated to require a twenty- to thirty-minute interview.

Questions relating to services not provided by individual local governments can of course be deleted. Some government services not covered in the questionnaire because they were outside the scope of this project were, however, identified in preliminary interviews as important to the business community. These include zoning and land development decisions, licensing, regulation of advertising signs, building codes, local "blue laws," special taxes, and the like. A government developing a business survey might want to include questions on these areas.

Method of Developing the Preliminary Questionnaire

The questionnaire in Appendix 2 was derived by the following means:

1. Ten "open-ended" interviews were held with individual businessmen for a variety of commercial establishments in the Washington, D.C., and Philadelphia areas. These businessmen were asked about their concerns and problems with local government services. These interviews indicated that, for the service areas listed above, business officials have the same kinds of concerns that persons speaking as householders have, plus much concern with zoning, planning, licensing, and building codes.
2. A major source of questions has been the questionnaire used for the survey of citizens. There are many similarities between the questions included in the citizen survey in Appendix 1 and those of the survey of businesses. Those questions with similar wording have been tested at least once in the citizen survey.
3. There are useful precedents for surveys of businesses in the area of crime control. Particularly important are the Bureau of the Census commercial victimization surveys undertaken for the Law Enforcement Assistance Administration (LEAA).[2] The Census survey and its procedures

are considerably more detailed and involve a much more costly approach than seems feasible for annual business surveys by most local governments. Governments with the resources to undertake more extensive surveys may want to use the Census questionnaire for the crime victimization questions rather than the shorter form presented here.
4. A number of suggestions for our questionnaire were provided by central staff personnel of four cities who reviewed early versions.

Some Preliminary Suggestions for Conducting the Survey

Who Should Be Included? From What Part of the Business Population Should the Sample Be Drawn?

There are a number of options. One is to include *all* kinds of businesses.[3] There are less complete, but somewhat more manageable, alternatives such as the following:

- Only "for profit" establishments;
- All profit-making firms except those considered to provide professional services (such as doctors, lawyers, consultants, accountants, and the like);
- Only profit-making firms that are the sole occupants of a building;
- Only profit-making establishments that sell retail goods or provide services directly to the public; and
- Only profit-making firms dealing with "walk-in" trade.

The following issues need to be considered in the selection:

1. For some businesses located in a building with a number of business establishments or in a shopping center, some services, such as solid waste collection, are provided collectively to the building or center. The interviewer, therefore, may need to ask some questions only of the main occupant, while other questions probably should be asked of all businesses.
2. Some of the businesses selected may receive such services as solid waste collection or security protection from private firms. Is the government in-

---

2. For example, see *Commercial Victimization Survey: Interviewers' Manual, City Sample,* September 1973, and *National Crime Survey; Central Cities Sample, Five Largest Cities, 1973: Survey Documentation,* May 1974, both published by the U.S. Department of Commerce, Bureau of the Census.

3. The Industry Code of the U.S. Department of Commerce provides a useful listing of the classifications of businesses from which choices might be made.

terested in their ratings on privately delivered services? Other businesses may provide their own services, in which case they probably should not be queried on quality because the government has no responsibility for them.

3. Some businesses, such as chain stores, have more than one location. Should stores under the same ownership be treated as separate firms—and possibly interviewed at more than one location—or should they be treated as one firm?

4. There remains the question of which person should be interviewed. Ideally, persons who are familiar with all of the services delivered, such as an owner, manager, or assistant manager, would be selected.

How Many Businesses Should Be Included in the Population to Be Surveyed?

The answer here will depend mainly on the type and number of business subgroups on which separate measurement information is wanted, the precision needed in the findings, and, of course, resource constraints.

1. At one extreme, no stratification may be needed, but rather the business community can be considered as a whole. In this case, even a sample of perhaps only 100 interviews would be sufficient to provide a reasonable representation of the total population of businesses.[4]

2. Another alternative is to group the responses by major locations in the city. This would permit identification of differences in perceived service levels by geographical area. If this is done, 100 interviews from each area might be sufficient.

3. A third alternative is to group responses by type of firm (such as retail, wholesale, or service). This classification could be as specific as "eating and drinking places," "cleaning businesses," "food stores," "apparel stores," and the like. As the number of subgroups increases, however, the total sample size also should be increased to provide perhaps 50 to 100 interviews from each category.

Our preliminary judgment is that a local government should limit its survey to only a few kinds of businesses or to three to five geographic areas of the city with at least 100 interviews from each.

How Should the Sample Be Selected?

There are a number of sources which could provide a listing of businesses from which a random sample can be drawn. For example:

4. Selection of sample sizes is discussed in Chapter 14.

1. *Local government lists of business establishments*, such as those used for licensing, taxing, or occupancy and property inspection purposes. Tax lists include profit-making firms in a city and are generally updated annually. The inspection lists include nonprofit organizations, but because requirements for inspection vary (for example, some businesses are inspected once a year, others every two years), licensing lists may be somewhat outdated. Moreover, some businesses that have been granted a license may no longer be operating in the city.

2. *Classified section of the local telephone directory.* Most local businesses are listed here, but there are two problems with using the directory. First, multiple listings for the same firm are common. For example, a single appliance store could be listed under "appliances," "refrigerators," "washers," "dryers," "freezers," "air conditioners," "service and repair," and so on. A random sample drawn without accounting for multiple listings will give those businesses so listed a greater chance of being selected. A second problem with the telephone directory is that it often includes establishments located outside the jurisdiction. However, most of these probably could be deleted before interviewing.

3. *Directories of businesses,* such as the Polk or Haines directories. The relative currency and comprehensiveness of these lists should be considered.

4. *Member lists of local and area merchant associations* (or the local chamber of commerce). These associations chiefly represent local retail establishments and probably will be the least complete source.

Local governments should evaluate each available list or directory for the following characteristics: its coverage of businesses; its currency; the completeness of its information for each business (address, telephone number, and name of manager); and the ease with which information it offers can be acquired and used.

Once a list has been settled on, the businesses should be selected in a statistically random way. As noted above, the government might want to set certain criteria for businesses before the selection process begins. For example, the sample could be restricted to certain types of businesses, and to those in business in certain locations for at least twelve months. If possible, the criteria should be examined for each business drawn for the sample in advance of any interviewing, and replacements selected when necessary to replace inappropriate ones.

How Should the Survey Be Conducted and Who Should Conduct It?

Three basic techniques exist, namely, personal interviews, telephone surveys, and mail surveys. If the resources for personal interviewing—usually the most expensive and time-consuming technique—are available, this method is generally preferred because its results are likely to be the most thoughtful and complete. If personal interviewing is used, an appointment should probably be arranged for the interview. The caller can also determine in advance of the interview whether the business establishment meets such requirements as length of time at the location or class of business to be included in the sample.

With use of the questionnaire recommended here (twenty to thirty minutes in length), telephone interviewing should also be feasible. It is less expensive and less time consuming than the personal interview because no travel time is involved. Appointments may still be necessary, as it is difficult to retain the businessperson's attention for a long telephone interview without advance notice and commitment.

With either telephone or personal interviewing, interruptions may occur, making it necessary to postpone completing the interview. Our own limited experience and that of others indicate that perhaps three to five contacts with a business are required to arrange for and complete the survey. A letter explaining in advance the purpose and use of the information to be gathered is likely to help gain business managers' cooperation both in initially agreeing to and in completing the interviews.

The mail survey, although the least expensive, is also probably the least reliable. Large percentages of those contacted may not respond.[5] Those persons who respond may well have opinions unrepresentative of the entire business community. The respondents may also be less likely to answer honestly if they feel their written responses could "float around city hall." Moreover, someone other than the desired respondents (owner, manager, or assistant manager) could complete the survey. These factors could have a marked effect on the findings. If the response rate is low (that is, if less than perhaps half of those who are mailed surveys complete and return them), the representativeness of the survey statistics would be questionable. But the mail interview might be used

in combination with one of the other two approaches, especially if a business manager preferred mailing in the completed questionnaire to scheduling a telephone or personal interview.

Governments should consider making this survey a joint government-business venture. Local business associations such as the chamber of commerce should be consulted; they could even be asked to help with such tasks as: selecting survey topics, pretesting candidate questions, selecting or preparing the list from which the sample is drawn, and, especially, requesting businesses to participate in the survey, thereby helping to obtain high response rates with the fewest contacts.

The interviewing itself can be conducted by professional survey personnel or, to reduce costs, by government personnel, volunteers, or even persons from business associations who have been trained by, and are supervised by, professional survey personnel.

Need for Confidentiality of Individual Responses

All businesses contacted should be assured that at no time will the list of businesses surveyed be made public nor will any response be identified with a particular business.

How Much Will the Survey Cost?

Costs will depend chiefly on the sample size, the method of interviewing, and the amount of analysis of the data collected. Because the survey procedures have not been tested, only rough estimates can be given. If extensive effort is not required to prepare the list from which the sample is drawn, a twenty- to thirty-minute, in-person survey of 300 business establishments using a questionnaire similar to that shown in Appendix 2 should cost approximately $5,000. Costs for a telephone survey would be slightly less. Cash outlays for the business survey will be reduced if, as suggested above, some of the work is done by current government employees or by volunteers. If government employees or volunteers are used for sample selection and interviewing, professional survey guidance should still be obtained to prepare the questionnaire (at least for the initial survey), to develop the specific procedures for selection of persons to be interviewed, and to train and monitor interviewers.

The above estimates do not include costs for de-

---

5. Typically, 75 percent or more of households surveyed by mail do not respond. The percentages of businesspersons responding could probably be increased if special efforts to increase the response rate (such as follow-up mailings or telephone calls) are made.

tailed development of the questionnaire, or for analysis of the results; preparation of basic tabulations of the results is included.

Validation of the Survey

Will the responses to the business survey actually represent the experiences and perceptions of the total population of business establishments in the community on various aspects of the quality of government services? It is extremely difficult to prove that the findings are valid, but certain steps can be taken to increase the likelihood that the findings accurately represent the experiences and views of the business community. Some of these steps are described in Chapter 14; they apply equally to surveys of business communities.

As indicated earlier, it is particularly important when undertaking a business survey to enlist the aid of local business associations to achieve maximum cooperation of the respondents. A high response rate will reduce the chance of bias stemming from an inability to interview some businesses in the sample. It is also very important that the survey procedure provide for anonymity of responses in order to encourage frank and honest answers without fear of retaliation or embarrassment to the respondent. A mail survey, especially one to be returned to city hall, might discourage frank, honest responses.

As yet, the questionnaire and survey procedures discussed in this chapter have not been field-tested; such testing should help develop sound procedures and provide some initial evidence on certain aspects of validity. In the end, however, each government that undertakes a survey will need to utilize the approaches outlined above and in Chapter 14 to make sure its own survey efforts are as sound as possible.

Chapter 16

On Measuring Local Government Efficiency: A Preliminary Examination

Measuring the effectiveness and quality of government services has been discussed in the preceding chapters. But it is also important for governments to measure their efficiency in using resources to produce these levels of public services. Ideally, each government would like to measure regularly the following: To what degree does the government produce as much as possible from its resources? Or alternatively, to what degree does it produce the output as inexpensively as it could? Few if any standards now exist for levels of efficiency, and there may never be precise standards. Nevertheless, regular measurement of various aspects of efficiency should be able to provide a reasonable perspective on the current level of efficiency and how it is changing over time for individual government services. This chapter tries to provide a framework to help governments answer these questions. It also attempts to identify the vital, but often neglected, relationship between effectiveness and efficiency.

Some governments have been conducting limited efficiency measurement for several years, generally by relating the amount of work accomplished to the amount of employee-hours or dollars expended.

The first part of this chapter presents a classification of the types of efficiency measures that local governments might use and identifies some of the principal problems. The second part presents a preliminary list of efficiency measures that local governments may wish to consider.

We have not tested procedures for obtaining data for these efficiency measures. However, because many of them draw on cost and workload data—often readily available—and some drawn on effectiveness data gathered by procedures discussed elsewhere in this book, additional testing is probably not critical in most cases. But important problems remain, and these will be discussed. Governments introducing these measures will need to reassess them periodically to determine whether their usefulness warrants the additional data collection and analysis efforts required.

Classifying Efficiency Measures

Five types of efficiency measures are described and illustrated below:

1. Output-input ratio measures, using workload data as the unit of output;
2. Output-input ratio measures, using effectiveness data as the unit of output;
3. Equipment and personnel utilization rates;
4. Combinations of the preceding types of measures;
5. Measures of relative change: "productivity indices."

The ratios in (1) and (2) presented here will generally be expressed as the "amount of output per unit of input," but, the ratios can be inverted and used in the form "cost per unit of output." In general, these forms are equivalent. Each government can decide which form it prefers.[1]

These five types of measures are complementary. As with measures of effectiveness, seldom do single measures of efficiency adequately portray efficiency for any major service area. Thus, more than one efficiency measure for any given government service should be considered in order to obtain an overall perspective on efficiency. Also, as with effectiveness measurement, in-depth analysis will generally be needed to determine why the efficiency level is as it is and what is responsible for any improvement or deterioration that may appear.

In examining efficiency in government, what often seems to be forgotten is that efficiency implies a certain level and quality of service. If the quality of service is not at least maintained, an increase in output-input ratios is not really an efficiency improvement. Thus, to obtain a complete picture of government performance, both effectiveness and efficiency measures need to be examined. Efficiency may appear to be improving (or worsening), while in reality the service quality may be deteriorating (or improving). For example, an increase in tons of refuse collected per dollar could result from accelerated worker effort—but at the expense of more litter scattering or missed collections. Improved output-input ratios that are achieved at the expense of the quality of the service is not improved efficiency.

Type 1:   Output-input ratio measures, using workload accomplished as the measure of output.

This kind of measure is familiar to most local governments, though even today there is surprisingly little regular measurement being undertaken. For many government activities, one or more physical workload units can usually be identified as the outputs. Examples of such outputs include tons of refuse collected, miles of street repaired, acres of park grass mowed, number of park trees trimmed, number of complaints or requests handled, and number of government vehicles serviced. These outputs can be related to the resources used in producing them. Normally dollars or employee-hours are used as the input units. They can thus be expressed

as ratios such as "the number of tons collected per dollar or per employee-hour."[2]

A variation of this type of measure, becoming increasingly used in local governments, is that of "work standards." In this variation, instead of "number of work units produced per employee-hour," one compares the "number of standard (expected) hours per actual employee hours." The numerator is determined by multiplying the number of actual units of output produced times a predetermined "standard" time assigned each unit of the output. This variation is applicable only to those activities for which work standards can be developed, generally the more repetitive activities. In effect the government estimates the amount of time a specific work activity "should" take (the "standard"), and actual performance is compared against the standard.[3]

"Costs per capita" for individual services have sometimes been used by individual jurisdictions. The U.S. Bureau of Census provides such data annually. Because of variations in the kinds and levels of service provided, however, it is particularly difficult to use these data to compare meaningfully one government's performance with that of others.[4] This form of measure seems most appropriate when a product is directly provided to persons or households, as is the case with waste collection and water supply. It seems less useful, and probably misleading for efficiency measurement purposes, to count all the population in the jurisdiction as being served when a significant part of the population may not actually use the particular service (as is likely to be the case with recreation or transit services).

In undertaking and using these measurements, it is necessary to consider the quality of the output. Improvement in the ratio of work accomplished per

2. Note that the amount of workload performed, such as tons of refuse collected, is not by itself a measure of efficiency. Also, the amount of workload *facing* a government (but not yet accomplished), even if divided by expenditures, is not an efficiency measure. Similarly, measures such as pupil-teacher ratios and ratios of the number of cases per caseworker reflect chiefly the amount of workload facing employees; they indicate nothing about output and thus are not measures of efficiency.

3. In general, work standards can be applied to those government activities that have each of the following three characteristics: (a) the product is sufficiently defined so that its presence or absence is clear; (b) the procedure for obtaining the product is sufficiently standardized so that the time requirements can be specified; and (c) specific quality standards are available so that the government can determine that the product has been adequately accomplished.

4. Also, in some instances, "dollars expended per capita" has been used as a ratio to *maximize*, not minimize; in these instances "dollars expended" is used as a proxy for *output*. These measures have been used in this way for such services as education and libraries. The use of dollars expended as an output measure begs the question as to what output was actually achieved. We recommend against the use of dollars as a proxy for output.

1. The term "productivity" has traditionally been used in the form "amount of output per unit of input." The term "efficiency" has, in typical government usage, often been expressed in the form of "cost per unit of output," that is, amount of input divided by the amount of output.

unit of input is not an improvement in efficiency if the level of service has deteriorated. When providing comparisons of this type of measure over time or among various work groups, and no statement is made to the contrary, the user of the data should be able to depend on the fact that the quality of the output has not been reduced. This means that a government should provide for some explicit assessment of that quality and report those findings along with the output-input ratios. Alternatively, one may utilize the second type of efficiency measure.

Type 2: Output-input ratio measures using effectiveness data as the measure of output.

The assumption here is that it is important to consider the real product of public services and not merely some physical output that happens to be easily measured. For example, should an inadequately patched pothole, or an arrest that was subsequently dropped because of inadequate police evidence, or the handling of a citizen request that was not satisfactorily resolved, be credited in counting output? We think not. For example, in the case of the defective pothole repair, the repair should not be included in the output until it is properly done, and the extra expense of the repatching should be included in the costs. Thus, this second type of efficiency measure attempts to consider explicitly the quality of service as part of the measure.

This kind of efficiency measure is seldom utilized in local government today, probably because of the general shortage of effectiveness data coupled with a lack of familiarity with this type of measure. As meaningful effectiveness data become available for government services, measures of this type will probably come into more general use.

Many of the effectiveness measures identified throughout this volume are candidates for the output portion of this efficiency measure. Some illustrations follow:

- To measure the efficiency of police in solving crimes, it is tempting to use the measure "number of arrests per dollar or per police-officer-hour" as the key measure of efficiency. But arrests can be of poor quality, and the possibility of encouraging perverse effects, such as harassment of citizens, is sufficiently great that another measure reflecting the quality of arrests seems preferable if not essential. A preferable efficiency measure is the "number of arrests *that pass the preliminary hearing* per dollar (or per police-officer-hour)."

(See Chapter 6 for a discussion of the procedures for measuring the number of arrests that pass the preliminary hearing.)

- For human resource treatment programs such as employment and training programs, physical and mental health treatment, vocational rehabilitation, offender rehabilitation, and social services such as family counseling, the meaningful output unit should be some form of "the number of clients *improved* per unit of resource." The typical current form, "number of clients *served* per unit of resource," says nothing about the results of the service provided, and its use as an efficiency measure is questionable.

- Another group of measures that fits into this classification is the "estimated number of households, citizens, or clients *satisfied* with the service (or a particular aspect of the service) per dollar or per employee-hour." This form of efficiency measure will be particularly important to those who believe that citizen, or client, satisfaction with services is a major product of government services. The output unit used here combines the conventional "number of persons served" with a measure of the percentage of citizens satisfied with the service. This information can be obtained with the use of systematic citizen or client surveys discussed in other chapters. The percentages obtained from the sample surveys can be projected to the appropriate total population to provide estimates of the total number of citizens who are satisfied.

This type of measure is subject to the problems that affect all effectiveness measures. For example, some highly desirable effectiveness measures are virtually impossible to obtain; prime examples are those that attempt to assess success of "prevention" activities, such as prevention of crimes, fires, traffic accidents, or illnesses. Thus, the ideal efficiency measure, "number of such events (crimes, fires, accidents, or illnesses) prevented per dollar or per employee-hour," is rarely measurable. (An effort to estimate these, however, can and should be made periodically in special studies.) In effectiveness measurement, the approach generally substituted is to measure the number of incidents not prevented— that is the number of crimes, fires, traffic accidents, or illnesses that do occur. These are useful and appropriate as measures of effectiveness, but constructing a ratio with these outputs related to dollars or employee-hours does not make sense. For example, the "number of crimes per dollar" or the "number of traffic accidents per dollar" are not meaningful efficiency ratios. If both the numerator (for example, the number of crimes) and the denominator (for example, the number of dollars) are reduced by 10 percent, the ratio will remain the same, implying that no improvement has occurred; in fact, there has obviously been improvement, because both costs and crimes are lower.

Effectiveness measures expressed as percentages, such as the percentage of clients satisfied with a particular service characteristic, are also generally inappropriate to use for these ratios. Such percentages should instead be converted to numbers of households or numbers of events, which can be used in the ratios.

Finally, a special type of effectiveness-to-input ratio is the benefit-cost (or cost-benefit) ratio. Here the output units (the benefits) are converted to monetary units that are presumed to represent in some way the monetary value of the benefits. These dollars are then divided by the costs of achieving the benefits (or the costs can be subtracted from the benefits) to give the benefit-cost ratios (or net benefits). These can be considered measures of efficiency. The attribution of dollars values to the various products of government services is complex and can involve very shaky assumptions, as, for example, in attributing dollar value to the time saved by a new highway. The principal use for these benefit-cost computations will probably be in special studies (if reasonable dollar value attributions can be made of the benefits) rather than for regular monitoring by a government.

Type 3.   Equipment and personnel utilization rates.

This is a common type of efficiency measure. It reflects the amount of specific resources of the government (equipment-hours or employee-hours) that are utilized (or not utilized) for potentially "productive" activities. This type of measure does *not* directly measure the amount of output obtained from these resources and thus should be considered only as "proxy" indicators. Yet, versions of it are likely to be useful for most government services. The general form of the measure is the ratio of the amount of the resource actually used to the amount potentially available.

In general, the more downtime a piece of government equipment has, or the larger proportion of time that a government employee is not utilized for operational duty, the less efficiently those resources are being used. "Total available hours" is the unit often used in the denominator of the ratio. In most cases it is impossible, as well as undesirable, to achieve 100-percent utilization of equipment or personnel. But generally, it is desirable to increase the percentage of time that they are utilized, at least up to some practical limit.

Closely related to "utilization" is "availability." Utilization and availability rates often will not be equivalent. A piece of equipment or an employee may be available for work but not be used. In practice, governments often collect data on obvious downtime such as time that a vehicle is in the shop being repaired. These statistics will not, however, capture the amount of time that the vehicle is available for use but unused because of lack of work or other scheduling problems. Preferably, this type of measure would focus on utilization, but as a practical matter it may often be measured more feasibly in terms of availability.

There are a number of variations. Some of the most common follow:

1. Percentage of available hours that each type of equipment (or employee) was utilized (or not utilized) for productive operation.
2. Average amount of utilization (or nonutilization or downtime) per piece of equipment (or employee).
3. Average percentage or average number of pieces of equipment (or employees) utilized (or not utilized).

These may also be expressed in a form which emphasizes preselected thresholds rather than averages:

4. Number of instances in which nonutilization of a piece of equipment (or employee) exceeded "x" hours.
5. Percentage of total hours that "y" or more pieces of equipment (or employees) were not utilized.

Here "x" and "y" are preselected threshold values.

This type of efficiency measure is somewhat complicated by the problem of backup equipment or personnel. The effect on government services of the breakdown of a piece of equipment, or the unavailability of personnel, will vary with the extent to which backup equipment, or personnel, is available. Similarly, if equipment breaks down at the end of a shift and is not scheduled for use in the next shift, its unavailability is of less consequence than if it breaks down during hours when it is needed. The same goes for an employee who is sick during slack work periods.

Note that measures of delays in serving citizens

have not been included under the term "efficiency measures." These measures are included in our classification as a measure of effectiveness, on the assumption that they represent a quality of the service to citizens, that is, promptness.

Two special variations are as follows:

1. In water supply, the "percentage of water that does not generate revenue or is otherwise not used 'productively'."
2. In public transit, the load factors, such as the ratio of actual passenger-miles to the total available capacity (seat-miles).

In the first case, resources have been used to treat and distribute the water; water lost due to such circumstances as leaks has not delivered a service. In the second case, seats for potential passengers have been transported from one point to another at some cost; if those seats were not filled, no service has been delivered by those seats.

Type 4.   Combination of the preceding types of measures.

Normally there will be more than one output measure relevant to the efficiency of a government service. Our general recommendation is to calculate and present each such relevant measure. It is tempting, however, to try to combine measures into a more comprehensive measure. An example of such a multiple measure is shown in Exhibit 16-1.[5] Such measures usually are more difficult to understand, and they tend to contain hidden value judgments about the relative importance of each factor in the index.

Type 5.   Measures of relative change: "productivity indices."

These indices are used to measure percentage changes from one year to a pre-selected base period. They measure relative efficiency rather than absolute efficiency. A productivity index can be constructed for any measure of any of the previous types. Specifically, a base year (or base period of

5. More complex approaches—more appropriate to in-depth analysis than to regular performance status monitoring—are possible. For example, statistical, multiple-regression analysis could be used to relate past output magnitudes to magnitudes of resources. The amount of resources actually used can then be inserted into the regression equation to estimate the effectiveness levels expected to be achieved with those resources. These can then be compared against actual outputs.

Exhibit 16-1
ILLUSTRATIVE EFFICIENCY MEASUREMENT PRESENTATION
(Solid waste collection)

DATA	1976	1977	CHANGE
1. Tons of solid waste collected	90,000	100,000	+10,000
2. Average litter cleanliness rating[1]	2.9	2.6	−0.3
3. Percentage of survey population expressing satisfaction with collection[1]	85%	80%	−5%[3]
4. Cost (unadjusted)	$1,200,000	$1,500,000	+$300,000
5. Cost (1976 dollars)	$1,200,000	$1,300,000	+$100,000
EFFICIENCY MEASURES[2]			
6. Workload per dollar (unadjusted)	75 tons per $ thousand	67 tons per $ thousand	−11%
7. Workload per dollar (1976 dollars)	75 tons per $ thousand	77 tons per $ thousand	+3%
8. Combined measure: $\frac{(1)\times(2)\times(3)}{(4)}$ (unadjusted dollars)	0.185	0.139	−25%
9. Combined measure: $\frac{(1)\times(2)\times(3)}{(5)}$ (1976 dollars)	0.185	0.160	−14%
10. Producivity index for Measure 9 (1976 base year)	100	86	−14%

1. For such procedures, see Chapter 2. The rating in line 2 is here based on a scale of 1 to 4, with 4 the cleanest.

2. The figures in line 7 indicate some improvement in efficiency, but line 6 suggests that cost increases such as wages have more than exceeded the efficiency gains. Efficiency, as indicated by the combined measures used, has gone down because of decreases in the street cleanliness ratings and decreased citizen satisfaction. Like most such complex measures, they are somewhat arbitrary and difficult to interpret. Measures such as these must be studied carefully before being accepted for use.

3. This change should be read: "5 percentage points."

Source: Adapted from Harry P. Hatry and Donald M. Fisk, *Improving Productivity and Productivity Measurement in Local Government* (Washington, D.C.: National Commission on Productivity, June 1971).

perhaps two or three years) could be used on any measure. The base period is given the value of 100. For example, if tons collected per employee-hour were 200 in the base year, and 225 in a subsequent year, the productivity index for the subsequent year would be $225/200 \times 100 = 112.5$—indicating 12.5 percent higher productivity. Indices can be calculated for each such efficiency measure. Line 10 in Exhibit 16-1 provides an example. By weighting different indices (such as by the relative amount of total employee-hours for each product in the base year), different government activities can be combined to form an overall index.

For many years U.S. Bureau of Labor Statistics has used such indices for tracking productivity in the private sector. The federal government has recently begun to use these indices for its own activities.[6]

Problems in Collecting Input Data

At first glance, it may seem that measuring the amounts of inputs is easy. Unfortunately, in actual practice many complications arise. Some of the chief issues follow:[7]

1. The figures representing the input resources—generally dollars or employee-hours—should ideally represent all the resources required to produce the outputs that are measured and only those. For example, for solid waste collection, estimates should include all the dollars or employee-hours involved in collection activities, but exclude costs for disposal. The total costs of any activity, the efficiency of which is being measured, should include employee-benefit costs (including full pension costs); costs of clerks, secretaries, and supervisors; costs of procuring and maintaining equipment; and costs of obtaining and maintaining necessary facilities. If it is desired to estimate the efficiency for subfunctions (such as solid waste collection for residential customers as distinct from collection for commercial customers), the problem of allocating costs or employee-hours becomes more difficult. Unfortunately, local government accounting systems in most jurisdictions do not automatically provide costs in the needed categories.

2. A further complication in the measurement of costs and employee-hours is the problem of shared costs. For example, solid waste collection and disposal activities may have some of the same supervisors and share some of the same facilities. Similarly, a single police officer may undertake crime prevention, apprehension, and perhaps traffic-control activities. Procedures are needed for allocating these joint costs if it is deemed desirable to examine separately the efficiency of these individual activities. The rules of allocation will probably have to be somewhat arbitrary.

3. Another difficult issue in cost measurement is how to handle capital and other investment costs. If investment costs are charged only to the year in which the costs are obligated or in which expenditures occur, the efficiency estimate for those years would be too low and for subsequent years, too high. Investment costs should probably be spread, over the years for which the investment is used, but the best method for doing this remains a matter for debate. Possible approaches are to use the appropriate annual debt service charges (if the funds were raised by borrowing) or, to use amortization procedures. Another approach is to estimate what it would cost to lease the piece of equipment or rent the facility and then use that figure as the cost for the year. If the municipality already leases the equipment or rents the facility, those costs should be readily available. In some cases, a city may already be using revolving funds; for example, a central garage may charge each agency for vehicle maintenance in such a way as to cover all the costs of the garage, including equipment and even facilities. If the city does not already use one of these procedures, one will be needed to estimate a fair share of the costs for each activity.

The easy way out—and the common practice—is to exclude capital costs from the measures and to consider only operating costs in the calculations. This means, however, that the efficiency measures will not be useful for comparisons between capital-intensive and labor-intensive practices. For example, output per *operating* cost dollar may have increased, but when the capital investment that led to reduced operating cost is considered, efficiency in terms of total expenditures may actually be found to have decreased.

4. Another problem occurs when cost comparisons are made over time. Changes may occur in price

6. For further information on the use of productivity indices in the government sector, see *Federal Productivity: Methods, Measurement, Results* (Washington, D.C.: General Accounting Office, August 1972); and *Government Productivity: Vol. 1, Productivity Trends and Current Efforts,* (Washington, D.C.: Joint Financial Management Improvement Program, July 1976).

7. This material is based in part on Harry P. Hatry and Donald M. Fisk, *Improving Productivity and Productivity Measurement in Local Governments* (Washington, D.C.: National Commission on Productivity, June 1971), especially pages 15-17.

levels, in accounting procedures, or in definitions of the costs. Such changes may require data adjustments. Cost data for different years can be adjusted for changes in price to indicate how "real" efficiency is changing in terms of quantity of physical resources used. Price indices should be applied to convert the dollar costs for each year to a base year. The question arises as to whether the government should use one overall deflator (an index of prices of all government items) or different deflators that permit the reflection of different mixes of inputs for each service area. The latter seems preferable, but it is more arduous. Because local governments are probably interested in both "real" changes and changes in output per actual dollar, unadjusted for price-level changes, it is recommended that both be calculated and presented. (See lines 6-9 of Exhibit 16-1 for an illustration of the use of such price indices.)

5. Both "output per employee-hour" and "output per dollar" (with dollars adjusted for price changes) seem desirable for measuring efficiency. The employee-hour measure produces major insights relative to the principal government input—that is, personnel. Dollar cost represents, at least roughly, all inputs and, thus, in effect permits simultaneous consideration of the efficiency of use of all resources, not just personnel.

Miscellaneous Issues

The Need to Avoid Overemphasizing Current Efficiency at the Expense of Future Performance

When a government undertakes to measure efficiency, there is a particular danger of encouraging excessive concern with current performance at the expense of future performance. If too much emphasis is put on current efficiency, expenditures aimed chiefly at improving future performance may be neglected. (This danger, of course, also exists for governments that are not measuring performance at all.) One way to alleviate this problem, as discussed earlier, is to avoid charging total investment and development costs to the current year's budget but to spread these costs over future years as well.

On occasion there may be government expenditures other than capital expenditures that are intended primarily to affect performance in future years. These can also be amortized or at least excluded from efficiency calculations for years prior to the period of their intended impact. For example,

costs for equipment overhaul and for long-range planning and development may fall into this category. Preventive maintenance is a similar cost, but to the extent that it is aimed mainly at helping operations within one year, it is appropriate to include such costs among current expenditures. Investments might be amortized over the first several years of their existence using accepted, private-sector kinds of accounting procedures.

Possible Problems in Interpreting Efficiency Data

Many factors can affect the values calculated for efficiency measures, even though the work force itself has not altered its pace or procedures. Substantial increases or decreases in the incoming workload can by themselves significantly affect efficiency values. The type of service provided by the government may change. In addition, differing external characteristics of neighborhoods (such as the terrain or resident population) make it difficult to compare various facilities or different units of workers in different areas.

These qualifications do not mean that examining efficiency is not useful, but rather that conclusions should not be jumped at or be based on only the gross efficiency data without careful consideration of likely causes. In some instances it is highly desirable to classify the workload in terms of its "difficulty." Displaying measurement results by categories of difficulty permits analysts to consider differences in mixes of workload difficulty when interpreting changes in efficiency measures. For example, data on measures involving solutions of crimes, such as "the number of arrests that pass preliminary hearing per police-officer-hour," should preferably be grouped to distinguish arrests relating to hard-to-solve crimes from those relatively easy to solve.

A special interpretation problem occurs if efficiency comparisons are made for periods of less than one year's duration. Efficiency measurements that cover a whole year can be compared with data from other years without concern regarding seasons. For shorter time periods, consideration of seasonal effects on efficiency will be necessary. After gaining experience, a government may choose to make statistical, seasonal adjustments to measured values so that efficiency comparisons can be made among time periods within a year.

Avoiding Excessive Efficiency Measurement

The number of activities and subactivities in government on which efficiency measurements can be undertaken seems almost endless. Examples exist of local governments engaging in very detailed efficiency measurement efforts that proved unable to survive their own tests of cost-effectiveness. Moreover, efforts requiring highly detailed time keeping can cause considerable annoyance to the personnel involved. Excessive data collection leads to knowing more and more about less and less, and should be avoided.

Illustrative Measures of Efficiency

In this section, a number of preliminary measures of efficiency of Types 1-3 are identified for the municipal services discussed in this report: solid waste collection and disposal, recreation, library services, crime control, fire protection, local transportation services, water supply, and handling of complaints and requests for services and information. (See page 233 for description of types.)

The measures shown here are illustrative. They are intended to provoke discussion by individual governments and their agencies and, we hope, more in-depth examinations and testing. Most of these measures have not been reviewed by operating agencies, and data collection procedures for many have not been tested. Some governments are already regularly collecting data on some of these efficiency measures, and many other governments are already collecting data that can be readily adapted for use in calculating some of these measures. Governments seeking to employ measures requiring effectiveness data would need to use the appropriate data collection procedures such as described in other chapters of this volume. As indicated in the section on data collection problems earlier in this chapter, calculating values for the relevant amounts of dollars or employee-hours poses some problems. Therefore, more effort by individual governments may be required before some of these measures will be fully operational.

The measures are listed by service area and are classified by type. Ratio measures are expressed in the form "output divided by input," but the inverse "input divided by output" generally provides equivalent information on efficiency. In most cases, the input units can be either dollars or employee-hours. They have been expressed here in terms of one or the other somewhat arbitrarily. Measures of utilization (Type 3) can be expressed either in terms of degree of utilization or nonutilization.

All the measures illustrated for any single service area are intended to be used together; they are complementary, not substitutes for each other. Together with effectiveness measures, measures such as these should provide a reasonably full perspective on the performance of those government services.

Individual governments should assess the desirability of using both individual efficiency and effectiveness measures by considering such criteria as the following:

1. Do the measures collectively cover all important aspects of the service activity? If not, improvements or deterioration in those aspects that are being measured should be kept in perspective. Users of efficiency measurement data should consider unmeasured aspects and not, for example, reward or penalize government personnel solely on aspects that can be quantified.
2. To what extent can the government affect the measured values? Particularly with measures that use effectiveness estimates for output calculations (Type 2 measures), a government will not have complete control over the measured values. If a government has little or no control, the measure will probably not be useful to it.
3. Is the measure understandable to users? The combination kind of measures (Type 4) are particularly likely to pose a comprehension problem, but other types of measures can as well.
4. Are the costs and personnel requirements to collect the data reasonable? Two problems are particularly worth noting: (a) For Type 2 measures, unless the government has an on-going effectiveness-measurement system (for example, regular citizen survey procedures), it may not be practical to collect such measurements solely for efficiency measurement. (b) It may be tempting, especially for Type 1 measures, to measure activities in increasing detail. If extensive daily activity reports are required, the costs of data processing can quickly become excessive.
5. Is there provision for analyzing the findings from the measurement process? The government should provide for the examination of changes in measured values; the following possibilities, among others, should be considered:
   a. The change may have occurred primarily because of an increase in workload without an accompanying increase in personnel or dollars, or
   b. The apparent improvement was achieved at the expense of reduced level or quality of the service.

Solid Waste Collection—Measures of Efficiency

Type 1:   *Output in units of workload ÷ input*
1-1   Tons collected per dollar.
1-2   Number of curb-miles of streets cleaned per dollar.
1-3   Number of large items hauled away (such as abandoned autos, refrigerators, etc.) per dollar.
1-4   Number of residential (or commercial) customers served per dollar.

Type 2:   *Output in units of "effectiveness" ÷ input*
2-1   Estimated number of total households and commercial customers satisfied with their collection services (as estimated from responses to a citizen survey and survey of businesses) per dollar.

Type 3:   *Utilization measures*
3-1   Average percentage of vehicles out of commission at any one time (during working hours).
3-2   Percentage of crew-shifts with shortage of personnel.

Solid Waste Disposal—Measures of Efficiency

Type 1:   *Output in units of workload ÷ input*
1-1   Number of tons disposed per dollar.
1-2   Number of tons disposed per acre (or per cubic yard of fill used). (Note: Here an input measure, other than dollars or employee-hours, that is, acreage, is used. Any scarce resource, in this case land, can be used as the input unit.)

Type 2:   *Output in units of "effectiveness" ÷ input*
2-1   Estimated number of site-days of environmental-hazard-free disposal per dollar.

Type 3:   *Utilization measures*
3-1   Percentage of working hours that major equipment is available.
3-2   Number of days that same-day cover was not achieved because of equipment failure or shortage of personnel.
3-3   Net revenues from recycling (for example, total value from products sold and heat recovered minus recycling operation costs).

Recreation—Measures of Efficiency

Type 1:   *Output in units of workload ÷ input*
1-1   Acres (or square feet of facility) maintained (mowed, cleaned, etc.) per dollar, for various types of facilities.[8] (If comparisons are made between facilities, adjustments are likely to be needed to account for differences in terrain, use levels, or other characteristics that lead to different maintenance requirements at different locations. If work standards are developed for different locations, the form "ratio of standard hours accomplished per employee-hour actually applied" would be appropriate.)[9]
1-2   Number of hours of operation per dollar, for individual programs or facilities.

Type 2:   *Output in units of "effectiveness" ÷ input*
2-1   Attendance (or visit) days per dollar, perhaps for individual programs or facilities.
2-2   Estimated number of different households using recreation services (at least once a year) per dollar, perhaps for individual programs or facilities (these estimates could be based on the participation rates obtained in an annual citizen survey—see Chapter 4).
2-3   Estimated number of total households satisfied with recreation services (as estimated by data from the annual citizen survey) per dollar.

Type 3:   *Utilization measures*
3-1   Major-equipment in-commission rates (perhaps calculated as the total number of equipment-days in commission divided by the total potential number of equipment-days).
3-2   Percentage of time facilities are closed for maintenance (percentages should be calculated for individual facilities such as swimming pools and tennis courts, as well as to provide an overall percentage).

Library Services—Measures of Efficiency

Type 1:   *Output in units of workload ÷ input*
1-1   Number of items circulated (books, records, and other items) per dollar, perhaps including in-library circulation (see Chapter 5).

8. This can be further split into more detailed work components to provide such measures as "acres of grass mowed per employee-hour," "number of trees maintained per employee-hour," "tons of litter removed per employee-hour," and "pieces of playground equipment maintained per dollar."
9. Work standards can be applied to many of the Type 1 measures illustrated in this chapter.

1-2   Number of items cataloged per employee-hour.

1-3   Number of items shelved per employee-hour.

1-4   Number of hours of operation per dollar.

Type 2:   *Output in units of "effectiveness" ÷ input*

2-1   Number of individual uses of library (including attendance counts plus telephone requests for information) per dollar.

2-2   Estimated number of different households (or persons) using library services at least once (as estimated from an annual citizen survey) per dollar.

2-3   Estimated number of households satisfied with library services (as estimated from the citizen survey) per dollar.

Type 3:   *Utilization measures*

None identified (but "usage" measures have already been included as Type 1 or Type 2 measures).

Crime Control—Measures of Efficiency

Type 1:   *Output in units of workload ÷ input*

1-1   Number of service calls responded to per hour of police-officer time—by type of call.

1-2   Number of investigations conducted per hour of police-officer time—by type of case.

1-3   Number of arrests per hour of police-officer time (but see Measure 2-1 below).

Type 2:   *Output in units of "effectiveness" ÷ input*

2-1   Number of felony arrests that pass preliminary hearing per police officer-hour—overall and by type of category. (Ideally, Measure 1-3 should be replaced by this measure because of the strong potential for abuse in the use of that measure; see discussion in Chapter 6.)

2-2   Estimated number of households reporting a reasonable feeling of security in walking their neighborhood at night (as estimated from citizen survey findings) per dollar.

2-3   Estimated number of nonvictimized households and commercial establishments per dollar. (The citizen survey could be used to provide estimates of the number of crime incidents not reported; see Chapter 6.)

Type 3:   *Utilization measures*

3-1   Percentage of total potentially available police-officer-time that is spent on "productive" purposes (productive time to exclude such time as waiting for car repair, waiting in courts, etc.).

3-2   Average percentage of police officers available for "productive" purposes.

3-3   Percentage of cases not investigated at all, by type of case.

Fire Protection—Measures of Efficiency

Type 1:   *Output in units of workload ÷ input*

1-1   Number of households and business establishments "protected" per dollar.

1-2   Number of fire prevention inspections per dollar—perhaps categorized as to whether inspections and costs are residential or commercial.

Type 2:   *Output in units of "effectiveness" ÷ input*

2-1   Number of fires fought for which less than a target amount of spread occurred per suppression dollar spent. (Target amount of spread would be defined relative to the size of the fire on arrival and possibly other relevant variables, such as occupancy type; see Chapter 7 for a discussion of these procedures.)

Type 3:   *Utilization measures*

3-1   Percentage of downtime of major fire equipment.

Local Transportation Services—Measures of Efficiency

Street Maintenance

Type 1:   *Output in units of workload ÷ input*

1-1   Number of miles (or lane-miles) of street maintained per dollar.

1-2   Number of repairs made (or number of square yards of repairs made) per employee-hour. (Individual street and maintenance activities might be distinguished separately as for example, "pothole repair with cold patch," "pothole repair with asphalt concrete," and "curb and gutter repair." If work standards are developed, the form "ratio of standard hours accomplished per employee-hour actually applied" would be appropriate.)

1-3   Number of square yards of street surface constructed per dollar.

Type 2: *Output in units of "effectiveness" ÷ input*
2-1 Number of streets maintained in rideability-condition "x" or better per dollar. (See Chapter 8 on local transportation for a discussion of procedures for assessing rideability).
2-2 Number of repairs made satisfactorily (for example, "patches lasting at least 'x' months after repair") per dollar.

Type 3: *Utilization measures*
3-1 Proportion of time that crews are "non-productive" (for such reasons as being in transit or waiting for materials).

Traffic
Type 1: *Output in units of workload ÷ input*
1-1 Number of signs installed per dollar.
1-2 Number of signals installed per dollar.
1-3 Number of feet of street markings laid per dollar.
1-4 Number of signs or signals repaired per dollar.

Type 2: *Output in units of "effectiveness" ÷ input*
2-1 Number of signs or signals maintained in acceptable operating condition per dollar.

Type 3: *Utilization measures*
3-1 Percentage of traffic signal time that signals were known to be defective.
3-2 Downtime of traffic signals from time signals were reported defective.
3-3 Average time to restore to service failed traffic signs or signals.

Public Transit—Measures of Efficiency
Type 1: *Output in units of workload ÷ input*
1-1 Number of vehicle-miles per dollar.
1-2 Number of transit vehicle-hours of operation per dollar.

Type 2: *Output in units of "effectiveness" ÷ input*
2-1 Number of passenger-trips per dollar.
2-2 Number of passenger-miles per dollar.
2-3 Estimated number of "satisfied" users (perhaps as estimated from an annual citizen survey) per dollar.

Type 3: *Utilization measures*
3-1 Average percentage of time transit vehicles are available as a percentage of potentially available hours, by type of vehicle.
3-2 Percentage of scheduled arrival times that are late or missed because of unavailable personnel or equipment.
3-3 Load factor: Ratio of actual passenger-miles to capacity, with capacity perhaps defined by seat-miles (this could be derived from a sampling of load factors at a representative cross section of times of day, days of the week, and seasons).
3-4 Amount of net operating deficit (or surplus) over costs (revenues would include fares and possibly subsidies; note that this measure has to be considered in relation to the jurisdiction's subsidy policy). This measure, as well as Measures 3-2 and 3-3, would be especially useful if the data can be calculated by route.

Water Supply—Measures of Efficiency
Type 1: *Output in units of workload ÷ input*
1-1 Number of gallons distributed per dollar.
1-2 Number of gallons treated per dollar.
1-3 Number of customers served per dollar (perhaps divided by residential and commercial customers).
1-4 Number of repairs completed per employee-hour, by type and size of repair.
1-5 Number of meters read per employee-hour.
1-6 Number of meters inspected per employee-hour.
1-7 Number of meters repaired per employee-hour.

Type 2: *Output in units of "effectiveness" ÷ input*[10]
2-1 Estimated number of customers indicating satisfaction with their water (as obtained from the annual citizen survey) per dollar.

Type 3: *Utilization measures*
3-1 Average percentage of downtime for major equipment as a percentage of total, potentially useful, equipment hours, by category of equipment.

---

10. Clearly, the amount of improvement between the quality of the incoming, untreated water and quality of the water supplied to consumers is a vital indicator of water supply effectiveness. We have not been able to identify a satisfactory efficiency measure covering this element. We hope others will be able to do so.

3-2   Percentage of water distributed that generates revenue or is otherwise used productively (such as for government uses, including fire fighting) as distinguished from leakage or other losses.

Handling of Citizen Complaints and Requests for Services and Information—Measures of Efficiency

Type 1:   *Output in units of workload ÷ input*
1-1   Number of complaints and requests for services and information handled per employee-hour or per dollar. (Note: It does not seem sufficiently useful to attempt to distinguish the dollar costs for complaints from those for services and

information, but this distinction could be feasible for employee-hours.)

Type 2:   *Output in units of "effectiveness" ÷ input*
2-1   Number of complaints and requests for services and information resolved satisfactorily (as estimated from an annual citizen survey, from a survey of complainants, or from examination of government records—see the data collection procedures discussed in Chapter 11). As in Type 1-1, because of difficulties in distinguishing dollar costs for each activity, it may not be feasible to distinguish complaints from requests for services and information.

Type 3:   *Utilization measures*
None identified.

Chapter 17

Some Implementation Suggestions

Although the research on which this report is based did not address the question of how best to implement effectiveness measurement procedures from an organizational viewpoint, we offer here some suggestions based on our experiences with the governments referred to throughout this report.[1]

Guidelines Based on Experiences to Date

1. *Involve the operating agencies in the development, implementation, and use of the measurement procedures.*

    Operating agencies contain the government employees who not only have considerable potential interest in the measurement findings, but who also can probably do most about the findings if they require action. Governments are therefore urged to involve individual agencies at all stages of the work, from the initial preparation of the measures and the development of data collection procedures to the review of the findings. This practice will greatly increase the likelihood that the procedures will work and that the information will be used.

    Involving agency employees is more easily said than done. Three problems have seemed particularly troublesome:

    a. *Interest by operating agencies in citizen-impact data is mixed.* In our trials, some organizations, such as park and recreation agencies, were quite interested in obtaining citizen feedback on their services. Others, however, were considerably more skeptical about the value of procedures calling for citizen ratings of aspects of their service.

    b. *There is a temptation for central staffs to be impatient.* They may not want to take the necessary, and often considerable, amount of time to work with agency personnel.

    c. *Agency staff time for analysis is limited or nonexistent.* Few local government agencies have staff analysts. Where analysts are present, the pressure of daily activities often prevents them from spending much time analyzing performance data. Agency managers can probably obtain many useful insights from even a brief examination of the measurement findings, but to gain a fuller perspective on the data, the use of trained analysts is desirable. (Some types of analyses that seem desirable were presented in Chapter 12.) The problem of scarcity of analytical staff looms less large when central staff analysts are available to help agencies.

2. *Use effectiveness measurement in a positive, constructive manner; make effectiveness measurement as rewarding and unthreatening as possible to government managers.*

    This is a tall order, since measurement implies evaluation and accountability, which often seem inherently threatening to those being evaluated. The cooperative approach to selection of measures and development of procedures suggested above will probably somewhat alleviate the concern. However, local gov-

---

1. Some additional implementation issues are discussed in Chapter 5 of our initial report. Chapter 14 of this report discusses some issues specifically relevant to citizen surveys, and the individual service area chapters discuss implementation issues on specific measurement procedures presenting special problems.

ernments are also urged to use the effectiveness measurement data not only to identify problem areas but also to provide appropriate commendations or rewards to those agencies and personnel for which the measurements point out major improvements, or maintenance of prior levels of service in the face of adverse external factors. When problems show up, it is important not to focus attention on attributing blame but rather on identifying constructive improvements.

3. *Provide specific incentives to government managers to participate constructively in evaluation-oriented activities.*

How to do this is by no means clear, but incentives are needed. Disincentives to evaluation currently predominate in most governments' systems of reward; for example, budget and staff size are important status symbols, but improvements in performance often lead to reduced budgets and staff. Potentially appropriate and practical rewards include the following:

- Favorable performance ratings,
- Formal commendations and public service awards,
- Reduction of selected management controls for those demonstrating high effectiveness and efficiency, and
- Monetary rewards such as merit increases or bonuses

The best single incentive for government management employees may be the *use* of the measurement information by top government management and the legislative body.

4. *Provide central staff leadership and management support to assist operating agencies in the development and use of measurement procedures.*

Central staff personnel will probably have to provide technical leadership for the agencies in establishing goals and objectives, in developing measures and implementing data collection activities, and in demonstrating central management's continuing high-priority view of effectiveness measurement. It seems likely that the central staff should also participate in analyzing measurement findings and helping the agencies (and possibly the local legislative body) use the information. In Nashville, St. Petersburg, and Palo Alto, central staff personnel provided analytical and coordination support to the operating agencies in developing the measurement procedures.

5. *Give considerable attention to maximizing the usefulness and application of the data produced by measurement procedures.*

The promise of usefulness is, of course, the justification for the effort and expense in implementing effectiveness measurement procedures. Some ways to increase the utility of the effectiveness data are suggested in Chapter 12. But failure to follow through on applying the data has been a major weakness in measurement efforts to date. Governments are urged to make formal provision for at least an annual review of the effectiveness measurement information and to delegate responsibility to specific staff members, probably on the central staff level, to analyze measurement findings and to work with agency personnel in reviewing and using them.

As illustrated in the exhibits in Chapter 12, the measurement findings should be summarized concisely and clearly. Each agency should be asked to identify any key problem areas indicated by the findings, to comment on areas in which significant progress has been made, and to recommend any follow-up that appears desirable. (Exhibit 12-6 illustrates how this information might be requested.) When agency recommendations are made, they should be carefully reviewed and feedback should be provided to individual agencies.

After the measurement data have been obtained for perhaps two or three years, the government should consider having agency managers set targets for the values of individual measures for the forthcoming year. At the end of each year, the actual outcomes would be compared to the targets as a basis for reviewing performance during that year.

The seriousness with which operating agencies treat effectiveness measurement will be greatly affected by the degree to which they perceive that central management (and the legislative body) takes it seriously.

6. *Work out a balance between client-oriented outcome measures and more agency-oriented activity (e.g., workload) measures.*

Designers of any system of effectiveness measurement will inevitably encounter a tug-of-war between measures oriented to citizen impact and those over which an operating agency feels it has more direct influence, especially measures of its immediate, physical output, that is, units of activity, or workload accomplished. Although citizens, upper-level management, and the legislative body will tend to be more interested in client-oriented measures, operating agency managers will more happily accept responsibility for the activity measures. In solid waste collection, for example, agency managers will usually be interested in and accept responsibility for measures of the amount of waste collected and the number of routes finished on time, but they will be less interested in measurements of the resulting cleanliness of the neighborhood (which can be at least partly affected by the behavior of the residents).

Both types of measures are useful for evaluating performance, but the measures of activity, such as workload accomplished, should not be mistaken for measures of the effectiveness of government services. The problem is that including activity measures under the label of measures of effectiveness may divert attention from real measures of outcome. When activity measures are included with effectiveness measures in performance reports, they should be labeled as activity measures and not as measures of effectiveness.

7. *If measurement resources are scarce, exclude, at least initially, government "support" services such as personnel, finance, purchasing, data processing, and motor vehicle repair.*

Measuring the effectiveness of services that directly affect the public should be of higher priority than support services, and handling these public services is likely to be enough work for any government entering the measurement field. But many of the principles and approaches discussed in this report do apply to support services as well, and support services might be added to the measurement effort in later stages.[2]

8. *Plan to institutionalize measurement activities.*

Difficulties in maintaining the measurement effort are likely to arise because some important data collection procedures, including the use of trained observers (see Chapter 13) and the citizen survey (see Chapter 14), require special resources and are not familiar to local governments. Special data collection procedures are likely to be the first items to be dropped when any short-term budget crunch occurs, particularly if no cost savings or effectiveness improvements attributable to the measurement system have been immediately demonstrated.

Later reinstitution, moreover, is likely to be difficult.

We recommend (a) that effectiveness measurement be incorporated into the formal, annual, budget-planning process (as by including the requirement for effectiveness information in the agency budget instructions), and (b) that after gaining favorable experience with the effectiveness measurement procedures, a local government should consider ordinances to require annual effectiveness measurement.[3]

With either of these two steps, effectiveness measurement procedures would have a firm basis for continuation and would not be so vulnerable as personnel come and go and as candidates for public office make an issue of "overhead" costs. In effect, we are arguing that collection of effectiveness measurement information should be instituted so as to be considered routine, in much the same way as the collection of expenditure data is considered routine. To ensure that effectiveness measurement is truly established, it will probably be necessary to make effectiveness information an integral part of the information regularly provided to the chief executive's office and the legislative body. It is also important to standardize and document measurement procedures, and to make sure that enough staff members know how to conduct measurements so that the turnover of one or two key persons will not halt the measurement effort.

9. *If measurement data are used to develop employee incentives, provide in advance for comprehensive discussion of the measures and measurement procedures.*

Thus far the local governments participating in this effort have tended to use the effectiveness measurement information primarily for management purposes that have not directly affected nonmanagement employees. Little reaction, positive or negative, has been forthcoming from the latter group. But management decisions on programs and policies based on effectiveness measurement information will eventually affect employees in those programs. If effectiveness information is used in the develop-

---

2. For example, obtaining feedback from the "clients" of each support service (that is, other government agencies receiving the services) on various aspects of the quality of the service (such as timeliness, correctness, and courteousness) is probably appropriate.

3. For example, the 1972 Milwaukee County General Ordinance Section 56.20 on welfare services contains the following: "Questionnaire as to Adequacy of Services: At least once a year the Department [of Public Welfare] shall offer to qualified recipients receiving care or services from an agency, or their respective guardians, a questionnaire regarding their impressions as to the adequacy and quality of the care or service provided to them by the Agency. Results of these questionnaires shall be tabulated annually by the Department according to Agency."

ment of specific employee incentives—be they monetary rewards or elements in productivity bargaining (see Chapter 12 for more discussion on this application)—individual employees and their labor organizations will become vitally concerned. They can be expected to raise major objections to such uses unless the government carefully discusses with them in advance the measurements and the incentives to head off problems before they develop.

10. *Some additional operational requirements.*

Experience thus far indicates that implementing a monitoring capability on a department level generally will require:

- Finding a team of interested persons who will be able to apply significant amounts of time over at least a year to work on the development and implementation of the measures.
- Overcoming both general inertia and specific objections of program managers. To accomplish this, top officials will have to make a strong commitment to the project, give it high priority, and find additional resources. Moreover, the project must minimize inconvenience to program managers at the same time that it involves them in developing measures and data collection procedures.
- Giving program managers sufficient support for data collection to enable them to provide accurate data.
- Winnowing all possible measures to produce a smaller selection of achievable measures. Many more measures of interest will be identified initially than can be implemented and analyzed.
- Reexamining collection procedures and verifying the data collected periodically after the system is implemented.

A Possible Strategy for Implementing a "System" for Monitoring Effectiveness

On the basis of the foregoing considerations, the following steps might be used for implementing procedures to monitor effectiveness:

1. Establish a working group consisting of a central staff and at least one member of each operating agency covered in the initial effort to: coordinate efforts, identify desired measures, develop measurement procedures, and follow through on implementation of the appropriate effectiveness measurement procedures.

2. Identify service objectives and an associated set of measures appropriate to each service area. The measures identified in this report can be used as a starting point.

3. Review existing data and data collection procedures for those that might be easily incorporated into the measurement effort. Consider new procedures such as use of trained observers, citizen surveys, and on-site surveys of users for those measures that are not obtainable from existing data.

4. Select a trial set of effectiveness measures and data collection procedures that appear to be feasible with the expectation that data on these measures will be obtained and tested for a period of two to three years.

5. Develop and implement the selected procedures, including necessary design of forms, selection of survey and sampling methods, training of personnel (such as trained observers), and pretesting of new procedures for clarity, feasibility, and reliability.

6. Develop a plan to use the data collected; this should include establishment of procedures for review, analysis, and presentation of findings. Establish links with continuing decision-making processes such as the preparation of the operating and capital budget, any management-by-objectives or other kind of performance assessment process (especially those for government managers), and any formal program evaluation or program analysis efforts.

7. Provide the measurement findings annually to management.

8. Prepare information on the costs of the measurement efforts including data collection and analysis.

9. Undertake collection of data on the measures for at least two to three years. Conduct annual reviews of the procedures after each of these years to determine significant problems and make necessary modifications, but do not expect full utility during this developmental period.

10. At the end of the three-year period, review the utility of the individual measures and the set as a whole. Revise those procedures displaying significant deficiencies; drop procedures that appear to have little use. Move toward institutionalization of the procedures that have proved their value so that collection will proceed without special go-ahead decisions each year.

APPENDICES

Many of the questions are preceded by a code in white letters and numbers on a black background. These codes relate to the specific effectiveness measures cited in earlier chapters. Note throughout that "Metro" is the local short term used for the metropolitan government. The coding is as follows: R = recreation; L = library; P = police (crime control); GT = general transportation (other than public transit); PT = public transit; SWC = solid waste collection; SWD = solid waste disposal; WS = water supply; CC = handling of citizen complaints; SI = handling of requests for services or information. For example, GT-12 at Question 3 indicates that this particular question is used to obtain information for Measure 12 in the general transportation chapter.

NASHVILLE-DAVIDSON COUNTY CITIZEN SURVEY

Hello, my name is . . . . I work for the Urban Observatory and I would like to speak to the youngest male (oldest female) 18 years of age or over who happens to be at home. (TO QUALIFIED RESPONDENT) The Metropolitan Government of Nashville-Davidson County has asked us to conduct an independent survey of citizens to help Metro improve its services. (SHOW I.D. AND LETTERS ONLY WHEN NECESSARY.) Here's the first question I'd like to ask:

(TIME INTERVIEW BEGAN: _____)

----

1. How long have you lived in Nashville or Davidson County?
(DO NOT READ RESPONSES)

12-1( ) Less than 3 months (TERMINATE)

2( ) 3 to 12 months
3( ) 1 to 5 years
4( ) More than 5 years
5( ) Don't know

----

2. Have you driven an automobile in Davidson County in the past 12 months?
(DO NOT READ RESPONSES)

13-1( ) Yes, I have driven

2( ) No, don't drive ⎱ (GO TO NO. 7)
3( ) Don't know ⎰

(NO. 3 TO NO. 6 DRIVERS ONLY)

GT-12

3. When you drive into downtown Nashville in the daytime to shop or for personal business, would you say finding a satisfactory parking space is hardly ever a problem, sometimes a problem, usually a problem, or don't you ever try to park downtown?

14-1( ) Hardly ever a problem
2( ) Sometimes a problem
3( ) Usually a problem
4( ) Don't park downtown
5( ) Don't know or don't remember

GT-14

4. While driving in Davidson County during the last 12 months, how often have you found pavement markings, such as the center lines, hard to see? Would you say this occurred rarely or never, once in a while, fairly often, or very often?

15-1( ) Rarely or never
2( ) Once in a while
3( ) Fairly often
4( ) Very often
5( ) Don't know

GT-14

5. Do you think Metro traffic signs, that is, its directional signs, stop signs, one-way signs, and so forth (but not including street name signs) are usu-

ally easy to see and understand quickly, sometimes hard to see or understand quickly, or often hard to see or understand quickly?

16-1( ) Usually easy to see and
        understand quickly   (GO TO NO. 6)

2( ) Sometimes hard to see
     or understand quickly ⎫
3( ) Often hard to see or   ⎬ (ASK 5a)
     understand quickly   ⎭

4( ) Don't know   (GO TO NO. 6)

GT-14

5a. What is the problem with the signs? (DO NOT READ RESPONSES—Check the response that comes closest to what respondent says.)

17-1( ) Blocked from view
2( ) Too small
3( ) Not at the same place on each intersection
4( ) Missing where they are needed
5( ) Hard to understand
6( ) Changed too often
7( ) Too many signs in same place
8( ) Other _____

6. In your personal experience during the past 12 months, would you say that enforcement of parking laws in Davidson County is generally too strict? Not strict enough? About right? Inconsistent?

18-1( ) Too strict
2( ) Not strict enough
3( ) About right
4( ) Inconsistent
5( ) Don't know

(ASK ALL FROM HERE ON)

GT-14

7. Do you think street name signs on streets and roads in Metro are usually easy to see and understand quickly, sometimes hard to see or understand quickly, or often hard to see or understand quickly?

19-1( ) Usually easy to see and understand quickly
2( ) Sometimes hard to see or understand quickly
3( ) Often hard to see or understand quickly
4( ) Don't know

GT-18

8. During the last 12 months, have you ever been bothered by traffic noise or construction noise in this neighborhood? (IF YES, ASK:) On the average, were you bothered by this noise almost daily, at least once a week, or only once in a while?

20-1( ) No, never   (GO TO NO. 9)

2( ) Yes, almost daily   ⎫
3( ) Yes, at least once a week ⎬ (ASK 8a)
4( ) Yes, only once in a while ⎭

5( ) Don't know   (GO TO NO. 9)

GT-18

8a. What seems to cause the most noise?
    (DO NOT READ RESPONSES)

21-1( ) No specific thing
2( ) General traffic
3( ) Motorcycles
4( ) Trucks
5( ) Construction
6( ) Other _____

GT-11

9. How would you rate the condition of street and road surfaces in your neighborhood? Are they in good condition all over, mostly good but a few bad spots here and there, or are there many bad spots?

22-1( ) Good condition all over
2( ) Mostly good but a few bad spots here and there
3( ) Many bad spots
4( ) Don't know

GT-21

10. Would you say the amount of street lighting at night in this neighborhood is about right, too low (need more lighting), too bright (more lighting than necessary), or no lighting is needed?

23-1( ) About right
2( ) Too low
3( ) Too bright
4( ) No lighting is needed
5( ) Don't know

GT-20

11. Would you say there are enough sidewalks in this neighborhood?

24-1( ) Yes, enough
2( ) No, (too few)
3( ) None exist and none needed
4( ) Don't know

GT-20

12. Are the sidewalks in this neighborhood generally in good condition?
    (DO NOT READ RESPONSES)

25-1( ) Yes
2( ) No
3( ) No sidewalks in this neighborhood
4( ) Don't know

PT-17

13. Now I have a few questions about *Metro bus service.* About how often have you ridden on Metro buses in the past 12 months? Would you say daily or almost daily; not daily, but at least once a week; occasionally, less than once a week; or not at all?

26-1( ) Daily or almost daily
2( ) Not daily, but at least
once a week   } (GO TO NO. 15)
3( ) Occasionally, less
than once a week

4( ) Not at all   } (ASK NO. 14)
5( ) Don't know

PT-17

14. Has anyone else in your household ridden on Metro buses in the past 12 months?

27-1( ) Yes
2( ) No   } (GO TO NO. 17)
3( ) Don't know

----

15. For most of the trips *you* make by bus, would you say the frequency of *your* bus service is excellent, good, fair, or poor? How about the reliability of *your* bus service; that is, buses running on schedule? How about . . . . ?
(ASK FOR 15c-15h REPEATING RATINGS WHEN NECESSARY.)

	Excellent	Good	Fair	Poor	Don't Know
PT-6 15a. Frequency of your bus service 28-	1( )	2( )	3( )	4( )	5( )
PT-6 15b. Reliability of your bus service— buses running on schedule 29-	1( )	2( )	3( )	4( )	5( )
PT-2 15c. Ability to get where you want to go in a reasonable length of time........ 30-	1( )	2( )	3( )	4( )	5( )
PT-6 15d. Ability to get schedule and routing information 31-	1( )	2( )	3( )	4( )	5( )
PT-8 15e. Bus drivers for helpfulness and courtesy 32-	1( )	2( )	3( )	4( )	5( )
PT-6 15f. Ability to get where you want to go without transferring 33-	1( )	2( )	3( )	4( )	5( )
PT-6 15g. Closeness of bus stop to your home 34-	1( )	2( )	3( )	4( )	5( )
PT-8 15h. Waiting conditions at bus stops you use 35-	1( )	2( )	3( )	4( )	5( )

----

16. Were the Metro buses on which you have ridden ever *uncomfortably hot or cold*? (IF YES, ASK:) Would you say this occurred very often, fairly often, or only once in a while? How about . . .? (REPEAT FOR 16b and 16c)

	No, Never	Very Often	Fairly Often	Once in a While	Don't Know
PT-8 16a. Uncomfortably hot or cold.......... 36-	1( )	2( )	3( )	4( )	5( )
PT-8 16b. Dirty or smelly..... 37-	1( )	2( )	3( )	4( )	5( )
PT-8 16c. Driven in a reckless or rough way 38-	1( )	2( )	3( )	4( )	5( )

(GO TO NO. 20)

----

17. Do you regularly travel more than ¼ mile to work? (IF YES, ASK:) About how far? (DO NOT READ RESPONSES)

39-1( ) No   (GO TO NO. 19)

2( ) ¼ to 1 mile
3( ) More than 1 but less
than 5 miles   } (ASK NO. 18)
4( ) More than 5 but less
than 10 miles
5( ) Over 10 miles

(NOTE: Include people who don't work regularly or who work at home in Response 1)

PT-3, 7, and 9

18. Different people have different reasons for *not traveling to work by bus.* Please tell me what are the two or three most important reasons why you do NOT travel to work by Metro bus more often?

40-( ) _____
41-( ) _____
42-( ) _____

18a.*Which of these is the *most important* reason? (DO NOT READ RESPONSES—Check the response that comes closest to what respondent says.)

43-1( ) Prefer to go by automobile
2( ) Service not frequent enough
3( ) Bus stop not close enough
4( ) Takes too long
5( ) Fares are too high
6( ) Poor waiting conditions at bus stops
7( ) Don't know schedules and routes
8( ) Don't like people who use buses
9( ) Other _____

(GO TO NO. 20)

----

*Chapter 9 suggests alternate wording for this question.

PT-3, 7, and 9

(ASK ONLY IF RESPONSE WAS "NO" TO NO. 17)

19. Different people have different reasons for not riding Metro buses. Please tell me what are the two or three *most important* reasons why you do not ride Metro buses more often?

　　44-( ) _____

　　45-( ) _____

　　46-( ) _____

19a.*Which of these is the *most* important reason? (DO NOT READ RESPONSES—Check the response that comes closest to what the respondent says.)

　　47-1( ) Prefer to go by automobile
　　　2( ) Service not frequent enough
　　　3( ) Bus stop not close enough
　　　4( ) Takes too long
　　　5( ) Fares are too high
　　　6( ) Poor waiting conditions at bus stops
　　　7( ) Don't know schedules and routes
　　　8( ) Don't like people who use buses
　　　9( ) Other _____

(ASK ALL FROM HERE ON)

PT-19

20. In general, would you rate the Metro bus service *available* to you and members of your household as excellent, good, fair, or poor?

　　48-1( ) Excellent
　　　2( ) Good
　　　3( ) Fair
　　　4( ) Poor
　　　5( ) Don't know

L-1, L-2

21. In the following questions on libraries, please consider only Metro (city and county) libraries and exclude university libraries. How would you evaluate Metro public library services? Would you rate them excellent, good, fair, or poor?

　　49-1( ) Excellent
　　　2( ) Good
　　　3( ) Fair
　　　4( ) Poor
　　　5( ) Don't know

L-4

22. Do you or any other member of this household have a library card for a Metro Public Library? (DO NOT READ RESPONSES)

　　50-1( ) Yes, have card
　　　2( ) No, don't have card
　　　3( ) Don't know

----

*Chapter 9 suggests alternate wording for this question.

L-2, L-3

23. Other than for group meetings, about how often during the past 12 months have you or members of your household (including children) used the Metro Public Library, including the Main Library, its branches, bookmobile, or telephone reference service? Would you say at least once a month, at least every 3 months, at least once last year, or not at all?

　　51-1( ) At least once a month
　　　2( ) At least once every ⎫ (ASK NO. 24)
　　　　　　3 months　　　　　　⎭
　　　3( ) At least once last year ⎫
　　　4( ) Not at all　　　　　　　⎪
　　　5( ) Don't know;　　　　　　⎬ (GO TO NO. 25)
　　　　　　don't remember　　　　⎭

----

24. Which one do you use most often? (Name and Location) _____

　　52-53( ) _____

24a. How would you rate this library on the following characteristics? Would you rate the hours of operation as excellent, good, fair, or poor? How about the availability of reading materials you wanted? How about ...?
(ASK FOR c-g, REPEATING RATINGS WHEN NECESSARY.)

	Excellent	Good	Fair	Poor	Don't Know

L-17
a. Hours of operation ...... 54-1( ) 2( ) 3( ) 4( ) 5( )

L-8
b. Availability of reading materials you wanted .. 55-1( ) 2( ) 3( ) 4( ) 5( )

L-12
c. Comfort and cleanliness .... 56-1( ) 2( ) 3( ) 4( ) 5( )

L-14
d. Convenience to your home .... 57-1( ) 2( ) 3( ) 4( ) 5( )

L-10
e. Helpfulness and courtesy of library personnel .... 58-1( ) 2( ) 3( ) 4( ) 5( )

L-9
f. Ease in finding and checking out library materials .... 59-1( ) 2( ) 3( ) 4( ) 5( )

L-14
g. Ease of parking .... 60-1( ) 2( ) 3( ) 4( ) 5( )

(GO TO NO. 26)

L-3

25. I am going to read a list of reasons *some* people have given for *not* using Metro libraries more often. Please tell me which, if any, generally are *true* for you or members of this household? Let's start with "Library does *not* have books I want," is this state-

ment generally *true* or generally *not true* for you or members of this household? How about "Too busy to go to the library"...True or Not True? How about....? (ASK FOR 25c-25l, REPEATING RATINGS WHEN NECESSARY.)

	True	Not True	Don't Know
a. Library does not have books or other items I want	61-1( )	2( )	3( )
b. Too busy to go to library	62-1( )	2( )	3( )
c. Not interested in library	63-1( )	2( )	3( )
d. Buy my own books and magazines	64-1( )	2( )	3( )
e. Health problems prevent my using the library	65-1( )	2( )	3( )
f. Not familiar with Metro's library services	66-1( )	2( )	3( )

L-18

g. Library not open right hours	67-1( )	2( )	3( )

L-15

h. Library hard to get to/no transportation	68-1( )	2( )	3( )

L-13

i. Library too noisy/too crowded	69-1( )	2( )	3( )
j. Poor staff service at library	70-1( )	2( )	3( )
k. Lack of adequate parking at library	71-1( )	2( )	3( )
l. Use libraries other than Metro's	72-1( )	2( )	3( )

L-3

25x. What would you say is the *most important* reason that you or members of your household do not use the Metro library system more often than you do? (DO NOT READ RESPONSES—Check the response that comes closest to what respondent says.)

73-1( ) Library does not have books or other items I want
2( ) Too busy to go to library
3( ) Not interested in library
4( ) Buy my own books and magazines
5( ) Health problems prevent my using the library
6( ) Don't know about the library
7( ) Library not open right hours
8( ) Library hard to get to/no transportation
9( ) Other _____

26. During the past 12 months have you or anyone in your household listened to WPLN, the Metro Library FM radio station? (IF YES, ASK:) How many times a week would you say your household listens?

74-1( ) 1 or 2 times
2( ) 3 or 4 times   } (GO TO NO. 27)
3( ) More than 4 times

4( ) No, never listens   } (ASK NO. 26a)
5( ) Don't know

26a. What is the main reason for not listening to WPLN? (DO NOT READ RESPONSES—Check the response that comes closest to what respondent says.)

75-1( ) Don't know about WPLN
2( ) Don't have an FM radio
3( ) Prefer other stations
4( ) Poor reception
5( ) Other _____

R-1

27. Now, we would also like to know how your household would rate the park and recreation opportunities in your immediate area. Would you rate them excellent, good, fair, or poor?

76-1( ) Excellent
2( ) Good
3( ) Fair
4( ) Poor
5( ) Don't know

P-17

28. Turning now to police protection and public safety, how safe would you feel walking alone in this neighborhood at night? Would you feel very safe, reasonably safe, somewhat unsafe, or very unsafe?

77-1( ) Very safe
2( ) Reasonably safe
3( ) Somewhat unsafe
4( ) Very unsafe
5( ) Don't know

P-17

29. Are there some parts of Davidson County where you would like to go at night but do not because you would not feel safe? (DO NOT READ RESPONSES)

78-1( ) Yes, some parts   (ASK NO. 29a)

2( ) No
3( ) Don't know   } (GO TO NO. 30)

29a. Which parts of the county are these?_____

79-80( ) _____

30. In the past 12 months, have you had any direct contact with the Metro Police for *any* reason such as calling for assistance, reporting a crime, or being stopped by police? (IF YES, ASK:) How many *total contacts* did you have with the Metro Police?

6-1( ) Yes, one contact
2( ) Yes, two contacts
3( ) Yes, three contacts
4( ) Yes, four or more contacts
5( ) No, no contacts
6( ) Don't remember

Comments _____

_____

P-2, P-3

31.* During the past 12 months in Davidson County, did anyone steal or use any vehicles belonging to you or to members of this household without permission? Do not include vehicles borrowed by other members of the household. (DO NOT READ RESPONSES)

7-1( ) Yes, did steal or use (ASK NO. 31a and b)
2( ) No
3( ) Don't know } (GO TO NO. 32)

P-2, P-3

31a. How many times did this occur? (DO NOT READ RESPONSES)

8-1( ) One
2( ) Two
3( ) Three
4( ) Four or more
5( ) Don't know

P-2, P-3

31b. Were all incidents reported to the Metro police? (IF NO, ASK:) How many were *not* reported? (DO NOT READ RESPONSES)

9-1( ) Yes (GO TO NO. 32)

2( ) No, one not reported
3( ) No, two not reported
4( ) No, three not reported
5( ) No, four or more not reported } (ASK NO. 31c)

6( ) Don't know (GO TO NO. 32)

P-2, P-3

31c. What was the *main reason* for *not* notifying the police? (DO NOT READ RESPONSES—Check the response that comes closest to what respondent says.)

10-1( ) Didn't want to go to court
2( ) Didn't think it was important enough
3( ) Didn't think it would do any good
4( ) Didn't want to get involved
5( ) Didn't want to get anybody in trouble
6( ) Afraid my insurance would go up or be cancelled
7( ) Other (specify) _____
8( ) Don't know, don't remember

P-2, P-3

32. In the past 12 months, did anyone break in or was there strong evidence someone tried to break into your home or garage? (DO NOT READ RESPONSES)

11-1( ) Yes, broke in
2( ) Yes, tried to break in } (ASK NO. 32a and b)

*Note that the following shorthand version might be substituted for Questions 31-36: "Were you a victim of any crime(s) in the past 12 months?" IF YES, "What crime(s)?" "How often?" "Were all incidents reported to the police?" IF NOT, "How many were not reported?" "What was the main reason for your not notifying the police?" Using this version of the questions would, however, require the interviewer or coder to subsequently categorize the information as Questions 31-36 do, if data on major categories of crime are desired.

3( ) No, neither
4( ) Don't know } (GO TO NO. 33)

P-2, P-3

32a. How many times did this occur? (Break-ins *or* attempted break-ins) (DO NOT READ RESPONSES)

12-1( ) One
2( ) Two
3( ) Three
4( ) Four or more
5( ) Don't know

P-2, P-3

32b. Were all incidents reported to Metro police? (IF NO, ASK:) How many were not reported? (DO NOT READ RESPONSES)

13-1( ) Yes, all reported (GO TO NO. 33)

2( ) No, one not reported
3( ) No, two not reported
4( ) No, three not reported
5( ) No, four or more not reported } (ASK NO. 32c)

6( ) Don't know (GO TO NO. 33)

P-2, P-3

32c. (IF ANY NOT REPORTED, ASK:) What was the main reason for *not* notifying the police? (DO NOT READ RESPONSES—Check the response that comes closest to what respondent says.)

14-1( ) Didn't want to go to court
2( ) Didn't think it was important enough
3( ) Didn't think it would do any good
4( ) Didn't want to get involved
5( ) Didn't want to get anybody in trouble
6( ) Afraid my insurance would go up or be cancelled
7( ) Other (specify) _____
8( ) Don't know; don't remember

P-2, P-3

33. To rob means to take something from a person by force, fear, or by the threat of force. Did anyone rob or try to rob you or a member of your household in the past 12 months in Nashville-Davidson? (DO NOT READ RESPONSES)

15-1( ) Yes (ASK NO. 33a and b)

2( ) No
3( ) Don't know } (GO TO NO. 34)

P-2, P-3

33a. (IF YES, ASK:) How many times did this occur? (DO NOT READ RESPONSES)

16-1( ) One
2( ) Two
3( ) Three
4( ) Four or more
5( ) Don't know

P-2, P-3

33b. Were all incidents reported to the Metro police? (IF NO, ASK:) How many were *not* reported? (DO NOT READ RESPONSES)

17-1( ) Yes   (GO TO NO. 34)

2( ) No, one not reported
3( ) No, two not reported
4( ) No, three not reported   } (ASK NO. 33c)
5( ) No, four or more
      not reported

6( ) Don't know   (GO TO NO. 34)

`P-2, P-3`

33c. (IF ANY NOT REPORTED, ASK:) What was the *main reason* for *not* notifying the police? (DO NOT READ RESPONSE—Check the reponse that comes the closest to what respondent says.)

18-1( ) Didn't want to go to court
2( ) Didn't think it was important enough
3( ) Didn't think it would do any good
4( ) Didn't want to get involved
5( ) Didn't want to get anybody in trouble
6( ) Afraid my insurance would go up or be cancelled
7( ) Other (specify) _____
8( ) Don't know; don't remember

`P-2, P-3`

34. Considering serious physical attacks to include such things as beatings, knifings, shootings, rapings, and so forth, in the last 12 months, were you or any members of your household seriously attacked in Nashville-Davidson County? (DO NOT READ RESPONSES)

19-1( ) Yes   (ASK NO. 34a and b)

2( ) No
3( ) Don't know   } (GO TO NO. 35)

`P-2, P-3`

34a. (IF YES, ASK:) How many times did this occur? (DO NOT READ RESPONSES)

20-1( ) One
2( ) Two
3( ) Three
4( ) Four or more
5( ) Don't know

`P-2, P-3`

34b. Were all incidents reported to the Metro police? (IF NO, ASK:) How many were *not* reported? (DO NOT READ RESPONSES)

21-1( ) Yes   (GO TO NO. 35)

2( ) No, one not reported
3( ) No, two not reported
4( ) No, three not reported   } (ASK NO. 34c)
5( ) No, four or more not
      reported

6( ) Don't know   (GO TO NO. 35)

`P-2, P-3`

34c. (IF ANY NOT REPORTED, ASK:) What was the *main reason* for not notifying the police? (DO NOT READ RESPONSES—Check the response that comes closest to what the respondent says.)

22-1( ) Didn't want to go to court
2( ) Didn't think it was important enough
3( ) Didn't think it would do any good
4( ) Didn't want to get involved
5( ) Didn't want to get anybody in trouble
6( ) Afraid my insurance would go up or be cancelled
7( ) Other (specify) _____
8( ) Don't know, don't remember

`P-2, P-3`

35. In the last 12 months, has anyone vandalized, that is intentionally damaged, your home, car, or other property or that of members of your household in Nashville-Davidson County? (DO NOT READ RESPONSES)

23-1( ) Yes   (ASK NO. 35a and b)

2( ) No
3( ) Don't know   } (GO TO NO. 36)

`P-2, P-3`

35a. (IF YES, ASK:) How many times did this occur? (DO NOT READ RESPONSES)

24-1( ) One
2( ) Two
3( ) Three
4( ) Four or more
5( ) Don't know

`P-2, P-3`

35b. Were all incidents reported to the Metro Police? (IF NO, ASK:) How many were *not* reported? (DO NOT READ RESPONSES)

25-1( ) Yes   (GO TO NO. 36)

2( ) No, one not reported
3( ) No, two not reported
4( ) No, three not reported   } (ASK NO. 35c)
5( ) No, four or more not
      reported

6( ) Don't know   (GO TO NO. 36)

`P-2, P-3`

35c. (IF ANY NOT REPORTED, ASK:) What was the *main reason* for *not* notifying the police? (DO NOT READ RESPONSES, BUT MARK *ONE* WHICH COMES CLOSEST TO REASON GIVEN BY RESPONDENT.)

26-1( ) Didn't want to go to court
2( ) Didn't think it was important enough
3( ) Didn't think it would do any good
4( ) Didn't want to get involved
5( ) Didn't want to get anybody in trouble
6( ) Afraid my insurance would go up or be cancelled
7( ) Other (specify) _____
8( ) Don't know, don't remember

`P-2, P-3`

36. In the last 12 months, has anyone committed any other crimes against you or any member of your household in Nashville-Davidson, such as stealing a

bicycle, or something from your car like hubcaps or packages, or something from your yard, or given you a bad check? (DO NOT READ RESPONSES)

27-1( ) Yes   (ASK NO. 36a-c)

2( ) No   ⎫
3( ) Don't know   ⎬ (GO TO NO. 37)

P-2, P-3

36a. (IF YES, ASK:) What were these crimes? _____

_____

28-( ) _____

P-2, P-3

36b. What was the total number of crimes committed? (DO NOT READ RESPONSES)

29-1( ) One
2( ) Two
3( ) Three
4( ) Four
5( ) Five
6( ) Six
7( ) Seven
8( ) Eight
9( ) More than nine. (Specify:)_____

P-2, P-3

36c. Were all incidents reported to the Metro Police? (IF NOT, ASK:) How many were *not* reported? (DO NOT READ RESPONSES)

30-1( ) Yes   (GO TO NO. 37)

2( ) No, one not reported   ⎫
3( ) No, two not reported   ⎪
4( ) No, three not reported   ⎬ (ASK NO. 36d)
5( ) No, four or more not   ⎪
        reported   ⎭

6( ) Don't know   (GO TO NO. 37)

P-2, P-3

36d. (IF ANY NOT REPORTED, ASK:) What was the main reason for *not* notifying the police? (DO NOT READ RESPONSES—Check the response that comes closest to what the respondent says.)

31-1( ) Didn't want to go to court
2( ) Didn't think it was important enough
3( ) Didn't think it would do any good
4( ) Didn't want to get involved
5( ) Didn't want to get anybody in trouble
6( ) Afraid my insurance would go up or be cancelled
7( ) Other (specify) _____
8( ) Don't know, don't remember

P-2, P-3

36x. *Coder* inserts total number of times household was victimized (that is, the sum of reported and unreported incidents for all police questions, 31-36)

32-0( ) No crimes
1( ) One crime
2( ) Two crimes
3( ) Three crimes

4( ) Four crimes
5( ) Five crimes
6( ) Six crimes
7( ) Seven crimes
8( ) Eight crimes
9( ) Nine or more crimes

P-2, P-3

36y. *Coder* inserts total number of *unreported* incidents. (Zero if all are reported)

33-0( ) No *unreported* crimes (all reported)
1( ) One *unreported* crime
2( ) Two *unreported* crimes
3( ) Three *unreported* crimes
4( ) Four *unreported* crimes
5( ) Five *unreported* crimes
6( ) Six *unreported* crimes
7( ) Seven *unreported* crimes
8( ) Eight *unreported* crimes
9( ) Nine or more *unreported* crimes

----

37. Did you receive any traffic tickets for a *moving violation* in Nashville-Davidson County during the past 12 months? (DO NOT READ RESPONSES)

34-1( ) Yes
2( ) No
3( ) Not a driver
4( ) Don't know

37a. In your personal experience, would you say the enforcement of traffic laws against *moving vehicles* in the County is generally too strict, generally not strict enough, about what it should be, or is it inconsistent?

35-1( ) Generally too strict
2( ) Generally not strict enough
3( ) About right
4( ) Inconsistent
5( ) Don't know

P-18

38. In your personal experience over the past 12 months, do you think the Metro Police were generally fair in their handling of people? (DO NOT READ RESPONSES)

36-1( ) Yes
2( ) No
3( ) Don't know

P-19

39. In your personal experience over the past 12 months, do you think the Metro Police were generally courteous in their dealings with people? (DO NOT READ RESPONSES)

37-1( ) Yes
2( ) No
3( ) Don't know

----

40. Do you think the amount of police patrolling in your neighborhood is too much, about right, or is not enough?

38-1( ) Too much
2( ) About right
3( ) Not enough
4( ) Don't know

P-22

41. On the whole, would you say the service provided to you and your household by the Metro Police over the past 12 months was excellent, good, fair, or poor?

39-1( ) Excellent
2( ) Good
3( ) Fair
4( ) Poor
5( ) Don't know

----

42. Did you personally appear in a court proceeding in Davidson County in the past 12 months as a witness, complainant, juror, or for any other reason other than as a spectator?

40-1( ) Yes   (ASK NO. 42a)

2( ) No   }
3( ) Don't know } (GO TO NO. 43)

42a. (IF YES) Based on your personal experience, would you rate the performance of the court system as very satisfactory, moderately satisfactory, or not satisfactory at all?

41-1( ) Very satisfactory   }
2( ) Moderately satisfactory } (GO TO NO. 43)

3( ) Not satisfactory   (ASK NO. 42b)
4( ) Don't know   (GO TO NO. 43)

42b. What was the major problem? (DO NOT READ RESPONSES, BUT MARK *ONE* WHICH COMES CLOSEST TO REASON GIVEN BY RESPONDENT.)

42-1( ) Inconvenient
2( ) Lack of fairness
3( ) Amount of time required
4( ) Not courteous
5( ) Other _____
6( ) Don't know

F-12

43. Turning to the area of fire protection. Were there any fires in your home in the past 12 months? (IF YES, ASK:) How many were there?

43-1( ) Yes, one   }
2( ) Yes, two   }
3( ) Yes, three   }
4( ) Yes, more than three } (ASK NO. 43a)
5( ) Yes, don't know how }
       many   }

6( ) No   }
7( ) Don't know, don't } (GO TO NO. 44)
       remember   }

F-12

43a. Was it (were all) reported to the Metro Fire Department or some other government agency? (DO NOT READ RESPONSES)

44-1( ) Yes, fire was reported   (GO TO NO. 45)
2( ) Not reported   (ASK NO. 43b)
3( ) Don't know if reported   (GO TO NO. 44)

F-12

43b. (IF NOT REPORTED, ASK:) What was the main reason for not reporting it (them)? (DO NOT READ RESPONSES—Check the response that comes closest to what respondent says)

45-1( ) Too small, didn't think it was important enough
2( ) Already out or almost out when fire first noticed
3( ) Handled by own fire defense (fire extinguisher, sprinkler system, hoses, etc.)
4( ) Didn't think it would do any good
5( ) Didn't want to get anybody in trouble
6( ) Afraid my (our) insurance would go up or be cancelled
7( ) Other _____
8( ) Don't know/don't remember

----

44. Have you or anyone in your household called the fire department for assistance of any kind or have you had any other firsthand contact with the fire department during the past 12 months (for example, watched a fire being fought or a fire prevention inspection at work)? (DO NOT READ RESPONSES)

46-1( ) No, no contact   (GO TO NO. 46)

2( ) Yes, called for assistance   }
3( ) Yes, other firsthand contact   }
       —watched a fire   }
4( ) Yes, other firsthand contact   }
       —watched a fire inspection   }
5( ) Yes, other firsthand contact   }
       —attended or heard fire   } (ASK NO. 45)
       department presentation   }
       (talk, lecture)   }
6( ) Yes, other firsthand contact   }
       —questioned in fire   }
       investigation   }
7( ) Yes, other firsthand contact   }
       —all other   }

8( ) Don't know   (GO TO NO. 46)

(ASK ONLY IF RESPONDENT HAS HAD CONTACT WITH THE FIRE DEPARTMENT)

F-18

45. How would you rate the overall service provided by the Metro Fire Department? Would you rate it as excellent, good, fair, or poor?

47-1( ) Excellent
2( ) Good
3( ) Fair

4( ) Poor
5( ) Don't know

(ASK ALL)
46. Would you allow a fireman to inspect your (home or apartment) to help you check for fire hazards? (DO NOT READ RESPONSES)

48-1( ) Yes
2( ) Probably yes
3( ) Probably no
4( ) No
5( ) Don't know

SWC-2

47. Turning now to neighborhood cleanliness, would you say your neighborhood is usually very clean, fairly clean, fairly dirty, or very dirty?

49-1( ) Very clean
2( ) Fairly clean
3( ) Fairly dirty
4( ) Very dirty
5( ) Don't know

(ASK QUESTION 48a-d ONLY OF PEOPLE WHO LIVE IN SINGLE FAMILY HOMES OR DUPLEXES)

SWC-2

48a. In the past 12 months, did the collectors ever miss picking up your trash and garbage on the scheduled pick-up days? (IF YES, ASK:) How many times would you say this occurred? (DO NOT READ RESPONSES)

50-1( ) No, never missed
2( ) Yes, 1 or 2 times
3( ) Yes, 3 or 4 times
4( ) Yes, 5 or 6 times
5( ) Yes, ___ times
6( ) Don't know; don't remember

SWC-13

48b. In the past 12 months, did the collectors ever spill or scatter trash or garbage? (IF YES, ASK:) How many times would you say this occurred? (DO NOT READ RESPONSES)

51-1( ) No, never spilled
2( ) Yes, 1 or 2 times
3( ) Yes, 3 or 4 times
4( ) Yes, 5 or 6 times
5( ) Yes, ___ times
6( ) Don't know, don't remember

SWC-14

48c. In the past 12 months, did the sanitation collectors ever damage your property when picking up trash and garbage? (IF YES, ASK:) What type of damage was it?

52-1( ) No damage   (GO TO NO. 49)
2( ) Yes, _____
      (IF DAMAGE TO TRASH OR GARBAGE CONTAINER, ASK NO. 48d)
3( ) Don't know   (GO TO NO. 49)

48d. Do you have a plastic or metal container?

53-1( ) Plastic
2( ) Metal
3( ) Other _____
4( ) Don't know

SWC-4

49. During the past 12 months, have collectors ever made so much noise it bothered you? (IF YES, ASK:) How many times did this occur and what type of noise was it? (DO NOT READ RESPONSES)

54-1( ) No, never
2( ) Yes, 1 or 2 times; type _____
3( ) Yes, 3 or 4 times; type _____
4( ) Yes, 4 or 5 times; type _____
5( ) Yes, ___ times; type _____
6( ) Don't know; don't remember

SWC-3

50. During the past 12 months, have you noticed widespread odors from uncollected garbage? (IF YES, ASK:) How often have you noticed odors? (DO NOT READ RESPONSES)

55-1( ) No, never
2( ) Yes, 1 or 2 times
3( ) Yes, 3 or 4 times
4( ) Yes, 5 or 6 times
5( ) Yes, ___ times
6( ) Don't know; don't remember

----

51. During the past 12 months have you had any problems with getting your tree limbs or brush picked up?

56-1( ) Yes
2( ) No
3( ) Don't know

SWC-9a

52. During the past 12 months, did you or members of your household see any rats on your block? (IF YES, ASK:) About how many times were rats seen? (DO NOT READ RESPONSES)

57-1( ) No, never
2( ) Yes, 1 or 2 times
3( ) Yes, 3 or 4 times
4( ) Yes, 5 or 6 times
5( ) Yes, ___ times
6( ) Don't know, don't remember

----

53. About how often over the past 12 months have you been seriously inconvenienced by standing water in the streets of your neighborhood after a rain storm? Would you say after almost every rain, only after every heavy rain, only after some heavy rain, never?

58-1( ) After *almost every* rain
2( ) Only after *every heavy* rain
3( ) Only after *some heavy* rains
4( ) Never
5( ) Don't know

54. About how often over the past 12 months have you been seriously inconvenienced by standing water on this property after a rain storm? Would you say after almost every rain, only after every *heavy* rain, only after *some* heavy rains, or never?

    59-1( ) After *almost every* rain
       2( ) Only after every *heavy* rain
       3( ) Only after some *heavy* rains
       4( ) Never
       5( ) Don't know

WS-4

55. Turning now to your drinking water. Do you consider the *taste, odor, appearance,* and *temperature* of your drinking water to be satisfactory or unsatisfactory?

    60-1( ) Satisfactory   (GO TO NO. 56)
       2( ) Unsatisfactory   (ASK NO. 55a-b)
       3( ) Don't know   (GO TO NO. 56)

WS-4

55a. What is the most important problem you have had with your water? (DO NOT READ RESPONSES—check reasons which come closest to that given by respondent)

    61-1( ) Chlorine taste or odor
       2( ) Sediment in water/water looks cloudy
       3( ) Water looks rusty
       4( ) Fluoride in water
       5( ) Bad taste
       6( ) Temperature
       7( ) Taste/odor (Other—specify) _____
       8( ) Appearance (Other—specify) _____

WS-4

55b. How often have you had this problem with your water in the last 12 months? Would you say it has always or usually been a problem, has been a problem a large number of times, a few times, or one or two isolated cases?

    62-1( ) Always or usually a problem
       2( ) A large number of times
       3( ) A few times
       4( ) One or two isolated cases

WS-8

56. During the past year, have there been any occasions when the *rate of flow* or *pressure* of your water caused you problems?

    63-1( ) Yes   (ASK NO. 56a)
       2( ) No
       3( ) Don't know } (GO TO NO. 57)

WS-8

56a. What was the problem you had? (DO NOT READ RESPONSES)

    64-1( ) Water shut off or reduced because of work on water lines or streets
       2( ) Always too low
       3( ) Pressure drops when washer or dishwasher in use

    4( ) Can't get good spray from shower/hose
    5( ) Other (specify) _____
    6( ) Don't know

WS-8

57. How many times over the past year were you without water for more than one hour? (DO NOT READ RESPONSES)

    65-1( ) None
       2( ) Once
       3( ) Two or three times
       4( ) Four or more times
       5( ) Don't know

CC-10

58.* Now that we're nearing the end of the survey, I would like to ask you a few questions about contacts you may have had with Metro. During the past 12 months, did you ever contact any Metro official to seek service or information or to complain about something like poor Metro services or a rude employee, or for *any* reason?

    66-1( )   Yes   (ASK NO. 58a)
       2( )   No
       3( )   Don't know; don't } (GO TO NO. 62)
            remember

CC-7, 8 and 9

58a. How many different problems or situations did you *complain* about to Metro officials during that period?

    67-1( ) None
       2( ) One
       3( ) Two
       4( ) Three
       5( ) Four
       6( ) Five
       7( ) Six
       8( ) More than six
       9( ) Don't know

59. Please describe briefly the nature of the 3 complaints or requests which were most *important* or *significant* to you over that period, starting with the most *important* one. (RECORD EACH ITEM ON A SEPARATE LINE BELOW)

    68-( ) A. _____
               _____

    69-( ) B. _____
               _____

    70-( ) C. _____
               _____

59a. Which department or official did you contact *initially* regarding _____ (READ ITEM A ABOVE)? (DO NOT READ RESPONSES)

---

*Note: Chapter 11 suggests an alternative set of questions on the handling of citizen complaints and requests for services and information, relating to Questions 58 through 63.

71-1( ) Mayor's office/City Hall
2( ) Councilman
3( ) Police
4( ) Sanitation
5( ) Streets/Public Works (excluding Sanitation)
6( ) Water and Sewers
7( ) Health
8( ) Welfare/Social Services
9( ) Other (specify) _____
0( ) Don't remember

59b. Were you ever told that Metro had no authority to deal with this matter, or that it was out of Metro's jurisdiction? For instance, because it was a private matter or a State responsibility? (DO NOT READ RESPONSES)

72-1( ) Yes
2( ) No
3( ) Don't remember
4( ) No response

CC-2 and 5, SI-2 and 5

59c. Were you generally satisfied with Metro's response? (IF DISSATISFIED, ASK:) What was the *main* thing or things you were dissatisfied with? (DO NOT READ RESPONSES—Check responses closest to what respondent says.)

73-1( ) Response not yet completed
2( ) Satisfied
3( ) Dissatisfied, never responded or corrected condition, or otherwise never provided the requested service or information
4( ) Dissatisfied, poor quality or incorrect response was provided
5( ) Dissatisfied, took too long to complete response, had to keep pressuring them to get results, etc.
6( ) Dissatisfied, too much run-around, red tape, etc.
7( ) Dissatisfied, personnel were discourteous, negative, etc.
8( ) Dissatisfied, other (specify) _____

_____

9( ) Don't know

(IF MORE THAN ONE ITEM WAS REPORTED UNDER 59, GO TO NO. 60a-c; OTHERWISE, GO TO NO. 62)

60a. Which department or official did you contact *initially* regarding _____? (READ ITEM B ABOVE IN QUESTION 59) (DO NOT READ RESPONSES)

74-1( ) Mayor's Office/City Hall
2( ) Councilman
3( ) Police
4( ) Sanitation
5( ) Streets/Public Works (excluding Sanitation)
6( ) Water and Sewers
7( ) Health
8( ) Welfare/Social Services
9( ) Other (specify) _____
0( ) Don't remember

60b. Were you ever told that Metro had no authority to deal with this matter, or that it was out of Metro's jurisdiction? For instance, because it was a private matter or a State responsibility? (DO NOT READ RESPONSES)

75-1( ) Yes
2( ) No
3( ) Don't remember
4( ) No response

CC-2 and 5, SI-2 and 5

60c. Were you generally satisfied or dissatisfied with Metro's response? (IF DISSATISFIED, ASK:) What was the *main* thing you were dissatisfied with? (DO NOT READ RESPONSES)

76-1( ) Response not yet completed
2( ) Satisfied
3( ) Dissatisfied, never responded or corrected condition, or otherwise never provided the requested service or information
4( ) Dissatisfied, poor quality or incorrect response was provided
5( ) Dissatisfied, took too long to complete request, had to keep pressuring them to get results, etc.
6( ) Dissatisfied, too much run-around, red tape, etc.
7( ) Dissatisfied, personnel were discourteous, negative, etc.
8( ) Dissatisfied, other (specify) _____

_____

9( ) Don't know

(IF THREE ITEMS WERE REPORTED UNDER NO. 59, ASK NO. 61a-c; OTHERWISE, GO TO NO. 62)

61a. Which department or official did you contact *initially* regarding _____ (READ ITEM C ABOVE IN QUESTION 59) (DO NOT READ RESPONSES)

77-1( ) Mayor's Office/City Hall
2( ) Councilman
3( ) Police
4( ) Sanitation
5( ) Streets/Public Works (excluding Sanitation)
6( ) Water and Sewers
7( ) Health
8( ) Welfare/Social Services
9( ) Other (specify) _____
0( ) Don't remember

61b. Were you ever told that Metro had no authority to deal with this matter, or that it was out of Metro's jurisdiction? For instance, because it was a private matter or a State responsibility?

78-1( ) Yes
2( ) No
3( ) Don't remember

CC-2 and 5, SI-2 and 5

61c. Were you generally satisfied or dissatisfied with Metro's response? (IF DISSATISFIED, ASK:) What was the *main* thing or things you were dissatisfied with?

79-1( ) Response not yet completed
2( ) Satisfied
3( ) Dissatisfied, never responded or corrected condition, or otherwise never provided the requested service or information
4( ) Dissatisfied, poor quality or incorrect response was provided
5( ) Dissatisfied, took too long to complete response, had to keep pressuring them to get results, etc.
6( ) Dissatisfied, too much run-around, red tape, etc.
7( ) Dissatisfied, personnel were discourteous, negative, etc.
8( ) Dissatisfied, other (specify) _____

_____

9( ) Don't know

CC-6, 7, 9 and 10

62. Thinking back over the past year, were there any *complaints* which you would have liked to have made to Metro officials but didn't?

80-1( ) Yes (ASK NO. 62a-b)

2( ) No
3( ) Don't know
4( ) No response
} (GO TO NO. 63)

62a. Please describe briefly the nature of those unreported complaints. (List up to two only.)

6-( ) #1 _____

_____

( ) #2 _____

_____

CC-6

62b. What was the MAIN reason or reasons you did *not* make the complaint(s)? (DO NOT READ RESPONSES)

7-1( ) Didn't think it would do any good
2( ) Expected or had previously experienced delays, run-around, red tape, etc.
3( ) Problem not important enough to complain about
4( ) No time, or just never got around to it
5( ) Thought officials already knew about problems or that someone else would report it
6( ) Contacted wrong department
7( ) Didn't know how or where to complain
8( ) Could not get through to appropriate Metro official
9( ) Other (specify) _____
0( ) Don't know

SI-6

63. Thinking back over the past year, were there any times you wanted to request services or information from the Metro government and didn't? (IF YES, ASK:) What was the *main* reason or reasons you didn't? (DO NOT READ RESPONSES)

8-1( ) No
2( ) Yes, didn't think it would do any good
3( ) Yes, unable to file request (no phone, unable to get to City Hall, etc.)

4( ) Yes, filing procedures too complex or too demanding
5( ) Yes, didn't know how or where to file a request
6( ) Yes, expected or had previously experienced run-around, delays, red tape, etc.
7( ) Yes, didn't want to bother anyone
8( ) Yes, other (specify) _____
9( ) Don't know

---

64. Do you feel you could have a say about the way the Metro Government is running things if you wanted to?

9-1( ) Yes
2( ) No
3( ) Don't know

---

65. In general, how good a job do you feel Metro Government is doing in meeting the needs of you and your family—excellent, adequate, somewhat inadequate, or very inadequate?

10-1( ) Excellent
2( ) Adequate
3( ) Somewhat inadequate
4( ) Very inadequate
5( ) Don't know

---

66. Finally, a few questions about you and your family. What are the ages of all the members of this household, including children?
Respondent's age _____ Ages of all other members of household _____

Respondent's Age
11-1( ) 18-24
2( ) 25-34
3( ) 35-49
4( ) 50-64
5( ) 65 and over
6( ) Other

---

67. Family Size. (NOTE TO INTERVIEWER: CHECK FAMILY SIZE BASED ON RESPONSES TO NO. 66)

12-1( ) 1
2( ) 2
3( ) 3
4( ) 4
5( ) 5
6( ) 6
7( ) 7 or more
8( ) Won't say

---

68. How many motor vehicles do you and members of this household own?

13-1( ) One
2( ) Two
3( ) Three or more
4( ) None
5( ) Don't know

(HAND CARD A)

69. Please give me the *letter* on this card which comes closest to your *total* household income before taxes last year? (DO NOT READ RESPONSES)

14-1( ) A—Under $3,000
  2( ) B—$3,000 to $4,999
  3( ) C—$5,000 to $7,999
  4( ) D—$8,000 to $9,999
  5( ) E—$10,000 to $14,999
  6( ) F—$15,000 and over
  7( ) Don't know
  8( ) Refused to say

---

70. What is the last grade or class *you completed* in school? (DO NOT READ RESPONSES)

15-1( ) Grade 8 or less
  2( ) High school, incomplete
  3( ) High school, complete
  4( ) Technical, trade or business school beyond high school
  5( ) College, incomplete
  6( ) College, complete
  7( ) Refused to say

---

71. So that my office may call you to check my work if it wants to, may I have your telephone number?

16-1( ) Number: _____
  2( ) Refused to give or doesn't know number
  3( ) No phone

---

72. (IF RESPONDENT GIVES NUMBER, ASK:) "Is this a listed phone number?"

17-1( ) Yes
  2( ) No or won't say

(NOTE TO INTERVIEWER: THIS COMPLETES THE QUESTIONS TO BE ASKED. THANK THE RESPONDENT. THEN ANSWER THE FOLLOWING QUESTIONS BASED ON YOUR OWN OBSERVATIONS.)

73. Check whether: Sidewalk in front of house.

18-1( ) Yes
  2( ) No

74. Check whether: Street light on block.

19-1( ) Yes
  2( ) No

75. Check whether interviewed:

20-1( ) White male
  2( ) White female
  3( ) Nonwhite male
  4( ) Nonwhite female

75x. *Sex*

21-1( ) Male
  2( ) Female

75y. *Race*

22-1( ) White
  2( ) Nonwhite

76. Check housing type:

23-1( ) Single family
  2( ) Duplex
  3( ) Multi-family, less than 4 units
  4( ) Multi-family, 4 or more units
  5( ) Residential hotel, rooming or boarding house
  6( ) Mobile home
  7( ) Other (specify) _____

77. Was interview completed in:

24-1( ) Primary household on first call
  2( ) Primary household on second call
  3( ) First alternate household
  4( ) Second alternate household
  5( ) Third alternate household
  6( ) Fourth alternate household
  7( ) Fifth or subsequent household

78. Address of primary household:
_____

79. Address of household interviewed (if different from primary).
_____

I hereby attest that this is a true and honest interview:
INTERVIEWER: _____ DATE: _____
                                       25-( )

TIME INTERVIEW ENDED: _____
AREA #: _____ CENSUS TRACT #: ____
  26-( )

Illustrative Questionnaire for Obtaining Feedback from the Business Community on the Quality of Government Services

(This questionnaire has *not* been tested.)

Many of the questions obtain data for specific measures of effectiveness as described in earlier chapters. A code in white letters and numbers on a black background refers to the chapter topic and measure number as follows: GT = general transportation; P = police (crime control); SWC = solid waste collection; WS = water supply; CC = handling citizen complaints; and SI = handling requests for service and information.

ILLUSTRATIVE DRAFT QUESTIONNAIRE FOR SURVEY OF BUSINESSES

NOTE: THIS SECTION IS TO BE COMPLETED BY THE INTERVIEWER BEFORE QUESTIONING THE RESPONDENT

ADDRESS: _____ DATE OF SURVEY: _____

A. Check type of business:

Retail
____Food or grocery store
____Eating and drinking
____General merchandise
____Apparel
____Automotive
____Furniture and appliances
____Drug and proprietary
____Liquor
____Other retail (specify____)
Manufacturing (specify type _____)

Service
____Cleaning establishments
____Auto repair or service
____Beauty or barber shops
____Hotels or motels
____General home or business service
____Other (specify ____)
Real Estate
____Apartments
____Other real estate
Wholesale

All others (specify _____
_____)

B. Service District (or other location code): _____

C. Is there a sidewalk in front of establishment?

____Yes
____No
____(Not applicable)

D. Is there a street light on block?

____Yes
____No
____(Not applicable)

E. Is there street parking in front of the establishment?

____Yes
____No
____(Not applicable)

F. Is there walk-in trade with the general public?

____Yes
____No

Time Survey Began _____

Hello, my name is . . . . . . I work for the . . . . . . and I would like to speak to: _____ (name of the person with whom the interview has been scheduled). The government of . . . . . . has asked us to conduct an independent survey of businesses to help it improve its services. Please be assured that all information will be kept strictly confidential; no names of persons or businesses will be identified.

The first question I'd like to ask is . . . .

Demographic Information
(IF NOT ESTABLISHED IN ADVANCE OF INTERVIEW, ASK)

----

1. What is your position in this business establishment?

____Owner or Partner
____Manager
____Assistant manager
____Other (specify) _____
____Not ascertained

1a. How long have you held this position?*

    ____Under 1 year (How many months____?)
    ____Over 1 year
    ____Not ascertained

2. How long has this business been in existence at this location?

    ____less than 1 year*
    ____1-3 years
    ____4-10 years
    ____11-20 years
    ____over 20 years

Now I'd like to ask you a few questions about your *local transportation services.*

3. Over the past 12 months, how would you rate the ability of the city public transit system to bring customers and employees to your business?
    (a) Customers?   (b) Employees?
    ____Excellent   ____Excellent
    ____Good   ____Good
    ____Fair   ____Fair
    ____Poor (Why?) ____   ____Poor (Why?) ____
    _____   _____
    ____Don't know ____   ____Don't know ____
    ____Not applicable

Streets and Sidewalks

GT-11

4. How would you rate the condition of the street in front of your business?

    ____Satisfactory (does not need improvement)
    ____Fair (needs minor improvement)
    ____Unsatisfactory (needs major improvement)
    ____No opinion.

(ASK ONLY IF THERE IS A SIDEWALK)

GT-20

5. How would you rate the condition of the sidewalk in front of your business:

    ____Satisfactory (does not need improvement)
    ____Fair (needs minor improvement)
    ____Unsatisfactory (needs major improvement)
    ____No opinion

GT-15

6a. How often in the past 12 months have your business or customers been inconvenienced by streets or sidewalks blocked by construction, delivery trucks, or refuse collection vehicles in the vicinity of your business?

    ____Never (GO TO NO. 7)

*To obtain opinions from persons with substantial experience with government services, the government might decide that it wants to interview only persons who have held the position for at least 1 year and businesses which have been at one location for at least 1 year.

    ____Very often
    ____Fairly often
    ____Once in a while
    ____Don't know (GO TO NO. 7)

6b. How was your business inconvenienced?

    ____Parking blocked
    ____Traffic tied up
    ____Sidewalk blocked
    ____Other (specify) _____

7a. During the past 12 months, were you, your customers, or employees ever bothered by traffic or construction noises occurring outside your business?

    ____No, never (GO TO NO. 8)
    ____Once in a while
    ____Frequently
    ____Don't know (GO TO NO. 8)

7b. What was the most annoying source of the noise?

    ____General vehicular traffic
    ____Buses
    ____Trucks
    ____Motorcycles
    ____Construction
    ____Emergency police, fire, or ambulance sounds
    ____Other (specify) _____
    ____Don't know/not sure

8. How adequate would you say the amount of public street lighting at night in your business area is?

    ____About right
    ____Not enough lighting
    ____Too much lighting; too bright
    ____Don't know
    ____No opinion

GT-12

9. How satisfactory is the availability of parking (public and private) for your customers and employees?

    ____Completely satisfactory (they can almost always find a place nearby at no cost/or reasonable cost)
    ____Usually satisfactory (they can usually find a place nearby)
    ____Often unsatisfactory (they are often unable to park nearby)
    ____Extremely unsatisfactory (they are almost never able to park nearby)
    ____Not applicable
    ____Don't know
    ____No opinion

10. How would you rate parking law enforcement along your block?

    ____About right (police use good judgment)
    ____Too strict
    ____Too lax (police allow too much illegal parking)
    ____Don't know
    ____Does not apply

Now, I would like to ask you a few questions about security and your local *police services.*

11. How safe do you feel while working in your business during the day?

_____Very safe
_____Reasonably safe
_____Somewhat unsafe
_____Very unsafe
_____Do not work during the day at this location
_____Don't know/no opinion

PT-17

12. How safe do you feel while working in your business at night?

_____Very safe
_____Reasonably safe
_____Somewhat unsafe
_____Very unsafe
_____Do not work at night at this location
_____Don't know/no opinion

13a. Do you employ or use any means of private security?

_____Yes
_____No (GO TO NO. 14)

13b. What type of private security do you use? (CHECK ALL THAT APPLY)

_____Burglar alarm system
_____Watchdog
_____Private security force or guards
_____Other (specify) _____

P-2 and 3

14a. In the past 12 months did anyone break into your business or attempt to illegally enter your business?

_____Yes
_____No (GO TO NO. 15)

14b. How many times did this occur in the past 12 months?

_____One
_____Two
_____Three
_____Four
_____Five
_____Six
_____Seven or more times (specify number_____)
_____Don't know

14c. Were all of these incidents reported to the police?

_____Yes (GO TO NO. 15)
_____No
_____Don't know

14d. (If no) How many were not reported?

_____One
_____Two
_____Three
_____Four
_____Five
_____Six
_____Seven or more
_____Don't know how many were not reported

14e. What were the major reasons for not reporting them?

_____Did not think it was important enough
_____Did not think it would do any good
_____Did not want to get involved or spend my time with the police and the courts
_____Did not want to get the person who did it in trouble
_____Afraid of adverse publicity in the media
_____Afraid of retaliation or that I would get in trouble
_____Other (specify) _____

P-2 and 3

15a. To rob means to take something from a person or business by force, fear, or threat of force. In the past 12 months, so far as you know, did anyone rob, or attempt to rob you, employees or customers on your premises (including your parking lot), or in the immediate vicinity of your business?

_____Yes
_____No (GO TO NO. 16)

(NOTE: REPEAT QUESTIONS 14(b)-(e))

P-2 and 3

16a. In the last 12 months, has anyone vandalized, that is intentionally damaged, your facility, business vehicles, or other business property?

_____Yes
_____No (GO TO NO. 17)

(NOTE: REPEAT QUESTIONS 14(b)-(e))

P-2 and 3

17a. During the last 12 months, do you know of any incidents of shoplifting from your establishment?

_____Yes
_____No (GO TO NO. 18)

(NOTE: REPEAT QUESTIONS 14(b)-(e))

P-2 and 3

18a. During the past 12 months, was your business the victim of any other crimes such as fraud, embezzlement, employee pilferage, theft of items outside the store, arson, or any other crime?

_____Yes
_____No (GO TO NO. 19)

18b. What were the major types of crimes that occurred?

1) _____
2) _____
3) _____

18c. How many incidents of each type of crime occurred in the past year?

1)__One   2)__One   3)__One
__Two   __Two   __Two
__Three   __Three   __Three
__Four   __Four   __Four
__Five   __Five   __Five
__Six   __Six   __Six
__Seven or more __Seven or more __Seven or more
__Don't know   __Don't know   __Don't know

18d. How many of each type of crime were not reported?

1)__One   2)__One   3)__One
__Two   __Two   __Two
__Three   __Three   __Three
__Four   __Four   __Four
__Five   __Five   __Five
__Six   __Six   __Six
__Seven or more __Seven or more __Seven or more
__Don't know   __Don't know   __Don't know

P-2 and 3

18e. What were the major reasons for not reporting them?

____Did not think it was important enough
____Did not think it would do any good
____Did not want to get involved or spend my time with police and the courts
____Did not want to get the person who did it in trouble
____Afraid of adverse publicity in the media
____Afraid of retaliation or that I would get in trouble
____Other (specify) _____

19a. During the past 12 months have you or your employees had any direct contact with police for any reason other than the above relating to your business, such as calling for assistance or being questioned by police?

____No (GO TO NO. 20)
____Yes
____Don't remember (know)

19b. How many contacts occurred?

____One
____Two
____Three
____Four
____Five
____Six
____Seven or more
____Don't know

19c. What were the main purposes?

1) _____
2) _____
3) _____

P-16

20. Over the past 12 months how would you rate the speed of the (name of city) police in responding to calls?

____Excellent
____Good
____Fair

____Poor (Why?) _____
____Don't know

P-19

21. How would you rate the courtesy of the police toward yourself and other persons in your establishment during the past 12 months?

____Excellent
____Good
____Fair
____Poor (Why?) _____
____Don't know

P-18

22. How would you rate the fairness of the police in dealing with your business during the past 12 months?

____Excellent
____Good
____Fair
____Poor (Why?) _____
____Don't know

P-22

23. Overall, how would you rate the police protection for your business?

____Excellent
____Good
____Fair
____Poor (Why?) _____
____Don't know

Now, I'd like to ask you some questions concerning *fire protection services.*

24a. During the past 12 months, was your facility inspected by the fire department?

____Yes
____No (GO TO NO. 25)

24b. How would you rate the adequacy of the inspection?

____Adequate
____Inadequate or underinspected (specify)_____
____Too extensive or too petty or particular
____Don't know

24c. How would you rate the courtesy of the fire inspectors?

____Excellent
____Good
____Fair
____Poor (Why?) _____
____Don't know

24d. Overall, do you feel that the inspections helped improve the fire safety of your establishment?

____Yes, quite a bit
____Yes, slightly
____No apparent help
____Don't know

25. How many times in the last 12 months was the fire department called to put out a fire or for emergency service?

    ____None   (GO TO NO. 26)
    ____One
    ____Two
    ____Three
    ____Four or more
    ____Don't know

25a. How would you rate the speed of the fire department in responding to the call(s) for service?

    ____Excellent
    ____Good
    ____Fair
    ____Poor (Why?) _____
    ____Don't know

25b. How would you rate the effectiveness of the fire department in extinguishing the fire(s)?

    ____Excellent
    ____Good
    ____Fair
    ____Poor (Why?) _____
    ____Don't know

SWC-2

26. Turning now to the cleanliness of the neighborhood and street where your business is located, would you say that the streets in this neighborhood are usually

    ____Very clean
    ____Fairly clean
    ____Fairly dirty
    ____Very dirty
    ____Don't know/no opinion

27a. Is there a publicly maintained alley beside or behind your business?

    ____Yes
    ____No (GO TO NO. 28)

SWC-2

27b. How would you rate the cleanliness of the alley in the past 12 months? Would you say it has usually been:

    ____Very clean
    ____Fairly clean
    ____Fairly dirty
    ____Very dirty
    ____Don't know

SWC-9

28a. During the past 12 months, did you or your employees see any rats outside of your establishment?

    ____Yes
    ____No (GO TO NO. 29)

SWC-9

28b. How many times during the past 12 months were rats seen?

    ____Once or twice
    ____Three or four times
    ____Five or six times
    ____More than six times
    ____Don't know how many times

(NOTE: THE FOLLOWING SECTION ASSUMES THAT THE LOCAL GOVERNMENT EITHER OPERATES, MONITORS, OR REGULATES COMMERCIAL REFUSE COLLECTION. IF NOT, QUESTIONS 29-33 MAY BE SKIPPED.)

SWC-12

29. In the past 12 months did the refuse collectors ever miss picking up your trash and/or garbage on scheduled pickup days? If yes, how many times did this occur?

    ____Yes, at least once a week
    ____Yes, at least once a month
    ____Yes, once every few months
    ____Yes, only once or twice
    ____Yes, don't know how many times
    ____No
    ____Don't know

SWC-13

30. In the past 12 months, did the collectors ever spill or scatter trash or garbage in the area of your business? How many times did this occur?

    ____Yes, at least once a week
    ____Yes, at least once a month
    ____Yes, once every few r..onths
    ____Yes, only once or twice
    ____Yes, don't know how many times
    ____No
    ____Don't know

SWC-14

31. In the past 12 months did the sanitation collectors ever damage your property when picking up trash and garbage? (IF YES, ASK:) What type of damage?

    ____No damage
    ____Yes (specify) _____
    ____Don't know

SWC-4

32. During the past 12 months, have refuse collectors—when collecting either your refuse or someone else's—ever made so much noise that it bothered you, your employees, or your customers? (IF YES, ASK:) How many times did this noise occur?

    ____Yes, at least once a week
    ____Yes, at least once a month
    ____Yes, once every few months
    ____Yes, only once or twice
    ____Yes, don't know how many times
    ____No
    ____Don't know

SWC-3

33. During the past 12 months, have you ever noticed odors from uncollected garbage? (IF YES, ASK:) How many times in the past 12 months have you noticed such odors?

____No
____Yes, one or two times
____Yes, three or four times
____Yes, five or six times
____Yes, more than six times
____Yes, don't know how many times
____Don't know

34. In the past 12 months, how many times has your establishment been inspected for cleanliness, health, or general sanitation purposes?

____None (GO TO NO. 36)
____One
____Two
____Three or more times
____Don't know

35a. How would you rate the adequacy of the inspection?

____Adequate
____Underinspected or inadequate
____Overinspected or too particular
____Don't know

35b
& c. How would you rate the courtesy and fairness of the inspectors?
b. *Courtesy*   c. *Fairness*
____Excellent   ____Excellent
____Good   ____Good
____Fair   ____Fair
____Poor (explain) ____   ____Poor (explain) ____
   _____   _____
____Don't know   ____Don't know

Now, I'd like to ask you some questions about your *storm drainage and water services.*

36. About how often over the past 12 months have you, your employees, or your customers been seriously inconvenienced by standing water or flooding in the immediate vicinity of your establishment after a rain storm?

____Never
____Only after *some* heavy rains
____Only after every *heavy* rain
____After almost every rain
____Don't know

WS-8

37. During the past 12 months, have there been any occasions when the rate of flow or pressure of your water caused inconvenience in your operations? Or do you not use the water for any commercial or business purposes?

____Yes
____No (GO TO NO. 38)

____Don't know (GO TO NO. 38)
____Not applicable—Don't use water for any commercial or business purposes (GO TO NO. 38)

WS-8

37a. What was the problem you had? (DO NOT READ THE RESPONSES)

____Water shut off or reduced because of work on water lines or streets
____Always too low
____Pressure drops when water-using machines (dishwasher, etc.) are in use
____Other (specify) _____
____Don't know

37b. On about how many working days did this occur in the past 12 months?

____One or two days
____3-10 days
____11-20 days
____More than 20 days (specify) _____
____Don't know

38. During the past 12 months, have you had any occasions of sewer stoppage, backup, or overflow? (IF YES, ASK:) About how often have these stoppages occurred during the past 12 months?

____No
____Yes, about one or two times a year
____Yes, more than 2 times a year/at most once a month
____Yes, more than once a month/at most once a week
____Yes, more than once a week
____Don't know

39. Overall, how would you rate your sewer facilities and sewer service?

____Excellent
____Good
____Fair
____Poor (explain) _____
____Don't know

Now that we are nearing the end of our survey, I'd like to ask you a few questions about *complaints, requests for service and information, and consumer affairs.*

CC-10

40a. In the past 12 months, have you ever called a city office to complain about something like poor city services or a rude city official, or for any other reason?

____No (GO TO NO. 41)
____Yes
____Don't know/don't remember

CC-7, 8 and 9

40b. How many different problems or complaints did you contact the city about in the past 12 months?

____One
____Two

____Three to five
____More than five
____Don't know/don't remember

40c. Please describe briefly the nature of your complaints, starting with the one you feel was most important.

1) _____
2) _____
3) _____

41a. Which departments or officials did you contact initially regarding these complaints?

____Mayor's Office/City Hall
____Councilmember
____Police
____Sanitation
____Streets/Public Works (excluding Sanitation)
____Water and Sewers
____Health
____Licenses & Inspections/Building Codes
____Other (specify) _____
____Don't know

CC-2 and CC-5

41b. Were you generally satisfied with the city's response to your complaints (IF DISSATISFIED, ASK:) What were the major reasons for your dissatisfaction? (DO NOT READ RESPONSES—CHECK RESPONSES CLOSEST TO RESPONDENT ANSWER.)

____Response not yet completed
____Satisfied
____Dissatisfied, never responded or corrected condition
____Dissatisfied, poor quality or incorrect response was provided
____Dissatisfied, took too long to complete response, had to keep pressuring them to get results, red tape, etc.
____Dissatisfied, personnel were discourteous, negative, etc.
____Dissatisfied, other (specify)_____
____Don't know

42a. During the past 12 months, have you ever contacted the city to seek service or information, such as having your water turned on, obtaining a building permit, etc.?

____No (GO TO NO. 43)
____Yes
____Don't know/don't remember

42b. How many different service or information requests did you contact the city for during the past 12 months?

____1-5
____6-10
____11-20
____More than 20
____Don't know how many

SI-2 and SI-5

42c. Were you generally satisfied with the city's response to your request? (IF DISSATISFIED, ASK:) What was the major reason for your dissatisfaction? (DO NOT READ RESPONSES—CHECK ONE OR MULTIPLE CLOSEST TO RESPONDENT'S ANSWER.)

____Response not yet completed
____Satisfied
____Dissatisfied, never responded or corrected condition
____Dissatisfied, poor quality or incorrect response was provided
____Dissatisfied, took too long to complete response, had to keep pressuring them to get results, red tape, etc.
____Dissatisfied, personnel were discourteous, negative, etc.
____Dissatisfied, other (specify)_____
____Don't know

CC-6 and SI-6

43a. Over the past 12 months have there been any complaints or requests for service or information related to your business which you would have liked to have made to city officials but didn't?

____No (GO TO NO. 44)
____Yes
____Don't know (GO TO NO. 44)

43b. Please describe briefly the nature of these items __

_____

CC-6 and SI-6

43c. Why didn't you communicate these to city officials?

____Didn't think it would do any good
____Unable to file request (could not get to City Hall, etc.)
____Filing procedures too complex or demanding
____Didn't know how or where to file complaint or request
____Expected—or had previously experienced—run-around, delay, red tape, etc.
____Item not important enough to contact city about
____No time, or just never got around to it
____Didn't want to bother anyone
____Thought someone else would contact city about it
____Other (specify) _____

44a. During the past 12 months, have you had any strong reason to suspect that pressure was put on your business or any of its employees by any city employee for financial or nonfinancial payments (not regular legal fees, charges, or taxes)? If so, which agency? (CHECK ALL THAT APPLY)*

____Never (GO TO NO. 45)
____Building Inspector

*It seems desirable to attempt to cover government employee "honesty" in their dealings with businessmen. Question 44a is an attempt to cover this very difficult issue. Preliminary interviews with businesspersons confirmed that this is a very sensitive area of questioning. If this version seems too "direct," a jurisdiction may prefer to change the wording or delete the question entirely. The specific wording shown here is illustrative only; careful attention to appropriate and useful wording will be needed before a final choice is made.

____Assessors
____Tax collectors
____Police
____Fire
____Sanitation
____Refused to say
____Other (specify) _____

44b. How many times did this occur?

____One
____Two
____Three
____Four or more
____Don't know how many times

44c. Would you describe the circumstances? _____
_____

CC-2 and 5, SI-2 and 5

45. Overall, how satisfied have you been with the out-comes of your contacts with the city government over the past 12 months?

____Very satisfied
____Fairly satisfied
____Somewhat dissatisfied
____Extremely dissatisfied
____Don't know/no opinion

CC-5, SI-5

46. Overall, how would you rate the courtesy of city of-ficials in the course of your contacts with city gov-ernment over the past 12 months?

____Very courteous
____Fairly courteous
____Somewhat discourteous
____Very discourteous
____Don't know/no opinion

(QUESTIONS 47-48 WOULD BE EXCLUDED IF NO LOCAL CONSUMER AFFAIRS OFFICE EXISTS.)

47a. During the past 12 months, has the Consumer Af-fairs Office contacted you or another employee for any reason relating to your business?

____No (GO TO NO. 49)
____Yes
____Don't know/don't remember

47b. Please describe briefly the circumstances of those dealings _____
_____

47c. Did you experience any problems in the course of your dealings with the Office of Consumer Affairs in the past 12 months? (IF YES, ASK:) Which of the following were problems for you?

____No
____Too much "run-around" or red tape involved
____Never resolved the problems or matters in-volved
____Unfair, biased against business and/or toward the consumer's position
____Unnecessarily hurt business, increased costs, etc.

____Personnel were discourteous
____Too "political" in their actions
____Procedures are too time consuming
____Other (specify) _____

48. Overall, are you satisfied with the usefulness, courtesy, and effectiveness of the Consumer Affairs Office, as you have experienced it or perceived it?

____Definitely yes
____Generally yes
____Generally no (explain) _____
____Definitely no (explain) _____
____Don't know

49. In general, how good a job do you feel government is doing in meeting the needs of your business?

____Excellent
____Good
____Fair
____Poor
____Don't know

50. Is there any other comment or problem that you would like to make about the services provided to you by your local government?

_____
_____

51a. Excluding yourself, approximately how many full-time and how many part-time employees did this facility have on the average during the past 12 months?

(Full-time)	(Part-time)
____None	____None
____1-10	____1-10
____11-30	____11-30
____31-50	____31-50
____More than 50	____More than 50

52. What are your regular business hours?

	From	To
Monday	____	____
Tuesday	____	____
Wednesday	____	____
Thursday	____	____
Friday	____	____
Saturday	____	____
Sunday	____	____

53. What were the approximate gross sales (of mer-chandise or services) at this establishment for the previous 12 months?

____None	____$100,000-499,999
____Under $25,000	____$500,000-999,999
____$25,000-99,999	____One million and above
	____Not known/would not answer

I hereby attest that this is a true and honest interview:
INTERVIEWER:_____ DATE: _____
TIME INTERVIEW ENDED: _____
AREA #:_____ CENSUS TRACT #:_____

COMPARISON OF CITIZEN PERCEPTION AND TRAINED OBSERVER CLEANLINESS RATINGS: THREE SETS OF OBSERVATIONS

A. DISTRICT OF COLUMBIA 1971 DATA FOR ONE AREA OF THE CITY.[1]

INSPECTOR RATING OF STREET*	CITIZEN OPINIONS							
	STREET CLEANLINESS				NEIGHBORHOOD CLEANLINESS			
	CLEAN	MOSTLY CLEAN	FAIRLY DIRTY	VERY DIRTY	CLEAN	MOSTLY CLEAN	FAIRLY DIRTY	VERY DIRTY
1, 1+, 2−	7	9	2	1	5	4	0	0
2, 2+, 3−	5	16	13	5	3	26	11	2
3, 3+, 4−	1	3	0	0	1	1	1	3
4	0	0	0	0	0	0	0	0

B. ST. PETERSBURG, FLORIDA[2]

SANITATION DISTRICT	HOUSEHOLD SURVEY RESULTS: PERCENTAGE RATING NEIGHBORHOOD AS "USUALLY DIRTY" OR "VERY DIRTY"	TRAINED OBSERVER RATING PERCENTAGE WORSE THAN 2.0*	
		STREETS	ALLEYS
A	4	0	0
B	5	1	0
C	10	13	3
D	20	29	18
Total city	13	5	13

C. NASHVILLE, TENNESSEE[3]

NEIGHBORHOOD	HOUSEHOLD SURVEY RESULTS: PERCENTAGE RATING NEIGHBORHOOD AS "USUALLY DIRTY" OR " VERY DIRTY"	TRAINED OBSERVER RATING PERCENTAGE WORSE THAN 2.0*		
		STREETS	YARDS	ALLEYS
A	2	28	12	—
B	4	33	8	—
C	5	6	6	—
D	6	8	6	—
E	9	31	27	—
F[4]	9	12	14	58
G	15	41	18	—
H[4]	15	14	25	86
I[4]	24	34	28	80
J[4]	27	37	51	91

1. These data are from the District of Columbia's 1971 trained observer ratings. Families were interviewed on a selection of blocks where inspector ratings had very recently been made. Broken lines show cases where general agreement seems to exist.

2. These data are derived from the citizen survey conducted in September 1973 and the visual inspections conducted in October 1973.

3. These data are derived from the citizen survey conducted in March 1974 and the visual inspections conducted in July-August 1974. Differences might be due to seasonal effects.

4. Urban areas of Nashville-Davidson County; the other areas are lightly populated, "rural" areas.

*In each case, the higher the trained observer rating, the dirtier. Rating "1" is very clean and "4" is very dirty.

Source: Louis H. Blair and Alfred I. Schwartz, *Measuring the Effectiveness of District of Columbia Solid Waste Collection Activities* (Washington, D.C.: The Urban Institute report to the District of Columbia, September 1971).

DETAILS ON TRAINED OBSERVER RATINGS OF SOLID WASTE DISPOSAL SITES

The trained observer rating procedure consists of two parts: (1) an external inspection of the entrance and selected perimeter points around the disposal or incineration area (to obtain ratings on appearance, odors, and noise), and (2) an internal inspection of the landfill or incineration area (to obtain ratings on the presence of airborne emissions such as smoke, dust, and ash; the presence of insects and rodents; and the presence of other health and safety hazards).

The following sections discuss these procedures. The scales used for each characteristic to be rated are shown in Exhibit 3-5, while Exhibit 3-4 illustrates the forms that could be used by inspectors to record the ratings needed.

MEASUREMENTS FOR THE EXTERNAL INSPECTION

External inspection should focus on perimeter points around the disposal site that represent points of maximum citizen contact with the site—in other words, points adjacent to or visible from transportation corridors or residential or commercial areas. Inspections should cover the appearance, odor, and noisiness of those points as they are affected by the disposal operations, whether landfill or incinerator.

Selection of the Perimeter Points

The perimeter points should be distributed around the site. These points should be kept far enough apart that the lines connecting them to the current fill area or to the incinerator do not form angles of less than 45 degrees,[1] which means a total of eight perimeter points at most. If one assumes that the site entrance always will be used as one perimeter point, there will be at most seven other perimeter points. In practice, most disposal sites are located so as to avoid citizen exposure to much of the perimeter. For example, the sites are located beside a bay, gorge, or some other physical feature that prevents exposure to citizens. Thus, the required number of perimeter points may be much less than eight, often only three or four.

[1] This limitation is aimed at holding down the number of observations required per inspection, while still assuring that problems noticeable to passing citizens will be discovered.

The perimeter points can be selected roughly from aerial photographs, which greatly aid the identification of symmetrically distributed points around the perimeter. The points then can be defined precisely by reference to prominent landmarks that are likely to remain in place for the foreseeable future (for example, a point on the highway shoulder that lines up with a billboard or street light). Because the perimeter points represent areas of maximum citizen contact or exposure to actual disposal operations, their locations may have to be changed when the current disposal activity is moved.

Cleanliness of Areas Near Site

The cleanliness of the perimeter point and its immediate area can be rated on a scale of 1.0 (clean, no litter) to 4.0 (extremely littered), using photographs and written descriptions similar to those for street and alley cleanliness ratings. (See Chapter 2 and Exhibit 2-2 in particular.) The perimeter point area to be rated for cleanliness may be defined as the open ground in a circle of, for example, a ten-yard radius from the selected perimeter point. Or the area might be some segment between a road and a fence surrounding the site. However, the area associated with a point should be readily located and small enough to be visible in its entirety from the point where the observer will be standing.

Appearance of the Site from Areas Nearby

The effects of blowing smoke, dust, and ash on site appearance are not dealt with here, because they will be covered in the internal inspection rating of smoke, dust, and ash conditions.

"Substantial general traffic" in an area, a term used in Exhibit 3-5 to define level 3 in the rating, will mean that the observer can see at least one car for every lane of traffic but not necessarily one car in each lane of traffic at all times.

Odors

The detection of disposal site odors can be extremely sensitive to wind speed and direction. Thus observers should take a few minutes to allow gusts of wind to blow in their direction from the site. This procedure is especially important if previous inspections or other information suggest that odors are likely to be a problem.[2]

Noise

Most of the noises associated with site operation will not be sufficiently near, loud, or shrill to be strongly offensive; thus a rating of 4 generally will not be needed. However, noise from vehicles entering and leaving the site may be a problem if sanitation trucks constitute the only traffic on the road. If there is uncertainty as to whether the rating should be 3 or 4, or if there are numerous complaints about noise, it may be desirable to check the noise level beside a nearby house or other structure. This check can be made either subjectively (with the human ear) or objectively (with a decibel meter). However, the procedure will not work so well if there are other major sources of noise in the area.

MEASUREMENTS FOR INTERNAL INSPECTIONS

Previous guidelines concerned measurements made outside the disposal site at points of public exposure. This section deals with measurements made within the disposal site area. For nonincinerator sites, the measurements should be made at the point of current disposal operations, at points of past or future disposal operations, and at points where citizens bringing refuse can be expected to come into contact with disposal operations. For incinerator sites, inspections probably should examine the following areas:

- Central receiving area (known as tipping area in incinerator operations),
- Citizen tipping area, where only private citizens may dump waste for processing, and
- Special receiving areas for receiving and processing hazardous or other special wastes; sorting and transferring areas where wastes can be separated by hand or transferred from processing or storage to vehicles; land disposal areas for processed residues or unprocessed special wastes.

Smoke, Dust, and Ash

Inspections for smoke, dust, and ash should be made in the current fill area for land disposal sites, in the tipping area and around the incinerator for incineration disposal sites. The principal finding is the presence or absence of smoke, dust, ash, or particulates in the air.

Further refinement of the term "visible smoke" used in defining level 4 in the scale could be achieved by making use of the Ringlemann scale, a procedure for rating the "blackness" of smoke. This rating generally is related to the degree of health hazard posed by the smoke and the degree to which smoke affects the appearance of surrounding areas. The Ringlemann scale consists of a series of reference grids of black lines on white; these correspond to ratings running from 1 to 4, which may be

used to assess the darkness of a stack plume. The scale is described in U.S. Bureau of Mines circular 7718, dated March 1955, and it has been reproduced in a number of other sources dealing with monitoring of stack emissions. Also, public health tests conducted on the Ringlemann procedure have established that consistent evaluations are possible by trained observers properly positioned with respect to stack, sun, and wind direction.

Ratings 3 and 4 distinguish between "intermittent" and "continuous" blowing of smoke, dust, or ash. Intermittent blowing is defined to mean that only a very small amount of airborne material is involved, even when substantial gusts of wind occur. Continuous blowing of smoke, dust, or ash means that trained observers standing in the area where the material is being blown have to shield their eyes and noses from the material.

Incinerators may have smoke and ash problems of short duration when the start-up process begins, or when the waste input stream is not properly mixed. Cities that find ratings of 4 at incinerator sites will want to consider these possible explanations and examine the actual duration of the problems. Also, ratings made at the start of the operating day should be noted as such.

Pests

Flies or mosquitoes are the insects most often present at disposal sites. Rats will probably be visible only at night; evidence will consist of rat droppings, burrows, or tracks. Disposal sites often are inspected by county and state health officials for pest control, and it may be possible to obtain ratings from these officials, who are likely to be well trained in what to look for and where to look.

Health Hazards

Health hazards consist of accumulations of exposed toxic wastes or wastes capable of harboring or supporting rats or insects. For the current and other general fill areas, this rating usually will be determined by the presence or absence of food wastes, since toxic wastes probably will not be accepted at the sites and large items are easy to cover. Measurement can generally be made only after hours, when the daily final cover of earth has been applied to the refuse. In looking for food wastes, the most common items are likely to be fruit wastes such as orange or lemon skins or banana peels and contaminated, greasy food wrappers.

In determining whether wastes are scattered or widespread, as required by the rating definitions for levels 3 and 3.5, the suggested procedure is to determine whether all or almost all of the individual waste items can be recognized by a visual scan. If wastes are so cluttered that they must be pulled apart to be counted, or if the observer must be right on top of the wastes in order to count them, then the waste in that area is considered widespread and should be rated at least 3.5.

If separate areas are maintained for bulky goods, hazardous and toxic wastes, or demolition waste, these areas will be able to receive ratings of 2 only if all wastes are covered.

Sewage solids handled at the landfill can present a health hazard if citizens come into contact with them or if drainage from them is not controlled. The latter problem can be dealt with as part of the general measurement of landfill impacts on water quality (see Measures 1-3 in Chapter 3).

---

[2]Observers rather than odorometers are recommended for the detection of odors. Experiments in developing standards for model odor control legislation at the local level have compared odorometer results with results of panels of citizens who simply used their noses. The studies showed the panel to be preferable, and they expressed considerable dissatisfaction with the meters. See Copley International Corporation, "A Study of the Social and Economic Impact of Odors—Phase III: Development and Evaluation of a Model Odor Control Ordinance," P.B.-223 589 (Washington, D.C.: National Technical Information Service, 1973).

Exhibit 4A-1
SOLID WASTE DISPOSAL SITE INSPECTION AND EVALUATION FORM
Sample City

Site inspected _____

Location _____

Perimeter point locations and directions for observation

(Rate cleanliness of each perimeter point in terms of litter within ten feet of where you stand)

(1) City limits sign near US 20 overpass on Santac Highway. When making observations of site, look toward site, keeping current fill area in the middle of your field of vision.

(2) At the WWWW billboard on US 20 opposite landfill site. When making observations of site, look toward site, keeping street lamp pole to the right of your field of vision.

(3) At the Joe's Restaurant billboard sign on US 20 opposite landfill site. When making observations of site, look toward site, keeping XYZ billboard to the right of your field of vision.

(4) Southeast corner of landfill. When making observations of site, look due northwest.

Weather conditions during inspection

(a) Current fill area inspection
Time/date _____
Temperature _____
Wind speed and direction _____
Humidity _____
Precipitation _____

(b) Other internal inspection
Time/date _____
Temperature _____
Wind speed and direction _____
Humidity _____
Precipitation _____

(c) External inspection
Time/date _____
Temperature _____
Wind speed and direction _____
Humidity _____
Precipitation _____

Phone number for weather _____

Inspectors: _____
_____
_____

External Inspection

CHARACTERISTIC	ENTRANCE	PERIMETER POINT NO. 1	PERIMETER POINT NO. 2	PERIMETER POINT NO. 3	PERIMETER POINT NO. 4	DEFINITIONS OF RATINGS
Cleanliness of areas near site	2	1	1	1	4	Assign ratings of 1, 2, 3, or 4, according to photographs used in the citywide street cleanliness ratings.
Appearance of site from areas nearby	1	4	2	2	2	1—No unattractive features in the foreground of the observer's field of vision. 2—Only unattractive features in view are raw earth or trucks. 3—Sanitation equipment other than trucks in view. 4—Uncovered refuse, paper blowing, or dust blowing toward point can be seen.
Odors	1	1	1	1	1	1—No odor detectable. 2—Odor detected that could be from site but cannot confirm, or it is indistinguishable from other odors in area. 3—Odor detected and confirmed as principally coming from site, but not offensive enough to cause an individual to seek to avoid it. 4—Odor detected, confirmed as principally coming from site, and is offensive enough to cause an individual to seek to avoid it.

(Continued on next page)

Exhibit 4A-1 continued

External Inspection

CHARACTERISTIC	ENTRANCE	PERIMETER POINT NO. 1	PERIMETER POINT NO. 2	PERIMETER POINT NO. 3	PERIMETER POINT NO. 4	DEFINITIONS OF RATINGS
Noise	1	1	1	1	1	1—No noise detectable. 2—Noise detected that could be from site but cannot confirm, or it is indistinguishable from other noises in area. 3—Noise detected, confirmed as principally coming from site, but is not offensive enough to cause an individual to seek to avoid it. 4—Noise detected, confirmed as principally coming from site, and is offensive enough to cause an individual to seek to avoid it.

Internal Inspection

CHARACTERISTIC	CURRENT FILL AREA	OTHER GENERAL FILL AREA	DEFINITIONS OF RATINGS
Smoke, dust, and ash	1	1	1—No blowing dust, no burning. 2—No blowing dust, no visible smoke escapes area of burning operation. 3—Considerable blowing dust *or* some visible smoke from burning does escape area of burning operations. 4—Visible smoke is escaping continuously or almost continuously from area of burning operations.
Pests	1	2	1—No evidence of rats or insects. 2—Evidence of insects but no evidence of rats. 3—Evidence of rats but no rats seen; 4—Rats seen.
Health hazards	2	3	1—No uncovered wastes. 2—A few scattered wastes but no food wastes, no hazardous or toxic wastes, no dead animals, and no bulky goods providing potential shelter for pests. 3—A few scattered items including some food wastes *or* some toxic or hazardous wastes *or* some dead animals *or* some bulky goods providing potential shelter for pests. 3.5—Widespread uncovered wastes but no piles of waste, and most of the ground is still visible. 4—Large areas of ground covered with wastes *or* some wastes in piles.
Other hazards	1	1	1—Restricted area not open to citizens. 2—Unrestricted area with no hazards. 3—Unrestricted area with some hazards but none likely to lead to serious injury. 4—Unrestricted area with some hazards capable of leading to serious injury.

Other Hazards

This rating should be made only if citizens are allowed access to the site to dispose of their trash, or if the site is not completely fenced off or otherwise controlled to keep citizens, particularly children, from the area. Certain parts of the disposal site may be closed off to the public while others, such as a tipping area for private citizens, may be open; in that case, ratings would be made only in the latter areas.

TIMING AND WEATHER CONDITIONS

Each inspection of landfill sites—or incineration sites with subsequent landfilling of the residue—normally will have to be performed in two parts. The evaluation of the current fill area can be done only *after* working hours, when wastes will be covered, if they ever are, and when rats are more likely to be visible. The evaluations at perimeter points can be done only during working hours, when odors and noises from operations may be detectable. The inspection of any internal areas where disposal operations are not currently being performed can be done at any time.

Temperature and humidity vary primarily by the season. If inspections are performed only quarterly or less frequently, they probably should be timed so that the temperature is at or above the seasonal average for that city. Probably the easiest way to be sure of measuring the most troublesome periods is to select the inspection day for a particular quarter from the two-week period that is historically the hottest for that quarter. If inspections are made only once a year, they should be made in the summer, when site problems are most noticeable.

Wind speed should be considered when inspections are infrequent (less often than once a month). Problems with blowing paper are aggravated as wind speeds increase, while odor problems are most noticeable at very low wind speeds, in the presence of temperature inversions. Wind speeds over 25 mph are likely to exaggerate blowing paper problems while obscuring odor problems; wind speeds under 4 mph are likely to conceal blowing paper problems. Inspectors should record the approximate wind speed. Any sizable shifts in the distribution of wind speeds during inspections from one year to the next should be considered when comparing the two years' ratings.

Precipitation should be noted because it can have an effect on site operations. For example, precipitation can make the ground difficult to drive on. Such effects result in the use of areas other than the designated current fill area and thus reduce the effectiveness of cover operations in covering all refuse. This, in turn, can affect the health hazard rating.

The inspection day should be selected randomly from all days the site is open during the rating period, except for the restrictions noted above for infrequent inspections. If inspections are done less often than once every two weeks and if, on the selected day, the wind speed is too high or too low during midday, inspection should be delayed until the appropriate conditions are met. This delay should involve no more than a day or two at the most.

ILLUSTRATIVE CITIZEN SURVEY QUESTIONNAIRE
ON RECREATION
(The 1973 St. Petersburg Questionnaire)

*INDICATES QUESTIONS THAT EVERYONE SURVEYED IS ASKED.

Hello, my name is _____. I work for the St. Petersburg Parks and Recreation Department. As mentioned in the letter we sent to your household this past week, we would like to know your opinion of the pools, parks, and recreational centers in your neighborhood.

(ONLY IF RESPONDENT MENTIONS THAT HE DID RECEIVE OR SEE THE LETTER SENT TO THE HOUSEHOLD OR THAT HE DID NOT RECEIVE OR SEE THE LETTER SENT, MARK APPROPRIATE RESPONSE)

Received letter   Yes ____   No ____

Is your telephone number _____?

Is your address _____?

(IF NO TO EITHER ADDRESS OR TELEPHONE CONCLUDE THE INTERVIEW.)

(IF THEY WISH TO VERIFY SURVEY, ASK THEM TO CALL _____ AT 894-2111, EXTENSION 269.)

(IF RESPONDENT IS TOO BUSY TO TALK NOW, SAY)

I'll call back later. What time is convenient for you? ____

(IF RESPONDENT AGREES TO INTERVIEW THEN CONTINUE)

*Q1. Are you 16 years or older?   Yes ____   No ____

*Q2. Are you a member of this household?
Yes ____   No ____

(IF RESPONDENT IS UNDER 16 YEARS, OR NOT A MEMBER OF THE HOUSEHOLD, SAY)

Is the mother or father of the household at home?

Yes ____   No ____

(IF NEITHER IS AT HOME, SAY)

Is some other adult at home?   Yes ____   No ____

(IF THE ADULT CANNOT BE REACHED ASK WHAT TIME AN ADULT WILL BE HOME. IF THERE IS NO ADULT, CONCLUDE THE INTERVIEW.)

*Q3. How would you rate the pool, park, and recreational opportunities in your neighborhood?

Excellent ____   Fair ____   No Opinion ____
Good ____   Poor ____   Don't know ____

(IF OPINION IS "POOR" ASK)

Would you tell me why you say that, please? ____
_____
_____

*Q4. Did anyone in your household use these facilities (NAME EACH FACILITY) during the past month?

(a) _____ Pool   Yes ____ No ____
     _____   Don't know ____
(b) _____ Park   Yes ____ No ____
     _____   Don't know ____
(c) _____ Center   Yes ____ No ____
                      Don't know ____

(IF YES TO a, b, OR c, ASK)

*Q5. Would you tell me which members of the household used these facilities and which members did not? I need to know the age and sex of each person, whether or not he or she used them.

(ENTER THE SEX AND AGE OF EACH HOUSEHOLD MEMBER ON THE SPREAD SHEET)

*Q6.　Did anyone in the household use any other public recreational facilities during the past month?

Yes ___　No ___　Don't know ___

(IF YES, ASK)
Which ones were they and who used them?

(ENTER OTHER FACILITIES ON SPREAD SHEET FOR EACH USER. IF NO ONE IN HOUSEHOLD USED ANY OTHER FACILITY (Q4 and Q6) GO TO Q13.)

(FOR Q7 THROUGH Q11 READ QUESTIONS FOR EACH HOUSEHOLD FACILITY USER AND ENTER ANSWER ON SPREAD SHEET BEFORE GOING ON TO NEXT HOUSEHOLD USER.)

Q7.　About how many times did (household member) use (facility name) in the past month?
(ENTER ON SPREAD SHEET)

Q8.　How many hours did he/she stay on the average?
(ENTER ON SPREAD SHEET)

Q9.　Which single activity does he/she enjoy doing most when he/she goes there?
(ENTER ON SPREAD SHEET)

Q10.　What means of transportation did he/she usually use to get there?

SPREAD SHEET

Q5		Q5 & Q6	Q7	Q8	Q9	Q10	Q11
SEX	AGE	FACILITY	NUMBER OF TIMES USED LAST MONTH	LENGTH OF STAY	ACTIVITY ENJOYED MOST	METHOD OF TRANSPORTATION	TRANSPORTATION TIME ONE-WAY
		Pool					
		park					
		center					
		Pool					
		park					
		center					
		Pool					
		park					
		center					
		Pool					
		park					
		center					

(ENTER ON SPREAD SHEET. USE CATEGORIES: WALK, CAR, CAB, PUBLIC BUS, BIKE, MOTOR-BIKE, OTHER.)

Q11. How many minutes does it take to get there on the average?

(ENTER ON SPREAD SHEET)

(Q12) IS FOR USERS ONLY)

Q12. How do you think your household members rate the facilities that they have used during the past month? (DO NOT READ)

(WRITE IN NAMES OF EACH FACILITY LISTED ON RATING TABLE)

(SURVEY ONLY THOSE FACILITIES WHERE NO ATTENDANCE BY ANYONE IN THE HOUSEHOLD. NAMES OF FACILITIES WILL BE PREVIOUSLY ENTERED FOR Q13 AND Q14.)

RATING TABLE

FACILITY NAME	CHARACTERISTICS	VERY GOOD	GOOD	FAIR	POOR	DON'T KNOW
	i) Hours of operation					
	ii) Cleanliness					
	iii) Condition of equipment					
	iv) Helpfulness and attitude of personnel					
	v) Amount of space					
	vi) Safety					
	vii) Overall rating					
	i) Hours of operation					
	ii) Cleanliness					
	iii) Condition of equipment					
	iv) Helpfulness and attitude of personnel					
	v) Amount of space					
	vi) Safety					
	vii) Overall rating					
	i) Hours of operation					
	ii) Cleanliness					
	iii) Condition of equipment					
	iv) Helpfulness and attitude of personnel					
	v) Amount of space					
	vi) Safety					
	vii) Overall rating					
	i) Hours of operation					
	ii) Cleanliness					
	iii) Condition of equipment					
	iv) Helpfulness and attitude of personnel					
	v) Amount of space					
	vi) Safety					
	vii) Overall rating					

*Q13. Would you give me the reasons why during the last month your household did not use

	(NAMES OF FACILITIES)	(REASONS)
a.	_____	_____
b.	_____	_____
c.	_____	_____

Q14. Let me read a list of possible reasons in case we have overlooked some. For (facility) . . . .

(READ REASONS. INDICATE RESPONSE BY CHECK MARK IN BOX.)

	NAMES OF FACILITIES		
	POOL	PARK	CENTER
a. Don't know about facility or its programs			
b. Not open the right times			
c. Too far away			
d. It's too crowded			
e. It's not attractive			
f. Costs too much to go there			
g. Too dangerous there			
h. Do not like other users			
i. Personal health			
j. Activities not interesting			
(IF CHECKED ASK WHAT WOULD BE INTERESTING)			
k. Too busy			
l. Other (SPECIFY)			

*Q15. Are there any recreational activities or programs that you would add or change in the city which would improve recreation for your household?

Yes___ No___ Don't know___ No opinion___

(IF YES)

What additions or changes would you make?

_____

_____

(IF RESPONSE IS "DON'T KNOW" THEN SUGGEST THESE CHANGES TO RESPONDENT)

Would you like to have more variety in the program being offered?

Yes ___ No ___ Don't know ___

(IF YES ASK)

What new programs would you like to see added?

_____

(POSSIBLE SUGGESTIONS INCLUDE: SEWING CLASSES, CARD GAMES, WRESTLING, JUDO, DANCING, ETC.)

Would you like to see more facilities available, such as:

Tennis courts	Yes ___	No ___
Ball diamonds	Yes ___	No ___
Handball courts	Yes ___	No ___
Swimming pools	Yes ___	No ___
Shuffleboard courts	Yes ___	No ___
Other _____		

*Q16. How many different people in your household have played golf in the last 12 months? _____

(IF RESPONDENT PLAYS GOLF ASK)

Q17. What kinds of waiting times do you experience?

Usually too long ___
Occasionally too long ___
Not usually a problem ___
Don't know ___

Q18. Has the cost of greens fees restricted your golfing:

A great deal ___
Somewhat ___
Not much ___
(DON'T READ) → Don't know ___

Now I have some general questions to complete the questionnaire. As mentioned in the letter, your replies will be strictly confidential.

*Q19. Does the household have a family vehicle like a car or truck?

Yes ___ No ___ Don't know___ Won't say ___

*Q20 What was the last grade or class the head of the household completed in school?

___Grade 8 or less
___High school, incomplete
___High school, completed
___Technical, trade or business
___College, university, incomplete
___College, university, graduate
___Don't know
___Won't say

*Q21. Do you own or are you buying or do you rent the place you live in?

___Own (buying)
___Rent
___Other
___Don't know
___Won't say

*Q22. How many years have you lived in the neighborhood? ___

Don't know ___ Won't say ___

*Q23. Can you tell me approximately what is the level of income for all members of your household, that is, before any taxes? What is the total annual income?

Below $5,000 ____
Between $5,000 and $10,000 ____
Between $10,000 and $15,000 ____

Over $15,000 ____
Don't know ____
Won't say ____

*Q24. Do you consider yourself of a White _____, Black _____, or of another race _____?
Don't know ____   Won't say ____

ILLUSTRATIVE SURVEY OF USERS OF RECREATION FACILITIES
(Adapted from Nashville and St. Petersburg user surveys)

Facility Name _____ Date_____

READ EACH QUESTION. CHOOSE AND CIRCLE THE NUMBER TO THE LEFT OF THE RESPONSE THAT BEST APPLIES TO YOU.

1. Where did you first find out about this facility?

   (1) Newspaper
   (2) Television
   (3) Friends and neighbors
   (4) City published information
   (5) Phone book
   (6) Other; specify _____

2. How did you get here?

   (1) Own car
   (2) Other person's car
   (3) Motorcycle
   (4) Bus
   (5) Bike
   (6) Walked
   (7) Other; specify _____

3. How long did it take to get here?

   (1) Less than 10 minutes
   (2) 10-19 minutes
   (3) 20-29 minutes
   (4) 30-39 minutes
   (5) 40-49 minutes
   (6) 50-59 minutes
   (7) 60 or more

4. About how often have you come here during the past 12 months?

   (1) This is my first visit
   (2) Almost daily
   (3) At least once a week
   (4) At least once a month
   (5) Less than once a month

5. How long do you usually stay at this facility?

   (1) Less than ½ hour
   (2) ½ or more, but not 1 hour
   (3) 1 hour or more, but not 2 hours
   (4) 2 hours or more, but not 4 hours
   (5) 4 hours or more

How would you rate the following?

	Excellent	Good	Fair	Poor
6. Hours of operation	1	2	3	4
7. Cleanliness	1	2	3	4
8. Condition of equipment	1	2	3	4
9. Availability of equipment	1	2	3	4
10. Amount of space (lack of crowdedness)	1	2	3	4
11. Safety conditions (including feeling of security)	1	2	3	4
12. Physical attractiveness	1	2	3	4
13. Variety of programs	1	2	3	4
14. Helpfulness and attitude of personnel	1	2	3	4
15. Parking area	1	2	3	4
16. Restrooms	1	2	3	4
17. Convenience to your home	1	2	3	4
18. Amount of supervision	1	2	3	4

19. Is there anything else you particularly like about this facility?

   _____

20. Is there anything else you particularly dislike about this facility?

   _____

21. How would you rate this facility overall?

   (1) Excellent
   (2) Good
   (3) Fair
   (4) Poor

22. Do you have any suggestions for improving this facility? _____
_____
_____

23. How long have you lived in _____?

    (1) Less than 3 months
    (2) 3-12 months
    (3) 1-5 years
    (4) More than 5 years
    (5) Not a resident

24. Home address (or nearest intersection to your home):

    _____

25. What is your age?

    (1) Less than 14
    (2) 14-18

    (3) 19-24
    (4) 25-34
    (5) 35-49
    (6) 50-64
    (7) Over 65

26. What is your sex and race?

    (1) White male
    (2) White female
    (3) Nonwhite male
    (4) Nonwhite female

27. Which of the following comes closest to your total household income before taxes last year?

    (1) Under $5,000
    (2) $5,000 to 7,999
    (3) $8,000 to 9,999
    (4) $10,000 to 14,999
    (5) $15,000 and over

ILLUSTRATIVE SET OF RECREATION QUESTIONS
FOR A MULTISERVICE CITIZEN SURVEY

(The questions are from the 1975 St. Petersburg Multiservice General Citizen Survey)

Q1.   Have you or any member of your household used any of St. Petersburg's Municipal Pools in the past 12 months? Parks? Recreational Centers? Playgrounds?

Q2.   Generally speaking, would you rate St. Petersburg Municipal Pools as: excellent, good, fair, or poor? (Asked only of users during the past 12 months.)

Q3.   Generally speaking, would you rate St. Petersburg Municipal Parks as: excellent, good, fair, or poor? (Asked only of users during the past 12 months.)

Q4.   Generally speaking, would you rate St. Petersburg Municipal Recreation Centers as: excellent, good, fair, or poor? (Asked only of users during the past 12 months.)

Q5.   Generally speaking, would you rate St. Petersburg Municipal Playgrounds as: excellent, good, fair, or poor? (Asked only of users during the past 12 months.)

Q6.   What is the main reason you have not used any of the St. Petersburg Municipal Pools? (Asked only of nonusers during the past 12 months.)

Q7.   What is the main reason you have not used any of the St. Petersburg Municipal Parks? (Asked only of nonusers during the past 12 months.)

Q8.   What is the main reason you have not used any of the St. Petersburg Municipal Recreation Centers? (Asked only of nonusers during the past 12 months.)

Q9.   What is the main reason you have not used any of the St. Petersburg Municipal Playgrounds? (Asked only of nonusers during the past 12 months.)

Q10. During the past 12 months have you or any member of your household attended any performance, sports event, show, exhibition, rock show, or other presentation or meeting at St. Petersburg's Bayfront Center? (IF YES, ASK:) Approximately how many times did you or they attend?

Q11. What would you say is the main reason(s) you and members of this household have not attended Bayfront Center activities and performances more often?

NOTE: 1. The response categories used for summarizing responses on Questions 6-9 were: (1) Don't know about them; (2) too crowded; (3) too hard to get to; (4) busy with other activities; (5) use private facilities; (6) age/health problems; (7) I don't enjoy; (8) other reasons; (9) don't know.

2. The response categories used for summarizing responses to Question 11 (the Bayfront Center usually has charges for admission and many events are at night) were: (1) Too old; health problems; (2) too busy; not enough time to go; (3) too expensive; don't have enough money; (4) prefer other activities; (5) don't go out, prefer to stay at home; (6) no transportation; too far; (7) afraid to go out at night; (8) just not interested; (9) don't know.

3. A problem with the use of these questions is the possibility that respondents are unable to distinguish the government's own facilities from those of other local governments, the state, or other providers. Thus, their responses may be affected by other facilities as well as those of the government doing the questioning.

LIBRARY USER SURVEY[1]

Form # M ML T J _____ Date _____ Time _____
     (1-4)   (5-6)   (7-10)

LIBRARY SURVEY

Dear Library User:
To help improve library service, we are surveying a sample of users. Please read each question, then choose and circle the number to the left of the response that best applies to you. It is NOT necesary to put your name on the survey form. The answers you provide will be kept strictly confidential. IF THIS IS YOUR FIRST VISIT TO A ST. PETERSBURG LIBRARY, PLEASE RETURN THE QUESTIONNAIRE TO THE ATTENDANT.

1. Which St. Petersburg library facilities have you used during the past 12 months? (Please circle all that apply.) (11-15)

   1. Main Library
   2. Mirror Lake
   3. Johnson
   4. Tyrone
   5. Mobile Unit

2. Do you or any other persons in your household have a St. Petersburg library card? (16)

   1. Yes
   2. No

3. What activity brought you to the library today? (please circle one) (17)

   1. Leisure-time material (reading/viewing/listening)
   2. School assignment
   3. Job-related reading or research
   4. Personal business/investment reading or research
   5. Attend a meeting
   6. Other (please specify) _____

---

1. This is the 1974 St. Petersburg, Florida, Library User Survey Questionnaire.

4. Did you come to: (Please circle one) (18)

   1. Use materials in the library?
   2. Check out materials?
   3. Both use *and* check out materials?
   4. Other: _____

5. About how often would you say that you have used *this* particular library during the past year? (Please circle *one*) (19)

   1. Almost daily
   2. At least once a week
   3. At least once a month
   4. At least once every 3 months
   5. At least once in the last year
   6. This is my first visit to this library. (If so, skip to Question 18)

6. About how long do you usually stay each time you visit the library? (20)

   1. Less than 15 minutes
   2. 15-30 minutes
   3. 30-60 minutes
   4. More than 60 minutes
      (Please estimate how long)_____

How would you rate this library in the following areas? (Please circle your answer)

	Excellent	Good	Fair	Poor	Don't Know
7. Hours of operation (21)	1	2	3	4	5
8. Days of operation (22)	1	2	3	4	5
9. Availability of material you want (23)	1	2	3	4	5
10. Comfort and cleanliness (24)	1	2	3	4	5
11. Convenience to your house (25)	1	2	3	4	5
12. Helpfulness and courtesy of library staff (26)	1	2	3	4	5
13. Ease in finding materials (27)	1	2	3	4	5
14. Ease in checking out materials (28)	1	2	3	4	5

	Excellent	Good	Fair	Poor	Don't Know
15. Ease of parking (29)	1	2	3	4	5
16. Reference help (30)	1	2	3	4	5
17. Overall service (31)	1	2	3	4	5

If you chose "excellent" or "poor" for any of your answers, please tell us why: _____

_____

18. About how far do you live from this library? (32)

   1. Less than 5 blocks (less than ½ mile)
   2. 5-10 blocks (½-1 mile)
   3. 10-20 blocks (1-2 miles)
   4. More than 20 blocks (over 2 miles)

19. What is the nearest street intersection to your home:

   _____

20. How did you get to this library today? (33)

   1. Car
   2. Bike
   3. Walked
   4. Bus
   5. Taxi
   6. Motorcycle
   7. Other: _____

21. Is there anything you particularly like about this library?

   _____
   _____

22. Is there anything you particularly dislike about this library?

   _____
   _____

23. What additions or changes would you like to see made in this library?

   _____
   _____

24. How long have you lived in St. Petersburg? (34)

   1. Less than 3 months
   2. 3 to 12 months
   3. 1 to 5 years
   4. More than 5 years
   5. Not a resident

25. Are you presently: (35-38)

   1. Student?
   2. Employed?
   3. Housewife?
   4. Retired?
   5. Other: _____

26. What is your age? (39)

   1. Under 13
   2. 13-17
   3. 18-34
   4. 35-49
   5. 50-64
   6. 65 and over

27. What is your sex? (40)

   1. Male
   2. Female

28. What is your race? (41)

   1. White
   2. Black
   3. Other

29. Here are four numbers that correspond to different family incomes during the past year. Please circle the one for your family or household: (42)

   1. Under $5,000
   2. $5,000-$9,999
   3. $10,000-$15,000
   4. Over $15,000

(CT____: 43-45)
THANK YOU!
Please place completed form in ballot box.

ILLUSTRATIVE WATER SERVICE USER QUESTIONNAIRE[1]

Hello, my name is _____. The *(name of city or county)* Water Department is surveying persons who have called the department to request service or to report a complaint over the past year. The department plans to use the survey results to help improve its services. Your answers will not be identified by name, so the answers you give will be completely confidential.

1. Our records show that you called about *(enter nature of service request or complaint)* on *(enter date of call).* Do you remember calling about service or a complaint at about that time?

   (1) Yes ____ (Go to 1b)
   (2) No ____ (Go to 1a)
   (3) Don't know ____ (Go to 1a)

1a. Is there anyone else in the household who might know about that call?

   (1) Yes ____ (Ask to speak to that person, then begin again with "Hello, . . .")
   (2) No ____ (STOP INTERVIEW)

1b. Was the reason for the call as I have stated?

   (1) Yes ____
   (2) No ____ (Enter correction:) _____
   (3) Don't know (STOP INTERVIEW)

1c. How many departments of the (city/county) did you have to call before someone was willing to check out your complaint?

   (1) One ____
   (2) Two ____

(3) Three or more ____
(4) No one agreed to check out complaint ____
(5) Other (Specify) _____
(6) Don't know ____
(7) No response ____

IF CALL *WAS NOT* ABOUT A *BILLING COMPLAINT*[2], GO TO QUESTION 2.

IF CALL *WAS* ABOUT A BILLING COMPLAINT[2], GO TO QUESTION 10.

2. How urgent did you consider your request to be? That is, did you feel that same-day service was required? Or, rather, that prompt service was required but not necessarily same-day service? Or that your request was not urgent?

   (1) Same-day service required ____
   (2) Prompt service required but same day service not required ____
   (3) Not urgent ____
   (4) Don't know ____
   (5) No response ____

3. Was the service you requested provided to your satisfaction? Were you completely satisfied, satisfied, dissatisfied, or completely dissatisfied?

   (1) Completely satisfied ____
   (2) Satisfied ____ } (Go to 8)

   (3) Dissatisfied ____
   (4) Completely dissatisfied ____ } (Go to 4)

   (5) Don't know ____ (STOP INTERVIEW)
   (6) No response ____

4. What was unsatisfactory?

   (1) Service refused or no service provided ____ (Go to 5)

---

1. These questions have not been field-tested. A local government choosing to undertake such a survey should review the questions for applicability and have the final questionnaire tested for clarity and understandability prior to full-scale implementation. Also, demographic questions should be included, such as length of residence in the community, type of housing unit, race, and income group. Sample questions of this type are included in the Recreation Users Survey, Appendix 5.

---

2. Nature of the call would already have been determined, as shown in Question 1, although the answer to Question 1b might indicate the call was about something else.

(2) Wrong service provided on
first service call ____

(3) Faulty or ineffective service
provided on first
service call ____   } (Go to 7)

(4) Other (Specify) _____
_____

(5) Don't know ____   }
(6) No response ____   } (Go to 8)

5. What was the reason you were given for their not
providing the service?

(1) City/county lacked authority or jurisdiction
over problem ____

(2) City/county lacked resources or technical
capability ____

(3) Denied that service was justified by stated facts
____

(4) Denied that facts of case were validly stated
____

(5) Promised service but never fulfilled promise
____

(6) Did not promise or refuse to give service but
never followed up ____

(7) Refused service with no reason given ____

(8) Other (Specify) _____

(9) Don't know ____

(10) No response ____

6. Were you satisfied that the explanation given was
reasonable?

(1) Yes, the explanation seemed reasonable ____
(2) No, the explanation seemed unreasonable ____
(3) Don't know ____
(4) No response ____

STOP THE INTERVIEW.

7. Did the Water Department provide the correct service in a later visit?

(1) Yes ____ (Go to 7a)

(2) No ____   }
(3) Don't know ____   } (Go to 8)
(4) No response ____   }

7a. How many service calls did the Water Department
make?

(1) Two ____
(2) Three ____
(3) Four or more ____
(4) Other (Specify) _____
(5) Don't know ____
(6) No response ____

8. What condition did the service personnel leave the
work area in? Was it cleaner than before they arrived, as clean as when they arrived, somewhat
messy, or very messy, or did they perform all their
work off your property?

(1) Cleaner than it was before they got here ____
(2) Kept it as clean as they found it ____
(3) Somewhat messy ____
(4) Very messy ____
(5) Did all work off my property ____

(6) Don't know ____
(7) No response ____

9. Was service provided conveniently for you, as far as
scheduling was concerned? Was it convenient, inconvenient, or extremely inconvenient, or were they
able to do all work without you present?

(1) Convenient ____   }
(2) Inconvenient ____   }
(3) Extremely inconvenient ____ }
(4) Did all work without me   } (Go to 11)
present ____   }
(5) Don't know ____   }
(6) No response ____   }

10. What was done about your complaint?

(1) Claimed bill correct after checking it ____
(2) Promised to check it but never followed up
____
(3) Refused to check billing complaint ____
(4) Acknowledged bill was too high and corrected
it ____
(5) Acknowledged bill was too high but refused to
correct it ____
(6) Acknowledged bill was too high and promised
to correct it but never followed up ____
(7) Claimed bill was too low after checking it ____
(8) Other (Specify) _____ ↓↓
(9) Don't know ____
(10) No response ____

11. How satisfied were you with the promptness of the
service personnel? Were you very satisfied,
satisfied, dissatisfied, or very dissatisfied?

(1) Very satisfied ____
(2) Satisfied ____
(3) Dissatisfied ____
(4) Very dissatisfied ____
(5) Don't know ____
(6) No response ____

12. Were the personnel you dealt with courteous?

(1) Yes ____
(2) No ____
(3) Don't know ____
(4) No response ____

13. How satisfied were you overall with the efforts on
your behalf? Were you very satisfied, satisfied, dissatisfied, or very dissatisfied?

(1) Very satisfied ____
(2) Satisfied ____
(3) Dissatisfied ____
(4) Very dissatisfied ____
(5) Don't know ____
(6) No response ____

14. How satisfied were you with the resolution of your
request? Were you very satisfied, satisfied, dissatisfied, or very dissatisfied?

(1) Very satisfied ____
(2) Satisfied ____
(3) Dissatisfied ____
(4) Very dissatisfied ____
(5) Don't know ____
(6) No response ____

WATER QUALITY CONTAMINATION ISSUES

The success of modern treatment methods in eliminating bacterial infections from the public water supply has meant that the principal health hazards remaining are much harder to detect. Infectious diseases display epidemic characteristics: large groups of persons are stricken within a short period of time, and exposure to the contaminated water carries with it a high probability of being stricken. As a result, both the events of illness and their cause are highly visible. With the virtual elimination of bacterial contamination, the principal health risks remaining are viruses and chemicals. Chemicals can pose acute, short-term threats in extremely high concentrations or long-term threats through accumulation; symptoms of short- and long-term effects differ markedly. Citizens and water service managers must answer some fundamental questions of values and intentions before desired treatment routines and appropriate measures of effectiveness can be specified:

1. What margin of safety should be chosen between expected level of exposure to the substance and the level of exposure required to damage health? For each contaminating substance, there is a body of research, often with great gaps and some contradictions, that constitutes the existing evidence on the effects of various levels of exposure. The evidence often includes studies of effects on laboratory animals (with the formula for transferring the results to human beings somewhat uncertain), reports of health incidents arising from accidental exposures (as in industrial accidents), and studies in which the mode of ingestion of the substance is different from that taken by drinking water (inhaling versus swallowing). All this tends to leave the relationship of risk to exposure rather fuzzy.
2. How much is more information worth? Viruses, so-called organic exotics (such as pesticides and herbicides), and to a lesser extent infectious bacteria, cannot be measured reliably and regularly at reasonable cost with today's technology. Some tests can be made reliably and regularly at reasonable cost and serve as indicators of the range of organics that are of concern, but some research suggests that the two

most widely used general indicators—coliform and carbon chloroform (or alcohol) extract—are not well correlated with the organic substances of real interest. Water service managers must decide how much value they place on extra detail and extraconfidence in the information they have regarding what is in the water.
3. What degree of contamination from other sources should be assumed in setting an acceptable level of contamination for the water supply? For chemical and radiological contaminants, the public water supply is only one, and rarely the most significant, source of exposure. Food and air generally contribute more exposure to chemical contaminants, and other natural and manmade sources generally contribute more exposure to radioactivity. Moreover, the fact that individuals differ widely in their average daily intake of water leads to some variability in the relationship between the concentration of a given substance in individuals.

For each of these questions, there is a range of vocal, informed opinion on how the risks and costs should be weighed. Although no single answer can be justified on the facts alone, there is a consensus on some of these points which we have attempted to reflect in our choice of measures by following the lead of the U.S. Public Health Service (PHS) Drinking Water Standards.

Standards. The PHS generally selects a limit that is below levels previously associated with illness. Large margins of safety are used. Yet the list of substances with limits is relatively short, since it contains only substances for which a substantial body of evidence exists—evidence sufficient not only to demonstrate the existence of a potential health risk, but also to support the establishment of a particular standard. Finally, in establishing standards for water quality, the PHS uses the average rate of water consumption and the average rate of exposure from other sources as a base. The PHS also attempts to use information on "background levels" of various substances—that is, the levels occurring in the absence of manmade pollution—as a guide to what exposure levels can be assumed to involve no significant health risk.

Frequency of Measurement. Another issue is the frequency of measurement needed to assure a given level of water quality. The PHS allows a relaxation of measurement frequency if the water source is strongly protected against contamination from industrial and municipal effluents or if repeated measurement indicates that the concentration of a particular substance is remaining well below the standard for that substance. But no water source—not even a well-shielded, deep, groundwater source—should be assumed to be clean. There is general agreement that if a routine survey turns up an unacceptably high concentration of some substance, there should be much more frequent measurement of that substance until the cause is identified and corrected and the concentration returns to an acceptable level.

In the following paragraphs each of the contaminants listed in the discussion of Measure 1 on page 160 of Chapter 10 is briefly discussed.

The use of certain groups of *coliform organisms* as indicators of bacterial contamination is the oldest and most heavily researched practice in the management of water safety. Coliform organisms enter bodies of water from the intestines of warmblooded animals in the same way disease bacteria of infected animals enter bodies of water. This is the basis for using coliform counts as indicators of bacterial contamination. The presence of the coliform group, however, is far from perfectly correlated with the presence of bacteria harmful to human beings. For that reason, measurement of residual chlorine in the distribution system is also widely used, since chlorine is known to be effective in killing disease-causing bacteria. The PHS recommendation, which is *not* part of its standards, is for a free chlorine residual of 0.2 ppm at the treatment plant and 0.05-0.1 ppm in the distribution system.[1]

The PHS standards for coliform tests include a recommended minimum number of tests per month in the distribution system, based on the population served. The standards, based on monthly testing, are contained in Public Health Service Publication No. 956, *Drinking Water Standards 1962.*

Carbon chloroform extract (CCE) is used as an indicator of general organic pollution because activated carbon is the best known substance for disinfecting water short of distillation. The unreliability of the test arises because both of the transfer processes—from water to carbon and from carbon to chloroform—permit the possibility that organic substances may be washed backwards; as a result, the extract may not reflect the total level of contamination. Moreover, because the extract contains a mixture of unidentified organic substances, it is unreliable to assign a particular degree of risk to a given level of CCE. The test is recommended because it is simple and practical. The recommended standard of 0.2 milligrams per liter (mg/l) was selected by the PHS based on CCE tests of water containing known substances in dangerous amounts. The American Water Works Association recommends a stricter standard of

0.04 mg/l. If the CCE standard is exceeded, the city will want to take further steps to identify the nature of the organic contamination so that the real risk may be determined.

Lead is a highly toxic, cumulative heavy metal. It enters the human body through tobacco, food, air, and water. The background level of lead in water ranges as high as .04 mg/l. The standard of .05 mg/l was selected by the PHS to compensate for assumed intakes of lead through tobacco, food, and air, given an assumed rate of water consumption. Apart from natural sources, lead enters the water supply primarily through the action of a high pH on lead and galvanized iron pipes and lead joints found in old buildings. Control of the pH level, as well as monitoring of the lead concentration at the treatment plant, is needed. A special study of lead and cadmium at the taps of old and substandard housing might be valuable, as private plumbing in such buildings is a major source of contamination.

Barium is a highly toxic substance that occurs naturally in brazil nuts and as a mineral salt (barite or barium sulfate) in some mineral springs. The PHS standard of 1.0 mg/l is based on air pollution standards for barium established by the American Conference of Government Industrial Hygienists and assumed rates of water consumption and bodily absorption of barium.

Cadmium is a highly toxic, cumulative substance associated with effluent from electroplating plants. It generally enters the water supply through the action of a high pH on galvanized iron pipes, in which cadmium is a contaminant. The PHS standard of .01 mg/l is set well below the lowest level of concentration known to have resulted in cadmium accumulation in the tissues.

Chromium (hexavalent) is included because chromium is known to be a carcinogenic substance when inhaled. Its carcinogenic properties when ingested are not known. There is little evidence of toxicity at high levels. Trivalent chromium, the primary form of chromium in food, is much less toxic than hexavalent chromium. The PHS standard of .05 mg/l was established in 1946, based on the lowest level detectable at that time.

Selenium is known to be toxic to both man and animals and to be carcinogenic when inhaled. the carcinogenic property is the primary reason cited by the PHS in lowering the 1946 standard of .05 mg/l to .01 mg/l in the 1962 standards.

Silver is a cumulative substance that can lead to permanent discoloration of the skin. The PHS limit of .05 mg/l is designed to ensure an acceptable upper bound on the body's lifetime retention of silver, based on an assumed rate of water consumption per day.

Arsenic is a highly toxic substance that lingers in the body for a long time. It is found in many foods as a result of its use as a poison in the control of pests. Using a large margin of safety relative to known dangerous levels of ingested arsenic, the PHS set a goal of .01 mg/l and a standard of .05 mg/l for arsenic.

Cyanide is another highly toxic substance that is often used as a poison. Since cyanide is quickly neutralized in the body, the cumulative effect is negligible. Chlorination of the water supply also will convert hydrogen cyanide to a form with only 5 percent of the toxicity. The PHS sets a goal of .01 mg/l, which is achievable by routine proper treatment, and a standard of .20

1. Edmund J Raubush, "Water Disinfection Practices in the United States," *Journal of the American Water Works Association,* (November, 1960), pp. 1416-1426, cited in Janice Crossland and Virginia Brodine, "Drinking Water," *Environment,* 15, April, 1973, pp. 11-19.

mg/l, which is one hundred times the human toxicity level and also provides security for several fish species with lower tolerances.

Zinc is a substance the primary effect of which is aesthetic, as it imparts an unpleasant taste to water. But, it also acts as a backup indicator of the presence of lead and cadmium, since zinc enters the water primarily through the action of a high pH on galvanized iron pipe. The PHS standard of 5 mg/l is designed to reflect this secondary indicator use and existing proportionate concentrations of zinc, lead, and cadmium in galvanized iron pipe. The lower American Water Works Association goal of 1 mg/l provides additional safety and a much reduced likelihood of taste effects.

Gross beta activity is an overall measure of radioactivity in the water supply. *Radium* and *strontium* are two specific contaminants that are known to enter the water supply through ore deposits and air pollution, respectively. The PHS standards of 1,000 picocuries (a picocurie is one trillionth of a curie) per liter of gross beta activity, 3 picocuries per liter of radium, and 10 picocuries per liter of strontium are based on Federal Radiation Council criteria on acceptable levels of human exposure to radioactivity, combined with assumed rates of water consumption. The American Water Works Association's lower goal of 100 picocuries per liter of gross beta activity reflects a greater margin of safety.

Fluoride is a substance that provides protection against tooth decay in regulated doses and causes problems for bones and teeth in much higher concentrations. The PHS has standards for communities that want to sustain dental-health-supporting fluoride levels and for communities that seek only to avoid harmful concentrations. The fluoride requirement for communities using it for dental-health support is based on the average air temperature. For nonusing communities, the fluoride standard is an upper bound not to be exceeded. The optimum concentration of fluoride drops as the air temperature rises, because the average amount of water consumed rises as the temperature rises.

Nitrate in well water has been associated with infantile poisoning in a wide variety of geographic locations. The fact that cases of poisoning from public water supplies are known indicates that some factors in the nitrate problem are yet to be discovered. Nitrate has no effects on persons over a few months old and there are no known economical treatment methods for removing excess nitrate. The PHS recommends that parents of infants be encouraged to use alternate water sources if the nitrate level of their water exceeds 45 mg/l.

Sodium can be a problem for persons on low-sodium diets because of heart conditions or other disease. To enable such persons to control their total sodium intake, new drinking-water standards will recommend that persons on low-sodium diets be notified to seek other water sources if the concentration exceeds 20 mg/l.

The measure of *residual chlorine* is a proxy measure for *bacterial decontamination.* The standards for residual chlorine are not so widely accepted as those for other measures on this list; no standards are available from the PHS. There are criteria available from the Environmental Protection Agency, but these are not considered to be on a par with PHS standards for other water properties. Because ozone can be used as an alternative to chlorine for treatment and because unacceptably high levels of chlorine are needed to affect viruses, this measure may be more readily dropped by localities than the other measures of water quality.

CITIZEN SURVEY QUESTIONS ON CITIZEN COMPLAINTS AND REQUESTS FOR SERVICES AND INFORMATION

Note: Symbols in white letters and numbers on a black background, appearing before many questions, refer to effectiveness measures in Chapter 11. Those coded "C" on citizen complaints are found in Exhibit 11-2; those coded "R" on requests for services and information are found in Exhibit 11-5.

C10

1. During the past 12 months did you ever get in touch with the city to complain about something like poor city services or a rude city employee or for *any* reason?

   1( ) Yes   (ASK 1a, 1b, 1c, 1d, 1e)

   2( ) No
   3( ) Don't know } (GO TO 2)

C7, C8, C9

1a. (IF YES TO 1) How many different problems or situations did you complain about to the city during that period? _____

C7, C8, C9, C10

1b. What were the problems or situations you complained about to the city?

   1. _____

   2. _____

   3. _____
      _____

(IF MORE THAN ONE COMPLAINT, ASK) Now, regarding the complaint you think was most important, will you tell me:

(IF ONLY ONE COMPLAINT, ASK)

1c. Which department or official did you contact *initially*?

1( ) Service and Information Center
2( ) Mayor or Councilman
3( ) City Manager's Office
4( ) Police
5( ) Other (specify): _____
6( ) Don't remember

1d. Were you ever told that the city had no authority to deal with this matter, or that it was out of its jurisdiction? For instance, because it was a private matter or a state responsibility?

1( ) Yes
2( ) No
3( ) Don't remember
4( ) No response

C2, C5

1e. Were you generally satisfied with the city's responses? (IF NO, ASK) What was the *main* thing you were dissatisfied with? (INTERVIEWER: MARK THE REASON *CLOSEST* TO THAT GIVEN BY RESPONDENT.)

1( ) Response not yet completed
2( ) Yes, satisfied
3( ) No, never responded to my request
4( ) No, never corrected problem
5( ) No, too much "run-around," "red tape"
6( ) No, had to keep pressuring them to get results
7( ) No, personnel were discourteous
8( ) No, information or service provided was wrong
9( ) No, other (specify): _____

10( ) Don't know

2. During the past 12 months, did you contact anyone with the city to seek service or information, such as having your water turned on, obtaining a building permit, and so forth?

   1( ) Yes   (ASK 2a, 2b, 2c, 2d)

2( ) No

3( ) Don't know } (GO TO 3)

2a. (IF YES TO 2) What services or information were you requesting?

1. _____
   _____
2. _____
   _____
3. _____
   _____

(IF MORE THAN ONE REQUEST, ASK) Now, regarding the request you think was most important, will you tell me:

(IF ONLY ONE REQUEST, ASK)

2b. Which department or official did you contact initially?

1( ) Service and Information Center
2( ) Mayor or Councilman
3( ) City Manager's Office
4( ) Police
5( ) Other (specify): _____
6( ) Don't remember

2c. Were you ever told that the city had no authority to deal with this matter, or that it was out of the city's jurisdiction—for instance, because it was a private matter or a state responsibility?

1( ) Yes
2( ) No
3( ) Don't remember
4( ) No response

R2, R5

2d. Were you generally satisfied with the city's response to your inquiries? (IF NO, ASK) What was the *main* reason you were dissatisfied? (INTERVIEWER: MARK THE REASON *CLOSEST* TO THE LISTED REASONS.)

1( ) Response not yet completed
2( ) Yes, satisfied
3( ) No, city *did not* provide requested service
4( ) No, city *could not* provide requested service
5( ) No, took too long to satisfy request
6( ) No, too much "run-around" or "red tape" involved
7( ) No, personnel were discourteous
8( ) No, information or service provided was wrong
9( ) Other (specify): _____

10( ) Don't know

C10

3. Thinking back over the past year, were there any complaints which you would have liked to have

made to city officials but didn't? (IF YES, ASK) What was the *main* reason you did *not* make the complaints? (INTERVIEWER: MARK REASON *CLOSEST* TO REASON GIVEN BY RESPONDENT.)

1( ) No   (GO TO 4)
2( ) Yes, didn't think it would do any good
3( ) Yes, problem not worth time or effort to complain about
4( ) Yes, thought officials already knew about problem
5( ) Yes, thought someone else had or would report problem
6( ) Yes, didn't know how or where to complain
7( ) Yes, was unable to complain (no phone, couldn't drive, etc.)
8( ) Yes, reported it to other people
9( ) Other (specify): _____

10( ) Don't know   (GO TO 4)

C6, C7, C9

3a. (IF YES TO 3) About how many unreported complaints did you have over that period?

C6, C7, C9, C10

3b. What were these complaints?

1. _____
   _____
2. _____
   _____
3. _____
   _____

R6

4. Thinking back over the past year, were there any times you wanted to request services or information from the government and didn't? (IF YES, ASK) What was the *main* reason or reasons you didn't? (DO NOT READ RESPONSES.)

1( ) No
2( ) Yes, didn't think it would do any good
3( ) Yes, unable to file request (no phone, unable to get to City Hall, etc.)
4( ) Yes, filing procedures too complex or too demanding
5( ) Yes, didn't know how or where to file a request
6( ) Yes, expected or had previously experienced run-around, delays, red tape, etc.
7( ) Yes, didn't want to bother anyone
8( ) Yes, other (specify): _____

9( ) Don't know

EXAMPLE OF A SURVEY OF COMPLAINANTS AND REQUESTERS OF SERVICES OR INFORMATION[1]

Note: Symbols in white on black background refer to effectiveness measures in Chapter 11. Those coded "C" on citizen complaints are found in Exhibit 11-2; those coded "R" on requests for services and information are found in Exhibit 11-5.

INTERVIEWER: BEFORE PLACING CALL, FILL IN THE FOLLOWING DATA AND THE BLANKS IN QUESTION 1, USING INFORMATION FROM THE COMPLAINT OR REQUEST RECORD. ATTACH A COPY OF THAT RECORD.

C3, C4, R3, R4

Check whether: ____ Complaint ____ Request for Service

Name of Citizen: _____ Telephone Number: _____
Address: _____
Response Time: ____ days. Neighborhood: _____
Time Interview Began: _____

Good afternoon. May I speak to _____. My name is _____ and I am calling for the city of _____. You recently contacted the city for (help) (service) (information), and we would like to know how you feel about the way your call was handled so that we may better serve *all* residents of _____. The information you give us will be strictly confidential.

1. Our records show that you contacted the city about _____ (ENTER NATURE OF REQUEST[2] OR COMPLAINT) on _____ (ENTER DATE). Do you remember calling about a request or a complaint at that time?

_____

1. Demographic questions on age, race, sex, and income—similar to those used in a general citizen survey—should be asked after Question 12 so that responses can be cross-tabulated by population subgroups.
2. The term "request" is used in this questionnaire to refer to a request for service *or* a request for information.

____Yes
____No   } TERMINATE INTERVIEW
____Don't know

1a. Was the reason for your contact as I stated? (IF "NO," ASK:) What was it?

____Yes
____No (ENTER CORRECTION:) _____
____Don't know (TERMINATE INTERVIEW)

C5, C7, R6

2. Overall, how easy would you say it was to report your (complaint) (request) to the proper city officials?[3] Was it

____Very easy
____Fairly easy
____Somewhat difficult
____Very difficult
____(Don't know)

3. How many times did you have to contact the city regarding this *same* matter?

____Once
____Twice
____Three times
____Four times
____Five or more
____Don't remember

3a. Which department or departments did you contact or deal with regarding this matter? (INTERVIEWER: IF NECESSARY, DETERMINE FIRST AND LAST DEPARTMENTS CONTACTED)

Initial Department: _____
Last Department (if different from above): _____
Others: _____
Don't know____

_____

3. The use of a question such as Number 2 for evaluating the accessibility of the complaint-processing mechanism was not discussed under Measure C7 but it is analogous to the procedure for requests described in conjunction with Measure R6.

`C2-4, R2-4`

4. How urgent do you regard your (complaint) (request)? Was

____Same or next day service required (Very Urgent)
____Response needed in 10 days (Moderately Urgent)
____Response not needed in 10 days (Not Urgent)
____(Don't know)

I would like to ask you a few questions now about the *final response* you received from the city with regard to your (complaint) (request).

5. As far as you can tell, has the city done all it is going to do with regard to your (request) (complaint)?

____Yes

____No ⎫
____Don't know ⎬ (GO TO #5d)

`C2, R2`

5a. How satisfied were you with the final outcome or resolution of your (complaint) (request)? Were you

____Very satisfied ⎫
____Satisfied ⎬ (GO TO #5d)

____Somewhat dissatisfied ⎫
____Very dissatisfied ⎬ (GO TO #5b)

____(Don't know) (GO TO #5d)

`C2, R2`

5b. (IF AT LEAST SOMEWHAT DISSATISFIED, ASK:) What was unsatisfactory about the outcome? (INTERVIEWER: MARK *ALL* RELEVANT RESPONSES)

____Never finally responded, refused to respond, could not respond (GO TO #5c)

____Referred me to another office or organization ⎫
____Response incomplete or never completed ⎪
____Response was erroneous ⎬ (GO TO #5d)
____Response was of poor quality or ineffective (problem not corrected) ⎪
____Other (specify):_____ ⎭

`C1, C2, R1, R2`

5c. (IF CITY DID NOT RESPOND, REFUSED TO RESPOND, OR COULD NOT RESPOND, ASK:) What reason was given for not doing anything about your (complaint) (request)? (INTERVIEWER: MARK CLOSEST REASON)

____Lacked authority or jurisdiction over matter
____Lacked resources or technical capability
____Denied facts of case were validly stated
____Denied any response was justified by facts
____Promised service but never fulfilled promise
____Refused service, no reason given
____Never responded at all, one way or the other
____Other (specify): _____
____Don't know/No response

`C2, R2`

5d. Were you satisfied with the city's explanation of its response?

____Yes, satisfied
____Partly satisfied
____No, not satisfied
____Explanation needed but not provided
____Explanation not needed or relevant
____Don't know

6. Were you contacted by someone from _____ (STATE *LAST* DEPARTMENT DEALT WITH, FROM QUESTION 3a) about your (complaint) (request)?

____Yes
____No
____Don't know or remember

Now I would like to ask about the way you were *treated* during your contacts with city personnel in regard to this matter.

`C5a, R5a`

7. Do you feel that your (complaint) (request) was handled fast enough?

____Yes
____No
____Don't know or remember

`C5b, R5b`

8. Were you inconvenienced by red tape or a run-around?

____Yes
____No
____Don't know or remember

`C5d, R5c`

9. Were the persons you dealt with fair in their treatment of you?

____Yes
____No
____Don't know or remember

`C5c, R5d`

10. Were you treated courteously?

____Yes
____No
____Don't remember

`C5c, R5d`

11. Were you satisfied with the efforts made by city personnel on your behalf?

____Yes
____No
____Don't know or remember

12. Do you have any general comments on the way the city handles citizen complaints and requests for services or information? _____
_____
_____

Thank you for your cooperation.
Date of Interview: _____
Time Interview Ended: _____

EXAMPLES OF GUIDELINES FOR TRAINED OBSERVER RATINGS[1]

DEFINITIONS

Abandoned automobile: A motor vehicle that is left unattended on public or private property, without current tags, and apparently totally inoperable—it may be on blocks, or have four flat tires, missing wheels, broken windows, and the like.

Alley: A roadway intended to provide access to the rear or side areas of lots or buildings in urban districts and not intended for through vehicular traffic. For the purpose of this survey, the edges of buildings and fences will be used to indicate alley boundaries. When no buildings or fences are present, utility poles will be considered to represent the boundaries, and when no utility poles are present, the alley boundaries will be considered to be five feet on each side of the edges of the alley's surface.

Block face: The area bounded by the property line and the street center line and the cross streets at each end of the block. Alleys shall be deemed to be on the block face if they may be entered from the block face or if they run parallel to the block face within the square block formed by the block face and three other streets.

Bulk items: Large, discarded objects such as stoves, refrigerators, sofas, other furniture, crates, tires, piles of lumber, or other items which would not bend easily or are otherwise too large to fit into a standard-size garbage can. Brush, rock, gravel, and abandoned automobiles are not considered bulk items.

Dirt and gravel: Loose rock, sand, dirt, heavy dust, or other such materials on a paved street that can be aesthetically displeasing and possibly unsafe.

Litter: An untidy array of small discarded objects such as scattered newspapers, wrappers or other scraps of paper, beverage or food containers, and the like. Materials in containers or in neat piles, apparently placed for refuse collection, are not considered litter. Grass clippings, limbs, leaves in bags, brush or parts of trees piled for collection are not considered litter. Any piles of wood or lumber, other than those mentioned above, will be counted as litter.

Pothole: A roughly circular depression in a street where surface pavement has been worn or washed away to create a hole with steep sides all around.

Rideability: The smoothness (or conversly the roughness) of the main surfaced portion of a street (not including the shoulder).

Road defects: An irregularity in street surface other than a pothole (including utility cuts, cracks, and manhole covers or other built-in equipment not flush with the street surface).

Sidewalk: A hard-surface walkway between the curbstone edge or the lateral lines of a roadway and the adjacent property lines. Curbstones are not included in the sidewalk area.

Signs: Markers designed to provide information and maintained by the city. Ratings are suggested for three categories of signs:
1. Stop signs;
2. Other traffic control signs including curve, intersection, and yield warnings; and signs indicating speed limits, pedestrian crossings, school zones, and school bus stops; and
3. Street name signs.
Note that parking signs and signs giving directions to specific places were not included in the procedure.

Street: There are two types of streets, those with curbstones and those without. Streets are delineated as follows: for streets with curbstones, from the center of the road to the curbstone, inclusive; for streets without curbstones, the area within the public right-of-way, which includes shoulders and ditches and is generally marked by utility poles. All fences and buildings are assumed to be on private property.

Vegetation (street): A growth of weeds or underbrush along a street. Only areas with a thick growth higher than two feet are reported as "weeds" by the trained observer.

Vegetation (yard): A growth of weeds or underbrush in the yard of a home or other building along a block face. Only areas with a thick growth more than two feet high are reported as "weeds—private property."

---

1. This appendix represents an adaptation of the manual prepared by Martha Groomes, Richard Caster, David Cushman, and John Logan of the Finance Office, Nashville-Davidson County Metropolitan Government, 1974.

STREET LITTER GRADES

Ratings for street litter are based on a scale of "1" (very clean) to "4" (very dirty) with the ratings defined by a set of photographs and further described in writing. Inspections are made bs an observer in an automobile. For streets with curbstones, street litter will be rated from the center of the street to the edge of the curbstone but not beyond it (that is, sidewalk litter is not counted). For streets with no curbstones, litter will be rated from the center of the street to the edge of the public right-of-way, usually indicated by utility poles; in all cases, fences and buildings will be considered to lie on private property.

Condition	Description (to supplement photographs)
1	Street completely clean or almost completely clean; two pieces of litter are permitted.
2	Street largely clean; a few pieces of litter observable, but only in the form of isolated discarded items. On a generally clean block face (number 1), a single accumulation of uncontained trash with a volume less than or equal to the volume of a large grocery bag that has not been set out for collection shall be rated as 2.
3	Lightly scattered litter along all or most of the street or one heavy pile of litter, but no accumulations of litter large enough to indicate dumping. On a generally clean block face (number 1) a single accumulation of litter that is larger than a number 2 accumulation but smaller than a thirty-gallon garbage can (and not set out for collection) shall be rated a number 3.
4	Heavily littered streets; litter accumulation in piles or heavy litter distributed down all or nearly all the block face. On a generally clean block face (number 1 or 2), a single accumulation of litter with a volume greater than that of a thirty-gallon garbage can (and not set out for collection) shall be rated a 4.

Note: Live vegetation and dirt are counted separately. Cut brush not piled for pickup and strewn so as to make the street unsightly is counted as street litter. Grass clippings are not considered litter and are not counted in any rating. Bulk items are not considered as litter in these ratings, but the number of bulk items that exist in the street is to be noted in the appropriate column.

ALLEY LITTER GRADES

Ratings for alley litter are based on a scale of 1 (very clean) to 4 (very dirty) with the points defined by a set of photographs and further described in writing. Inspection is made by an observer from an automobile. The alley parallel to the block face should be rated if possible. If no alley runs parallel to the block face, the alley intersecting the block face is to be rated. If bulk items are present in the alley, the number of such items shall be included in the proper column, and will not be counted as litter.

Condition	Description (to supplement photographs)
1	Alley is completely clean or almost completely clean (two pieces of litter are acceptable).
2	Alley largely clean, a few pieces of litter observable, but only in the form of isolated discarded items. On a generally clean alley (number 1), a single accumulation of uncontained trash with a volume less than or equal to the volume of a large grocery bag that has not been set out for collection shall be rated as 2.
3	Lightly scattered litter along all or most of the alley or one heavy pile, but no large accumulations of litter such as might indicate dumping. On a generally clean alley (number 1), a single accumulation of litter that is larger than a number 2 accumulation but smaller than a thirty-gallon garbage can (and not set out for collection) shall be rated a number 3.
4	Heavily littered alley; litter accumulation in piles or heavy litter distributed down all or nearly all the alley. On a generally clean alley (number 1 or 2), a single accumulation of uncontained litter with a volume greater than that of a thirty-gallon garbage can not set out for collection shall be rated a 4.

Note: Bulk items are not considered litter in these ratings, but the number of bulk items that exist in the alley is to be noted in the appropriate column.

YARD LITTER GRADES

Ratings for yard litter are based on a scale of 1 (very clean) to 4 (very dirty) with the points defined by a set of photographs and further described in writing. Inspections are made by an observer from an automobile. Yard litter is rated only for front yards, which are bounded by the edge of the street and the front of house or other buildings on that yard.

Condition	Description (to supplement photographs)
1	Yards completely clean or almost completely clean (two pieces of litter in a yard on block face are acceptable).
2	Yards generally clean, but some isolated pieces of litter visible in less than one-half of the yards on the block face. On a generally clean block face (number 1), a single uncontained accumulation of litter with a volume less than or equal to the volume of a large grocery bag shall be rated as 2.
3	Yards in the area are generally littered. (Some litter in one-half or more of the yards on the block face.) On a generally clean block face (number 1 or 2), a single uncontained accumulation of litter larger than a number 2 accumulation but smaller than or equal to the volume of a thirty-gallon garbage can shall be rated a 3.
4	Yards in the area are heavily littered; litter in almost every yard on block face. On a generally clean block face (number 1), a single uncontained accumulation of litter with a volume greater than that of a thirty-gallon garbage can shall be rated a 4.

Note: Bulk items are not considered as litter in these ratings, but the number of bulk items present in the yards on the block face is to be noted in the appropriate column.

STREET RIDEABILITY GRADES

Ratings of streets for smoothness of ride are made by visual inspection from an automobile.

Condition	Description
1	Probably smooth rideability (that is, appears to be smooth).
	a. No noticeable defects.
	b. One or two minor defects (small bump, crack, or hole).
	c. Many small cracks apparent but no noticeable affect on rideability.
2	Slightly bumpy rideability (bumps appear in photos).
	a. Several minor defects or minor potholes, but none appears severe.
	b. A large single bump or many minor bumps.
3	Considerably bumpy rideability: Much of the street is broken up, but no single hazard is apparent.
4	Potential safety hazard (or severe jolt) present (one or more large potholes or other major defects).

Note: A large pothole is defined here as a hole 3½ inches deep and at least 12 inches across. A major defect is defined as an abrupt change of street surface level greater than 3½ inches. A minor defect is defined as less than 3½ inches deep or less than about 12 inches in diameter.

SIDEWALK CONDITION GRADES

The "walkability" of sidewalks—the degree of walking comfort and safety for pedestrians—is rated visually from an automobile. Ratings shall indicate the worst portion of the sidewalk, and shall not include nonstructural defects, such as heavy litter or limbs on the sidewalk. Grates, water meters, driveway indentations, and other intentional sidewalk interruptions will not cause downgrading if level with sidewalk and in good condition. Pebble and brick surfaces are also acceptable if in good condition.

Condition	Description
1	No visual signs of walking discomfort. Some hairline cracks may be present, but surface still presents a smooth appearance with no perturbations likely to cause pedestrians to stumble.
2	Some visual signs of minor walking discomfort but not hazardous.
	a. Sidewalk is basically good but has a severe side-to-side slope or other minor deterioration which could cause walking discomfort.
	b. Sidewalk has some breaks or unevenness less than 1½ inches high or deep, or holes deeper but too narrow to catch even a child's foot.
3	One or more potential hazards or many signs of severe walking discomfort. A hazard is an abrupt rise or depression measuring more than 1½ inches above or below the sidewalk surface.

STOP-SIGN CONDITION GRADES

Visual ratings of readability and appearance of stop signs are made from an automobile.

Condition	Description
1	Conveniently visible[2]
	a. Sign head and support in good condition (tilted, twisted, or bent less than 5°); and
	b. Sign not defaced in any manner; and
	c. Sign continuously unobscured for the last 200 feet.
2	Visible but somewhat inconvenient to see.
	a. Sign head or support slightly tilted; sign twisted, bent (between 5° and 30°) but readable; or
	b. Sign partially obscured, or intermittently obscured within the last 200 feet of approach; or
	c. Sign defaced but still readable.
3	Missing, ambiguous, difficult to see or not visible.
	a. Sign broken off pole or otherwise missing, or major part defaced and difficult to read;
	b. Sign tilted, twisted, or bent more than 30°; or
	c. Sign totally obscured by a tree, bush, brush, pole, another sign, or other object so that it cannot be seen from the observer's position for the last 200 feet of approach.

Note: Intermittent observation of a stop sign can be ignored in the rating if there is a "stop ahead" sign present and in good condition. That is, the stop sign could be rated a 1 even though intermittently obscured under such circumstances.

STREET-NAME SIGN GRADES (And All Regulatory Signs Except for Stop Signs)

A visual rating of readability and appearance made to be used for all regulatory signs other than stop can be made from an automobile.

Condition	Description
1	Conveniently visible.
	a. Sign head and support in good condition (tilted, twisted, or bent less than 5°); and
	b. Sign not defaced in any manner; and
	c. Sign continuously unobscured for the last 50 feet.
2	Visible but somewhat inconvenient to read or find, or unpleasant to see.
	a. Sign head or support slightly tilted, twisted, or bent (between 5° and 30°), but visible even though inconvenient or unpleasant to see; or
	b. Sign partially obscured, or intermittently obscured within the last 50 feet; or
	c. Sign defaced but still readable.
3	Missing, ambiguous, difficult to see or read.

---

2. These are very strict conditions for a stop sign, which is designed by shape, color, lettering, and reflectivity to be visible even when badly tilted or partially defaced or obscured. But it simplifies the rating system if the same degrees of tilt are used for all signs.

a. No sign on any corner of the intersection; or
b. Sign broken off pole; or
c. Sign tilted, twisted, or bent more than 30°; or
d. Sign ambiguous, misleading, or incorrect (sign twisted 45° to 90°, or with wrong street name);[3] or
e. Sign totally obscured by a tree, bush, brush, pole, another sign, or other objects so that it cannot be read from the car continuously within the last 50 feet of approach; or
f. Printing on sign is not legible.

INSTRUCTIONS FOR CODING DRIVER'S FORM (see Exhibit 13A-1)

Columns	Instructions
1-4	Month and day of the inspection. Use four digits; for example, June 6 is written as 0606.
5	Code for inspector. Single digit to identify each inspector.
6	Hour of day as the whole hour or a code for the hour.
7-11	Unique identifier. It can consist of the last two digits of the census tract and a three-digit number for the block face listing.
12-15	Modified census tract number. Address range and street name for block face. This should be preselected and entered before starting inspections.
16	Street type.
	1—Freeway
	2—Expressway
	3—Proposed Scenic Roads
	4—Major Streets and Roads
	5—Secondary Streets and Roads
	6—Minor Streets and Roads
17-19	Rating for street rideability.[4]
20-22	Rating for stop sign.[4]
23-25	Rating for other traffic control signs.[4]
26-28	Rating for street name sign.[4]
29	Enter code 9 if visibility is blocked at the end of the block face; otherwise, leave blank.
30	Enter card number 1.

INSTRUCTIONS FOR CODING RIDER'S INSPECTION FORM (see Exhibit 13A-2)

Columns	Instructions
1-4	Month and day of the inspection. Use four digits, for example, June 6 is written as 0606.
5	Code for inspector.
6	Hour of day as the whole hour, or a code for the hour.
7-11	Unique identifier. It can consist of the last two digits of the census tract and the three-digit number for the block face being inspected.
12-15	Modified census tract number. Enter the address range and the street name for block face being inspected.
16-18	Rating for road litter.[4]
19	Code for bulk items present.
	1—One bulk item
	2—Two bulk items
	3—Three bulk items
	9—More than three bulk items
20	Enter code 9 if heavy vegetation exists on street or roadway; otherwise, leave blank.
21	Enter code 9 if heavy dirt or gravel exists on street or roadway; otherwise, leave blank.
22	Enter code if there is an abandoned automobile on street or roadway; otherwise, leave blank.
	1—One abandoned auto
	2—Two abandoned autos
	3—Three abandoned autos
	4—More than three abandoned autos
23	Enter code 9 if the lane of traffic is blocked; otherwise, leave blank.
24-26	Rating for yard litter.[4]
27	Enter code if a bulk item is present in any yard; otherwise, leave blank.
	1—One bulk item
	2—Two bulk items
	3—Three bulk items
	9—More than three bulk items
28	Enter code 9 if heavy vegetation is observed in the yards on the block face; otherwise, leave blank.
29	Enter code 9 if there is an abandoned automobile in the yards on the block face; otherwise, leave blank.
30-32	Rating for sidewalk walkability.[4] If no sidewalk, leave blank.
33	Enter code for type of sidewalk surface. If no sidewalk, leave blank.
	1—Concrete
	2—Pebble
	3—Asphalt
	4—Brick
	5—Mixed
	6—Other
34-36	Enter rating for alley litter.[4] If no alley, leave blank.
37	Enter card number 2.

---

3. A sign twisted 90°, that is, turned around, may appear normal at first glance.

4. These ratings must consist of one digit followed by a decimal and another digit.

Exhibit 13A-1
DRIVER'S INSPECTION FORM

Date	Inspector	Hour of day	Unique Identi-fier	Census Tract	Street Name and Range of Address	Type	Rideabil-ity	Signs			Visibility Blocked	Alley Litter	Card No.	Comments
								Stop	Other Traffic	Street Name Signs				

Source: Trained Observer Inspection Form, Finance Office, Metropolitan Nashville-Davidson County, 1974.

Exhibit 13A-2
RIDER'S INSPECTION FORM

Date	Inspector	Hour of day	Unique identi-fier	Census Tract	Street name and address	Road litter	Bulk	Weeds	Dirt	Abandoned Auto	Blocked Lane	Yard litter	Bulk	Weeds	Abandoned Auto	Side-walks	Type	Alley litter	Card No.	Comments

Source: Trained Observer Inspection Form, Finance Office, Metropolitan Nashville-Davidson County, 1974.

ILLUSTRATIVE GUIDELINES FOR THE CITIZEN SURVEY PROCESS

This appendix first briefly discusses the basic steps in the citizen survey process and then identifies a number of elements a government should consider in its contractual arrangements for a survey.[1]

BASIC STEPS

Five steps are generally required to develop citizen surveys, particularly surveys intended for obtaining service effectiveness information.

Step 1. Prepare a draft questionnaire. It is highly desirable that operating agencies participate in its preparation. The Nashville questionnaire (provided in Appendix 1) or the similar St. Petersburg questionnaire (included in our initial report) can be used as starting points for a local government's development of its own questionnaire.

There are a number of pitfalls in developing the questionnaire. The professional survey organization that undertakes the interviewing should "pretest" the questionnaire to work out the final specific wording. Exhibit 14A provides some general criteria that may be helpful in deciding whether a particular question or question topic is appropriate for a government citizen survey aimed at service effectiveness measurement.

Step 2. Identify the major population subgroups for which the government wants to obtain data. The number of such classifications and the number of categories within each are needed for determining both the size of the sample and the nature of the coding that will be needed. As a rule of thumb, the sample size should be large enough to provide approximately 100 (or more) respondents in most categories. For example, if the government has funds for a total sample of only 600, then it should have no more than about six geographical areas, six age groupings, or the like, on which it expects to obtain data. The government may find it will need to combine some groups, or provide for "stratified" sampling, to assure that each remaining group will be covered by an adequate subsample.

Step 3. Design a Request for Proposal for a professional survey organization to administer the survey. Elements to consider in contractual arrangements for a citizen survey are discussed later in this appendix.

Step 4. Select the contractor and undertake the proposed process. Both universities and survey firms should probably be included in the bidders' list. Try if possible to find organizations that have had experience with governments.[2]

Step 5. After the survey has been undertaken and the findings have been obtained, provide for analysis of the data, including analyses by operating agencies whose services are included in the survey. Prepare a summary of findings for use by the chief executive, the council, and citizens. Some suggestions for handling survey findings follow. (This step and some illustrative formats are discussed further in Chapter 12.)

SOME CONSIDERATIONS REGARDING THE SURVEY FINDINGS

1. A number of products should be prepared from the survey data. These include (a) a summary of the findings on each question with relevant cross-tabulations by particular clientele groups, and (b) a comparison of the demographic characteristics of the sample with the latest demographic data on characteristics of the total population of the jurisdiction, to estimate how representative the sample was of the total population.

2. Some local governments may be tempted to provide a summary report which either by selective presenta-

---

1. There is a growing literature on sample surveys. A number of items are listed in the selected bibliography.

2. Finding firms to bid may be a problem in some localities. Check with other local governments, city and county planning agencies, local universities, and professional associations in the survey field, especially those with codes of ethics and professional-level meetings and publications, such as the American Association of Public Opinion Research, American Marketing Association, the Association for Consumer Research, and the Market Research Association. Some of these issue geographically classified directories. Check the local classified telephone directory (both for regional offices of nationally recognized firms as well as local firms), but screen out organizations without the needed skills or professional approach. A survey professional, perhaps from a nearby university, might help in this screening process.

Exhibit 14A

CHECKLIST OF CRITERIA FOR DECIDING WHETHER A PARTICULAR QUESTION SHOULD BE INCLUDED IN THE CITIZEN SURVEY AIMED AT SERVICE EFFECTIVENESS MEASUREMENT

1. The information cannot be obtained as accurately by other practical means.

2. The information cannot be obtained as inexpensively by other means.

3. The information is sufficiently important to merit the time and expense of inclusion in the survey. Interviewing time and cost are not the only considerations. Each additional question will generate added data to be tabulated, displayed, and analyzed. Marginal questions can overload the government's capacity to consider the data.

4. The question is of direct relevance to measuring service effectiveness; that is, it provides information on (a) service effectiveness, (b) respondent characteristics, or (c) conditions that can help to explain why the level of effectiveness is as it is.[1]

5. The question will be understandable to respondents.

6. There will be enough respondents appropriate to answer the questions asked in the sample size chosen to provide statistical information. Some questions are intended to be asked only of those who have previously indicated that they fall into a particular category. For example, only those who have made a complaint to the government would be asked how satisfied they were with the handling of the complaint. To ensure that the information obtained has at least minimum precision, surveyers should probably set a minimum of perhaps fifty appropriate respondents. Thus, in the foregoing example, the government should estimate that a minimum of fifty persons of those interviewed will have made a complaint before including the question asking for a satisfaction rating.

7. Citizens are competent to respond to the questions so that their information will be meaningful; that is, they can be expected to make a reasonably informed response on the question. (In general, questions encouraging "hearsay" evidence or questions that presume special or technical knowledge, should be avoided.)

1. Some governments also may want to include questions that seek citizen opinions on current issues. Because such questions are particularly susceptible to unintentional bias, special care should be given to how they are worded.

tion or by wording "plays down" apparent deficiencies. (For example, in a statement that "only 20 percent of the respondents found their neighborhoods to be dirty," the word *only* is a value judgment and should be avoided.) In the long run, a professional approach that presents the material as objectively as possible is best. A government, however, is likely to want to make some judgments as to whether a condition identified is "good" or "bad." Such judgments should be identified as opinions and carefully distinguished from the actual data. The basic cross-tabulations should be made available so that users of the information can see the results for themselves if they wish.

3. Finally, the government should make the findings conveniently available throughout the community. One method is that used by the city of St. Petersburg, where copies of the report containing the complete survey results were placed in the public libraries.

ELEMENTS FOR INCLUSION IN SURVEY CONTRACTUAL ARRANGEMENTS

The following section identifies some of the major elements that should be addressed explicitly when contracting for a citizen survey. Each should be discussed with potential contractors. Each also should be considered for inclusion in a Request for Proposal so that contractors can bid on an appropriate and reasonably common basis. These same elements also should be considered for inclusion in the final contractual agreement.

Even if the local government decides to administer the citizen survey itself, it will need to consider explicitly most of these elements prior to undertaking the survey. However, it is recommended that the local government employ a professional expert to help at least with its first citizen survey.

Elements discussed below include: (1) the minimum number of interviews to be completed; (2) the sampling method; (3) the role of the contractor in development of the questionnaire; (4) specification of how the interviews will be conducted; (5) pretesting of the questionnaire; (6) provision for verification of a certain percentage of the interviews; (7) maintenance of confidentiality of responses; (8) special coding to be done by the contractor; (9) comparison of sample versus total population characteristics; (10) products to be provided to the government; (11) the time schedule for the work; (12) the survey firms' credentials; and (13) cost quotations. Chapter 14 provides additional discussion of some of these issues.

1. *The minimum number of interviews to be completed.* This number is determined by considerations such as cost, the degree of precision sought, and the number of different clientele groupings within the jurisdiction for which the government seeks data (area of residence, age group, sex, race, income group, and so forth). We suggest somewhat arbitrarily that a minimum of about 100 interviews be sought for each clientele group.[3] Thus, if a city wants information on each of six neighborhood groups, it should seek about 600 interviews.

3. Roughly speaking, sample sizes of 100, if randomly chosen, would mean precision such that if 20 percent of the sample had given a particular rating on a specific question, we could have 90-percent confidence that the percentage for the total population actually falls between 13 percent and 27 percent. If two population groups with sample sizes of 100 each reported 20 percent and 10 percent respectively, there would be less than a 10-percent probability that a difference as large as that observed was the luck of the draw rather than a real difference. Survey organizations can supply tables showing the trade-offs of precision versus sample size so that each government can judge for itself what minimum sample sizes are appropriate. Unfortunately, there appears to be no literature available to provide guidance as to the amount of precision needed for the variety of potential decisions that might be affected by various precision levels.

The degree of precision needed is a very complex question, the resolution of which is beyond this report. Nevertheless, important judgments on precision are implied in the selection of sample size. The precision obtainable from population group samples of 100 or even somewhat less can, for most uses of these data, probably provide information that is sufficiently precise—at least as accurate as much other information currently available to local officials. Where funds permit, larger samples would be desirable. Note that the Gallup and Harris polls use samples of approximately 1,500 adults, often categorized by age group, sex, race, education levels, or whatever, to represent the complete adult population of the United States.

2. *Sampling method.* The principal concern is to obtain interviews that are at least roughly representative of the population. The contractor should fully specify the sampling method that will be used. (Any professional firm should be willing to describe completely the methods that it uses for its sampling process.) There are a number of options such as completely random sampling, cluster sampling, clusters with quotas, and multistage sampling designs. Although some of these issues will not be discussed here because they are primarily technical, a few points require government consideration:

a. An important question is what will be done about those households selected for interviews whose occupants are not at home. For at-home and telephone interviews, the minimum number of call-backs and time of call-backs to be made should be specified. More call-backs entail higher cost, but yield greater confidence that the sample interviewed represents the population from which the sample was drawn. More call-backs are practical for telephone interviewing—even up to six or more—than are practical for at-home interviewing.

A "noncall-back" approach used by some survey organizations is an option for at-home interviewing for the type of survey under consideration here. When no eligible respondent is available at the original target home, the interviewer, though still bound by quotas to obtain a representative age-sex distribution, goes to the next home instead. This procedure will reduce costs considerably. If properly done, the evidence (provided by election results) suggests that this approach is likely to be adequate.[4]

b. Because the citizen survey discussed in this report includes a number of questions about conditions in the respondent's own neighborhood, "cluster" sampling should be avoided. That is, if the city undertakes 600 interviews in 100 clusters of six, the responses from the six households in a cluster on these neighborhood questions may be closely correlated, thus perhaps providing a sample of 100 independent observations rather than 600.[5] Avoiding clusters will,

however, by increasing the travel time for the interviewers, increase the interviewing cost. Note that this problem arises only for at-home, not telephone, interviewing.

c. The approximate distribution of interviews by day of the week and hour of the day should also be made explicit by the bidding firm. This is particularly important when, as will usually be the case, the method of selecting the person to be interviewed depends on who is home at the time. The only methods exempt from this problem would be those relatively expensive ones that use specific, preselected individuals and require considerable effort to find them at home. Moreover, instead of concentrating the interviewing on weekdays and normal working hours, interviewers should schedule some interviewing for weekends and early evening times. This practice should produce a more representative sample because it avoids interviewing an excessive proportion of persons who are normally at home during the day. In St. Petersburg, for example, interviewing was conducted between 2:00 p.m. and 8:30 p.m. on weekdays and all day on weekends.

d. An important decision for at-home interviewing is the choice of listings from which the sample will be randomly drawn. The survey firm probably should draw the sample, but the government should approve the list from which it will be drawn. The government will want to assure that the listing is reasonably current and covers the great majority of the population. Special problems may arise in covering mobile homes or new housing developments not included in the available listing of households. Another problem might arise from using a listing such as tax assessors' block books, which include only specific street addresses. Some procedure must then be used that allows for adequate representation of multiple dwelling units (such as apartment houses) at a single address.

e. Another decision is who should be interviewed once a dwelling unit is selected for the sample. In general, because of cost constraints, only one adult will be interviewed per household. (This will somewhat undercount adults from households with more than one adult, but this problem could be partly compensated for if responses are weighted according to the number of adults in each household.) It is also necessary to specify what age group is to be included in the interviews. For the information sought in the questionnaires illustrated in these reports, it is probably most appropriate to interview only persons eighteen years old or older.[6] (In Palo Alto those sixteen years old or older were interviewed with no apparent problems.)

Still another decision concerns which adult to interview at a household in cases presenting a practical option. For some questions in the survey, an adult who takes care of the home may be the most informed person, for others, the "working" head of the household. A representation by age and sex groupings is suggested on grounds that the subject matter of the questionnaire needs a cross section of adult

---

4. However, there remains the nagging concern that those seldom at home would have different experiences with, and perceptions about, government services than those found at home by the interviewers. The extent of such a potential bias is not known. See Chapter 14 for further discussion.

5. This problem becomes even more troublesome for comparisons of different neighborhood areas. If the community is divided into six neighborhood areas with about 100 interviews in each, clusters of six would mean that only about seventeen blocks in each area would be covered.

6. For some services, such as recreation and libraries, it would be desirable to obtain information from juveniles as well. Juveniles could be included in surveys of users of specific government facilities, but probably should be excluded from the multiservice citizen survey discussed here.

viewpoints. Each local government should make its choice after considering the specific questions to be included and the information it wants.

3. *Role of the contractor in developing the questionnaire.* It is assumed here that the local government rather than the contractor will undertake the major effort in developing the questionnaire, perhaps using as a starting point questionnaires such as those included or cited in this report. Nevertheless, the contractor, after pretesting results, should work out the final wording of the questions. Also the survey firm will normally want to put the questionnaire into its own format to provide for ease of editing, coding, and keypunching. The contractor and government should agree on the final wording of questions. In essence, the government is responsible for content and the contractor for technique.

4. *Specification of how the interviews will be conducted.* Either at-home or telephone interviews, or a combination, seem appropriate for a survey that is no more than an average of thirty minutes in length. Longer questionnaires of the type discussed here may also be feasible but they have not been tested during the project period.[7] Mail interviews do not seem appropriate because of the questionnaire's length and the tendency of respondents not to answer at all or to answer only some questions, thereby increasing considerably the possibility that the results will not be representative of the whole community.[8] Jurisdictions having a significant proportion of families without telephones should avoid telephone interviews or supplement them with at-home interviews. In a telephone survey, care should be taken to cover families with unlisted telephone numbers; a random digit dialing approach can be employed to select respondents from the complete population of households with telephones.

Jurisdictions with large proportions of ethnic and language groups may also need to ensure that interviewers will be able to communicate with such groups.

5. *Questionnaire pretesting.* A pretest of the questionnaire is essential to check on the adequacy of the wording. The minimum amount of pretesting should be specified. About twenty-five interviews are probably enough if no significant problems show up.

The questions on the sample questionnaires contained or cited in this report for St. Petersburg and Nashville were pretested and used a number of times. But even if these questionnaires appear to another jurisdiction to be appropriate as currently worded, pretesting should still be undertaken in the jurisdiction in which the

questionnaire is to be used to detect any local language problems or situational differences. Any questions modified for use, or new ones added, should be tested before use.

6. *Verification of a certain proportion of the interviews.* The survey organization should provide for verification of at least a small percentage of the interviews. Verification is a process in which someone other than the original interviewer, perhaps the field supervisor, calls back a household to check responses to a few carefully chosen questions. This process should give assurance that the interviews have been accomplished correctly. Provision should be made for correcting any problems found. Verification rates of perhaps 10 percent for each interviewer are probably adequate. An early review of completed interviews will help spot any particularly careless or inaccurate interviewers.

7. *Confidentiality of responses.* It is vital that adequate provision be made to assure anonymity of individual respondents. Interviewers should be required to assure interviewees of the confidentiality of their responses at the beginning of each interview. All reputable survey firms—or the government, if it undertakes the interviewing itself—will protect the names and identifying characteristics of all respondents.

The government will probably want a copy of the deck of punch cards or tape containing the basic information received from the individual questionnaire. The nature of the survey, however, does not require the government to have information that would permit identifying specific individuals interviewed.[9] No names should be included on the deck and location of residence should identify the individual only down to a geographic area of the city or neighborhood service area, perhaps a census tract. Names and addresses should probably be destroyed after verification is completed.

The effort to protect the confidentiality of the respondents should not be confused with the question of releasability of the survey data. Since one purpose of the survey is to increase accountability, the grouped survey data, regardless of the findings, should be made public—unless some circumstance arises that clearly invalidates the survey.

8. *Special coding to be done by the contractor.* The questionnaire may require special coding after the interview is completed. Generally the government will have established code categories prior to the interviewing. (This will be particularly true for repeat surveys.) In some instances, however, this coding may be deferred or some interpretation may be required that the interviewer cannot do "on the spot." For example, it may be necessary to translate resident addresses to a special area-of-residence code. The survey organizations should be clearly notified in advance about such special coding requirements. For the purposes of the surveys discussed here, open-ended questions should be kept to a minimum; coding can require significant added effort and cost.

9. *Comparison of demographic characteristics of the sample versus those of the total population.* Proper sampling is intended to provide survey responses that

---

7. In seventeen telephone interviews tried in Nashville, interviews averaged thirty minutes; there were no early terminations and only one refusal.

8. However, another possibility is an initial mailing of the questionnaire with adequate provision for follow-up by telephone or at-home interviews to obtain reasonably high response rates. To our knowledge such an approach has not been tested on a survey of this subject matter. On the question of what are appropriate response rates, again there are no clear guidelines. However, the federal government has established a ground rule that any proposed statistical data collection activity "having an expected response rate of less than 50 percent will be disapproved." It also indicated that data collections for statistical purposes should have a response rate of 75 percent; those with expected response rates of less than 75 percent require "special justification." See "Memo to the Heads of Executive Departments and Establishments: President's Reporting Burden Reduction Program," September 1, 1976.

---

9. Freedom-of-information laws (including "sunshine" laws) do not make identities of survey respondents public information.

are representative of the whole population. One approach to determine whether the sample is reasonably representative is to compare available demographic characteristics of the sample against known values for these characteristics for the whole population from which the sample is drawn.

For at-home interviews, after drawing the sample and before interviewing, a partial determination of whether the sample is representative should be made. Normally, at this stage the primary characteristic available for comparison will be the geographic distribution of those in the sample rather than personal characteristics such as age, sex, or race. The sample's geographical distribution can be compared against the latest jurisdiction population-distribution figures. If these examinations show significant variations between the geographical distribution of the sample and that of the whole population, the contractor should be requested to review the sampling procedures and make appropriate corrections.

For all modes of interviewing, at the end of the survey other characteristics obtained for the sample from the questionnaires, such as age group, sex, race, and income class, should be compared against the latest available figures for the whole population from which the sample was drawn (generally all persons eighteen years or older). The results of this comparison should be provided in the final report to the government to provide information on the degree of representativeness of the sample.

Note that the usefulness of census data for comparisons declines with age. In fact, late in the period between censuses, the sample drawn may be more up to date than the census data, especially in areas of rapid growth.

10. *Products to be provided to the government.* Survey firms would normally be asked to provide some or all of the following:

a. A deck of the punch cards or tape with the questionnaire information. Even though the government may have the survey firm make the main tabulations, government analysts may later require special cross-tabulations or further examination of the data. In addition, the questionnaires themselves should be accessible to the government (but not with names and addresses of respondents attached) so that responses, such as those to open-ended questions, are available.

b. A report describing in detail the methodology used, a guide to the use of the data with the deck of computer cards, any comparisons made of the sample and total population characteristics, and whatever can be said about the precision of the findings.

c. A copy of the questionnaire (or its equivalent) showing overall jurisdiction percentages and sample sizes.

d. Specified tabulations of survey results. Although a government with its own computer capability may prefer to undertake these tabulations itself, most are likely to find it convenient to have the contractor provide at least some tabulations. The government can request (1) a complete set of cross-tabulations of each demographic characteristic against each of the other questions or (2) a selected set of tabulations. Findings should be expressed as percentages of particular client groups responding in each category. To facilitate judging the precision of the findings, the sample size for each client group should also be displayed. (Exhibit 12-4 in Chapter 12 presents our recommended summary format for each question.)

e. A detailed analysis identifying the highlights of the findings prior to government review. Many governments may choose to undertake this step themselves.[10] When this is publicly released, all basic tabulations—not only the highlights—should be made available to the interested public, perhaps by putting them on display in public libraries.

11. *The schedule for the work.* Completion dates should be specified, but the government itself can delay the contractor by refusing to grant final approval of the questionnaire wording after the pretest. Illustrative time periods are four weeks for pretest and modifications, three weeks for conducting up to perhaps 1,000 interviews, and four weeks for providing the final tabulations—a total of approximately three months. This schedule assumes that both the proposed questionnaire and selected population sample will need little revision and that detailed analysis of findings is not included.

Interviewing took more than two weeks in St. Petersburg for 626 completed interviews; about three weeks in Nashville for 1,002 completed interviews; and one week in Palo Alto for 574 completed interviews.

12. *The survey firm's credentials.* Background information on the firm and its interviewers should be examined before the contract is awarded. In cases involving bidders who have not previously worked for the local government, previous clients of the bidder should be consulted regarding the firm's performance, including the specific nature of the survey work performed; the timeliness, thoroughness, and quality of the product; and the apparent success with interviewees. Qualifications of the specific members of the firm who will be involved with the survey, especially the field coordinator and data-processing specialist, should be examined carefully. Firms with experience will usually have a stable group of regular interviewers. For both at-home and telephone interviewing, most survey firms use female interviewers primarily, but not exclusively. (Female interviewers appear to be substantially more successful than males in achieving cooperation from respondents in both kinds of interviews. In Nashville, for example, refusal rates were two and one-half times as high for male interviewees as for females.)

13. *Cost quotations.* Costs will depend on the decisions made regarding the issues discussed previously. The contractor's degree of responsibility should be established with regard to drawing the sample, wording the questionnaire, coding open-ended questions, keypunching, tabulating, and analyzing results. The local government might request cost estimates based on a small number of alternative arrangements such as vari-

---

10. For examples of such presentations, see St. Petersburg Office of Management and Budget, *Multi-Service Citizen Survey for the City of St. Petersburg,* 1973, 1974 and 1975 editions (January 1974); Nashville-Davidson County Metropolitan Government Department of Finance, *How Well Is Metro Doing?* 1974 and 1976 editions; and Finance and Public Works Committee, Palo Alto, "Staff Reports to the City Council," regarding the citizen survey, May 23, June 6, and July 11, 1974; Zeeland, Michigan, Office of City Superintendent, 1976 *Multi-Service Citizen Survey for Zeeland, Michigan,* 1976; and Sioux City, Iowa, *1976 Multi-Service Citizen Survey Report,* in five parts, 1976 and 1977.

ous numbers of interviews, different sampling methods, or different outputs desired.

For the type and length of survey described in these reports, costs could probably be kept within a range of $10 to $15 per interview for telephone interviewing (in 1976 prices). At-home interviewing is likely to add at least an additional $5 per interview. These costs include pre-testing, final questionnaire preparation and printing, in-terviewing, editing, coding, card-punching, and initial summary tabulations. These estimates assume that no extensive effort is required for developing the question-naire or for developing the list of households from which the sample is to be drawn.[11]

11. For further discussion of survey costs, see Chapter 14; Webb and Hatry, *Obtaining Citizen Feedback*; and Weiss and Hatry, *An Introduction to Sample Surveys*.

Selected Bibliography

Solid Waste Collection (Chapter 2)

Blair, Louis H., and Alfred I. Schwartz. *How Clean Is Our City?* Washington, D.C.: The Urban Institute, 1972.

————. "Measuring the Effectiveness of District of Columbia Solid Waste Collection Activities." 4 vols. Washington, D.C.: The Urban Institute, 1971.

Blair, Louis H., Harry P. Hatry, and P. A. Don Vito. *Measuring the Effectiveness of Local Government Services: Solid Waste Collection.* Washington, D.C.: The Urban Institute, 1970. Available through National Technical Information Service.

District of Columbia, Office of Environmental Services. "Solid Waste Litter Visual Inspection and Reporting System," by E. M. Melgaard. May 1974.

Fund for the City of New York. "Project Scorecard: Purpose, Function, Method, and Structure." New York, N.Y., 1975.

Messer Associates, Inc. *Measures of Effectiveness of Refuse Storage, Collection, and Transportation Practices.* EPA-670/2-74-082. Cincinnati: U.S. Environmental Protection Agency, November 1974.

Savannah, Georgia, Office of the City Manager. "City of Savannah Community Renewal Program." June 1973.

U.S. Environmental Protection Agency. *Decision-Makers' Guide in Solid Waste Management.* 2nd ed. Washington, D.C.: U.S. Government Printing Office, 1976.

The Urban Institute. *Challenge of Productivity Diversity: Improving Productivity Measurement and Evaluation in Local Governments.* Part II: "Measuring Solid Waste Collection Productivity." Prepared for the National Commission on Productivity. Washington, D.C.: The Urban Institute, June 1972.

Solid Waste Disposal (Chapter 3)

American Public Health Association. *Standard Methods for the Examination of Water and Wastewater.* 13th ed. Washington, D.C.: American Public Health Association, 1971.

American Public Works Association. *Municipal Refuse Disposal.* 3rd ed. Chicago: Public Administration Service, 1970.

Blair, Louis H., and Alfred I. Schwartz. *How Clean Is Our City?* Washington, D.C.: The Urban Institute, 1972.

U.S. Department of Health, Education and Welfare, Public Health Service. "Control of Domestic Rats and Mice," by Bayard F. Bjornson, Harry D. Pratt, and Kent S. Littig. Washington, D.C.: U.S. Government Printing Office, 1970.

————. "Municipal-Scale Incinerator Design and Operation," by Jack DeMarco, Daniel J. Keller, Jerold Leckman, and James L. Newton. Washington, D.C.: U.S. Government Printing Office, 1973.

U.S. Environmental Protection Agency. *Decision-Makers' Guide in Solid Waste Management,* 2nd ed. Washington, D.C.: U.S. Government Printing Office, 1976.

————. "Sanitary Landfill Design, Construction and Evaluation," by Maxwell J. Wilcomb and H. Lanier Hickman, Jr. Washington, D.C.: U.S. Government Printing Office, 1971.

Recreation Services (Chapter 4)

Buechner, Robert D. *National Park Recreation and Open Space Standards.* National Recreation and Park Association, 1970.

Burton, Thomas L. *Experiments in Recreation Research.* Totowa, N.J.: Rowman and Littlefield, 1971.

Butler, George. "Summer Playground Attendance Formula." *Recreation,* April 1961.

Dunn, Diana R. *Open Space and Recreation Opportunity in America's Inner Cities: A Summary of an Analysis of Low-Income, High Density, Inner-City Residents and Their Non-Commercial Leisure Resources in Twenty-Five Cities Over 250,000 Population.* NTIS PB 235-121-AS. Springfield, Va.: National Technical Information Service, 1974.

Ferriss, Abbott L. "Applications of Recreation Surveys." *Public Opinion Quarterly* 27:443-454, Fall 1963.

Fisk, Donald M., and Cynthia A. Lancer. *Equality of Distribution of Recreation Services: A Case Study of*

Washington, D.C. Washington, D.C.: The Urban Institute, July 1974.

Gold, Seymour M. *Urban Recreation Planning.* Philadelphia: Lea and Febiger, 1973.

Hatry, Harry P., and Diana R. Dunn. *Measuring the Effectiveness of Local Government Services: Recreation.* Washington, D.C.: The Urban Institute, 1971.

International City Management Association. *Municipal Recreation Administration.* 4th ed. Chicago, 1960.

Lucas, Robert C. "Bias in Estimating Recreationists' Length of Stay From Sample Interviews." *Journal of Forestry* 61, no. 12:912-914.

Lutzin, Sidney G., and Edward H. Storey, eds. *Managing Municipal Leisure Services.* Washington, D.C.: International City Management Association, 1973.

Nashville-Davidson County Metropolitan Government, Board of Parks and Recreation. "Summary Report of Citizen Surveys of Metro Park and Recreation Opportunities in Nashville-Davidson County." May 1974.

Nashville-Davidson County Metropolitan Government, Urban Observatory. *Leisure Services: The Measurement of Program Performance.* Nashville: The Urban Observatory, June 1974.

Philadelphia. "School Site Standards Study." August 1969.

Staley, Edwin J. "Determining Neighborhood Recreation Priorities: An Instrument." *Journal of Leisure Research,* Winter 1969.

U.S. Department of Agriculture, Forest Service. *A Comparison of Four Survey Techniques Used in Outdoor Recreation Research,* by Elwood L. Shafer, Jr., and John F. Hamilton. Research Paper NE-86. 1967.

———. *Instructions for Using Traffic Counters to Estimate Recreation Visits and Use on Developed Sites,* by George A. James, April 1966.

———. *Sampling Procedures for Estimating Mass and Dispersed Types of Recreation Use on Large Areas,* by George A. James and Robert K. Henley. Research Paper SE-31. March 1968.

U.S. Department of the Interior, Bureau of Outdoor Recreation. *COMPARE: A System for Optimizing Federal and Federally Assisted Recreation Programs.* 1968; rev. 1969, 1970.

———. *How Effective Are Your Community Recreation Services?* by Donald M. Fisk. Washington, D.C.: U.S. Government Printing Office, April 1973.

U.S. Outdoor Recreation Resource Review Commission. *The Quality of Outdoor Recreation: As Evidenced by Citizen Satisfaction.* Washington, D.C.: U.S. Government Printing Office, 1962.

Verhoven, Peter J., Jr., ed. *An Evaluation of Policy-Related Research in the Field of Municipal Recreation and Parks.* Arlington, Va.: National Recreation and Parks Association, July 1975.

Library Services (Chapter 5)

DeProspo, Ernest R., Ellen Altman, and Kenneth E. Beasley. *Performance Measures for Public Libraries.* Chicago: American Library Association–Public Library Association, 1973.

DeProspo, Ernest R., Ellen Altman, Phil M. Clark, and Ellen Connor Clark. *A Data Gathering and Instructional Manual for Performance Measures in Public Libraries.* Chicago: Oberon Press, 1976.

Drott, M. Carl. "Random Sampling: A Tool for Library Research." *College and Research Libraries* 30, no. 2 (March 1969).

Lipsman, Claire K. *The Disadvantaged and Library Effectiveness.* Chicago: American Library Association, 1972.

Little, Arthur D., and John S. Bolles. *The Urban Central Library: Development Alternatives for San Francisco.* San Francisco: Arthur D. Little, Inc., and John S. Bolles Associates, December 1970.

Monat, William et al. *The Public Library and Its Community: A Study of the Impact of Library Services in Five Pennsylvania Cities.* Pennsylvania State Library Monograph Series no. 7. Institute of Public Administration, Pennsylvania State University, 1967.

Newhouse, Joseph P., and Arthur J. Alexander. *An Economic Analysis of Public Library Services.* Santa Monica, Calif.: The Rand Corporation, February 1972.

St. Petersburg, Florida. "General Citizen Survey." September 1973.

———. "Report On Library User Survey 1974." Management Improvement Department, October 1974.

Tauber, Maurice, and Irlene Roemer Stephens, eds. *Library Surveys.* New York: Columbia University Press, 1967.

Wasserman, Paul, and Mary Lee Bundy, eds. *Reader in Library Administration.* Washington, D.C.: NCR Microcard Editions, 1968.

Wheeler, Joseph L., and Herbert Goldhor. *Practical Administration of Public Libraries.* New York: R. R. Bowker Co., 1969.

Crime Control (Chapter 6)

Albright, Ellen, Martin A. Baum, Brenda Forman, Sol Gems, David Jaffe, Frank C. Jordan, Jr., Ruth Katz, and Philip A. Sinsky. *Criminal Justice Research: Evaluation in Criminal Justice Programs, Guidelines and Examples.* Washington, D.C.: U.S. Government Printing Office, June 1973.

Alprin, Geoffrey. "D.C.'s Case Review Section Studies: The 'No-Paper' Phenomenon." *The Police Chief,* April 1973.

Beaton, W. Patrick. "The Determinants of Police Protection Expenditures." *National Tax Journal* 27, no. 2 (June 1974).

Bertram, Deborah K. and Alexander Vargo. "Response Time Analysis Study: Preliminary Findings on Robbery in Kansas City." *The Police Chief,* May 1976.

Biderman, Albert D. "Surveys of Population Samples for Estimating Crime Incidence." *Annals of American Academy of Political and Social Science* 374, November 1967.

Bloch, Peter B., and David Specht. *Neighborhood Team Policing.* Washington, D.C.: National Institute of Law Enforcement and Criminal Justice, December 1973.

Blumstein, Alfred. *Seriousness Weights in an Index of Crime.* Pittsburgh: Carnegie-Mellon University, Urban Systems Institute, January 1974.

Bozza, Charles M. "Motivations Guiding Policemen in the

Arrest Process." *Journal of Police Science and Administration* 1, 1973.

Chaiken, Jan M., Michael W. Lawless, and Keith A. Stevenson. *The Impact of Police Activity on Crime: Robberies on the New York City Subway System.* New York: New York City Rand Institute, January 1974 (R-1424-NYC).

Council on Municipal Performance. "City Crime." *Municipal Performance Report.* May-June 1973, with June 1974 supplement. Also discussed in "City Crime: Report of Council on Municipal Performance." *Criminal Law Bulletin* 9, no. 7, 1973.

Disser, L. R., and Roland M. Kissinger. "Inspection: A Management Tool." *The Police Chief,* August 1975.

Dodge, Richard W., and Anthony G. Turner. "Methodological Foundations for Establishing a National Survey of Victimization." Speech presented at the American Statistical Association meeting, August 23-26, 1971.

Farmer, David J. "Fact vs. Fact: A Selective View of Police Research in the United States." *The Police Journal,* April 1976.

Greenwood, Peter W. *An Analysis of the Apprehension Activities of the New York City Police Department.* R-529. New York: New York City Rand Institute, September 1970.

Hatry, Harry P. "Wrestling With Police Crime Control Productivity Measurement." *Readings on Productivity in Policing.* Washington, D.C.: The Police Foundation, 1975.

Hindlang, Michael J. "The Uniform Crime Reports Revisited." *Journal of Criminal Justice* 2, no. 1, Spring 1974.

Jones, E. Terrence. "Evaluating Everyday Policies: Police Activity and Crime Incidence." *Urban Affairs Quarterly* 8, no. 1, March 1973.

———. "The Impact of Crime Rate Changes on Police Protection Expenditures in American Cities." *Criminology* 2, no. 4, February 1974.

Kansas City, Missouri. *Annual Report of the Kansas City, Missouri, Police Department.* 1970.

Kelling, George L., Tony Pate, Duane Dieckman, and Charles E. Brown. *The Kansas City Preventive Patrol Experiment: A Summary Report* and *The Kansas City Preventive Patrol Experiment: A Technical Report.* Washington, D.C.: Police Foundation, 1974.

Maltz, Michael D. "Crime Statistics: A Mathematical Perspective." *Journal of Criminal Justice* 3:174-194, 1975.

New York, New York. *City of New York Police Department Evaluation Guide.* n.d. (c. 1974).

Ostrom, Elinor. "On the Meaning and Measurement of Output and Efficiency in the Provision of Urban Police Services." *Journal of Criminal Justice* 1, no. 2, Summer 1973.

Parks, Roger B. "Complementary Measures of Police Performance: Citizen Appraisals and Police-Generated Data." *Studies in Political Theory and Policy Analysis.* Bloomington: Indiana University Department of Political Science, 1973.

Parnas, Raymond. "Police Discretion and Diversion of Incidents of Intra-Family Violence." *Law and Contemporary Problems: Police Practices.* Duke University. Vol. 36, Autumn 1971.

Press, S. James. *Some Effects of an Increase in Police*

Manpower in the 20th Precinct of New York City. R-704. New York: New York City Rand Institute, October 1971.

Schaenman, Philip S. "Police Productivity Measurement: Initial Approaches and Practical Problems." *Proceedings of the Criminal Justice Symposium Focusing on Police Productivity,* Lehigh University, July 19, 1974.

Schmid, Calvin F. "Urban Crime Areas: Parts I and II." *American Sociological Review* 25, nos. 4 and 5, August and October 1960.

Schnelle, John F., Robert E. Kirchner, Joe D. Casey, and Thomas H. Shriver. "Evaluation of the Quality of Police Arrests by District Attorney Ratings." *The Police Chief,* January 1977.

Schuessler, Karl, and Gerald Slatin. "Sources of Variation in U.S. City Crime, 1950 and 1969." *Journal of Research in Crime and Delinquency* 1, no. 2, July 1964.

Sellin, Johan Thorsten, and Marvin E. Wolfgang. *The Measurement of Delinquency.* New York: John Wiley and Sons, 1964.

Sunnyvale, California, Public Safety Department. *Investigation Control and Management System,* by Charles T. Crabtree. 1973.

Tuchfarber, Alfred J., and William R. Klecka. *Random Digit Dialing: Lowering the Cost of Victimization Surveys.* Washington, D.C.: Police Foundation, December 1976.

The Urban Institute. *The Challenge of Productivity Diversity: Improving Local Government Productivity Measurement and Evaluation, Part III: Measuring Police-Crime Control Productivity.* PB223117. Washington, D.C.: National Commission on Productivity, National Technical Information Service, June 1972.

U.S. Department of Justice, Federal Bureau of Investigation. *Crime in the United States: Uniform Reports, 1974.* Washington, D.C.: U.S. Government Printing Office, November 1975.

———. *Uniform Crime Reporting Handbook: How to Prepare Uniform Crime Reports.* Washington, D.C.: U.S. Government Printing Office, January 1974.

U.S. Department of Justice, Law Enforcement Assistance Administration, National Institute of Law Enforcement and Criminal Justice. *Crimes and Victims: A Report on the Dayton-San Jose Pilot Survey of Victimization.* Washington, D.C.: U.S. Government Printing Office, June 1974.

———. "Criminal Victimization Surveys in the Nation's Five Largest Cities." Washington, D.C.: U.S. Government Printing Office, April 1975.

———. "Evaluation of Crime Control Programs," by Michael D. Maltz. Washington, D.C.: U.S. Government Printing Office, April 1972.

U.S. National Commission on Productivity. *Opportunities for Improving Productivity in Police Services.* Washington, D.C.: U.S. Government Printing Office, 1973.

U.S. President's Commission on Law Enforcement and Administration of Justice. *The Challenge of Crime in a Free Society.* Washington, D.C.: U.S. Government Printing Office, 1967.

Zeisel, Hans. "The Future of Law Enforcement Statistics: A Summary View." *Federal Statistics: Report of the President's Commission.* Vol. 2. Washington, D.C.: U.S. Government Printing Office, 1971.

Fire Protection (Chapter 7)

Fyffe, David E., and Ronald L. Rardin. *An Evaluation of Policy-Related Research in Fire Protection Service Management.* Atlanta: Georgia Institute of Technology, October 1974.

International City Management Association. *Municipal Fire Administration.* Chicago: International City Management Association, 1967.

Schaenman, Philip S., John R. Hall, Jr., Alfred Schainblatt, Joe Swartz, and Michael Karter. *Measuring Local Fire Protection Outcomes: Some Potential Improvements.* Washington, D.C.: The Urban Institute and National Fire Protection Association, forthcoming.

Schaenman, Philip S., and Joe Swartz. "Measuring Fire Protection Productivity in Local Government." National Fire Protection Association, October 1974.

Transportation (Chapters 8 and 9)

Boots, Andrew J., III, Grace Dawson, William Silverman, and Harry P. Hatry. *Inequality of Local Government Services: A Case Study of Neighborhood Roads.* Washington, D.C.: The Urban Institute, 1972.

Carroll, Susan. "An Analysis of the Relationship Between Citizen Perceptions and Unobtrusive Measures of Street Conditions." Technical Report no. M-10, Workshop on Political Theory and Policy Analysis. Bloomington: Indiana University, 1975.

"Driving Time Studies: A Procedure Guide." Stock no. 3253. American Automobile Association, Traffic Engineering Division, June 1963.

Ferguson, Earl. *Final Report on National Science Foundation Grant No. GR-43107.* Stillwater: Department of Industrial Engineering, Oklahoma State University, September 1975.

Green, Vernon. "An Analysis of the Relationship Between Citizen Perceptions and Physical Measures of Street Lighting." Workshop in Political Theory and Analysis, n.d. Research Report no. 7. Bloomington: Indiana University Department of Political Science.

Metropolitan Washington Council of Governments. "1975 Metro Area Travel Times—Auto and Transit." Washington, D.C., April 1976.

Ostrom, Elinor, and Roger B. Parks. "Measuring Urban Services: A Multi-Mode Approach." The Workshop on Political Theory and Policy Analysis, Department of Political Science. Bloomington: Indiana University, September 1975.

Rich, Richard. "The Development of Residential Street Roughness Indicator as a Mode of Measurement for the Survey of Residential Street Services." Research Report no. 6. Bloomington: Indiana University Department of Political Science, n.d.

Schultz, T. J. "Noise Assessment Guidelines—Technical Background." Prepared for the U.S. Department of Housing and Urban Development by Bolt, Beranek, and Newman. Washington, D.C.: U.S. Government Printing Office, 1972.

Schultz, T. J., and Nancy M. McMann. *Noise Assessment Guidelines.* Prepared for the U.S. Department of Housing and Urban Development by Bolt, Beranek, and Newman. Washington, D.C.: U.S. Government Printing Office, 1971.

Spokane, Washington, Transportation Study Division. "1973 Travel Time Inventory and Analysis." Spokane Regional Planning Conference, March 1974.

Walker, William P. "Speed and Travel Time Measurement in Urban Areas." *Traffic Speed and Volume Measurements.* Highway Research Bulletin 156. Washington, D.C., 1956.

Winnie, Richard E., and Harry P. Hatry. *Measuring the Effectiveness of Local Government Services: Transportation.* Washington, D.C.: The Urban Institute, 1972.

Water Supply (Chapter 10)

American Public Health Association. *Standard Methods for the Examination of Water and Wastewater.* 13th ed. Washington, D.C.: American Public Health Association, 1971.

American Water Works Association. "AWWA Statement of Policy on Public Water Supply Matters." New York: American Water Works Association, October 1972.

International City Management Association. *Municipal Fire Administration.* Chicago: International City Management Association, 1967.

U.S. Department of Health, Education and Welfare, Public Health Service. "Public Health Service Drinking Water Standards 1962." Washington, D.C.: Government Printing Office, 1962.

Handling Citizen Complaints and Requests for Service and Information (Chapter 11)

Charlottesville, Virginia. "Measurements of Effectiveness for Processing of Citizen Complaints." Memo to the City Manager, 1973.

Council on Municipal Performance. "City Hall Ears." *COMP News,* no. 3, April 19, 1976.

Frank, Bernard. "Ombudsman Survey: July 1, 1974-June 30, 1975." Allentown, Pa.: Ombudsman Committee, American Bar Association, n.d.

Gelhorn, Walter. *When Americans Complain.* Cambridge, Mass.: Harvard University Press, 1966.

Greiner, John M. "Urban Response Times: A Model of City Government Reactions to Citizen Letters." Master's thesis, University of Pennsylvania, October 1970 (rev. October 1972).

Gusdorf, Nigel, John D. C. Little, Chandler H. Stevens, and Peter Tropp. "Puerto Rico's Citizen Feedback System." Technical Report no. 59. Cambridge, Mass.: Operations Research Center, Massachusetts Institute of Technology, April 1971.

316

International City Management Association. "Anonymity of Complainants." Management Information Service, no. 168. Washington, D.C., January 1958.

Krendel, Ezra S. "A Case Study of Citizen Complaints as Social Indicators." IEEE Transactions on Systems Science and Cybernetics, vol. SSC-6, no. 4:265-272, October 1970.

Lindvall, Thomas, and Edward Radford. "Measurement of Annoyance Due to Exposure to Environmental Factors." Environmental Research 6:1-36 (1973).

Little, John D. C., Thomas B. Sheridan, Chandler H. Stevens, and Peter Tropp. "Citizen Feedback Components and Systems." Technical Report no. 76. Cambridge, Mass.: Operations Research Center, Massachusetts Institute of Technology, June 1972.

Los Angeles Technical Services Corporation. Measures of Effectiveness: City of Dallas. Los Angeles, May 1973.

Nebraska, Office of the State Ombudsman. "Second Annual Report of the Nebraska Ombudsman, 1972." January 15, 1973.

New York, New York, Office of the Mayor. "Citizen Feedback: An Analysis of Complaint Handling in New York City," by John A. Kaiser. April 1971.

———. "Guidelines for the Establishment and Monitoring of Services and Complaint Response Standards." June 1972.

———. "Referral of Misdirected Complaints and Requests." June 1, 1972.

———. "Guidelines for the Establishment of Services and Complaint Response Standards Within City Agencies," by Timothy W. Costello. March 28, 1972.

Seattle-King County, Washington, Office of the Ombudsman. "First Annual Report to the King County Council, the Seattle City Council, and the Office of Economic Opportunity." August 1972.

Sunnyvale, California. "City Services Effectiveness Measurement Procedures: Citizen's Complaints," by Camille Cates. Memo to the City Manager, December 19, 1973.

Tibbles, Lance, and John H. Hollands. Buffalo Citizen's Administrative Service: An Ombudsman Demonstration Project. Berkeley: Institute of Governmental Studies, University of California, 1970.

Wyner, Alan J. The Nebraska Ombudsman: Innovation in State Government. Berkeley: Institute of Governmental Studies, University of California, 1974.

Reports on Orange, California and Flint, Michigan." Washington, D.C.: Labor-Management Relations Service, December 1974.

Greiner, John M., Roger Dahl, Harry P. Hatry, and Annie Millar. "Monetary Incentives and Work Standards for Public Employees." Washington, D.C.: The Urban Institute, 1977.

Gueron, Joseph and Binyork Ouyang. "UI-MCTAB, A Multiple Crosstab Program." Washington, D.C.: The Urban Institute, August, 1974.

Hatry, Harry P., and Donald M. Fisk. Improving Productivity and Productivity Measurement in Local Governments. Washington, D.C.: National Commission on Productivity, June 1971.

International City Management Association. Improving Effectiveness: Responsive Public Services. Municipal Innovation Series no. 10. Washington, D.C.: International City Management Association, June 1976.

Nashville-Davidson County Metropolitan Government, Department of Finance. How Well Is Metro Doing? 1974 and 1976 editions.

Neubacher, James. Detroit Sanitation Productivity—Everyone Wins: Strengthening Local Government Through Better Labor Relations, no. 18. Washington, D.C.: Labor-Management Relations Service, November 1973.

Research Triangle Institute. "Case Study No. 10: Effectiveness Measurement Methods: Urban Institute." Research Triangle Park, N.C., 1975.

Rogers, Michael P. "Assessing Public Recreation Needs." Ann Arbor, Mich.: U.S. Bureau of Outdoor Recreation, November 1974.

Schaenman, Philip S., John R. Hall, Jr., Alfred Schainblatt, Joe Swartz, and Michael Karter. Measuring Local Fire Protection Outcomes: Some Potential Improvements. Washington, D.C.: The Urban Institute and National Fire Protection Association, forthcoming.

U.S. General Accounting Office, Comptroller General of the United States. "Standard for Audit of Governmental Organizations, Programs, Activities, and Functions." 1972.

U.S. General Accounting Office. Federal Productivity: Methods Measurement Results. Washington, D.C.: Government Printing Office, August 1972.

U.S. Office of Management and Budget, Joint Financial Management Program. Government Productivity, vol. 1, Productivity Trends and Current Efforts. Washington, D.C.: July 1976.

Using Effectiveness Measurement Information (Chapter 12)

Boots, Andrew J., Grace Dawson, William Silverman, and Harry P. Hatry. "Inequality in Local Government Services: A Case Study of Neighborhood Roads." Washington, D.C.: The Urban Institute, 1972.

Fisk, Donald M. and Cynthia A. Lancer. "Equality of Distribution of Recreation Services: A Case Study of Washington, D.C." Washington, D.C.: The Urban Institute, July 1974.

Greiner, John M. "Tying City Pay to Performance: Early

The Multiservice Citizen Survey (Chapter 14)

Abramson, J. H. Survey Methods in Community Medicine. London: Churchill Livingstone, 1974.

Babbie, Earl R. Survey Research Methods. Belmont, Calif.: Wadsworth Publishing Co., 1973.

Cahalan, Don. "Correlates of Respondent Accuracy in the Denver Validity Survey." Public Opinion Quarterly 32, no. 4, Winter 1968-69.

Clausen, Aage R. "Response Validity: Vote Report." *Public Opinion Quarterly* 32, no. 4, Winter 1968-69.

deBerge, Earl, and Conrad Joyner. "Opinion Polls or . . . How to Ask Right Questions of Right People at the Right Time." *Public Management* 48, no. 11, November 1966.

———. "Opinion Research Comes to Tucson." *Public Management* 48, no. 10, October 1966.

Dillman, Don A., Jean Gorton Gallegos, and James H. Frey. "Reducing Refusal Rates for Telephone Interviews." *Public Opinion Quarterly* 40, no. 1, Spring 1976.

Donald, Marjorie N. "Implications of Non-Response for the Interpretation of Mail Questionnaire Data." *Public Opinion Quarterly* 24, no. 1, Spring 1960.

Gueron, Joseph, and Binyork Ouyang. "UI-MCTAB, A Multiple Crosstab Program." Washington, D.C.: The Urban Institute, August 1974.

Hochstim, Joseph R. "A Critical Comparison of Three Strategies of Collecting Data from Households." *Journal of the American Statistical Association* 52, no. 319, September 1967.

International City Management Association. *Using Citizen Surveys: Three Approaches.* Municipal Innovation Series no. 15. Washington, D.C.: International City Management Association, February 1977.

Lagay, Bruce W. "Assessing Bias: A Comparison of Two Methods." *Public Opinion Quarterly* 30, no. 4, Winter 1970.

Leuthold, David, and Raymond Scheele. "Patterns of Bias in Samples Based on Telephone Directories." *Public Opinion Quarterly* 35, no. 2, Summer 1971.

Lehnen, Robert G.: "Assessing Reliability in Sample Surveys." *Public Opinion Quarterly* 35, no. 4, Winter 1971-72.

Levy, Clifford V. *A Primer for Community Research.* San Francisco: Far West Research, Inc., 1972.

Little, John D. C., et al. *Citizen Feedback Components and Systems.* Operations Research Center Technical Report no. 76. Cambridge, Mass.: Massachusetts Institute of Technology, 1972.

Mazer, Larry, and Kenneth Andrews. "A Municipality Surveys Its Citizens." *Popular Government* 41, no. 1, Summer 1975.

Nashville-Davidson County Metropolitan Government, Department of Finance. *How Well Is Metro Doing?* 1974 and 1976 editions.

Nemanich, Dorothy, and Diane O'Rourke. *A Manual for the Coding of Survey Data.* Dubuque, Iowa: Kendall/Hunt, Survey Research Laboratory, 1975.

Olsen, Marvin E.: "Alienation and Political Opinions." *Public Opinion Quarterly* 29, no. 2, Summer 1965.

O'Neill, Harry W. "Response Style Influence in Public Opinion Surveys." *Public Opinion Quarterly* 31, no. 1, Spring 1967.

Parry, Hugh J., and Helen M. Crossley. "Validity of Responses to Survey Questions." *Public Opinion Quarterly* 14, no. 1, Spring 1950.

"Questions Often Asked About Published Polls." *Gallup Opinion Index,* May 1970.

St. Petersburg Office of Management and Budget. *Multi-Service Citizen Survey for the City of St. Petersburg.* 1973, 1974, and 1975 editions.

Saroff, Jerome R., and Alberta Z. Levitan. *Survey Manual for Comprehensive Urban Planning.* Anchorage, Alaska: Development Research Associates, Inc., 1969.

Sioux City, Iowa. "1976 Multi-Service Citizen Survey Report." In five parts, 1976 and 1977.

Slonim, Morris J. *Sampling in a Nutshell.* New York: Simon and Schuster, 1960.

Tuchfarber, Alfred J., and William R. Klecka. *Random Digit Dialing: Lowering the Cost of Victimization Surveys.* Washington, D.C.: Police Foundation, December 1976.

U.S. Civil Service Commission, Personnel Research and Development Center. *Construction of Questionnaires.* Technical Study TS—7-73-1. July 1973.

U.S. Department of Commerce. *Supplemental Courses for Case Studies in Surveys and Censuses: Sampling Lectures.* ISP Supplemental Course, series no. 1, 1968.

U.S. Department of Health, Education and Welfare. "Reporting of Hospitalization in the Health Interview Survey." *Vital and Health Statistics,* series 2, no. 6, July 1965.

———. "Optimum Recall Period for Reporting Persons Injured in Motor Vehicle Accidents." *Vital and Health Statistics,* series 2, no. 50, April 1972.

U.S. Department of Justice, Law Enforcement Assistance Administration, National Institute of Law Enforcement and Criminal Justice, Statistics Division. "San Jose Methods Test of Known Crime Victims." Statistics Technical Report no. 1.

U.S. Executive Office of the President, Bureau of the Budget. *Household Survey Manual.* 1969.

U.S. Interstate Commerce Commission, Bureau of Economics. *Guidelines for the Presentation of the Results of Sample Studies,* Statement no. 71-1. Washington, D.C.: U.S. Government Printing Office, February 1971.

Weaver, Charles N., and Carol L. Swanson. "Validity of Reported Date of Birth, Salary, and Seniority." *Public Opinion Quarterly* 38, no. 1, Spring 1974.

Webb, Kenneth, and Harry P. Hatry. *Obtaining Citizen Feedback.* Washington, D.C.: The Urban Institute, 1973.

Weiss, Carol H., and Harry P. Hatry. *An Introduction to Sample Surveys for Government Managers.* Washington, D.C.: The Urban Institute, 1971.

Wheeler, Michael. "Political Polling: The German Shepherd Factor." *The Washington Monthly,* April 1976.

"Winnetka/Austin: Surveys Net Citizen Response." *Public Management* 51, no. 5, May 1969.

Zeeland, Michigan, Office of City Superintendent. "1976 Multi-Service Citizen Survey for Zeeland, Michigan." 1976.

MAR 1 5 1993

Cover photography: William Cady